Red Famine

ANNE APPLEBAUM

Red Famine

Stalin's War on Ukraine

ALLEN LANE
an imprint of
PENGUIN BOOKS

ALLEN LANE

UK | USA | Canada | Ireland | Australia
India | New Zealand | South Africa

Allen Lane is part of the Penguin Random House group of companies
whose addresses can be found at global.penguinrandomhouse.com

First published 2017
003

Copyright © Anne Applebaum, 2017

The moral right of the author has been asserted

Set in 10.5/14 pt Sabon LT Std
Typeset by Jouve (UK), Milton Keynes
Printed in Great Britain by Clays Ltd, St Ives plc

A CIP catalogue record for this book is available from the British Library

ISBN: 978–0–241–00380–0

Жертвам
To the victims

Contents

List of Illustrations

List of Maps

1054

KYIVAN RUS'

Baltic Sea

Black Sea

1582

POLISH-LITHUANIAN COMMONWEALTH

Baltic Sea

Black Sea

1795

RUSSIAN EMPIRE

PRUSSIA

AUSTRO-HUNGARIAN EMPIRE

OTTOMAN EMPIRE

Baltic Sea

Black Sea

FINLAND

SWEDEN

ESTONIA

Stockholm

Riga

LATVIA

LITHUANIA

Baltic Sea

Memel

EAST PRUSSIA

Danzig

Berlin

Warsaw

Bug

Brest-Litovsk

P O L A N D

Elbe

Oder

Lublin

Volodymyr Volynskyi

Tešin

Vistula

Prague

Lviv

C Z E C H O S L O V A K I A

Carpathian

Vienna

AUSTRIA

Budapest

HUNGARY

Danube

Belgrade

YUGOSLAVIA

Sarajevo

Adriatic Sea

Sofia

The Soviet Union and Eastern Europe, 1922

USSR
Soviet republic
Other national border

Petrograd

Kazan

RUSSIA

Moscow

Ryazan

Saratov

Minsk

Mogilev

Voronezh

Gomel

BELARUS

Kursk

Don

Volga

Kyiv

Kharkiv

Tsaritsyn

Dnieper

UKRAINE

Dniester

Rostov

Mountains

Odessa

Krasnodar

ROMANIA

CRIMEA

Novorossiisk

Sochi

Sevastopol

GEORGIA

Bucharest

Black Sea

Batumi

BULGARIA

TURKEY

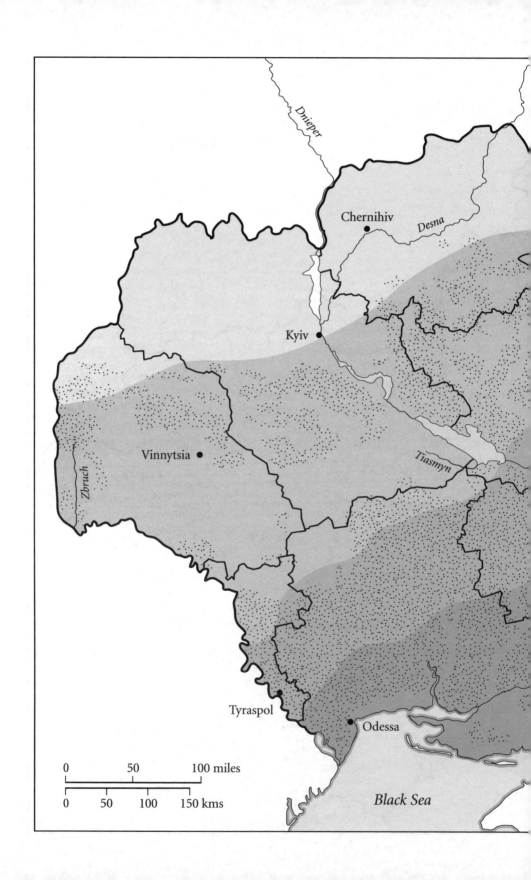

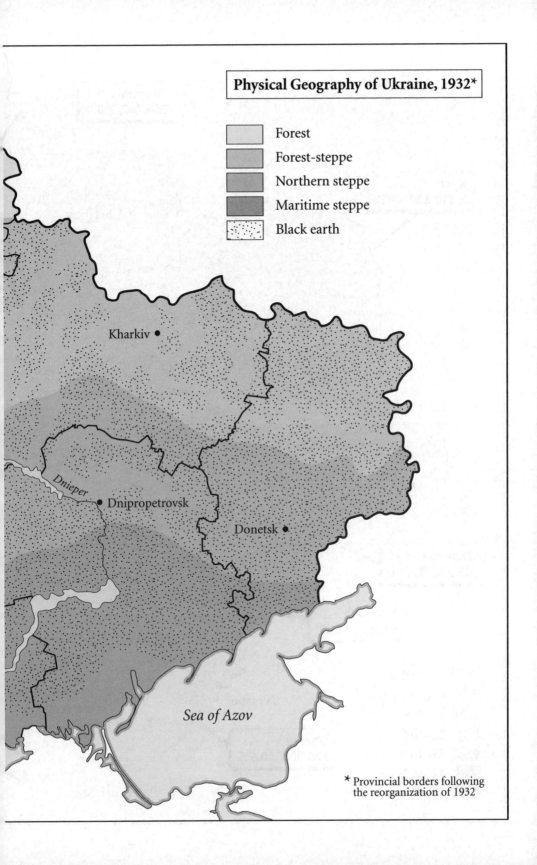

Physical Geography of Ukraine, 1932*

Forest
Forest-steppe
Northern steppe
Maritime steppe
Black earth

Kharkiv •

Dnieper
• Dnipropetrovsk

Donetsk •

Sea of Azov

* Provincial borders following
the reorganization of 1932

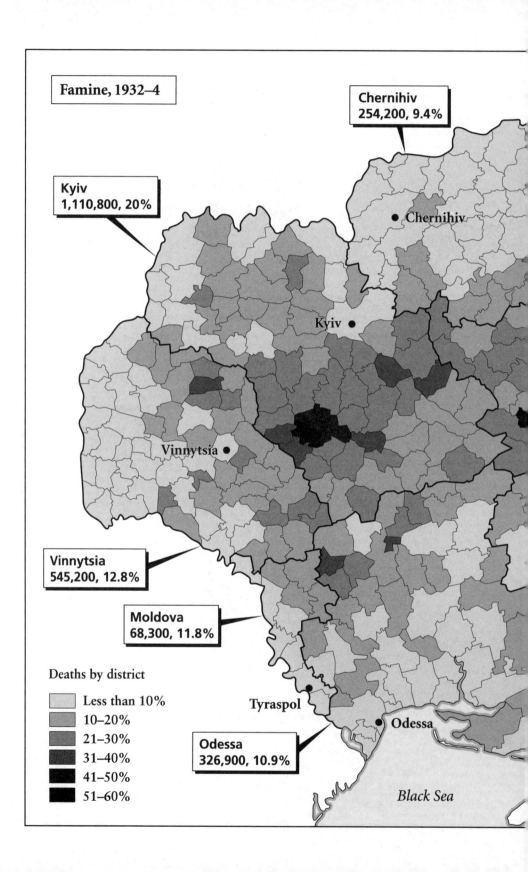

Famine, 1932–4

Chernihiv
254,200, 9.4%

Kyiv
1,110,800, 20%

● Chernihiv

Kyiv ●

Vinnytsia ●

Vinnytsia
545,200, 12.8%

Moldova
68,300, 11.8%

Deaths by district

Less than 10%
10–20%
21–30%
31–40%
41–50%
51–60%

Tyraspol ●

● Odessa

Odessa
326,900, 10.9%

Black Sea

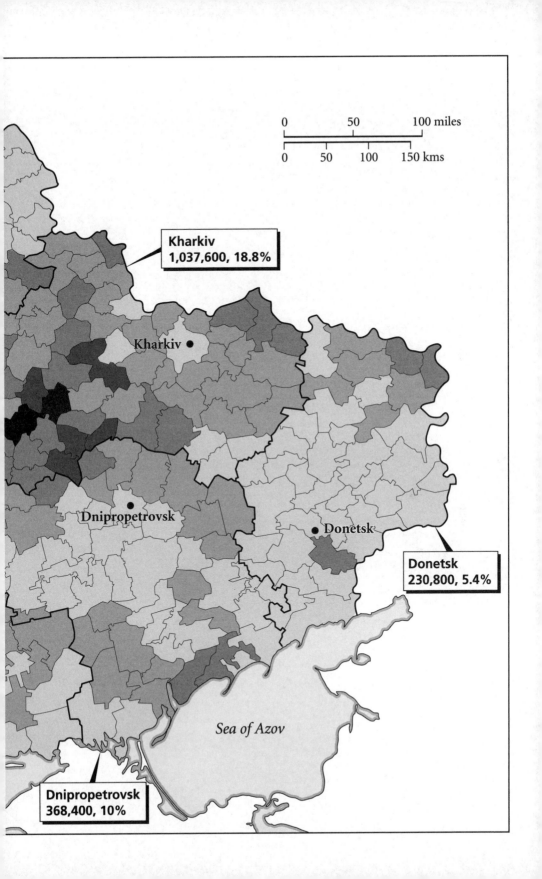

Kharkiv
1,037,600, 18.8%

Kharkiv ●

Dnipropetrovsk ●

● Donetsk

Donetsk
230,800, 5.4%

Dnipropetrovsk
368,400, 10%

Sea of Azov

0   50   100 miles

0   50   100   150 kms

Acknowledgements

Without the encouragement, advice and support of Professor Serhii Plokhii and his colleagues at the Harvard Ukrainian Research Institute, this book would not have been written. The scholars at HURI understood a decade ago that new archival discoveries merited a new approach to the history of the Holodomor – and they were right. Different members of staff helped at different times, but I owe special thanks to Oleh Wolowyna and Kostyantyn Bondarenko of the MAPA project at Harvard, who have done extraordinary work on statistics, demographics, numbers and maps.

I also owe an enormous debt to Marta Baziuk of the Holodomor Research and Education Consortium in Toronto, as well as her Kyiv-based counterpart, Lyudmyla Hrynevych of the Holodomor Ukrainian Research Centre, both of whom shared their profound knowledge of the subject with great generosity. Many thanks to the documentary filmmaker Andrew Tkach and Vladyslav Berkovsky of the TsDKFFA photographic archive for assistance with photographs. Professor Andrea Graziosi at the University of Naples helped shape the original outline and acted as a sounding board all the way through the project. Two extraordinary young historians, Daria Mattingly and Tetiana Boriak, provided research assistance from Kyiv and other cities in Ukraine. Ian Crookston and Professor Oksana Mykhed, two brilliant former Harvard graduate students, read the text for accuracy of sourcing and transliteration. A host of other Ukrainian historians offered suggestions and let me borrow their books or unpublished articles. They are all listed in the preface, but I'd like especially to thank Iurii Shapoval and Hennadii Boriak here again. I am grateful to the colleagues who read early versions of the manuscript, including

Geoffrey Hosking, Bogdan Klid, Lubomyr Luciuk and Frank Sysyn. Many thanks to Nigel Colley and Russ Chelak for help with the story of Gareth Jones. I am also indebted to Roman Procyk of the Ukrainian Studies Fund and to its benefactors, especially Luba Kladko, Dr Maria Fischer Slysh, Arkadi Mulak-Yatzkivsky and Ivan and Helena Panczak, as well as the Semenenko Fund of the W. K. Lypynsky East European Research Institute.

As in the past, Stuart Proffitt at Penguin in London and Kris Puopolo in New York made a brilliant, transatlantic publishing team, and Georges Borchardt was a superb agent. This is now the third book I've been able to write with the help of this same trio. I will always be grateful to them. Richard Duguid managed the production of this book from London with customary efficiency, while Richard Mason was an excellent and meticulous copyeditor.

My final thanks go to Radek, Tadziu and Alexander – with love.

A NOTE ON TRANSLITERATION

The transliteration of Ukrainian names and place names in this book follows the standard set out by the Harvard Ukrainian Research Institute. The Library of Congress transliteration rules for Ukrainian names and place names are followed strictly in the endnotes; in the text, names and place names are written without primes, since that seems more familiar to an English reader. Russian and Belarusian place names are transliterated according to the rules of those languages. A few well-known names and place names, including Moscow and Odessa, have been left in their better-known forms, also to make them recognizable to English-language readers.

Preface

The warning signs were ample. By the early spring of 1932, the peasants of Ukraine were beginning to starve. Secret police reports and letters from the grain-growing districts all across the Soviet Union – the North Caucasus, the Volga region, western Siberia – spoke of children swollen with hunger; of families eating grass and acorns; of peasants fleeing their homes in search of food. In March a medical commission found corpses lying on the street in a village near Odessa. No one was strong enough to bury them. In another village local authorities were trying to conceal the mortality from outsiders. They denied what was happening, even as it was unfolding before their visitors' eyes.[1]

Some wrote directly to the Kremlin, asking for an explanation:

> Honourable Comrade Stalin, is there a Soviet government law stating that villagers should go hungry? Because we, collective farm workers, have not had a slice of bread in our farm since January 1 . . . How can we build a socialist peoples' economy when we are condemned to starving to death, as the harvest is still four months away? What did we die for on the battlefronts? To go hungry, to see our children die in pangs of hunger?[2]

Others found it impossible to believe the Soviet state could be responsible:

> Every day, ten to twenty families die from famine in the villages, children run off and railway stations are overflowing with fleeing villagers. There are no horses or livestock left in the countryside . . . The bourgeoisie has created a genuine famine here, part of the capitalist plan to set the entire peasant class against the Soviet government.[3]

But the bourgeoisie had not created the famine. The Soviet Union's disastrous decision to force peasants to give up their land and join collective farms; the eviction of 'kulaks', the wealthier peasants, from their homes; the chaos that followed; these policies, all ultimately the responsibility of Joseph Stalin, the General Secretary of the Soviet Communist Party, had led the countryside to the brink of starvation. Throughout the spring and summer of 1932, many of Stalin's colleagues sent him urgent messages from all around the USSR, describing the crisis. Communist Party leaders in Ukraine were especially desperate, and several wrote him long letters, begging him for help.

Many of them believed, in the late summer of 1932, that a greater tragedy could still be avoided. The regime could have asked for international assistance, as it had during a previous famine in 1921. It could have halted grain exports, or stopped the punishing grain requisitions altogether. It could have offered aid to peasants in starving regions – and to a degree it did, but not nearly enough.

Instead, in the autumn of 1932, the Soviet Politburo, the elite leadership of the Soviet Communist Party, took a series of decisions that widened and deepened the famine in the Ukrainian countryside and at the same time prevented peasants from leaving the republic in search of food. At the height of the crisis, organized teams of policemen and party activists, motivated by hunger, fear and a decade of hateful and conspiratorial rhetoric, entered peasant households and took everything edible: potatoes, beets, squash, beans, peas, anything in the oven and anything in the cupboard, farm animals and pets.

The result was a catastrophe: At least 5 million people perished of hunger between 1931 and 1934 all across the Soviet Union. Among them were more than 3.9 million Ukrainians. In acknowledgement of its scale, the famine of 1932–3 was described in émigré publications at the time and later as the *Holodomor*, a term derived from the Ukrainian words for hunger – *holod* – and extermination – *mor*.[4]

But famine was only half the story. While peasants were dying in the countryside, the Soviet secret police simultaneously launched an attack on the Ukrainian intellectual and political elites. As the famine spread, a campaign of slander and repression was launched against Ukrainian intellectuals, professors, museum curators, writers, artists, priests, theologians, public officials and bureaucrats.

Anyone connected to the short-lived Ukrainian People's Republic, which had existed for a few months from June 1917, anyone who had promoted the Ukrainian language or Ukrainian history, anyone with an independent literary or artistic career, was liable to be publicly vilified, jailed, sent to a labour camp or executed. Unable to watch what was happening, Mykola Skrypnyk, one of the best-known leaders of the Ukrainian Communist Party, committed suicide in 1933. He was not alone.

Taken together, these two policies – the Holodomor in the winter and spring of 1933 and the repression of the Ukrainian intellectual and political class in the months that followed – brought about the Sovietization of Ukraine, the destruction of the Ukrainian national idea, and the neutering of any Ukrainian challenge to Soviet unity. Raphael Lemkin, the Polish-Jewish lawyer who invented the word 'genocide', spoke of Ukraine in this era as the 'classic example' of his concept: 'It is a case of genocide, of destruction, not of individuals only, but of a culture and a nation.' Since Lemkin first coined the term, 'genocide' has come to be used in a narrower, more legalistic way. It has also become a controversial touchstone, a concept used by both Russians and Ukrainians, as well as by different groups within Ukraine, to make political arguments. For that reason, a separate discussion of the Holodomor as a 'genocide' – as well as Lemkin's Ukrainian connections and influences – forms part of the epilogue to this book.

The central subject is more concrete: what actually happened in Ukraine between the years 1917 and 1934? In particular, what happened in the autumn, winter and spring of 1932–3? What chain of events, and what mentality, led to the famine? Who was responsible? How does this terrible episode fit into the broader history of Ukraine and of the Ukrainian national movement?

Just as importantly: what happened afterwards? The Sovietization of Ukraine did not begin with the famine and did not end with it. Arrests of Ukrainian intellectuals and leaders continued through the 1930s. For more than half a century after that, successive Soviet leaders continued to push back harshly against Ukrainian nationalism in whatever form it took, whether as post-war insurgency or as dissent in the 1980s. During those years Sovietization often took the form of

Russification: the Ukrainian language was demoted, Ukrainian history was not taught.

Above all, the history of the famine of 1932–3 was not taught. Instead, between 1933 and 1991 the USSR simply refused to acknowledge that any famine had ever taken place. The Soviet state destroyed local archives, made sure that death records did not allude to starvation, even altered publicly available census data in order to conceal what had happened.[5] As long as the USSR existed, it was not possible to write a fully documented history of the famine and the accompanying repression.

But in 1991 Stalin's worst fear came to pass. Ukraine did declare independence. The Soviet Union did come to an end, partly as the result of Ukraine's decision to leave it. A sovereign Ukraine came into being for the first time in history, along with a new generation of Ukrainian historians, archivists, journalists and publishers. Thanks to their efforts, the complete story of the famine of 1932–3 can now be told.

This book begins in 1917, with the Ukrainian revolution and the Ukrainian national movement that was destroyed in 1932–3. It ends in the present, with a discussion of the ongoing politics of memory in Ukraine. It focuses on the famine in Ukraine, which, although part of a wider Soviet famine, had unique causes and attributes. The historian Andrea Graziosi has noted that nobody confuses the general history of 'Nazi atrocities' with the very specific story of Hitler's persecution of Jews or gypsies. By the same logic, this book discusses the Soviet-wide famines between 1930 and 1934 – which also led to high death rates, especially in Kazakhstan and particular provinces of Russia – but focuses more directly on the specific tragedy of Ukraine.[6]

The book also reflects a quarter-century's worth of scholarship on Ukraine. In the early 1980s, Robert Conquest compiled everything then publicly available about the famine, and the book he published in 1986, *The Harvest of Sorrow*, still stands as a landmark in writing about the Soviet Union. But in the three decades since the end of the USSR and the emergence of a sovereign Ukraine, several broad national campaigns to collect oral history and memoirs have yielded thousands of new testimonies from all over the country.[7] During that same time period, archives in Kyiv – unlike those in Moscow – have become accessible and easy to use; the percentage of unclassified material in Ukraine is one of the highest in Europe. Ukrainian government funding has encouraged scholars to publish collections of documents, which have made research even more straightforward.[8] Established scholars on the famine and on the Stalinist period in Ukraine – among them Olga Bertelsen, Hennadii Boriak, Vasyl Danylenko, Lyudmyla Hrynevych, Roman Krutsyk, Stanislav Kulchytsky, Yuri Mytsyk, Vasyl Marochko, Heorhii Papakin, Ruslan Pyrih, Yuri Shapoval, Volodymyr Serhiichuk, Valerii Vasylyev, Oleksandra Veselova and Hennadii Yefimenko – have produced multiple books and monographs, including collections of reprinted documents as well as oral history. Oleh Wolowyna and a team of demographers – Oleksander Hladun, Natalia Levchuk, Omelian Rudnytsky – have at last begun to do the difficult work of establishing the numbers of victims. The Harvard Ukrainian Research Institute has worked with many of these scholars to publish and publicize their work.

The Holodomor Research and Education Consortium in Toronto, led by Marta Baziuk, and its partner organization in Ukraine, led by Lyudmyla Hrynevych, continue to fund new scholarship. Younger scholars are opening new lines of inquiry too. Daria Mattingly's research on the motives and background of the people who confiscated food from starving peasants and Tetiana Boriak's work on oral history both stand out; they also contributed important research to this book. Western scholars have made new contributions too. Lynne Viola's archival work on collectivization and the subsequent peasant rebellion have altered the perceptions of the 1930s. Terry Martin was the first to reveal the chronology of the decisions Stalin took in the autumn of 1932 – and Timothy Snyder and Andrea Graziosi were among the first to recognize their significance. Serhii Plokhii and his team at Harvard have launched an unusual effort to map the famine, the better to understand how it happened. I am grateful to all of these for the scholarship and in some cases the friendship that contributed so much to this project.

Perhaps if this book had been written in a different era, this very brief introduction to a complex subject could end here. But because the famine destroyed the Ukrainian national movement, because that movement was revived in 1991, and because the leaders of modern Russia still challenge the legitimacy of the Ukrainian state, I should note here that I first discussed the need for a new history of the famine with colleagues at the Harvard Ukrainian Research Institute in 2010. Viktor Yanukovych had just been elected president of Ukraine, with Russian backing and support. Ukraine then attracted little political attention from the rest of Europe, and almost no press coverage at all. At that moment, there was no reason to think that a fresh examination of 1932–3 would be interpreted as a political statement of any kind.

The Maidan revolution of 2014, Yanukovych's decision to shoot at protesters and then flee the country, the Russian invasion and annexation of Crimea, the Russian invasion of eastern Ukraine and the accompanying Russian propaganda campaign – all unexpectedly put Ukraine at the centre of international politics while I was working on this book. My research on Ukraine was actually delayed by events in that country, both because I wrote about them and because my Ukrainian colleagues were so transfixed by what was happening. But while the events of that year put Ukraine at the heart of world politics, this book was not written in reaction to them. Nor is it an argument for or against any Ukrainian politician or party, or a reaction to what is happening in Ukraine today. It is instead an attempt to tell the story of the famine using new archives, new testimony and new research, to draw together the work of the extraordinary scholars listed above.

This is not to say that the Ukrainian revolution, the early years of Soviet Ukraine, the mass repression of the Ukrainian elite as well as the Holodomor do not have a relationship to current events. On the contrary: they are the crucial backstory that underlies and explains them. The famine and its legacy play an enormous role in contemporary Russian and Ukrainian arguments about their identity, their relationship and their shared Soviet experience. But before describing those arguments or weighing their merits, it is important to understand, first, what actually happened.

Introduction
The Ukrainian Question

When I am dead, bury me	Як умру, то поховайте
In my beloved Ukraine,	Мене на могилі
My tomb upon a grave mound high	Серед степу широкого
Amid the spreading plain,	На Вкраїні милій,
So that the fields, the boundless steppes,	Щоб лани широкополі,
The Dnieper's plunging shore	І Дніпро, і кручі
My eyes could see, my ears could hear	Було видно, було чути,
The mighty river roar.	Як реве ревучий.

Taras Shevchenko, 'Zapovit' ('Testament'), 1845[1]

For centuries, the geography of Ukraine shaped the destiny of Ukraine. The Carpathian Mountains marked the border in the southwest, but the gentle forests and fields in the northwestern part of the country could not stop invading armies, and neither could the wide open steppe in the east. All of Ukraine's great cities – Dnipropetrovsk and Odessa, Donetsk and Kharkiv, Poltava and Cherkasy and of course Kyiv, the ancient capital – lie in the East European Plain, a flatland that stretches across most of the country. Nikolai Gogol, a Ukrainian who wrote in Russian, once observed that the Dnieper River flows through the centre of Ukraine and forms a basin. From there 'the rivers all branch out from the centre; not a single one of them flows along the border or serves as a natural border with neighbouring nations.' This fact had political consequences: 'Had there been a natural border of mountains or sea on one side, the people who settled here would have carried on their political way of life and would have formed a separate nation.'[2]

The absence of natural borders helps explain why Ukrainians failed, until the late twentieth century, to establish a sovereign Ukrainian state. By the late Middle Ages, there was a distinct Ukrainian language, with Slavic roots, related to but distinct from both Polish and Russian, much as Italian is related to but distinct from Spanish or French. Ukrainians had their own food, their own customs and local traditions, their own villains, heroes and legends. Like other European nations, Ukraine's sense of identity sharpened during the eighteenth and nineteenth centuries. But for most of its history the territory we now call Ukraine was, like Ireland or Slovakia, a colony that formed part of other European land empires.

Ukraine – the word means 'borderland' in both Russian and Polish – belonged to the Russian empire between the eighteenth and twentieth centuries. Prior to that, the same lands belonged to Poland, or rather the Polish-Lithuanian Commonwealth, which inherited them in 1569 from the Grand Duchy of Lithuania. Earlier still, Ukrainian lands lay at the heart of Kyivan Rus', the medieval state in the ninth century formed by Slavic tribes and a Viking nobility, and, in the memories of the region, an almost mythical kingdom that Russians, Belarusians and Ukrainians all claim as their ancestor.

Over many centuries, imperial armies battled over Ukraine, sometimes with Ukrainian-speaking troops on both sides of the front lines. Polish hussars fought Turkish janissaries for control of what is now the Ukrainian town of Khotyn in 1621. The troops of the Russian tsar fought those of the Austro-Hungarian emperor in 1914 in Galicia. Hitler's armies fought against Stalin's in Kyiv, Lviv, Odessa and Sevastopol between 1941 and 1945.

The battle for control of Ukrainian territory always had an intellectual component as well. Ever since Europeans began to debate the meaning of nations and nationalism, historians, writers, journalists, poets and ethnographers have argued over the extent of Ukraine and the nature of the Ukrainians. From the time of their first contacts in the early Middle Ages, Poles always acknowledged that the Ukrainians were linguistically and culturally separate from themselves, even when they were part of the same state. Many of the Ukrainians who accepted Polish aristocratic titles in the sixteenth and seventeenth centuries remained Orthodox Christians, not Roman Catholics; Ukrainian peasants spoke a language that the Poles called 'Ruthenian', and were always described as having different customs, different music, different food.

Although at their imperial zenith they were more reluctant to acknowledge it, Muscovites also felt instinctively that Ukraine, which they sometimes called 'southern Russia' or 'little Russia', differed from their northern homeland too. An early Russian traveller, Prince Ivan Dolgorukov, wrote in 1810 of the moment when his party finally 'entered the borders of the Ukraine. My thoughts turned to [Bohdan] Khmelnytsky and [Ivan] Mazepa' – early Ukrainian national leaders – 'and the alleys of trees disappeared . . . everywhere, without exception, there were clay huts, and there was no other accommodation'.[3] The historian Serhiy Bilenky has observed that nineteenth-century Russians often had the same paternalistic attitude to Ukraine that northern Europeans at the time had towards Italy. Ukraine was an idealized, alternative nation, more primitive and at the same time more authentic, more emotional, more poetic than Russia.[4] Poles also remained nostalgic for 'their' Ukrainian lands long after they had been lost, making them the subject of romantic poetry and fiction.

Yet even while acknowledging the differences, both Poles and Russians also sought at times to undermine or deny the existence of a Ukrainian nation. 'The history of Little Russia is like a tributary entering the main river of Russian history,' wrote Vissarion Belinsky, a leading theorist of nineteenth-century Russian nationalism. 'Little Russians were always a tribe and never a people and still less – a state.'[5] Russian scholars and bureaucrats treated the Ukrainian language as 'a dialect, or half a dialect, or a mode of speech of the all-Russian language, in one word a *patois*, and as such had no right to an independent existence'.[6] Unofficially, Russian writers used it to indicate colloquial or peasant speech.[7] Polish writers, meanwhile, tended to stress the 'emptiness' of the territory to the east, often describing the Ukrainian lands as an 'uncivilized frontier, into which they brought culture and state formations'.[8] The Poles used the expression *dzikie pola*, 'wild fields', to describe the empty lands of eastern Ukraine, a region that functioned, in their national imagination, much as the Wild West did in America.[9]

Solid economic reasons lay behind these attitudes. The Greek historian Herodotus himself wrote about Ukraine's famous 'black earth', the rich soil that is especially fertile in the lower part of the Dnieper

River basin: 'No better crops grow anywhere than along its banks, and where grain is not sown, the grass is the most luxuriant in the world.'[10] The black-earth district encompasses about two-thirds of modern Ukraine – spreading from there into Russia and Kazakhstan – and, along with a relatively mild climate, makes it possible for Ukraine to produce two harvests every year. 'Winter wheat' is planted in the autumn, and harvested in July and August; spring grains are planted in April and May, and harvested in October and November. The crops yielded by Ukraine's exceptionally fertile land have long inspired ambitious traders. From the late Middle Ages, Polish merchants had brought Ukrainian grain northwards into the trade routes of the Baltic Sea. Polish princes and nobles set up what were, in modern parlance, early enterprise zones, offering exemptions from tax and military service to peasants who were willing to farm and develop Ukrainian land.[11] The desire to hold on to such valuable property often lay behind the colonialist arguments: neither the Poles nor the Russians wanted to concede that their agricultural breadbasket had an independent identity.

Nevertheless, quite apart from what their neighbours thought, a separate and distinct Ukrainian identity did take shape in the territories that now form modern Ukraine. From the end of the Middle Ages onwards, the people of this region shared a sense of who they were, often, though not always, defining themselves in opposition to occupying foreigners, whether Polish or Russian. Like the Russians and the Belarusians, they traced their history back to the kings and queens of Kyivan Rus', and many felt themselves to be part of a great East Slavic civilization. Others identified themselves as underdogs or rebels, particularly admiring the great revolts of the Zaporozhian Cossacks, led by Bohdan Khmelnytsky, against Polish rule in the seventeenth century, and by Ivan Mazepa against Russian rule at the beginning of the eighteenth century. The Ukrainian Cossacks – self-governing, semi-military communities with their own internal laws – were the first Ukrainians to transform that sense of identity and grievance into concrete political projects, winning unusual privileges and a degree of autonomy from the tsars. Memorably (certainly later generations of Russian and Soviet leaders never forgot it), Ukrainian Cossacks joined the Polish army in its march on Moscow in 1610 and again in 1618, taking part in a siege of the city and helping ensure that the Polish-Russian conflict of that era ended, at least for a time, advantageously for Poland. Later, the tsars gave both the Ukrainian Cossacks and Russian-speaking Don Cossacks special status in order to keep them loyal to the Russian empire, with which they were allowed to preserve a particular identity. Their privileges guaranteed that they did not revolt. But Khmelnytsky and Mazepa left their mark on Polish and Russian memory, and on European history and literature too. 'L'Ukraine a toujours aspiré à être libre,' wrote Voltaire after news of Mazepa's rebellion spread to France: 'Ukraine has always aspired to be free.'[12]

During the centuries of colonial rule different regions of Ukraine did acquire different characters. The inhabitants of eastern Ukraine, who were longer under Russian control, spoke a version of Ukrainian that was slightly closer to Russian; they were also more likely to be Russian Orthodox Christians, following rites that descended from Byzantium, under a hierarchy led by Moscow. The inhabitants of Galicia, as well as Volhynia and Podolia, lived longer under Polish control and, after the partitions of Poland at the end of the eighteenth century, that of Austria-Hungary. They spoke a more 'Polish' version of the language and were more likely to be Roman Catholics or Greek Catholics, a faith that uses rites similar to the Orthodox Church yet respects the authority of the Roman pope.

But because the borders between all of the regional powers shifted many times, members of both faiths lived, and still live, on both sides of the dividing line between former Russian and former Polish territories. By the nineteenth century, when Italians, Germans and other Europeans also began to identify themselves as peoples of modern nations, the intellectuals debating 'Ukrainianness' in Ukraine were both Orthodox and Catholic, and lived in both 'eastern' and 'western' Ukraine. Despite differences in grammar and orthography, language unified Ukrainians across the region too. The use of the Cyrillic alphabet kept Ukrainian distinct from Polish, which is written in the Latin alphabet. (At one point the Habsburgs tried to impose a Latin script, but it failed to take hold.) The Ukrainian version of Cyrillic also kept it distinct from Russian, retaining enough differences, including some extra letters, to prevent the languages from becoming too close.

For much of Ukraine's history, Ukrainian was spoken mostly in the countryside. As Ukraine was a colony of Poland, and then Russia and Austria-Hungary, Ukraine's major cities – as Trotsky once observed – became centres of colonial control, islands of Russian, Polish or Jewish culture in a sea of Ukrainian peasantry. Well into the twentieth century, the cities and the countryside were thus divided by language: most urban Ukrainians spoke Russian, Polish or Yiddish, whereas rural Ukrainians spoke Ukrainian. Jews, if they did not speak Yiddish, often preferred Russian, the language of the state and of commerce. The peasants identified the cities with wealth, capitalism and 'foreign' – mostly Russian – influence. Urban Ukraine, by contrast, thought of the countryside as backward and primitive.

These divisions also meant the promotion of 'Ukrainianness' created conflict with Ukraine's colonial rulers, as well as with the inhabitants of the Jewish shtetls who had made their home in the territory of the old Polish-Lithuanian Commonwealth since the Middle Ages. Khmelnytsky's uprising included a mass pogrom, during which thousands – perhaps tens of thousands – of Jews were murdered. By the beginning of the nineteenth century, Ukrainians rarely saw the Jews as their most important rivals – Ukrainian poets and intellectuals mostly reserved their anger for Russians and Poles – but the widespread anti-semitism of the Russian empire inevitably affected Ukrainian-Jewish relations too.

The link between the language and the countryside also meant that the Ukrainian national movement always had a strong 'peasant' flavour. As in other parts of Europe, the intellectuals who led Ukraine's national awakening often began by rediscovering the language and customs of the countryside. Folklorists and linguists recorded the art, poetry and everyday speech of the Ukrainian peasantry. Although not taught in state schools, Ukrainian became the language of choice for a certain kind of rebellious, anti-establishment Ukrainian writer or artist. Patriotic private Sunday schools began to teach it too. It was never employed in official transactions, yet the language was used in private correspondence, and in poetry. In 1840, Taras Shevchenko, born an orphaned serf in 1814, published *Kobzar* – the word means 'minstrel' – the first truly outstanding collection of Ukrainian verse. Shevchenko's poetry combined romantic nationalism and an idealized picture of the countryside with anger at social injustice, and it set the tone for many of the arguments that were to come. In one of his most famous poems, 'Zapovit' ('Testament'), he asked to be buried on the banks of the Dnieper River:

Oh bury me, then rise ye up	Поховайте та вставайте,
And break your heavy chains	Кайдани порвіте
And water with the tyrants' blood	І вражою злою кров'ю
The freedom you have gained . . .	Волю окропіте . . .[13]

The importance of the peasantry also meant that from the very beginning the Ukrainian national awakening was synonymous with populist and what would later be called 'left wing' opposition to the Russian and Polish-speaking merchants, landowners and aristocracy. For that reason, it rapidly gathered strength following the emancipation of the serfs across imperial Russia under Tsar Alexander II in 1861. Freedom for the peasants was, in effect, freedom for Ukrainians, and a blow to their Russian and Polish masters. The pressure for a more powerful Ukrainian identity was, even then, also pressure for greater political and economic equality, as the imperial ruling class well understood.

Because it was never linked to state institutions, the Ukrainian national awakening was also, from its earliest days, expressed through the formation of a wide range of autonomous voluntary and charitable organizations, early examples of what we now call 'civil society'. For a brief few years following the serfs' emancipation, 'Ukrainophiles' inspired younger Ukrainians to form self-help and study groups, to organize the publication of periodicals and newspapers, to found schools and Sunday schools and to spread literacy among the peasantry. National aspirations manifested themselves in calls for intellectual freedom, mass education, and upward mobility for the peasantry. In this sense, the Ukrainian national movement was from the earliest days influenced by similar movements in the West, containing strands of Western socialism as well as Western liberalism and conservatism.

This brief moment did not last. As soon as it began to gather strength, the Ukrainian national movement, alongside other national movements, was perceived by Moscow as a potential threat to the unity of imperial Russia. Like the Georgians, the Chechens and other groups who sought autonomy within the empire, the Ukrainians challenged the supremacy of the Russian language and a Russian interpretation of history that described Ukraine as 'southwest Russia', a mere province without any national identity. They also threatened to empower the peasants further at a time when they were already gaining economic influence. A wealthier, more literate and better-organized Ukrainian peasantry might also demand greater political rights.

The Ukrainian language was a primary target. During the Russian empire's first great educational reform in 1804, Tsar Alexander I permitted some non-Russian, languages to be used in the new state schools but not Ukrainian, ostensibly on the grounds that it was not a 'language' but rather a dialect.[14] In fact, Russian officials were perfectly clear, as their Soviet successors would be, about the political justification for this ban – which lasted until 1917 – and the threat that the Ukrainian language posed to the central government. The governor-general of Kyiv, Podolia and Volyn declared in 1881 that using the Ukrainian language and textbooks in schools could lead to its use in higher education and eventually in legislation, the courts and public administration, thus creating 'numerous complications and dangerous alterations to the unified Russian state'.[15]

The restrictions on the use of Ukrainian limited the impact of the national movement. They also resulted in widespread illiteracy. Many peasants, educated in Russian, a language they barely understood, made little progress. A Poltava teacher in the early twentieth century complained that students 'quickly forgot what they had been taught' if they were forced to study in Russian. Others reported that Ukrainian students in Russian-language schools were 'demoralized', grew bored with school, and became 'hooligans'.[16] Discrimination also led to Russification: for everybody who lived in Ukraine – Jews, Germans and other national minorities as well as Ukrainians – the path to higher social status was a Russian-speaking one. Until the 1917 revolution, government jobs, professional jobs and business deals required an education in Russian, not Ukrainian. In practice, this meant that Ukrainians who were politically, economically or intellectually ambitious needed to communicate in Russian.

To prevent the Ukrainian national movement from growing, the Russian state also banned Ukrainian organizations from 'both civil society and the body politic ... as a guarantee against political instability'.[17] In 1876, Tsar Alexander II issued a decree outlawing Ukrainian books and periodicals and prohibiting the use of Ukrainian in theatres, even in musical libretti. He also discouraged or banned the new voluntary organizations, and provided subsidies to pro-Russian newspapers and pro-Russian organizations instead. The sharp hostility to Ukrainian media and Ukrainian civil society later espoused by the Soviet regime – and, much later, by the post-Soviet Russian government as well – thus had a clear precedent in the second half of the nineteenth century.[18]

Industrialization deepened the pressure for Russification as well, since the construction of factories brought outsiders to Ukrainian cities from elsewhere in the Russian empire. By 1917 only one-fifth of the inhabitants of Kyiv spoke Ukrainian.[19] The discovery of coal and the rapid development of heavy industry had a particularly dramatic impact on Donbas, the mining and manufacturing region on the eastern edge of Ukraine. The leading industrialists in the region were mostly Russians, with a few notable foreigners mixed in: John Hughes, a Welshman, founded the city now known as Donetsk, originally called 'Yuzivka' in his honour. Russian became the working language of the Donetsk factories. Conflicts often broke out between Russian and Ukrainian workers, sometimes taking the 'most wild forms of knife fights' and pitched battles.[20]

Across the imperial border in Galicia, the mixed Ukrainian-Polish province of the Austro-Hungarian empire, the nationalist movement struggled much less. The Austrian state gave Ukrainians in the empire far more autonomy and freedom than did Russia or later the USSR, not least because they regarded the Ukrainians as (from their point of view) useful competition for the Poles. In 1868 patriotic Ukrainians in Lviv formed Prosvita, a cultural society that eventually had dozens of affiliates all around the country. From 1899 the Ukrainian National Democratic Party operated freely in Galicia too, sending elected representatives to the parliament in Vienna. To this day, the former headquarters of a Ukrainian self-help society is one of the most impressive nineteenth-century buildings in Lviv. A spectacular piece of architectural fusion, the building incorporates stylized Ukrainian folk decorations into a *Jugendstil* facade, creating a perfect hybrid of Vienna and Galicia.

But even inside the Russian empire, the years just before the revolution of 1917 were in many ways positive for Ukraine. The Ukrainian peasantry took part enthusiastically in the early twentieth-century modernization of imperial Russia. On the eve of the First World War, they were rapidly gaining political awareness and had grown sceptical of the imperial state. A wave of peasant revolts ricocheted across both Ukraine and Russia in 1902; peasants played a major role in the 1905 revolution as well. The ensuing riots set off a chain reaction of unrest, unsettled Tsar Nicholas II, and led to the introduction of some civil and political rights in Ukraine, including the right to use the Ukrainian language in public.[21]

When both the Russian and Austro-Hungarian empires collapsed, unexpectedly, in 1917 and 1918 respectively, many Ukrainians thought they would finally be able to establish a state. That hope was quickly extinguished in the territory that had been ruled by the Habsburgs. After a brief but bloody Polish-Ukrainian military conflict that cost 15,000 Ukrainian and 10,000 Polish lives, the multi-ethnic territory of western Ukraine, including Galicia as well as Lviv, its most important city, was integrated into modern Poland. There it remained from 1919 to 1939.

The aftermath of the February 1917 revolution in St Petersburg was more complicated. The dissolution of the Russian empire briefly put power in the hands of the Ukrainian national movement in Kyiv – but at a moment when none of the country's leaders, civilian or military, were yet ready to assume full responsibility for it. When the politicians gathered at Versailles in 1919 drew the borders of new states – among them modern Poland, Austria, Czechoslovakia and Yugoslavia – Ukraine would not be among them. Still, the moment would not be entirely lost. As Richard Pipes has written, Ukraine's declaration of independence on 26 January 1918 'marked not the *dénouement* of the process of nation-forming in the Ukraine, but rather its serious beginning'.[22] The tumultuous few months of independence and the vigorous debate about national identity would change Ukraine for ever.

I

The Ukrainian Revolution, 1917

Ukrainian people! Your future is in your own hands. In this hour of trial, of total disorder and of collapse, prove by your unanimity and statesmanship that you, a nation of grain producers, can proudly and with dignity take your place as the equal of any organized powerful nation.

The Central Rada's First Universal, 1917[1]

We shall not enter the kingdom of socialism in white gloves on a polished floor.

Leon Trotsky, 1917[2]

In later years there would be bigger demonstrations, more eloquent speakers, more professional slogans. But the march that took place in Kyiv on the Sunday morning of 1 April 1917 was extraordinary because it was the first of its kind. Never before had the Ukrainian national movement shown itself in such force on the territory of what had been the Russian empire. But only weeks after the February revolution had toppled Tsar Nicholas II, anything seemed possible.

There were flags, blue and yellow for Ukraine as well as red for the socialist cause. The crowd, composed of children, soldiers, factory workers, marching bands and officials, carried banners – 'A free Ukraine in a free Russia!' or, using an ancient Cossack military title, 'Independent Ukraine with its own hetman!' Some carried portraits of the national poet, Taras Shevchenko. One after another, speakers called for the crowd to support the newly established Central

Rada – the 'central council' – which had formed a few days earlier and now claimed authority to rule Ukraine.

Finally, the man who had just been elected chairman of the Central Rada stepped up to the podium. Mykhailo Hrushevsky, bearded and bespectacled, was one of the intellectuals who had first put Ukraine at the centre of its own history. The author of the ten-volume *History of Ukraine-Rus'*, as well as many other books, Hrushevsky had turned to political activism at the very end of the nineteenth century when in December 1899, and in exile, he helped found the Ukrainian National Democratic Party in Habsburg Galicia. He returned to work in the Russian empire in 1905, but in 1914 he was arrested and once again went into exile. In the wake of the revolution, he had returned to Kyiv in triumph. The crowd now welcomed him with vigorous cheers: *Slava batkovi Hrushevskomu*, or 'Glory to Father Hrushevsky!'[3] He responded in kind: 'Let us all swear at this great moment as one man to take up the great cause unanimously, with one accord, and not to rest or cease our labour until we build that free Ukraine!' The crowd shouted back: 'We swear!'[4]

From the perspective of the present, the image of a historian as the leader of a national movement seems odd. But at the time it did not seem unusual at all. From the nineteenth century onwards, Ukrainian historians, like their counterparts in many of Europe's smaller nations, had deliberately set out to recover and articulate a national history that had long been subsumed into that of larger empires. From there, it was a short step to actual political activism. Just as Shevchenko had linked 'Ukrainianness' to the peasants' struggle against oppression, Hrushevsky's books also stressed the role of the 'people' in the political history of Ukraine, and emphasized the centrality of their resistance to various forms of tyranny. It was only logical that he should want to inspire the same people to act in the politics of the present, both in words and deeds. He was particularly interested in galvanizing peasants, and had written a Ukrainian history book, *About Old Times in Ukraine*, especially for a peasant audience. In 1917 it was reprinted three times.[5]

Hrushevsky was by no means the only intellectual whose literary and cultural output promoted the sovereignty of Ukraine. Heorhii Narbut, a graphic artist, also returned to Kyiv in 1917. He helped found the Ukrainian Academy of Fine Arts and designed a Ukrainian coat of arms, banknotes and stamps.[6] Volodymyr Vynnychenko, another member of the Central Rada, was a novelist and poet as well as a political figure. Without sovereignty – and without an actual state that could support politicians and bureaucrats – national feelings could only be channelled through literature and art. This was true all across Europe: before they attained statehood, poets, artists and writers had played important roles in the establishment of Polish, Italian and German national identity. Inside the Russian empire, both the Baltic States, which became independent in 1918, and Georgia and Armenia, which did not, experienced similar national revivals. The centrality of intellectuals to all of these national projects was fully understood at the time by their proponents and opponents alike. It explains why imperial Russia had banned Ukrainian books, schools and culture, and why their repression would later be of central concern to both Lenin and Stalin.

Although they began as self-appointed spokesmen for the national cause, the intellectuals of the Central Rada did seek democratic legitimacy. Operating out of a grand, white, neoclassical building in central Kyiv – appropriately, it had been previously used for meetings of the Ukrainian Club, a group of nationalist writers and civic activists – the Central Rada convened an All-Ukrainian National Congress on 19 April 1917.[7] More than 1,500 people, all elected one way or another by local councils and factories, converged on the National Philharmonic concert hall in Kyiv to offer their support for the new Ukrainian government. Further congresses of veterans, peasants and workers were held in Kyiv that summer.

The Central Rada also sought to build coalitions with a range of political groups, including Jewish and other minority organizations. Even the radical left wing of the Ukrainian Socialist Revolutionary Party – a large peasant populist party known as *Borotbysty* after its newspaper *Borotba* ('Struggle') – came to support the Central Rada. Some of the peasantry did too. Between 1914 and 1918 the army of the Russian tsar had contained more than 3 million Ukrainian conscripts, and the Austro-Hungarian army had included an additional 250,000. Many of these peasant-soldiers had shot at one another across the muddy trenches of Galicia.[8] But after the war ended, some

300,000 men who had been serving in 'Ukrainianized' battalions, composed of Ukrainian peasants, declared their loyalty to the new state. Some brought back weapons and joined the new Central Rada militia. They were motivated by a desire to return to their homeland, but also by the new Ukrainian government's promises of revolutionary change and national renewal.[9]

In subsequent months the Central Rada did enjoy some popular success, not least thanks to its radical rhetoric. Reflecting the left-wing ideals of the times, it proposed compulsory land reform, the redistribution of property from large landowners, both monasteries and private estates, to the peasants. 'No one can know better what we need and what laws are best for us,' declared the Central Rada in June 1917 in the first of a series of 'Universals', manifestos addressed to a broad audience:

> No one can know better than our peasants how to manage their own land. Therefore, we wish that after all the lands throughout Russia held by the nobility, the state, the monasteries and the tsar, have been confiscated and have become the property of the people, and after a law concerning this has been enacted by the All-Russian constituent assembly, the right to administer Ukrainian lands shall belong to us, to our Ukrainian assembly . . . They elected us, the Ukrainian Central Rada, from among their midst and directed us . . . to create a new order in free autonomous Ukraine.[10]

That same Universal called for 'autonomy'. In November, the third and final Universal would declare the independence of the Ukrainian National Republic and call for elections to a constituent assembly.[11]

Although some people predictably opposed it, the revival of the Ukrainian language was also popular, especially among the peasantry. As it had in the past, Ukrainian again became synonymous with economic and political liberation: once officials and bureaucrats began to speak Ukrainian, peasants had access to courts and government offices. The public use of their native language also became a source of pride, serving as a 'profound base of emotional support' for the national movement.[12] An explosion of dictionaries and orthographies followed. Between 1917 and 1919, Ukrainian printers published fifty-nine books devoted to the Ukrainian language, as compared to a total of eleven during the entire preceding century. Among them were three Ukrainian-Russian dictionaries and fifteen Russian-Ukrainian ones. Heavy demand for the latter came from the large number of Russian speakers who suddenly had to get by in Ukrainian, not a prospect that they all enjoyed.[13]

During its brief existence, the Ukrainian government also had some diplomatic successes, many of which subsequently faded from memory. Following its declaration of independence on 26 January 1918, the Ukrainian Republic's twenty-eight-year-old Foreign Minister, Oleksandr Shulhyn (also a historian by training), won de facto recognition for his state from all of the main European powers, including France, Great Britain, Austria-Hungary, Germany, Bulgaria, Turkey and even Soviet Russia. In December the United States sent a diplomat to open a consulate in Kyiv.[14] In February 1918 a delegation of Ukrainian officials at Brest-Litovsk concluded a peace treaty with the Central Powers, a deal separate from the better-known one signed by the new leaders of Soviet Russia a few weeks later. The young Ukrainian delegation impressed everyone. One of their German interlocutors remembered that 'they behaved bravely, and in their stubbornness forced [the German negotiator] to agree to everything that was important from their national point of view'.[15]

But it was insufficient: the spread of national consciousness, foreign recognition and even the Brest-Litovsk treaty were not enough to build the Ukrainian state. The Central Rada's proposed reforms – especially its plans to take land from estate owners without compensation – brought about confusion and chaos in the countryside. The public parades, the flags and the freedom that Hrushevsky and his followers greeted with so much optimism in the spring of 1917 did not lead to the creation of a functioning bureaucracy, a public administration to enforce its reforms or an army effective enough to repel invasion and protect its borders. By the end of 1917 all the military powers of the region, including the brand-new Red Army, the White Armies of the old regime, and troops from Germany and Austria, were making plans to occupy Ukraine. To different degrees, each of them would attack Ukrainian nationalists, Ukrainian nationalism and even the Ukrainian language along with Ukrainian land.

*

Lenin authorized the first Soviet assault on Ukraine in January 1918, and briefly set up an anti-Ukrainian regime in Kyiv in February, of which more later. This first Soviet attempt to conquer Ukraine ended within a few weeks when the German and Austrian armies arrived and declared they intended to 'enforce' the treaty of Brest-Litovsk. Instead of saving the liberal legislators of the Central Rada, however, they threw their support behind Pavlo Skoropadsky, a Ukrainian general who dressed in dramatic uniforms, complete with Cossack swords and hats.

For a few months Skoropadsky gave a sliver of hope to adherents of the old regime while maintaining some of the attributes of Ukrainian autonomy. He founded the first Ukrainian Academy of Science and the first national library, and used Ukrainian in official business. He identified himself as a Ukrainian, taking the title of 'hetman'. But at the same time Skoropadsky brought back tsarist laws and tsarist officials, and advocated reintegration with a future Russian state. Under Skoropadsky's rule, Kyiv even became, briefly, a haven for refugees from Moscow and St Petersburg. In his satirical novel *White Guard* (1926), Mikhail Bulgakov, who lived in Kyiv during that era, remembered them:

> Gray-haired bankers and their wives had fled, as had smooth operators who had left their trusty assistants in Moscow . . . Journalists had fled, from Moscow and St. Petersburg, venal, greedy cowards. Demimondaines. Virtuous ladies from aristocratic families. Their gentle daughters. Pale Petersburg debauchees with lips painted carmine red. Secretaries to department directors fled, poets and usurers, gendarmes and actresses from the imperial theatres.[16]

Skoropadsky also reinforced the old ownership laws and withdrew promises of land reform. Unsurprisingly, this decision was deeply unpopular among the peasantry, who 'hated that very same Hetman as though he were a mad dog' and didn't want to hear about reform from 'bastard lords'.[17] Opposition to what was quickly perceived as a German puppet government began to organize itself into various militant forms: 'Ex-colonels, self-styled generals, Cossack *otamany* and *batky* [local warlords] blossomed like wild roses in this revolutionary summertime.'[18]

By the middle of 1918 the national movement had regrouped under the leadership of Symon Petliura, a social democrat with a talent for paramilitary organization. His contemporaries were of radically different minds about him. Some perceived him as a would-be dictator, others as a prophet before his time. Bulgakov, who disliked the idea of Ukrainian nationalism, dismissed Petliura as 'a legend, a mirage . . . a word that combined unslaked fury, and the thirst for peasant vengeance'.[19] As a young man Petliura had impressed Serhii Yefremov, an activist contemporary, with his 'boastfulness, doctrinairism and flippancy'. Later, Yefremov reversed his views and declared that Petliura had evolved into 'the only unquestionably honest person' produced by the Ukrainian revolution. While others gave up or engaged in petty infighting, 'only Petliura stood his ground and did not waver'.[20] Petliura himself later wrote that he wanted the whole truth about his actions revealed: 'the negative aspects of my personality, my actions, must be illuminated, not covered up . . . For me, the judgement of history has begun. I am not afraid of it.'[21]

History's judgement of Petliura has remained ambivalent. Certainly he was brave enough to seize an opportunity, reckoning that the end of the First World War gave Ukraine's national movement one more chance. As German troops withdrew from the country, he patched together some of the 'ex-colonels, self-styled generals, Cossack *otamany* and *batky*' into a pro-Ukrainian force known as the Directory, and laid siege to the capital. Although the Russian-language press reviled the Directory as 'bands of thieves' and called their coup a 'scandal', Skoropadsky's forces crumbled with amazing speed, almost without fighting.[22] On 14 December 1918, Petliura's troops marched into a surprised Kyiv, Odessa and Mykolaiv, and power changed hands yet again.

The Directory's rule would be short and violent, not least because Petliura never managed to obtain complete legitimacy and could not enforce the rule of law. Economically, the Directory, like the Central Rada before it, was far to the left. Reflecting the increasingly radical views of its supporters, the leadership convened not a parliament but a 'Workers' Congress' from representatives of the peasants, the workers and the working intelligentsia. But Petliura's peasant army was the true source of his authority and, in the words of one of his opponents, it made for 'neither a good government nor a good army'.[23] Many of its members were 'adventurers' who wore a wide variety of uniforms and Cossack costumes and were perfectly capable of pulling out their revolvers to rob anyone who simply looked wealthy. The inhabitants of bourgeois Kyiv took turns standing sentry outside their apartment blocks.[24]

Inside the city one of the few policies that the Directory 'not only declared but carried out', in the snide words of one memoirist, was the removal of Russian-language signs in Kyiv and their replacement with Ukrainian ones: 'Russian wasn't even allowed to remain alongside Ukrainian.' Allegedly, this wholesale change was ordered because many of the Directory's troops came from Galicia, spoke very little Russian, and were horrified to find themselves at sea in a Russian-speaking city. The result was that 'for a few jolly days, the whole city was changed into an artists' workshop', and the deep connection between language and power was driven home to the residents of Kyiv once again.[25]

Outside the capital, Petliura controlled very little territory. Bulgakov described the Kyiv of this era as a city that had 'police . . . a ministry, even an army, and newspapers of various names, but what was going on around them, in the real Ukraine, which was bigger than France and had tens of millions of people in it – no one knew that'.[26] Richard Pipes writes that in Kyiv 'edicts were issued, cabinet crises were resolved, diplomatic talks were carried on – but the rest of the country lived its own existence where the only effective regime was that of the gun'.[27]

By the end of 1919 the national movement, launched with so much energy and hope, was in disarray. Hrushevsky, forced out of Kyiv by the fighting, would soon go abroad.[28] Ukrainians themselves were profoundly divided along many lines, between those who supported the old order and those who did not; those who preferred to stay linked to Russia and those who did not; those who supported land reform and those who did not. The competition over language had intensified and become irreconcilably bitter. The refugees from Moscow and St Petersburg were already moving on to Crimea, Odessa and exile.[29] But the greatest political divide – and the one that would shape the course of the subsequent decades – was between those who shared the ideals of the Ukrainian national movement and those who supported the Bolsheviks, a revolutionary group with a very different ideology altogether.

At the beginning of 1917, the Bolsheviks were a small minority party in Russia, the radical faction of what had been the Marxist Russian Social Democratic and Labour Party. But they spent the year agitating in the Russian streets, using simple slogans such as 'Land, Bread and Peace' designed to appeal to the widest numbers of soldiers, workers and peasants. Their coup d'état in October (7 November according to the 'new calendar' they later adopted) put them in power amidst conditions of total chaos. Led by Lenin, a paranoid, conspiratorial and fundamentally undemocratic man, the Bolsheviks believed themselves to be the 'vanguard of the proletariat'; they would call their regime the 'dictatorship of the proletariat'. They sought absolute power, and eventually abolished all other political parties and opponents through terror, violence and vicious propaganda campaigns.

In early 1917 the Bolsheviks had even fewer followers in Ukraine. The party had 22,000 Ukrainian members, most of whom were in the large cities and industrial centres of Donetsk and Kryvyi Rih. Few spoke Ukrainian. More than half considered themselves to be Russians. About one in six was Jewish. A tiny number, including a few who would later play major roles in the Soviet Ukrainian government, did believe in the possibility of an autonomous, Bolshevik Ukraine. But Heorhii Piatakov – who was born in Ukraine but did not consider himself to be Ukrainian – spoke for the majority when he told a meeting of Kyiv Bolsheviks in June 1917, just a few weeks after Hrushevsky's speech, that 'we should not support the Ukrainians'. Ukraine, he explained, was not a 'distinct economic region'. More to the point, Russia relied on Ukraine's sugar, grain and coal, and Russia was Piatakov's priority.[30]

The sentiment was not new: disdain for the very idea of a Ukrainian state had been an integral part of Bolshevik thinking even before the revolution. In large part this was simply because all of the leading Bolsheviks, among them Lenin, Stalin, Trotsky, Piatakov, Zinoviev,

Kamenev and Bukharin, were men raised and educated in the Russian empire, and the Russian empire did not recognize such a thing as 'Ukraine' in the province that they knew as 'Southwest Russia'. The city of Kyiv was, to them, the ancient capital of Kyivan Rus', the kingdom that they remembered as the ancestor of Russia. In school, in the press and in daily life they would have absorbed Russia's prejudices against a language that was widely described as a dialect of Russian, and a people widely perceived as primitive former serfs.

All Russian political parties at the time, from the Bolsheviks to the centrists to the far right, shared this contempt. Many refused to use the name 'Ukraine' at all.[31] Even Russian liberals refused to recognize the legitimacy of the Ukrainian national movement. This blind spot – and the consequent refusal of any Russian groups to create an anti-Bolshevik coalition with the Ukrainians – was ultimately one of the reasons why the White Armies failed to win the civil war.[32]

In addition to their national prejudice, the Bolsheviks had particular political reasons for disliking the idea of Ukrainian independence. Ukraine was still overwhelmingly a peasant nation, and according to the Marxist theory that the Bolshevik leadership constantly read and discussed, peasants were at best an ambivalent asset. In an 1852 essay Marx famously explained that they were not a 'class' and thus had no class consciousness: 'They are consequently incapable of enforcing their class interest in their own names, whether through a parliament or through a convention. They cannot represent themselves, they must be represented.'[33]

Although Marx believed that peasants had no important role in the coming revolution, Lenin, who was more pragmatic, modified these views to a degree. He thought that the peasants were indeed potentially revolutionary – he approved of their desire for radical land reform – but believed that they needed to be guided by the more progressive working class. 'Not all peasants fighting for land and freedom are fully aware of what their struggle implies,' he wrote in 1905. Class-conscious workers would need to teach them that real revolution required not just land reform but the 'fight against the rule of capital'. Ominously, Lenin also suspected that many farmers of small-holdings, because they owned property, actually thought like capitalist smallholders. This explained why 'not all small peasants join the ranks of fighters for socialism'.[34] This idea – that the smallest landowners, later called kulaks, were a fundamentally counter-revolutionary, capitalist force – would have great consequences some years later.

The Bolsheviks' ambivalence about nationalism also led them to be suspicious of Ukraine's drive for independence. Both Marx and Lenin had convoluted and constantly evolving views of nationalism, which they sometimes saw as a revolutionary force and at other times as a distraction from the real goal of universal socialism. Marx understood that the democratic revolutions of 1848 had been inspired in part by national feelings, but he believed these 'bourgeois nationalist' sentiments to be a temporary phenomenon, a mere stage on the road to communist internationalism. As the state faded away, so, somehow, would nations and national sentiments. 'The supremacy of the proletariat will cause them to vanish still faster.'[35]

Lenin also argued for cultural autonomy and national self-determination, except when it didn't suit him. Even before the revolution, he disapproved of non-Russian language schools, whether Yiddish or Ukrainian, on the grounds that they would create unhelpful divisions within the working class.[36] Although he theoretically favoured granting the right of secession to the non-Russian regions of the Russian empire, which included Georgia, Armenia and the Central Asian states, he seems not to have seriously believed it would ever happen. Besides, recognition of the 'right' of secession didn't mean that Lenin supported secession itself. In the case of Ukraine, he approved of Ukrainian nationalism when it opposed the tsar or the Provisional Government in 1917, and disapproved of it when he thought it threatened the unity of the Russian and Ukrainian proletariat.[37]

To this complicated ideological puzzle, Stalin would add his own thoughts. He was the party's expert on nationalities, and was initially far less flexible than Lenin. Stalin's essay, 'Marxism and the National Question', had argued in 1913 that nationalism was a distraction from the cause of socialism, and that comrades 'must work solidly and indefatigably against the fog of nationalism, no matter from what quarter it proceeds'.[38] By 1925 his thoughts had evolved further into an argument about nationalism as an essentially peasant force. National movements, he declared, needed peasants in order to exist: 'The peasant question is the basis, the quintessence, of the national question. That explains the fact that the peasantry constitutes the main army of the national movement, that there is no powerful national movement without the peasant army . . .'[39]

That argument, which clearly reflected his observation of events in Ukraine, would become more significant later. For if there is no powerful national movement without the peasant army, then someone who wished to destroy a national movement might well want to begin by destroying the peasantry.

In the end, ideology would matter less to the Bolsheviks than their personal experiences in Ukraine, and especially of the civil war there. For everyone in the Communist Party, the civil war era was a true watershed, personally as well as politically. At the beginning of 1917 few of them had much to show for their lives. They were obscure ideologues, unsuccessful by any standard. If they earned any money, it was by writing for illegal newspapers; they had been in and out of prison, they had complicated personal lives, they had no experience of government or management.

Unexpectedly, the Russian revolution put them at the centre of international events. It also brought them fame and power for the very first time. It rescued them from obscurity, and validated their ideology. The success of the revolution proved, to the Bolshevik leaders as well as to many others, that Marx and Lenin had been right.

But the revolution also quickly forced them to defend their power, presenting them not just with ideological counter-revolutionaries but with a real and very bloody counter-revolution, one that had to be immediately defeated. The subsequent civil war forced them to create an army, a political police force and a propaganda machine. Above all, the civil war taught the Bolsheviks lessons about nationalism, economic policy, food distribution and violence, upon which they later drew. The Bolsheviks' experiences in Ukraine were also very different from their experiences in Russia, including a spectacular defeat that nearly toppled their nascent state. Many subsequent Bolshevik attitudes towards Ukraine, including their lack of faith in the loyalty of the peasantry, their suspicion of Ukrainian intellectuals, and their dislike of the Ukrainian Communist Party, have their origins in this period.

Indeed, the experience of the civil war, especially the civil war in Ukraine, shaped the views of Stalin himself. On the eve of the Russian Revolution, Stalin was in his late thirties, with little to show for his life. He had 'no money, no permanent residence, and no profession other than punditry', as a recent biographer has written.[40] Born in Georgia, educated in a seminary, his reputation in the underground rested on his talent for robbing banks. He had been in and out of prison several times. At the time of the February revolution in 1917, he was in exile in a village north of the Arctic Circle. When Tsar Nicholas II was deposed, Stalin returned to Petrograd (the name of St Petersburg, the Russian capital, had been Russified in 1914, and would be changed to Leningrad in 1924).

The Bolshevik coup d'état in October 1917 unseated the Provisional Government and brought Stalin his first, glorious taste of real political power.[41] As the People's Commissar for Nationalities, he was a member of the first Bolshevik government. In that role he was directly responsible for negotiating with all the non-Russian nations and peoples who had belonged to the Russian empire – and, more importantly, for convincing, or forcing, them to submit to Soviet rule. In his dealings with Ukraine he had two clear and immediate priorities, both dictated by the extremity of the situation. The first was to undermine the national movement, clearly the Bolsheviks' most important rival in Ukraine. The second was to get hold of Ukrainian grain. He embarked on both of those tasks only days after the Bolsheviks took power.

Already in December 1917, in the pages of *Pravda*, Stalin was denouncing the Central Rada's Third Universal, the manifesto that had proclaimed the Ukrainian People's Republic and laid out the borders of Ukraine. Who, he asked rhetorically, would support an independent Ukraine:

Big landowners in Ukraine, then Aleksei Kaledin [a White Army general] and his 'military government' on the Don, i.e. Cossack landowners . . . behind both lurks the great Russian bourgeoisie which

used to be a furious enemy of all demands of the Ukrainian people,
but which now supports the Central Rada . . .

By contrast, 'all Ukrainian workers and the poorest section of the
peasantry' opposed the Central Rada, he claimed, which was hardly
the truth either.[42]

Stalin followed up his public denunciations of the Central Rada
with what would later be termed 'active measures', intended to destabilize the Ukrainian government. Local Bolsheviks tried to
establish so-called independent 'Soviet republics' in Donetsk-Kryvyi
Rih, Odessa, Tavriia and the Don province – tiny, Moscow-backed
mini-states, which were of course not independent at all.[43] The Bolsheviks also attempted to stage a coup in Kyiv; after that failed, they
created an 'alternative' Central Executive Committee of Ukraine and
then a 'Soviet government' in Kharkiv, a more reliably Russian-
speaking city. Later, they would make Kharkiv the capital of Ukraine,
even though, in 1918, only a handful of Kharkiv Bolshevik leaders
spoke Ukrainian.[44]

As the Bolsheviks consolidated their rule in Russia, the Red Army
kept pushing south. Finally, on 9 February 1918, even as the Central
Rada leaders were negotiating in Brest-Litovsk, Kyiv fell to Bolshevik
forces for the first time. This first, brief, Bolshevik occupation brought
with it not only communist ideology but also a clearly Russian
agenda. General Mikhail Muraviev, the commanding officer, declared
he was bringing back Russian rule from the 'far North', and ordered
the immediate execution of suspected nationalists. His men shot anyone heard speaking Ukrainian in public and destroyed any evidence
of Ukrainian rule, including the Ukrainian street signs that had
replaced Russian street signs only weeks before.[45] The 1918 Bolshevik
bombardment of the Ukrainian capital deliberately targeted Hrushevsky's home, library and collections of ancient documents.[46]

Although the Bolsheviks controlled Kyiv for just a few weeks, this
first occupation also gave Lenin a taste of what Ukraine could bring
to the communist project. Desperate to feed the revolutionary workers who had brought him to power, he immediately sent the Red
Army to Ukraine accompanied by 'requisition detachments', teams of
men instructed to confiscate the peasants' grain. He named Sergo

Ordzhonikidze, a leading Georgian Bolshevik, as 'extraordinary pleni-potentiary commissar' in charge of requisitioning Ukrainian grain.[47] *Pravda*'s editorial board trumpeted these soldiers' success, and assured its urban Russian readers that the Soviet leadership had already begun to take 'extraordinary measures' to procure grain from the peasants.[48]

Behind the scenes, Lenin's telegrams to the Ukrainian front could hardly have been more explicit. 'For God's sake,' he wrote in January 1918, 'use all energy and all revolutionary measures to send grain, grain and more grain!! Otherwise Petrograd may starve to death. Use special trains and special detachments. Collect and store. Escort the trains. Inform us every day. For God's sake!'[49] The rapid loss of Ukraine to the German and Austrian armies in early March infuriated Moscow. A furious Stalin denounced not only the Ukrainian national movement and its recalcitrant peasant supporters but also the Ukrainian Bolsheviks, who had fled Kharkiv and set up another messy 'Soviet Ukrainian government in exile' just over the Russian border in Rostov. Instinctively, he disliked the idea of 'Ukrainian Bolsheviks', and felt they should give up their efforts to create a separate party. From Moscow, he attacked the Rostov group: 'Enough playing at a government and a republic. It's time to stop that game; enough is enough.'[50]

In response, one of the few Ukrainian speakers in Rostov sent a protest note to the Council of People's Commissars in Moscow. Stalin's statement, wrote Mykola Skrypnyk, had helped 'discredit Soviet power in Ukraine'. Skrypnyk did believe in the possibility of 'Ukrainian Bolshevism' and was an early champion of what would later be called 'national communism', the belief that communism could have separate forms in separate countries and was not incompatible with national sentiment in Ukraine. He argued that the brief rule of the Central Rada had created a real desire for Ukrainian sovereignty, and proposed that the Bolsheviks should recognize and incorporate that desire too. The Soviet government, he argued, should not 'base their decisions on the opinion of some people's commissar of the Russian federation, but should instead listen to the masses, the working people of Ukraine'.[51]

In the short run, Skrypnyk won this exchange, but not because the

Bolsheviks had decided to listen to the masses or the working people. In the wake of his first defeat in Ukraine, Lenin had simply decided to adopt different tactics. Using the methods of what would (much later, though in a similar context) be called 'hybrid warfare', he ordered his forces to re-enter Ukraine in disguise. They were to hide the fact that they were a Russian force fighting for a unified Bolshevik Russia. Instead, they called themselves a 'Soviet Ukrainian liberation movement', precisely in order to confuse nationalists. The idea was to use nationalist rhetoric cynically, in order to convince people to accept Soviet power. In a telegram to the Red Army commander on the ground, Lenin explained:

> With the advance of our troops to the west and into Ukraine, regional provisional Soviet governments are created whose task it is to strengthen the local Soviets. This circumstance has the advantage of taking away from the chauvinists of Ukraine, Lithuania, Latvia and Estonia the possibility of regarding the advance of our detachments as occupation and creates a favourable atmosphere for a further advance of our troops.[52]

Military commanders, in other words, were responsible for helping to create the pro-Soviet 'national' governments that would welcome them. The idea, as Lenin explained, was to ensure that the population of Ukraine would treat them as 'liberators', and not as foreign occupiers.

At no point in 1918, or later, did Lenin, Stalin, or anyone else in the Bolshevik leadership ever believe that any Soviet-Ukrainian state would enjoy true sovereignty. The Ukrainian revolutionary council formed on 17 November included Piatakov and Volodymyr Zatonskyi, both pro-Moscow 'Ukrainian' officials – as well as Volodymyr Antonov-Ovsienko, the Red Army's military commander in Ukraine, and Stalin himself. The 'Provisional Revolutionary government of Ukraine', formed on 28 November, was led by Christian Rakovsky, who was Bulgarian by origin. Among other things, Rakovsky declared that all demands to make Ukrainian the official language of the country were 'injurious to the Ukrainian revolution'.[53]

The general disorder made it easy to carry out this hybrid war. The Red Army began its assault on the republic at exactly the same time as the Bolsheviks began to negotiate an agreement with Petliura. The officials of the Directory furiously denounced this two-faced policy: Georgii Chicherin, the Bolshevik People's Commissar for Foreign Affairs, blandly replied that Moscow had nothing to do with the troops moving onto Ukrainian soil. He blamed the military action on that territory on 'the army of the Ukrainian Soviet government which is completely independent'.[54]

The Directory protested that this was a flat-out lie. They could see perfectly well that the 'army of the Ukrainian Soviet government' was in actual fact the Red Army. But the Directory went on protesting, right up until January 1919 when the Red Army forced the Ukrainian government to withdraw from Kyiv altogether.[55]

The second Bolshevik occupation of Ukraine began in January and would last for six months. During that period Moscow never controlled the whole territory of what later became the Ukrainian Republic. Even in districts where the Bolsheviks exercised authority in the towns and cities, the villages often remained under the sway of local partisan leaders or 'otamans', some loyal to Petliura and some not. In many places Bolshevik authority hardly extended beyond the train stations. Nevertheless, even that short period of partial rule gave the Bolshevik leaders of the Ukrainian Soviet Republic the opportunity to show their true colours. Whatever theoretical independence the Ukrainian communist leaders had on paper, they had none in practice.

Moreover, whatever ideas they had about Ukraine's economic development were also quickly overwhelmed by another priority. No considerations of Marxist theory, no arguments about nationalism or sovereignty, mattered as much to the Bolsheviks in that year as the need to feed the workers of Moscow and Petrograd. By 1919, Lenin's telegram – 'For God's sake, use all energy and all revolutionary measures to send grain, grain and more grain!!!' – had become the single most important description of Bolshevik attitudes and practice in Ukraine.

The Bolshevik obsession with food was no accident: The Russian empire had been struggling with food supplies ever since the outbreak of the First World War. At the beginning of the conflict with Germany, imperial Russia centralized and nationalized its food distribution system, creating administrative chaos and shortages. A Special Council for Discussing and Coordinating Measures for Food Supply, a state food distribution organization and a clear precedent for the Soviet organizations that followed, was put in control. Instead of ameliorating the situation, the Special Council's drive to 'eliminate middlemen' and to create a supposedly more efficient, non-capitalist form of grain distribution had actually exacerbated the supply crisis.[56]

The resulting food shortages sparked the February revolution in 1917 and propelled the Bolsheviks to power a few months later. Morgan Philips Price, a British journalist, described the atmosphere of that year:

> Involuntarily the conversation seemed to be drifting on to one main topic, which was evidently engaging the attention of all: bread and peace . . . Everyone knew that the railways were no longer equal to the transport burden, that the cereals formerly exported to Western Europe were now more than absorbed by the army, that the cultivated area had fallen 10 per cent last year, and was certain to fall more this spring, that the workmen of several big towns had been several days without bread, while Grand Dukes and profiteers had large stores in their houses.[57]

Price saw women queuing for rations: 'Their pale faces and anxious eyes betrayed the fear that some calamity was approaching.'[58] He visited the barracks of one of the Moscow regiments, where he found that 'food rations were the subject of debate, and someone with a louder voice and more initiative than the rest proposed a delegation of three to the commanding officer to demand the immediate increase of these rations'. From food rations, the group moved on to the war, and then to the ownership of land: 'This embryo Soldiers' Soviet had, at any rate, become a centre for exchange of views on subjects which till yesterday were forbidden to all outside the charmed circle of the ruling caste. The next stage of the Revolution had been reached.'

Later, Price observed that hunger, at least in its early stages, made people 'more rapacious'. The lack of food led people to question the system, to demand change, even to call for violence.[59]

The link between food and power was something that the

Bolsheviks also understood very well. Both before, during and after the revolution, all sides also realized that constant shortages made food supplies a hugely significant political tool. Whoever had bread had followers, soldiers, loyal friends. Whoever could not feed his people lost support rapidly. In 1921, when an American relief mission was negotiating to enter the Soviet Union, one of its representatives told the Soviet negotiator (and later Foreign Minister), Maksim Litvinov, that 'we do not come to fight Russia, we come to feed'. According to an American journalist, Litvinov responded very succinctly, in English: 'Yes, but food is a *veppon* . . .'[60]

Lenin thought so too. But the revolutionary leader did not therefore conclude that the Special Council's nationalized food distribution system was wrong. Instead, he decided that its methods were insufficiently harsh, especially in Ukraine. In 1919, Rakovsky, the Bolshevik leader in charge of Ukraine, echoed this sentiment in a frank comment to a party congress. 'We went into the Ukraine at a time when Soviet Russia went through a very serious production crisis,' he explained: 'our aim was to exploit it to the utmost to relieve the crisis'.[61] From the very beginning of their rule, the Bolsheviks assumed that the exploitation of Ukraine was the price that had to be paid in order to maintain control of Russia. As one of them wrote years later, 'the fate of the revolution depended on our ability to reliably supply the proletariat and the army with bread'.[62]

The urgent need for grain spawned an extreme set of policies, known then and later as 'War Communism'. Launched in Russia in 1918 and brought to Ukraine after the second Bolshevik invasion in early 1919, War Communism meant the militarization of all economic relationships. In the countryside, the system was very simple: take control of grain, at gunpoint, and then redistribute it to soldiers, factory workers, party members and others deemed 'essential' by the state.

In 1918 many would have found this system familiar. The Russian imperial government, tormented by wartime food shortages, had begun to confiscate grain at gunpoint – a policy known as *prodrazvyorstka* – as early as 1916. In March 1917 the Provisional Government had also decreed that peasants should sell all grain to the state at prices dictated by the state, with the exception of what they needed for their own sowing and consumption.[63] The Bolsheviks followed suit. In May 1918 the Council of People's Commissars followed up on tsarist policy and established a 'food-supply dictatorship'. The Commissariat of Food Supply created a 'food-supply army', which was to be deployed on the 'food-supply front'.[64]

But despite the militarized language, in practice War Communism meant that most people went hungry. To obtain any food at all, in the years between 1916 and 1918 the majority of Russians and Ukrainians used the black market, not the non-existent state companies.[65] In Boris Pasternak's *Doctor Zhivago*, the doctor's wife seeks food and fuel in post-revolutionary Moscow by 'wandering the nearby lanes, where *muzhiks* [peasants] sometimes turned up from their suburban villages with vegetables and potatoes. You had to catch them. Peasants carrying loads were arrested.' Eventually she found a man selling green birch logs, and exchanged them for a 'small mirrored wardrobe'. The peasant took it as a present for his wife. The two made 'future arrangements about potatoes'.[66] Such was the interaction between city and countryside in the years of War Communism.

City-country barter remained an enduring part of the economic system for many years after that. Even in 1921, when the civil war was technically over, an American charitable delegation visiting Moscow discovered a very similar set of arrangements. On Kuznetskii Most, once an important commercial street, old women and children were selling fruit from baskets outside the empty, shuttered shops. Vegetables and meat were unavailable except in the open-air markets. In the evening the Americans discovered the source of these goods. Returning to the railway car where they were due to spend the night, they watched a 'perfect mob' of men, women and children push and shove one another in order to get onto a train heading out of the city. What they deemed a 'very fantastic sight in the half twilight' was in fact the Russian food distribution network, thousands of individual traders going back and forth from the cities to the countryside.[67]

During those years these illegal markets gave many people access to food, especially individuals not on special government lists. But the Bolsheviks not only refused to accept these street bazaars, they blamed them for the continuing crisis. Year after year the Soviet leadership was surprised by the hunger and shortages that their 'confiscate and redistribute' system had created. But because state intervention was supposed to make people richer, not poorer, and because the Bolsheviks never blamed any failure on their own policies, let alone on their rigid ideology, they instead zeroed in on the small traders and black marketeers – 'speculators' – who made their living by physically carrying food from farms into towns. In January 1919, Lenin himself would denounce them as ideological enemies:

> All talk on this theme [private trade], all attempts to encourage it are a great danger, a retreat, a step back from the socialist construction that the Commissariat of Food is carrying out amid unbelievable difficulties in a struggle with millions of speculators left to us by capitalism.

From there, he needed to make only a short logical leap to the denunciation of the peasants who sold grain to these 'speculators'. Lenin, already suspicious of the peasantry as an insufficiently revolutionary class, was perfectly clear about the danger of urban-rural trade:

> The peasant must choose: free trade in grain – which means speculation in grain; freedom for the rich to get richer and the poor to get poorer and starve; the return of the absolute landowners and the capitalists; and the severing of the union of the peasants and workers – or delivery of his grain surpluses to the state at fixed prices.[68]

But words were not enough. Faced with widespread hunger, the Bolsheviks took more extreme measures. Usually, historians ascribe Lenin's turn towards political violence in 1918 – a set of policies known as the Red Terror – to his struggle against his political opponents.[69] But even before the Red Terror was formally declared in September, and even before he ordered mass arrests and executions, Lenin was already discarding law and precedent in response to economic disaster: the workers of Moscow and Petrograd were down to one ounce of bread per day. Morgan Philips Price observed that Soviet authorities were barely able to feed the delegates during the Congress of Soviets in the winter of 1918: 'Only a very few wagons of flour had arrived during the week at the Petrograd railway stations.'[70] Worse, 'complaints in the working-class quarters of Moscow began to be loud. The Bolshevik regime must get food or go, one used to hear.'[71]

In the spring of 1918 these conditions inspired Lenin's first *chrezvychaishchina* – a phrase translated by one scholar as 'a special condition in public life when any feeling of legality is lost and arbitrariness in power prevails'.[72] Extraordinary measures, or *chrezvychainye mery*, were needed to fight the peasantry whom Lenin accused of holding back surplus grain for their own purposes. To force the peasants to give up their grain and to fight the counterrevolution, Lenin also eventually created the *chrezvychainaia komissiia* – the 'extraordinary commission', also known as the Che-Ka, or Cheka. This was the first name given to the Soviet secret police, later known as the GPU, the OGPU, the NKVD and finally the KGB.

The emergency subsumed everything else. Lenin ordered anyone not directly involved in the military conflict in the spring and summer of 1918 to bring food back to the capital. Stalin was put in charge of 'provisions matters in southern Russia', a task that suddenly mattered a lot more than his tasks as Nationalities Commissar. He set out for Tsaritsyn, a city on the Volga, accompanied by two armoured trains and 450 Red Army soldiers. His assignment: to collect grain for Moscow. His first telegram to Lenin, sent on 7 July, reported that he had discovered a 'bacchanalia of profiteering'. He set out his strategy: 'we won't show mercy to anyone, not to ourselves, not to others – but we will bring you bread.'[73]

In subsequent years Stalin's Tsaritsyn escapade was mostly remembered for the fact that it inspired his first public quarrel with the man who would become his great rival, Leon Trotsky. But in the context of Stalin's later policy in Ukraine, it had another kind of significance: the brutal tactics he used to procure grain in Tsaritsyn presaged those he would employ to procure grain in Ukraine more than a decade later. Within days of arriving in the city Stalin created a revolutionary military council, established a Cheka division, and began to 'cleanse' Tsaritsyn of counter-revolutionaries. Denouncing the local generals as 'bourgeois specialists' and 'lifeless pen-pushers, completely ill-suited to civil war', he took them and others into custody and placed them on a barge in the centre of the Volga.[74] In conjunction with several units of Bolshevik troops from Donetsk, and with the help of Klement Voroshilov and Sergo Ordzhonikidze, two men who would remain close associates, Stalin authorized arrests and beatings on a broad scale, followed by mass executions. Red Army thugs robbed local merchants and peasants of their grain; the Cheka then fabricated criminal cases against them – another harbinger of what was to come – and caught up random people in the sweep as well.[75]

But the grain was put on trains for the north – which meant that, from Stalin's point of view, this particularly brutal form of War Communism was successful. The populace of Tsaritsyn paid a huge price and, at least in Trotsky's view, so did the army.[76] After Trotsky protested against Stalin's behaviour in Tsaritsyn, Lenin eventually removed Stalin from the city. But his time there remained important to Stalin, so much so that in 1925 he renamed Tsaritsyn 'Stalingrad'.

During their second occupation of Ukraine in 1919, the Bolsheviks never had the same degree of control as Stalin had over Tsaritsyn. But over the six months when they were at least nominally in charge of the republic, they went as far as they could. All of their obsessions – their hatred of trade, private property, nationalism, the peasantry – were on full display in Ukraine. But their particular obsession with food, and with food collection in Ukraine, overshadowed almost every other decision they made.

When they arrived in Kyiv for the second time, the Bolsheviks moved very quickly. They immediately dropped the pretence that they were a force for 'Ukrainian liberation'. Instead, they once again followed the precedent set by the tsars: they banned Ukrainian newspapers, stopped the use of Ukrainian in schools, and shut down Ukrainian theatres. The Cheka carried out rapid arrests of Ukrainian intellectuals, who were accused of 'separatism'. Rakovsky, the Ukrainian party boss, refused to use or even to recognize the Ukrainian language. Pavlo Khrystiuk, a Ukrainian Socialist Revolutionary, later remembered that 'Russian troops', many drawn from the ranks of the old imperial police, once again 'shot anyone in Kyiv who spoke Ukrainian and considered himself a Ukrainian'. Hateful, anti-Ukrainian rhetoric became a standard part of Bolshevik language in Kyiv: 'The unemployed, hungry, toiling masses simply joined the army, they were paid well for their service and provided with "rations" for their families. It wasn't difficult to raise the "morale" of this army. All one had to say was that our "brothers" are starving because of the Ukrainian-*Khokhly* [a derogatory term for Ukrainians]. This is how our "comrades" lit the fires of hatred for Ukrainians.'[77]

As in Russia, they also confiscated large estates and used some of the land to create collective farms and other state-owned agricultural enterprises, yet another harbinger of future policy. But although the Moscow Bolsheviks were keen to try these experiments, the Ukrainian communists were not. More to the point, neither were the Ukrainian peasants. Russia did have a tradition of communal agriculture, and the majority of Russian peasants held land jointly in rural communes (known as the *obschina*, or *mir*). But only a quarter of Ukrainian peasants followed the same custom. Most were individual farmers, either landholders or their employees, who owned their land, houses and livestock.[78]

When spontaneously offered the chance to join collective farms in 1919, very few Ukrainian peasants accepted. And although the new Soviet regime organized some 550 collective and state farms in Ukraine in 1919, they were mostly unpopular and unsuccessful: almost all of them were dissolved soon afterwards. The vast majority of the confiscated land was instead redistributed. Peasants received smaller parcels in the western and central part of Ukraine, larger parcels in the steppe regions of the south and east. Small landowners who controlled between 120 and 250 acres kept their property. Although no one said so, this was a tacit admission that Ukraine's private landowners produced more grain with greater efficiency.[79]

But in 1919 grain was still a far bigger priority for Lenin than the conversion of Ukrainians to the benefits of collective farming. Whenever the republic was discussed, that was his primary concern: 'at every mention of Ukraine Lenin asked how many [kilos of grain] there were, how many could be taken from there or how many had already been taken'.[80] He was encouraged in his obsession by Alexander Shlikhter, a Bolshevik with revolutionary credentials who was named People's Commissar of Food Collection in Ukraine in late 1918. By early 1919, Shlikhter had already placed every person, institute and agency associated with food production in Ukraine under his personal control.[81] A native of Poltava, in east-central Ukraine,

Shlikhter thought that the food-producing potential of his birthplace was huge, though he did not imagine that the beneficiaries would be Ukrainians: 'We have a target, to procure 100 million poods [1.6 million kilos] through grain requisition ... 100 million for starving Russia, for Russia which is now under threat of international intervention from the East. This is a colossal number, but rich Ukraine, bread-producing Ukraine will help . . .'[82]

These numbers were plucked from the sky; later, Shlikhter would be asked for 50 million poods, but the reduction didn't matter since he couldn't collect anything close to that number.[83] Certainly he found it impossible to purchase grain. As one observer remembered, the peasants refused to give up their produce to lazy city-dwellers in exchange for 'Kerensky money' [the currency created in February 1917] or Ukrainian karbovantsi: 'There was scarcely a home which did not own bales of worthless paper money.'[84] Although the peasants would have happily bartered their grain for clothing or tools, Russia was barely producing any manufactured goods and Shlikhter had nothing to give them.

Force was again the only solution. But instead of deploying the crude violence that Stalin had used in Tsaritsyn, Shlikhter chose a more sophisticated form of violence. He created a new class system in the villages, first naming and identifying new categories of peasants, and then encouraging antagonism between them. Previously, class distinctions in Ukrainian villages had not been well defined or meaningful; Trotsky himself once said the peasantry 'constitutes that protoplasm out of which new classes have been differentiated in the past'.[85] As noted, only a minority of Ukrainian villages followed the practice, more common in Russia, of holding land communally. In most, there was a rough division between people who owned land and were considered hard workers, and those who did not own land or who for whatever reason – bad luck, drink – were considered to be poor workers. But the distinction was blurry. Members of the same family could belong to different groups, and peasants could move up or down this short ladder very quickly.[86]

The Bolsheviks, with their rigid Marxist training and hierarchical way of seeing the world, insisted on more formal markers. Eventually they would define three categories of peasant: kulaks, or wealthy peasants; *seredniaks*, or middle peasants; and *bedniaks*, or poor peasants. But at this stage they sought mainly to define who would be the victims of their revolution and who would be the beneficiaries.

In part, Shlikhter created a class division through the launch of an ideological struggle against the 'kulaks', or 'kurkuls' (literally 'fists' in Ukrainian). The term had been rare in Ukrainian villages before the revolution; if used at all, it simply implied someone who was doing well, or someone who could afford to hire others to work, but not necessarily someone wealthy.[87] Although the Bolsheviks always argued about how to identify kulaks – eventually the term would simply become political – they had no trouble vilifying them as the main obstacle to grain collection, or attacking them as exploiters of the poorer peasants and obstacles to Soviet power. Very quickly, the kulaks became one of the most important Bolshevik scapegoats, the group blamed most often for the failure of Bolshevik agriculture and food distribution.

While attacking the kulaks, Shlikhter simultaneously created a new class of allies through the institution of 'poor peasants' committees' – *komitety nezamozhnykh selian*, otherwise known as *komnezamy* (*kombedy* in Russian). The *komnezamy* would later play a role in the Ukrainian famine, but their origins lay in this immediate, post-revolutionary moment, in Shlikhter's first grain collection campaign. Under his direction, Red Army soldiers and Russian agitators moved from village to village, recruiting the least successful, least productive, most opportunistic peasants and offering them power, privileges, and land confiscated from their neighbours. In exchange, these carefully recruited collaborators were expected to find and confiscate the 'grain surpluses' of their neighbours. These mandatory grain collections – or *prodrazvyorstka* – created overwhelming anger and resentment, neither of which ever really went away.[88]

These two newly created village groups defined one another as mortal enemies. The kulaks understood perfectly well that the *komnezamy* had been set up to destroy them; the *komnezamy* equally understood perfectly well that their future status depended upon their ability to destroy the kulaks. They were willing to exact harsh punishments on their neighbours in order to do so. Iosyp Nyzhnyk, a loyal member of the poor peasants' committee in Velyke Ustia,

Chernihiv province, joined a *komnezam* in January 1918, after returning home from the front. As he recalled later, there were fifty members of the local committee. Tasked with confiscating land from their wealthier neighbours, they unsurprisingly met with fierce resistance. In response, a handful of *komnezam* members formed an armed 'revolutionary committee', which, Nyzhnyk recalled, imposed immediate, drastic measures: '*kulaks* and religious groups were banned from holding meetings without the permission of the revolutionary committee, weapons were confiscated from kulaks, guards were placed around the village and secret surveillance of the kulaks was set up as well'.[89]

Not all of these measures were ordered or sanctioned from above. But by telling the poor peasants' committees that their welfare depended on robbing the kulaks, Shlikhter knew that he was instigating a vicious class war. The *komnezamy*, he wrote later, were meant to 'bring the socialist revolution into the countryside' by ensuring the 'destruction of the political and economic rule of the kulak'.[90] Another Bolshevik stated it clearly at a party meeting in 1918: 'You, peasant comrades, must know that here now in the Ukraine, there are many rich kulaks, very many, and they are well organized, and when we start founding our communes in the countryside . . . these kulaks will put up a great opposition.'[91]

At one of the low moments of the civil war, in March 1918, Trotsky told a meeting of the Soviet and Trade Unions that food had to be 'requisitioned for the Red Army at all costs'. Moreover, he seemed positively enthusiastic about the consequences: 'If the requisition meant civil war between the kulaks and the poorer elements of the villages, then long live this civil war!'[92] A decade later Stalin would use the same rhetoric. But even in 1919 the Bolsheviks were actively seeking to deepen divisions inside the villages, to use anger and resentment to further their policy.

Shlikhter did not invent this form of grassroots revolution: Lenin had earlier tried it in Russia, in 1918, but it had failed. The poor peasants' committees in Russia had not only been unpopular – Russian peasants were even less inclined than Ukrainians to think of themselves using strict class divisions, preferring to regard their neighbours as 'fellow villagers' – but also corrupt. The committees were quick to use what grain they confiscated for their own benefit, and in many Russian districts they deteriorated into 'networks of corruption and distortion'.[93] Shlikhter knew the political risks of repeating this policy in Ukraine, where the peasantry were less sympathetic to the Bolsheviks. Nevertheless, under the slogan 'Bread for the Fighters, for the Salvation of the Revolution!', Shlikhter put huge pressure on the *komnezamy* to collect grain using whatever means they could.

They were not his only tactic: Shlikhter also offered commissions to private groups or warlords. According to official records, eighty-seven separate grain collection teams arrived in Ukraine from Russia in the first half of 1919, deploying 2,500 people. The total number, if soldiers and other unofficial participants were counted, may have been higher.[94] Others came from within Ukraine, from cities as well as from local criminal networks. Just like the collectivization brigades that would be sent into the countryside from the cities in 1929, many members of these teams were urban followers of the Bolsheviks, if not Russian then Russian-speaking. Whatever their ethnic origin, peasants regarded these militarized collection teams as 'foreigners', outsiders who deserved no more consideration than the German and Austrian soldiers who had tried the same tactics a year earlier. Unsurprisingly, the peasants fought back, as Shlikhter also admitted: 'Figuratively speaking, one could say that every *pood* of requisitioned grain was tinged with drops of workers' blood.'[95]

Peasants were not the only instigators of class violence, or the only victims. The Cheka also pursued a harsh and rigid campaign in Ukraine against political enemies. The secret police arrested not only Ukrainian nationalists but merchants, bankers, capitalists and the bourgeoisie, both *haute* and *petite*; former imperial officers, former imperial civil servants, former political leaders; aristocrats and their families; anarchists, socialists and members of any other left-wing parties who failed to toe the Bolshevik line. In Ukraine the latter were particularly important. The *Borotbysty*, the radical left wing of the Ukrainian Socialist Revolutionary Party, had a strong following in the Ukrainian countryside. But although the *Borotbysty* were very close to the Bolsheviks ideologically – they also favoured radical land reform, for example – they were excluded from the government and treated with suspicion because they had cooperated with the Central Rada.

The list of Bolshevik enemies also included the neighbouring Don and Kuban Cossacks, whose territory straddled Russia and Ukraine and who, like the Zaporozhian Cossacks in southern Ukraine, had always enjoyed a large measure of autonomy. Many Cossack *stanitsas* – the name given to their self-governing communities – sided with the White Russian imperial armies during the revolution, and some reacted even more radically. The Kuban Rada, the ruling organization of the most Ukrainian-speaking Kuban Cossacks, declared itself the sovereign ruling body in Kuban in April 1917, then fought against the Bolsheviks from October, and even proclaimed an independent Kuban People's Republic in January 1918. At the height of the civil war in 1918, the Russian-speaking Don Cossacks also declared independence and founded the Don Republic, a romantic gesture that won them no friends in Moscow. The Bolsheviks repeatedly described them as 'instinctive counter-revolutionaries' and 'lackeys of the imperial regime'.

In January 1919, after the Red Army entered the Don province, the Bolshevik leadership issued an order designed to dispose of the Cossack problem altogether. Soldiers received orders 'to conduct mass terror against wealthy Cossacks, exterminating them totally; to conduct merciless mass terror against all those Cossacks who participated, directly or indirectly, in the struggle against Soviet power . . . To confiscate grain and compel storage of all surpluses at designated points'.[96]

Josef Reingold, the Chekist in charge, euphemistically referred to this program as 'de-cossackization'. In fact, it was a massacre: some 12,000 people were murdered after being 'sentenced' by revolutionary tribunals consisting of a *troika* of officials – a Red Army commissar and two party members – who issued rapid-fire death sentences. A form of ethnic cleansing followed the slaughter: 'reliable' workers and peasants were imported in order to 'dilute' the Don Cossack identity further.[97] This was one of the first Soviet uses of mass violence and mass movement of people for the purposes of social engineering. It was an important precedent for later Soviet policy, especially in Ukraine. The term 'de-cossackization' itself may have been the inspiration for 'de-kulakization', which would be so central to Soviet policy a decade later.

But the policy backfired. By mid-March, Cossacks in the

Veshenskaia *stanitsa*, many of whom had originally cooperated with the Red Army, were in full revolt.[98] Across Ukraine, Red Army commanders were intensely worried. Antonov-Ovsienko, the Red Army leader in the region, twice wrote letters to Lenin and the Central Committee asking for a relaxation of Soviet policy, and particularly for more cooperation with local groups and Ukrainian national leaders. He suggested that the Ukrainian Soviet government be expanded to include social democrats and *Borotbysty*, who had more support among the peasantry than the Bolsheviks. He called for an end to the grain requisitions, and for concessions to the Ukrainian peasants who were deserting the Red Army in droves.

Nobody in Moscow was listening. The harsh rhetoric continued. The grain collection policy remained in place. It was unsuccessful: Shlikhter only managed to dispatch some 8.5 million poods of grain – 139,000 metric tonnes – to Russia, a tiny fraction of what Lenin had demanded.[99]

The Bolsheviks were expelled from Kyiv for the second time in August 1919. In their wake, the largest and most violent peasant uprising in modern European history exploded across the countryside.

2

Rebellion, 1919

Ukrainian people, take the power in your hands! Let there be
no dictators, neither of person nor party! Long live the dictatorship of the working people! Long live the calloused hands
of the peasants and workers! Down with political speculators! Down with the violence of the Right! Down with the
violence of the Left!

Otaman Matvii Hryhoriev, 1919[1]

Great was the year and terrible the year of Our Lord 1918,
but more terrible still was 1919.

Mikhail Bulgakov, 1926[2]

When Nestor Makhno was christened, the priest's clothing was said to
have caught fire. This, the peasants said, was a sign: he was destined to
become a great bandit. When Makhno's first son was born, he had a
mouth full of teeth. This, the peasants said, was also a sign: it meant
that he was the Antichrist.[3] Makhno's son died, and the story of
Makhno's own christening faded. But the wildly contradictory rumours
that swirled around Makhno, the most powerful and probably the
most charismatic of the Ukrainian peasant leaders who arose out of
the chaos of 1919, continued well after his death. Trotsky memorably
described Makhno's followers as 'kulak plunderers' who 'throw dust
in the eyes of the most benighted and backward peasants'.[4] Piotr Arshinov, a Russian anarchist and admirer of Makhno, described him as the
man who brought unity to the 'revolutionary insurrectionary movement of the Ukrainian peasants and workers'. When 'throughout the

immense stretches of the Ukraine, the masses seethed, rushing into revolt and struggle', Makhno 'drew up the plan for the struggle, and coined the slogans of the day'.[5]

Parting the mists and myths that surround the Ukrainian peasant revolt of 1918–20 is not easy, if only because a large number of the leading protagonists, Makhno among them, played so many roles and changed sides so many times. Originally, Makhno was a revolutionary activist from Zaporizhia in southeastern Ukraine. Arrested several times by the tsarist police, he spent the years 1908–17 in a Moscow prison. There he befriended Arshinov, among others, and became indoctrinated in the ideology of anarchism. This philosophy, although radical and opposed to the status quo in equal measures, never aligned precisely either with the Bolsheviks or the Ukrainian nationalists: Makhno wanted to destroy the state, not empower it. Released in 1917 after the February revolution, he returned to Zaporizhia and began organizing a Peasants' Union. This grew rapidly into a rowdy peasant army which controlled what Trotsky described in disgust as the 'little known state' of Huliaipole, the territory around Makhno's home village that refused to recognize the authority of Kyiv.

Sometimes called the Black Army – they fought under the black anarchist flag – and at other times referred to as Makhnovists (*Makhnovshchyna*), Makhno's men originally took up arms against both Pavlo Skoropadsky and his German and Austrian allies, as well as Symon Petliura and his Ukrainian nationalist forces. Some of their anger was purely local: among other things, they identified the Mennonite landowners of eastern Ukraine as 'German' exploiters who deserved to be stripped of their property. But they did have broader goals. Sympathizing neither with the 'Whites' nor with the Ukrainian Central Rada, Makhno's anarchists allied themselves initially with the Bolsheviks. His forces helped the Bolsheviks establish the first, brief Bolshevik Ukrainian government in early 1918.

Unsurprisingly, relations broke down. Makhno's anarchism hardly sat well with the controlling instincts of the Bolsheviks. Their authoritarian methods didn't appeal to him either. By 1920, Makhno was calling on Red Army soldiers to desert:

We drove out the Austro-German tyrants, smashed the Denikinist [Imperial Russian] hangmen, fought against Petliura; now we are fighting the domination of the commissar authority, the dictatorship of the Bolshevik-Communist Party: it has laid its iron hand on the entire life of the working people; the peasants and workers of the Ukraine are groaning under its yoke ... But we consider you, comrades in the Red Army, our blood brothers, together with whom we would like to carry on the struggle for genuine liberation, for the true Soviet system without the pressure of parties or authorities.[6]

Despite Trotsky's scorn, those sentiments proved popular well beyond Huliaipole. The idea that Ukrainians stood for the 'true Soviet system without the pressure of parties or authorities' – socialism without Bolshevism – was widespread and deeply appealing, affecting many people who knew nothing about Makhno. Like the Kronstadt sailors and Tambov peasants who also staged rebellions in 1920 and 1921, tens of thousands of rural Ukrainians wanted a socialist revolution but not the centralized power and repression emanating from Moscow. A leaflet passed around in central Ukraine, addressed to 'Comrade Red Army Men', put it succinctly:

You are led into Ukraine by Russian and Jewish commissar communists who tell you they are fighting for Soviet power in Ukraine but who in fact are conquering Ukraine. They tell you they lead you against rich Ukrainian peasants but in fact they are fighting against poor Ukrainian peasants and workers ...

Ukrainian peasants and workers cannot tolerate the conquest and pillage of Ukraine by Russian armies; they cannot tolerate the oppression of the Ukrainian language and culture as occurred under Tsarist rule ...

Brothers, don't turn your weapons against the peasants and workers of Ukraine but against your commissar communists who torture your unfortunate people as well.[7]

An observer who visited Ukraine on a Red Cross mission at the time paraphrased Ukrainian thinking like this:

A special peasant phraseology was formed: 'We are Bolsheviks,' said the peasants in the Ukraine, 'but not communists. The Bolsheviks gave us land, while the communists take away our grain without giving us anything for it. We will not allow the Red Army to hang the commune about our necks. Down with the commune! Long live the Bolsheviks!'[8]

So confused was the terminology at the time that those sentences could easily have been written the other way around: 'Down with the Bolsheviks! Long live the commune!' But the point was clear: the Ukrainian peasants had wanted one form of revolution, but had got something else altogether.

Similarly left-wing, equally revolutionary and anti-Bolshevik language also appealed to the followers of Matvii Hryhoriev, another charismatic leader who emerged from the chaos of 1919. On the surface, Hryhoriev could not have been more different from Makhno. A Cossack and a former member of the Russian imperial army, he had initially supported the Skoropadsky regime, which granted him the rank of colonel. Disillusion then set in, and his ambition grew. Hryhoriev gathered around him a band of loyal followers – 117 separate partisan bands, by one account, including between 6,000 and 8,000 soldiers – allied himself with a similarly idiosyncratic group of peasant commanders, and transferred his support from the German puppet regime to Petliura.[9]

The Directory, the national force led by Petliura, granted Hryhoriev the title of 'Otaman of Zaporizhia, Oleksandriia, Kherson and Tavryda'. A braggart and a blusterer, Hryhoriev, like Makhno, used the language of the radical left. He equated the German and Austrian occupiers with the hated 'bourgeoisie' who had connived to keep Ukraine poor. In one ultimatum, issued in the autumn of 1918, he declared:

> I, Otaman Hryhoriev, in the name of the partisans whom I command, rising against the yoke of bourgeoisie, in clear conscience declare to you that you have appeared here in Ukraine as blind instruments in the hands of your bourgeoisie, that you are not democrats, but traitors of all European democrats.[10]

When it became clear that the Directory would fall to the Red Army, Hryhoriev quickly changed sides again and joined forces with the

Bolsheviks. This alliance was even more unstable than the pact between Makhno and the Red Army. One Soviet war correspondent travelling with Hryhoriev's men observed with trepidation the irregular organization of the troops, their fondness for looting, and the anti-semitism 'embedded in the consciousness' of the soldiers. He quoted some of the commanders joking about the day they would once again take up arms against the 'communist-Jews'.[11] This kind of talk didn't, he feared, bode well for a long-term alliance with the Bolsheviks.

It didn't work in the short term either. Communications between Hryhoriev and the Red Army commanders frequently broke down, especially when he wanted them to do so. Cooperation eventually ceased altogether and in May 1919, Hryhoriev finally called upon his followers to revolt against the Soviet regime that was still then clinging to power in Kyiv. His grandiose statement was a complete mishmash of ideas – nationalist, anarchist, socialist, communist – that probably reflected quite accurately the feelings of Ukrainian peasants who had already watched several armies tramp across their soil:

> Let there be no dictators, neither of person or party! Long live the
> dictatorship of the working people! Long live the calloused hands of
> the peasants and workers! Down with political speculators! Down
> with the violence of the Right! Down with the violence of the Left![12]

The Bolsheviks responded to this rhetoric with their own. They denounced the 'kulak uprising', the 'kulak bandits' and the 'kulak traitors'. Evidently the word 'kulak' had already acquired a broader meaning, well beyond 'rich peasant'. As early as 1919, anyone who had extra stores of grain – and anyone who opposed Soviet power – could be damned by it. A decade later, Stalin would not need to invent a new word for the same sort of enemy.[13]

But flinging insults didn't help the Soviet cause in 1919. By early summer, both Hryhoriev and Makhno had broken away from the Bolsheviks once and for all, as had a host of other partisans, atamans and local leaders, all of whom agreed upon only one thing: their revolutionary aspirations for land and self-government had been thwarted by Ukrainian nationalists, by Germans and above all by the Bolsheviks. Lured by the slogan, 'For Soviet Power, without Communists!', peasant soldiers deserted the Red Army in droves and joined other groups. Oleksandr Shlikhter counted ninety-three 'counter-revolutionary attacks' in the month of April alone.[14] By another reckoning, there were 328 separate revolts in June, incidents of peasant attacks on Soviet officials or the Red Army. In the month of July, Christian Rakovsky counted more than 200 anti-Bolshevik rebellions within twenty days.[15]

The word 'chaos' fails to explain or encompass what happened next. Makhno and Hryhoriev fought the Red Army, the White Army, the Directory – and eventually one another. A meeting of rebel forces turned into a shootout in July after Makhno's deputy pulled a gun on Hryhoriev, murdering him along with several aides. Anton Denikin, the White general, began a new campaign, first taking Stalin's beloved Tsaritsyn and then advancing into Ukraine, capturing Kharkiv and Katerynoslav (Dnipropetrovsk) in June. A month later he took Poltava too. Meanwhile, Petliura's forces advanced from the west and retook Kyiv, only to lose the city again soon afterwards.

All told, Kyiv changed hands more than a dozen times in 1919 alone. Richard Pipes has memorably described that year in Ukraine as 'a period of complete anarchy':

> The entire territory fell apart into innumerable regions isolated from each other and the rest of the world, dominated by armed bands of peasants or freebooters who looted and murdered with utter impunity . . . None of the authorities which claimed Ukraine during the year following the deposition of Skoropadsky ever exercised actual sovereignty. The Communists, who all along anxiously watched the developments there and did everything in their power to seize control for themselves, fared no better than their Ukrainian nationalist and White Russian competitors.[16]

For ordinary people, lawlessness meant that they were constantly preyed upon. Heinrich Epp, one of Ukraine's Mennonite minority, remembered that his community was at the mercy of whoever passed through:

> Most of the time we were without any real government for all intents and purposes. There were no laws or police . . . During the day it was

mainly the local Russian nationals from the region or young men who visited us repeatedly. Each time they took something which caught their fancy as their own property . . . But far more fearful were the nights, when the so-called bandits came, for such visits rarely passed without some life being given as sacrifice.[17]

Each change of power was accompanied by a change in policy. Whenever Denikin's White Army took over a region, it returned confiscated property to landowners. Following in the tsarist tradition, it also shut down Ukrainian libraries, cultural centres, newspapers and schools. Derisively, Denikin's men spoke not of Ukraine but of 'Little Russia', and thus successfully alienated any Ukrainian forces who might have joined them.[18]

Whenever the Red Army took over, Bolshevik commissars organized a slaughter of the 'aristocracy' and the 'bourgeoisie' – which could just mean anyone who opposed them – and once again empowered the poor peasants' committees, helping them to rob their wealthier neighbours. In Odessa, Bolshevik leaders armed 2,400 criminals, put them under the control of the city's most famous crime boss, Misha the Jap – a character in Isaac Babel's stories – and let them plunder the city.[19] In Kyiv stories were told of a torturer named Rosa:

She would cause a captured soldier to be tied to nails driven into the wall, and would then sit a few feet away from him with a revolver in her hand. She would treat him to a little talk about the proletariat, punctuating her remarks every ten minutes by shooting at and smashing his main joints one after the other.[20]

Meanwhile, Makhno's 10,000-man cavalry and 40,000 foot soldiers, dragging their artillery around on wheeled carts, undermined whoever was in power. All told, his Black Army killed more than 18,000 of Denikin's soldiers, severely weakened his forces, and possibly robbed him of what could have been a victory against the Bolsheviks.[21] In the regions they occupied, including the Mennonite German settlements of southern Ukraine, some of Makhno's men also attacked civilians with an abandon that seemed unhinged. In his memoir – evocatively entitled 'The Day the World Ended: December

7, 1919, Steinbach, Russia' – Epp remembered going from house to house in the village of Steinbach, and finding that all the inhabitants had been murdered. At each one, he opened the door and found corpses:

> The next place was Hildebrandts – my cousin Maria . . . Here I saw a scene of indescribable horror that I will never forget as long as I live. Mrs Hildebrandt lay in the small bedroom just inside the door to the corner room, completely unclothed. One of her arms had been chopped off and lay on the floor in the middle of the room. Her youngest baby lay dead in the cradle. Its neck had been hacked off. The woman was one of those who had been raped, before or after her murder.

As Epp stood there, mourning his friends and family, peasants began to gather in the village:

> The robbery now commenced: all property, movable or unmovable, dead or alive, now went over into their hands. In one place, I witnessed a woman turn a dead body over onto its back and tear off his coat. She dealt with the corpse as if it were a head of livestock.[22]

Atrocities committed by one side fuelled the anger of the others. When the White Army took over Kharkiv in August 1919, it exhumed the bodies of officers recently buried in shallow trenches in a public park. They found evidence that the men 'while still alive, had actually had their shoulder badges nailed on to the flesh. In some cases live coals had been pressed into their stomachs, and a number appeared to have been scalped.' Of course the revelations spurred on those who wanted revenge.[23]

Conflicts not only broke out between armies and ethnic groups, but also within villages. In Velyke Ustia, Chernihiv province, violence between the 'poor peasants' committee' and the 'kulaks' erupted during elections to the local village council:

> The *komnezam* members got ready, they were deciding who should nominate whom, who should nominate candidates for the presidium, how the vote should be counted and other details . . . but the kulaks also got ready, and started nominating kulak agents. Seeing that the poor and middle peasants were standing together and winning over

kulak agents, the kulaks started a fistfight in the building, trying at least to disrupt the meeting; but the *komnezam* activists did not hold back, they began to put down the fighting and tossed the bullies out of the window. The meeting went on as it was supposed to, under full democracy.[24]

Soon after, the same *komnezam* members were attacking kulaks and forcibly taking their bread, 'in order to give it to the organs of Soviet power'. They also took part in the 'fight against banditry', battling what they called 'kulak bands' of various kinds and at one point calling in the militia to help. Together, one remembered, 'the militia and the *komnezam* activists caught the bandits near the cemetery. During the shooting, the bandits hid themselves, after which they never again appeared in the village and soon were completely liquidated.'[25]

Massacre followed massacre in repetitive cycles. The peasants' resistance infuriated the Bolsheviks, not least because it confounded their historical determinism: the poor were supposed to support them, not fight against them. Conscious that they were a minority fighting against the majority, the Bolsheviks increased their brutality, sometimes demanding the murder of hundreds of peasants in exchange for one dead communist, or calling for the entire adult male population of a village to be wiped out.[26]

The tragedies of those terrible years would remain in local memory for decades afterwards, feeding the desire for revenge on all sides. But some of the most brutal violence was inflicted on a group that sought to stay as far away from the conflict as possible.

In the autumn of 1914 a young Russian soldier named Maksim wrote a cheerful letter home to his family from the Austrian front. He opened with reverent respect for his father and all his relatives, as well as a wish that 'the Lord God gives you good health and all of the happiness in the world'. But he continued with concern. His unit had suffered a defeat, which he blamed on Jewish spies who had, he believed, set up an underground telephone line in order to feed information to the enemy. Since then, he and his comrades had been 'plundering and beating the Jews as they deserve, for they just want to trick all of us'.[27]

Of course, Maksim wasn't the first to come up with the idea that Jews were traitors: anti-semitism was rife throughout the imperial army in 1914, as indeed it was rife throughout Russian society, even at the very highest levels. Tsar Nicholas II was a particularly enthusiastic anti-semite, for whom Jews symbolized everything hateful about the modern world. The emperor once defined a newspaper as a place were 'some Jew or another sits . . . making it his business to stir up passions of people against each other'.[28] During his reign the *okhrana*, the imperial secret police, had produced the 'Protocols of the Elders of Zion', a notorious forgery that depicted a Jewish plot to govern the world. The state had also had a hand in inspiring a wave of pogroms across Russia in 1905. Given that general attitude, it is not surprising that the army leadership in 1914 suspected Jews of 'consorting with the enemy through the use of underground telephones and airplanes' and supplying German troops with gold smuggled across the front line in the stomachs of cattle and the eggs of geese.[29] Swirling conspiracy theories about Jewish treachery supplied a plausible explanation for unpalatable facts: the defeat of a unit, the loss of a division, the poor performance of the entire army.

This same belief in Jewish treachery, common enough before the February revolution, laid the groundwork for a series of appalling massacres in the years that followed. Between 1918 and 1920 combatants on all sides – White, Directory, Polish and Bolshevik – murdered at least 50,000 Jews in more than 1,300 pogroms across Ukraine, according to the most widely accepted studies, though some put the death toll as high as 200,000. Tens of thousands were injured and raped as well. Many shtetls were burnt to the ground. Many Jewish communities were blackmailed out of all their worldly goods by soldiers who threatened to kill them unless they paid up. In the town of Proskuriv (now Khmelnytskyi) a riot started by the Bolsheviks led to the deaths of 1,600 people over the course of two days. Thousands of Jews fled the violence only to die of hunger and disease in Kyiv. When Denikin's troops left the city in December 1919, some 2,500 Jewish corpses were found in makeshift refugee shelters.[30]

A complete explanation for this infamous wave of anti-semitic violence is beyond the scope of this book, especially since so much of the evidence was long ago cherry-picked by authors seeking to prove a case for or against the Bolsheviks, the White Army or the Directory. From a wide range of sources it is clear that there were perpetrators on all sides. Hryhoriev made little pretence about his virulent anti-semitism; Denikin and his generals enthusiastically carried out pogroms in retaliation against the 'Jewish' Cheka and the 'Jewish' Bolsheviks. A British journalist who travelled for a time with Denikin recorded that the White general's officers and men, in line with their tsarist upbringing, 'laid practically all the blame for their country's troubles on the Hebrew':

> They held that the whole cataclysm has been engineered by some great and mysterious secret society of international Jews who in the pay and at the orders of Germany had seized the psychological moment and snatched the reins of government ... Among Denikin's officers this idea was an obsession of such terrible bitterness and insistency as to lead them into making statements of the wildest and most fantastic character.[31]

By contrast, Petliura is not known to have used anti-semitic language. He was a former member of the Central Rada, which had deliberately included Jews among its leaders; more than once he went out of his way to discourage anti-semitism in his own ranks: 'Because Christ commands it, we urge everyone to help the Jewish sufferers,' he declared. During his brief tenure in power his government had granted autonomous status to the Jews of Ukraine, encouraged Jewish political parties, and funded Yiddish publications.[32]

But his Directory soldiers felt varying levels of loyalty to their commander, and the results on the ground were often different. A Red Cross committee met one of Petliura's generals in Berdychiv in 1921: 'In a cynical fashion he abused the whole of Jewry and accused them of lending support to the Bolsheviks.'[33] The same committee told another general that the Directory leadership had ordered a halt to the pogroms. In response, he replied that 'the Directory was a puppet in the hands of the diplomats, most of whom were Jews', and that he would do as he pleased.[34]

The Bolshevik leadership also formally opposed pogroms, though that didn't stop Red Army soldiers from blackmailing Jewish communities or stealing their money. Lenin was informed that Red Army soldiers in Zhytomyr province were 'destroying the Jewish population in their path, looting and murdering', in October 1920. Despite his arguments to the contrary, followers of Makhno were also responsible for attacks on Jews, as were some Polish soldiers.[35]

But the violence was greatest in areas that were not under any political control at all. The worst damage was inflicted by disintegrating military units or bandits with little sense of allegiance to anybody.[36] One testimony, written by a Jewish trader, Symon Leib-Rabynovych, describes what happened in the village of Pichky, near Radomysl, when twenty members of 'Struk's gang' took over in 1919. On the first evening the Jews of the village were taken hostage until they agreed to pay 1,800 roubles. A few days later most of them fled temporarily, following a Bolshevik attack on the village. When they returned, they discovered that their homes had been plundered and their possessions distributed among their neighbours. Leib-Rabynovych went to one of them and asked for his feather bed back:

> He fell on me like a wild beast; how did I dare to demand of him, the head man of the village? He would arrest me and hand me over to the Strukists as a communist. I saw that some change had taken place in my neighbour. He had previously been peaceable, and extraordinarily conscientious, and had always been kind to me. I understood that I could not stay any longer in the village. I had to get away to save my life.[37]

Leib-Rabynovych escaped. The next day the Struk gang took the entire Jewish population of the village out into the field, stripped all of them of their clothes and possessions, demanded money, and murdered those who could not pay.

Similar scenes unfolded in Makariv, a large village in the Kyiv district, over the course of 1919. The first attack was organized by one of the local warlords. His gang, which one memoirist described as a band of 'barefoot teenagers, armed with rifles', appeared in the village in June. The Jews vanished 'like mice to their holes'; the young people, 'having amused themselves with their bullets', began destroying the stalls in the bazaar. Their leader, Matviienko, encouraged the local peasants to join in. Eventually the Jews agreed to negotiate:

> '50,000,' said Matviienko.
> 'We'll get it.'

'In two hours,' he added gloomily.

They fulfilled the demand.[38]

A few days later Matviienko came back for more, this time taking valuables and clothes as well. A few weeks after that he demanded six local Jews as hostages: he wanted to trade them for his brother, who had been captured by Bolsheviks fighting in the area. When the Jews asked why it had to be them, he shrugged: 'Communists are yids, and all yids are communists.' Six Jews were taken; two weeks later Matviienko demanded that the community provide another 150,000 roubles to buy them back. Soon after, the local villagers decided to play the same game, and began demanding money and hostages too. Then the Bolsheviks arrived, with new demands; then Matviienko came back. The Jews sent a delegation to him, and this time he shot them all on the spot. After that, his men went through the village, looking for Jews and killing those they found: 'In total, about 100 people were killed. Naturally, all of the property was stolen.'[39]

The violence against Jews left its mark on those who witnessed it, perpetrated it or experienced it. The pogroms, like the civil war itself, contributed to the brutalization of the population, which quickly learned to conform to the will of men with guns. The methods used in the pogroms would also find echoes in the drive to collect grain in 1921, when Lenin proposed to take hostages in order to force peasants to hand over their supplies. They also haunted the collectivization campaign a decade later, when the kulaks were terrorized using exactly the same methods that had been used in 1919. Like the Jews, kulaks would be rounded up, stripped to their underclothes, blackmailed out of their possessions, mocked and humiliated, and sometimes shot.

The pogroms also foreshadowed later events in another sense. Much as they would one day use history, journalism and politics to cover up the famine and to twist the facts of Ukrainian history, Soviet propagandists also sought to use the pogroms to discredit the Ukrainian national movement. For decades, Soviet historians characterized Petliura as little more than an anti-semite. They denied the Bolshevik role in pogroms; they denied that either the Directory or the Central Rada before it had ever represented a real national movement at all.

Instead, they linked Ukrainian nationalism to looting, killing and above all pogroms. Great efforts were made to gather 'testimony' against Petliura and the generals who were associated with him, and to publish it in different languages.[40] Petliura himself was murdered in Paris in 1926 by a Russian Jew, Sholom Schwartzbard, who claimed to be taking revenge for the pogroms. Even if Schwartzbard wasn't a direct Soviet agent, as many thought at the time, he was certainly inspired by Soviet propaganda that demonized Petliura.

The Ukrainian community in Paris and elsewhere fought back. They published several Directory pamphlets as well as Petliura's own proclamations from 1919 calling on Ukrainian soldiers to defend Jews.[41] They didn't, of course, also explain that many of Petliura's own generals had pursued a very different policy, in defiance of their leader. Of all the many things that were lost in the propaganda war between the Soviet Union and Ukrainian nationalism, none disappeared more quickly than nuance.

The Ukrainian peasant uprising devastated the countryside and created divisions that would never heal. It also altered, profoundly, the Bolshevik perceptions of Ukraine. If the Bolsheviks had previously been inclined to dismiss Ukraine as 'Southwest Russia', a province of no real interest except for its rich soil and abundant food, the experiences of 1919 taught them to see Ukraine as potentially dangerous and explosive, and Ukrainian peasants and intellectuals as threats to Soviet power.

The rebellion also taught them to see Ukraine as a source of future military threats, for it was thanks to the chaos in Ukraine that Denikin's last campaign nearly succeeded. Following the bloody summer of 1919, Denikin seized Kyiv in August. He took Kursk on 20 September and Orel on 13 October. He came within 200 kilometres of Moscow – so close that he might have taken the city. Had Denikin formed an alliance with Ukrainian national forces he might well have toppled the Bolshevik regime before it really got started. Yet his unpopular land policies, his opposition to Ukrainian institutions, and his officers' brutal tactics instead provoked Ukrainian partisans to attack his supply lines. His hold on Ukrainian territory weakened rapidly and so he withdrew.

But Deniken's offensive also paved the way for one more attack on

Bolshevik power. As the White Army pulled back, Petliura prepared one last stand in concert with Józef Piłsudski, the Polish national leader who had just helped his own country re-establish sovereignty. Unlike Denikin, Piłsudski did not seek to occupy central or eastern Ukraine. Although he did incorporate what is now western Ukraine into the new Polish republic, he also hoped to establish a strong Ukrainian state that would serve as a counterweight to Soviet Russia. The agreement made by the two leaders began 'with the deep conviction that every nation possesses the right to determine its own fate and to decide upon its relationship with its neighbours'.[42] Piłsudski himself issued a proclamation to the Ukrainians, using language that the Bolsheviks would long remember:

> The armies of the Polish Republic, on my orders, have advanced deep into Ukraine. I want the inhabitants of this country to know that Polish troops will remove from your lands the invader against whom you have risen up in arms to defend your homes against violence, conquest and pillage. Polish troops will remain in Ukraine only until the rightful Ukrainian government assumes power.[43]

The Poles and the Ukrainians began their joint campaign in the spring of 1920 and at first faced little resistance. On 7 May, Piłsudski's army occupied Kyiv, which was so poorly defended that his soldiers entered the city riding tram cars. Belatedly, another White Army commander, General Peter Wrangel, agreed to join them from his base in Crimea.

Their occupation was short. On 13 June the Red Army forced Polish troops to retreat. By early August it was just outside Warsaw. Piłsudski pushed them back, following a battle remembered later as the 'Miracle on the Vistula'. Polish troops again advanced into Ukraine, but ultimately failed to create an independent Ukrainian state. Piłsudski signed an armistice in October and concluded a border treaty between Poland and the Soviet Union the following year.[44]

But even after the Poles withdrew and the remnants of the White Army, stranded in Crimea, scrambled onto boats and sailed across the Black Sea, the problem of Ukraine loomed large in the Bolshevik imagination. Trotsky, in a letter to his colleagues, explained that peace would be difficult to enforce there. For although the Red Army had won a military victory, there had been no ideological revolution in Ukraine: 'Soviet power in Ukraine has held its ground up to now (and it has not held it well) chiefly by the authority of Moscow, by the Great Russian communists and by the Russian Red Army.'[45] The implication was clear: force, not persuasion, had finally pacified Ukraine. And force might one day be needed again.

The security threat waned, in other words, but the ideological threat remained. Ukrainian nationalism had been defeated militarily, but it remained attractive to the Ukrainian-speaking middle class, intelligentsia and a large part of the peasantry. Worse, it threatened the unity of the Soviet state, which was still struggling to find ways of accommodating national differences. Most ominously of all, nationalism had the power to attract foreign allies, particularly across the border in Poland.

The Ukrainian rebellion also posed a broader threat to the Bolshevik project. The radical, anarchic, anti-Bolshevik rhetoric used during the peasant uprising had reflected something real. Millions of Ukrainian peasants had wanted a socialist revolution, but not a Bolshevik revolution – and certainly not one directed from Moscow. Although their leaders represented a wide range of views, from anarchist to monarchist, villagers across the country expressed a coherent set of beliefs. They wanted to vote for their own representatives, not for communists. They wanted big landowners dispossessed, but they wished to farm that land themselves. They did not want to return to the 'second serfdom' represented by collective farms. They sought respect for their religion, language and customs. They wanted to be able to sell their grain to traders, and they hated the enforced requisition of their produce.[46]

This critique – socialist but not authoritarian, communist but not Bolshevik – would resonate strongly throughout the 1920s, finding a spokesman, among others, in Trotsky himself. But the first and most damaging appearance of the anti-Soviet 'left' was in Ukraine. The 'cruel lesson of 1919', as the Ukrainian peasant revolt came to be called, loomed over the Bolsheviks for many years afterwards.[47]

3
Famine and Truce, the 1920s

We must teach these people a lesson right now, so that they will not even dare to think of resistance in the coming decades.

Lenin, in a letter to Vyacheslav Molotov, 1922[1]

Since our literature can at last follow its own path of development ... we must not, on any account, follow the Russian ... Russian literature has been burdening us for ages, it has trained us to imitate it slavishly.

Mykola Khvylovy, 1925[2]

The truce with Piłsudski as well as the defeat of Denikin, the Directory and a wide array of rebels, finally allowed the Bolsheviks to force an uneven peace on Ukraine in the course of 1920–1. The bloodshed did not stop right away: Makhno's Black Army kept on fighting through the summer of 1921, and some of Petliura's forces were still fighting that autumn even though Petliura himself had fled. The Cheka killed 444 rural rebel leaders in Ukraine during the first half of that year, and reckoned that thousands of 'bandits' still roamed the countryside.[3] Felix Dzerzhinsky, the Cheka's gloomy founder, personally brought 1,400 men to Ukraine to help his local allies finish them off.[4]

Ukraine's new rulers, not trusting the mood in Kyiv, moved the republican capital east to Kharkiv, a city further from the Polish border, closer to Russia, and with a large, Russian-speaking proletariat. The Red Army divisions stationed in Ukraine retained their foreign character, with the majority of soldiers hailing from Russian districts far away. In a 1921 speech the Red Army's top commander in Ukraine and Crimea, Mikhail Frunze, described the Ukraine-based Red Army as 85 per cent Russian and only 9 per cent Ukrainian. (The rest consisted of 'other nationalities', including Poles and Belarusians.)[5]

The shaky 'peace' did not bring prosperity either. Waves of violence had displaced people and destroyed villages, towns, roads and railroads. The politics and policies of the Bolsheviks had rendered the economy nearly dysfunctional. The abolition of trade, the nationalization of industry, the failed experiments with collectivization and the use of forced labour had all taken their toll. 'Industry was dead,' wrote one observer:

> Trade existed only in violation of Soviet law. Agriculture, still in the process of communization, had almost reached the point where what it produced, if evenly distributed, was scarcely enough to maintain the people of the country. Administrative chaos and physical deterioration of rail and river transport made distribution impossible. Hunger, starvation, disease were increasing.[6]

Prospects for the future were hardly any better. This time a Ukrainian government, directed by the Ukrainian Communist Party – a separate entity from the Soviet Communist Party, with its own Politburo and Central Committee – was formally in charge. But in practice, policy was made in Moscow, and it sounded much the same as in the past. At the national level, Trotsky called for the militarization of the economy, the use of forced labour brigades and requisitioning, the same tactics deployed in the months following the 1917 revolution.[7] During a visit to Kharkiv, Stalin announced the creation of a 'Ukrainian Labour Army'. In a speech to the Ukrainian Communist Party in 1920, he argued that the military tactics used to win the civil war could be applied to the economy: 'We shall now have to promote economic non-commissioned officers and officers from the ranks of the workers to teach the people how to battle against economic disruption and build a new economy ... this requires training "officers of labour".'[8]

But the renewed language of War Communism held no attraction for Soviet peasants, and 'officers of labour' offering lessons in the 'new economy' could hardly have inspired them either. In practice, the end of the civil war brought back Shlikhter's hated *prodrazvyorstka*, the mandatory food confiscation, as well as the *komnezamy*, the poor peasants' committees in Ukraine. The party was taking no chances: it wanted once again to strengthen its hand against the wealthier peasants and to ensure some control over the village soviets (the Bolshevik name for village councils), many of which were led by the same village elders as in the past.

To the peasants, the newly reinforced requisitioning committees seemed to have no scruples. Their members, now veterans of the brutal peasant uprising, were clearly working to gain privileges and protection in a devastated and hungry world. Their behaviour was described by one peasant very succinctly: 'If they want, they take the grain; if they like it, they arrest; what they want, they do.'[9] Another remembered that nobody seemed to control the committees at all: 'The *komnezamy* were left to themselves and were guided in all their actions by their "revolutionary" self-consciousness.' Those further up the chain of command deliberately reinforced this sense of impunity. The party authorities told one local committee that anyone who showed any signs of 'kulak counter-revolution' should be locked up for fifteen days. If that didn't work – then 'shoot them'.[10]

The cruelty they used was no secret. During a confidential meeting in the summer of 1920, the Soviet 'procurements commissars', the men tasked with organizing the collection of grain, considered the 'impact of the requisitions on the population'. After a long debate, they made a decision: 'no matter how heavy the requisitions can be for local inhabitants . . . state interests must anyway come first'.[11]

This harsh attitude created a harsh response. Matvii Havryliuk, a peasant who worked as a grain requisitioner in 1921, remembered the violent emotions of this period in testimony he gave a decade later:

In 1921, when the state needed food, I worked in the food procurement squad collecting bread from the kulaks in our village and then in five villages in Ruzhyn district and helped the army squads, deployed outside the village, catch those who would spread kulak unrest. Despite this very trying time, when kulaks did not want to submit any grain and even threatened to kill me and my family, I persevered and stayed vigilant on behalf of the Soviet power. I requisitioned grain under the supervision of special plenipotentiary Bredykhin [from the Cheka] who rated my work highly. From that moment on I learnt to work in the village, how to organize poor peasant masses, to motivate them to participate in the campaign. Siding with Soviet power right from the beginning made me an enemy of the kulaks in the village too. I always fought with the kulaks . . . they care about their own interests rather than those of the state.[12]

Thanks to the 'perseverance' and 'vigilance' of men like Havryliuk, the great grain collections of 1920 spared nobody. Lenin's instructions explicitly called for the requisitioning of all grain, even that needed for immediate consumption and for planting next year's harvest, and there were many people willing to carry out his orders.[13]

In response, the peasants' enthusiasm for growing, sowing and storing grain plunged. Their ability to produce would have been very low in any case: across Ukraine and Russia, up to a third of young men had been mobilized to fight in the First World War. Even more had joined the armies of the civil war, on one side or another, and hundreds of thousands had not returned. Many villages lacked sufficient numbers of men fit to work the fields. But even those who had returned and could work had no incentive to produce extra grain that they knew would be confiscated.

As a result, the peasants sowed far less land in both Ukraine and Russia in the spring of 1920 than they had at any time in the recent past.[14] And even that land wasn't particularly fruitful, for that spring turned out to be 'hot and almost rainless', as one observer wrote: 'the land at the time of the spring planting was caked and dry'. Very little rain fell that summer or the following winter either.[15] As a result, between a fifth and a quarter of the grain sown in the summer of 1921 withered on the stalk.[16] The drought eventually struck about half of the food-producing areas in the country, of which roughly a fifth experienced total crop failure.[17]

By itself, the bad weather would certainly have caused hardship, as bad weather had in the past. But when combined with the confiscatory food collection policies, the absence of able-bodied men and the acres of unsown land, it proved catastrophic. The twenty most productive agricultural provinces in imperial Russia had annually produced 20 million tonnes of grain before the revolution. In 1920 they produced just 8.45 million tonnes, and by 1921 they were down to 2.9 million.[18] In the Stavropol province of the Northern Caucasus, almost the entire crop disappeared.[19] In southern Ukraine the drop was especially dramatic. In 1921 the amount of grain harvested in the province of Odessa dropped to 12.9 per cent of previous levels. The southeastern provinces of Katerynoslav, Zaporizhia and Mykolaiv produced between 3.7 per cent and 5.1 per cent of their normal crop. In other words, some 95 per cent of the normal harvest had failed to materialize.[20]

Historically, both Russian and Ukrainian peasants had survived periodic bad weather and frequent droughts through the careful preservation and storage of surplus grain. But in the spring of 1921 there was no surplus grain: it had all been confiscated. Instead, food shortages quickly resulted in famine in the Russian Volga provinces – the wide swath of territory along the middle and lower part of the Volga River – in the Urals and southern Ukraine. As the peasants grew hungry, many left home in search of food. More than 440,000 refugees fled the Volga region alone, some mistakenly making their way to Ukraine. Poorly informed officials even deliberately directed orphans from starving Russia towards Ukraine, but when they arrived they found no orphanages and no food.[21]

Just as they would a decade later, peasants began to eat dogs, rats and insects; they boiled grass and leaves; there were incidents of cannibalism.[22] A group of refugees who managed to board a train to Riga from Saratov, a Volga river port at the heart of the famine district, described life in the city:

> Old garbage carts collected the dead daily as they used to collect garbage . . . we saw many cases of bubonic plague in the streets. This never was mentioned by the Soviet press, the officials attempting to keep knowledge of this plague from the public . . .
>
> The Soviet government reports the peasants are abandoning their children. This is not true. It is correct that some parents turn over their children to the state, which promises to care for them and does not. Others throw their children into the Volga, preferring to see them

drown rather than be brought up in the communist faith, which they believe is an anti-Christ doctrine.[23]

Just as they would a decade later, starving people sought to escape the barren countryside and instead gathered within makeshift refugee camps in cities and around train stations, living in discarded boxcars and 'huddled together in compact masses like a seal colony, mothers and young close together'.[24] An American journalist, F. A. Mackenzie, described the scene at Samara station:

> Here were lads, gaunt and tall, thin beyond any conception a Westerner can have of thinness, covered with rags and dirt. Here were old women, some of them sitting half-conscious on the ground, dazed by their hunger, their misery and their misfortune . . . Here were pallid mothers seeking to feed dying babies from their milkless breasts. Were a new Dante to come among us, he could write a new *Inferno* after visiting one of these railway stations.[25]

But in one extremely important sense this first Soviet famine did differ from the famine that was to follow a decade later: in 1921 mass hunger was not kept secret. More importantly, the regime tried to help the starving. *Pravda* itself announced the existence of famine when on 21 June it declared that 25 million people were going hungry in the Soviet Union. Soon after, the regime sanctioned the creation of an 'All-Russian Famine Committee' made up of non-Bolshevik political and cultural figures. Local self-help committees were created to assist the starving.[26] International appeals for aid followed, most prominently from the writer Maxim Gorky, who led a campaign addressed 'To All Honest People', in the name of all that was best in Russian culture. 'Gloomy days have come to the country of Tolstoy, Dostoevsky, Mendeleev, Pavlov, Mussorgsky, Glinka,' he wrote, and called for contributions. Gorky's list of Russian luminaries conspicuously left out the names of Lenin and Trotsky.[27] Extraordinarily – given how paranoid they would become about the diaspora in the years that followed – the Ukrainian Communist Party even discussed asking for help from Ukrainians who had emigrated to Canada and the United States.[28]

This public, international appeal for help, the only one of its kind in Soviet history, produced fast results. Several relief organizations, including the International Red Cross and the Jewish Joint Distribution Committee (known as the JDC, or simply 'Joint'), would eventually contribute to the relief effort, as would the Nansen Mission, a European effort put together by the Norwegian explorer and humanitarian Fridtjof Nansen. But the most important source of immediate aid was the American Relief Administration (ARA), which was already operating in Europe in the spring of 1921. Founded by future president Herbert Hoover, the ARA had successfully distributed more than $1 billion in food and medical relief across Europe in the nine months following the 1918 armistice.[29] Upon hearing Gorky's appeal, Hoover, an astute student of Bolshevik ideology, leapt at the opportunity to expand his aid network into Russia.

Before entering the country, he demanded the release of all Americans held in Soviet prisons, as well as immunity from prosecution for all Americans working for the ARA. Hoover worried that ARA personnel had to control the process or aid would be stolen. He also worried, not without cause, that Americans in Russia could be accused of espionage (and they were indeed collecting information, sending it home and using diplomatic mail to do so).[30] Lenin fumed and called Hoover 'impudent and a liar' for making such demands and raged against the 'rank duplicity' of 'America, Hoover and the League of Nations Council'. He declared that 'Hoover must be punished, he must be *slapped in the face publicly*, for *all the world* to see', an astonishing statement given how much aid he was about to receive. But the scale of the famine was such that Lenin eventually yielded.[31]

In September 1921 an advance party of ARA relief workers reached the city of Kazan on the Volga, where they found poverty of a kind they had never seen before, even in ravaged Europe. On the streets they met 'pitiful-looking figures dressed in rags and begging for a piece of bread in the name of Christ'. In the orphanages they found 'emaciated little skeletons, whose gaunt faces and toothpick legs . . . testified to the truth of the report that they were dying off daily by the dozen'.[32] By the summer of 1922 the Americans were feeding 11 million people every day and delivering care packages to hundreds of thousands. To stop epidemics they provided $8 million worth of medicine as well.[33] Once their efforts were underway, the independent Russian famine relief committee was quietly dissolved: Lenin didn't want any Russian organization not directly run by the Communist Party to gain credibility by participating in the distribution of food. But the American aid project, amplified by contributions from other foreign organizations, was allowed to go ahead, saving millions of lives.

Yet even within this ostensibly outward-looking, genuine and robust response, there were some discordant notes. Throughout the whole disaster the Soviet leadership – just as it would a decade later – never relinquished its desire for hard currency. Even as the famine raged, the Bolsheviks secretly sold gold, artworks and jewellery abroad in order to buy guns, ammunition and industrial machinery. By the autumn of 1922 they began openly selling food on foreign markets too, even while hunger remained widespread and foreign aid was still coming in.[34] This was no secret: Hoover fulminated against the cynicism of a government that knew people were starving, and yet exported food in order to 'secure machinery and materials for the economic improvement of the survivors'.[35] A few months afterwards the ARA left Russia for precisely this reason.

As it would a decade later, the authorities' reaction to the famine also differed between Russia and Ukraine. Like their Russian colleagues, the Ukrainian communists set up a famine committee. But the purpose of the committee was not, at first, to help Ukrainians.[36] In its September 1921 resolution 'on the campaign against hunger', the Politburo noted that many districts in northern Ukraine could be 'fully provided by their provincial and county funds'. It therefore instructed the Ukrainian famine committee to direct any surplus Ukrainian grain – and there was some, in the northern parts of the republic not affected by the famine – to the starving Russian provinces of Tsaritsyn, Uralsk, Saratov and Simbirsk, not to the starving people of southern Ukraine.[37] At about the same time Lenin wrote to Rakovsky, then still the leader of the Ukrainian Bolsheviks, to remind him that he was expecting food and cattle from Kyiv and Kharkiv to be sent to Russia too.[38]

By late autumn 1921, with food shortages worsening, Lenin's tactics sharpened. Although he had already halted food collections in the worst-affected parts of Russia, the Soviet leader ordered even more pressure to be put on peasants in better-off provinces; Ukraine, despite the disaster in its southern and eastern provinces, was deemed to be one. Lenin sent frequent requests to Kharkiv for more grain.[39] He also suggested new tactics: those who refused to turn over grain should face fines and prison – or worse.

In November, Lenin specifically ordered 'harsh revolutionary methods', including the taking of hostages, to be used against peasants who refused to hand over their grain. This form of blackmail, used with such powerful effect against the Jews during the civil war and the pogroms, was now deployed to facilitate collection of this precious commodity. Lenin gave the grain collection teams and *komnezamy* a clear order: 'In every village take between 15 and 20 hostages, and, in case of unmet quotas, put them all up against the wall.' If that tactic failed, hostages were to be shot as 'enemies of the state'.[40] Pressure from above was accompanied by propaganda below. In the Mykolaiv province of southern Ukraine, where famine was already beginning to bite, posters exhorted 'Workers of Mykolaiv, help the starving of the Volga.'[41]

The men of the ARA also noticed Lenin's different treatment of Ukraine and Russia, and recorded it in their notes and memoirs. Initially, the authorities in Moscow did not tell the Americans about food shortages in Ukraine at all. The organization instead learned of the famine in southern Ukraine from the Joint Distribution Committee, which received reports of mass starvation there and passed them on to the ARA and others.

More peculiarly, the ARA's first requests for permission to visit Ukraine were turned down on the grounds that northwestern Ukraine was still producing plenty of grain and the republic had no need of special help. When two ARA officials finally managed to travel to Kharkiv in November 1921, they were met with a cool welcome. Mykola Skrypnyk, at that time the Ukrainian Commissar of Internal Affairs, received the Americans and told them they could not operate in the republic because Ukraine, unlike Russia, did not have an agreement with the ARA. The men were 'partly amused, partly irritated', and insisted that they were interested in famine relief, not politics. Skrypnyk responded that Ukraine was a sovereign state, and not part of Russia: 'you are mixing in politics when you differentiate between the two republics; when you treat with one, and refuse to do so with the other, when you regard one as a sovereign state and the other as a subject state.'[42] Given that Ukraine was at that time contributing to the relief of the Soviet famine, was subject to Soviet laws and confiscatory Soviet agricultural policy, Skrypnyk's insistence on Ukrainian sovereignty in the matter of famine relief was absurd.

Only when starvation in the southern provinces of Ukraine was so widespread that it could not be ignored did the Moscow party bosses and their Ukrainian colleagues relent. In January 1922 the Ukrainian Politburo finally agreed to work with the ARA, as well as with other European and American famine relief organizations. Feelings of trust were still lacking: the Politburo empowered Comrades Rakovsky and Vasilii Mantsev to negotiate with foreign donors, but also to 'take measures' against relief organizations that might turn out to be covers for espionage.[43] Years later Soviet citizens who had worked for the ARA became objects of suspicion: in 1935 an Odessa woman was sentenced as a counter-revolutionary, in part because she had worked with the Americans who sought to relieve the famine in her city.[44] Despite the general ill will, ARA soup kitchens nevertheless began to operate across southern and eastern Ukraine as well as Crimea in the winter and spring of 1922.[45] The Ukrainian Red Cross contributed to the effort too, as did the Joint Distribution Committee, which provided food and other aid to victims of the pogroms.[46]

Inevitably, all the foreign organizations operated under restrictions. The Nansen Mission was forced to work through Soviet institutions instead of using its own personnel. The Joint Distribution Committee did send its own employees, but all of them had to promise to 'refrain from expressions of opinion on national or international politics' and 'do nothing that shall in the slightest way aid or abet any section or element of people over and above any other section or element'.[47] Antisemitism hampered the Committee's relief programme; posters, leaflets and other objects bearing its logo were often quickly removed or confiscated by the authorities. The ARA was sometimes banned from particular places with little advance notice. At one point its officials were told to keep away from the industrial city of Kryvyi Rih, probably because partisans were still operating there. Soviet authorities feared the influence of Americans in territory that was not quite pacified.[48]

Eventually, aid reached Ukraine, food became more available, and death rates slowed. By the end of 1923 the crisis seemed to be under control. But the delay in the delivery of aid had caused tens of thousands of unnecessary deaths. Many wondered, both at the time and later, why it had happened. The ARA's members discussed it among themselves and wrote about it years later. Most believed that the initial Soviet opposition to their relief programme in Ukraine was politically inspired. Southern Ukraine, one of the worst-hit regions in the whole of the USSR, had also been a Makhno and Cossack stronghold. Perhaps Soviet authorities were 'willing to let the Ukraine suffer, rather than take the chance of new uprisings which might follow foreign contact', the Americans mused.[49] Aware that they were perceived as spies, the Americans also thought that the regime expected them to act as provocateurs. They may well have been right.

More recently, some Ukrainian scholars have offered an even more pointed political explanation: perhaps the Soviet authorities actually used the famine instrumentally, as they would in 1932, to put an end to the Ukrainian peasant rebellion.[50] This thesis cannot be proven: there is no evidence of a premeditated plan to starve the Ukrainian peasants in 1920–1. At the same time, it is true that if Moscow had indeed been using its agricultural policy to put down rebellion, it could hardly have done so more efficiently. The grain requisition system broke up communities, severed relationships, and forced peasants to leave home in search of food. Starvation weakened and demoralized those who remained, forcing them to abandon the armed struggle.[51] Even at the time, many noted that conditions were particularly bad in Huliaipole, the home province of Makhno. The territories where he held power in the south were among the most devastated, first by the crop failure and then by the lack of famine relief.[52]

Certainly the regime did use the famine – as it would a decade later – to strike hard at the Ukrainian religious hierarchy. In the name of famine relief, the state forced Ukrainian churches to give gold objects, icons and other valuables to the state. But behind the scenes, party leaders, including Skrypnyk, who led the collection drive, hoped that they could use the policy to create tensions between the newly formed Ukrainian Autocephalous Orthodox Church and its main rival, which was still loyal to the Moscow patriarchate. Over

many weeks the Ukrainian Politburo discussed these Church 'dona-
tions', inquired after them, and interested itself in their sale abroad.[53]
In 1922, Lenin, who was then already ill, sent a letter to Vyacheslav
Molotov, who preceded Stalin in the leadership of the Communist
Party secretariat. The letter, arguing that the famine offered a unique
opportunity to seize Church property, was to be passed on to party
members. The Church's sacrifice of valuable objects could, Lenin
wrote, have an important political impact:

> Now and only now, when people are being eaten in famine-stricken
> areas, and hundreds, if not thousands, of corpses lie on the roads, we
> can (and therefore must) pursue the removal of church property with
> the most frenzied and ruthless energy and not hesitate to put down the
> least opposition. Now and only now, the vast majority of peasants will
> either be on our side, or at least will not be in a position to support to
> any decisive degree this handful of [reactionary] clergy and reaction-
> ary urban petty bourgeoisie, who are willing and able to attempt to
> oppose this Soviet decree with a policy of force.[54]

This, Lenin explained, was a time to teach the peasants, the clergy
and other political opponents a 'lesson', so that 'for the coming decades they will not dare think about any resistance'.[55]

But the extent of the famine did frighten the Bolsheviks. Food
shortages might possibly have helped to end peasant rebellions in
Ukraine, but elsewhere they fuelled them. In the Russian province of
Tambov, food requisitioning sparked the Antonov rebellion, one of
the most serious anti-Bolshevik uprisings of the era. Food shortages
also helped inspire the infamous Kronstadt rebellion, during which
the Red Army fired on sailors who had played an important role in
the revolution. Over the course of three years some 33.5 million
people were affected by famine or food shortages – 26 million in Russia, 7.5 million in Ukraine – though precise death rates are difficult to
calculate because nobody was keeping track of the numbers.[56] In
Ukraine the best guesses put the number of deaths between 250,000
and 500,000 for southern Ukraine, the hardest-hit region.[57] In the
USSR as a whole the ARA estimated that 2 million people had died;
a Soviet publication produced soon after the famine concluded that 5
million had died.[58]

These numbers shook the regime's confidence. The Bolsheviks feared that they were blamed for the disaster – and indeed they were. One survivor of the 1932–3 famine later remembered meeting a peasant from the Dnipropetrovsk province in 1922 and hearing of the famine there. The man explained what had happened that year in no uncertain terms: 'The Bolsheviks robbed people, took horses and oxen. There is no bread. People are dying of hunger.'[59]

By 1922 the Bolsheviks knew that they were unpopular in the countryside and especially the Ukrainian countryside. The expropriation of food had led to shortages, protest and finally starvation, all across the nascent USSR. Their rejection of everything that looked or sounded 'Ukrainian' had helped keep nationalist, anti-Bolshevik anger alive in Ukraine.

In response, the regime changed course and adopted two dramatically new policies, both intended to win back the support of the recalcitrant Soviet peasants, and especially recalcitrant Ukrainian peasants with nationalist sentiments. Lenin's 'New Economic Policy', which put an end to compulsory grain collection and temporarily legalized free trade, is the better remembered of the two. But in 1923, Moscow also launched a new 'indigenization' policy (*korenizatsiia*) designed to appeal to the Soviet federal state's non-Russian minorities. It gave official status and even priority to their national languages, promoted their national culture, and offered what was in effect an affirmative-action policy, replacing Russian cadres from Moscow with ethnic nationals. The policy was known in Ukraine as 'Ukrainization', a word that had actually been coined by Hrushevsky, who had called for the Ukrainization of the Russian-speaking state apparatus back in 1907.[60] Hrushevsky (who was long gone from politics by the early 1920s) had wanted to use the language to solidify support for national independence. The goal of Lenin's 1923 policy was precisely the opposite: he hoped to make Soviet power seem less foreign to Ukrainians, and thus reduce their demands for sovereignty.

To the purists, both of these strategies represented a step 'backwards', away from Marxist-Leninist ideals, and many refused to believe that they would be permanent. One senior Bolshevik, Grigorii Zinoviev, called the New Economic Policy 'a temporary deviation' and a 'clearing of the land for a new and decisive attack of labor against the front of international capitalism'.[61] Lenin himself, when explaining the New Economic Policy to the party's political educators in October 1921, used the expression 'strategic retreat'. When discussing the policy, he often sounded almost apologetic. He told one group of educators that Soviet economic policy had so far been based on a mistaken assumption, namely that 'the peasants would provide us with the required quantity of grain, which we could distribute among the factories and thus achieve communist production and distribution'.[62] Because the peasantry had not yet reached the correct level of political evolution, some retrenchment was now required. Once they became enlightened, it might be possible to try more advanced communist economic policies once again.

To those who had believed in a unified, homogenized, Russian-speaking workers' state, the very notion of 'Ukrainization' was similarly disheartening. Rakovsky, who was still leader of the Ukrainian Council of People's Commissars in 1921, declared that widespread use of the Ukrainian language would mean a return to the 'rule of the Ukrainian petit-bourgeois intelligentsia and the Ukrainian kulaks'. His deputy, Dmytro Lebed, argued even more forcefully that the teaching of Ukrainian was reactionary, because it was an inferior language of the village, whereas Russian was the superior language of the city. In an essay outlining his 'Theory of the Two Cultures', Lebed conceded that there might be a reason to teach peasant children in Ukrainian, since it was their native language. Later, however, they should all study Russian, in order to help them eventually merge with the Russian proletariat.[63]

Beneath their fears of the 'reactionary' and 'kulak' Ukrainian language, Rakovsky, Lebed and the other Russophone Bolsheviks in Ukraine had a mixed set of motives. Once again, there was an element of Russian chauvinism in all of their thinking: Ukraine had been a Russian colony throughout their lives, and it was difficult for any of them to imagine it as anything else. Ukrainian, to many of them, was a 'barnyard' language. As the Ukrainian communist Volodymyr Zatonskyi complained, 'it is an old habit of comrades to look upon Ukraine as Little Russia, as part of the Russian empire – a habit that has been drummed into you throughout the millennia of the existence of Russian imperialism'.[64] Others had deeper objections and argued that Ukrainian was actually a 'counter-revolutionary language'. Scarred by the peasant revolt, they had a well-founded fear of Ukrainian nationalism, which they identified with the Ukrainian language. Zatonskyi again explained: 'Precisely in the year 1919 ... there was a certain suspicion regarding the Ukrainian language. Such feelings were widespread, even in circles of the revolutionary proletariat and peasantry of undeniably proletarian origin.'[65]

Their prejudice against all things Ukrainian of course had an ideological source too: the Bolsheviks were committed to a heavily centralized state and the destruction of independent institutions, whether economic, political or cultural. Intuitively, they understood that the autonomy of any Soviet province or republic could become an obstacle to total power. Class solidarity, not national solidarity, was supposed to guide the way. As another communist leader put it: 'I think that if we concern ourselves with the culture of every nation individually, then this will be an unhealthy national vestige.'[66]

Still, both of the new policies had enthusiastic supporters at the highest levels. The New Economic Policy found a champion in the Bolshevik intellectual Nikolai Bukharin, who came to believe that the USSR would reach the higher stages of socialism through market relations, and who argued forcefully against grain requisitioning.[67] Partly thanks to his support, and to Lenin's support in the months before his death in January 1924, the New Economic Policy – widely known by the acronym NEP – briefly evolved into a form of what Lenin called 'state capitalism'. Under the new system, markets functioned, but only under heavy state control. The state abolished the *prodrazvyorstka*, the mandatory grain procurement, and replaced it with a tax. Peasants began to sell grain again in the traditional way – that is, for money. Small traders – 'NEP men' – also bought and sold grain and thus organized its distribution, as they had for many centuries. At this very elementary level, a market economy was restored and food gradually became more available.

Ukrainization had real advocates too. After the experience of the peasant rebellions, Lenin himself said in 1919 that it would be a 'profound and dangerous error' to ignore nationalist sentiment in Ukraine.[68] In February 1920, as the third and final Bolshevik occupation of Ukraine got underway, he sent a telegram to Stalin, telling him to hire interpreters for the Red Army in Ukraine and to 'oblige unconditionally all their officers to accept applications and other documents in the Ukrainian language'.[69] Lenin did not want to lose Ukraine again, and if that meant indulging Ukrainian national emotions, then he would do so.

Inside Ukraine, the moment of the 'national communists' had arrived. Optimistically, they argued that Ukrainian national feelings would enhance the revolution, and that Ukrainization and Sovietization were not just compatible but mutually reinforcing. Skrypnyk – the same Ukrainian official whose resistance to American aid had so surprised the men from the ARA – was the most enthusiastic of all. Ever since he had served as Lenin's envoy to Ukraine in December 1917, Skrypnyk had been arguing that the hostility between the Russian-speaking proletariat and the Ukrainian-speaking peasantry was counter-productive.[70] His views were echoed by Zatonskyi, who told his fellow Bolsheviks in 1921 that they had missed the nationalist moment: 'When the dark peasant masses rose up and became conscious of themselves, when the peasant who had previously looked at himself and his language with scorn put up his chin and started demanding more – we didn't make use of it.' As a result, the national revolution had been hijacked by the bourgeoisie: 'We should say it straight: that was our great mistake.'[71]

Oleksandr Shumskyi and other members of the far left Borotbyst group, which had secured so much popularity in 1917–18, also joined the ranks of the national communists after 1920.[72] By the standards of the USSR at the time, Shumskyi's position was unusual. Although socialists, Mensheviks, anarchists and Socialist Revolutionaries were already under investigation or arrest all over the Soviet Union, Moscow made an exception in Ukraine for a few of the Borotbyst group, who were brought into the Soviet fold. Lenin hoped that they would align their peasant supporters with the Bolsheviks and add a touch of native authenticity to the new regime.

Shumskyi himself suspected that he was serving as a form of camouflage, but he accepted the arrangement and agreed to serve as Commissar of Education in Ukraine. Skrypnyk became Commissar of Justice. In the summer of 1923 the Central Committee of the

Ukrainian Communist Party – the wider body of leaders, beneath the Politburo – passed its first decree on Ukrainization. The authorities in Kharkiv recognized Ukrainian as the majority language in the republic, and required all state employees to become bilingual within a year.[73]

Through these changes, Ukraine's national communists hoped to make Soviet communism seem more native, to make it look less like a Russian imposition. They also hoped to encourage the Ukrainian intellectual elite to be more sympathetic, and even to make Soviet Ukraine attractive to the ethnic Ukrainians who lived across the border in Poland and Czechoslovakia. The USSR was always looking out for foreign revolutions that it could support. To most people it looked as if Moscow had fully thrown its weight behind these policies, and for a few short years many sincerely believed that they might work.

In March 1924, nearly seven years after his triumphant speech to the flag-waving crowds in Kyiv, Mykhailo Hrushevsky returned to Ukraine. After fleeing the country in 1919, he had lived for a time in Vienna. For a couple of years he contemplated moves to Prague or Lviv, even Oxford or Princeton. He negotiated with the Bolsheviks and seems to have sought a political role.

Although he did not find one, Hrushevsky decided to come back anyway, returning to Ukraine as a 'private person' and a scholar. No one doubted the symbolic significance of his decision, including the Ukrainian communists. Between January and June 1921 the Ukrainian Politburo had discussed Hrushevsky and his possible return no fewer than four times.[74] Many of the Ukrainian national leaders who remained in exile denounced his decision as a 'legitimization' of Bolshevik rule; the Bolsheviks celebrated it for the same reason. It was proof that their policy was working. Later, they would claim he had begged to return, having repented of his previous counter-revolutionary activity.[75]

But Hrushevsky himself said repeatedly that he had made no concessions. He was returning, he said, because he believed that a Ukrainian political revival first required a Ukrainian cultural revival, and he thought that such a thing might now be possible. Restricted though he might be in the Soviet Union, Hrushevsky could not miss this moment, so pregnant with possibilities for Ukraine. 'One must think how to avoid allowing cultural life to backslide,' he wrote to a colleague. 'So far, both government and society are holding their own.'[76] Not everyone in the Ukrainian administration felt the same way: as soon as he arrived back in his homeland, the secret police began to construct what would become a massive surveillance operation all around him, recruiting dozens of people to report on his movements and his thinking.[77] Hrushevsky may not have known the details of this operation, but he surely suspected something like it: before his return, he had asked both the Ukrainian Communist Party and the government to write him letters guaranteeing him immunity from political prosecution.[78]

Nevertheless, on the surface the Bolsheviks accepted his presence, and he accepted the Bolsheviks. Hrushevsky received state support to set up a new institute for historical studies in Kyiv under the banner of the All-Ukrainian Academy of Sciences – *Vseukraïnska Akademiia Nauk* – best known by its Ukrainian acronym, VUAN. He went back to work on his multi-volume *History of Ukraine-Rus'*, began editing a journal, and encouraged younger colleagues in their work.[79]

Hrushevsky's return set the tone for a period of genuine intellectual and cultural ferment in Ukraine. For a few brief years his fellow historians at VUAN produced monographs on nineteenth-century Ukrainian peasant rebellions and the history of Ukrainian nationalist sentiment.[80] The Ukrainian Autocephalous Orthodox Church declared itself fully independent in 1921; it rejected the authority of the Moscow patriarchate, decentralized the hierarchy, revived Ukrainian liturgy, and anointed a leader, Metropolitan Vasyl Lypkivskyi. Artists and architects in Kharkiv experimented with Cubism, Constructivism and Futurism, just like their counterparts in Moscow and Paris. Ukrainian architects built the first skyscraper complex in Europe, a cluster of buildings that included government offices, a library and a hotel. Years later, Borys Kosarev, an artist, set designer, and one of the stars of Kharkiv modernism, remembered that in Kharkiv 'new theatres opened regularly. Performances were accompanied by heated debate.' Kosarev worked on one production created to mark the opening of a tractor-production plant: 'The plant was built by discharged Red Army soldiers and peasants from remote villages – our potential spectators. The task was to tell them the truth about their reality, as well as to create a fascinating performance. But first the spectators had to be lured in.'[81]

Meanwhile, young Ukrainian literati dreamed of inventing whole new forms of artistic experience. One literary group, Hart ('The Tempering'), sought to 'unite the proletarian writers of Ukraine' the better to create 'one international, communist culture'. Not that its leaders, former Borotbysts, were sure what such a thing would look like in reality:

> We do not know whether, during Communism, emotions will disap-
> pear, whether the human being will change to such an extent that he
> will become a luminous globe consisting of the head and brain only,
> or whether new and transformed emotions will come into being.
> Therefore we do not know precisely what form art will assume under
> Communism . . .[82]

Another organization, Pluh ('The Plough'), sought to cultivate peasant writers, in the hope that they could help awaken the creativity of rural Ukraine. They started rural reading circles and sent evangelistic envoys into the countryside. Their literary programme proclaimed the group's goal to be the 'creation of broad pictures, works with universal themes, dealing primarily with the life of the revolutionary peasantry'.[83] They also established one of the first writers' colonies in Ukraine, an apartment compound in Kharkiv where writers and journalists could live together.[84]

The Ukrainian intelligentsia also had, for the first time, the resources and the legal status that they needed in order to standardize their own language. Because Ukrainian had never before been the official language of a modern state, not everybody agreed upon proper usage. Ukrainians in the western half of the country had borrowed many words and spelling habits from Polish, whereas in the eastern half they borrowed from Russian. For the first time in its history the Ukrainian Academy of Sciences set up an orthography division to iron out the differences, and began work on a definitive Russian-Ukrainian dictionary. In 1925 the Ukrainian Council of People's Commissars also created a special orthographic commission to formalize and standardize the language, under the leadership first of

Shumskyi, and then of Skrypnyk. After many months of debate, the commission's work culminated in a conference, held in Kharkiv in the spring of 1927, to which Skrypnyk invited leading scholars from Lviv, which was part of Poland. The resulting 'Kharkiv orthography', finally published in 1929, proved acceptable to both eastern and western Ukrainians. It was intended to become the standard textbook for those living inside the Ukrainian Republic as well as those outside its borders.[85]

As their confidence rose, some of the Ukrainian leadership also began to seek to spread Ukrainian culture beyond the country's formal borders, partly with Moscow's support. The Stalinist leadership particularly approved of Kharkiv's efforts to exert its influence on the Ukrainians across the border in Poland. Shumskyi served as liaison to the Communist Party of western Ukraine, meaning the territories that then belonged to Poland. Stalin personally received a delegation from western Ukraine in 1925, and of course it was hoped that these West Ukrainian communists would help destabilize the Polish state.[86] Things became more complicated when some of the national communists grew interested in the nearly 8 million Ukrainian speakers living across their eastern border in Russia, and especially the 915,000 living in the neighbouring North Caucasian district of Kuban. From 1925 onwards the Ukrainian leadership grew more enthusiastic in its pursuit of national links in Russia, agitating for more Ukrainian-language schools there and even seeking to change the republic's eastern border in order to include more Ukrainian-speaking territory.

Although the alarmed authorities in the North Caucasus successfully resisted all but the most minimal border change, they were forced to relent on schools after a Central Committee investigation into the political mood of the Cossacks found evidence of 'mass counter-revolutionary work' and general dissatisfaction. To placate them, Moscow granted the Cossacks all across Ukraine and Russia recognition as a national minority. Because the Kuban Cossacks spoke Ukrainian, they too had the right to open Ukrainian-language schools.[87]

This 'high' cultural activism was accompanied by what was referred to as 'low' Ukrainization, meaning the promotion of the Ukrainian language in ordinary life – in the media, in public debate, and above all in schools. Just before the start of the school year in 1923, the republican government decreed that all Ukrainian schoolchildren should be taught in their own language, using a new educational pro-gramme designed to 'cultivate a new generation of loyal citizens'.[88] The idea was to make the peasantry both literate and Soviet. By absorbing Marxist thought in Ukrainian, they would come to feel like an integral part of the USSR. In order to promote the language more widely and faster, Skrypnyk even imported 1,500 school-teachers from Poland, where Ukrainian-language schools had been in existence for longer and where the teaching of Ukrainian was more entrenched.[89]

These decisions had a significant impact. The percentage of books published in Ukrainian doubled between 1923 and 1929, and the number of Ukrainian-language newspapers and periodicals grew rap-idly as well. So did the number of Ukrainian schools. In 1923 just over half of schools in the republic taught children in Ukrainian. A decade later the figure had risen to 88 per cent.[90]

In many places the change went even deeper than language. Petro Hryhorenko, a schoolboy at the time – the son of peasants, he became a Soviet general, and later a dissident – remembered the era as one of real enlightenment. Two of the teachers in his village founded a branch of Prosvita, the nineteenth-century Ukrainian cultural organ-ization, which had been revived: 'In their house I first saw and heard played the Ukrainian national musical instrument, the bandura. From them I learned of *Kobzar*, written by the great Ukrainian poet Taras Hryhorovych Shevchenko. And from them I learned that I belonged to the same nationality as the great Shevchenko, that I was Ukrainian.'[91] At the time Hryhorenko perceived no conflict between his 'Ukrainian' identity and the ideals of the Bolsheviks: 'Love for my culture and my people mingled in my mind with the dream of univer-sal happiness, international unity and the unlimited "power of labor".' His Prosvita club eventually founded a Komsomol cell, and he eventually became an active communist.[92]

Others trod a similar path. Ukrainization launched a broad fash-ion for folk music, and hundreds of young Ukrainians, both urban and rural, formed bandura ensembles that performed traditional songs at public events. Sometimes the songs, with their Christian and anti-Russian echoes, had to be toned down and 'secularized'. But their romantic appeal seemed to move young people, including those like Hryhorenko who had not grown up with them.[93]

Romantic legends of the past inspired many. One headmaster in Kyiv was so moved to teach children the language of Ukrainian poetry that he christened his school Taras Shevchenko Kyiv Labour School No. 1, and put Ukraine's national poet at the centre of the curriculum. He encouraged the school's pupils to keep journals, to write down their thoughts and to draw pictures in response to Shevchenko's poetry. They also performed skits about the poet at the local workers' club, and interviewed the school janitor, whose father had met the poet, for the school newspaper.[94] In all of these projects the slogans calling for social justice derived from Shevchenko, not Marx. That some of Shevchenko's verse had anti-Russian overtones seemed, at the time, not to matter: his words were interpreted as opposition to the Russian empire, not to the Russian nation, and allowed to stand.

Still, cracks in the scheme were visible very early. Not all of the schools officially deemed 'Ukrainian-speaking' necessarily taught the language very well. The majority of teachers were still native Russian speakers, and few of them found it easy to make the switch – or wanted to. In rural schools, teachers who spoke bad Ukrainian were instructing pupils who also spoke bad Ukrainian; both might end up speaking an ungrammatical mix of languages. Attempts to verify the skills of teachers met with many forms of passive resistance. Teachers would refuse to be tested, protest that they had no time to acquire fluency or complain, no doubt accurately, about inadequate text-books. It was hard to disprove their claims, since many members of the commissions set up to check on the teachers' aptitudes could not themselves speak Ukrainian either.[95]

Some resisted more actively. Many people didn't want their children to be educated in Ukrainian, on the grounds that they would be handicapped when attempting to enter higher education, where Russian was still dominant.[96] Bureaucrats also resisted efforts to make the state apparatus use Ukrainian. Despite being theoretically required to speak Ukrainian, party officials often shirked the task with impunity. By the second half of the decade the regional party committee in Odessa, a Russophone city, had established courses in Ukrainian for 300 party apparatchiks. Only 226 actually registered, and of that number only 75 attended regularly. Even fewer paid the required fees. The organizers of the programme harassed the recalcitrant pupils to pay up, which could hardly have encouraged them to attend, and complained constantly that they had lost money.[97]

The party's failure even to train its own officials in the language hinted at something deeper. By the mid-1920s the USSR had already become a strict police state, one that, if it had wanted to do so, could have cracked down hard on party members who refused to learn Ukrainian. But in truth the police state was already quietly pursuing another set of policies. Even as Hrushevsky, Shumskyi, Skrypnyk and other advocates of an independent Ukrainian identity rose to prominence in cultural and educational ministries, a very different group of officials were rising alongside them. Pro-Soviet, Russian speaking – and, often, Russian, Jewish or even Latvian or Polish by 'ethnicity' – Ukraine's political policemen were far more likely to be devoted to Stalin than to any abstract idea of the Ukrainian nation. As the decade wore on, their allegiances would begin to show.

Of the Ukrainian policemen who came of age in the 1920s, the most loyal, and in many other ways the most notable, was Vsevolod Balytsky.[98] Born in 1892 in Verkhniodniprovsk, a small city on the Dnieper River, Balytsky spent most of his childhood in the industrial city of Luhansk, where his father was an accountant in a factory. Raised in the Russian-speaking world of the Ukrainian industrial intelligentsia – rumour had it that he was even of aristocratic origin – Balytsky described himself in a 1922 document as 'Russian', though later he changed his national designation to 'Ukrainian'. Only much later, at the time of his arrest during the 'great terror' of 1937, did he declare himself 'Russian' once again.

In fact, Balytsky's national sympathies had always been less important to him than his political sympathies. He was radicalized as a teenager, and later claimed to have been 'in contact with the revolutionary movement in Luhansk' from the age of seventeen. He went to law school in Moscow, and in 1913 joined the Menshevik Party, the Bolsheviks' rivals, a fact that he later tried to strike out of his biography. He switched sides and became a Bolshevik in 1915, joining the party early enough to count as a true believer. Tall and blonde, he was given to dramatic gestures and radical declarations. After being drafted into the army to fight in the First World War, he conducted 'revolutionary agitation' among other soldiers. When the revolution finally broke out in February 1917, he ran one of the bloody 'people's tribunals' in the Caucasus. Perhaps it was there that he acquired his taste for identifying, purging and murdering class enemies. Violence, in Balytsky's rhetoric, was often associated with cleansing and purifying, with ridding the party of 'termites' and 'pollution'.

Balytsky's belief in the cleansing power of political violence motivated him to return to Ukraine, and to join the Ukrainian Cheka, in 1919. In February of that year he published a poem in the Ukrainian *Izvestiya*:

> There, where even yesterday life was so joyous
> Flows the river of blood
> And so? There where it flows
> There will be no mercy
> Nothing will save you, nothing![99]

Soon after his return, Balytsky had the opportunity to see the 'river of blood' he had imagined. He played an active role in resisting the peasant rebellion of 1919. Fighting alongside the Red Army, he took part in the mass murder of hostages, before being forced out of the republic altogether. For a few weeks he wound up in Gomel, in the southeastern corner of the Republic of Belarus, in what must have felt like a major setback. Just as he had been preparing to take his place among the leaders of Ukraine, he found himself stranded in a distant provincial city, once again leading a revolutionary tribunal. Nevertheless, he stuck to his goal even at the edge of the war zone, arresting and shooting counter-revolutionaries, speculators and others who seemed to pose a threat to Soviet forces.

Eventually, Balytsky returned to Ukraine, where he triumphantly helped Dzerzhinsky 'clean up' in the wake of the White Army's retreat. He travelled a good deal around the republic at this time, and at one point accidentally walked into a band of Makhno partisans. According to his own account, the insurgents immediately arrested him and marched him to the edge of the village to be shot. But one of their commanders, apparently impressed by Balytsky's aristocratic bearing, stopped them from killing him. After a brief interrogation, the partisan chief decided to let him go. A few years later Balytsky returned the favour. After Bolshevik forces captured the same commander, Balytsky allegedly commuted his death sentence.[100]

After the fighting died down, Balytsky was rewarded for his loyalty. In 1923 he became commander of the Ukrainian Cheka. Taking the lead from his colleagues in Moscow, who were then busy prosecuting the Bolsheviks' socialist opponents, he helped organize the first trial of Ukrainian Socialist Revolutionaries. In this period the courts handed down relatively mild sentences and many of the accused received pardons.

Quietly, Balytsky's power and influence kept growing. In 1925, at his insistence, the Ukrainian Politburo signed a series of decrees strengthening the Ukrainian secret police, whose name was changed first to GPU – the State Political Directorate – and then to OGPU – the Joint State Political Directorate.[101] Among other things he convinced the Politburo to protect the salaries of his departments' employees. Even as the cultural influence of the Ukrainian intelligentsia was its height and the power of the peasants was at their greatest, Balytsky, Ukrainian by birth but Russian-speaking and Soviet by sympathy, was building the loyalty of quite a different team, preparing them to play a large role in the future of Ukraine.

4

The Double Crisis, 1927–9

Glavlit instructs you to take all measures to completely bar
the appearance in the press of any dispatches (articles, items,
etc) that refer to difficulties or interruptions in the supply of
grain for the country as they could, without sufficient
grounds, cause panic and derail measures being taken by the
government to overcome temporary difficulties in the matter
of grain procurements and supplies for the country.

Mailgram to all units from the information
department of the OGPU, 1927[1]

It is not possible that there is no bread. If they gave us rifles
we would find some.

Comment overheard by a secret police informer, 1927[2]

War Communism had failed. The radical workers' state had not
brought prosperity to the workers. But by the latter part of the 1920s,
Lenin's New Economic Policy was failing too.

Theoretically, markets were free. But in practice, the state was not
content to leave them alone. Officials, suspicious of the traders profit-
ing from the sale of grain, interfered constantly by circulating
aggressive, 'anti-speculator' propaganda and imposing heavy regu-
lations. They set high prices for industrial goods and low prices for
agricultural products (hence the designation 'scissors crisis'), which
created an imbalance. Some traders offered to buy grain at low
'state' prices, others offered high 'private' prices. Many peasants
who could not get the higher prices did not sell at all. Instead they

preferred – logically – to store their grain, feed it to their livestock, and wait for the prices to go up.

This new crisis came as a shock. Food supplies had gradually been improving since the famine of 1921–3. A poor grain harvest in 1924 led once again to widespread hunger, but the peasants still had beets, potatoes, and their cows and pigs to rely upon. The moratorium on enforced grain collection, which was still then in place, meant that peasants were willing to plant during the following spring.[3]

By 1927 the system looked shaky again. In that year the state obtained (according to its own unreliable counting methods) 5.4 million tonnes of grain. But the food distribution agencies that handed out strictly rationed bread loaves to the urban proletariat and the bureaucracy had been counting on 7.7 million tonnes.[4] In an all-union survey, the OGPU reported 'crushing mobs and shouting matches' in the queues for food all across the USSR. The same secret survey quoted the wife of a factory worker: 'the whole day is killed just for 10 pounds of flour, your husband comes home from work and dinner isn't ready'. Ominously, some of the complaining had a political edge. In the city of Tver, police found a proclamation calling for a strike: 'There's no butter, flour became available only recently, there's no kerosene, the people have been duped.'[5] Paul Scheffer, the Moscow correspondent for *Berliner Tageblatt*, reported 'waiting lines in front of the shops everywhere in the Soviet Union' and extraordinarily high prices. His ominous thought: 'Might one not say, in comment on all such things, that they are "like the winter of 1917" in Germany?'[6] Eugene Lyons, freshly posted to Moscow as the correspondent for United Press International, also described the queues he saw in the winter of 1927–8:

> Everywhere these ragged lines, chiefly of women, stretched from shop doors, under clouds of visible breath; patient, bovine, scarcely grumbling . . . Bread, which constitutes the larger half of the ordinary Russian's diet, became a 'deficit product'.[7]

For the Communist Party the crisis threatened to overshadow an important anniversary: ten years after the revolution, living standards in the Soviet Union were still lower than they had been under the tsars. Food of all kinds was obsessively rationed – workers received food coupons according to their status – and very scarce. So sensitive was information about grain production that five months before the anniversary celebrations, in May 1927, the OGPU forbade all Soviet newspapers from writing about any 'difficulties or interruptions in the supply of grain to the country as they could . . . cause panic'.[8]

The renewed food crisis also came at a critical moment in the Communist Party's own internal power struggle. Since Lenin's death in 1924, Stalin had been organizing support inside the Communist Party, marshalling his forces against Trotsky, his main rival. To do so, he had sided with the 'Rightists', most notably Nikolai Bukharin – who supported the principles of the New Economic Policy, limited free commerce and cooperation with the peasants – against Trotsky's 'Leftists', who warned that the policy would create a new capitalist class and enrich the kulaks in the countryside. But in 1927 he flipped his politics: having satisfactorily disposed of the 'Leftists' – Trotsky was by now in disgrace, and would soon be in exile – Stalin now began preparing an attack on the 'Rightists', Bukharin and the New Economic Policy. In other words, Stalin used the grain crisis, as well as the general economic dissatisfaction, not only to radicalize Soviet policy, but also to complete the destruction of this group of rivals.

From the Kremlin's standpoint, 1927 was also an important year in foreign policy. For the previous several years, the OGPU had been expanding its spy network throughout Europe with great enthusiasm. But in 1927 the Soviet Union's foreign spies suffered some embarrassing setbacks. Major Soviet espionage operations were uncovered in Poland, Turkey, China and France, among other places. In London, the British government broke off diplomatic relations with the USSR after uncovering an operation described by the Home Secretary in the House of Commons as 'one of the most complete and one of the most nefarious spy systems that it has ever been my lot to meet'.[9]

At the same time the newly expanded Soviet espionage service uncovered what it claimed to be evidence of Japanese territorial designs on the Soviet Far East. Poland was assumed to have ongoing designs on the USSR as well, especially after Marshal Piłsudski's successful coup d'état in 1926 brought the victor of the Polish-Bolshevik war back to power. Ironically, Poland did secretly sponsor some schemes to promote Ukrainian nationalism in the 1920s, with some support from Japanese diplomats, but there is no evidence that Stalin knew about it.[10] His suspicions were focused instead on non-existent Polish and Japanese spy networks and what was, at best, some very superficial Polish-Japanese military collaboration.[11]

Taken together all these incidents did seem threatening, especially to Soviet leaders who still remembered the bitterness of the fighting a decade earlier. In a *Pravda* article in July 1927, Stalin warned of the 'real and material threat of a new war in general, and a war against the USSR in particular'. Unconnected stories were presented in newspapers and public speeches as a looming conspiracy.[12] The accompanying propaganda campaign prepared Soviet society for wartime conditions and more austerity, and sought to inspire greater loyalty to the communist system at the same time.[13]

Responding both to the apparent threat of hostilities as well as to the more realistic prospect of mass food riots, the OGPU proposed a list of harsh new policies in October 1927. Among other things the secret police wanted the right to 'hold accountable' private grain traders who were 'speculating' in scarce goods and inflating prices.[14] The Politburo also called for an immediate transfer of industrial goods to the countryside (a carrot among the many sticks); the collection of back taxes; the freezing of grain prices; and the direct involvement of local party officials in the collection of grain.[15]

None of these changes had any significant impact. In early January 1928 the Soviet Central Committee observed that despite their orders, 'no breakthrough was visible' in the collection of grain. To solve the problem, Stalin told party bosses to 'rapidly mobilize all of the party's best forces', to make local party leaders 'personally responsible' for grain collection, to organize a propaganda campaign that would point clearly at those who were failing, and to apply 'harsh punishments' to those who were refusing to pay their taxes, especially if they were kulaks.[16] Eventually, the state would fine peasants who could not deliver grain, charging them up to five times its monetary value. Those who refused to pay these fines could have their property confiscated and sold at auction.[17]

The language Stalin now used was militaristic. He spoke of 'mobilization' and 'fronts', as well as of 'enemies' and 'danger'. The kulaks and the speculators had, he said, 'taken advantage of the goodwill and the slow workings of our organizations and broken through the front on the bread market, raised prices and created a wait-and-see mood among the peasants, which has paralysed the grain collection even more'. In the face of this threat it would be a terrible mistake to move softly or slowly. Instead, the kulaks and traders had to be separated from the other peasants, and hit hard with arrests:

> Only with that kind of policy will the middle-income peasants understand that the possibility of higher prices is a lie invented by speculators, that the kulak and the speculator are enemies of Soviet power, that linking their own fate with the fate of speculators and kulaks is dangerous.[18]

At about this time Stalin and the rest of the Soviet leadership also brought back the phrase *chrezvychainye mery*, 'extraordinary measures', as well as the *chrezvychaishchina*, a state of emergency, words still redolent of Tsaritsyn, the Red Terror and the civil war. And along with the language of the civil war, the tactics of the civil war – the violence Stalin had deployed in Tsaritsyn ten years earlier – returned too.

In early January, Genrikh Yagoda, now the chairman of the OGPU, issued abrupt instructions to immediately arrest 'the most prominent private grain procurement agents and most inveterate grain merchants . . . who are disrupting set procurement and market prices'. In practice, anyone making a living trading grain was now liable to be reclassified as a criminal. By the middle of the month more than five hundred people had been imprisoned across Ukraine, and more investigations were underway. In Cherkasy, Mariupol and Kharkhiv, among other places, police discovered many tonnes of grain that had been kept back because peasants had, quite rationally, been waiting for prices to rise. The police pounced upon this evidence of conspiracy.[19]

The OGPU meanwhile concluded that some of the dealers concealing this grain were aware of police repression and seeking actively to avoid it. Many had moved their grain to prevent being arrested; others, hoping for the wave of repression to subside, were paying peasants to hold onto grain in order to wait for a better moment.[20] The OGPU ended all this activity with a blunt decree on 19 January: anyone who refused to sell grain to the state at the agreed price would be arrested and tried.[21] With that order the New Economic Policy effectively came to an end.

The grain traders were useful scapegoats. But in truth, Soviet economic policy in the 1920s had rested on a fundamental contradiction, and even ordinary people could see it. At the beginning of 1929, Semen Ivanisov, an educated peasant from Zaporizhia in southern Ukraine, wrote a letter to a friend who was a party official. The letter praised Lenin, who had once written of the 'indispensable link' between workers and peasants. But Ivanisov feared that Lenin's sentiments had been forgotten. 'What do we see now? The correct relationship with the peasantry, a relationship of allies – it doesn't exist.'

Instead, wrote Ivanisov, he and his fellow peasants were now in an impossible situation. If they worked hard and built up their farms then they became kulaks, 'enemies of the people'. But if they took the other option and remained *bedniaks*, poor peasants – then they were worse off than the 'American peasants' with whom they were supposed to be competing. There seemed no way out of the trap. 'What shall we do,' Ivanisov asked his friend, 'how shall we live?' His own situation was deteriorating. 'Now we have to sell our cows, without that there is nothing. At home there are tears, endless shouting, suffering, curses. I would suggest that if you should go soon and visit a peasant family and listen, you would say: this isn't life, but rather hard labour, hell, worse than the devil knows what. That's all.'[22]

Ivanisov, like many others, faced an impossible choice: ideologically approved poverty on the one hand, or dangerously unacceptable wealth on the other. The peasants knew that if they worked badly, they would go hungry. If they worked well, they would be punished by the state. Even Maurice Hindus, the American journalist who generally admired the USSR, could see the problem: 'When therefore a man came into possession of two or three horses, as many or a few more cows, about half a dozen pigs, and when he raised three or four hundred poods of rye or wheat, he fell into the category of kulak.'[23] Once a peasant became wealthy and successful he became an enemy. Farmers who were too efficient or effective immediately became figures of suspicion. Even girls stayed away, Hindus recorded: 'Nobody wants to marry a rich man nowadays.'[24] Eugene Lyons in Moscow noted that 'the more industrious, more unscrupulous and more prosperous peasants' were all under huge pressure. The writer Mikhail Sholokhov, in his novel *Virgin Soil Upturned*, also depicted a character whose farm had simply prospered too much:

> I sowed twelve, then twenty, and even thirty hectares, think of that! I worked, and my son and his wife. I only hired a labourer a couple of times at the busiest season. What was the Soviet government's order in those years? Sow as much as you can! And now ... I'm afraid. I'm afraid that because of my thirty hectares they'll drag me through the needle's eye, and call me a kulak.[25]

Thus had the Soviet Union comprehensively destroyed the peasants' incentive to produce more grain.

Perhaps not all of the Bolsheviks understood this contradiction. But Stalin certainly did, and in the winter of 1928 he and his most senior comrades decided to take it on directly. The Politburo sent one of its members, Anastas Mikoyan, to the North Caucasus in order to uncover the source of the food shortages. Molotov went to Ukraine. Stalin himself decided to go to Siberia.

The records of Stalin's three-week trip are revealing. In the reports he wrote afterwards, he observed that most of his party colleagues on the ground – some of whom still dared to argue with him – were convinced that the grain shortage could be solved by technical changes, for example by offering the peasants more manufactured goods in exchange for grain. But would a better supply of shoes for peasant children really fix the longer-term problem? At a meeting with Siberian party leaders, Stalin, clad in a brand-new sheepskin coat, unexpectedly began to think aloud about the deep flaws of Soviet agriculture. After the revolution, he reminded them, peasants had occupied and divided up the private estates of aristocrats and monasteries, thus creating hundreds of thousands of tiny, unproductive farms and similar numbers of poor peasants. But this was precisely the problem: kulaks – rich farmers – were so much more productive than their poor neighbours because they had held on to bigger properties.

The strength of the wealthy farmer, Stalin concluded, lay 'in the fact that his farming is large scale'. Larger farms were more efficient, more productive, more amenable to modern technology. Ivanisov had spotted the same problem: over time the most successful farmers became wealthier and accumulated more land, which raised their productivity. But by doing so they became kulaks, and therefore ideologically unacceptable.

What should be done about this? Stalin's ideology would not let him conclude that successful farmers should be allowed to accumulate more land and build up major estates, as had happened in every other society in history. It was impossible, unimaginable, that a communist state could contain major landowners, or even wealthy farmers. But Stalin also understood that persecution of successful peasants would not lead to higher grain production either. His conclusion: collective farming was the only solution. 'Unification of small and tiny peasant household farms into large collective farms . . . for us is the only path.'[26] The USSR needed large, state-owned farms. The peasants had to give up their privately owned land, pool their resources, and join them.

Collectivization had, as noted, been tried on a small scale and mostly abandoned in 1918–19. But it aligned with several other Marxist ideas and had some advocates in the Communist Party, so the idea had remained in the air. Some hoped that the creation of collectively owned communal farms – kolkhoz – would 'proletarianize' the peasantry, making farmers into wage labourers who would begin to think and act like workers. During a discussion of the subject in 1929 one advocate explained that 'the large kolkhoz – and this is entirely clear to everyone – must in its type be a production economy similar to our socialist factories and state farms'.[27] The collectivization propaganda also contained more than a whiff of the Soviet cult of science and of the machine, the belief that modern technology, increased efficiency and rationalized management techniques could solve all problems. Land would be shared. Farming equipment would also be shared. In the name of efficiency, tractors and combine harvesters would be controlled by state-owned Machine Tractor Stations, which would lease them out as needed to the collective farms.

Collectivization and centrally planned agriculture also matched Stalin's plans for Soviet industry. In 1928 the Soviet government would approve its first 'Five-Year Plan', an economic programme that mandated a massive, unprecedented 20 per cent annual increase in industrial output, the adoption of the seven-day week – workers would rest in shifts, so that factories would never have to close – and a new ethic of workplace competition. Foremen, labourers and managers alike vied with one another to fulfil, or even to over-fulfil, the plan. The massive increase in industrial investment created thousands of new working-class jobs, many of which would be taken by peasants forced off their land. It also created an urgent need for coal, iron and natural resources of all kinds, many of which could only be found in the far north or far east of the USSR. These resources would also be mined by peasants made redundant by collectivization.

The 'emergency methods', the collectivization drive and rapid industrialization quickly became Stalin's signature policies. This 'Great Turnaround' or 'Great Upheaval', as it became known, represented a return to the principles of War Communism and, in practice, a second revolution. Because the new policies represented a clear departure from ideas that Stalin and others had been advocating for several years, and because his main party rivals were bitter opponents of collectivization in particular, he became deeply invested, both personally and politically, in their success. Eventually, Stalin would personally redraft the collectivization orders so as to implement them as radically and rapidly as possible.[28]

In the wake of Stalin's visit, the Siberian OGPU realized that they had to ensure their leader's success. Instead of waiting for contributions from the peasants as they had done in the past, they abandoned any pretence of rule of law, sent agents into the countryside, searched and arrested farmers and took their grain, just as they had in the days of the civil war. 'Comrade Stalin gave us our motto,' declared one local grain collector: 'Press, beat, squeeze.'[29] They got results. Even before he had returned to Moscow, Stalin sent a telegram to his colleagues, declaring success: 'We greet the Central Committee with 80 million poods [1.31 million metric tonnes] of grain for January. This is a great victory for the Party.' February, he claimed, would be the 'most important fighting month in Siberia'.[30]

Buoyed by these reports, Stalin intensified the argument for collectivization at two tumultuous Central Committee meetings in the spring and summer of 1928. In the speeches he made at the time, it is clear that he was, in part, pushing hard for the policy change precisely because it was opposed by his remaining serious party rivals, especially Bukharin, whom he now denounced as a 'Right-Opportunist'. Even apart from its ramifications in the countryside, the collectivization policy was an ideological tool that established Stalin as the indisputable leader of the party. Eventually, the acceptance of his policy would invest him with authority and legitimacy inside the party. His opponents would recant their dissent.[31]

In the spring and summer of 1928 the reverse was also true: Stalin used the internal party conflict in order to build up an ideological case for the collectivization drive. At the July plenum, he argued, infamously, that the exploitation of the peasants was the key to the industrialization of the USSR: 'You know that for hundreds of years England squeezed the juice out of all its colonies, from every continent, and thus injected extra investment into its industry.' The USSR could not take that same path, Stalin argued. Nor, he declared, could it rely on foreign loans. The only remaining solution was, in effect, for the country to 'colonize' its own peasants: squeeze them harder and invest this 'internal accumulation' into Soviet industry. To support this transformation, peasants would have to pay 'a tribute' so that the Soviet Union could 'further develop the rate of industrial growth':

> This situation, one must say, is unpleasant. But we wouldn't be Bolsheviks if we skated over this matter and closed our eyes to the fact that without this additional tax on the peasants, unfortunately, our industry and our country will not be able to manage.

As for the 'emergency methods' that were causing so much pain, these had already 'saved the country from a general economic crisis . . . we would now have a serious crisis of the whole national economy, starvation in the cities, starvation in the army'. Those who opposed them 'are dangerous people'. The once-lauded 'tight link' between the peasants and the working class was no longer necessary: 'the only class which holds power is the proletariat'.[32]

Stalin's language was deeply rooted in his Marxist understanding of economics. He had arrived at the 'solution' of rapid collectivization not by accident, but after a careful logical process. He had determined that the peasantry would have to be sacrificed in order to industrialize the USSR, and he was prepared to force millions off their land. He had knowingly decided that they would have to pay 'tribute' to the workers' state, and he knew that they would suffer in the process.

Was forced collectivization, accompanied by violence, really the only solution? Of course not. Other options were open to the Soviet leadership. Bukharin, for example, believed in voluntary collectivization and raising the price of bread.[33] But Stalin's understanding of Soviet agriculture, his fanatical commitment to his ideology and his own experiences – especially his faith in the efficacy of terror – made mass, forced collectivization appear to him inevitable and unavoidable. He would now stake his personal reputation on the success of this policy.

The New Economic Policy was not the only inconsistent Bolshevik policy, nor was it the only one to hit a crisis point in 1927. 'Ukrainization' also contained within itself a profound contradiction, which became obvious around this time. On the one hand, the policy was essentially instrumental: the Bolsheviks in Moscow created it in order to placate Ukrainian nationalists, to convince them that Soviet Ukraine really was a Ukrainian state, and to draw them in to Soviet power structures. Yet to succeed, Ukrainization could not *appear* to be instrumental: if Ukrainian nationalists were to become loyal citizens of the USSR, they needed to believe that Ukrainization was real.[34]

In order to win over Ukrainian nationalists, the Soviet state was therefore obliged to appoint ethnic Ukrainians to leading positions in the country, to fund the teaching of Ukrainian, and to allow the development of an 'authentic' Ukrainian national art and literature that would be regarded as distinct and different from Russian or Soviet culture. But these actions did not placate the nationalists. Instead, they encouraged them to demand more rapid change. Eventually, they encouraged them to question the primacy of Moscow altogether.

The loudest noises of discontent came from the literary world, where ambitions were expanding rapidly. Both the Hart and Pluh groups, like the rest of the Soviet artistic avant-garde, survived only briefly. In January 1926 they were folded into a more explicitly political organization, the Free Academy of Proletarian Literature, *Vilna Akademiia Proletarskoï Literatury*, known by its Ukrainian acronym, VAPLITE. The group's leader, Mykola Khvylovyi, had joined the Bolsheviks during the civil war and even belonged briefly to the Cheka. But his identification with Ukraine afforded him some distance from the Moscow Bolsheviks, and he began to develop in a different direction. Eschewing provincialism, 'backwardness' and the peasantry, railing against the 'servile psychology' of his compatriots, Khvylovyi aspired instead for Ukraine to develop an urban literary culture. He sought to identify Ukraine with Europe, not Russia, and by 1925 he was willing to say so:

> Since our literature can at last follow its own path of development, we are faced with the question: by which of the world's literatures should we set our course? On no account by the Russian. This is definite and unconditional. Our political union must not be confused with literature. Ukrainian poetry must flee as quickly as possible from Russian literature and its styles ... the point is that Russian literature has weighed down upon us for centuries as master of the situation, it has conditioned our psyche to play the slavish imitator ...[35]

The Ukrainian artist Mykhailo Boichuk, a modernist who had been part of the revolutionary avant-garde, had come to a similar conclusion around this time. Ukraine should construct a 'great wall' on its border with Russia, as the Chinese had done, 'a barrier even for birds', so that Ukrainian culture stood a chance of developing by itself.[36]

An echo of that language appeared in the Ukrainian press, which was becoming evangelistic about spreading the benefits of Ukrainization beyond the country's borders. As we have seen, the state approved of the idea that Soviet Ukraine should begin to exercise influence on Ukrainian speakers abroad, particularly in Poland. But in 1927, Soviet Ukraine also began looking to exercise influence on Ukrainians in Russia, and in particular on those in Kuban, a province of the North Caucasus where Ukrainian speakers outnumbered Russian speakers by two to one, and three to one in the countryside. The republic's government newspaper published a series of twelve articles on Kuban and the North Caucasus, describing the history of Ukrainian influence in the province and the warm feelings that Ukrainians in Kuban felt for their brethren in Ukraine.

The series of articles openly advocated Ukrainization, infuriating the Russophone communists who ruled Kuban. Soon after, they arrested and prosecuted a group of alleged saboteurs, accusing them of advocating the transfer of Kuban to Ukraine. One confessed, or was made to confess, that he had been inspired by articles in the Ukrainian press.[37] Fears that the region might become 'Ukrainianized', and thus to the Bolsheviks politically unreliable, would have fatal significance a few years later.

Discontent was also simmering within the Ukrainian political class, which objected to the heavy-handed role Moscow continued to play in the affairs of the republic's communists. In April 1925, less than two years after the first decree on Ukrainization, the Soviet Communist Party abruptly sacked the leader of the Ukrainian Communist Party, Emmanuel Kviring, who had been an open opponent of Ukrainization, and replaced him with Lazar Kaganovich, one of Stalin's closest colleagues. Although Kaganovich had been born in Kyiv province, he spoke Ukrainian poorly. He was also Jewish, had spent most of his career in Russia, and was perceived in Ukraine not as a native Ukrainian but as an advocate for the Russian Bolsheviks.

Ostensibly, Kaganovich arrived with a plan to speed up the process of Ukrainization. During his three years in charge of the Ukrainian Communist Party (he was replaced in 1928 by Stanislav Kosior) he would in practice continue to encourage 'low' Ukrainization – the elimination of the bureaucratic obstacles to the use of the language – because the Bolsheviks still thought that was necessary to keep Ukrainian speakers loyal to the regime. But his suspicion of 'high' Ukrainization – culture, literature, theatre – turned quickly into real antagonism, irritating his new colleagues. Soon after Kaganovich's appointment, Oleksandr Shumskyi, the Commissar of Education, met with Stalin. He complained about the new Ukrainian party secretary and demanded the appointment of a 'real' Ukrainian in Kaganovich's place. A few months later Shumskyi also complained to the Ukrainian

Politburo about unnamed Ukrainian communists – 'unprincipled and hypocritical, slavishly two-faced and traitorously sycophantic' – who paid lip service to Ukraine but in truth would do anything to please the Russians in order to 'get a position'.

Shumskyi's confidence – in himself, his position, in Moscow's commitment to Ukrainian culture – was remarkably high, given that the ground was already beginning to shift under his feet. As Kaganovich oriented himself in Ukrainian affairs, he grew increasingly alarmed by what he saw and heard. He was astonished to discover that Hrushevsky, a man who had 'served in a series of governments' – meaning non-Bolshevik ones – was still walking freely on the streets of Kyiv. Elsewhere in the USSR such people were long behind bars. The more aggressive writings of the Ukrainian literati, especially Khvylovyi's call for Ukrainian poetry to 'flee as quickly as possible from Russian literature and its styles', shocked Stalin's envoy too.[38] So did the writer's frequently repeated slogan, *'Het vid Moskvy!'* ('Away from Moscow!'). Kaganovich sent a few choice Khvylovyi quotations to Stalin, who was predictably outraged, denounced the 'extreme views', and fulminated against Comrade Shumskyi for failing to understand that 'only by combatting such extremisms is it possible to transform the rising Ukrainian culture and Ukrainian social life into a Soviet culture and a Soviet social life'.[39]

Stalin had no need to alert his other ally in Ukraine to his concerns, for he already shared them. By that time, Vsevolod Balytsky had run the Ukrainian OGPU for several years, mostly keeping his activities shrouded in mystery. Although in charge of what was technically a Ukrainian party organization, Balytsky kept quiet about his surveillance of leading cultural figures and politicians, never making regular reports to the Ukrainian Council of Ministers or to local administrators. He even blocked a propaganda film intended to laud the work of his agents, on the grounds that it would reveal too many secrets. He remained loyal not to the Republic of Ukraine but to the Communist Party leadership in Moscow, and he demanded the same of his subordinates: 'If the order is given to shoot into the crowd and you refuse,' he told them at one point, 'then I will shoot all of you. You must conform without objection to my commands, I will permit no protests.' At the same time Balytsky worked hard to improve their salaries and privileges, as well as his own. Presumably it was at about this time that he acquired the taste for jewellery and fine art, which would be discovered in his possession at the time of his death.[40]

By 1925, Balytsky had also convinced the Ukrainian Politburo to set up a commission to monitor the activities of 'Ukrainian intellectuals', particularly those linked to the Academy of Sciences. In 1926 the OGPU produced a report 'on Ukrainian separatism' that recommended close observation of anyone with past links to any 'Ukrainian anti-Soviet movements'.[41] The nationalists had stopped conducting an open struggle against the Soviet state, but that 'does not mean that they have been fully reconciled to the existing situation and have sincerely abandoned their hostile intentions'.[42] Perhaps, the authors mused, the nationalists had changed not ideology but tactics:

> Their hopes to overthrow Soviet power failed. The nationalists were forced to accept Soviet power as an unavoidable fact. Therefore, a new battle tactic was forged. They will use the new weapon of 'cultural work' against Soviet power . . . In general, representatives of Ukrainian nationalism work without rest to embed nationalist feelings in the masses . . .[43]

Kaganovich, who would have read all these reports, concluded that these nationalists, among them the former Borotbysts, had not 'come over to our side' because they were true Bolsheviks, but rather because they were 'calculating that they would re-orient us'. The Soviet programme of Ukrainization had, he feared, failed to Sovietize Ukraine. Instead, it had emboldened the enemies of the USSR, turning them into a 'hostile force' that threatened Soviet society from within: by allowing Ukrainian nationalists to remain in power, the Bolsheviks had nurtured the seeds of a new opposition.[44]

Balytsky, with the skill of a trained conspiracy theorist, detected an even deeper plot. He suspected that the Ukrainian nationalists were not merely enemies: they were also traitors, a 'fifth column' that had infiltrated its way into the Soviet system on behalf of foreign powers. In a report entitled 'On the Strength of the Counter-Revolution in Ukraine', he traced the origins of this secret force to the coup carried out by Piłsudski in Poland in May 1926. 'Anti-Soviet elements' in Ukraine had, he explained, 'seen in the figure of Piłsudski an old ally of Petliura', and had been inspired once again to fight for the bourgeois-nationalist cause. The destruction of this elaborate plot would require a 'vast operation to strangle anti-Soviet Ukrainian activity'.[45]

As 1926 turned to 1927, the vast operation began. Stalin kicked off a wave of attacks on Shumskyi, denouncing him by name. One by one the other members of the Ukrainian Communist Party Central Committee also denounced Shumskyi, censured him and insulted him, both at party meetings and in the press. He had to resign as Commissar of Education, and from a host of other institutions as well, including the orthographic commission tasked with writing the Ukrainian language dictionary. Khvylovyi was also attacked and expelled from VAPLITE; the literary organization was forcibly dissolved and replaced with a more 'pro-Soviet' – in other words controlled and penetrated – union of proletarian writers, the All-Ukrainian Union of the Workers of Communist Culture. 'Shumskyism' and 'Khvylovyism' became buzzwords for dangerous nationalist deviations. In subsequent months and years association with either one of them became toxic.

The attacks on Shumskyi and Khvylovyi were only the loudest manifestations of the political pressure that began to affect other Ukrainian intellectuals as well. Hrushevsky, under heavy surveillance since his return to Kyiv, began to have trouble getting his books published.[46] Suddenly, he encountered difficulties in travelling abroad – the informers watching him were convinced he was planning to defect – and an OGPU plot would soon prevent him from becoming president of the Academy of Sciences.[47]

The OGPU also stepped up its surveillance campaign. One of its informers heard a Ukrainian professor predicting a war between the Soviet Union and Poland and arguing, allegedly, that Ukrainians should 'use the conflict to strengthen themselves'. A further informer claimed that another professor believed that 'Ukrainization' would raise national awareness to such an extent that soon – within two or three years – Ukraine would separate itself from Russia. The OGPU also recorded Ukrainian intellectuals worrying that the republic would soon fall into the hands of 'foreign' elements – that is, Russians and Jews.[48] These accusations filtered into the language of the leadership. At a special plenum in the spring of 1927, Skrypnyk, who had now replaced Shumskyi as Commissar of Education, echoed the general paranoia about foreign enemies and denounced both Shumskyi and Khvylovyi for collaborating with 'fascist' Poland.[49]

By the end of 1927, Balytsky was ready to proclaim the existence of a broader conspiracy: in Ukraine the Communist Party was facing opposition of an unprecedented kind. Acting both openly and subversively, people with links to anti-Bolshevik parties were working inside Soviet institutions in order to hide their true allegiance. Many remained in contact with 'foreigners' who were actively seeking to launch a counter-revolution, just as they had done in 1919.

Not accidentally, this wave of accusations coincided with the food shortages and discontent of 1927, as well as the ten-year anniversary of the revolution. Someone, after all, had to be blamed for the slow pace of Soviet growth – and it would not be Stalin.

In 1927 the OGPU had begun looking for a 'case' that could launch a new campaign against the saboteurs and foreign agents who were allegedly holding back the USSR. In the spring of 1928 they found one. In the Russian town of Shakhty – just to the east of Ukraine, in the North Caucasus, on the edge of the Donbas coal basin – the OGPU 'discovered' a conspiracy of engineers who allegedly were aiming to destroy the coal industry, in league with manipulative foreign powers. A few of them had indeed come from abroad and in due course more than two dozen German engineers were arrested, along with similar numbers of Soviet colleagues. The secret police also believed they would find connections between members of the workforce and the former owners of factories who had lost their property in the revolution and were supposedly plotting to get it back, as well as links to other foreign powers, including Poland.

The result was an elaborate show trial, the first of many. Dozens of foreign journalists attended the court in Shakhty in southwest Russia every day, along with the German ambassador and other prominent guests. The chief prosecutor, Nikolai Krylenko – an advocate of 'socialist justice', the theory that politics matter more than rule of law – lectured the spellbound audience about the 'vampires' who had sucked the blood of the working class. 'This was Revolutionary

Justice,' wrote Eugene Lyons, 'its flaming eyes wide open, its flaming sword poised to strike.'[50] Not all of the testimony went quite the way it was supposed to. One of the witnesses, Nekrasov, failed to appear. His lawyer explained that Nekrasov 'was suffering hallucinations and had been placed in a padded cell, where he screamed about rifles pointed at his heart and suffered paroxysms'.[51] One of the German engineers openly declared he had made his 'confession' only under duress.[52] Nevertheless, five of the engineers accused of 'wrecking' were sentenced to death, and forty-four received prison sentences. Newspapers across Russia covered the trial in great detail. Party functionaries everywhere got the message: if you don't obey, this too can be your fate. In practice, 'the Shakhty engineers were essentially on trial not as individuals but as members of a class'.[53] Anyone with education, expertise, technical experience was now under suspicion.

Because so many foreigners were involved, the Shakhty trial enjoyed huge notoriety abroad. Foreign diplomats rightly interpreted it as a signal that the New Economic Policy had been abandoned and that bigger changes were coming. But inside the Soviet Union almost as much attention was paid to a second show trial: that of the Union for the Liberation of Ukraine, the *Spilka Vyzvolennia Ukraïny* or SVU, an organization which seems to have been entirely fictional. A group with a similar name had been founded in Lviv in 1914 – it later developed small branches in Vienna and Berlin before fading away – and had propagated the Ukrainian cause among prisoners of war. But the Soviet version was invented by Balytsky's Ukrainian OGPU. The goal was clear: the arrest of Ukrainian intellectuals who might secretly harbour a belief in Ukrainian independence, and the destruction of that belief once and for all.[54]

The SVU trial was just as well prepared as the Shakhty trial, and had equally broad aims.[55] The first arrests were made in the spring of 1929. Eventually, the OGPU detained 30,000 people – intellectuals, artists, technical experts, writers and scientists – and publicly tried forty-five of them at the Kharkhiv Opera House in the spring of 1930. The most prominent was Serhii Yefremov, a literary critic, historian, vice-president of the Ukrainian Academy of Sciences and a former deputy chairman of the Central Rada. Yefremov had already been under public attack for many months, on the grounds that he had published an article in a Ukrainian-language newspaper based across the Polish border in Lviv. Others on trial included professors, lecturers, editors, laboratory assistants, as well as linguists, doctors, lawyers, theologians and chemical engineers.[56] Several others had also been Central Rada politicians; nearly half were either priests or the sons of priests.[57]

Teachers and students were particular targets. Among them was the director of the Taras Shevchenko Kyiv Labour School No. 1, which had so assiduously organized its curriculum around the verse of Ukraine's national poet. The director and four of his colleagues were arrested on the grounds that they had supposedly excluded the children of Jews and workers from the school, had catered exclusively to the 'bourgeois nationalists', and had collected funds for a monument to Petliura. Leaders of student organizations, including some that had allegedly recruited kulak children by reading Shevchenko's poetry, were also arrested and tried. The state seemed to fear that many Ukrainians would be seduced by nationalist poetry, a paranoia that would last until the 1980s.[58]

The Ukrainian Autocephalous Orthodox Church was another target. Its success – at its height it had 6 million followers and thirty bishops – had inspired suspicion. Balytsky's secret police had picked up 'clues' about the Church's real nature. Informers had reported, for example, that Church leaders secretly told peasants to stay faithful to the Ukrainian cause.[59] During the SVU trial the state openly accused the Church of preparing a revolt:

> the Ukrainian counter-revolution defeated on the battlefields of the civil war hid in the underground and began to organize partisans, to undermine the construction of Soviet power and to launch an uprising against the worker-peasant state. One of the most important roles in this uprising was to be played by the Autocephalous Church, created by the leaders and ideologists of the Petliura movement.[60]

Two Church leaders – brothers, one of them a former member of the Central Rada – were among the group of accused at the SVU trial. Thousands of others, priests as well as ordinary believers, were swept up in the mass arrests that followed.

The occupations of the other defendants varied widely. The state

1. 'From this day forth, the Ukrainian People's Republic becomes independent, subject to no one, a Free, Sovereign State of the Ukrainian People.' The Central Rada declares independence, Fourth Universal, 9 January 1918.

2. Heorhiy Narbut designed the Ukrainian coat-of-arms, stamps and banknotes as well as this cover of the cultural journal *Nashe Mynule*, which means 'Our Past'.

3. An independence rally in 1917 on Khreshchatyk, Kyiv's main street – also the site of the Maidan demonstrations in 2014.

4-5. Mykhailo Hrushevsky, one of the leading figures in the Ukrainian national revival, and the cover of his landmark *History of Ukraine*, published in 1917.

NATIONALISTS AND ANARCHISTS

6. Symon Petliura (*centre right*), commander of the Ukrainian Directory, with Polish leader Józef Piłsudski (*centre left*), Stanislaviv, 1920. Memories of this Ukrainian–Polish alliance haunted Stalin for many years.

7. Nestor Makhno, whose anarchist Black Army fought Ukrainian, Bolshevik and White armies alike.

8. Pavlo Skoropadsky (*centre*), who took the Cossack title *hetman* and ruled Ukraine with German backing in 1918.

COMMUNISTS

9. Oleksandr Shumskyi, the *Borotbyst* party leader who joined the Bolsheviks before being expelled for nationalism. Arrested during the famine.

10. Mykola Skrypnyk, the leading 'national communist'. Killed himself during the famine.

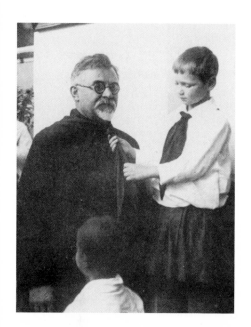

11. Hryhorii Petrovskii with a member of the 'Pioneer' youth group, putting on a Pioneer tie. Leader of the Ukrainian republican government during the famine.

12. Vsevelod Balytsky, OGPU. Leader of the Ukrainian secret police during the famine.

13. An auction of 'kulak' property.

14. A 'kulak' family on their way to exile.

15. Confiscating icons, Kharkiv.

16. Discarded churchbells, Zhytomyr. They were later melted down.

17. Poor peasants beside the ruins of a burned house.

clearly wanted the group to represent a broad swath of the Ukrainian national intelligentsia, in order to slander as many of them as possible. The indictment accused the SVU of plotting the overthrow of Soviet power in Ukraine, 'with the assistance of a foreign bourgeois state' – Poland – so as to 'restore the capitalist order in the form of the Ukrainian People's Republic'. During the trial the journal *Bilshovyk Ukraïny* (*Ukrainian Bolshevik*) put it even more bluntly: 'the proletarian court is examining a case not only of the Petliurite scum, but also judging in historical retrospect all of Ukrainian nationalism, nationalistic parties, their treacherous policies, their unworthy ideas of bourgeois independence, of Ukraine's independence'. One of the defendants, a student named Borys Matushevsky, later recalled hearing similar language from his interrogator. 'We have to put the Ukrainian intelligentsia on its knees, this is our task – and it will be carried out; those whom we do not [put on their knees] we will shoot!'[61]

Stalin personally helped write the trial scenario, sending memoranda about it to the Ukrainian leadership. In one of them he expressed a particular paranoia that would repeat itself many years later, during the 'Doctors' Plot' investigations of the early 1950s. 'We think that not only the insurgent and terrorist actions of the accused must be enlarged upon during the trial,' he wrote to the Ukrainian communist leadership, 'but also the medical tricks, the goal of which was the murder of responsible workers.' That order resulted in the arrest of Arkadii Barbar, a well-known Kyiv physician and professor of medicine. No evidence was produced against him, even during the trial. But Stalin's desire to punish 'the counter-revolutionary part of the specialists who seek to poison and murder communist patients' was all that mattered.[62]

The trial itself was farcical. The case against Yefremov derived almost entirely from notes in his diary, whose existence was revealed to the police by another defendant. But although it contained a few entries that sniped at some of Ukraine's communist leaders, the diary didn't mention a clandestine organization at all. It contained no evidence of foreign contacts or revolutionary conspiracies. Yefremov nevertheless 'confessed', after being told that there was no other way to save his wife from arrest and torture. An informer placed in his cell reported back on his behaviour:

Yefremov returned from the interrogation very upset and to my question, 'How's it going?' he replied: 'I have never been in such a loathsome and pitiful and stupid state. It would be better if they took me right away and finished me off than this torment every day with their interrogations . . . I would be very glad if there truly had been such an organization with all those people and details they are attaching to it today. Then I would say everything and that would be the end of it . . . But here I have to tell them about details about which I know nothing . . .' It should be added that here during this conversation Yefremov was very upset, completely exhausted, and spoke with tremor in his voice and tears in his eyes.[63]

In the end Yefremov wrote a 120-page confession of his 'crimes'; he repeated the same invented stories during the Kharkiv Opera House show trial. Others did the same. A Ukrainian writer, Borys Antonenko, later said of another defendant that 'even if one were to believe all of his statements, during the trial he looked like an operetta chieftain without an army and fellow thinkers'. Another called the trial 'a theatre within a theatre'. The writer Kost Turkalo, possibly the only defendant to survive the trial, his subsequent imprisonment and the Second World War, later described the scene:

It began with the interrogation of the defendants, each of them being given a chance by the presiding justice to say whether he had received a copy of the bill of indictment and, if so, whether he pleaded guilty or not. When all had been put through this ordeal, the justice began to read publicly the whole of the bill of indictment, the reading continuing for more than two days, because the bill was a 230-page book. This book was also given a special name by the defendants, they called it the 'libretto of the grand SVU opera' . . . Everyone was perfectly aware of the court's attitude. It was plain that all details of the trial and its final outcome were planned ahead, and that it was necessary only for propaganda purposes abroad and for the fanatical party followers and some deluded citizenry at home.[64]

All of the defendants were ultimately found guilty. Most received Gulag or prison sentences, and many were later shot during a wave of prison executions in 1938. But the purge didn't end there. Between

1929 and 1934 the OGPU in Ukraine would 'discover' three more nationalist conspiracies: The 'Ukrainian National Centre' (Ukraïnskyi Natsionalnyi Tsentr, or UNT), the 'Ukrainian Military Organization' (Ukraïnska Viiskova Orhanizatsiia, or UVO) and the 'Organization of Ukrainian Nationalists' (Orhanizatsiia Ukraïnskykh Natsionalistiv, or OUN). The UVO and OUN were real organizations – both were active across the border in Poland, where they resisted Polish rule in western Ukraine – but their influence in Ukraine was vastly exaggerated. All these cases kept acquiring new aspects, and were eventually twisted to include anyone whom the political police wanted to arrest, right to the end of the 1930s.[65]

Like the SVU investigation, these cases also had support at the highest levels, and the incentive to expand them was strong. OGPU officers who 'discovered' nationalist conspiracies in Ukraine received promotions. In the spring of 1931 those who specialized in these issues received their own special department within the secret police, the Secret Political Department of the OGPU in Ukraine (the *sekretno-politychnyi viddil*, or SPV). The SPV then created special sections to monitor the Ukrainian Academy of Science, to track the 60,000 Ukrainians who had moved to the USSR from Poland, and to look into a huge range of literary groups and publishers, university professors, high-school teachers and other 'suspicious' groups as well. In 1930 the OGPU even announced that it had discovered a conspiracy of 'counter-revolutionary veterinarians and bacteriologists' who were allegedly poisoning wells and murdering livestock.[66]

Each of these cases was accompanied by a substantial public disinformation campaign. From 1927 onwards the Soviet press was filled with slogans denouncing the 'Ukrainian counter-revolution' and 'Ukrainian bourgeois nationalism'. The public campaigns were intended to affect their victims, and they did: public shaming played an important role in the campaign to 'break' arrestees and get them to confess to crimes they had not committed – and, of course, to silence and terrify everyone who knew them. In the atmosphere of hysteria and hatred any criticism of the Communist Party or any of its policies, including its agricultural policies, could be used as evidence that the critic was a nationalist, a fascist, a traitor, a saboteur or a spy.[67]

*

At a great distance in space and time, the problem of Ukrainian national aspirations might appear to be quite different from the problem of resistance to Soviet grain procurement. The former involved intellectuals, writers and others who felt continued loyalty to the idea of Ukraine as an independent or even semi-independent state. The latter concerned peasants who feared impoverishment at the hands of the USSR. But in the late 1920s there is overwhelming evidence to show that the two became interlinked, at least in the minds of Stalin and the secret police who worked with him.

Famously, Stalin had explicitly linked the 'national question' and the 'peasant question' more than once. In his memorable 1925 speech he had declared that 'the peasantry constitutes the main army of the national movement, that there is no powerful national movement without the peasant army'. In the same lecture he also chided a comrade for failing to take this dangerous combination seriously, for refusing to see the 'profoundly popular and profoundly revolutionary character of the national movement'.[68] Although he did not specifically mention Ukraine by name, Ukraine was the Soviet republic which, at the time, had the largest national movement and the most numerous peasantry, as Stalin well knew.

Even in his theoretical comments, in other words, Stalin saw the danger of 'peasant armies' united behind a national banner. His Bolshevik colleague Mikhail Kalinin made the same point, though Kalinin also repeated a solution offered by the advocates of collectivization: turn the peasants into a proletariat. That way they would lose their attachment to a particular place or nation: 'The national question is purely a peasant question ... the best way to eliminate nationality is a massive factory with thousands of workers ... which like a millstone grinds up all nationalities and forges a new nationality. This nationality is the universal proletariat.'[69]

In practice, the OGPU also anticipated a specific danger to the Soviet state from the Ukrainian peasantry, one that was not theoretical at all. Under economic pressure, the peasants had erupted in revolt in 1918–20. Now, as collectivization loomed, the same provinces were about to be put under economic pressure again. Unsurprisingly, the OGPU feared a repeat of those years, so much so that its officers, echoing Stalin, also began using language lifted straight out of the civil war era.[70]

In a certain sense the OGPU's fears were well founded. Among other things, its tasks included the regular collection of information on the 'political moods' and opinions of ordinary people. It was therefore well aware of how much the new policies on grain collection – essentially a revival of the old ones – would be loathed by those upon whom they were about to be inflicted, especially in Ukraine.

The OGPU were equally aware of discontent among educated Ukrainians in the cities, and they feared the connection between the two disgruntled groups. In 1927 the OGPU reported, among other things, that a former Ukrainian Communist Party member of the Central Committee had been overheard denouncing Moscow's 'colonialist' policies towards Ukraine.[71] They observed a 'chauvinist' crowd caught up in 'national-independent' feelings present yellow and blue flowers – the colours of the Ukrainian flag – to two famous Ukrainian musicians after a concert in Odessa.[72] The OGPU took note of an anonymous letter mailed to a newspaper that described the peasants as 'slaves' who were oppressed beneath the 'Muscovite-Jewish boot' and the 'Tsars from the Cheka'. The same letter warned the editorial board not to read too much into the nation's silence: the Ukrainians had not 'forgotten everything'.[73] Police informers in Zhytomyr even heard teachers complaining that Ukrainian food and resources were being sent to Russia. The teachers agreed that the peasants would surely revolt against such practices: 'It's only necessary to find leaders from among the peasants themselves, in whom the peasant masses could believe.'[74]

Even more worrying was the evidence that some peasants, frightened by the constant drumbeat of war propaganda, were hoping that an invasion might save them from a new round of grain requisitions. Rumours that the Poles were soon to cross the border inspired peasants in the village of Mykhailivka to start stockpiling food, emptying the local cooperative shop of its provisions. A local newspaper printed a letter describing the panic:

> Everyone is crying, and reports arrive as if by telegraph: 'The Poles are already in Velykyi Bobryk!' 'Bobryk has already been taken!' 'They are advancing directly on Mykhailivka!' No one knows what to do – flee or stay.[75]

Secret police reports recorded peasants telling one another that 'in two months the Poles will arrive in Ukraine, and that will be the end of grain requisitions' or that 'We have no grain because the authorities are shipping it to Moscow, and they are shipping it out because they know that they will soon lose Ukraine. Well, never mind, the time is coming for them to take to their heels.' Polish, German and Jewish residents of Ukraine meanwhile began plotting to leave. 'The Germans in Russia are outcasts; we need to go to America', members of that minority told one another: 'It is better to be a good farmer in America than a bad one in Russia and be called a kulak.' Ethnic Poles were reportedly excited by news that the Polish army was conducting military exercises across the border, and taking 'malicious pleasure at the prospect of an impending change of government'.[76]

Knowing or at least guessing at what was to come after collectivization, the secret police expected opposition to increase among urban Ukrainians as well as peasants. Their ideology anticipated this resistance: as the class struggle intensified, the bourgeoisie would naturally fight even harder against the revolution. The OGPU knew it was their job to ensure that the revolution triumphed nevertheless.

In October 1928 two senior OGPU officers, Terentii Derybas and A. Austrin, tried to sketch out the nature of the problem in a wide-ranging report for their superiors, entitled 'Anti-Soviet Movements in the Countryside'. They started by recounting the searing experiences of the civil war all across the USSR, which had forged so many of their careers. 'In the history of the struggle of the organs of the Cheka-OGPU against counter-revolution, the fight against counter-revolutionary manifestations in the countryside played a significant role,' they began. The two officers went on to recall how the 'kulaks and the rural bourgeoisie', led by anti-Soviet parties, had fought the Bolsheviks during the 'kulak uprising' of 1918–19 – in other words, the great peasant revolts led by Petliura, Makhno, Hryhoriev and others. They observed that these peasant movements had subsided during the early 1920s; but they also suspected that they were again gathering strength, taking new forms and using new slogans. In short, the old peasant uprising might return in a new form.

The officers had observed, or said they had observed, a new phenomenon: 'urban anti-Soviet intelligentsia' were making greater efforts than ever before to link up with 'anti-Soviet movements of the kulaks'. Thanks to this expanding relationship between the city and the countryside, they wrote, little cells of opposition had emerged around the country – even within the ranks of the Red Army. The officers were particularly worried by the periodic calls for a peasants' trade union, or for a class-based peasant party – a counterpoint to the workers' party – which the OGPU's informers now heard, or thought they had heard, with alarming frequency all across the Soviet countryside. They had counted 139 calls for a peasants' union in 1925. In 1927 the number had risen to 2,312.

Despite the fact that Symon Petliura himself was now dead – murdered two years earlier by an assassin's bullet in Paris – the memory of how his forces had once conquered Kyiv, backed by Polish forces, was never far from the two officers' thoughts:

> Notably reanimated in recent days are the Petliurists, who are trying to make Ukraine into a beachhead for a future imperialist campaign in the USSR. There is no doubt that the government of Piłsudski stands behind the Petliurist UNR [Ukrainian People's Republic movement] but it would be incorrect to explain the revival of Petliurists in the Ukrainian Republic as simply an intrigue of the Polish government and UNR. The Petliurists, promoting chauvinist and anti-semitic slogans and attracting the masses with the existence of an independent [Ukrainian national] republic, can become an organizational centre which can unite a wide range of anti-Soviet organizations in the villages and among the urban petit-bourgeoisie under a unified national flag, in order to carry out a joint attack on Soviet power.[77]

Even with hindsight it is impossible to judge the veracity of this report. Links between anti-Soviet intellectuals and anti-Soviet peasants in Ukraine may well have been a significant phenomenon, and calls for a peasants' union may also have been spreading. Certainly the secret police reports include multiple examples of political ferment. In late 1927 the newspaper *Vesti* received an anonymous letter from the 'Farmers' Union of Ukraine', sent from a fake address in 'Petliura Street, Kyiv', declaring 'we can no longer bear the rule of communists'. The letter ended with a verse from the Ukrainian national anthem, 'Ukraine has not died yet'. At about the same time the OGPU found leaflets floating around Ukraine, allegedly printed by the 'Ukrainian revolutionary committee', a body that called on the peasants to prepare themselves for the 'day when the rule of the Moscow Bolsheviks will end' and the Ukrainian People's Republic would return.[78]

But these theories could also have been produced or pumped up by the OGPU's collective imagination. Some of the parties and leaflets may also have been produced by the secret police themselves. One of their techniques, learned from their tsarist predecessors, was to create fake opposition movements and organizations designed to tempt potential dissidents into exposing themselves by joining them.

Still, even if these beliefs in a city-country conspiracy were paranoid, they were not illogical. The Bolsheviks' own experience of revolution taught them that revolutions emerge from the link between intellectuals and workers. So why shouldn't a new revolution now emerge from the link between Ukrainian nationalist-intellectuals and peasants? And why mightn't such a movement grow very quickly? After all, that was roughly what had happened in 1919, when the peasant rebellion, seemingly coming from nowhere, had exploded all across Ukraine. Some of the leaders of that movement had certainly had national aspirations, and their rebellion had indeed paved the way for a foreign 'imperialist' invasion.

At the beginning of 1928 the two OGPU officers writing this ponderous essay clearly remembered these events, the tenth anniversary of which was so near. Armed with daily reports of 'anti-Soviet' whispers, leaflets and worse, they had to assume that the danger of another explosion in Ukraine was real. Having anticipated the rise of urban-rural nationalism, the OGPU investigated it, sought it out, and recorded the evidence, real or false. Even before the collectivization drive had properly begun, in other words, the Soviet secret police and Soviet leadership already perceived any Ukrainian resistance to grain collection as evidence of a political plot against the USSR.

Very quickly, the OGPU's expectations were fulfilled: all across the USSR peasants objected to the confiscation of their property, arbitrary arrests, the criminalization of 'grain hoarding' and the imposition of fines. Reports of resistance flooded in from Siberia and the North Caucasus as well as Ukraine, everywhere where 'emergency methods' were applied with vigour. 'Moscow,' recalled Eugene Lyons, 'buzzed with rumors of localized rebellion in the Kuban, Ukraine, and other sections ... When the press was permitted to speak more openly, many of the rumours appeared to be true. From all sections of the country came reports of local communists, visiting grain agents and tax collectors assaulted and murdered.'[79] In some places anger led to real violence. In January 1928 the OGPU arrested six people in a town near Odessa for beating up the secretary of a collective farm. Another group of rebels were arrested in southern Ukraine for thrashing a tax collector.[80]

For some Ukrainians this was not resistance, but rather a struggle for survival. The harvests of 1928–9 were poor. Fluctuating weather and rain during the harvesting season meant that the quantity of grain produced in the winter and spring harvests was well below average. As in 1921, political pressure meant that peasants had very little grain in reserve. Food once again became scarce, especially in the steppe region of southeastern Ukraine – but grain collection continued at the same pace. At least 23,000 people died directly of hunger in the scarcely remembered smaller famine of 1928–9, and another 80,000 died from disease and other knock-on effects of starvation.[81]

In many ways, this smaller famine was a 'dress rehearsal', marking a transition point between the disaster of 1921 and the larger famine of 1932–3. The Soviet Union did not call for international involvement, as it had in 1921. Nor did Moscow provide grain or other food aid. Instead, the USSR left the problem to the Ukrainian communists to solve. In July 1928 the Ukrainian government did create a republican commission to help 'victims of the famine'. The commission granted loans to peasants for the purchase of seeds (which had to be paid back), provided some food aid (in return for public work), offered some meals and medical assistance to children. But news of the famine was kept to a minimum. In about a third of cases death certificates for victims of starvation listed other causes. And at no point in 1928–9 did anyone in the leadership question whether the 'emergency methods' themselves were the source of the problem.[82]

Instead, throughout 1928 the OGPU continued to search for evidence of counter-revolutionary activity. Its officers noted the discovery of 'anti-Soviet leaflets' in several parts of rural Ukraine, produced by 'Petliura-friendly circles'. They recorded 'anti-Soviet' comments in the Ukrainian countryside. 'It's better to burn your bread rather than give it to the Bolsheviks', one peasant was heard to declare.[83] The Soviet leadership believed that many Ukrainians were preparing for outside invasion, and the Ukrainian OGPU was happy to provide them with evidence. Balytsky told Kaganovich in the summer of 1928 that internal dissent in Ukraine was by definition connected to foreign actors:

> One may consider as established the circumstance that the degree of activity of internal chauvinist elements corresponds directly to the complexity and acuteness of the USSR's international status. They proceed from the fundamental thesis that the breakup of the USSR is inevitable, and with this catastrophe Ukraine will be able to gain independence.[84]

Worse, there was evidence of discontent among Red Army troops in the Ukrainian military district, the vast majority of whom were peasants. Knowing how poor the conditions were for their families, they talked about abandoning their units, joining partisan groups, even fighting for peasants' rights. The historian Lyudmyla Hrynevych has compiled a striking list of overheard complaints, all made in May 1928:

> 'In the event of war, the forests will be overflowing with bandits' (80th Infantry Division)
>
> 'As soon as war breaks out, all these organizations will fall apart, and the peasantry will go to fight for its rights' (44th Infantry Division)
>
> 'In the event of war, we will turn our bayonets against those who are flaying the skin off the peasants' (51st Infantry Division)
>
> 'As soon as war breaks out, we will throw down our rifles and scatter to our homes' (Communications Company of the 17th Infantry Corps)[85]

Because the 'political mood' in Ukraine was thought to be so bad, in 1928 the OGPU also began to monitor closely anyone who might *potentially* become the leader of a peasant uprising or a Ukrainian liberation movement. An informer reported that Hryhorii

Kholodnyi, head of the Institute of Ukrainian Scientific Language, told colleagues he believed the police were arresting anyone who had close ties to the villages or who was well regarded among the peasantry. His comments triggered a search for precisely the kind of person that Kholodnyi described. And thus did one of the victims' hypotheses about the wave of arrests become one of the OGPU's working theories. Kholodnyi was eventually arrested himself as part of the SVU case. He spent eight years in the Gulag before being shot in 1938.[86]

But the OGPU now identified another potential scapegoat: the Ukrainian Communist Party itself. While Stalin was in Siberia in 1928, Molotov made a similar trip to Ukraine. Upon his return to Moscow, he told the Politburo that the news was not good. Ukraine – which, Molotov observed, accounted for 37 per cent of the entire grain collection plan for the Soviet Union – was already collecting less and less grain every month. He blamed not just the kulaks and speculators, but the Ukrainian communists. The Ukrainian Party, he complained, had underestimated the grain deficit. 'Elementary discipline' was lacking in the provinces. Local officials were setting their own grain collection targets, regardless of the 'all-Union' targets and requests sent from Kyiv. Some of these local officials didn't even seem to care about his visit, Molotov observed with all the outrage he could muster: they had evidently decided these 'emergency measures' amounted to a 'mini-storm' that would soon pass.[87]

The idea that some local communist parties were more than merely ineffective also began to appear in OGPU reports soon afterwards. Another account spoke of 'khvostism' – from the Russian for 'tail', meaning to be behind events – and 'inactivity' among party members. It also accused them of offering 'incorrect explanations of the goals of the [grain procurement] campaign' and harbouring unwarranted sympathy for kulaks. Some lower-level officials, the report stated, were actually refusing to procure grain or carry out any orders at all.[88] OGPU informers even recorded the grumblings of Marchenko and Lebedenko, two local officials. The former objected to Molotov himself. The man was a Russian who lived in Moscow, Marchenko grumbled: his visit was evidence that the Ukrainian Republic was nothing but a 'fiction', and that the Ukrainian communists were mere puppets. Lebedenko went further: 'The Bolsheviks have never robbed Ukraine as thoroughly and as cynically as they do now. Without question, there will be famine . . .'[89]

Instead of addressing the problem, the Soviet Communist Party sought to eliminate the dissidents. In November 1928 the state conducted a purge of the *komnezamy*, the committees of poor peasants, kicking out those members who were insufficiently enthusiastic. Purges of the Ukrainian Communist Party also took place that year. These were not the lethal purges of 1937–8; the point was not to kill people, but to eliminate potential troublemakers, and to create the atmosphere of insecurity and tension that would persuade party members to carry out the difficult task of collectivization in the months to come.[90] In practice, Moscow was also accumulating the evidence it might need in the future. Collectivization was coming. And if it failed in Ukraine, Moscow could force the Ukrainian Communist Party to shoulder the blame.

Wild rumours now swept across the countryside. Ukrainians were afraid of a new wave of requisitions, famine, economic collapse, or war. The peasants told one another that the grain requisitions had become harsher because the Soviet Union owed money to foreign governments. Many started to bury their grain underground. Some refused to sell anything for paper money. Others began hoarding whatever goods they could buy.[91] In this atmosphere – of conspiracy, hysteria, uncertainty, suspicion – collectivization began.

5

Collectivization: Revolution in the Countryside, 1930

Green corn waves new shoots
Though planted not long ago
Our brigadier sports new boots
While we barefoot go.

Collective farm song, 1930s[1]

The words 'liquidation of the kulaks' carry few implications of human agony. It seems a formula of social engineering and has an impersonal and metallic ring. But for those who saw the process at close range the phrase is freighted with horror . . .

Eugene Lyons, Assignment in Utopia, *1937*[2]

In the winter of 1929 outsiders came to Miron Dolot's village on the banks of the Tiasmyn River in central Ukraine. It was a large village by the standards of the time, with about eight hundred families, a church and a central square. Villagers owned their own house and land, but most of those houses had thatched roofs and the plots were tiny. Few farmers possessed more than fifty acres, but they felt, by the standards of the time, comfortably off.

As Dolot remembered it, the presence of the Soviet state in his village in the 1920s had been minimal. 'We were completely free in our movements. We took pleasure trips and travelled freely looking for jobs. We went to big cities and neighboring towns to attend weddings, church bazaars, and funerals. No one asked us for documents or questioned us about our destinations.'[3] Others remembered the era before collectivization in the same way. The Soviet Union was in charge, but not every aspect of life was controlled by the state, and peasants lived much as they had in the past. They farmed the land, ran small businesses, traded and bartered. A woman from Poltava remembered that her parents, 'very industrious people and religious', had owned ten hectares of land and earned money doing other odd jobs too: 'My father was a good carpenter. He also knew many other crafts.'[4]

Politics had remained loose and decentralized: 'The Ukrainian government did not dictate in the 1920s and say that a particular school had to be Ukrainian or Russian, because that decision was made in the locale itself.'[5] Villages were self-governing, much as they always had been. Tension between the adherents of Bolshevism and the more traditional peasants remained, but the various groups tried to accommodate one another. In Pylypivka, this is how a group of boys prepared to go carolling on Christmas Day:

> the boys made a star [traditional for carollers] and thought about how to design it. After some debate, a decision was made: on one side of the star, an icon of the Mother of God would be featured, while on the other, a five-pointed [Soviet] star. In addition, they learned not only old carols, but also new ones. They made a plan: when they were approaching a communist's house, they would display the five-pointed star and sing the new carols, but when they approached the house of a religious man, they would display the side with the icon of the Mother of God, and would sing [old carols].[6]

But the outsiders who came to Dolot's village that December brought with them a different set of ideas about how life there should be lived. Loose organization was to be replaced by strict control. Entrepreneurial farmers would become paid labourers. Independence was to be replaced with strict regulation. Above all, in the name of efficiency, collective farms, owned jointly by the commune or the state, were to replace all private farms. As Stalin had said in Siberia, the 'unification of small and tiny peasant household farms into large collective farms . . . for us is the only path'.[7]

Eventually, there would be different types of collective farm with different degrees of communal ownership. But most would require their members to give up their private property – their land as well as horses, cattle, other livestock and tools – and to turn all of it over to the collective.[8] Some peasants would remain in their houses, but others would eventually live in houses or barracks owned by the collective, and would eat all of their meals in a common dining room.[9] None of them would own anything of importance, including tractors, which were to be leased from centralized, state-owned Machine Tractor Stations that would manage their purchase and upkeep. Peasants would not earn their own money, but would rather be paid day wages, *trudodni*, often receiving for their labour not cash but food and other goods, and those in small quantities.

Supposedly, all of this was to come about spontaneously, as the result of a great upswell of rural enthusiasm. In November 1929, Stalin lauded the collectivization 'movement', which he claimed was 'sweeping the country':

> radical change ... has taken place in the development of our agriculture from small, backward *individual* farming to large-scale, advanced *collective* agriculture, to cultivation of the land in common ... the new and decisive feature of the peasant collective farm movement is that the peasants are joining the collective farms not in separate groups, as was formerly the case, but in whole villages, whole regions, whole districts and even whole provinces.[10]

But in practice, the policy was pushed hard from above. In the week starting 10 November 1929 the party's Central Committee met in Moscow and resolved to 'speed-up the process of collectivization of peasant households' by sending party cadres into the villages to set up new communal farms and persuade peasants to join them. The same resolution condemned the opponents of collectivization and expelled their leader, Nikolai Bukharin – Stalin's most important political opponent by that time – from the Politburo. A few weeks later the People's Commissariat for Agriculture declared that all of the grain-producing regions of the USSR would be collectivized within three years.[11]

The men and women who showed up in Dolot's village that winter were the first tangible evidence of the new policy. At first, the villagers didn't take them seriously: 'Their personal appearance amused us. Their pale faces and their clothes were totally out of place in our village surroundings. Walking carefully to avoid getting snow on their polished shoes, they were an alien presence among us.' Their leader, Comrade Zeitlin, treated the peasants rudely and seemed to know nothing of their ways. Supposedly, he mistook a calf for a colt. A farmer pointed out his mistake. 'Colt or calf,' he replied, 'it does not matter. The world proletarian revolution won't suffer because of that.'[12]

Comrade Zeitlin was, in the language of the time, a 'Twenty-Five Thousander' – a 'Thousander' for short – meaning that he was one of approximately 25,000 working-class, urban *aktivists* recruited at the end of 1929, following the Central Committee's resolution, to help carry out the collectivization of Soviet agriculture. The physical manifestation of the Marxist-Leninist belief that the working class would be an 'agent of historical consciousness', these urban activists were enticed into the countryside with a campaign that had the feel of a 'military recruitment drive in the initial stages of a patriotic war'.[13] Newspapers published photographs of these 'worker-volunteers', and factories held meetings to celebrate them. Competition to join their ranks was, at least according to official sources, quite fierce. One volunteer, a former Red partisan, later made an explicit comparison to the bloody battles of the previous decade: 'Here now before me arises an image of '19, when I was in the same district, climbing along snowdrifts with rifle in hand and blizzard raging, like now. I feel that I am young again . . .'[14]

The motivations of the urban men and women themselves were mixed. Some sought advancement, some hoped for material rewards. Many felt genuine revolutionary fervour, stoked by constant, angry, repetitive propaganda. Others felt fear as well, as the newspapers wrote constantly about imminent war. Urban food shortages, all too real, were widely blamed on the peasants, and the Twenty-Five Thousanders knew that too. Even in 1929 many Soviet citizens already believed that recalcitrant peasants posed a very real threat to themselves, and to the future of their revolution. This powerful belief enabled them to do things that 'bourgeois morality' would have once described as evil.

One of the people gripped by this revolutionary fervour was Lev

Kopelev, a Twenty-Five Thousander who played an unusual role in the history of Soviet letters. Kopelev was born in Kyiv to an educated Jewish family, studied in Kharkiv, spoke Ukrainian as well as Russian, but identified himself as 'Soviet'. Much later, in 1945, he was arrested and sent to the Gulag. He survived, befriended the writer Alexander Solzhenitsyn, became a model for one of Solzhenitsyn's characters, wrote powerful memoirs of his own, and became a prominent dissident. But in 1929 he was a true believer:

> With the rest of my generation, I firmly believed that the ends justified the means. Our great goal was the universal triumph of Communism, and for the sake of the goal everything was permissible – to lie, to steal, to destroy hundreds of thousands and even millions of people, all those who were hindering our work or could hinder it, everyone who stood in the way. And to hesitate or doubt about all this was to give in to 'intellectual squeamishness' and 'stupid liberalism', the attributes of people who 'could not see the forest for the trees'.[15]

He was not alone. In 1929, Maurice Hindus, the American socialist, received a letter from a Russian friend, Nadya, who did not yet have the benefit of Kopelev's hindsight. She wrote in a state of ecstatic excitement:

> I am off in villages with a group of other brigadiers, organizing *kolkhozy*. It is a tremendous job, but we are making amazing progress . . . I am confident that in time not a peasant will remain on his own land. We shall yet smash the last vestiges of capitalism and forever rid ourselves of exploitation . . . The very air here is afire with a new spirit and a new energy.[16]

Kopelev, Nadya and others like them were bolstered by a sense of grievance. The Bolsheviks had made extraordinary promises to people, offering wealth, happiness, land ownership, power. But the revolution and the civil war had been violent and disorienting, and the promises had not been kept. Ten years after the revolution, many people were disappointed. They needed an explanation for the hollowness of the Bolshevik triumph. The Communist Party offered them a scapegoat, and urged them to feel no mercy. Mikhail Sholokhov, in his novel *Virgin Soil Upturned*, painted a telling portrait of one such disappointed fanatic. Davidov was a Twenty-Five Thou-sander who had come to collectivize the peasants at any cost. When, at one point, a farmer tentatively suggested that he had been too cruel to the village kulaks, he lashed back: 'You're sorry for them . . . you feel pity for them. And have they had pity for us? Have our enemies ever wept over the tears of our children? Did they ever weep over the orphans of those they killed?'[17]

It was with this kind of attitude that, after very brief training sessions – usually no more than a couple of weeks – the urban volun-teers set out for the villages. But although they boarded trains in Leningrad, Moscow or Kyiv while listening to the strains of revol-utionary music and the echoes of patriotic speeches, as they moved into the countryside the music faded away. One brigadier wrote later, 'They saw us off with a triumphal march, they met us with a funeral dirge.'[18] It was at this moment in time that the Stalinist rhetoric of progress clashed headlong with the reality of Ukrainian and Russian peasant life.

The trains ran more slowly as they entered the countryside: not every provincial railway manager was enthusiastic about the new urban activists. In Ukraine most of these volunteer outsiders were Russian speakers, either from Russia or from Ukrainian cities; in either case they seemed equally foreign to the Ukrainian-speaking peasants. When they arrived in provincial capitals, the activists sometimes found that the reception was hostile, which was unsur-prising. To local peasants who had just recovered from the shortages and hunger of the summer of 1929, the newcomers would have seemed indistinguishable from the soldiers and activists who had come to the Ukrainian countryside to expropriate grain a decade earlier.

Nor was their task simple. Initially, collectivization was supposed to be voluntary. The activists were simply meant to argue and harangue, and in the process persuade. Village meetings were held, and these agitators also went from house to house. Antonina Solo-vieva, an urban activist and Komsomol member in the Urals, remembered the collectivization drive with nostalgia:

The objective was to talk individual peasants into joining the collective farm; to make sure that the collective farm was ready to begin sowing; and, most important, to find out where and by whom state grain was being hidden ... We would spend long evenings around a small table with a weakly flickering kerosene lamp at some collective farm headquarters, or by a burning stove in some poor peasants' hut.[19]

But while the objectives might have been clear, the lines of command were not. Many different groups had some responsibility for the implementation of collectivization, including the local communist parties, the Komsomol (the communist youth organization), the Young Pioneers (the communist children's organization), the remaining Committees of Poor Peasants, the Central Control Commission, the Workers' and Peasants' Inspectorate, the Collective Farm Centre (*kolkhoz-tsentr*), the trade unions and, of course, the secret police. Other state officials, most notably teachers – educators of the new generation – were involved too.

All these local authorities, already burdened with chaotic chains of command and conflicting priorities, had mixed feelings about these young enthusiasts who had no experience in farming, agriculture or even of country life, while the young urban enthusiasts had mixed feelings about the local authorities too. Many documents from the period cite complaints about the local village councils, which were alleged to be dragging their feet or otherwise obstructing the work of the volunteers sent from the outside. Clearly the village councils were inefficient. But they may also have wanted to protect their neighbours from the harsh impact of orders issued by fanatical young outsiders.[20]

The peasant farmers themselves, whether or not they were classified as kulaks, were even less enthusiastic about the urban activists. The oral historian William Noll, interviewing Ukrainians in the 1980s, found that folk memories of the Twenty-Five Thousanders were still strong. As in Dolot's description, they were remembered as incompetent: they used the wrong seeds for the soil, gave bad advice, knew nothing about the countryside.[21] They were also remembered as foreign, Russians or Jews. Oleksandr Honcharenko, a young man at the time, later recalled – incorrectly, since many of his subjects came from Ukrainian cities – that the Twenty-Five Thousanders were 'all Russians'. He also remembered that in his village in Cherkasy province the brigadier – 'obviously' a Russian – was rejected immediately: 'He came to convince the peasants how wonderful life was under the Soviets. But, who listened? No one. This liar made his way from one end of the village to the other. No one wanted anything to do with him.'[22]

Of course the urban activists were unpopular not just because they seemed 'foreign', but because their policy was unpopular – profoundly so, as the next chapter will explain. But if a small number of peasants eventually came, like Kopelev, to sympathize with their views, most had the opposite reaction. If anything, the peasants' stubborn opposition made the activists angrier, more prone to violence, and more convinced of the rightness of their cause. In January 1930, Genrikh Yagoda, the deputy director of the secret police at the time, told his senior staff that resistance would be fierce. The kulak 'understands perfectly well that he will perish with collectivization and therefore he renders more and more brutal and fierce resistance, as we see already, [ranging] from insurrectionary plots and counter-revolutionary kulak organizations to arson and terror'.[23]

This notion trickled down to the villages, where the emissaries of the working class saw the peasants' unfriendliness as evidence of the 'kulak counter-revolutionary tendencies' that they had been warned to expect. Much of the subsequent cruelty can be explained by this clash between what the urban activists wanted and the very different reality in the countryside itself.

They also had to prove themselves and their loyalty. 'Your task,' a local communist told Antonina Solovieva, 'is to engage in agitational work among the village youth . . . and to find out where the kulaks are hiding the grain and who is wrecking agricultural machinery.' In addition, 'you will need to talk to these people and explain party policies and collectivization to them'. Solovieva, then a young student, had a moment of doubt: 'This was a huge task; were we up to it? We really knew nothing about these things; we did not know how to begin.' Resolved to prove herself – 'there was no time to lose' – she had no incentive to be kind.[24]

*

There is no doubt that the collectivization drive was ordered by Moscow, imposed 'from above', and that it was Stalin's personal policy, as first outlined on his trip to Siberia at the end of 1928. Nor is there any doubt that collectivization was first brought to the countryside by urban outsiders who were culturally alien and, in the case of Ukraine, linguistically and often ethnically alien as well. But the collectivization drive did find some supporters among both local officials and peasants. Just as Aleksandr Shlikhter had set poor villagers against wealthier ones in the immediate aftermath of the revolution, the Bolsheviks yet again sought to empower one group of peasants so that they could exploit their neighbours on behalf of the state.

As soon as they arrived, the outside agitators began to identify and elevate local collaborators – the *aktiv* – who could help them to do just that. Pasha Angelina, later a celebrated 'shock worker' and one of the first female tractor-drivers in the USSR, wrote a highly politicized memoir of collectivization in Starobesheve, her village in Donetsk province. The memoir is notable for its rigid conformity to the socialist realist template – being a predictable tale of the triumph of the Communist Party over all obstacles – as well as for the genuine hatred evoked in her wooden prose. Although she gave few details, Angelina and her family had played an active part in forcing their neighbours to join the new collective farms: 'Those were difficult days, filled with tension and fierce class struggle. It was only after defeating the kulaks and chasing them off the land that we, the poor, felt truly in charge.' Neither she nor her parents and siblings felt any remorse:

> We went after the 'kurkuls' who were strong and ruthless in their hatred of everything new . . . Our family, and many families like ours, had been working for the kulaks for many generations. We realized that it was impossible for us to live on the same earth as those bloodsuckers. The kulaks stood between us and the good life, and no amount of persuasion, constraint or ordinary taxation was sufficient to move them out of the way. Once again, the party understood our needs and showed us the solution. Through Comrade Stalin, the party told us: 'Move from limiting the kulaks to the liquidation of the kulaks as a class . . .'[25]

She and her siblings were not alone. A Ukrainian secret police report from February 1930 described with enthusiasm the crowds of poor and so-called 'middle' peasants, who were rather less impoverished, gathering with 'red flags and revolutionary songs' in some villages to oversee collectivization.[26] Some of these local participants were former members of the 'committees of poor peasants', exactly the same people who had led the grain requisition drives in 1918–20 and felt some loyalty to the Soviet system. Matvii Havryliuk, who had worked as a requisitioner in 1921 despite the kulaks 'threatening to kill me and my family', leapt at the chance to rejoin the struggle: 'All of 1930 I was an agitator, participated in the brigades . . . I even found those kulaks who tried to avoid de-kulakization by hiding in the woods. I personally brought them to justice.'[27]

Others sought to use the new revolutionary situation to improve their status. As the OGPU itself recognized, many of the 'poor peasants' were in fact 'criminal elements' who saw a way to profit off the misfortune of their neighbours.[28] Sergo Ordzhonikidze, the OGPU boss who travelled back and forth between Ukraine and Moscow at this time, worried that the authorities relied too much upon people with no background or experience: 'We take a Komsomol member, we add two or three poor peasants and we call this an "aktiv", and this aktiv conducts the affairs of the village.'[29]

Like the Twenty-Five Thousanders themselves, some of these local collaborators found Bolshevik ideology appealing. They believed the promises of a 'better life', a phrase that must have meant full stomachs to some and something more mystical to others, and they thought that the destruction of the party's 'enemies' could make the better life arrive faster. As in 1918, collectivization would eventually help create a new rural elite, one that felt confident about its right to rule. Activists argued, even years later, that despite the opposition, the collectivization was 'for the greater good'.[30] Many, though not all, would be rewarded with jobs and better rations. The strengthening of this new elite also helped, in turn, to intimidate the opponents of collectivization further. An OGPU report from Ukraine in March 1930 explained, approvingly, that 'the activity of the village masses was so great that throughout the period of the operation there was no need to call on the armed forces.' Thanks to the 'enthusiasm and activity' of local volunteers, opponents of collectivization felt abandoned and alone. This, according to the OGPU, removed the incentive for resistance and demoralized those under arrest.[31]

It is impossible to know, from the evidence available, just how much of the 'enthusiasm and activity' was real. The existing memoirs hint that many of those who joined the collectivization brigades, perhaps even the majority, were neither enthusiastic nor cynical nor criminal, but simply afraid: they felt that they had no option but to join in. They were afraid of being hurt or being beaten, of going hungry, of being named as 'kulaks' or enemies themselves. Komsomol members received direct orders to participate, and may have believed that it was impossible to refuse.[32] One later remembered, 'once all of the students and teachers who were Komsomol and party members were ordered to surround one of the villages to prevent anyone from escaping while [secret police vans] drove the peasants out of the village to the heated box-cars of the trains waiting to deport them'.[33] A teacher recalled that 'all teachers were considered helpers in the socialization of the village, so that we were automatically recruited as activists to encourage people to join the collective farms'. Those who refused could lose their property or be transported to another village.[34]

To those who opposed them, these collaborators were 'lazy loiterers' or 'thieves' who hoped to profit from the misfortune of others.[35] But many of the local perpetrators would have been as terrorized and traumatized as their victims, intimidated by the same undertones of violence and the language of threat. And when famine took hold, some of them would become victims themselves.

One morning in January 1930, not long after the Twenty-Five Thousanders had arrived in Dolot's village, the peasants awoke to discover that several of their most prominent citizens – a teacher, a clerk, a store owner and several relatively wealthy farmers, all among the most respected members of the community – had been arrested. Immediately afterwards, the wives of the arrested men were evicted from their homes along with their children. One of the women, the wife of a farmer known as Uncle Tymish, tried to fight back after they grabbed her:

She struggled and pulled their hair. She was finally dragged out of the house and thrown onto the sleigh. While two men held her, the children were brought out. A few of their possessions were thrown onto the sleigh and it moved off. Still restrained by the two officials, Uncle Tymish's wife and his children, wailing and shouting, disappeared in the winter haze.[36]

Within days of deporting this prosperous farmer and his wife – whether to Siberia or to another part of Ukraine nobody knew – the men from Moscow had occupied Uncle Tymish's house and refitted it to serve as a district office.

What Dolot had witnessed was the beginning of 'de-kulakization' – the ugly, bureaucratic term that was shorthand for the 'elimination of the kulaks as a class'.[37] But who was a kulak? As noted, this term was not traditional everywhere in the USSR, and certainly not in Ukraine. Although widely used in newspapers, by agitators and by authorities of all kinds since the fall of Tsar Nicholas II, it had always been vague and ill-defined. In her memoir of the Russian Revolution, Ekaterina Olitskaia noted that in the civil war era:

Anyone who expressed discontent was a kulak. Peasant families that had never used hired labor were put down as kulaks. A household that had two cows, a cow and a calf or a pair of horses was considered kulak. Villages that refused to give up excess grain or expose kulaks were raided by punitive detachments. So peasants had special meetings to decide who was going to be a kulak. I was astonished by all this, but the peasants explained: 'We were ordered to uncover kulaks, so what else can we do?' . . . To spare the children they usually chose childless bachelors.[38]

In 1929, just as in 1919, the notion of a 'wealthy' peasant remained a relative thing. In a poor village, 'wealthy' could mean a man with two pigs instead of one. A 'wealthy' peasant might also be one who inspired dislike or envy among his neighbours – or who acquired enemies among the village rulers or the local communists.

As the state demands to 'eliminate the kulaks as a class' became a priority, Ukrainian authorities felt the need to find a better definition. In August 1929 the Ukrainian Council of People's Commissars issued a decree identifying the 'symptoms' of kulak farms: a farm that regularly hired labour; a farm that contained a mill, a tannery, brick factory or other small 'industrial' plant; a farm that rented buildings or agricultural implements on a regular basis. Any farm whose owners or managers involved themselves in trade, usury, or any other activity that produced 'unearned income' was certainly run by kulaks too.[39]

Over time, this economic definition would evolve. Needing to explain how it was possible that people who did not employ hired labour or rent property could still oppose collectivization, the authorities invented a new term. The *podkulachniki*, the 'under-kulaks' – or perhaps better translated as 'kulak agents' – were poor peasants who were somehow under the influence of a kulak relative, employer, neighbour or friend. A *podkulachnik* might be a poor man who had had wealthier parents and thus inherited some kind of kulak essence. Alternatively, he might have been somehow duped or misled into opposing the Bolsheviks, and could not be re-educated.[40]

Other poor peasants became kulaks simply because they refused to join the collective farm. Maurice Hindus stood in the back of the room while a visiting party member harangued a gathering of women in the Belarusian village of Bolshoe Bykovo about the so-called benefits of joining the collective farm: 'They would have to bother hardly at all with their babies, he declared, for these would be cared for in well-equipped nurseries. They would not have to roast over ovens, for community kitchens would do all the cooking . . .'

The response to this tirade was silence – and then a 'babel of shouts'. Finally, one of the women spat at the whole gathering: 'Only pigs have come here; I might as well go home.' A local agitator shouted back: 'What do we see? What do we hear? One of our citizens, a poor woman, but one with a decided kulak quirk in her mind, has just called us pigs!' In other words, it was not her wealth that defined the woman as 'kulak' – or rather as a person with a 'kulak quirk in her mind' – but her opposition to collectivization.[41]

The definition, infinitely adaptable, seemed to expand most easily to encompass the smaller ethnic groups who lived in the USSR, including Poles and Germans, both of whom had a distinct presence in Ukraine. In 1929 and 1930 many Ukrainian officials believed that all of the ethnic Germans in Ukraine, who had been there since the eighteenth century, should be classified as kulaks. In practice, they were de-kulakized and deported at about three times the rate of ethnic Ukrainians, and were often targeted for special abuse. 'Wherever you destructive insects have settled in our land,' a collective farm boss told one group of ethnic German villagers, 'no God will drop manna from heaven to help you, and nowhere will anyone hear your miserable complaints.'[42] Jews, by contrast, were very rarely classified as kulaks. Although many were arrested as speculators, very few of them owned land, since the Russian empire had restricted their ability to own property.

Initially, some in the OGPU were uneasy about how quickly the definition of 'kulak' evolved. In a note to Stalin written in March 1930, Yagoda feared that 'middle-income peasants, poor peasants, and even farm labourers and workers' were falling into the 'kulak' category. So were former 'red partisans' and the families of Red Army soldiers. In the Central Volga province, 'middle and poor peasants' were counted as 'dyed-in-the-wool kulaks'. In Ukraine, Yagoda complained, poor peasants were counted as kulaks merely on the grounds that they were 'babblers' or troublemakers. In the Central Black Earth province – one of the Russian administrative districts to the north of Ukraine – the list of kulaks was found to contain three poor peasants and a day labourer, the declassé son of a merchant.[43]

Yet the OGPU was itself responsible for the rapidly expanding definition: in large part, the numbers of people identified as kulaks kept increasing because Moscow said the numbers had to go up. Orders to liquidate the kulaks came accompanied by numbers and lists: how many should be removed, how many exiled, how many sent to the newly expanding concentration camps of the Gulag, how many re-settled in other villages. Policemen on the ground were responsible for meeting these quotas, whether they were able to identify kulaks or not. And if they couldn't find them, then they would have to be created.

Like the central planners of the same era, the OGPU was nothing if not ambitious. Of all the grain-growing regions of the USSR, Ukraine was expected to deliver the most kulaks: 15,000 of the most 'diehard and active kulaks' were to be arrested, 30,000–35,000 kulak families were to be exiled, and all 50,000 were to be removed to the Northern Krai, the northern Russian region near Arkhangelsk on the

White Sea. By contrast, the comparable kulak numbers from Belarus were 4,000–5,000, 6,000–7,000 and 12,000. From the Central Black Earth province 3,000–5,000 were arrested, 10,000–25,000 were to be exiled, and a total of 20,000 were to be resettled. The high numbers for Ukraine may have reflected the higher percentage of peasants there. They may also have reflected Moscow's perception that the Ukraine's peasants remained the greatest source of political threat.[44]

The need to meet these high numbers also meant that anti-kulak rhetoric tended to become more extreme over time, not more moderate. As early as January 1930 an OGPU operative used the term 'kulak-White-Guard-bandits' to describe opponents of collectivization, thus stigmatizing the kulaks not only as class enemies but as national enemies – agents of the 'White Guard' – and criminals.[45] Language also quickly became more extreme on the ground. In Dolot's village one mandatory meeting ended in chaos after villagers refused to sign up for the collective farm. The brigade 'propagandist' urged them on, but no one responded:

'Come on! It's late,' he urged us. 'The sooner you sign in, the sooner you go home.' No one moved. All sat silently. The chairman, bewildered and nervous, whispered something in the propagandist's ear . . . We kept our silence. This irritated the officials, especially the chairman. A moment after the propagandist finished his admonishment, the chairman rushed from behind the table, grabbed the first man before him, and shook him hard. 'You . . . you, enemy of the people!' he shouted, his voice choking with rage. 'What are you waiting for? Maybe Petliura?'[46]

The immediate association of 'Petliura', a name that invoked the anti-Soviet rebellion, was, again, not accidental: to the agitators, anyone who didn't join the collective farm must by definition be part of the counter-revolution, part of the defeated Ukrainian national movement, part of one of the many 'enemies' of the Soviet regime.

Nor were these mere insults. As de-kulakization began in earnest, the vicious language had practical consequences: once a peasant was named a 'kulak', he was automatically a traitor, an enemy and a non-citizen. He lost his property rights, his legal standing, his home and his place of work. His possessions no longer belonged to him;

expropriation often followed. The *aktiv*, in conjunction with the agitators and the police, could and did confiscate kulak homes, tools and livestock with impunity.

In principle, the new collective farms were the beneficiaries of this mass theft. One report to the authorities from the Collective Farm Centre from February 1930 speaks approvingly of the 'decisive methods' being deployed by those prosecuting the battle against the wealthy farmers: 'confiscation of kulak property ... means of production, equipment, livestock and feed. Houses of kulaks are being used for communal organizations or as barracks for farm labourers.'[47]

In practice, de-kulakization quickly evolved into plunder. Some kulak property was confiscated and then sold to the public at improvised auctions. Clothes and trinkets were piled up on carts in village squares, and peasants were invited to bid on their neighbours' possessions:

> I can see the scene as clearly as if it were happening right now: a girl, a member of the Komsomol, is standing in front of the village soviet and conducting an 'auction'. She would pick up some miserable piece of clothing from the pile of goods confiscated from some 'kulak', wave it in the air and ask: 'Who's going to make an offer for this thing?'[48]

Much property was simply stolen outright. At one village near Kharkiv twelve farms were 'de-kulakized'. This meant that, on the appointed day, a mob of 400 peasants carrying red flags marched towards the designated farms. They arrived, ripped apart the huts and took what they wanted. One of the mob leaders seized the hat off a kulak's head and the coat off his body, and walked away wearing both of them.[49] In another village the collective farm and the collective farm boss simply divided all the confiscated property between them.[50] Some called this form of theft War Communism, in another nod to the past.[51]

At times, expropriation was fast and violent. In the Chernihiv province, the local brigades threw a peasant family out of their home in the dead of winter. The entire family was undressed on the road, driven to an unheated building and told it would be their new home.[52] In the Bereznehuvate district, a twelve-year-old girl was left with only a single shirt. A baby was stripped of its clothes and thrown into the street along with its mother. An activists' brigade took away a teenage girl's underwear, and left her naked in the street as well.[53]

In other cases de-kulakization was drawn out over many months. When one peasant refused to join his local collective farm, the authorities made him pay: 'They taxed us more and more. They took away the cow, yet they imposed tax quotas on butter, cheese, and milk, which we didn't have anymore!' When the family had nothing left to give, the brigade leaders arrived to seize whatever was left:

> They began to break into our grain bins where we kept the seed. They would drive up in their horse-drawn carts, load up the carts, taking everything. After the seed, they started taking our clothes. The confiscation happened in stages ... They took all our winter clothes, the sheepskin coats, and cloaks, as well as other clothes. Then they started taking the clothes off our backs.

Finally, in the winter, the local *aktiv* threw the family out of the house, exiled the father, and split the children up among relatives.[54]

In some instances expropriation took place through the means of heavy, retrospective taxation. One peasant donated his livestock to the collective farm. He worked there for a year, but then tried to take his cows back: his children were starving and he needed the milk. He was allowed to do so, but the following day he was asked to pay the heavy taxes required of the 'individual' peasant. To do so, he had to sell a cow, two goats and some clothes. Taxes kept increasing anyway, until the family finally had to sell the house and move into a barn where they slept on hay. Eventually they escaped, blending into the urban landscape of Leningrad.[55]

As collectivization progressed, so did the propaganda campaign. In places where efforts seemed to be flagging, the Red Army would make occasional appearances. Soldiers would march down streets, conduct exercises, fire into the air. Cavalry would ride through the streets at full gallop. Urban agitprop teams sometimes made an appearance as well, 'a few hundred people from neighboring cities [marching] in orderly columns ... ordinary industrial workers, students, office clerks'. They were there to demonstrate the cities' support for collectivization, and they brought propaganda films, improvised theatre and 'unceasing noise'.[56] Although ostensibly intended to show

solidarity between the country and the city, their presence also underlined the pointlessness of dissent. The peasants were to understand
that the urban working class supported collectivization, and that dissent would win them no allies.

Under pressure to fulfil quotas, inspired and terrified by the propaganda machine, the collectivization brigades sometimes resorted to
outright intimidation and torture. Both memoirs and archives record
multiple examples of 'persuasion' involving threats, harassment and
physical violence. In one Russian village a brigade raped two kulak
women and forced an elderly man to dance and sing before beating
him up. In another Russian village an older man was forced to
undress, remove his boots, and march around the room until he collapsed. An OGPU report told of other forms of torture too: 'In the
village of Novooleksandrivka, secretary Erokhin from the Komsomol cell forced a middle peasant to pull the end of a noose that had
been thrown around his neck. The peasant was gasping for breath,
the secretary mocked him, saying, "Here's some water, drink it." '[57]

In Poltava province the daughter of another kulak recalled that her
father was locked in a cold storage room and deprived of food and
drink. For three days he ate only the snow that issued through the
chinks in the wall. On the third day he agreed to join the collective
farm.[58] In Sumy the local brigade leaders set up their headquarters in
one of the villagers' huts. A handful of them sat in the sitting room; a
gun lay on a table in front of them. One by one, recalcitrant peasants
were marched into the room and asked to join the collective farm.
Anyone who refused was shown the revolver – and if that failed, he
was marched to an isolation cell in another village with the words
'malicious hoarder of state grain' written in chalk on his back.[59]

There were many casual cruelties. In one Ukrainian village, brigades burned down the home of two recently orphaned sisters. The
elder girl went to work at the collective farm, and was forbidden to
care for her younger sibling when she became very ill. No pity was
shown to either girl. Instead, neighbours scavenged the charred
remains of their house for firewood, and helped themselves to their
remaining possessions.[60]

Nevertheless, the same extreme circumstances that generated fear
and hatred also sometimes brought out bravery, kindness and

sympathy in people. Even the OGPU saw it. One of its officers observed, with some concern, that 'due to a lack of mass explanatory work, some poor and middle peasants have treated the kulaks with either sympathy or indifference, and in isolated cases, with pity, helping them with lodgings and providing physical and material assistance'. In one village, the OGPU observed how '50 poor peasants, without putting up resistance to the expropriation, wept with the kulaks and helped them take out their household belongings and also [helped] with lodging them.'[61]

From the officer's point of view, the peasants who 'wept with the kulaks' before inviting them into their home were proof that 'mass explanatory work' – vicious propaganda – had failed. But they also proved that even in an atmosphere of violence and hysteria, some people, in some places, managed to preserve their humanity.

Once identified as enemies and robbed of their possessions, the kulaks met a variety of fates. Some were allowed to stay in their villages, where they were given the worst and most inaccessible land. If they continued to refuse to join the collective farm, they often had their tools confiscated, as well as their livestock. They were called names such as *odnoosibnyk*, or singleton, which eventually became insults.[62] When famine struck later on, they were often the first to die.

To keep them away from their friends and neighbours, some kulaks were given plots of land in other parts of the country, or even in the same districts but distant from their old farms and with worse soil. Henrikh Pidvysotsky's family was sent to the Urals: 'We lived there for one summer and spent almost the entire fall walking back on foot.'[63] A Ukrainian government order in late 1930 commanded kulaks to be expropriated and moved to 'the farthest away and least comfortable' land inside the republic.[64]

To avoid that fate many escaped. In a few cases neighbours or local officials helped them to sell their property, or even quietly gave some of it back to ease their journey.[65] Those who could do so made their way to cities. Some 10 million peasants entered the Soviet industrial workforce in the years 1928–32; many, perhaps most, were forced or persuaded to do so by collectivization and de-kulakization.[66] Whereas unemployment had been a problem in some cities just a year or two earlier, factories scrambling to meet their Five Year Plan targets in 1930 were desperate for workers, and not as concerned by their social origins as they were meant to be.

For those kulaks coming from the villages of Ukraine, the most obvious destination was the coalmining and industrial centre of Donbas, in the southeastern corner of the republic. Donbas was expanding rapidly, and it had long had a reputation as the 'wild East', a land of Cossacks and adventurers. In tsarist Russia, Donbas had attracted runaway serfs, religious dissidents, criminals and black marketeers.[67] By 1930 it seemed an obvious destination for anyone who wanted to conceal their 'kulak' origins. Oleksandr Honcharenko later remembered avoiding arrest by 'hiding' in the Donbas: as 'everyone knew,' he wrote 'they were not hunting down kulaks in the Donbas'. Honcharenko believed this was deliberate: Soviet authorities wanted the good workers to go to the factories while the 'riffraff' stayed behind on the collective farms.[68] Even later on, after laws required peasants to have living permits, it was still sometimes possible to flout the rules in Donbas. The work in mines and heavy factories was difficult and dangerous, and the authorities were willing to turn a blind eye to their employees' past.[69]

Some officials still tracked their progress. In Mykolaiv province the authorities recorded the flight of 172 kulak families and their arrival in the industrial quarters of Donbas where they were 'living in working-class apartments and conducting anti-Soviet agitation among the workers'. In Sumy province hundreds of kulaks were also considered to be suspicious because they had 'refused' to sow their land, preferring instead to abandon it and move away, allegedly destroying their farm machinery too.[70]

But the overwhelming number of kulaks wound up much further away from home. Between 1930 and 1933 over 2 million peasants were exiled to Siberia, northern Russia, Central Asia and other underpopulated regions of the Soviet Union, where they lived as 'special exiles', forbidden to leave their designated villages.[71] The story of this vast movement of people is separate from the story of collectivization and famine, though no less tragic. This was the first of what would be several mass Soviet deportations in the 1930s and 1940s, and the most chaotic. Whole families were loaded into boxcars, transported hundreds of miles, and often left in fields with no food or shelter, since no preparations had been made for their arrival. Others were abandoned in Central Asian villages where suspicious Kazakhs either deigned to help them or didn't. Many died on the way, or during the first winter, in settlements with no access to the outside world.

Almost everywhere the facilities were primitive and the local officials were disorganized and neglectful. At what would eventually become a labour camp in the Arkhangelsk region, one prisoner arrived to find 'neither barracks, nor a village. There were tents, on the side, for the guards and for the equipment. There weren't many people, perhaps one and a half thousand. The majority were middle-aged peasants, former *kulaks*. And criminals.'[72] In February 1930 the Politburo itself urgently discussed the fact that Siberia was unprepared for such large numbers of prisoners, not to mention their wives and children. The OGPU, it was decided, would divide the exiles into groups of no more than 60,000 families. Ukraine, Belarus and the other regions with high numbers of kulaks were asked to coordinate their activities accordingly.[73]

In time, the large numbers of deported kulaks would fuel the rapid expansion of the Soviet forced labour system, the chain of camps that eventually became known as the Gulag. Between 1930 and 1933 at least 100,000 kulaks were sent directly into the Gulag, and the system grew, in part, in order to accommodate them.[74] In this era the relatively small group of 'political' camps on the Solovetsky islands expanded across the far north and east. Under the leadership of the OGPU, the Gulag launched a series of ambitious industrial projects: the White Sea canal, the coalmines of Vorkuta, the goldmines of Kolyma – all enterprises made possible by the sudden availability of plentiful forced labour.[75] Conversely, in some regions ambitious local leaders sought to increase the supply of forced labour in order to expand their industrial projects. In the Urals local bureaucrats may have sought an increase in the number of kulaks precisely because they needed men to work in the local coalmines and metallurgical plants, all of which now had to meet the impossible requirements of the Five Year Plan.[76]

In due course the kulaks met the same wide variety of fates as other Gulag prisoners and Soviet deportees. Some starved to death, others were murdered as 'enemies' in the Great Terror of 1937. Some remained in the cities or at the industrial sites to which they had been deported, integrating seamlessly into Soviet working-class culture. Others wound up in the Red Army and fought the Nazis. A few acknowledged that exile saved them from the famine of 1932–3: in the 1980s one Ukrainian peasant told an oral historian he was lucky to have been sent to Siberia, because it meant he could bring his family there when food shortages began.[77]

Most of the kulaks never returned to their villages. They stayed in Siberia or in Donbas, stopped farming, blended into the working class. Thus did Stalinist policy successfully remove the most prosperous, the most effective and the most defiant farmers from the Soviet countryside.

De-kulakization was the most spectacular of the many tools used to force the revolution in the countryside. But it was accompanied by an equally powerful ideological attack on the 'system' that the kulaks supposedly represented, and that the collective farms were meant to replace: the economic structure of the village as well as the social and moral order, symbolized by village churches, priests and religious symbols of all kinds. Religious repression in the USSR began in 1917 and lasted until 1991, but in Ukraine it reached its brutal height during collectivization. It was not coincidental that the Politburo's January 1930 decree on collectivization also ordered churches to be closed and priests arrested: the Soviet leaders knew that a revolution in the countryside's class and economic structure also required a revolution in its habits, its customs and its morality.

The assault on religion was part of collectivization from the beginning. All across Ukraine, the same brigades that organized collectivization also ordered peasants to take down church bells and destroy them, to melt down the bells into metal, to burn church property, to wreck icons.[78] Priests were mocked and holy places were desecrated. Oleksandr Honcharenko has described an agitator who 'donned the priest's vestments, took hold of the chandelier and started clowning around in the church, stomping all over the iconostasis'.[79] Many eyewitnesses – from Odessa, Cherkasy and Zhytomyr provinces in Ukraine among others – remembered this desecration for years afterwards, especially the silencing of the bells.[80] A priest's wife, born in Poltava province, described the assault on her village bell tower: 'When a man went up to remove the bell and the bell fell to the ground and ran, out, all the people burst into tears. Everyone was weeping and saying goodbye to the bell, because that was the last time that the bell rang . . .'

After that the *aktiv* smashed the church icons too. In due course her husband was arrested, along with many other priests: 'They took him away and we were left alone, my son was fatherless.'[81] Other priests were forced out of their parishes. Many were deported along with the kulaks, or else forced to change jobs. Priests shed their cassocks and became manual labourers or factory workers.[82]

The state accompanied the destruction of the physical symbols of religion and the repression of priests with a wave of angry, anti-religious propaganda and attacks on the rituals of religion as well as those of peasant life in general. In rural and urban schools children were told not to believe in God. The state banned traditional holidays – Christmas, Easter, saints' days – as well as Sunday services, replacing them with Bolshevik celebrations such as May Day and the anniversary of the revolution. It also organized atheist lectures and anti-religious meetings. The whole cycle of traditional peasant life – christenings, weddings, funerals – was disrupted. The authorities promoted 'getting together' instead of marriage, a status marked by a visit to a registry office rather than a church, and with no traditional feast or celebration afterwards.[83]

Within a decade musical traditions were lost too. Traditionally, young people had gathered together at somebody's house, unmarried girls helping out with weaving or embroidering while boys sang and played music. This custom of *dosvitky* – 'till dawn' – celebrations gradually ceased, as did Sunday dances and other informal musical gatherings. Young people were told instead to meet in the Komsomol, and formal concerts replaced the spontaneous village music-making.[84]

At the same time the institution of the *kobzar* – the traditional wandering minstrel, playing the bandura, who had once been a staple of Ukrainian village life – disappeared so abruptly that many long believed they had been arrested en masse. There is no documentary evidence of this (though Dmitry Shostakovich referred to it in his memoirs), but it is not unthinkable. Still, even without a deliberate murder, the *kobzars* would have fallen foul of the passport laws passed in 1932; later the famine would have killed many, since they would not have had easy access to ration cards. Inevitably, they would also have attracted the attention of the police. Many of their traditional songs retold Cossack legends, and had anti-Russian overtones that acquired anti-Soviet overtones after the revolution. In 1930 an alert citizen in Kharkiv wrote an indignant letter to a local newspaper, claiming that he had heard a minstrel at a bazaar recite anti-Lenin (and anti-semitic) rhyming couplets, and sing an anti-Soviet song:

> Winter asks the Frost
> Whether the kolkhoz has boots
> There are no boots just sandals,
> The kolkhoz will disintegrate.[85]

The song (which rhymes in Ukrainian) must have been popular, because two ethnographers recorded another man, a blind *kobzar*, singing exactly the same one at a bazaar in Kremenchuk. When policemen came to arrest him, he sang another verse:

> Oh see, good folks,
> What world has arrived now:
> The policeman has become
> A guide for a blindman.[86]

The official dislike of the *kobzar* and the bandura was no surprise: like court jesters in Shakespeare's day, they had always expressed impolitic thoughts and ideas, sometimes singing of things that could not be spoken. In the heated atmosphere of collectivization, when everyone was in search of enemies, this form of humour – along with the nostalgia and emotion that folk music evoked in Ukraine – was intolerable. A Red Army colonel in Kyiv complained about it to a colleague:

> Why is it that when I listen to a piano concert, a violin concert or a symphony orchestra, or a choir, I always notice that the audience listens politely? But when they listen to the women's bandura choir, and

they get to singing the *dumy* [epic ballads], then I see tears welling up in the eyes of the Red Army soldiers? You know, these banduras have a Petliurist soul.[87]

Folk music inspired an emotional attachment to Ukraine and evoked memories of village life. No wonder the Soviet state wanted to destroy both of them.

The joint attack on the churches and village rituals had an ideological justification. The Bolsheviks were committed atheists who believed that churches were an integral part of the old regime. They were also revolutionaries who wanted to destroy even the memory of another kind of society. Churches – where villagers had gathered over many decades or centuries – remained a potent symbol of the link between the present and the past. In most Russian and many Ukrainian cities, the Bolsheviks had immediately sacked churches – between 1918 and 1930 they shut down more than 10,000 churches across the USSR, turning them into warehouses, cinemas, museums or garages.[88] By the early 1930s few urban churches were still functioning as places of worship. The fact that they had continued to exist in so many villages was one of the things that made the peasants seem suspicious to urbanites, and especially to the urban agitators who arrived to help carry out collectivization.

Churches also served a social function, especially in poorer villages that had few other social institutions. They provided a physical meeting place that was not controlled by the state, and at times were centres of opposition to it. During a series of violent peasant riots in Ryazan province, near Moscow, church bells had served as a call to arms, warning the farmers that the brigadiers and soldiers from the capital had arrived.[89] Above all, the church was an institutional umbrella under which people could organize themselves for charitable and social endeavours. During the 1921 famine Ukrainian priests and church institutions had helped organize assistance for the starving.

Once the churches were gone, no independent bodies in the countryside remained capable of motivating or organizing volunteers.[90] The church's place in the cultural and educational life of the village was taken instead by state institutions – 'houses of culture', registry offices, Soviet schools – under the control of the Communist Party. Churches were eliminated in order to prevent them from becoming a source of opposition; in practice, their absence also meant that they could not be a source of aid or comfort when people began to die from hunger.

Whether they had volunteered to join communal farms or had been forced, whether they joined the campaign or opposed it, collectivization was a point of no return for all the inhabitants of the Soviet countryside. Villagers who had participated in acts of violence found it difficult to return to the old status quo. Long-standing friendships and social relationships were destroyed by unforgivable acts. The attitude to the village, to work and to life changed for ever. Petro Hryhorenko was shocked to discover, on a trip into the countryside in 1930, that his formerly hard-working neighbours had lost their desire even to bring in their own harvest:

> Arkhanhelka, an enormous steppe village consisting of more than 2,000 farmhouses, was dead during the height of the harvest season. Eight men worked one thresher for one shift daily. The remaining workers – men, women and young people – sat around or lay in the shade. When I tried to start conversations people replied slowly and with total indifference. If I told them that the grain was falling from the wheat stalks and perishing they would reply, 'Of course, it will perish.' Their feeling must have been terribly strong for them to go to the extreme of leaving the grain in the fields.[91]

Family relationships changed too. Fathers, deprived of property, could no longer bequeath land to their sons and lost authority. Before collectivization it was very unusual for parents to abandon children, but afterwards mothers and fathers often went to seek work in the city, returning sporadically or not at all.[92] As elsewhere in the USSR, children were instructed to denounce their parents, and were questioned at school about what was going on at home.[93] Traditions of village self-rule came to an abrupt end too. Before collectivization, local men chose their own leaders; after collectivization, farcical 'elections' were still held, with candidates making speeches exhorting their neighbours to join the great Soviet project. But everyone knew that the outcome was determined in advance, guaranteed by the omnipresent police.[94]

Finally, and perhaps most ominously, collectivization left the peasants economically dependent on the state. Once the collective farms were established, nobody who lived on them had any means of earning a salary. The farm bosses distributed food products and other goods according to the quality and quantity of work. Theoretically, the system was supposed to provide an incentive to work. In practice, it also meant that peasants had no cash, no way to purchase food, and no mobility. Anyone who left without permission or refused to work could be deprived of his or her ration. When their family cows and garden plots were taken away, as they would be during the autumn and winter of 1932–3, the peasants had nothing left at all.[95]

By itself, collectivization need not have led to a famine on the scale of the one that took place in 1932–3. But the methods used to collectivize the peasants destroyed the ethical structure of the countryside as well as the economic order. Old values – respect for property, for dignity, for human life – disappeared. In their place the Bolsheviks had instilled the rudiments of an ideology that was about to become lethal.

6

Rebellion, 1930

Comrades! I call on you to defend your property and the property of the people. Be prepared for the first and the last call. The rivers and seas will dry up and water will flow on to the high Kurgan and blood will flow in the streams and the land will rise up in high whirlwinds ... I call on you to defend each other, don't go into the collective farm, don't believe the gossips ... Comrades, remember the past, when you lived freely, everyone lived well, poor and rich, now all live poorly.

Anonymous proclamation, 1930[1]

If we had not immediately taken measures against violations of the party line, we would have had a wide wave of insurrectionary peasant uprisings, a good part of our lower officials would have been slaughtered by the peasants.

Central Committee secret memorandum, 1930[2]

In just a few short months during the winter of 1929–30 the Soviet state carried out a second revolution in the countryside, for many more profound and more shocking than the original Bolshevik revolution itself. All across the USSR, local leaders, successful farmers, priests and village elders were deposed, expropriated, arrested or deported. Entire village populations were forced to give up their land, their livestock, and sometimes their homes in order to join collective farms. Churches were destroyed, icons smashed and bells broken.

The result was rapid, massive, sometimes chaotic and often violent resistance. But properly speaking, it is incorrect to say that resistance *followed* collectivization, since resistance of various kinds actually accompanied every stage of de-kulakization and collectivization, from the grain requisitions of 1928 to the deportations of 1930, continuing throughout 1931 and 1932, until hunger and repression finally rendered further defiance impossible. From the beginning, resistance helped shape the nature of collectivization: because peasants refused to cooperate, the idealistic young agitators from outside and their local allies grew angrier, their methods became more extreme and their violence harsher. Resistance, especially in Ukraine, also raised alarm bells at the highest level. To anyone who remembered the peasant rebellion of 1918–19, the rebellion of 1930 seemed both familiar and dangerous.

At different stages the rebellion took different forms. The initial refusal to join collective farms was itself a form of resistance. Many Ukrainian peasants did not trust the Soviet state that they had fought against only ten years earlier. Parts of Ukraine were just recovering from the famine and food shortage of 1929; with no tradition of jointly owned land, the peasants had good reason to believe that outsiders would make things worse rather than better. All across the USSR peasants felt attached to their cows, horses and tools, which they did not want to surrender to some uncertain entity. Even in Russia, where there was a tradition of communally owned farmland, peasants were suspicious of collective farms, which had an uncertain future and an unfamiliar organization. The Soviet state had proposed rapid policy changes before, and sometimes unwound them with equal speed. Some remembered that the disarray of the civil war years had given way to the more 'reasonable' New Economic Policy, and assumed collectivization was another short-lived Soviet fad that would soon disappear.

Peasants also had reason to fear that, even if they went along with it, worse could follow. In his first report to Moscow for the year 1930, Vsevolod Balytsky noted that many middle-income peasants – farmers who were not kulaks but not quite the poorest either – had been overheard saying that 'after the kulaks, they will de-kulakize us too'.[3]

Outright refusal was often followed by immediate action. Ordered to hand over their livestock to collective farms that they did not trust, peasants began to slaughter cows, pigs, sheep and even horses. They ate the meat, salted it, sold it or concealed it – anything to prevent the collective farms from getting hold of it. All across the Soviet Union, in all the rural districts, slaughterhouses suddenly began working overtime. Mikhail Sholokhov penned a famous fictional portrait of a livestock bloodbath:

> Hardly had darkness fallen when the brief and stifled bleating of a sheep, the mortal scream of a pig or the bellowing of a calf would be heard piercing the silence. Not only those who joined the collective farm, but individual farmers also slaughtered. They killed oxen, sheep, pigs, even cows; they slaughtered animals kept for breeding ... the dogs began to drag entrails and guts about the village, the cellars and granaries were filled with meat ... 'Kill, it's not ours now!' 'Kill, they'll take it for the meat collection tax if you don't!' 'Kill, for you won't taste meat in the collective farm!'[4]

This most visceral and immediate form of resistance continued well into the following year and beyond. Between 1928 and 1933 the numbers of cattle and horses in the USSR dropped by nearly half. From 26 million pigs, the number went down to 12 million. From 146 million sheep and goats, the total dropped to 50 million.[5]

Those who did not slaughter their animals protected them ferociously. In one village the OGPU observed a mob attempting to beat up a Komsomol member who was trying to lead away a horse. In another village a group of twenty women, armed with clubs, raided a collective farm to take back their horses. In yet another, peasants burned a barn full of horses to the ground, preferring to see their animals dead rather than confiscated.[6] Peasants were heard to declare that it was 'better to destroy everything' rather than let the authorities have their property.[7]

In a few cases peasants simply released their animals into the streets rather than hand them over. In the North Caucasian village of Ekaterinovka one farmer set his chestnut mare free to wander the streets, carrying the sign 'please take, whoever wants'. One report on this incident indignantly described the horse as playing the role of a 'kulak agitator': the mare was 'wandering around the village for two days already, provoking curiosity, laughter and panic'.[8]

Both the killing of animals and the resistance to their confiscation was entirely personal: peasants feared losing their wealth, their food, their entire future. But the authorities perceived the slaughter as purely political: it was deliberate 'sabotage', motivated by counter-revolutionary thinking – and they punished the saboteurs accordingly. One man who refused to give his cow to the collective farm and killed it instead was forced to walk around the village with the dead cow's head tied to his neck. The local brigade leaders wanted to 'show the entire village what can happen, what everybody can expect later on'.[9] More commonly, those who slaughtered their livestock were automatically categorized as 'kulaks', if they had not been so designated already, with all of the consequences: loss of property, arrest, deportation.

Unsurprisingly, demands for seed grain produced similar reactions. The memory of the grain confiscations, shortages and famines of the previous decade were still strong. One woman, a young girl at the time, remembered the day that her father abruptly came home and locked her in the house. She sat at the window and saw dozens of people, mostly women, running across her courtyard towards the railway station. Not long afterward, she saw them come back, dragging sacks of grain. Later, her father told her that people from the surrounding villages had attacked the grain storage bins at the town's railways station – bins containing their own grain – and had begun removing the contents. Although the local security guards failed to prevent them from entering the storage area, additional police troops arrived from Poltava. Horses trampled the 'thieves'. A few people escaped with some grain, but most were left with nothing.[10] This was not unusual: in a report covering sixteen Ukrainian districts the OGPU noted that the riots following the 'collectivization' of seed grain led to the deaths of thirty-five people 'from our side' – meaning the police and authorities. Another thirty-seven were wounded and 314 were beaten. In the exchange twenty-six rioters – described by police as 'counter-revolutionaries' – were killed as well.[11]

But if police viewed the rioters as political agents rather than desperately poor people who feared starvation, it was equally true that the rioters viewed the government as a hostile force, or worse. To some, the collectivization policy was the ultimate betrayal of the revolution, proof that the Bolsheviks intended to impose a 'second serfdom' and rule like the nineteenth-century tsars. In 1919 similar fears had helped inspire the anti-Bolshevik sentiments of the peasant rebellion. Now they were frequently expressed, so much so that the OGPU gleaned them from informers. In the Russian Central Black Earth district OGPU sources heard one peasant declare, 'The communists deceived us in their revolution, all land was given out to work for free and now they take the last cow.' In the Middle Volga province another said, 'They said to me "revolution", I didn't understand but now [I] understand that such a revolution means to take everything from the peasants and leave them hungry and naked.' In Ukraine a peasant declared, 'They push us into the collective farm so that we will be eternal slaves.'[12] Many decades later, Mikhail Gorbachev, the last General Secretary of the Soviet Communist Party and the grandson of kulaks, described the collective farms as 'serfdom'. In order for the memory of collective farms as a 'second serfdom' to have had such a long life, it must have been deeply rooted.[13]

But to some people the regime quickly became far more than just an ordinary earthly enemy. In the past, fears of the apocalypse and expectations of the end of the world had periodically swept through the Russian and Ukrainian countryside, where religious cults and magical practice had been present for centuries. The 1917 revolution inspired another wave of religious mania. Throughout the 1920s dire prophecies were common, as were omens and miracles. In Voronezh province, pilgrims flocked to see trees that had unexpectedly burst into bloom: their 'regeneration' was taken as a sign of a change to come.[14] In Ukraine a crowd gathered to watch a rusty icon on the road to Kharkiv 'come to life', taking on shape and colour.[15]

In 1929–30 some Soviet peasants, appalled by the attacks on churches and priests, once again became convinced that the Soviet Union was the Antichrist – and that collective farm managers were therefore his representatives. Priests told their parishioners that the

Antichrist was taking their food, or that the Antichrist was trying to destroy them.[16] In line with those beliefs, peasants rejected the collective farms not merely for material or political reasons, but for spiritual ones: they feared eternal damnation. The state was attacking the Church; group prayers, singing and church services became a form of opposition. One local official recorded the words of a Ukrainian farmer: 'You will be forced to work on Sundays if you go into the collective farm, [they] will put the seal of Antichrist on your forehead and arms. Now already the kingdom of Antichrist is begun and to go into the collective farm is a big sin. About this it is written in the bible.'[17] Members of the Catholic minority in Ukraine were affected by the same spirit: in the ethnic German village of Kandel, the local bishop, Antonius Zerr, began to offer counsel and even ordain priests in secret, in defiance of anti-religious laws.[18]

Buffered sometimes by faith, sometimes by anger at the theft of their possessions, the peasants grew bolder. In response to the Soviet propaganda songs that they heard played over and over again – songs with refrains such as 'Our burdens have lightened! Our lives have gladdened!' – they began to write their own:

> Hey, our harvest knows no limits or measures.
> It grows, ripens, and even spills over onto the earth,
> Boundless over the fields . . . While the patrolling pioneers
> Come out to guard the ripening wheat-ears of grain.[19]

Songs and poetry of resistance were passed from village to village. According to one inhabitant of the Dnipropetrovsk province, they were sometimes even printed and bound into small booklets.[20] Graffiti formed a part of the culture of resistance too: one Ukrainian peasant later remembered inscriptions appearing on the walls of houses: 'Down with Stalin', 'Down with Communists'. They were wiped off, and the next day they appeared again. Eventually, two men were arrested as members of the 'organization' that had written them.[21]

Protest also took the form of escape, not just from the countryside but from the Soviet Union itself. Already in January 1930 guards caught three peasants in the Kamianets-Podilskyi border province trying to cross the Polish-Ukrainian border.[22] A month later, a group of 400 peasants from several villages marched towards the border shouting 'We don't want collectives, we're going to Poland!' Along the way they attacked and beat up anyone who stood in their way, until they were finally stopped by border guards. The following day another crowd from the same group of villages marched towards the border, also shouting that they would ask for help from the Poles. They too were stopped by guards, this time only 400 metres from the border. Secret police also recorded several attempts to raid grain warehouses near the border. Peasants who lived close to the border seem to have been inspired by the proximity of the 'normal' life of their neighbours on the other side.[23]

Inevitably, these spontaneous protests, church meetings and border marches gave way to organized violence. All across the USSR – but with significantly higher numbers in Ukraine – people who saw that they were about to lose their possessions and possibly their lives took matters into their own hands. The OGPU archives record what happened next.

In Sumy province thirteen 'kulaks' took the weapons they had saved from the civil war, slipped into the forest and became partisans. Near Bila Tserkva, in Kyiv province, another ex-partisan was, according to a secret police report, organizing an armed band. Pasha Angelina, the female tractor-driver who had so delighted in the downfall of her kulak neighbours, felt this violence first hand:

> In the summer of 1929, when my brother, Kostia, my sister, Lelia and I were walking to a Komsomol meeting in the neighboring village of Novobesheve, somebody shot at us with a sawed-off shotgun . . . I will never forget how we ran, barefoot, through the prickly grass, our hearts beating wildly with fear.[24]

The OGPU responded immediately to these early 'terrorist incidents'. By 6 February 1930, only a few months after collectivization had been formally launched in November, the Soviet secret police had already arrested 15,985 people across the Soviet Union for 'counter-revolutionary activity' in the countryside. Of that number, about a third were Ukrainians. Between 12 and 17 February the secret police across the USSR made another 18,000 arrests. Those hauled into prison were accused of planning organized armed uprisings, of 'recruiting' rebels among the poor and middle peasants, and even of seeking contacts with the peasant soldiers in the Red Army, in order to alienate them from the government and convert them to the kulak cause.[25]

None of this news was sufficient to convince Stalin to abandon collectivization or to reconsider whether it was a good idea to force farmers into collective farms they detested. The situation still seemed as if it was under control. Nevertheless, he was worried enough by these initial reports to tone down the collectivization rhetoric – with unexpected results.

'Dizzy with Success'. That was the title of an article written by Stalin and published in *Pravda* on 2 March 1930. The phrase might well have been borrowed from Josef Reingold, the Chekist who had used the same expression in 1919 to bring a halt to the bloody repression of the Don Cossacks. But whether or not he hinted at any such allusion, Stalin certainly did not intend any irony. 'Dizzy with Success' began with a long tribute to the great achievements of collectivization. Not only was the policy going well, he declared, it was proceeding far better and far more quickly than expected. The USSR had already 'overfulfilled' the Five Year Plan for collectivization, he declared: 'Even our enemies are forced to admit that the successes are substantial.' After only a few weeks the countryside had already made a 'radical turn . . . towards socialism'. An extraordinary amount had been accomplished – so much so that perhaps it was time to slow the pace of change. Even such a great achievement had drawbacks, he warned:

> Such successes sometimes induce a spirit of vanity and conceit . . . People not infrequently become intoxicated by such successes, they become dizzy with success, lose all sense of proportion and the capacity to understand realities . . . adventurist attempts are made to solve all questions of socialist construction in a trice . . . Hence the party's task is to wage a determined struggle against these sentiments, which are dangerous and harmful to our cause, and to drive them out of the party.[26]

Collectivization, Stalin disingenuously reminded the cadres, was intended to be 'voluntary'. It was not supposed to require force. It might not progress uniformly: not every region would be able to collectivize at the same pace. Because of the enormous enthusiasm, he feared these principles had been forgotten. Some excesses had occurred.

Of course, neither Stalin nor anyone else back in Moscow took responsibility for these 'excesses', either then or later. Nor did he give any real details. The murders and beatings, the children left outside in the snow with no clothes – all of this naturally went unmentioned. Instead, Stalin shifted the blame for any mistakes squarely onto the shoulders of local party members, the men and women on the lowest rung of the hierarchy, who had 'become dizzy with success and for the moment have lost clearness of mind and sobriety of vision'. He mocked them for using militaristic language – which was, of course, an echo of his own – and condemned their 'blockheaded' attempts to lump different kinds of farms together. He even took them to task for removing church bells: 'Who benefits by these distortions, this bureaucratic decreeing of the collective farm movement, these unworthy threats against the peasants? Nobody, except our enemies!'[27]

Why did he write this article? By the time it appeared, Stalin would have seen the secret police accounts of rebellion, resistance and armed attacks on party members. He may also have known that at least some of the Communist Party leadership in both Russia and Ukraine had doubts about the policy. Although these critics only began to speak openly some months later, Stalin might already have sensed the potential for a backlash against him in the wake of a failed or chaotic drive to collectivization, so he sought someone else to blame. The lowest party officials – the local leaders, the village bosses – made the perfect target: they were far away, they were nameless, and they were powerless. The letter neatly shifted the responsibility for what was clearly a disastrous policy away from him, and onto a social group far from Moscow.

Ostensibly, the article was also conciliatory. Stalin seemed to be seeking at least a temporary halt to the worst excesses of his policy. In the wake of the article some genuine concessions were made as well: the Central Committee decided, for example, to allow peasants to keep a family cow, some poultry, and their own kitchen gardens.[28] But if these gestures were meant to stop the rebellion then they back-fired. Far from calming the peasants, 'Dizzy with Success' inspired a new wave of insurrection, a vast array of armed and unarmed resist-ance. One official christened this movement 'March Fever', but that expression was misleading: it implies that the protest wave was a brief illness, or perhaps a form of temporary insanity. What began to happen was in fact far more profound. 'What the state labelled a fever,' wrote Lynne Viola, 'was in fact a massive peasant rebellion, reasoned in cause and content.'[29]

The impact was immediate. All across the USSR party officials read and discussed Stalin's article at party meetings and with one another. In Myron Dolot's village, as in many villages, a local activist read the 'Dizzy with Success' article aloud to the villagers. As he was explaining that mistakes had been made, that errors had been com-mitted, and that party members had made grave miscalculations, 'the assembled crowd was deathly still'. Then the activist added his own view: the Jews within the party were at fault, not the party itself. This explanation neatly exempted himself and his comrades from blame. 'What happened next,' wrote Dolot, 'was a spontaneous riot.' 'Away with you!' one man shouted. 'We've had enough of you,' cried another. 'We have been duped! Let's get our horses and cows out of that stinking collective farm before it's too late!' In a disorganized wave the villagers ran to get their livestock, tripping over one another in the dark. About twenty peasants were shot in the subsequent chaos.[30]

In the days that followed, similar riots broke out all across the Soviet Union, and in a few places they acquired new layers of sophis-tication. The first signs of organized opposition that had so worried Balytsky in January became, by March, April and May, a real move-ment. The riots quickly became organized – sometimes very well organized – and they acquired a much more obvious political charac-ter. Men and women across the USSR, but especially and most numerously from Ukraine, attacked, beat and murdered activists in the spring of 1930. They organized raids on warehouses and grain storage containers. They broke locks, stole grain and other food, and distributed it around villages. They set fire to collective and Soviet property. They attacked 'collaborators'. In one village those who were 'not satisfied with the regime . . . burnt down the houses of the [collective farm] activists'.[31] The activist who had 'donned the priest's vestments' and stomped on the iconostasis was found dead in a ditch the following day.'[32]

There was little pity for the victims. One man who had played in a local concert band remembered being asked to play at the funerals of 'Twenty-Five Thousanders' who had been murdered by peasants. 'For us it was a happy event because every time somebody was killed, they would take us to the village, give us some food and then we would play at the funeral. And we were looking forward every time to the next funeral, because that meant food for us.'[33]

Some of the angriest protests took the form of *babski bunty*, a phrase that literally translates as 'women's revolts' or 'riots', though the word *baba* connotes not just a woman but a peasant woman, and implies something uncouth and irrational. Women had organized protests in the USSR before, in 1927 and 1928. But these riots had focused on food shortages, not politics. As one secret policeman wrote about those earlier protests, 'In this period, demonstrations with the participation of women didn't have, as a rule, any kind of clearly defined anti-Soviet character: crowds or groups of women gathered at state and cooperative organizations, demanding bread.'[34]

In the spring of 1930 the peasant women's inchoate demand for bread turned into equally rudimentary attacks on the men who had confiscated it. Crowds of women mobbed activists, Soviet officials and visiting dignitaries, demanding their property back. They shouted and chanted, sang songs and hurled threats. Others took matters into their own hands. In one Ukrainian village a young girl watched her mother, along with other 'hungry women', break the locks of the collective farm storehouse and take the stored grain; local officials, intimidated by the mob, called in provincial party officials and Komsomol members to help arrest the women and recover the grain. They remained in prison for two weeks.[35] In another Ukrainian village a boy watched activists go from house to house claiming property on behalf of the collective farm. In response, a group of women stormed the farm and demanded everything back: 'One woman grabs her plough; the other her horse; a third, the cow.' Soldiers, or possibly secret police troops – the memoirist isn't clear – then 'came and chased all of these women away ... all of the confiscated items, agricultural implements and horses, once again became part of the collective farm'.[36] In early March 1930 some 500 ethnic German women from three different villages also spent a week demonstrating, demanding their property back from the collective farms and preventing them from functioning.[37]

Sometimes the crowds went even further. The OGPU itself recorded an incident in Mariupol province in Ukraine, which began when a 'mob' of 300 women descended on the village council and demanded the key to the village church, which had been turned into an administrative building. The women then shouted that Naumenko, the boss of the village soviet, had broken down the door of a member of the church council. When he denied doing so, 'The women sat him on a wagon (tachanka) and forcibly took him to the man's house, where it was established that he had indeed been present. The mob decided to hold an impromptu trial.'

The women then forced Naumenko to sign a paper promising to free the churchman – and then attempted a citizens' arrest of a local party official, Filomynov. They publicly mocked both officials, spitting in their eyes and face, calling the communist officials 'bandits, thieves and White guards'. The two men were freed only by the intervention of the OGPU. For several days afterwards, crowds armed with sticks and clubs continued to meet in front of local administrative buildings, demanding their property back. The rebellion was finally put down, and the peasants were 'pacified'. But nobody believed that the Soviet state had won them over.[38]

There were many such incidents. By the end of March 1930 the OGPU had recorded 2,000 'mass' protests, the majority of which were exclusively female, in Ukraine alone.[39] At the Ukrainian Party Congress in the summer of 1930 several speakers referred to the problem. Kaganovich, no longer head of the Ukrainian Communist Party but still keenly interested in Ukrainian affairs, declared that women had played the 'most "advanced" role in the reaction against the collective farm'.[40] The OGPU explained this phenomenon, naturally, as evidence of the influence of the 'kulak-anti-Soviet element' on their ignorant wives and daughters. More propaganda work and agitation among peasant women would surely solve the problem.[41]

The OGPU also suspected that women were protesting precisely because they knew that they were less likely to be arrested. They may have been right: even without bringing in the men, women could attack officials – even physically attack them – with far less fear of retribution. Women's protest also offered a 'legitimate' way for men to join: if activists arrived to fight peasant women, then the village men could leap in to defend them on the grounds that they were defending the honour of their wives, mothers and daughters.

Not all of them needed a pretext. Many Ukrainian men had, in recent memory, taken up arms against hated rulers. As they had done during the civil war, some began to organize themselves into partisan units. As one remembered, 'Rifle fire was heard at night. Partisan groups operated out of the forests. It was a typical peasant uprising. The village soviet was destroyed. Heads of the village soviet either fled or ran the risk of being killed.'[42] Many local communists failed to escape and were killed on the spot.

The violence was real, and it was widespread. Soviet documents from 1930 record 13,794 'incidents of terror' and 13,754 'mass protests', of which the largest number took place in Ukraine and were caused, in the OGPU's own view, by collectivization and de-kulakization.[43] The local records of the secret police in Ukraine are both more emotive and more precise about the rebellions on their territory. Despite prior attempts to confiscate weapons, they noted that peasants still had them: shotguns and rifles, kept in storage since the civil war period, as well as pikes and staves. In the spring of 1930 they began once again using them in a coordinated fashion. Balytsky did not doubt that he was witnessing the same kind of 'anti-Soviet activity' that had taken place in Ukraine in the past. 'Kulak counter-revolutionary activists have not stopped their struggle,' he declared, 'but are rather fortifying their position.' Between 20 January and 9 February his men arrested 11,865 people, including members of 'counter-revolutionary organizations and groups', people who were preparing to carry out 'armed revolution' as well as those who could become the 'ideologists' of such a revolution. Anybody with any foreign links – especially links to Poland – was suspicious because they might receive 'active assistance' from abroad. The secret police also focused on those who were using anything that sounded like a 'Ukrainian-chauvinist' or 'Petliurite' slogan, and identified three major groups of such activists in Dnipropetrovsk, Kharkiv and Kremenchuk provinces, all important centres of strife during the civil war era.[44]

Towards the middle of March the situation had worsened. On 9 March, Balytsky reported 'mass uprisings' in sixteen districts of Ukraine. Most had been 'pacified' by the time of his report, but in Shepetivka district in the western part of the country, 'anti-Soviet and criminal elements', some in groups as large as 300 to 500 people, had armed themselves with sawn-off shotguns, hunting rifles and axes. The Shepetivka peasants had been fighting since February, when Balytsky himself had arrived in the district. On his orders the OGPU had brought in cavalry units, armed with machine guns and backed up by border guards and militia.[45] Balytsky claimed the OGPU had broken up the gang, but they had killed a Komsomol leader and were holding other communist leaders hostage; he feared the gang had made contact with another armed gang in a neighbouring district.[46] Within only a few weeks of the publication of 'Dizzy with Success', the rebellion seemed very close to spinning out of control.

Reading through the archival documentation of the 1930 rebellions, it is not always easy to separate fact from fiction. How well organized was the dissent in reality? How much were the secret policemen inventing conspiracies where none existed? How much were they 'finding' the nationalist movements that they were seeking? To what extent were they inventing a problem that they could later claim to have solved? The OGPU had, after all, invented the fictitious SVU only a year earlier. A few years later, Soviet secret policemen would manufacture hundreds of thousands of false accusations in the course of the Great Terror of 1937–8.

The archival accounts of the 1930 rebellion do at times sound deliberately embroidered, as if the OGPU was trying to show Moscow that it was faithfully following orders. In February 1930, for example, the OGPU conducted an operation against 'counter-revolutionary kulak-white guard and bandit elements' all across the Soviet Union, again arresting the largest numbers in Ukraine, where they identified seventy-eight individual cells of 'anti-Soviet activists'. Among the most serious were the 'Petliurivska' bandits whom they believed had been organizing an armed uprising in the Kremenchuk district in central Ukraine, scheduled to take place in the spring of 1930. They identified the leader, 'Manko' – a name suspiciously similar to 'Makhno' - as a 'former Petliura officer' who had entered Ukraine illegally, crossing the Polish border in 1924.

The report on the operation quoted Manko: 'When the state authorities carry out collectivization, they will ensure their influence over the masses, their eyes will be everywhere, as a result of which it will be difficult to approach them and our organizational efforts will lead to failure.' His group was also said to have 'set as its goal the creation of an independent Ukraine on the basis of the right to private ownership of land' and the preservation of the Cossack class. Allegedly, Manko intended to launch an attack on the city of Kremenchuk by starting fires outside the town and taking over the train station and the telegraph office.[47]

Other groups were believed to harbour similar goals. Some were said to have links with one another, others were suspected of sowing traitorous ideas within the Red Army. Yet another group, in the western districts of Ukraine, had created a 'kulak-Petliurite' organization that was supposedly conducting 'counter-revolutionary agitation' and spreading 'provocative rumours' as well. The same report recorded the arrest of 420 members of 'counter-revolutionary organizations and groups' in the North Caucasus region, in the course of only five days, as well as arrests in the Volga regions too.[48] Balytsky himself recorded his visit to Tulchyn district in the spring of 1930, where he found armed rebels, trenches around the villages, and peasants shouting 'Down with the Soviets' and singing 'Ukraine has not yet died', the anthem of the Ukrainian People's Republic in the era of the Central Rada.[49]

The tone of these accounts can seem exaggerated and hysterical. Yet both documentary and memoir evidence does show that not all of these movements were invented. There was real violence, well organized and nationalist in character. In a number of places it was armed and contagious, spreading from village to village as peasants gained confidence from the actions and slogans of their neighbours.

In mid-March 1930, for example, a string of villages in the Tulchyn district staged protests, one following the next. The archival reports are clear: peasants were shouting, 'We don't want leaders who rob peasants!' and 'Down with the communists, who are leading the country to disaster!' Even when they didn't kill the local authorities, they drove them out of office. In 343 villages, peasants elected their own 'starostas', or traditional village elders, and refused to cooperate with the communists.[50] In many places they also fired Soviet teachers, banned cooperatives and announced the return of free trade. Some of the villagers began to talk about organizing armed resistance, and a few passed around leaflets that the OGPU described darkly as having 'an anti-Soviet character'. At one meeting those gathered called for property to be given back to the 'kulaks', and for the liquidation of the collective farms. On several occasions, rebels reportedly sang the national anthem. The victory in Tulchyn was short-lived: the OGPU blamed 'Petliurists' and called for 'operational measures'. The province was duly divided into sectors, and each sector was assigned an armed OGPU cavalry unit.[51] Balytsky told a colleague that he had been instructed, by Stalin himself, 'not to make speeches but to act decisively'.[52]

In several places the rebellions were not only genuinely political, they were also genuinely led by people who had played some role in the peasant rebellions, the Ukrainian national movement or the civil war. Certainly this was the case in Pavlohrad, a district in the Dnipropetrovsk province of eastern Ukraine, whose armed rebellion has now been extensively documented.[53] Even before the 'March fever' rebellions, the authorities expected violence in Pavlohrad itself, a town originally founded as a Cossack base. In the nineteenth century one of the villages in the Pavlohrad district took part in a revolt against local gentry; in 1919 many in the district had supported Makhno.[54] Anticipating violence after collectivization, local police in February 1930 arrested seventy-nine people and executed twenty-one of them for plotting rebellion.

Even after that several Pavlohrad leaders with prior military experience were still willing to resist. In March 1930, Kyrylo Shopin, a former soldier in the army of Hetman Skoropadsky, escaped arrest and began travelling through the region. He went from village to village encouraging peasants to revolt. Some of those who would eventually join him had previously fought for Petliura or Makhno.

Shopin's efforts paid off in early April, when representatives from around the region met in Bohdanivka and began to plan their uprising. Many of those present had lost possessions during collectivization, and were partly motivated by the belief that they could get them back. But they had political goals as well, and they used political slogans: 'Down with Soviet power' and 'Let's fight for a different kind of freedom.' After the first group meeting small rebel cells formed, somewhat chaotically, around the nearby countryside. On 4 April many of their members began arriving in Osadchi, a small hamlet near Bohdanivka, hoping to join the rebellion and expecting to be given weapons.

Precautions were taken: the rebels agreed that if the revolt were to fail, everyone who joined should claim that he had been forced against his will to take part. Their leaders tried to reach out to the soldiers of the Pavlohrad district militia, in the hopes that they would sign on as well. They outlined a plan: March on Pavlohrad, gather weapons, use them to storm Dnipropetrovsk and, eventually, take over the rest of Ukraine. From the documentation – the interrogations, investigations, memoirs, accounts written afterwards – it seems clear that the participants in the Pavlohrad uprising were convinced that they could succeed. All over Ukraine, they told one another, abused peasants would rise up and join them.

On 5 April they began their rebellion in Osadchi, where they murdered the local Soviet and party activists, and then moved on quickly to nearby villages, where others joined them. Arriving in Bohdanivka at mid-day, they rang the church bells, took control of a key bridge, and began fighting the local militia. Over the course of the day, the insurgents killed several dozen government figures, including party members, Komsomol members, village councillors and others. Towards the end of the day they managed to cut the telephone lines, but it was too late: the head of the village council had already tele-graphed to Pavlohrad for help.

The Pavlohrad militia, which had not taken up the rebels' call to join them, arrived in the evening. The rebellious peasants retreated, but in the meantime another group of insurgents had taken over the village council and party buildings in a nearby village, Ternivka. Finally, on 6 April, an armed OGPU unit arrived in Bohdanivka from Dnipropetrovsk – 200 men, fifty-eight on horseback. Balytsky had given them explicit orders, using the strongest language possible: 'liquidate these counter-revolutionary bands'.

In the end, the fighting lasted no more than two days. Although the insurgents had killed several dozen government figures, including party members, Komsomol members, village councillors and others, the peasant army never really had a chance. The mostly illiterate leaders had no communications or logistics, and not enough weapons. They were easily overpowered, arrested and killed. Thirteen of them died, a handful were badly injured.

More than 300 were detained, of whom 210 were convicted in a trial which, unlike the SVU trial, was firmly closed to the public: the party could not risk staging a 'show trial' for a genuine rebellion. The witnesses could not be so easily manipulated, the story could not be retold in such a way as to hide what had really happened: poor peasants, led by men with genuine military backgrounds, had taken up arms against the state. Nor could the survivors be allowed to live to tell the true story. On 20 May twenty-seven of them were executed.

The Pavlohrad rebellion was unusually brutal, but it was not unique. In March the OGPU had also been surprised by a rebellion in Kryvyi Rih province in eastern Ukraine, a region that had a 'nearly 100 percent' collectivization record and was considered docile. Although the arrest and deportations there had been 'accompanied by some negative phenomenon', according to an OGPU report, de-kulakization had been enthusiastically supported by poorer and middle-income peasants.

But a 'change of mood' followed orders to confiscate seed grain in anticipation of the spring sowing season. One local peasant was heard to declare that the collection of seed grain meant that 'all bread will be taken out of Ukraine, and Ukraine will be left with nothing'. In another village someone expressed the fear that 'they will take our last grain and leave the peasants starving'. Following Stalin's 'Dizzy with Success' article, the OGPU men blamed ill humour on over-enthusiastic Kryvyi Rih officials putting pressure on peasants who were not 'kulaks'. One set of officials had reportedly confiscated some 'dirty linen' from a poor peasant, and demanded milk and lard for his brigade; others had broken down the doors of peasant cottages, stripped the inhabitants and thrown them out on the street. In response, a mob of women gathered around a local party activist and shouted that Stalin had said that the collective farms were to be organized 'voluntarily'. Others organized petitions demanding their land back, or had rushed to the collective farms to reclaim equipment and livestock.

Some of their demands went further. 'Under the influence of anti-Soviet and kulak agitation', the OGPU reported, peasants in the village of Shyroke made a series of 'counter-revolutionary political demands'. Finally, on 14 March, a mob of 500 men and women surrounded the local government offices and demanded the return of seed grain, the dissolution of the Komsomol, the restitution of property confiscated or forcibly 'donated' to the collective farm, and the refund of monetary fines paid to the local authorities.[55]

Once again, the documentation makes clear that all these rebellions, in Tulchyn, Pavlohrad, Kryvyi Rih and elsewhere, were real. They represented an organized reaction to a much-hated policy, as well as to the violence used to enforce it; some of the people who led the revolts were, unsurprisingly, people who had opposed Soviet rule all along.

But even if the rebellions were real, the OGPU's explanation of their sources and influence is harder to believe. The secret policemen in Stalin's Soviet Union could not tell their superiors that their policy was failing, or that honest Soviet citizens opposed it for understandable reasons. Instead, they had to imply the influence of class enemies and foreigners, inventing or exaggerating links and connections. The report on Kryvyi Rih, for example, attributed all the violence to 'anti-Soviet elements, kulaks and relatives of kulaks': Karpuk, a

'refugee from Poland'; Lisohor, the brother of an exiled kulak; Kras-
ulia, a bootmaker, and thus a man who owned a bit of property.[56]
All of them belonged to suspect categories: people with foreign connections, with previously arrested family members, with any property
at all.

Over and over again, officials also sought explanations for the
strength of the rebellion in the province's history, drawing attention
especially to the rebellions of 1918–20. At one point, the OGPU
assigned a group of officers to work across several districts, citing the
'especially important political significance of the border zones and
the historical past of these regions'. Among them were the districts of
Volyn, Berdychiv, Mogilev, Vinnytsia, Kamianets and Odessa, all sites
of major fighting in the previous decade.[57] Balytsky noted elsewhere
that special care had to be taken in one region because it was the
territory of the 'Zabolotny gang', one of the partisan units during the
civil war.[58]

This obsession with the civil war past was not unique to Ukraine.
It spread to include the North Caucasus, where Soviet authorities also
attributed violent resistance to collectivization to the influence of
Cossacks as well as Ukrainian nationalists. It also encompassed Siberia and the Urals, where Soviet secret policemen targeted 'former
White Guard officers'. Violent resistance to collectivization in Central Asia, Kazakhstan, Tatarstan and Bashkiria was also immediately
understood to be anti-Soviet and counter-revolutionary – again, not
without reason. In the Fergana region of Central Asia, Red Army
troops arrived to pacify the Basmachi guerrilla movement. Although
it had been repressed a few years earlier, the movement was revived
by anger at collectivization. Violent struggles also followed collectivization in the Caucasian autonomous republics of Chechnya and
Dagestan.[59]

But in Ukraine the strength of nationalism in the cities made this
anger in the countryside more dangerous. In 1930, OGPU analysts
returned repeatedly to the matter of city-country contacts, and to
the links between intellectuals and peasants predicted in 1929.
Some of these may have been real; others were clearly invented. On
21 March, Balytsky sent a report to Stanislav Kosior, the general
secretary of the Ukrainian Communist Party, and to Yagoda, now

the boss of the OGPU: in a village in the Vinnytsia district, he had discovered a link between leaders of the local uprising and the SVU. Allegedly, a rebel there had declared, 'After the liquidation of the SVU it is necessary to work according to other methods – to incite the ignorant masses to revolt.' Other SVU members were 'discovered' in Vinnytsia in subsequent days. Balytsky congratulated himself for finding them, and indeed for predicting the influence of the SVU – an organization that he himself had conjured into existence. The cells, he wrote, 'correctly confirm the SVU's strong links with active cadres of rural counter-revolution and SVU's expectations for an uprising in 1930–31'. He patted himself on the back: 'it was only the timely liquidation of the SVU that disorganized the splinters of the organization, forcing them to act at their personal fear and risk'. Perhaps this is how Balytsky escaped criticism for failing to stop the rural uprisings: had he not rid Ukraine of the non-existent SVU, he was arguing, they might have been worse.[60]

During subsequent months the police kept up the search for new and undiscovered conspiracies. Even after the SVU had supposedly been rounded up, the OGPU was still anticipating the 'strengthening of links between counter-revolutionary elements in the city and the countryside', claiming that a wide range of rural organizations had their headquarters in towns. Counter-revolutionaries from the cities were allegedly roaming around Ukraine; in the western provinces of the republic, 'a range of counter-revolutionary organizations (mainly Petliurite) liquidated in Ukraine ... were tightly linked to Poland'.[61]

The search for the SVU and 'Petliurites' would continue well into the end of the decade. In retrospect, it is clear that 1932 and 1933 were really the beginning of the great wave of terror that peaked all across the USSR in 1937 and 1938. All of the elements of the 'Great Terror' – the suspicion, the hysterical propaganda, the mass arrests made according to centrally planned schemes – were already on display in Ukraine on the eve of the famine. Indeed, Moscow's paranoia about the counter-revolutionary potential of Ukraine continued after the Second World War, and into the 1970s and 1980s. It was taught to every successive generation of secret policemen, from the OGPU to the NKVD to the KGB, as well as every successive generation of party leaders. Perhaps it even helped mould the thinking of the post-Soviet elite, long after the USSR ceased to exist.

7

Collectivization Fails, 1931–2

We could lose Ukraine . . .

Stalin to Kaganovich, August 1932[1]

The secret policemen triumphed. Although the protests slowed the progress of collectivization, the state fought back with mass arrests, mass deportations, mass repression. The Communist Party waited – and then pressed ahead. The temperate language of Stalin's 'Dizzy with Success' article turned out to be just that: language. The same policies continued, and even grew harsher.

In July 1930, just a few months after the angriest 'March fever' protests, the Politburo itself set new targets: up to 70 per cent of households in the main grain-growing regions, Ukraine among them, were to join collective farms by September 1931. In December 1930, eager to prove their enthusiasm, Politburo members raised that same target to 80 per cent of households.[2] A Central Committee resolution again confirmed that in certain regions – Ukraine, as well as the Northern Caucasus and the Lower and Middle Volga provinces – the achievement of this goal would require the 'liquidation of the kulaks as a class'.[3]

All through the subsequent autumn sowing and the winter harvests, and again during the spring sowing and summer harvest – pressure on the peasants continued. Taxes on peasants who remained on their own land remained high. Deportations to the fast-expanding camps of the Gulag increased. Food shortages became permanent. In the summer of 1930 secret police reports again identified the first signs of starvation, as people once more began to suffer from diseases caused by hunger. A driver weakened by lack of food fell from his tractor in one Ukrainian village; in another, people were beginning to swell with hunger. In the course of a few months 15,000 peasants in the North Caucasus abandoned their farms to look for work in the cities. In Crimea people began eating horse feed, which made them ill.[4]

Threatened by violence and afraid of hunger, hundreds of thousands of peasants finally relinquished their land, animals and machines to the collective farms. But just because they had been forced to move, they did not become enthusiastic collective farmers overnight. The fruits of their labour no longer belonged to them; the grain they sowed and harvested was now requisitioned by the authorities.

Collectivization also meant that peasants had lost their ability to make decisions about their lives. Like the serfs of old, they were forced to accept a special legal status, including controls on their movement: all collective farmers, *kolkhozniks*, would eventually need to seek permission to work outside the village. Instead of deciding when to reap, sow and sell, kolkhozniks had to follow decisions made by the local representatives of Soviet power. They did not earn regular salaries but were paid *trudodni* or day wages, which often meant payment in kind – grain, potatoes or other products – rather than cash. They lost their ability to govern themselves too, as collective farm bosses and their entourages supplanted the traditional village councils.

As a result, men and women who had so recently been self-reliant farmers now worked as little as possible. Farm machines were not maintained and frequently broke down. In August 1930 some 3,600 tractors out of 16,790 in Ukraine were in need of repair. The problem was cynically blamed on 'class struggle' and 'wreckers' who were allegedly sabotaging the farm machinery.[5]

Even when peasants did sow and till the fields, they often did their work without the care and enthusiasm they had shown in the past. Collective farms produced dramatically less than they could or should have done. Everyone tried to borrow or take from the collective as much as possible: after all, the state's grain belonged to 'no one'. Men and women who would never have considered stealing in the past now had no compunction about taking from state organizations that no one owned or respected. This form of 'everyday resistance' was not unique to the peasantry.[6] Working as little as possible, stealing public property, failing to care for state-owned equipment and machinery – these were the methods by which underpaid, underfed and unmotivated Soviet workers of all kinds got along.

Peasants also continued to abandon the collective farms for work in the cities – the OGPU quoted one saying 'it's impossible to tolerate this any more'. They divided up the land or the harvested grain among themselves instead of sharing it out with others. In a few places the authorities observed that kulaks ejected from their own farms banded together to form what the authorities called 'kulak collectives'. Working together, they 'tried to win sympathy from the local population and to demonstrate their superiority to the other collective farms'. This too was seen as a form of anti-Soviet activity.[7]

Attacks on shops and grain warehouses continued too. In May 1930 a crowd of several thousand people – mostly women – from outside Odessa swarmed into the city and attacked several state-run grocery stores as well as a restaurant. Mounted policemen were sent in to restore order, and several arrests were made. The unrest was significant enough to appear in the reports of both the Turkish and the Japanese consuls in Odessa – and those reports were significant enough to alarm the OGPU. Although the police had responded promptly, the Japanese observed, 'the general atmosphere in the town remains agitated'.[8]

Nevertheless, the summer of 1930 seemed, from the perspective of Moscow, to mark a moment of victory. Despite the evidence of suffering and the reports of chaos, the illusion that collectivization would still be a 'success', dizzy or otherwise, persisted through the end of 1930. There are many arguments about whether the published figures for that year – and indeed subsequent years – were real, falsified, or simply mistaken. But there is no question that the state claimed, and Stalin appears to have believed, that 1930 was a high point. The official statistics decreed that 83.5 million tonnes of grain had been collected in 1930, a notable rise over 1929 – a year of famine and bad weather – when the comparable figure was 71.7 million tonnes.[9] Convinced that collectivization was now on the path to success, the Kremlin made what would turn out to be a disastrous and callous decision: to increase the export of grain, as well as of other food products, out of the Soviet Union in exchange for hard currency.

Grain export was of course not new. As we have seen, in 1920 the Bolsheviks had reckoned grain to be one of the safest goods to sell to the West, since doing so required no interaction with 'capitalists'.[10] Nor was it the only source of hard currency. Funds also came in from the sale of art, furniture, jewellery, icons and other objects confiscated from 'the bourgeoisie' and the Church. In July 1930 the state also opened the 'Torgsin' chain of hard currency shops (from *torgovlia s inostrantsami* or 'trade with foreigners'), originally created to attract foreign visitors forbidden to spend foreign money elsewhere but later accessible to Soviet citizens. Goods in them were available to those who had tsarist-era gold coins; during the famine they would become a means of survival for peasants who had saved gold objects or even had foreign currency transferred to them from relatives abroad.[11]

But grain was still the most lucrative export, especially since the timber trade had run into trouble; reports (which were accurate) that convict labour produced Soviet timber had led to calls for boycotts in a number of Western countries. The level of grain exports duly rose throughout the 1920s. Britain bought 26,799 tonnes of wheat from the USSR in 1924; by 1926–7 that had risen to 138,486 tonnes. Exports to Italy, Turkey and the Netherlands grew as well. Between 1929 and 1931, Soviet grain exports to Germany tripled.[12]

As exports rose, the Soviet leadership perceived that they brought more than just hard currency. Foreshadowing the future Soviet (and Russian) use of gas as a weapon of influence, the Bolsheviks also began asking for political favours in response to large shipments of relatively low-priced grain. In 1920 they demanded that, in exchange for grain, the Latvians recognize the Soviet Republic of Ukraine. In 1922 the Soviet government told the British Foreign Secretary, Lord Curzon, that unless Britain signed a peace treaty with Soviet Russia, it would cut off the supply of grain to British markets. Some speculate that in the late 1920s the Soviet Union began dumping grain at low prices for geopolitical reasons: Stalin hoped to damage Western capitalism. By 1930 one German newspaper was arguing for trade barriers to stop the flood of 'cheap Russian produce'. At a League of Nations gathering in 1931 the Soviet Foreign Minister, Maksim Litvinov, smugly boasted that 'I am enjoying a special status here thanks to the fact that the country I represent not only does not suffer from economic crisis, but is on the contrary living through an unprecedented moment in its economic life.'[13]

The desire to maintain this 'special status' was intense, but domestic pressure for more imports was enormous as well. In the cities and on new building sites, Stalin's drive for industrialization was intensifying. To meet the extraordinarily ambitious targets of the first Five Year Plan, Soviet factories urgently required machines, parts, tools and other things available only for hard currency. In a letter to Molotov in July 1930, Stalin was already writing of the need to 'force the export of grain . . . this is the key'. In August, fearing that American grain would soon flood the market, he again urged speed: 'if we don't export 130–150 million poods [2.1–2.4 million tonnes] our currency situation may become desperate. Once again: we must force the export of grain with all of our strength.'[14]

Elsewhere Stalin spoke of the risk that a lack of hard currency posed to the metallurgical and machine-building industries, and of the need to obtain a foothold in the international market. He also railed against the 'know-it-alls' in the export department who advised waiting for prices to rise, and who should be thrown out by the scruff of their necks: 'to wait, we would need currency reserves. And we haven't got any.'[15] In September 1930, Anastas Mikoyan – now Commissar for Internal and External Trade – wrote a note to the head of the grain export enterprise, urging him to conclude longer-term export agreements with European companies, although this would mean 'holding back some reserves for them'.[16] A few weeks later the Politburo discussed increasing food exports to fascist Italy, and even taking credit from Italian banks to finance them.[17]

The result of this urgent policy directive would be a far higher rate of grain export in 1930 – 4.8 million tonnes, up from 170,000 tonnes in 1929 – and an even higher rate in 1931, 5.2 million tonnes.[18] These numbers were a relatively small fraction of the more than 83 million tonnes, with higher totals in future, that Stalin believed should be harvested. But when less than that came in, they represented food that would not be available to Soviet citizens – and certainly not to the peasants who produced it.

The optimism that followed the 1930 summer harvest did not last. The autumn sowing season was delayed by the general confusion – peasants were still joining, leaving and rejoining the collective farms – and by uncertainty over who controlled which pieces of land. The spring sowing of 1931 was hampered by shortages of horses, tractors and seeds. Worse, the spring was cool, and there was less rain than in some other years, especially in the east. The Volga region, Siberia and Kazakhstan all suffered from bouts of drought, as did central Ukraine. By itself the weather might not have created a crisis. But, as in 1921, poor conditions combined with the chaos of Soviet policy meant that farmers could not produce what the state demanded from them. Some were already finding it difficult to produce enough even to feed themselves.[19]

By the summer of 1931 bureaucrats and activists at all levels were once again warning of trouble to come. The OGPU in Ukraine predicted the loss of a 'significant part of the harvest'. Aside from the weather problems, their report described unprepared storage containers, as well as tractors and other machinery in poor condition: 'In not a single region have district plans been brought to individual villages and collective farms ... No mass-educational work or organizational preparation for the harvest has been conducted at the local level.'[20] Multiple reports – some sent directly to Stalin – described the poor working practices of the collective farms and their inefficient methods.[21]

Throughout the summer and autumn a flurry of letters and directives circulated in Moscow and Kharkiv, all expressing the fear that grain collection would go badly, especially in Ukraine – or even that Ukrainian peasants would not sow at all. On 17 June, Stalin and Molotov sent out an order, jointly signed, demanding that the Ukrainian leadership ensure that 'unsown fields be sown', and bluntly calling on the Ukrainian Communist Party to mobilize all existing resources: 'Please inform us of the results by June 25th.'[22]

But the situation was not better by that date, or even by the autumn. By September it was already clear that the 1931 harvest would be smaller than that of the previous year, not larger as expected.[23] The Soviet leadership was particularly concerned that the country would not meet its export quotas. In the middle of the month Molotov sent a secret telegram to the Communist Party leaders in the North Caucasus, declaring that grain collection for purposes of export was proceeding 'disgustingly slowly'.[24] By late autumn it was clear that grain collection all across the USSR would fall short of the targets; the official harvest total for 1931–2 would eventually come to 69.5 million tonnes, instead of the 83 million-plus expected.[25]

Soviet exports would be hit if the numbers didn't rise. Worse, people in the cities would once again have no bread. The leader of Kyiv province had already written a begging letter to Mikoyan, who was at the time the People's Commissar of Trade: 'For two weeks we haven't distributed any rationed meat, no one brings us any fish, potatoes only sometimes.' As a result, 'the mood of the workers is agitated; the rural poor have no bread. Industrial productivity is on the edge of a serious crisis.' Please, he asked, could someone 'supply Kyiv quickly with bread according to the established norms'.[26] In Moscow no meat was available at all.[27]

Everybody understood, at some level, that collectivization was itself the source of the new shortages. Stalin himself had received reports explaining exactly what was wrong with the collective farms, describing their inefficiency in great detail. One official from the Central Black Earth province even wrote him a daring defence of private property: 'How to explain this enormous drop in collective farm production? It's impossible to explain it, except to say that the material interest in and responsibility for the losses, and for the low quality of work, don't affect each individual collective farmer directly . . .'[28]

The missing feeling of 'responsibility', destroyed by collectivization, would plague Soviet agriculture (and indeed Soviet industry) as long as it existed. But although this was already clear as early as 1931, it was not possible to question the policy because it was already too closely associated with Stalin himself. He had staked his leadership of the party on collectivization and he had defeated his rivals in the course of fighting for it. He could not be wrong. A large chunk of the Central Committee plenum in October was therefore devoted to a search for alternative scapegoats. Since Stalin could not be responsible, and since senior party officials did not want to be, responsibility for the looming disaster was again sought further down the hierarchy.

Echoing the 'Dizzy with Success' accusations, Stanislav Kosior – since 1928 the General Secretary of the Ukrainian Communist Party, as well as a member of the Soviet Politburo – blamed the lower levels of the party hierarchy for the harvest failures. Ukrainian officials, he explained, had gone into the rural districts. They had personally talked to the directors of the machine tractor stations. They had directly accused them of failing to put their energy into collecting grain. But even so, many had 'fallen captive' to the idea that the state's demands for grain were too high. For they had returned to Kharkiv and Moscow from their sojourns into the countryside with the wrong message for the leadership: the peasants were very hungry and needed more food.

As a good Bolshevik, Kosior could only see this demand in conspiratorial terms. 'Even our communists and often our twenty-five thousanders had come to believe the fiction about hungry peasants,' he declared. Worse, 'among the twenty-five thousanders there has appeared a whole array of alien elements'. The result: 'Not only did they not fight, not only did they fail to organize the collective farm masses in the struggle for bread against the class enemy, they often followed along with this peasant mood, sometimes out of gullibility, and sometimes consciously.' Suspect party members had already been expelled from the Ukrainian Communist Party: 'In the countryside we need genuine Bolsheviks, who will fight for the construction of socialism, for the collective farm, for the interests of our Soviet state, and not for kulak nonsense.'[29]

As they so often did when their policies failed, the authorities also blamed 'sabotage'. During the Shakhty trial in 1928 they had focused on mining engineers in order to explain production failures in heavy industry. Now they sought agricultural specialists to blame. In the spring of 1931 secret police operatives in the western Ukrainian city of Vinnytsia disclosed and eliminated a 'saboteur counter-revolutionary organization', the 'Peasants' Labour Party of Podolia'. Most of the sixteen people arrested for 'organized acts of sabotage in all sectors of agriculture: planning, land administration, crediting, machine supplies etc' were agronomists. Most had been members of the Podolian branch of the All-Ukrainian Agricultural Society, an institution set up in the more optimistic year of 1923. Now they stood accused of seeking the 'overthrow of Soviet rule and the establishment of a bourgeois democratic republic'.

Although none of their biographies appeared obviously counter-revolutionary, they were educated people who had connections in both town and country – precisely the category of suspect that interested the OGPU most. Stepan Cherniavsky was an agronomist who had been working for the Ukrainian government since the days of Petliura, and had been chairman of the Podolia Land Office. Iukhym Pidkui-Mukha had been secretary of the same organization. Ivan Oliinyk had been a professor at the Agricultural Institute in Kamianets-Podilskyi. Others worked on agricultural credit issues or as experts in various fields of agriculture and husbandry. Not only could this educated, accomplished group be blamed for the multiple agricultural failures, its members could also be plausibly accused of spreading counter-revolutionary ideas among the rural peasants in the countryside. The trial was heavily covered by the Soviet press; most of the accused would spend between three and ten years in the Gulag.[30]

This search for scapegoats was effective, but only in a narrow sense: the arrest of the 'enemy' agronomists and the expulsion of some party members helped explain Ukraine's failure to meet its quotas, at least to the rest of the party, but it did not produce more grain. Angry telegrams from Moscow did not produce more grain.[31] Nor did Mikoyan's declaration, in October 1931, that the year's plan still had to be fulfilled, whatever the weather, so any regions unaffected by drought should contribute more. This was perhaps unfair, as even he conceded – 'people are working hard . . . and now we demand more' – but it hardly mattered, since this order could not make more bread appear on the shelves either.[32]

Both threats and persuasion were failing. That left coercion – and in December 1931, Stalin and Molotov made coercion the policy: collective farms that had not met their grain quotas would have to repay any outstanding loans, and return any tractors or other equipment that had been leased to them from the machine tractor stations. Their spare cash – including that intended to buy seeds – would be confiscated. Molotov, dispatched to Kharkiv to explain the new rules, showed little mercy. He pushed aside any complaints about bad weather and a poor harvest. The problem was not lack of grain, he told the Ukrainian party leaders: the problem was that they were incompetent. They were badly organized, they had failed to mobilize, and they had not managed to collect as much grain as they should have done. In the districts he harangued collective farm leaders, calling them 'agents of the kulaks'. He repeated Stalin's threat to take away their tractors while at the same time dangling the promise of more manufactured goods for farms that met the state targets. Upon returning to Moscow, Molotov and Stalin sent another missive to Kosior, who was on vacation in Sochi. They ordered him back to Ukraine and demanded that he force the republic to meet the grain requirements as planned.[33]

In the wake of this acrimonious meeting, the Ukrainian Politburo met again at the end of December. Once more the Ukrainian communists paid lip service to the Five Year Plan. They agreed to collect 8.3 million tonnes of grain, although everyone in the room must have known that it was impossible. They declared that they themselves would go out to the villages to supervise the procurement, although each one of them must have known that would make no difference either. To increase the efficiency of the whole operation, they reorganized Ukraine into six collection districts, and put a single party leader in charge of each one. All of them must have felt deep anxiety about the task ahead.

Perhaps they were reassured by the news that each district boss would receive emergency powers, including the power to sack anyone who stood in the way of fulfilling the plan: anyone who failed would be able to place some of the blame, yet again, on scapegoats.[34] But at the same time the stakes were raised. The harvest had been unsatisfactory in the Urals, the Volga, Kazakhstan and western Siberia. That meant the Ukrainians and others in the western USSR would have to collect not only their original grain quota, but also an extra amount of seed grain, to be used for spring planting in other regions. To an impossible quota, in other words, the state had added an even more impossible new demand.[35]

In the spring of 1932 desperate officials, anxious for their jobs and even their lives, aware that a new famine might be on its way, began to collect grain wherever and however they could. Mass confiscations occurred all across the USSR. In Ukraine they took on an almost fanatical intensity. Visiting the Moldovan autonomous republic that was then part of Ukraine, a *Pravda* correspondent was shocked to discover the lengths to which grain procurement officials would now go.[36] In a private letter to a colleague, he wrote of 'openly counter-revolutionary attacks' on the peasantry: 'The searches are usually conducted at night, and they search fiercely, deadly seriously. There is a village just on the border with Romania where not a single house has not had its stove destroyed.'

Worse, anyone found in possession of any bread or grain at all – even the poorest of peasants – was dragged from his or her home and stripped of their possessions, just as had happened to the kulaks in the months before. But this was unusual: 'Very rarely did they find a more or less solid amount, usually the searches finished with the confiscation of the very last few pieces of bread in the smallest possible amount.'[37] No one in authority questioned the wisdom of this behaviour: the fact that the OGPU and Communist Party officials allowed journalists, even those loyal to the regime, to observe the confiscation of grain meant that, at the highest levels, they were convinced of the legitimacy of what they were doing.

Local party leaders, their careers on the line, organized groups of activists and sent them, village by village, to begin confiscating whatever grain they could find. A peasant in the village of Sobolivka, in the western part of Ukraine, wrote to his Polish relatives describing how this worked:

The authorities do as follows: they send the so-called brigades which come to a man or a farmer and conduct a search so thorough they even look through the ground with sharp metal tools, through the walls with matches, in the garden, in the straw roof, and if they find even half a pood, they take it away on the horse wagon. This passes for life here ... Dear brother Ignacy, if it is possible, I ask you to send me a package, as it is very needed. There is nothing to eat and one must eat.[38]

All these methods recalled the events of the past: in the days of 'War Communism' the Red Army had searched peasants' property with similar violence, and with similar disregard for their lives. But they also foreshadowed the immediate future: these were the first of what would be thousands of many intense, destructive searches, conducted by activists all across Ukraine a year later, in the winter of 1932-3. The use of violence, the smashing of walls and furniture in search of hidden grain – these were a harbinger of what was to come.

The pockets of real starvation all across the USSR were an ominous warning too. Reports from the Volga district, the Caucasus and Kazakhstan already spoke of starving children, people too weak to work, whole districts deprived of bread. In Ukraine the situation of several villages in Odessa province was so dramatic that in March the local party leaders in Zynovïvskyi district sent a medical team to investigate. The doctors were stunned by what they found. In the village of Kozyrivka half the inhabitants had died of hunger. On the day of their visit 100 households remained out of 365, and the rest 'are emptying': 'Quite a few of the remaining huts are being taken apart, the window and door frames are being used as fuel.' The family of Ivan Myronenko – seven people, including three school-age children – were surviving 'entirely on carrion'. When the team entered their hut, the Myronenkos were eating boiled horsehide together with a 'stinking yellow liquid' made from the broth. Nearby, the inspectors met the Koval family that had four children. On entering the hut, they found Maria Koval boiling the bones of a dead horse. An elderly woman lay on a bed, asking for medicine 'in order to die more quickly'.[39]

In the village of Tarasivka the situation was not much better. Here the number of households had halved, from 400 to 200. Corpses lay on the street, as there was no one to bury them. The medical team

was told that this had become normal in villages where corpses sometimes went untouched for three or four days. The doctors visited a
home where the father was 'yellow, emaciated, barely able to stand
on his feet'.[40] With equal horror the group reported that provincial,
district, village and party officials 'try not to notice the incidence of
starvation, and try not to speak about it'. The local leaders were actually 'hiding' the rising mortality. This too was a pattern that would
soon be repeated.[41]

The OGPU in Ukraine had no illusions about what was happening.
In the first quarter of 1932, their operatives recorded that eighty-three
Ukrainians had become swollen with hunger, and that six had died.
Informers also reported on sporadic food shortages in the Kharkiv, Kyiv,
Odessa, Dnipropetrovsk and Vinnytsia provinces. Horses were observed
to be dying at a high rate too; across Ukraine their numbers had dropped
by more than half since collectivization.[42] The leaders of one collective
farm jointly informed party authorities that they were losing up to four
horses a day to starvation and overwork. Worse, they were unable to
prevent the peasants from eating them. 'We have several times warned
the kolkhozniks not to eat the carcasses, but they answer: "We're going
to die anyway from hunger, and we'll eat the carcasses, even those of
infected cattle. You can shoot us if you want." '[43]

Letters flooded into the party offices, and especially to Stalin. 'It's
horrible, having children and not being able to raise them in civilized
conditions – better not to have them,' one woman wrote to him from
Nyzhniodniprovsk.[44] A party member wrote of collection teams entering the huts of poor and middle peasants who had 'filled all of their
grain requisition obligations', yet taking all the rest of their grain,
'leaving nothing to eat, nothing for the fall sowing'.[45] Another wrote:

> Dear Stalin,
> Please answer me, why are the collective farmers on the collective
> farms swelling with hunger and eating dead horses? I got a holiday
> and went to Zynovïvskyi district, where I saw for myself how people
> are eating horses . . .[46]

In the spring of 1932 secret police informers also began, for the first
time in a decade, to use the word 'famine' in describing the situation
in Ukrainian villages.[47] The republican government in Kharkiv also

began to act as if it understood that the threat of hunger was very real. Government grain warehouses released more than 2,000 tonnes of millet in April, to help those 'in the most difficult situations'.[48] A month later the Kyiv provincial government discussed the provision of extra food to thirty districts, particularly for the children.[49] They also decided to send emergency grain supplies immediately to two districts where the need was extreme.[50]

The sense of impending crisis affected the foreigners living in Ukraine too. The Polish consul in Kyiv cabled to Warsaw his observations of 'severe food shortages' in many villages. He had seen people collapsing on the streets from starvation in Vinnytsia and Uman.[51] The German consul reported that he had received appeals from members of the German minority, who were petitioning to be recognized as citizens in order to emigrate: 'There is not enough bread, villagers are forced to eat unacceptable ersatz [food] ... villagers who are underfed at the collective farms and workers whose rations are insufficient are begging for food.'[52]

Given the scale of the food shortages it was hardly surprising that the peasants balked, that spring, and, as in 1921, refused to sow their land: if they planted their last remaining kernels of seed grain, then they would have nothing to eat. They must also have known that whatever they did manage to grow would be confiscated. In April 1932 the OGPU raised the alarm: more than 40,000 households were not going to plant anything at all.[53] As hunger spread, many were too weak to work in the fields. The empty fields were no secret: *Visti VUTsVK*, the main newspaper of the Ukrainian republican government, openly reported that only about two-thirds of Ukrainian fields had been sown that spring.[54]

No unbiased observer, at that moment, could possibly have believed that Ukraine had any chance of meeting Moscow's demands for grain that year. The food supply was clearly going to drop. The grain for export was not going to materialize. And many, many people were going to starve.

In the spring of 1932 a few high-ranking Ukrainian communists finally gathered the courage to call for a drastic change of direction. In February, Hryhorii Petrovskyi – an 'Old Bolshevik', a party member since before the revolution, member of the Ukrainian Polit-buro and chairman of Ukraine's Supreme Soviet – wrote a short letter to his colleagues. He did not name scapegoats, and did not seek to explain away shortages as 'temporary' or imaginary. Instead, he observed the lack of food in 'not only villages but also working-class towns' all across Ukraine, in Kyiv and Vinnytsia provinces as well as Odessa, Dnipropetrovsk and Kharkiv.

Petrovskyi made a list of suggestions: write a letter to the Central Committee, describing the 'drastic shortages of produce for the pop-ulation and feed for livestock'; ask it to halt grain collections in Ukraine and restore free exchange of goods 'according to the law'; call upon the Red Cross and other emergency relief organizations to pool their resources, as they had in 1921, in order to rescue people in the worst affected areas, especially children; mobilize organizations within the Ukrainian republic to help out famine-struck regions. Bluntly, he declared that the Soviet state should expect to collect nothing in Ukraine at all in 1932. In order to feed hungry Ukrainian peasants, any food harvested should remain inside the republic.[55]

The Ukrainian party leadership heeded Petrovskyi's call. In March, reversing their earlier statements, party officials abruptly told local lead-ers to stop collecting grain. Despite having not met the spring quotas, the peasants should concentrate on sowing the next season's crop.[56] Encour-aged by these signs from the top, several Ukrainians officials lower down the hierarchy refused to comply with demands from other republics and other state institutions for Ukrainian grain. One official, having been asked to send 1,000 tonnes of grain to the Urals, wrote back that this was 'impossible'. A request to send beans and peas was refused as well.[57]

The ensuing arguments – within the Moscow leadership, the Ukrainian Communist Party in Kharkiv, and between Moscow and Kharkiv – were murky and guarded, even confusing and contradic-tory. The potential for widespread famine was by now well understood on all sides. But, again, Stalin's personal responsibility for the col-lectivization policy – he had conceived and argued for it, backed and stood by it – was perfectly well understood too. To oppose it openly, let alone imply that it had somehow failed, sounded like a criticism of the leader himself. Everyone knew that the provision of food aid to Ukraine was a tacit admission of Stalin's failure – yet if the Ukrainian peasants were not spared their grain and encouraged to sow their crops, everyone also knew that catastrophe would follow.

Different leaders tried different strategies, choosing their words carefully. On 26 April, Kosior wrote a long, exceedingly cautious letter to Stalin on the general situation in the Ukrainian countryside, rather downplaying the problems. He had, he said, just been to visit several of the southern districts. Despite all the negative reports he was certain that the 1932 harvest would surpass that of the previous year, mostly because the weather had improved. Contradicting his colleagues' fearful missives, he declared that 'all conversation about "famine" in Ukraine must be categorically abandoned'. Yes, 'serious mistakes had been made in carrying out the grain collection' in a few provinces, but he expected them to be rectified. Kosior also conceded that there had been some 'incidents' in Kyiv province, where certain protests of a 'Petliurite' character had taken place: hungry peasants were refusing to sow any grain. But he assured Stalin that all was well. The state had offered a bit of food aid to those provinces, including some millet, corn and horse feed. This little hiccup prompted him to ask for a favour: because of these small disruptions, some 'extra help' might be useful in some other parts of Ukraine. For this 'we will be obliged to turn once again to the Central Committee'.[58]

Kosior was delicately asking for food aid, in other words, but only for a few districts, only in a limited quantity, and only because some counter-revolutionaries had disrupted the sowing season with their political protests. He and other Ukrainian communist leaders had reason to believe that Stalin would look favourably upon such carefully worded requests. Throughout the spring of 1932 the Soviet leader had several times seemed open to changing the policy. He told Kaganovich that more industrial goods ought to be made available to peasants, the better to inspire them. He had offered some small shipments of cereals in April to ease the food shortages.[59] Even as exports to Western countries continued, he had authorized secret purchases of corn, wheat and other grain from the Far East and Persia, demonstrating that he knew there were shortages inside the USSR.[60] He had backed a Politburo decision to authorize another small shipment of grain to Odessa province.[61] Stalin had even toyed with the idea that the grain procurement plans all across the USSR were 'too mechanical' and ought to be adjusted for regional weather and other local factors. Both Kaganovich and Molotov would reiterate that point later in the summer.[62]

But in April his tone shifted: Stalin had received some alarming material on the political situation in Ukraine. The archives don't record exactly what it was he read, though it is possible to guess. Perhaps it was the 'Petliurite' protests to which Kosior alluded, or a report from the Pavlohrad district. Perhaps it was a report on the mood within the Communist Party itself. Balytsky's OGPU was diligently collecting informers' reports from the countryside, recording in particular the dissatisfaction of party members, their dislike of collectivization, and their resentment of Moscow. Later that autumn he would present Stalin with a list of angry remarks from Ukrainian party officials, reported by informers, and descriptions of party members turning in their party cards; it may be that Stalin saw something similar that spring. Whatever it was, Stalin lashed out on 26 April in a letter to Kosior: 'Judging from this material, it seems that in several places in Ukraine, Soviet power has ceased to exist. Is this really true? Is the situation in the countryside really that terrible? Where are the GPU organs, what are they doing? Could you verify this case and report back to the Central Committee on what measures you've taken?'[63]

Prompted by whatever had provoked his note, Stalin immediately withdrew the millet and other food aid to Ukraine. He also demanded that the Ukrainian Communist Party maintain its policy of confiscating tractors and other equipment from underperforming farms. He did not want any generous gestures to be misinterpreted as an independent action of the Ukrainian leadership, and he certainly didn't want them to be seen as a 'demonstration against Moscow and the Soviet Communist Party'.[64] He was deeply concerned about the Ukrainian party's reliability. Using language that illustrates how far the Soviet state had gone in the direction of personal tyranny, he told Kaganovich and Molotov that the local leaders were insufficiently loyal. 'Pay serious attention to Ukraine,' he wrote to both of them on 2 June: '[Vlas] Chubar [head of the Ukrainian government], through his rotten and opportunistic nature, and Kosior, through his rotten diplomacy . . . and his criminally light-minded attitude to affairs, are completely ruining Ukraine. These comrades are not up to leading today's Ukraine.'[65]

These 'rotten' and reviled leaders did nevertheless make one last appeal. On 10 June, Petrovskyi wrote the frankest letter of all. He had just been to visit several rural districts where people were beginning to starve. He had faced down the starving peasants himself:

We knew beforehand that fulfilling state grain procurements in Ukraine would be difficult, but what I have seen in the countryside indicates that we have greatly overdone it, we have tried too hard. I was in many villages and saw a considerable part of the countryside engulfed in famine. There aren't many, but there are people swollen from starvation, mainly poor peasants and even middle peasants. They are eating food scraps from the bottom of the barrel, if any are available. During big meetings in the villages, the peasants of course curse me, old women cry and men sometimes do also. Sometimes the criticism of the worsening situation becomes very deep and broad – Why did they create an artificial famine? After all, we had a good harvest. Why did they take away all of the sowing seeds? That did not happen even under the old regime. We didn't have that even under the old regime. Why are Ukrainians forced to make treacherous journeys to find bread in less fertile regions? Why isn't bread being brought here? and so on . . . It's difficult, in these conditions, to offer an explanation. You obviously condemn those who committed excesses, but generally feel like a carp squirming on a frying pan . . .[66]

Theft was increasing in the villages, Petrovskyi explained. In the shops he had been unable to buy bread, sugar or anything else. Prices were rising, and 'speculation' was spreading. Local offices were refusing to sell train tickets, and they didn't know why. Each one of these facts was 'being used against the party, and against the collective farms', he wrote, and he finished with a plea for aid: 'To conclude, I ask again that you consider all methods and resources available to provide urgent food aid to Ukrainian villages, and to supply buckwheat for sowing as quickly as possible, in order to make up for what has not been sown.'[67]

On the same day Chubar, the Ukrainian leader, also wrote a long letter to Stalin and Molotov, describing the poor spring harvest and the pockets of famine: 'It is now possible to count at least 100 districts in need of food aid.' Like Petrovskyi, Chubar had been in the countryside. Like Kosior, he avoided putting direct blame on state policy, instead attributing the crisis to the 'poor planning and management' of the harvest. But he was absolutely clear about what was happening: 'In March and April, there were tens of thousands of malnourished, starving and swollen people dying from famine in every village; children abandoned by their parents and orphans appeared. District and provincial governments provided food relief from internal reserves, but growing despair and the psychology of famine resulted in more appeals for help.'

He came to the same conclusion: It was time to end the 'unrealistic' grain procurement policies. 'Even some of those collective farms which had already fulfilled their quota received demands to fulfill it a second or even a third time.'[68]

Kaganovich forwarded the two letters to Stalin. He told him that he found Chubar's note to have a more 'businesslike and self-critical character'. Petrovskyi's letter by contrast, contained an element of 'rot'. Kaganovich particularly disliked the Ukrainian leader's criticism of the Soviet Communist Party and, by implication, of Stalin. Nevertheless, he supported their request: it was time to offer some help to Ukraine.[69] Molotov also wrote to Stalin and suggested that Soviet grain exports might, for a time, be curtailed, so as to provide Ukraine with some food aid.[70]

Stalin argued back. From the tone of his letter it is clear that he could not (or did not want to) believe that there really was insufficient grain in Ukraine:

> I did not like the letters from Chubar and Petrovskyi. The former spouts 'self-criticism' in order to secure a million more poods of bread from Moscow, the latter is feigning sainthood, claiming victimization from the [Central Committee] in order to reduce grain procurement levels. Neither one nor the other is acceptable. Chubar is mistaken if he thinks that self-criticism is required for securing outside 'help' and not for mobilizing the forces and resources within Ukraine. In my opinion, Ukraine has been given more than enough . . .[71]

Stalin was of course talking about 'giving' grain to Ukraine that had been taken from the country in the first place. But no one challenged him. On

16 June, Kaganovich once again wrote to Stalin that 'This year's harvest campaign will be especially difficult, particularly in Ukraine. Unfortunately, Ukraine is not sufficiently prepared for it.'[72] But he did not speak, as his Ukrainian colleagues had done, of sending mass food aid.

Instead, in the summer of 1932, the policies that could have prevented mass famine in Ukraine were quietly abandoned. Some grain was granted to Kyiv and Odessa, though not as much as had been requested. No horses or tractors were included.[73] Kosior told local party bosses that there was enough to help just 'twenty districts' – out of more than 600: 'Quickly inform by telegram which districts in your province should be on that list.'[74]

Even as hunger spread, the state continued to issue plans and orders designed to maintain the export of grain abroad. In March 1932, Moscow told Kharkiv that Ukrainian officials would be 'made personally responsible for the export of rye from the Odessa port'. The Council of People's Commissars urged all enterprises involved in export to improve the quality of their barrels and containers and the storage for goods heading abroad.[75] To Ukrainians watching food leaving their hungry republic, the export policy seemed crazy, even suicidal. Mykola Kostyrko, an engineer who lived in Odessa at the time, remembered 'foreign vessels' coming into the port: 'they exported everything in order to get foreign capital for the "needs of the state" to buy tractors and for propaganda abroad'. At one point, he remembered, longshoremen in Odessa refused to load pigs onto a ship. A detachment of Red Army soldiers was sent to do it for them.[76]

An employee of the Italian consulate in Odessa also recorded widespread anger at the export policy: 'there is no [vegetable] oil here, even while oil, and seed used for its production, are being sent abroad'.[77] Public anger at the exports was no secret to the Communist Party either. In April 1932 the Ukrainian party leadership had agreed never to discuss the matter publicly, as it would only create 'unhealthy moods'.[78] By the year's end export levels did fall dramatically – from 5.2 million to 1.73 million tonnes.[79] The value to the state dropped dramatically as well, from 203.5 million rubles in 1931 to 88.1 million in 1932.[80] But the shipments abroad never stopped altogether.

The mood inside the party itself did not improve either. In July, Molotov and Kaganovich again arrived in Ukraine, with the goal once more of overriding any remaining objections. They had direct orders from Stalin, who wrote to them on 2 July, repeating his concerns about Ukraine and its leadership: 'Pay more serious attention to Ukraine. Chubar's deterioration and opportunistic nature, Kosior's rotten diplomacy ... and a criminally reckless approach to affairs will lose Ukraine in the end.'[81]

They used the Third Party Conference – a grim affair – to make their point. All the Ukrainians present objected, as far as they dared, to the quota assigned to their country. Some local leaders were quite blunt. The first secretary of a district in the Kharkiv province pointed out that, thanks to the absence of reserves and seed grain, there were 'food shortages' in his area.[82] One of his counterparts in Kyiv province complained even more bluntly that the collection brigades doomed peasants to death: the party, he said, was guilty of 'distortions' in its agricultural policy.[83] A comrade from the Melitopol district complained that the central plan often did not bear any relationship to the situation of specific collective farms and that the centre seemed to prepare plans without consulting the local peasants.[84] Roman Terekhov, from Kharkiv province, declared that every district knew perfectly well that the plans were badly made, that work was poorly organized, and that 'huge losses' had resulted, leading to 'food shortages' in at least twenty-five districts.[85]

Although he didn't repeat his call to end the grain procurement policy altogether, Mykola Skrypnyk, the Commissar of Education, was also quite blunt. Ukraine simply could not and would not produce the requisite amount of grain. The plan would not be fulfilled: 'this is a huge, shameful failure'.[86] Both Petrovskyi and Chubar spoke of 'shortages' and 'failures' as well.[87] What they were asking for, however, was a reduction in the amount of grain Ukraine was required to produce.

Molotov and Kaganovich refused to yield. Molotov told the Ukrainian communists that they had become 'whisperers and capitulators'.[88] Later, the two men told Stalin that they had turned down a Ukrainian resolution calling for lower quotas: 'We categorically rejected a revision of the plan, demanded the mobilization of party forces to combat losses and the squander of grain and to invigorate collective farms.'[89] The result was that instead of pulling back, the conference passed a resolution recognizing as 'correct' the unrealistic, impossible 5.8 million tonne (356 million pood) plan, and resolved to 'adopt it for unconditional fulfilment'.[90]

Molotov and Kaganovich also described the mood of the Communist Party leadership in Kharkiv as 'more favourable' than they had anticipated, by which they seem to have meant that the Ukrainians were still amenable to taking orders.[91] Carefully, the two men suggested to Stalin that the seriousness of the situation remain concealed: 'In order not to give any information to the foreign press, we have to publish only modest criticism in our own press, without any information about the situation in the bad districts.'[92] Accordingly, the official line remained positive. A few weeks after the conference, the Soviet government and the Communist Party jointly declared 'complete victory' in agriculture. The 'bourgeois theory' that the USSR would have to revert to capitalism and markets had been 'battered and smashed into dust'.[93]

There is no doubt that Stalin knew, by this point, that 5.8 million tonnes was an unrealistic figure. On 25 July he told Kaganovich that he intended to allow the 'suffering' collective farms in Ukraine to get by with reduced quotas. He had, he wrote, avoided speaking of a reduction in grain collection before, because he wanted to avoid 'demoralizing' the Ukrainians further or disrupting the harvest. He intended instead to wait until later to make the announcement, hoping to 'stimulate' the peasants during the harvest season – and to appear benevolent – by offering a small reduction of 30 million poods (490,000 tonnes) or 'as a last resort' (those words were underlined) 40 million poods (655,000 tonnes). Kaganovich wrote back in agreement: 'Now is not the time to tell the Ukrainians' about the decrease. It was better to let them worry about meeting an impossible demand.[94]

Before this game could play itself out, Stalin was once again distracted by bad news from across the Soviet Union – and some especially bad news from Ukraine. All through the summer, the OGPU had been reporting growing levels of theft. People were stealing from railroads, shops, enterprises, and above all from collective farms. This was hardly surprising: collective farm workers (and factory workers too) often felt that state property belonged to no one and so there was no harm in taking it. More to the point, they were very hungry. That's the clear implication of a report the OGPU filed in July, describing a worrying trend: many peasants were beginning to harvest grain prematurely, and secretly, and then keeping it for themselves. One report came from Central Volga province:

> On the night of 9 July, five women were found in the fields cutting the ears of wheat. When an attempt was made to detain the women, they fled in different directions. The guard fired twice with a hunting gun. One of the collective farm women who fled was severely wounded (she died several hours later) . . .

On that same night, in the same village, a watchman also discovered a crowd of 'fifteen thieves on horseback with sacks of stolen grain'. This group of 'thieves' fared better than the five women. After they put up violent resistance, the watchman took fright and escaped.[95]

As so often in the past, Stalin found a political interpretation for these acts of desperation. On vacation in Sochi – having travelled on a 'train well-stocked with fine provisions' – he wrote several letters to Kaganovich on the subject.[96] The two of them confirmed one another's views. The state and its policies were not a danger to the starving peasants – but the starving peasants were a great danger to the state. 'Kulaks, the de-kulakized and anti-Soviet elements all steal,' Stalin told Kaganovich. 'Crime must be punished with ten years or capital punishment', and there should be no amnesty: 'Without these (and similar) draconian socialist measures it is impossible to establish new social discipline, and without such discipline it is impossible to strengthen and defend our new order.'[97]

A few days later, in another set of letters to Kaganovich and Molotov, he elaborated further, clearly having thought about the matter some more during his seaside holiday. A new law, he now worried, was an insufficient deterrent. In order to get people to stop stealing food, the law must be supported by a propaganda campaign fully grounded in Marxist theory. Capitalism had defeated feudalism because capitalism ensured that private property was protected by the state; Socialism, in turn, could defeat capitalism only if it declared public property – cooperative, collective, state property – to be sacred and inviolable too. The very survival of socialism might well depend on whether or not the state could prevent 'anti-social, kulak-capitalistic elements' from stealing public property.[98]

Stalin's obsessive belief in Marxist theory once again triumphed over what he would have called 'bourgeois morality'. On 7 August 1932 the USSR duly passed an edict draconian even by Soviet standards. It began with a declaration:

Public property (state, kolkhoz, cooperative) [is] the basis of the Soviet system; it is sacred and inviolable, and those attempting to steal public property must be considered enemies of the people ... the decisive struggle against plunderers of public property is the foremost obligation of every organ of Soviet administration.

It continued with a definition, and a conclusion:

The Central Executive Committee and Soviet of People's Commissars of the USSR hereby resolve ...

1) To regard the property of kolkhozes and cooperatives (harvest in stores, etc.) as tantamount to state property.

2) To apply as a punitive measure for plundering (thievery) of kolkhoz and collective property the highest measure of social defence: execution with the confiscation of all property, which may be substituted ... by the deprivation of freedom for a period of no fewer than ten years.[99]

The theft of tiny amounts of food, in other words, could be punished by ten years in a labour camp – or death. Such punishments had hitherto been reserved for acts of high treason. Now, a peasant woman who stole a few grains of wheat from a collective farm would be treated like a military officer who had betrayed the country during wartime. The law had no precedent, even in the USSR. Only a few months earlier, the Russian republican Supreme Court had punished a person who had stolen wheat from a collective farm field with just one year of forced labour.[100]

As Stalin wished, an educational press campaign followed. Two weeks after the decree, *Pravda* published an account of the case of 'the female kulak Grybanova', who had been stealing grain from the fields of the 'Red Builder' collective farm. She was sentenced to be shot. The Ukrainian press reported in detail on three cases tried in Odessa, including an account of a husband and wife who were both shot for 'pilfering'.[101] Other published stories included the case of a peasant shot for possessing a small quantity of wheat gleaned by his ten-year-old daughter.[102]

This extraordinary law took an extraordinary toll. By the end of 1932, within less than six months of the law's passage, 4,500 people had been executed for breaking it. Far more – over 100,000 people – had received ten-year sentences in labour camps. This preference for long camp sentences over capital punishment, dictated from above, was clearly pragmatic: forced labourers could get to work on the Gulag system's vast new industrial projects – mines, factories, logging operations – that were just getting underway.[103]

In subsequent weeks and months, thousands of peasants flooded into the camp system, victims of the 7 August law. According to official figures (which do not reflect all arrests), the number of Gulag inmates nearly doubled between 1932 and 1934, from 260,000 to 510,000. The camp system had neither the resources nor the organizational capacity to cope with this huge influx of people, many of whom arrived already emaciated by hunger. As a result, deaths in the Gulag also climbed from 4.81 per cent in 1932 to 15.3 per cent in 1933.[104] Others may have been saved by their incarceration. Years later, Susannah Pechora, a Gulag prisoner in a later period, recalled meeting a fellow prisoner, a former peasant. Upon being given her meagre daily ration, the woman sighed and stroked the small, hard chunk of bread. 'Khlebushka, my little bit of bread,' she purred, 'and to think that they give you to us every day!'[105]

Theft was not Stalin's only concern in the summer of 1932. Soon after passage of the 7 August law, he received a startling document from the Ukrainian secret police. The historian Terry Martin, the first to identify its significance, has called this document 'extraordinary and unique'.[106] Stalin may have seen comparable reports before. This one may have been similar to the material that had caused his outburst in April, when he had demanded to know whether 'Soviet power has ceased to exist' in some parts of Ukraine. But this time, with a new food crisis building, his reaction was even harsher.

Normally, the OGPU sent Stalin reports written in careful prose and filled with stock phrases about enemies and conspiracies. But in August 1932 the Ukrainian secret police sent him a straightforward set of quotations without commentary. The quotations were all collected from informers and attributed to Ukrainian party members operating at district level, all of whom were bitterly opposed to the grain requisition campaign. Normally, this kind of raw material would serve as the basis for a more elaborate report. This time, the raw material itself was striking enough that it was sent on its own.

Almost all the evidence in the document expressed direct defiance of Moscow's orders. 'I will not obey this [grain requisition] plan', one party member was quoted as saying: 'I do not want to accept this plan. I will not complete this grain requisition plan.' And after that, the secret policemen recorded, he 'put his party card on the table and left the room'.

Another had a similar reaction: 'It will be difficult to fight for the completion of this grain requisitions plan, but I know a way out of this difficulty – I'll send my party card to the local council, and then I will be free.'

And a third: 'We will not accept the grain requisitions plan, since in its current form it cannot be fulfilled. And to again force the people to starve is criminal. For me it is better to turn in my Party card than to doom the collective farmers to starve through deceit.'

And a fourth: 'I see that this plan dooms me. I will ask the party cell to remove me from my job, since otherwise I will soon be excluded from the party for failing to cope with my work and failing to fulfil the party's tasks.'[107]

Had they been deliberately trying to prejudice the Soviet leader against Ukraine, the men of the OGPU could not have chosen a better way, for the report confirmed all of Stalin's worst fears. He had long perceived a clear connection between the grain collection problem in Ukraine and the threat of nationalism in the republic. Now he heard a clear echo of the events of the previous decade: the civil war, the peasant revolt, the Bolshevik setback. His response, in a letter to Kaganovich, was harsh:

The chief thing now is Ukraine. Things in Ukraine are terrible. It's terrible in the party. They say that in some parts of Ukraine (it seems, Kyiv and Dnipropetrovsk) around 50 district committees have spoken out against the grain requisition plan, considering it unrealistic. In other district committees, it appears the situation is no better. What is this? This is not the party, not a parliament, this is a caricature of a parliament . . .

If we don't make an effort now to improve the situation in Ukraine, we may lose Ukraine. Keep in mind that Piłsudski is not daydreaming, and his agents in Ukraine are many times stronger than Redens or Kosior think. Keep in mind that the Ukrainian Communist Party includes more than a few rotten elements, conscious and unconscious Petliurites as well as direct agents of Piłsudski. As soon as things get worse, these elements will not be slow in opening a front within (and without) the party against the party. The worst thing is that the Ukrainians simply do not see this danger . . .[108]

Stalin went on to list all the changes that he wanted to make in the Ukrainian Communist Party. He wanted to remove Stanislav Redens, the head of the Ukrainian secret police (and his brother-in-law). He wanted to transfer Balytsky, his reliable ally, back to Ukraine from Moscow, where he had briefly served as deputy leader of the OGPU, an order that would be carried out in October. He wanted Kaganovich himself to take full responsibility for the Ukrainian Communist Party once again: 'Give yourself the task of quickly transforming Ukraine into a true fortress of the USSR, a truly model republic. We won't spare money on this task.'[109] He believed that this was the moment to revive tactics deployed in the past: 'Lenin was right in saying that a person who does not have the courage to swim against the current when necessary cannot be a real Bolshevik leader . . .'

He also believed that time was short: 'Without these and similar measures (ideological and political work in Ukraine, above all in her border districts and so forth) I repeat – we could lose Ukraine . . .'[110]

For Stalin, who remembered the civil war in Ukraine, the loss of the republic was an exceedingly dangerous prospect. In 1919 a peasant revolt in Ukraine had brought the White Army within a few days' march of Moscow; in 1920 chaos in Ukraine had brought the Polish army deep into Soviet territory. The USSR could not afford to lose Ukraine again.

8

Famine Decisions, 1932:
Requisitions, Blacklists and
Borders

> Like the Jews that Moses led out of Egyptian slavery, the
> half-savage, stupid, ponderous people of the Russian
> villages . . . will die out, and a new tribe will take their place –
> literate, sensible, hearty people.
>
> *Maxim Gorky*, On the Russian Peasant, *1922*[1]

Sometime in the early hours of 9 November 1932 – two days after the
solemn celebrations of the fifteenth anniversary of the revolution –
Nadezhda Sergeevna Alliluyeva, Stalin's wife, shot herself with a
small pistol. She died instantly.

A few hours later a doctor examined her corpse and declared the
cause of death to be 'an open wound to the heart'. Soon afterwards,
after exchanging a few sharp words with Molotov and Kaganovich,
the doctor changed his mind. On her death certificate he listed the
cause of death as 'acute appendicitis'. The politics behind this change
would have been perfectly clear to Stalin's inner circle: in the autumn
of 1932 all of them knew that Nadya's suicide, whatever its real
causes, would be interpreted as a form of political protest – even as
an anguished outcry against the spreading famine.[2]

Rightly or wrongly, this is indeed how Nadya's suicide was remembered. Years later their daughter Svetlana wrote of her mother's
'terrible, devastating disillusionment' with her father and his politics.[3] A talkative Ossetian who met Nadya at a student party in 1929
recalled her sympathy for Stalin's most important opponent, Bukharin, who opposed collectivization and lost his Politburo seat, and
eventually his life, for doing so.[4] The famine had been a common
topic of conversation among their fellow students at the Industrial

Academy, and several people there heard her denouncing collectivization. In the last months of her life she suffered from migraine headaches, stomach pains, rapid mood swings and bouts of hysteria. Retrospectively, these maladies have been attributed to acute depression. At the time they were described, in whispers, as symptoms of bad conscience, of disappointment and of despair.[5]

Certainly others in Stalin's immediate entourage were unhappy about the famine. Peeking through the lace curtains of their well-appointed trains, many senior Bolsheviks saw things that summer that horrified them, and a few of them were brave enough to tell their leader about it. In August 1932, while Stalin was still in Sochi, he had received a letter from Klement Voroshilov, soon to become Commissar of Defence:

> Across the Stavropol region, I saw all the fields uncultivated. We were expecting a good harvest but didn't get it . . . Across the Ukraine from my train window, the truth is that it looks even less cultivated than the North Caucasus . . . Sorry to tell you such things during your holiday but I can't be silent.[6]

Another senior military figure, the civil war hero Semyon Budyonny, also wrote to Stalin from his train: 'Looking at people from the windows of the train, I see very tired people in old worn clothes, our horses are skin and bone.'[7] When Kira Alliluyeva, Nadezhda's niece, travelled to Kharkiv to visit her uncle – Stanislav Redens, then head of the Ukrainian OGPU – she too saw beggars at the train stations, emaciated people with swollen bellies. She told her mother, who told Stalin. He dismissed the story: 'She's a child, she makes things up.'[8]

Others who were less intimate with the Soviet leader saw or heard the same things. Bukharin had by now recanted his views: in December 1930 he had declared that he now understood the need for the destruction of the kulaks and for a 'direct break with the old structure'.[9] But others had not. Martemyan Ryutin, a Moscow party boss, was one of them. Ryutin had been evicted from the party in 1930 for 'expounding right-opportunist views', but unlike Bukharin he had refused to recant. Ryutin was arrested and then released. But he kept in touch with other would-be dissidents, and in the spring of 1932 he invited a dozen of them to help him write a statement of opposition.

In August the group met in a Moscow suburb to put the finishing touches to a political platform calling for change, as well as a shorter 'Appeal to all Party Members'.[10] Both documents were copied and circulated, by hand and by post, in Moscow, Kharkiv and other cities.

'Ryutin's Platform', as it came to be known, denounced Stalin in no uncertain terms. The authors called him an 'unscrupulous political intriguer', mocked him for his pretensions to be Lenin's successor, and accused him of having terrorized workers and peasants alike. Above all, Ryutin was angered by Stalin's attack on the Soviet countryside. The policy of 'all-out collectivization', Ryutin declared, had not been voluntary, as the propaganda claimed, and it was not a success. On the contrary:

> It is founded on direct and indirect forms of the most severe coercion, designed to force the peasants to join the collective farms. It is founded not on an improvement in their condition, but on their direct and indirect expropriation and massive impoverishment ... outcries directed by Stalin at the kulaks at the present time are only a method of terrorizing the masses and concealing his own bankruptcy.

These were not just mistakes, wrote Ryutin, but crimes. He called on his fellow dissidents to organize a revolt:

> In the struggle to destroy Stalin's dictatorship, we must in the main rely not on the old leaders but on new forces. These forces exist, these forces will quickly grow. New leaders will inevitably arise, new organizers of the masses, new authorities ... A struggle gives birth to leaders and heroes. We must begin to take action.[11]

This was distinctly Bolshevik language, which may help explain why Stalin, when he read it, took it so seriously. He had seen revolutionary passion before, and he knew it could be triggered again. After an informer tipped off the OGPU in September, he showed no mercy. Within days the Communist Party expelled and arrested twenty-one people, including the son of Hryhorii Petrovskyi, the chairman of the Ukrainian Supreme Soviet, as well as Ryutin himself. All were condemned as counter-revolutionaries. All were executed, as were, in due course, Ryutin's wife and two adult sons.[12] In later years, to have read 'Ryutin's Platform', or even to have heard of it, became a capital crime.

Stalin must have assumed that Ryutin's views were nevertheless widely shared, especially at the lower levels of the party and among people who had daily contact with the hungry rural population, for the Ryutin affair sharpened his sensitivity to other signs of discontent. Throughout the summer of 1932 he had been reading the reports from across the Soviet Union, including the disturbing ones from Ukraine. More arrived in early September. In the North Caucasus the OGPU claimed to have discovered a counter-revolutionary group that objected to Soviet policy because 'the pace of all-out collectivization has been too rapid'.[13] Across the USSR secret policemen were warning their superiors about 'new tactics practised by the kulaks', now including 'fake' complaints of famine. They were advised to investigate: 'where a case of feigning hunger is brought to light, the perpetrators are to be considered counter-revolutionary elements'.[14]

Nadya's death, the Ryutin affair, the worrying letters from close colleagues, the stark missives from the field – all this fed Stalin's growing paranoia that autumn. Discontent was seething all around him, and the prospect of counter-revolution suddenly seemed real. Historians have long thought that the events of the summer and autumn of 1932 were the catalyst for the mass arrests and executions of 1937–8, later known as the Great Terror.[15] But they also formed the immediate backdrop to an extraordinary set of decisions affecting Ukraine.

That autumn it would still have been possible to turn back. The Kremlin could have offered food aid to Ukraine and the other grain-growing regions of the USSR, as the regime had done in 1921 and as it had begun to do, in fits and starts, already that year. The state could have redistributed all available resources, or imported food from abroad. It could even have asked, as it had also done in 1921, for help from abroad.

Instead, Stalin began using stark language about Ukraine as well as the North Caucasus, the Russian province that was heavily Ukrainian. 'Give yourself the task of quickly transforming Ukraine into a true fortress of the USSR, a truly model republic', were Stalin's words to Kaganovich in August. 'Curse out the North Caucasus leadership for their bad work on grain requisitions,' he declared.[16] Others echoed his words on the ground. Early in October, Stanislav Kosior, General Secretary of the Ukrainian Communist Party, accused district officials who could not collect enough grain of harbouring ' 'right-wing attitudes'. A few days later, after a week in which the Ukrainian provinces produced only 18 per cent of their grain quota, the Ukrainian Politburo sent a panicked letter to local leaders warning them that there was 'little time left' and calling for 'an end to the calm attitude of party and state agencies'.[17] Soon after that, Molotov arrived in Kharkiv and Kaganovich headed to the North Caucasus to 'struggle with the class enemy who sabotaged the grain collection and the sowing'.[18]

By November 1932 it was nevertheless clear that the autumn harvest would not meet the plan. It came in 40 per cent lower than the planners had expected in the USSR as a whole, and 60 per cent lower in Ukraine.[19] Intriguingly, the overall drop in production was not as dramatic as it had been in 1921, and over the next few years it remained about the same. All across the USSR the total grain harvest for 1931–2 was 69.5 million tonnes (down from 83.5 million in 1930–1); for 1932–3 the total was 69.9 million tonnes. In 1933–4 the USSR harvested 68.4 million tonnes, and in 1934–5 the total was 67.6 million. But the state's unrealistic demands on the peasants – the expectation that they meet unattainable goals – created the perception of total failure. The insistence that the peasants deliver grain that Stalin believed *should* exist created, in turn, a humanitarian catastrophe.[20]

Stalin's policies that autumn led inexorably to famine all across the grain-growing regions of the USSR. But in November and December 1932 he twisted the knife further in Ukraine, deliberately creating a deeper crisis. Step by step, using bureaucratic language and dull legal terminology, the Soviet leadership, aided by their cowed Ukrainian counterparts, launched a famine within the famine, a disaster specifically targeted at Ukraine and Ukrainians.

Several sets of directives that autumn, on requisitions, blacklisted farms and villages, border controls and the end of Ukrainization – along with an information blockade and extraordinary searches, designed to remove everything edible from the homes of millions of peasants – created the famine now remembered as the Holodomor. The Holodomor, in turn, delivered the predictable result: the Ukrainian national movement disappeared completely from Soviet politics and public life. The 'cruel lesson of 1919' had been learned, and Stalin intended never to repeat it.

REQUISITIONS

In July 1932, Stalin had toyed with the idea of reducing his unrealistic demands for grain from Ukraine in order to appear more benevolent. In the autumn, as it became clear that Ukraine would not come anywhere near the required number, he changed his tactics. Ukraine could indeed be 'allowed' to produce less than required, even by 70 million poods (1.1 million tonnes). But this meant that every bit of the remaining quota – which was still unrealistic – had to be collected. On 29 October, Molotov sent a telegram to Stalin confirming what he had told the Ukrainians: the remaining plan had to be 'fulfilled unconditionally, completely, not lowering it by an ounce'.[21]

On 18 November the Ukrainian communists carried out his wishes. The party issued a resolution declaring that 'the full delivery of grain procurement plans is the principal duty of all collective farms', to be prioritized above and beyond anything else, including the collection of grain reserves, seed reserves, animal fodder and, ominously, daily food supplies. In practice, both individual and collective farmers were forbidden from holding back anything at all. Even those allowed to keep grain in the past had to give it back. Any collective farmer who produced grain for his family on a private plot now had to turn that over too.[22] No excuses were accepted.

A few weeks after this order was issued, Kaganovich arrived in Ukraine to ensure that it was carried out. Following another tumultuous Politburo meeting, this one lasting until 4 a.m., he posted a telegram to Stalin. Myriad Ukrainian communists had begged for the peasants to be allowed some reserves for their own consumption, as well as some seeds for the next season's crop, but he assured Stalin that he had stood firm: 'We are convinced that this "preoccupation" with reserves, including seed reserves, is seriously hampering and undermining the entire grain procurement plan.'[23] Two days later, on 24 December, the Ukrainian Communist Party gave up trying to resist. The leadership conceded completely and gave all under-performing collective farms 'five days to ship, without exception, all collective farm reserves, including sowing seeds'.[24]

Grain was not the only food that Moscow now determined to squeeze out of Ukraine. During past years of poor harvests and bad weather, peasants had survived thanks to their livestock and to veg-etables grown in their kitchen gardens. Following the bad harvest in 1924, Soviet agronomists noted that the dairy and poultry industries actually expanded.[25] But in the autumn of 1932 underperforming private farmers and collective farms not only had to give up their seed reserves, they also had to pay a meat penalty – a 'fifteen-month quota of meat from collectivized and privately owned livestock' – as well as a potato penalty, comprising a 'one-year potato quota'. In practice, this law forced families to relinquish whatever potatoes they had stored away, and to turn over their remaining livestock, including the family cows that they had been allowed to keep since March 1930.[26]

To ensure that nobody protested or resisted those orders, Stalin sent a telegram to the Ukrainian Communist Party leaders in Kharkiv on 1 January 1933 demanding that the party use the 7 August law on 'theft of state property' to prosecute collective and individual farmers in Ukraine who were allegedly hiding grain.[27] The historian Stanislav Kulchytsky has argued that this telegram, coming from the party leader himself at that overwrought moment, was a signal to begin mass searches and persecutions. His view is an interpretation, rather than solid proof: Stalin never wrote down, or never preserved, any document ordering famine. But in practice that telegram forced Ukrainian peasants to make a fatal choice. They could give up their grain reserves and die of starvation, or they could keep some grain reserves hidden and risk arrest, execution or the confiscation of the rest of their food – after which they would also die of starvation.[28]

Two and a half weeks later the Soviet government issued another order that seems, at first glance, to have been intended to soften the blow. In an oddly worded statement, the Council of Ministers denounced the irregular methods of food collection that had been used all across the country – the plans, the plan failures, the supplementary plans – and called, instead, for peasants to pay a tax, in the form of a fixed percentage of their production. But there was one caveat: the tax was to take effect only in the summer of 1933. Until then the deadly requisitions would continue.[29] In other words, Stalin knew that the methods being used were damaging, and he knew they would fail. But he allowed them to continue for several fatal months, during which time millions died.[30]

Certainly during the winter of 1933 he did not offer any additional food aid, nor did he ease up on grain collection. Grain exports continued to flow out of the USSR, albeit more slowly than in the past. Since the spring of 1932 Soviet foreign trade officials had complained about the drop in the quantity of grain for export. In Odessa those responsible for shipping also complained that they were receiving poor-quality and poorly packed grain. Soviet officials had in the past been specifically instructed to take Western businessmen out to dinner and to flatter them, as a way of making up for the fact that grain shipments were late or non-existent.[31] Such gestures may well have been required in 1932, for export levels did sink that year, as noted earlier.[32]

But the number never fell to zero. Nor did exports of other kinds of food stop either. In 1932 the USSR exported more than 3,500 tonnes of butter and 586 tonnes of bacon from Ukraine alone. In 1933 the numbers rose to 5,433 tonnes of butter and 1,037 tonnes of bacon. In both years Soviet exporters continued to ship eggs, poultry, apples, nuts, honey, jam, canned fish, canned vegetables and canned meat, food that could have helped to feed Ukraine.[33]

BLACKLISTS

In November and December 1932, as the significance of the new 'unconditional' requisition orders was sinking in, the Ukrainian Communist Party enlarged and formalized the republic's system of blacklists. The term 'blacklist' (*chorna doshka*, which translates more literally as 'black board') was not new. From their very earliest days in power, the Bolsheviks had grappled with the problem of low productivity. Since neither bosses nor workers in state companies had any market incentives to work hard or well, the state created elaborate schemes of reward and punishment. Among other things, many factories began to place the names of their most successful workers on 'red boards', and those of the least successful workers on 'black boards'. In March 1920, Stalin himself gave a speech in Donbas and referred specifically to the need to 'favour one group over another' and to reward 'red medals' to the work brigade leaders, 'as in a military operation'. At the same time, those comrades who were avoiding work must be 'pulled by the hair': 'For them we need black boards'. During the civil war, in 1919–21, the Bolsheviks had placed whole villages on blacklists if they failed to fulfil grain requisition requirements.[34]

In 1932 the blacklist returned as a tool for the reinforcement of grain procurement policy. Although they were used to some degree in all the other grain-producing regions of the USSR, blacklists were applied earlier, more widely and more rigorously in Ukraine. From the beginning of that year, provincial and local authorities had begun to blacklist collective farms, cooperatives and even whole villages that had failed to meet their grain quotas, and to subject them to a range of punishments and sanctions. In late summer local leaders expanded the blacklists. In November the practice became ubiquitous, spreading to include villages and collective farms in almost every district of Ukraine.[35]

All across the republic, the names of blacklisted villages appeared in newspapers, along with the percentage of the grain quota they had achieved. One such article, for example, simply entitled 'The Black List', appeared in the Poltava province in September 1932, with a black border around it. The list contained seven villages, each of which had produced between 10.7 per cent and 14.2 per cent of the yearly plan.[36]

Because records were kept separately in each province of Ukraine, the total number of blacklisted entities is hard to determine. But by the end of the year there were hundreds and possibly thousands of villages, collective farms and independent farms on blacklists all across the republic.[37] At least seventy-nine districts were entirely blacklisted, and 174 districts were partially blacklisted, nearly half of the total in the entire republic.[38] Although the names were compiled by local leaders, Moscow took a keen interest in the process. Kaganovich personally pushed for the system of blacklisting to be spread to the Kuban, the historically Cossack and majority Ukrainian-speaking province of the North Caucasus.[39] Kuban had attracted negative attention a few years earlier, when enthusiasts of Ukrainiz-ation had begun promoting the language there. Kaganovich himself now took charge of a commission set up to combat the combined prob-lem of grain deliveries and national sentiments there. On 4 November the leadership of the North Caucasus duly published a blacklist of fifteen Cossack settlements (*stanitsy*).

A series of sanctions on blacklisted farms and villages followed. In a telegram sent to all the provinces the Ukrainian Central Committee banned blacklisted districts that had failed to meet grain targets from purchasing any manufactured or industrial goods. In the initial order an exception was made for kerosene, salt and matches. Two weeks later, in a telegram from Moscow, Molotov ordered Kosior to ban the deliv-ery of those three items too. After the ban went into effect, any peasant who might possess food would soon have great difficulties cooking it.[40]

A complete ban on trade came next. Earlier in 1932 an edict had forbidden peasants from trading grain and meat products if their farms had not met requisition quotas. Now, districts which had failed to meet the grain procurement targets – and this included most of Ukraine – could no longer legally trade grain, seeds, flour or bread in any form at all. Anyone caught trading anything was liable to be arrested. Policemen seized grain or bread from bazaars. The peasants who lived on underperforming farms could neither purchase grain, barter for grain, nor legally obtain or possess grain at all.

The Politburo's next decree purged 'counter-revolutionary ele-ments' in blacklisted communities. Local activists in Kuban won the right to conduct their own 'trials' of local saboteurs, and in the weeks that followed they deported 45,000 people and imported demobilized Red Army soldiers and other outsiders to replace them.[41] Kaganovich was in no doubt about the purpose of the Kuban blacklist. As he wrote to Stalin, he wanted 'all Kuban Cossacks to know that in 1921 the Terek Cossacks who resisted were deported. Just like now – we cannot allow them on Kuban land, its golden land, to refuse to sow and to obstruct us instead.'[42]

The blacklists also served as a lesson in the folly of resistance in Ukraine. Unlike Russia and Belarus, where the term 'blacklist' was confined to grain producers, in Ukraine it could be applied to almost any entity. Whole districts were blacklisted. Machine tractor stations, timber companies and all kinds of provincial enterprises only distantly connected to grain production were blacklisted. As one historian has written, 'the blacklist became a universal weapon aimed at all rural residents' in Ukraine.[43] Blacklisting affected not just peasants but artisans, nurses, teachers, clerks, civil servants, anyone who lived in a blacklisted village or worked in a blacklisted enterprise.

As the number of people affected increased, the definition of what it meant to be 'blacklisted' would also evolve. Like everyone in the regions that had not met the grain targets, those on the blacklists were prohibited from receiving any manufactured goods whatsoever – including, thanks to Molotov, kerosene, salt and matches. The activists also forced them to hand back to the central authorities any manufactured goods – clothes, furniture, tools – they had stored in shops and warehouses.

Financial sanctions then also followed: blacklisted farms and enterprises could no longer receive credit of any kind. If they had outstanding loans they had to repay them early. In some cases all of their money was confiscated: the state could close their bank accounts and force their employees to pay their collective debts. The state prohibited the milling of grain, making it impossible to prepare flour (even if any grain could be obtained) in order to bake bread. Blacklisted farms could not receive the services of the machine tractor stations, which meant that all farm work had to be done by hand or with livestock.[44] In some places the blacklists were enforced by special brigades or teams of soldiers or secret policemen who blocked trade to the village, farm or district.[45]

Sometimes particular farms received extra sanctions. After the village of Horodyshche, in Voroshilov district, Donetsk province, was blacklisted in November 1932, local authorities noticed that the rules weren't having much impact. Horodyshche was near the large railway station of Debaltseve where a good deal of illicit trading took place. Many of the villagers were craftsmen or worked in nearby mines, they had a wide range of contacts as well as private plots of land, and they were finding ways to get hold of the products they needed. Worse, Horodyshche had a suspect history: during the civil war, the local party committee report noted, the village had hosted many 'groups of bandits, horse thieves and the like'. Collectivization had 'encountered active resistance' in the town as well, thanks to a 'large kulak community'. The district leaders decided to tighten the rules just for Horodyshche. They demanded the early return of a 23,500-ruble loan that had been borrowed by the collective farm. They seized three tractors. They confiscated all of the village's seed stock. They levied meat 'fines' – which meant the confiscation of livestock – and confiscated the miners' garden plots. They arranged for 150 people to be dismissed from their jobs in local factories, because their families had failed to hand over grain. Finally, they arrested and put on trial the collective farm leadership, and warned all of the village residents that if 'sabotage' did not cease, they would be deported and replaced with 'conscientious collective farmers'. Their houses would be confiscated and given to 'industrial laborers in need of accommodations'.[46]

Ostensibly, the blacklists were designed to persuade the peasants sanctioned by them to work harder and produce more grain. In practice, they had quite a different impact. With no grain, no livestock, no tools, no money and no credit, with no ability to trade or even to leave their places of work, the inhabitants of blacklisted villages could not grow, prepare or purchase anything to eat at all.

BORDERS

As Ukrainian peasants grew more hungry, another problem arose: how to prevent starving people from leaving their homes in search of something to eat.

The issue was not a new one. Already in 1931 the OGPU had been warning of a 'systematic' exodus of peasants from Ukrainian villages, and the numbers had continued to rise.[47] Their own statistics showed the number of rural workers dropping rapidly as thousands of people escaped the collective farms.[48] In January 1932 the problem grew suddenly worse. In a report sent to Stalin, Vsevolod Balytsky, still the head of the Ukrainian OGPU, reckoned that more than 30,000 people had left the Ukrainian Republic during the previous month.[49] A year later the Ukrainian OGPU produced an even more alarming tally: between 15 December 1932 and 2 February 1933 nearly 95,000 peasants had left their homes. The OGPU stopped short of admitting that people were leaving because they were starving – 'most of those fleeing are private farmers and kulaks who have failed to fulfil their grain procurement obligations and are afraid of facing repression' – but they did concede that some of the escapees had 'concerns over problems with food supplies'.[50]

Some were crossing the Ukrainian border to search for food in Russia. 'When their potatoes were gone,' one Ukrainian worker remembered, 'people began to go to the Russian villages and to exchange their clothing for food. Interestingly enough, beyond Kharkiv where the Russian territory starts there was no hunger.'[51] Indeed, officials in Russian districts along the Ukrainian border had already begun complaining of the Ukrainian influx in early 1932. 'Crowds' of individuals, whole families with small children and old people were pouring over the border, looking to buy or beg for bread: 'The situation is becoming dangerous,' wrote one Russian local official. His letter also spoke of the 'moral' threat from the hungry arrivals and the rise of theft.[52]

A few weeks later a group of Belarusian workers wrote a letter to the Ukrainian Communist Party. They protested that starving Ukrainians were blocking their roads and railways:

It's shameful, when you look at these wandering, starving Ukrainians, and when you ask, why don't they stay at work, they answer that there aren't any seeds to sow and there's nothing to do at their collective farms and the supplies are bad . . . a fact is a fact, millions of people are wandering naked, starving in the woods, stations, towns and farms of Belarus, begging for a piece of bread.[53]

But the Ukrainians kept leaving, not least because there really was more food available in Russia and Belarus. At the end of October 1932 one young girl's father made it all the way to Leningrad. Departing in secret, in the middle of the night, her family managed to join him weeks later, travelling through stations packed with starving Ukrainians. 'At that time neither Moscow nor other cities close to it were starving,' she remembered. 'Only Ukraine was honoured with this crown of thorns.' By making the arduous trip to the far north, the entire family survived.[54]

Others made it out as well: in January 1933 the OGPU observed that 16,500 long-distance tickets had been purchased at Lozova station and 15,000 at Sumy, both towns in Kharkiv province in the northern part of Ukraine.[55] Tens of thousands of others were trying to leave with them. By the end of 1932, stations all across Ukraine were already crowded with emaciated, ragged people, trying to beg food and tickets from passengers, since many of them had no money. A boy who travelled to join his mother at that time saw corpses at the Kharkiv railway station, and watched a young girl grab chicken bones off the floor of the station buffet and begin gnawing them. Those who did manage to board a train hid themselves beneath benches; the conductors threw them off, but more kept getting on.[56] These same crowds had disturbed Voroshilov, Budyonny and Kira Alliluyeva in the summer of 1932. In the autumn of 1932 and winter of 1933 their numbers only grew larger.

Others left by ship. One of several unusually observant Italian consuls, this one in the city of Batumi, Georgia, on the Black Sea coast, reckoned in January 1933 that 'every steamship that arrives from Odessa – three arrive per week – usually delivers one to two thousand Ukrainians'. Previously, the Ukrainians seemed to have been looking to buy food in Batumi, to purchase flour or seeds that they could eat at home or else sell at a profit. But in the late autumn, the mass movement of people had taken on the character of a refugee influx, with thousands seeking to settle 'where the means of existence and opportunities to obtain food are more abundant'.[57]

As in 1930, some peasants tried to leave the country as well. Maria Błażejewska, an ethnic Pole, entered Poland from Ukraine in October 1932 by pretending to be a washerwoman. While laundering clothes in the Zbruch River, which then served as the border, she slipped across to the other side. Two of her sons made the dangerous crossing with her; a third had already been deported to the Far East. 'From 1931,' she told the Polish border police, 'life in Soviet Russia ... turned into unbearable torture because the Soviet authorities began taking almost all the grain and the livestock away from us, leaving me only a very small amount which did not suffice even for the most modest standard of living.'[58] Leon Woźniak, aged fifteen, also escaped in October: 'We were driven away from our own house ... both my brother and I worked in the forests, yet with this we could not make a living. Because presently all work has ceased and I was dying of hunger, on 15 October, together with my mother Małgorzata and my brother Bronisław, I escaped from Soviet Russia into Poland.'[59]

Others tried to escape the same way, but failed in the attempt. A few months after Maria and Leon slipped over the border, a group of sixty people tried to cross the Zbruch River together. Only fourteen succeeded; the rest drowned or were shot by border guards. Another 250 families would try to cross the border during the winter of 1932–3. By December 1932 the Polish Interior Ministry had established a special commission for Ukrainian refugees, including a representative of the Red Cross and one from the League of Nations.[60]

Still others tried to walk, ride or get onto trains heading into Ukrainian cities. If they had left early enough, if they had relatives to meet them, and if they were strong enough to work, they sometimes succeeded. Many 'kulaks' had earlier escaped deportation by moving to Kyiv and Kharkiv as well as to the mines and factories of Donetsk. But by late 1932 the numbers of people began to multiply, and the cities, especially Kyiv, Kharkiv and Odessa, could no longer cope. In the autumn of 1932 one memoirist recalled an 'uneasy mood' in Kharkiv:

> There was no food. There were long lines, and there was much noise in newspapers about the grain procurements, about the way the anti-Soviet element, the so-called 'kurkuls' or 'kulaks' were supposedly hiding grain from the government ... Bread, which could be obtained with ration cards, was sold only irregularly. Lines began to form at night, but were often dispersed by the militia. In order to mask the situation, bread was issued not in shops but out in the open.[61]

As more peasants drifted into the centre of Kharkiv, things grew worse. They were easily identifiable by their ragged clothes and bare feet: thanks to the *trudodni* system of rationing, they had no money, and no way to buy either food or clothing. Instinctively, the city-dwellers, who themselves had very little food and also relied on rationing, stayed away from them. By the winter, the peasants in the city were hardly better off than those who had remained at home:

> Many villagers roamed the streets there. You met them everywhere. They were of various ages – old, young, children, and infants. Their state of physical deterioration was evident in the slow way they moved their bodies. The light was extinguished from the downcast eyes on the haggard and occasionally swollen faces. They were hungry, exhausted, ragged, filthy, cold and unwashed. Some of them dared to knock on people's doors or maybe on someone's window, and some could barely stretch out their begging hands. Others yet were sitting against the walls, and they were motionless and speechless.[62]

Another memoirist remembered the peasants in the marketplaces:

> The mothers with babies in their arms made the strongest impression. They seldom mingled with the others. I remember seeing one such mother who looked more like a shadow than a human being. She was standing by the side of the road, and her little skeleton of a child, instead of suckling her mother's empty breast, sucked its own small knuckles thinly covered with translucent skin. I have no idea how many of the unfortunates I saw managed to survive. Every morning on my way to work I saw bodies on the pavements, in ditches, under a bush or a tree, which were later carried away.[63]

As a result of the influx, municipal authorities found themselves simultaneously trying to cope with several different kinds of crisis. Orphans began to crowd into city orphanages, as many parents left their children behind in the hope that they would survive. Dead bodies caused a sanitary crisis. In January 1933 the city of Kyiv had to remove 400 corpses from the streets. In February the number rose to 518, and in just the first eight days of March there were 248.[64] These were only the official numbers. Multiple witnesses in Kyiv and

Kharkiv recall the trucks cruising the city at that time, the men pulling the dead off the streets and loading them onto their vehicles in a manner which suggested that no one would give much thought to counting them.

The beggars from the countryside added to the pressure on city residents who were also running short of food. Tempers inside Kharkiv rose particularly quickly. That spring the Italian consul reported that several thousand people had attacked the militiamen assigned to distribute bread in one suburb of the city. In another part of town an enraged mob attacked two bakeries, stole the flour and wrecked the buildings. Police began to use special, preventative measures in response. At about 4 a.m. one morning, the consul reported, Kharkiv police blocked the side streets around a bakery where hundreds of people had been waiting all night for the doors to open. They beat the crowd back and forced the people towards the train station. They then pushed them onto trains and drove them out of the city.

The influx was further demoralizing the countryside, because the vast migration made life more difficult for those who remained. In desperation, one Communist Party member from Vinnytsia wrote a letter to Stalin in the autumn of 1932 begging for help:

> All the peasants are moving and leaving the villages, to save themselves from starvation. In the villages, ten to twenty families die from hunger every day, the children run away to wherever they can, all of the train stations are full of peasants trying to get out. In the countryside neither horses nor cows remain. Starving peasant-collective farm workers leave everything and disappear . . . it is impossible to speak of fulfilling the sowing campaign, because the small percentage of peasants who remain are wasting away from hunger.[65]

What really concerned the Soviet authorities was the political significance of this mass movement of people. All across the Soviet Union, in the far north and far east, in the Ukrainian-speaking territories of Poland and in Ukraine itself, itinerant Ukrainians were not only spreading news of the famine, they were bringing their allegedly counter-revolutionary attitudes along with them. As their numbers increased dramatically, the Soviet government finally declared there could no longer be any doubt: 'the flight of villagers and the exodus

from Ukraine last year and this year is [being] organized by the enemies of the Soviet government . . . and agents of Poland with the goal
of spreading propaganda among the peasants'.

A solution was found. In January 1933, Stalin and Molotov simply
closed the borders of Ukraine. Any Ukrainian peasant found outside
the republic was returned to his or her place of origin. Train tickets were
no longer sold to Ukrainian villagers. Only those who had permission
could leave home – and permission was, of course, denied.[66] The borders of the heavily Ukrainian North Caucasus district were also closed,
and in February the Lower Volga district was also blocked.[67] The border closures remained in place throughout the famine.

Separately, work continued on an internal passport system, which
was finally set up in December 1932. In practice, this meant that anyone who resided in the city needed a special passport, a residence
document – and peasants were explicitly prevented from obtaining
them. In conjunction with this new law, Kharkiv, Kyiv and Odessa
were all to be cleared of 'excess elements' from the countryside.[68]
City-dwellers were reassured: the new measures would facilitate 'the
unburdening of the cities and the purging of kulak criminal
elements'.[69]

These restrictions were implemented with unprecedented speed.
Within days the OGPU had sent reinforcements from Moscow. Cordons appeared on the roads leading out of Ukraine and along major
highways entering the cities. Between 22 and 30 January 1933, Genrikh Yagoda, the OGPU's boss, told Stalin and Molotov that his men
had caught 24,961 people trying to cross the borders, of whom two-
thirds came from Ukraine and almost all the rest from the North
Caucasus. The majority were sent back home, though nearly eight
thousand were being detained under police investigation and more
than a thousand had already been arrested.[70]

By their own account, Yagoda's Ukrainian colleagues were even
busier. In February they reported that they had established an 'unconditional ban on issuing any travel document', so that no peasant
could legally leave his or her village. In addition, they had created
'mobile patrols' that had detained more than 3,800 people found on
the roads and over 16,000 people on the railways. They had mobilized

'secret agents' and 'village activists' to uncover 'exodus organizers' and help arrest them.[71]

The effect was stark, as if Ukraine and Russia now had a visible border. A Polish diplomat who travelled by car from Kharkiv to Moscow in May 1933 was struck by it:

> What intrigued me most during the whole journey was the difference between what villages looked like in Ukraine and the neighboring [Russian] Black Earth province ... Ukrainian villages are in decay, they are empty, deserted and miserable, cottages half-demolished, with roofs blown down; no new houses in sight, children and old people are more like skeletons, no sight of livestock ... When I found myself in [Russia] afterwards I had the impression of crossing the border from the state of the Soviets to Western Europe.[72]

To preserve a semblance of order, policemen also began to remove any peasants who had made it into the cities. Vasily Grossman – the Soviet writer who grew up in Ukraine, worked in Donbas, and knew of the famine as it was happening – remembered that 'blocks were put on the roads to prevent peasants from getting into Kyiv. But they used bypasses, forests, swamps to get there.'[73] Those who made it did so by 'cutting through' the cordons, and hacking through the underbrush.[74] But even those who found their way into the queues for bread did not necessarily last long, as another Kyiv resident remembered: 'The police would take villagers from these lines, load them on trucks and take them out of the city.'[75]

Halyna Kyrychenko saw police remove people from bread queues in Kharkiv too. They were put onto trucks, she remembered, and driven so far out of town that they could not return: 'being exhausted, they died somewhere on the road'. Police also seized people on the streets who seemed to be trying to buy or barter for bread, since to do so was suspicious: city-dwellers had access to ration cards and workers with the proper registration ate their meals in canteens. Kyrychenko herself, then aged thirteen, several times escaped from police.[76]

Urban Ukrainians saw what was happening, and spread rumours about it. Mariia Umanska's father told her that he had helped pick up peasants and their children off the streets of Kharkiv. The authorities had promised him that they would be fed and taken home, but he had heard a different story: at night, the living and the dead would be loaded onto trucks, driven to a ravine outside of town and thrown into it: 'They said that the ground stirred.'[77] Olena Kobylko heard the same story: peasants found on the streets of Kharkiv were supposedly 'carried out in a freight train behind the city to a field so that they die there unseen by anybody', and then, alive or dead, were thrown into pits.[78]

These stories surely filtered back to the villages, as they were intended to do. Peasants knew that if they left home without the permission of the local authorities, they could be returned by force. Lev Kopelev's conclusion was stark: 'The passport system laid an administrative and judicial cornerstone for the new serfdom [and] tied down the peasantry as it had been before the emancipation of 1861.'[79]

9

Famine Decisions, 1932: The End of Ukrainization

> They placed their talents at the service of the kulaks and Ukrainian counter-revolutionary nationalists and have not even now shown such symptoms of artistic change as would prove that they are ready to serve fully with their art the interests of the Party, the Soviet government and the workers of the great socialist fatherland – the USSR.
>
> *Ivan Mykytenko, explaining why some Ukrainian writers had been turned down for membership of the Writers' Union, 1934.*[1]

To anyone who knew the Ukrainian countryside it would have been clear, in the autumn of 1932, that widespread famine was coming, and that many people would die. Such an extraordinary catastrophe required an extraordinary justification. In December that is exactly what the Politburo provided. Just as it was publicly publishing the new decrees on food requisition and blacklists, the Politburo also issued, on 14 and 15 December respectively, two secret decrees that explicitly blamed Ukrainization for the requisitions failure.

In the context of the broader, 1932–3 Soviet famine, these two decrees are unique, as are the events that followed them. There were, it is true, other regions that received special treatment. Suspicion of their loyalty probably contributed to higher death rates among peasants in the Volga provinces, where some of the policies used in Ukraine, including mass arrests of communist leaders, were also deployed, though not at the same level as in Ukraine.[2] In Kazakhstan the regime blocked traditional nomadic routes and requisitioned livestock to feed the Russian cities, creating terrible suffering among the ethnic Kazakh nomads. More than a third of the entire population, 1.5 million people, perished during a famine that barely touched the Slavic population of Kazakhstan. This assault on the nomads, sometimes called 'sedentarization', was another form of Sovietization and a clear attack on a recalcitrant ethnic group.[3] But nowhere else were agricultural failures linked so explicitly to questions of national language or culture as they were in both Ukraine and in the North Caucasus, with its large Ukrainian-speaking population.

The first decree blamed the failure to procure grain in both Ukraine and the North Caucasus on the 'poor efforts and absence of revolutionary vigilance' in local and regional Communist Parties. Although pretending to be loyal to the USSR, these lower-level party committees had allegedly been 'infiltrated by counter-revolutionary elements – kulaks, former officers, Petliurites, supporters of the Kuban Rada, etc.'. They were secret traitors, and they had ensconced themselves in the very heart of the party and state bureaucracy:

> They have managed to find their way into collective farms as directors and other influential members of administration, accountants, store-keepers, foremen at threshing floors etc. They have succeeded in infiltrating village soviets, land management bodies, cooperative societies, and are now trying to direct the work of these organizations contrary to the interests of the proletarian state and the party policy, as well as to organize a counter-revolutionary movement and the sabotage of the harvest and sowing campaigns ...
>
> The worst enemies of the party, working class and the collective farm peasantry are saboteurs of grain procurement who have party membership cards in their pockets. To please kulaks and other anti-Soviet elements, they organize state fraud, double-dealing, and the failure of the tasks set by the party and government.[4]

The policy of Ukrainization was at fault: it had been carried out 'mechanically', the decree explained, without taking proper notice of the purposes it served. Instead of furthering the interests of the USSR, Ukrainization had allowed 'bourgeois-nationalist elements, Petliurites and others' to create secret counter-revolutionary cells within the state apparatus. Nor was this merely a problem for Ukraine. The decree also inveighed against the 'irresponsible non-Bolshevik "Ukrainization" in the North Caucasus', which provided 'the enemies of Soviet power' with a legitimate cover.[5]

Kulaks, former White officers, Cossacks and members of the Kuban Rada – those who had fought, during the civil war, for an independent Cossack state in Kuban – were all blamed. They were named and linked together as 'Ukrainians', or at least as the beneficiaries of Ukrainization.

The second decree echoed the first but extended the ban on Ukrainization further, to the Far East, Kazakhstan, Central Asia, the Central Black Earth province and 'other areas of the USSR' that might have been infected with Ukrainian nationalism. The Soviet government issued this supplement in order to 'condemn the suggestions made by individual Ukrainian comrades about the mandatory Ukrainization of entire areas of the USSR' and to authorize an immediate halt to any Ukrainization anywhere. The regions named were ordered to stop printing Ukrainian newspapers and books immediately, and to impose Russian as the main language of school instruction.[6]

The two decrees provided an explanation for the grain crisis and named scapegoats. They also set off an immediate mass purge of Ukrainian Communist Party officials, as well as verbal and then physical attacks on university professors, schoolteachers, academics and intellectuals – anyone who had promoted the Ukrainian national idea. During the following year all of the institutions connected to Ukrainian culture were purged, shut down, or transformed: universities, academies, galleries, clubs.

The decrees established a direct link between the assault on Ukrainian national identity and the famine. The same secret police organization carried them out. The same officials oversaw the propaganda that described them. From the point of view of the state, they were part of the same project.

PURGING THE UKRAINIAN PARTY

The OGPU often devised fantastical conspiracy theories about its enemies. But the opposition to the grain requisition policies in the lower-level leadership of the Ukrainian Communist Party was real. In November 1932 the reports on party dissatisfaction that had prompted Stalin to declare that 'things in Ukraine are terrible' were updated and recirculated. Hundreds of Ukrainian party members regularly and repeatedly opposed the grain requisitions and the blacklists, both verbally and in practice.

At times, their pleas were emotional. One party member in the town of Svatove declared his views openly in a long letter to his local party committee. 'I remember how from my first day in the Komsomol, in 1921, I yearned and went to work with a feeling that the party line is right and I am right,' he wrote. But in 1929 he had begun to have doubts. And when people began to starve, he felt he had to protest: 'The general party line is wrong and its implementation led to poverty in the countryside, to forced proletarianization in agriculture, which is confirmed by our train stations and the appearance in the cities of entire masses of homeless orphans.'[7] Others clearly perceived the new requisitions as an attack on the republic itself. 'They could make mistakes in 10 or 20 districts', one local party secretary was heard to say, 'but to make mistakes in all districts of Ukraine – this means that something is wrong.'[8]

Such expressions of doubt unsettled the Soviet leadership. For if communists no longer supported the official policy, then who would carry it out? Nobody took this problem more seriously than Stalin himself. After consulting with Balytsky, whom he met twice in November 1932, Stalin sent out a letter addressed to all party leaders, national, regional and local, all across the country, declaring war on the traitors inside the party. 'An enemy with a party card in his pocket should be punished more harshly than an enemy without a party card,' he proclaimed:

> The organizers of sabotage are in the majority of instances 'communists', that is people who have a party card in their pocket but have

long ago remade themselves and broken with the party. These are the same swindlers and crooks who conduct kulak policy under the false flag of their 'agreement' with the general line of the party.[9]

By that time, high-level change had already begun. Stalin had sent Balytsky back to run the secret police in Ukraine, ending his brief sojourn at headquarters in Moscow. He had also sent Pavlo Postyshev, a former Kharkiv party boss, back to Ukraine after a stint running the propaganda office at the Central Committee in Moscow. In subsequent months Postyshev functioned as Stalin's direct emissary, a kind of governor-general of Ukraine. Stalin also removed Vlas Chubar from the Ukrainian leadership, though he allowed Stanislav Kosior and Hryhorii Petrovskyi to stay (the former was arrested in 1938 and executed in 1939; the latter managed to survive until the 1950s).[10] In the winter of 1932–3 he launched a new wave of investigations, prosecutions and arrests of the low-level Ukrainian Communist Party members who had dared to protest. The result of this purge, which took place at the same time as the famine, was to make the Ukrainian Communist Party a tool of Moscow, with no autonomy or any ability to take decisions on its own.[11]

Local leaders paid a high price for honesty. In the village of Orikhiv, for example, the local communists had tried to tell the truth. 'We are party members and should be candid,' they told colleagues in Kharkiv: 'the plan is unrealistic and we won't fulfil it. We'll get to 45–50 per cent.'[12] Years later, when the Orikhiv case was re-examined – in 1964, during the brief period known as 'the Khrushchev thaw' – witness after witness declared that the Orikhiv communists did not fulfil the plan because it was an impossible task: their fields simply did not produce that much grain. One of them, Mykhailo Nesterenko, a former collective farm boss, remembered how much pressure there had been in those years 'The fact of the matter is that the word "sabotage" in those years was a meaningless word. For the tiniest defect, they called us bosses saboteurs, and threatened us with repression.'[13]

At the time, such thoughts were treasonous, and several Orikhiv party officials were arrested and sentenced. Some spent long terms in the Gulag. Many never returned home. The OGPU justified these extreme punishments by giving their actions a deeper interpretation:

although they pretended to be party members, communists such as those in Orikhiv secretly planned to overthrow the state. The Orikhiv communists had followed the 'kulak path of betrayal of the party and the workers' state, the path of sabotage, of demoralization of the collective farms, of organized sabotage of the grain collection, all the while concealing their kulak-thievery beneath the pretence of "agreement" with the general party line'.[14]

One of those sentenced – Maria Skypyan-Basylevych, a party bureaucrat who spent ten years in the Gulag – declared, thirty years later, that 'absolutely innocent people had suffered, honest and principled communists'.[15] But in 1933 the Orikhiv arrests sent out a strong message: party members themselves were not immune from prosecution. Anybody, however apparently loyal, however good a communist, could now become a scapegoat if he or she dared to disagree with the authorities.

The language used to condemn the Orikhiv communists was applied all over the republic. On 18 November, the same day the Ukrainian Politburo called for the confiscation of all remaining stores of grain, it also issued a decree 'on the liquidation of counter-revolutionary nests and the defeat of kulak groups'. In blacklisted villages, 'kulaks, Petliurites, pogromists and other counter-revolutionary elements' were slated for arrest.[16] Four days later the Soviet Politburo in Moscow resolved to establish death sentences for party and collective farm leaders who had failed to meet grain targets. A special 'troika' of Ukrainian officials, including Kosior, received the authority to order executions. They were also under instructions to report their decisions to Moscow every ten days.[17]

They moved quickly. Within four days the OGPU discovered not only widespread dissatisfaction but evidence of a 'kulak-Petliurite' conspiracy in 243 Ukrainian districts.[18] The secret police arrested 14,230 people in November 1932 alone; the total number of arrests for that year was 27,000, enough to eviscerate the party at the grass-roots level.[19] Even young people who were not yet members of the party fell under a cloud: between late 1932 and early 1934 the Komsomol expelled 18,638 of its members.[20]

As the arrests progressed, the language of the OGPU grew even more shrill. 'The operational strike against internal-collective farm anti-Soviet groups continues at a rapid pace', declared the Ukrainian OGPU's operational bulletin in December 1932:

> The counter-revolutionary activities of uncovered and liquidated groups on collective farms had consisted of undermining important agricultural campaigns, especially grain procurement; of squandering, concealing and hiding grain; and of anti-collective farm and anti-Soviet agitation ... The overwhelming majority of liquidated internal-collective farm groups were closely influenced by kulak and counter-revolutionary groups, especially Petliurite elements that corrupted the collective farms and their administrative apparatus ...[21]

The fictitious 'conspiracy' also grew denser, more complex, and more closely linked to the rebellions of the past. Many of those arrested, especially in November and December, were the chairmen or leaders of collective farms; others were accountants or clerks. The names of the arrested were often listed with their real or imagined links and credentials too: 'former Petliurite commander'; 'son of a trader, whose mother has been sent to the North'; 'former landowner'; 'former active participant in Petliurite and Makhno bands'. Their 'crimes' always involved the supposed theft of bread, criticism of the grain collection campaign, or other activities that somehow explained the harvest failure in Ukraine.[22] Yet their motives were described not merely as political but also as counter-revolutionary. They were said to have been influenced by Makhno, Petliura, the SVU, by class-hostile elements, kulaks, or some other past revolutionary movement.

In a few cases the past and the present were explicitly linked. The authorities in the village of Kostiantynivka, in Odessa province, arrested Tymofii Pykal in December 1932 on the grounds of his present behaviour as well as his past connections. In the account of the case Pykal was quoted telling his fellow farmers not to hand over grain: 'This year Soviet authorities are going to take all of our bread, we will all collapse from hunger if we give away our bread.' At the same time the police noted that Pykal had been a 'commander of a unit during the peasant uprising' a decade earlier. He was arrested under the infamous Ukrainian article 54-10 – 'anti-Soviet agitation and propaganda' – and sent away to be sentenced.

Petro Ovcharenko, the inhabitant of another village in Odessa province, met a similar fate. Ovcharenko was simultaneously accused in December 1932 of having 'organized a sectarian group' in the past as well as 'systematic agitation against the grain collection plans'. Supposedly, he had been overheard asking, 'Why do we need these plans? Who has the right to collect our grain and leave us to starve? We won't hand over our grain . . .'[23]

By the end of the year, the 'conspiracy' had acquired international aspects too. In late December, Balytsky revealed the existence of a plot, a 'Polish-Petliurite insurgent underground encompassing 67 local districts in Ukraine'. In February 1933 he wrote again of the 'counter-revolutionary insurgent underground, linked to foreigners and foreign espionage, mainly the Polish general staff'.[24] Balytsky's Russian colleagues reinforced this particular brand of conspiracy thinking early in that year, when the Soviet OGPU organs in Moscow prepared an even more elaborate report 'on the uncovered and eradicated kulak-White-Army-insurgent counter-revolutionary organizations' not only in Ukraine but – following the December 1932 decrees – in the Northern Caucasus, the Central Black Earth province and the Urals.

The Moscow report went even beyond Balytsky's fantastical claims, claiming that it had found links between the underperforming collective farms and the 'Russian All-Military Union', an organization of exiled former tsarist officers led by Piotr Wrangel, a White Army general. In Ukraine the OGPU had captured a 'kulak' named Barylnykov, who had supposedly been sent by Wrangel from Paris to agitate against grain procurements and collectivization. They had also found '23 Polish-Petliurite representatives'; a 'widely established insurgent underground' in the western districts of Ukraine as well as Donbas, supposedly linked to a 'Warsaw-based' Ukrainian government in exile; a 'kulak-White Army diversion group' connected to Romanian intelligence; and, in Kuban, organizations with links to 'Cossack centres of White emigrés'. These various groups were accused, among other things, of distributing political leaflets; carrying out arson attacks against kolkhoz property; destroying a poultry farm and killing 11,000 birds; setting up links with foreign counter-revolutionary organizations using sailors as agents; and, of course, sabotaging the harvest and stealing grain.[25]

While the low-level party resistance had been real, these vast international connections were, even by OGPU standards, absurd. Poland had signed a non-aggression pact with the USSR in July 1932.[26] The White Army generals named in the reports were already semi-retired and living in Paris, old men with no real reach or influence in the USSR. Petliura was long dead.

But the accusations cooked up by Balytsky and the OGPU chief, Genrikh Yagoda, weren't designed to reflect the truth. The discovery of this vast political conspiracy provided an explanation: why the harvest was failing, why people were hungry, why the Soviet agricultural policy, so closely and intimately linked with Stalin, was failing. To reinforce the point, Stalin personally sent out a letter at the end of December to the members and candidate members of the Central Committee, as well as to party leaders at the republican, provincial and local levels. Attached were lengthy, wordy, legal documents detailing the 'sabotage of the grain collection in Kharkiv and Dnipropetrovsk provinces' as well as the activity of 'wrecking groups in Kuban'. Lists of guilty officials, with their crimes, were tacked on to the end.[27]

The tale of the conspiracy also provided those who remained in the party with an ideological justification for what they were about to do. The deadly new decrees could not be enforced by Moscow alone. The policy would require local collaborators. Within a few weeks thousands of people would be required to carry out policies leading to the starvation of their neighbours. They would need multiple motivations: fear of arrest, fear of starvation – as well as hysteria, suspicion and hatred of their enemies.

PURGING THE NATIONAL MOVEMENT: 'THE EXECUTED RENAISSANCE'

The Ukrainian Communist Party was the immediate victim of the December decrees. But the orders linking Ukrainization to grain requisition also marked the end of the Ukrainian national movement in the Soviet Union.

In fact, the situation of national cultural leaders had already deteriorated significantly by the autumn of 1932. Since the orchestrated outcry against 'Shumskyism' in 1927, the lives of many of those associated with Ukrainian culture had grown more precarious. Mykhailo Hrushevsky had remained under assault both in ways that he could see and in ways that he could not. His secret police detail had deliberately encouraged animosity all around him, goading his friends into becoming critics. His funding had dried up. A new school of Marxist historians now attacked his books on Ukrainian history, arguing that he paid insufficient attention to the story of the working class and showed too much interest in the evolution of Ukrainian identity.

The OGPU finally arrested Hrushevsky in the spring of 1931 while he was on a trip to Moscow. They brought him to Ukraine, where Balytsky personally decided to send Ukraine's greatest historian into exile rather than to prison. The OGPU returned him to Russia, and told him to stay there. Soon afterwards the authorities organized three public debates designed to delegitimize his work altogether. These 'show trials' were staged with great pomp and circumstance in three buildings associated with the national movement: the Kyiv opera house, the former Central Rada building and the Academy of Sciences. They 'unmasked' Hrushevsky as an active enemy agent, a 'Ukrainian bourgeois nationalist and fascist allegedly working toward the separation of Ukraine from the USSR and its subjugation by the capitalist West'.[28] His name disappeared from public life, and he never returned to Ukraine. He died under what many still believe to be suspicious circumstances in the Caucasian resort town of Kislovodsk in 1934.

In the months following the Hrushevsky trials, the national communists – the faithful Bolsheviks who had believed they could inspire Ukraine's peasants and workers with both Ukrainian culture and Soviet rhetoric – all met a similar fate. Mykola Skrypnyk, who had led the charge against Shumsky, acquiesced in the denunciations of Hrushevsky and faithfully toed the party line, was now the primary victim. In January 1933 the party abolished the Ukrainian history and language courses that Skrypnyk had established in Ukraine's universities. In February, Skrypnyk was forced to defend himself against the charge that he had tried to 'Ukrainize' Russian children by force. In March, while the famine was raging in the countryside, Postyshev, in his role as Stalin's de facto spokesman in Ukraine, forced through a decree eliminating Ukrainian textbooks as well as school lessons tailored to Ukrainian children.[29]

Skrypnyk's school system now lay in ruins. In June, Postyshev accused him of having made theoretical 'mistakes' at the People's Commissariat of Education. But Postyshev also went further:

> these [theoretical errors] are trivial in comparison to that wrecking that took place in the education organs that aimed at the confusion of our youth with an ideology hostile to the proletariat ... [As a result] Ukrainization often was put into the hands of Petliurite swine, and these enemies with party cards in their pockets hid behind your broad back as a member of the Ukrainian Politburo, and you often defended them. You should have talked about that. That is the main issue.

Postyshev didn't call Skrypnyk himself a 'hidden enemy', but he came very close.[30] Soon after, a series of articles in the communist press attacked Skrypnyk's language and linguistics policy, including his brand-new Ukrainian orthography, compiled over many years with the input of scholars from across the Ukrainian-speaking world.[31] At a Politburo meeting on 7 July, Skrypnyk protested to a roomful of his colleagues against all these charges. They formally rebuffed his comments: 'Skrypnyk has not completed his obligation to give the Central Committee a short letter admitting his errors.' But by then he had walked out of the Politburo meeting, returned home and shot himself.[32]

The noose was tightening around others as well, especially the Ukrainian artists and writers who had taken up residence at the Budynok 'Slovo', the House of Writers, the apartment block reserved for cultural figures in Kharkiv. Since 1930 the Budynok 'Slovo' had been the focus of almost hysterical OGPU surveillance. Minders watched the building at all times; police conducted regular searches of the sixty-eight apartments and broke up any chance courtyard conversations involving more than three people, on the grounds that they might be illegal 'organizational' meetings, planning a plot. One writer, Ostap Vyshnia, stopped leaving his apartment altogether; another, Mykola Bazhan, slept every night in his clothes, preparing to be hauled away.

Arrests began to empty the building, creating an atmosphere that was particularly painful to Mykola Khvylovyi, the writer whose calls for a 'European' literature in Ukraine had so shocked Kaganovich and Stalin. By then, Khvylovyi had withdrawn or retracted much of his more provocative work, including his famous slogan, 'Away from Moscow!' He had also travelled around the decimated countryside and witnessed the growing numbers of starving peasants, and he returned to Kharkiv devastated. He told a friend that the famine he had witnessed was a purely political construction, 'designed to solve a very dangerous Ukrainian problem all at once'. To Khvylovyi, the link between the deadly grain requisition policy and the crackdown on Ukrainian culture was already clear. The secret police watching him also wrote that after his return from the famine districts, 'his emotions had possessed him more than anything else'. The arrest of one of his close friends, the writer Mykhailo Ialovyi, seems to have finally tipped him over the edge. In the hours before he too shot himself, he composed a suicide note. In it he spoke of 'the murder of a generation . . . for what? Because we were the most sincere communists? I don't understand.' His conclusion: 'Long live communism. Long live the construction of socialism. Long live the Communist Party.'[33]

Khvylovyi's death made a bad situation worse: informers in the Budynok 'Slovo' told their OGPU minders that the writer's remaining friends looked upon his suicide as an 'act of heroism'. Others complained bitterly that there could be no protests during his funeral, because the party would 'control all speeches in advance'. The informers' conclusion: 'Anti-Soviet elements from academic research institutes and the Ukrainian intelligentsia are using the death of Khvylovyi as a new occasion for counter-revolutionary plotting.' More arrests followed; among the new victims was Oleksandr Shumskyi. A few months later a party journal lumped Khvylovyi, Shumskyi and Skrypnyk together: all of them wanted to 'break Soviet Ukraine away from the USSR and turn it into an imperialist colony'.[34]

By then, the purge of Skrypnyk's Commissariat of Education was well underway. The ground had been prepared back in 1927, when an OGPU investigation into their political views had concluded that teachers, like collective farm workers, were hiding their 'anti-Soviet views' behind a facade of support for the state.[35] During the SVU trials of 1929 and 1930 thousands were accused of counter-revolutionary conspiracy.[36] But after Skrypnyk's resignation and suicide the systematic sacking of Ukrainian teachers, professors and education bureaucrats progressed to its logical conclusion. In 1933 all the regional heads of education departments were fired, along with the vast majority of local education bureaucrats. Some 4,000 Ukrainian teachers were named as 'class-hostile enemies'. Out of twenty-nine directors of pedagogical institutes, eighteen were dismissed.[37] Across the republic anyone with any conceivable link to nationalism – or anyone with an imaginary link to anything that might resemble nationalism – lost his job. Many were subsequently arrested.

By any standard the number of victims was very large: in the course of two years, 1932 and 1933 – the years of the famine – the same Soviet secret police responsible for overseeing the hunger in the countryside would arrest nearly 200,000 people in the republic of Ukraine.[38] But even this figure, as large as it is, underrates the catastrophic impact of this targeted purge on specific institutions and branches of society, especially education, culture, religion and publishing. In essence, the 200,000 represented an entire generation of educated, patriotic Ukrainians. In the Ukrainian context this 1932–3 purge was similar in scale to the 'Great Terror' of 1937–8, which eradicated most of the Soviet leadership and would take many Ukrainian victims too.[39]

During the crucial years 1932–3 whole institutions – the Polish pedagogical institute, a German secondary school – were shut down or else cleansed entirely of faculty and staff.[40] University faculties and publishing houses were shut down. Forty staff employed by the Ukrainian National Library were arrested as 'national-fascist wreckers'.[41] All the remaining departments of the Ukrainian Academy of Sciences were liquidated.[42] The Ukrainian Academy of Agricultural Sciences lost between 80 and 90 per cent of its presidium. Other organizations similarly wiped out in 1933 included the editorial board of the Ukrainian Soviet Encyclopedia, the Geodesic Administration, the Cinema Studio, the Chamber of Weights and Measures, the Institute of Soviet Law in Kharkiv and many others. Two hundred 'nationalistic' Ukrainian plays were banned, along with a couple of dozen 'nationalistic' Ukrainian translations of world classics.[43]

Particularly poignant was the fate of the pedagogical institute in Nizhyn, Chernihiv province, whose origins dated back to the early nineteenth century, and whose graduates included Nikolai Gogol. In the second half of 1933 a special Central Committee commission investigated the institute and 'uncovered' a vast web of suspicious elements residing in its classical buildings. The findings were ominous: the institute's journal was said to be full of dangerous examples of nationalism, the professors were propagating the now unacceptable works of Hrushevsky, the researchers were idealizing the Cossack leaders of the past. The chair of the Soviet history department had ignored the role of class struggle in Ukrainian history, and was forced to publicly retract his views; the chair of the economics department had supported an 'anti-Leninist' theory of economic crisis. After absorbing this report, the local party cell dismissed the heads of many departments – including the departments of biology, history and economics – and closed the institute's museum and journal. The Nizhyn institute survived, but was renamed and repopulated with completely different teachers.[44]

Others took the hint. Although the Ukrainization policy continued to exist on paper, in practice the Russian language returned to dominance in both higher education and public life. Millions assumed that any association with Ukrainian language or history was toxic, even dangerous, as well as 'backwards' and inferior. The city government of Donetsk dropped its use of Ukrainian; factory newspapers that had been publishing in Ukrainian switched to Russian.[45] The universities of Odessa, which had recently adopted Ukrainian, also went back to teaching in Russian. Ambitious students openly sought to avoid studying Ukrainian, preferring to be educated in Russian, the language that gave them greater access and more career opportunities.[46]

Some now feared to use Ukrainian at all. The director of the fine arts academy in Odessa, which taught most of its courses in Ukrainian, put it most clearly: 'After the Skrypnyk affair, every one switched back to Russian fearing that otherwise they would be labeled a Ukrainian nationalist.'[47] Similar forces engulfed the local museums, as well as the little periodicals devoted to regional studies and Ukrainian history. Most lost their funding, and they began to disappear too.[48]

A similar wave of repression washed over the Church. The Ukrainian Autocephalous Orthodox Church, established in 1921 as an independent branch of Orthodoxy, had already been badly weakened during the SVU trials of 1929, when many of its leaders had been arrested and condemned. In February 1930, at the height of the peasant rebellion, the USSR had adopted its decree on 'the fight against new counter-revolutionary elements in governing bodies of the religious unions' and, as noted, promoted the theft of bells and icons as well as the arrests of priests.

Between 1931 and 1936 thousands of churches – three-quarters of those in the country – ceased to function altogether. Many would be physically demolished: between 1934 and 1937 sixty-nine churches were destroyed in Kyiv alone. Both churches and synagogues were converted to other uses. The buildings, hungry peasants were told, were needed to serve as 'granaries'. The result was that by 1936 services took place in only 1,116 churches in the entire Ukrainian Republic. In many large provinces – Donetsk, Vinnytsia, Mikolaiv – there were no Orthodox churches left at all. In others – Luhansk, Poltava, Kharkiv – there was but a single church in use.[49]

The city of Kyiv also suffered. Because many Kyiv buildings were associated with past moments of national triumph, they too became the focus of the anti-national assault in the aftermath of the famine. In its professional journal the Architects' Union of the USSR criticized the city's architecture for embodying 'class hostile ideology'. A special government commission was created to carry out the socialist reconstruction of Kyiv; Balytsky and Postyshev both participated.[50] By 1935 the committee had approved a 'general plan' for the city, which would turn 'a city of churches and monasteries into an architecturally complete, real socialist center of the Soviet Ukraine'.[51] Only a few years earlier the Ukrainian Academy of Sciences had proposed creating a historical preservation zone, a 'Kyiv Acropolis' in the most ancient part of the city. But in 1935 the city instead destroyed dozens of architectural monuments, including Orthodox and Jewish cemeteries as well as churches and ecclesiastical structures. The graves and monuments of literary and political personalities from the nineteenth and early twentieth centuries disappeared from Kyiv too.[52] Allegedly, Postyshev believed that this vandalism would help the party combat the bourgeois nationalism inspired by this 'historical junk'.[53]

The destruction of the buildings was accompanied by an attack on the people who understood them best: a whole generation of art historians and curators. People who had dedicated their lives to the causes of art and knowledge met horrifying ends. Mykhailo Pavlenko of the Kyiv painting gallery was arrested in 1934 and shot in 1937, after three years spent living in exile. Fedir Kozubovskyi, director of the Institute of the History of Material Culture in Kyiv, was shot in 1938; before that, he was driven to such despair during his interrogation that he asked for poison to alleviate his suffering. Pavlo Pototsky, an art collector who had donated his paintings to the Historical Museum, was arrested at age eighty-one. He died of a heart attack inside the Lubyanka, the notorious Moscow prison.[54]

Once the people and the monuments were out of the way, the attack on their books followed. On 15 December 1934 the authorities published a list of banned authors, decreeing that all their books, for all years and in all languages, must be removed from libraries, shops, educational institutions and warehouses. Eventually, four such lists would be published, containing works by Ukrainian writers, poets, critics, historians, sociologists, art historians, and anyone else who had been arrested. In other words, the extermination of the intellectual class was accompanied by the extermination of their words and ideas.[55]

Finally, the new cultural establishment attacked the Ukrainian language itself, starting with Skrypnyk's dictionary, the fruit of so much careful collaboration: it relied too much on pre-revolutionary sources, it neglected new revolutionary, 'Soviet' words, it included language components that had a 'class enemy character'. Its authors represented the 'language theory of bourgeois nationalism', they 'continued the tradition of the Union for the Liberation of Ukraine [SVU]', they had to be purged from their various institutions. Many were arrested, later murdered.[56]

The abolition of the dictionary led to linguistic changes in official and academic documents, in literature and school textbooks. The Ukrainian letter 'g' (Г) was dropped, a change that made the language seem 'closer' to Russian. Foreign words were given Russian forms instead of Ukrainian ones. Ukrainian periodicals received lists of 'words not to be used' and 'words to be used', with the former including more 'Ukrainian' words, and the latter sounding more Russian. Some of these changes would be reversed again, in 1937, when the 'Great Terror' let to the arrest of the remaining Ukrainian linguists, including those who had enforced the 1934 changes. By the end of the decade chaos reigned, as the linguist George Shevelov has written:

> Teachers were confused and frightened, and students were bewildered. Not to follow the new trend was criminal, but to follow it was impossible, because of the lack of information. Instability seemed to be an inherent feature of the Ukrainian language, in contrast to Russian, which suffered no upheaval of any kind. The already damaged prestige of Ukrainian sank further.[57]

The situation would be stabilized somewhat after Nikita Khrushchev became the first party secretary in Ukraine in 1939. But by then the experts were imprisoned or dead; neither their books nor their carefully produced grammars were ever revived in Soviet Ukraine.

IO

Famine Decisions, 1932: The Searches and the Searchers

I'm no longer under a spell, I can see now that the kulaks were human beings. But why was my heart so frozen at the time? When such terrible things were being done, when such suffering was going on all around me? And the truth is that I truly didn't think of them as human beings. 'They're not human beings, they're kulak trash' – that's what I heard again and again, that's what everyone kept repeating . . .

Vasily Grossman, Everything Flows, *1961*[1]

Long before collectivization began, the phenomenon of the violent expropriator – a man who brandished a gun, spouted slogans and demanded food – was familiar in Soviet Ukraine. Such men had appeared in 1918 and 1919, looking for grain to feed their armies. They had appeared again in 1920, when the Bolsheviks returned to power. They came back in 1928 and 1929, as a new wave of food shortages began. In the winter of 1932–3 they were back again, but their behaviour had changed.

Unlike the other measures aimed at Ukraine in 1932–3, no written instructions governing the behaviour of activists have ever been found. Perhaps they were not put to paper, or perhaps they were destroyed along with other archival materials from Ukraine in this period, which, at the provincial and district level, are far sparser than those from the same period in Russia. Nevertheless, a remarkably consistent oral history record shows a sharp change in activists' behaviour on the eve of the Holodomor.

That winter the teams operating in villages all across Ukraine began to search not just for grain but for anything and everything edible. They were specifically equipped to do so with special tools, long metal rods, sometimes topped by hooks, that could be used to prod any surface in search of grain. The peasants had many different names for these instruments, calling them iron wires, cudgels, metal sticks, sharp sticks, rods, lances, spears and spokes.[2] Thousands of witnesses have described how they were used to search ovens, beds, cradles, walls, trunks, chimneys, attics, roofs and cellars; to pry behind icons, in barrels, in hollow tree trunks, in doghouses, down wells and beneath piles of garbage. The men and women who used them stopped at nothing, even trawling through cemeteries, barns, empty houses and orchards.[3]

Like the requisitioners of the past, they were looking for grain. But in addition they also took fruit from trees, seeds and vegetables from kitchen gardens – beets, pumpkins, cabbages, tomatoes – as well as honey and beehives, butter and milk, meat and sausage.[4] Olha Tsymbaliuk remembered that the brigades took 'flour, cereals, everything stored in pots, clothes, cattle. It was impossible to hide. They searched with metal rods ... they searched in stoves, broke floors and tore away walls.'[5] Anastasiia Pavlenko recalled that they took a bead necklace from her mother's neck, assuming it contained something edible.[6] Larysa Shevchuk saw activists take away beet and poppy seedlings that her grandmother was cultivating to plant in her vegetable garden.[7]

Maria Bendryk from Cherkasy province wrote that the activists 'came and took everything. They looked in kitchen storage tins, took away one person's kidney beans, another person's dried crusts. They shook them out and took them away.'[8] In Kirovohrad province, Leonid Vernydub saw the brigade take down three corn cobs that had been hanging from the ceiling to dry, in preparation for use as seeds in the following year. They also took 'kidney beans, cereals, flour and even dried fruits for making compote'.[9]

In Chernihiv province Mariia Kozhedub saw teams of people taking not only the buckwheat soup, but the pot that it had been cooking in. They also took 'milk, eggs, potatoes, chickens ... they had iron rods and used them to search for hidden food. Those who were clever hid their food in the forest; everything hidden in a house or barn could be found.'[10]

In many places the activists also led away the cows that many families had been allowed to keep, even those who lived on collective farms, since 1930. Sometimes this loss was remembered more vividly, and with more sorrow, than even the deaths of people. A teenage peasant girl wept and held on to the horns of her family cow as it was led away.[11] A father and son guarded their cow with guns and pitchforks to prevent it from being taken.[12] 'Whoever had a cow could survive,' Hanna Maslianchuk from Vinnytsia remembered. Her family managed to keep theirs, and lived; the neighbours did not have one, became swollen from hunger and died.[13] Unable to get or purchase fodder, families made huge efforts to keep their cows alive, even feeding them thatch from their own roofs.[14]

The activists took other kinds of livestock too, including pigs and poultry, and sometimes dogs and cats. In Kyiv province Mykola Patrynchuk saw activists take 'all our food . . . they even killed our dog and put it dead on a cart'.[15] Many other survivors speak of dogs being taken or killed, so much so that the hunt for dogs – perhaps to stop them from barking or biting – almost took on the aspect of a sport: 'I can never forget, so long as I live, how they drove their two vehicles, each carrying eight to twelve men . . . they were riding with their legs hung over the sides, and with their rifles they went from yard to yard to kill all the dogs. After this, when they had destroyed all the dogs, they started gathering all the food . . .'[16]

The activists also had instructions to return, to surprise people in order to catch them unaware and with their food unguarded. In many places the brigades came more than once. Families were searched, and then searched again to make sure that nothing remained. 'They came three times,' one woman remembered, 'until there was nothing left. Then they stopped coming.'[17] Brigades sometimes arrived at different times of day or night, determined to catch whoever had food red-handed.[18] If it happened that a family was eating a meagre dinner, the activists sometimes took bread off the table.[19] If it happened that soup was cooking, they pulled it off the stove and tossed out the contents. Then they demanded to know how it was possible the family still had something to put in the soup.[20]

People who seemed able to eat were searched with special vigour; those who weren't starving were by definition suspicious. One survivor remembered that her family had once managed to get hold of

18. What collectivization was supposed to be: women voting to join a collective farm.

19. Peasants listening to the radio during a break from fieldwork.

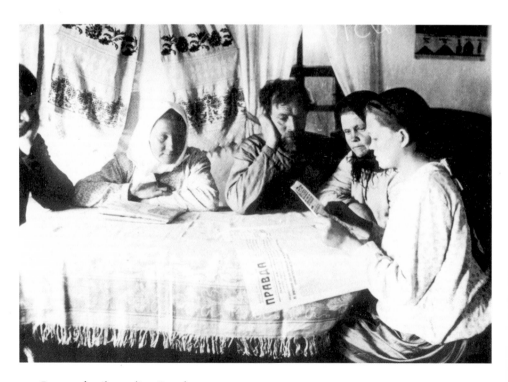

20. Peasant family reading *Pravda*.

21. A bountiful tomato harvest.

22. Workers from a local factory 'voluntarily' help bring in the harvest.

23. An activist brigade finds grain buried underground. The leader is holding one of the long iron rods used in the searches.

24. An activist brigade shows off sacks of grain and corn they've discovered.

25. Guarding the fields
on horseback.

26. Guarding the grain stores with a gun.

27. Peasants leaving home in search of food.

28. An abandoned peasant house.

29. Starving people by the side of a road.

30. A starving family on waste ground.

31. Peasant girl. One of Alexander Wienerberger's most famous photographs.

some flour and used it to bake bread during the night. Their home was instantly visited by a brigade that had detected the noise and sounds of cooking in the house. They entered by force and grabbed the bread directly out of the oven.[21] Another survivor described how the brigade 'watched chimneys from a hill: when they saw smoke, they went to that house and took whatever was being cooked.'[22] Yet another family received a parcel from a relative containing rice, sugar, millet and shoes. A few hours later a brigade arrived and took everything except the shoes.[23]

But the activists also learned, over time, to identify the places where peasants might hide food. Because many people buried their grain in the ground, brigades began looking for signs of fresh digging, using their iron rods to poke into the earth.[24] One survivor remembered that her mother put some millet in a bag, hid it up a chimney, and covered it with cement. But the cement was new, and so the millet was discovered. A neighbour, meanwhile, hid flour beneath her baby's cradle, but that too was found: 'She was crying and begging them to leave it because the baby would die of hunger, but they, the crucifiers, took it all the same.'[25]

Even when not out on raiding parties, the brigades and their leaders collected information about food and who might have it. Informers were recruited to help out the activists. In some villages special boxes were set up where people could deposit anonymous confessions or information as to the whereabouts of their neighbours' hidden grain.[26] Hanna Sukhenko remembered that it was 'popular' to inform, because when a person found someone else's food, he or she was given up to a third of it as a reward.[27] Local civil servants were expected to contribute too. Ihor Buhaievych's family survived in Poltava province because his mother, who had found work in Leningrad, regularly sent home packages of dried bread crusts. But the packages attracted the suspicion of the post office boss, who came to the house accompanied by an activist to find out what was in them. The activist confiscated half of the bread crusts.[28]

Others were secretly paid: Halyna Omelchenko remembered a local man, deployed as a spy, who watched her family closely and provided information about their behaviour to the authorities.[29] Mykola Mylov remembered a neighbour who came one day and looked around his house. The following day activists arrived and confiscated his food. Mylov asked the neighbour whether he had informed on him: 'Of course it was me, do you think I am afraid to confess? I have now received two sacks of wheat, my six children will not go hungry.'[30] There were many similar examples of how starvation was used to make peasants complicit.

The brigades also asked for money. All peasants were still subject to the 1929 law, which instructed them to pay fines of up to five times the value of grain that they could not produce. Inhabitants of blacklisted villages were meant to hand over their savings too. Collecting these sums had long been a problem: in his diary for December 1932, Lazar Kaganovich, Stalin's close associate in Ukraine, noted that the individual farmers in Ukraine had been fined 7.8 million rubles, but that only 1.9 million had been collected. Vlas Chubar had weakly argued that this was because they had 'nothing to sell'.[31] But in the autumn of 1932 auctions of furniture and other goods were arranged so that peasants could pay these sums: 'When a peasant paid the tax, then another, bigger tax was put on him. Father could not pay this additional tax, so an auction was called . . . a storehouse, a shed were sold.'[32] Sometimes these demands had little to do with past payments: in one village anyone who had relatives in the United States was asked to hand over the money they were presumed to have received from abroad.[33]

During searches for both food and money, violence was frequently used. One woman from Chernihiv province remembered:

> During the search, the activists asked where was our gold and our grain. Mother replied that she had neither. She was tortured. Her fingers were put in a door and the door was closed. Her fingers broke, blood ran, she lost consciousness. Water was poured over her head, and she was tortured again. They beat her, put a needle under her fingernails . . .[34]

Two sisters from Zhytomyr province witnessed a similar attack on their father:

> Our father hid three buckets of barley in the attic and our mother stealthily made porridge in the evening to keep us alive. Then somebody must

have denounced us, they took everything and brutally beat our father for not giving up that barley during the searches . . . they held his fingers and slammed the door to break them, they swore at him and kicked him on the floor. It left us numb to see him beaten and sworn at like that, we were a proper family, always spoke quietly in our father's presence . . .[35]

In Vinnytsia province a blacksmith was brought to the village committee after stealing wheat ears to feed his three children: 'they beat him, tortured him, twisted his head completely back to front and threw him down the stairs'.[36] In Dnipropetrovsk province men were held inside hot stoves until they confessed to hiding grain.[37] As during collectivization, peasants found concealing food were robbed of their remaining possessions, evicted from their homes, and thrown into the snow without any clothes.[38]

Imprisonment was another tool. In one village peasants who could not come up with any grain were thrown into the 'cooler' by the chairman of the village soviet. The 'cooler' was simply the back room of the village hall, with no beds or benches – and no food. Peasants simply sat there on the ground, hungry, unless their relatives could help feed them. 'Men and women were kept there together; they all lay side by side on the straw.'[39]

Some recalled that, in addition to taking the food, brigades went out of their way to spoil it. In Horodyshche – the blacklisted village subjected to so much special attention – a survivor recalled that activists spoiled grain with water so that it turned black, sprouted, and was then thrown into a local ravine. They also poured carbolic acid onto salted fish, which the peasants ate anyway.[40] Another family saw that all the stolen food taken from their home was rendered useless for human consumption: 'They had a big sack with them, and they poured everything all together – seeds, flour, wheat – into that sack. Only pigs would be able to eat it, because everything was mixed.'[41] Most thought that this behaviour was simply a form of sadism: 'When anything was discovered they scattered it on the floor and enjoyed the sight of weeping children gathering grains of lentils or beans from the dirt.'[42]

To ensure that starving peasants did not 'rob' the fields of whatever grain was growing in them, the brigade leaders also sent guards on horseback – usually villagers bribed to assist, with promises of food – to watch the fields, or else set up watchtowers beside them, to ensure that nobody stole anything from them. Armed guards – again, many were villagers – were placed in front of barns and other places where grain was stored. Now that there was so little food left, the 7 August law against gleaners began to make a difference. In the late autumn of 1932, 'we continued to search for food by gleaning wheat ears from harvested fields,' one Poltava man remembered. 'But gleaning was prohibited, and we were chased and whipped by overseers on horseback.'[43] People were punished for stealing frozen beets, sprouted grain, even wheat from their own private plots.[44] Outside a sugar-beet factory in Kyiv province bloody corpses lay unburied beside the piles of unprocessed beets to warn off others wanting to steal them.[45]

To prevent their family from dying of hunger, some peasants sent small children into the fields to hunt for leftover grain, hoping they would escape notice. 'We children would run to the collective farm stubble-field to gather up the stalks,' remembered Kostiantyn Mochulsky, then aged eight. 'Mounted patrolmen would chase after the children, slashing at them with rawhide whips. But I collected some ten kilograms of grain.'[46] Some failed to evade the overseers. A girl from Kharkiv province once succeeded in quietly gathering some wheat ears, but on the way home from the fields she met three young Komsomol members. They took her wheat and beat her 'so severely that there were bruises on my shoulders and lower legs long afterwards'.[47] Perhaps she was lucky: another survivor remembered a young girl who was shot on the spot for gleaning leftover potatoes.[48]

The possession and preparation of food, even the milling of grain, became suspect. In Cherkasy province activists broke all the millstones in the village of Tymoshivka. The locals assumed that this was 'so that there would be no place to grind a handful of grain, even if there were some left somewhere'.[49] They also broke the millstones in another Cherkasy village, Stari Babany. The peasants there thought their millstones had been broken in order to get more money out of them, as they would then have to take their grain to the collective farm and pay if they wanted it to be ground.[50]

As the weeks dragged on, just being alive attracted suspicion: if a family was alive, that meant it had food. But if they had food, then they should have given it up – and if they had failed to give it up, then they were kulaks, Petliurites, Polish agents, enemies. A brigade searching the home of Mykhailo Balanovskyi in Cherkasy province demanded to know 'how it is possible that no one in this family has yet died?'[51] A brigade searching through the roof thatch at the home of Hryhorii Moroz in Sumy province failed to find any food and demanded to know: 'With the help of what do you live?'[52] With each passing day, demands became angrier, the language ruder: Why haven't you disappeared yet? Why haven't you dropped dead yet? *Why are you alive at all?*[53]

Years and decades later, survivors found different ways of describing the groups of men and a very few women who had come to their homes and removed their food, knowing that they would starve. In oral histories the groups have sometimes been described as 'activists', 'Komsomol', 'confiscators' or 'murderers'; as an 'iron brigade,' a 'red team', 'red caravan' or 'red broom' that swept the village. Sometimes they were called *komnezamy*, after the 'poor peasants' committees' set up in 1919, and often their members were *komnezamy* veterans. Special brigades were called 'tugboats' – *buksyrnyky* – because they were dragging the village towards the quota. Sometimes they are remembered, simply, as 'Russians', 'foreign' or 'Jewish'.[54]

In practice, the brigades in the autumn of 1932 and winter of 1933 were almost always composites. As in 1930, they often included members from different organizations: the local party leadership and the provincial government, the Komsomol, the civil service, the secret police. This was deliberate. If all the institutions in the countryside participated, then all bore some responsibility for the results. Their membership frequently overlapped with the grain collection teams of the past, and they often included some of the same activists who had helped carry out collectivization, as well as people who had been members of the 'poor peasants' committees' as far back as 1920.

But there were some differences. Their numbers were greater: on 11 November 1932 the Ukrainian Communist Party called for the creation of no fewer than 1,100 new activist brigades by 1 December – that is, within three weeks. That was the first of what would be several attempts to increase the numbers of people dedicated to enforcing the requisitions policy. As time went on, extra manpower would be required not only to collect food but to protect fields and crops from starving peasants, to prevent people from entering train stations or crossing borders, and eventually to bury the dead.[55]

Their task was also different from what it had been in 1930. These new brigades were not carrying out an agricultural reform, or even pretending to do so: they were taking food away from starving families, as well as anything valuable that could have been exchanged for food, and, in some cases, any implements that could be used to prepare it. For that reason their nature and their motivation require closer examination.

Often, as in the past, there were at least one or two outsiders in an activist group, people not originally from the village, the province, or even the republic. A handful of these were former 'Twenty-Five Thousanders', about a third of whom had remained in the countryside after 1930, working on collective farms, on machine tractor stations or in the party bureaucracy.[56] But fresh activists were also deliberately sent from outside the republic at this time. In December 1932, Kaganovich visited Voznesensk in southern Ukraine and told a group of party activists that they were not tough enough: 'A Ukrainian saying has it that "you should twist, but not overtwist".' But they have decided 'not to twist at all'. The goal, he explained frankly, was to put villages in such a panic 'that the peasants themselves give away their hiding places'.[57]

That same month Kaganovich also sent Stalin a telegram complaining about the 'unreliability' of the Ukrainian members of the grain collection brigades, and calling for Russians from the Russian Republic to help. A month later the order was executed.[58] One former activist remembers first encountering 'young men, speaking Russian' in the village of Krupoderentsi. They were there, he was told, because 'the authorities did not trust the local party activists to do the job'.[59]

Some of the outsiders were 'foreign' in a different sense. Although they were activists, students or teachers from Ukrainian universities, they seemed, as during collectivization, like foreigners to the peasants. Some were collectivization veterans, but many of them had come to the countryside for the first time in 1932 and 1933, ignorant of what they would find. Students at Kharkiv University were sent out on 'voluntary' stints to help with grain collection in 1933, and were shocked to discover the truth. 'You look as if you've seen ghosts,' the student Viktor Kravchenko said to a friend who had just come back from the Poltava area. 'I have,' the man responded, and turned his gaze away.[60]

Kravchenko himself went to the countryside soon afterwards – he was told that village authorities needed an 'injection of Bolshevik iron' – and quickly saw the gap between propaganda and reality. The 'kulaks' were not rich, they were starving. The countryside was not wealthy, it was a wasteland: 'Large quantities of implements and machinery, which had once been cared for like so many jewels by their private owners, now lay scattered under the open skies, dirty, rusting and out of repair. Emaciated cows and horses, crusted with manure, wandered through the yard. Chickens, geese and ducks were digging in flocks in the unthreshed grain.'[61]

At the time Kravchenko did not protest. As he explained years later, he had, like the Twenty-Five Thousanders before him, deliberately allowed himself to succumb to a form of intellectual blindness. Kravchenko spoke for many when he described it: 'To spare yourself mental agony you veil unpleasant truths from view by half-closing your eyes – and your mind. You make panicky excuses and shrug off knowledge with words like exaggeration and hysteria.'[62] The language of the propaganda also helped mask reality:

> We communists, among ourselves, steered around the subject; or we dealt with it in the high-flown euphemisms of party lingo. We spoke of the 'peasant front' and 'kulak menace', 'village socialism' and 'class resistance'. In order to live with ourselves we had to smear the reality out of recognition with verbal camouflage.[63]

Like Kravchenko, Lev Kopelev also joined one of the grain confiscation brigades in December 1932. Having participated in collectivization, he was mentally prepared. At the time he was a journalist of sorts, writing articles for a Kharkiv factory newspaper. Upon arrival in Myrhorod, in Poltava province, he gave evening lectures to the peasants, 'mustachioed men in fur jackets, in grey caftans, young lads dreamily indifferent or sullen with contempt'. Every other day he and some colleagues put out a newsletter, containing 'statistics on the grain delivery, reproaches to the unconscientious peasants, curses to the exposed saboteurs'. But the agitation quickly failed, and the searches began.

Teams made up of several young collective farmers, the village Soviet and Kopelev himself would 'search the hut, barn, yard and take away all the stores of seed, lead away the cow, the horse, the pigs'. They would take anything valuable as well: icons, winter coats, carpets, money. Although the women 'howled hysterically' clinging to their family heirlooms, the searches continued. Hand over the grain, the activists told them, and eventually you will get it all back. Kopelev himself found the task 'excruciating', but he also learned that constant repetition of hateful propaganda helped him steel himself to the task at hand: 'I persuaded myself, explained to myself. I mustn't give in to debilitating pity. We were realizing historical necessity. We were performing our revolutionary duty. We were obtaining grain for the socialist fatherland. For the five-year plan.'[64]

Propaganda also helped persuade many activists to think of the peasants as second-class citizens, even second-class human beings – if they were even human beings at all. Peasants already seemed alien to most city-dwellers. Now their deep poverty and even their starvation made them unlikeable, inhuman. Bolshevik ideology implied they would soon disappear. The French writer Georges Simenon, who visited Odessa in the spring of 1933, was told by one man that the *malheureux*, the 'unfortunates' that he saw begging for food in the streets, were not to be pitied: 'Those are kulaks, peasants who have not adapted to the regime . . . there is nothing for them but to die.' There was no need for pity: they would soon be replaced by tractors, which could do the work of ten men. The brave new world would not have space for so many useless people.[65]

This sentiment also found an echo in Andrey Platonov's absurdist play about the famine, *Fourteen Little Red Huts* (1933). 'What use are we to the state like this,' one starving character says to another: 'The State would be better off if there were sea here, not people. At least the sea has fish in it.'[66] Platonov's language reflected what he found in the official press. All through the previous two years these uncouth, illiterate, backward and ultimately redundant inhabitants of the countryside had been firmly and repeatedly accused of blocking the progress of the forward-looking proletariat. Over and over again Soviet newspapers had explained that food shortages in the cities were not caused by collectivization, but rather by greedy peasants who were keeping their produce to themselves. Years later Kopelev explained to an interviewer:

> I was among those who believed that you had to shake up the village to get it to give up the grain ... That the villagers had no conscious-ness or awareness, that they were backward. That they care only about their property, that they don't care for the workers. That they are not interested in the general problems of the construction of social-ism and the fulfilment of the five-year plan ...
>
> This is what I was taught in school, in the Komsomol, that's what I read in newspapers and what I was told in meetings. All young men thought like that.[67]

Like others in the party, he believed that 'the villagers were hiding bread and meat'. All around him, others were similarly hostile. Kopelev paraphrased his generation's views like this: 'I am a real prol-etarian and I don't have enough bread. And you, you country bumpkin, you buckwheat sower, you don't know how to work but you've got pork fat in your pocket.'[68]

The city party bosses who recruited activists to go into the villages relied on exactly the same sentiments. Advertisements for 'soldiers to fight on the bread front' appeared everywhere in towns where there were food shortages.[69] Activists repeated the same language as they carried out their food collections: 'They kept shouting that we had to make up our quota: Go off and die, but Russia will be saved!'[70] In his memoir Kopelev described how this poisonous language even infected one of the villagers, a young peasant woman, herself very hungry, who voluntarily brought a kilogram and a half of wheat to feed the activist brigade. 'That black-haired fellow said the workers were very hungry, their kids didn't have any bread. So I brought as much as I was able. The last of my grain.'[71]

But the vast majority of members of the brigades that searched vil-lages for food in 1932–3 were not outsiders. Nor were they motivated by hatred of Ukrainian peasants, because they were Ukrainian peasants themselves. More importantly, they were the neighbours of the people whose food they stole: local collective farm bosses, members of the village council, teachers and doctors, civil servants, Komsomol leaders, former members of the 'poor peasants' committees' from 1919, former participants in de-kulakization. As in other historic genocides, they were persuaded to kill people whom they knew extremely well.

At the highest level these local activists were not considered to be entirely trustworthy. The outsiders sent to assist them were partly there in order to make sure they did their jobs. Frequently, they were told to search not in their own villages but in neighbouring ones, where they would not personally know the peasants whose food they were confiscating.[72] The fear that collection brigades would become too sympathetic to their victims was often discussed by the Ukrainian leadership. 'There is a need to change the members more often,' Chubar observed at one point, 'because they quickly grow accustomed to the locals and cover up for them.'[73]

Both memoir and documentary evidence also shows that many local activists refused to carry out orders that they knew would kill their neighbours. Mykola Musiichuk, a Communist Party member in Vinnytsia since 1925, appointed to a grain collection committee in 1932, lost his party card for refusing to take grain from peasants' private pots and jars. Two days later he hanged himself.[74] In the village of Toporyshche, Dmytro Slyniuk, the boss of the local collective farm, actually took grain away from activists after they had already confiscated it, had it milled, and then distributed the flour to starving peasants. He lost his job for doing so.[75] In the village of Bashtanka, Vira Kyrychenko's father was asked to join a brigade but refused. He was locked up for three days, then went to the city of Mykolaiv to look unsuccessfully for work. Eventually he died of hunger. Vira's brother was made the same offer: he too refused, was arrested and beaten so badly that he died after being released.[76] Years later peasants recounted how brothers and fathers were exiled, executed or beaten for refusing to cooperate.[77]

Yet many did collaborate, in different ways and at different levels, and out of a mix of motives. Some had no choice. One girl aged thirteen joined a brigade directly from her school classroom; activists arrived, ordered her to come with them, and took her to carry out searches. She had no chance to tell her parents and spent a week carrying out orders, searching for grain.[78]

She and others like her believed they had no choice, or were afraid that refusal would mean arrest or even death. The majority of the thousands of long prison sentences handed out to Ukrainian communists at that time were for people who had failed, sometimes deliberately, to put pressure on their neighbours to give up all their food. By the time of the grain collections, Balytsky's purge of the Ukrainian Communist Party had begun, and leaders at every level knew that they were at risk of arrest and execution. The party trials were discussed openly in the newspapers. The names of those arrested were printed in the party bulletins that were sent out to the village and district party offices.[79] Nobody with any links to the party wanted to share their fate.

Fear was reinforced by memories of past violence. Almost everyone in Ukraine had been brutalized by successive waves of political change. Except for the very youngest, all of them remembered the pogroms and mass murders during the civil war just thirteen years earlier. Everyone recalled the more recent cruelty of de-kulakization as well.[80] Many had already exercised power over their neighbours, and they knew what was to be gained from it. The leader of Kopelev's brigade, Bubyr, was the consumptive son of a landless peasant who had been 'orphaned early'. Bubyr had participated in punishment squads during the revolution, worked for the Komsomol since 1921, taken part in collectivization and de-kulakization, and clearly enjoyed the power he had to threaten his neighbours. Matvii Havryliuk, a member of the 'poor peasants' committee' in the village of Toporyshche, had been part of a brigade in 1921, 'collecting bread from kulaks', as he later told a court, and working to 'organize poor peasant masses'. He had taken an active role in de-kulakization, was an agitator for collectivization, and an enthusiastic participant in the house searches that led to the famine. He knew well the people he was starving to death but he felt no empathy for them: 'I had nothing in common with the kulaks, and the proof can be found in the fact that they have always been against me.'[81]

As the peasants began to starve in the winter and spring of 1933, hunger became the most important motivator of all. In a devastated world, where food was scarce and possessions were few, desperate people confiscated their neighbours' food in order to eat it. Often it was hard to distinguish the behaviour of the brigades from that of criminal gangs. 'They robbed everyone and lived well,' remembered Maryna Korobska from Dnipropetrovsk province: 'They wore what they had stolen from people, and ate our food.'[82]

Even those who didn't openly steal hoped to gain some advantage. As noted, informers had an expectation of reward. In some districts, activists received a percentage of what they collected outright. The 2 December law on blacklists contained an order to 'issue a directive on bonuses to activists who find hidden grain'.[83] A decision from the Dnipropetrovsk provincial council in February 1933 recommended that brigade members be given '10–15 per cent' of what they collected outright, and other provinces issued similar instructions.[84] Everyone knew that working with the party might bring with it access to food or to ration cards, or to other people who had them. Kateryna Iaroshenko, also from Dnipropetrovsk province, survived the famine because her father was a party leader who had access to a special Communist Party shop providing grain and sugar.[85] The highest party officials also had ration cards, which enabled them to make purchases that were impossible for others. Privileges were also extended to their children, as those less fortunate remembered: 'There was a special school for the children of the bosses. There was a canteen inside . . . breathtaking smells spread from that kitchen, I wept because of them, with such tears!'[86]

Others believed that they would receive food, but were deceived, as one Poltava man remembered: 'Of those who went with rods and searched for food, half died of hunger. They were promised they would get food if they searched for food. They received nothing!'[87] Another survivor remembered that brigade members who stole food and kept it in their homes were horrified when they too were searched. Activists from one village would be sent to search the homes in another village, and would not necessarily spare their fellow collaborators.[88] Some of the perpetrators were even met with violence from the neighbours they had robbed. In the space of just three weeks in December 1932, nine local officials were murdered in Kyiv province alone; there were eight other murder attempts, and eleven cases of arson, when peasants had tried to burn down the homes of brigade members.[89] Even children carried out small acts of revenge. The son of an activist in Novopokrovka, Dnipropetrovsk province, hid his loaves of white bread from the other children at his school, but to no avail. He was beaten up by his classmates anyway.[90]

As winter turned to spring, and the lack of food took its toll, the vast majority of peasants ceased to fight back. Even those who had rebelled in 1930 stayed silent. The reason for this was physical, not psychological. A starving person is simply too weak to fight back. Hunger overwhelms even the urge to object.

Whether they were locals or outsiders, all those who carried out orders to confiscate food did so with a sense of impunity. They may have felt some personal sense of guilt in the years that followed, or they may have been aware of the anger and despair of the peasants whom they left to starve. But they were also certain that their actions were sanctioned at the very highest levels. Over and over again they had been told that their starving neighbours were kulak agents, dangerous enemy elements. In November 1932 the Ukrainian Communist Party instructed its members to repeat this language again. 'Simultaneously', while they were using legal and physical repression, the party and its collection brigades must act: 'Against thieves, ruffians and bread thieves, against those who deceive the proletarian state and the collective farmers . . . we must raise the hatred of the collective farm masses, we must ensure that the entire mass of collective farmers denigrate these people as kulak agents and class enemies.'[91] With those instructions ringing in their ears, grain collectors not only did not fear punishment for their behaviour, they expected rewards.

The curious story of Andrii Richytskyi illustrates the problem very well, for he is one of the very few exceptions to this rule. Richytskyi, by the time he became a district plenipotentiary, had already been a participant in many of the intellectual and political movements of his time. As a young man he had been part of the 1919 peasant uprising, operating with one of the partisan groups, at least according to his police record. Later he was a Socialist Revolutionary, before seeing the light and becoming an ardent communist, though as a leader of the Ukrainian Communist Party, one of the 'national communist' parties that initially opposed the Bolsheviks. Later still he was a biographer of the poet Taras Shevchenko and the first translator of Karl Marx into Ukrainian. In 1931, Richytskyi had participated in the orchestrated attacks on Mykhailo Hrushevsky, 'unmasking' the famous historian as a bourgeois enemy of socialism.[92] Despite these efforts to ingratiate himself with the regime, Richytskyi's complicated history of political engagement made him a suspicious figure in the Ukraine of the early 1930s, and in November 1933 he was arrested as part of the case against the fictitious 'Ukrainian Military Organization'.[93]

Richytskyi's trial in March 1934 focused on his short career as a grain collector and the leader of an activist brigade in Arbuzynka, Mykolaiv province, from December 1932 until the end of February 1933. The investigation into his activities during those three months was thorough, running into hundreds of pages and more than forty witnesses. The court accused Richytskyi and other local leaders, most notably Ivan Kobzar, secretary of the district party committee, of counter-revolution, distorting the party line, and deliberately using excessive violence in order to create 'disaffection'.

In fact, the documentation shows that Richytskyi, Kobzar and the other local leaders behaved no differently from thousands of other communist officials in Ukraine in that same era. Richytskyi had been sent to Arbuzynka precisely because he already had a successful track record as a grain collector in Vinnytsia province. Even before that, in 1930, he had served as a grain collector in Ukraine's Moldovan autonomous republic – one of the places that used brutal methods very early – and received a medal for his efforts. Upon arrival in his new workplace, he immediately began to form a brigade that would force the peasants of Arbuzynka to meet their targets as well.

His intentions became clear on his very first night, as one farmer testified. Richytskyi gathered the village leaders together in a room, closed the door, and 'started shouting that all the collective farmers are Petliurites and we should beat them until the grain is gathered'. When some objected, he shouted again: 'Do you know who is speaking to you? A member of the government, a member of the Central Committee, a candidate member of the Politburo.' He then called for the creation of a brigade, which would act differently from all others before it: 'every house, after this brigade enters it, should require capital refurbishment. It should have no oven and no roof.'

Several local secret police informers and officers joined the brigade. So did two well-known criminals, as was common practice; again, the police selected such people for their known ruthlessness. One of them was Spyrydon Velychko, who had been expelled from one of the local collective farms for theft in September 1932. Velychko was allowed to join the brigade because he was willing to inform on his fellow collective farmers and reveal where they had hidden their grain. He understood that this was a quid pro quo, and in his case it worked: 'He wasn't forgotten during the famine', according to the testimony. In other words, he did not starve.

In the weeks following Richytskyi's arrival, the new Arbuzynka brigade added some twists to the traditional methods of collecting grain. They detained recalcitrant peasants in a cellar, sometimes for two or three days, with little or no food. They beat them regularly, until they revealed the location of their grain. They subjected others to a form of public shaming: stripped of their clothes, peasants were placed in barrels and driven from village to village as 'examples' for others not to follow. If neither of those methods worked, then Richytskyi's team resorted to even more spectacular punishments. After confiscating peasants' property – underwear, frying pans, shoes – they simply destroyed their houses altogether.

They used other kinds of violence and torture as well. One local man described how Richytskyi's methods worked in one case: 'After I discovered four hiding places for grain at one farmer's place, I brought the man to the village council. Richytskyi beat him up, shouting "Do you know, for hiding bread you will be shot?" The man shouted back: "I don't care, we will die anyway." On another occasion several brigade members poured kerosene onto a cat, set it alight and threw it into the cellar where men, women and children were being held. Sexual coercion was also used as a weapon: one brigade member told several women that in exchange for sex with him, they would not have to give up their grain.

The accusations of abuse appear to have been designed to blame the violence, retrospectively, on rogue elements, to minimize the party's role in these crimes. But Richytskyi had a strong defence: he had followed clear orders – and had been consistently rewarded for doing so. In his testimony he explained that when he came to Arbuzynka he discovered that the decrees of autumn 1932 had not actually been applied. The local communists had not begun to confiscate all the peasants' food or make them pay 'taxes' if their grain quotas fell short. They had not evicted anyone from their homes. These were precisely the methods that Richytskyi had used successfully in Vinnytsia, with the approval of higher authorities, and upon arrival in Arbuzynka he had resolved to repeat them.

Richytskyi also declared that Kaganovich himself had reinforced his faith in these methods. On 24 December 1932, Richytskyi and Kobzar, the local party leader, attended the meeting with Kaganovich in the village of Voznesensk. The two men clearly heard this senior Soviet figure tell the assembled party officials that they were not tough enough. They even heard the order, quoted previously, that their task was to put villages into such a panic 'that the peasants themselves give away their hiding places'.[94] At that meeting – which ended at 4 a.m. – they signed an agreement to collect 12,000 tonnes of grain by 1 February 1933. Richytskyi testified that he had been inspired by this speech. It persuaded him that the village should drop its old 'ineffective' grain procurement methods and adopt harsher techniques.

Nor was Kaganovich the only high-level party figure to drive home this point. In the second half of January a Ukrainian Politburo leader, Volodymyr Zatonskyi, had visited Arbuzynka and was more than satisfied with the brutal work of the brigade. Zatonskyi specifically approved of their 'concentrated strikes' on peasants, along with fines, evictions and arrests. These were necessary to 'scare others'. Richytskyi openly admitted that he had been inspired by this language to destroy peasant houses: 'I reckoned that for a greater effect, the houses that were about to be confiscated should be ruined. So that people would see this with their own eyes.'

Richytskyi's trial was a curious one, not least because he made his points forcefully, sometimes over the objections of a prosecutor who tried to dismiss his arguments. It is not clear who ordered the investigation, or why it was allowed to happen; generally speaking, it was

very rare for perpetrators of the famine to face any kind of retribution at all.[95] No doubt it happened for reasons related to Richytskyi's
patchwork career, which drew the attention of OGPU officers looking for secret nationalists and closet counter-revolutionaries. He was
sentenced to death in 1934.

Richytskyi's testimony nevertheless removes any doubt about the
prevailing moral atmosphere at the time. Far from being an outlier or
a criminal, he felt himself to be very much in the mainstream. He and
the other brigade members had good reason to believe that the party
leadership, at the very highest levels, sanctioned extreme cruelty and
supported the removal of food and possessions from the peasantry.
There was no misunderstanding at all.

11

Starvation: Spring and Summer, 1933

How could we resist when we had no strength to go outside?
Mariia Dziuba, Poltava province, 1933[1]

Not one of them was guilty of anything; but they belonged to
a class that was guilty of everything.
Ilya Ehrenburg, 1934[2]

The starvation of a human body, once it begins, always follows the same course. In the first phase, the body consumes its stores of glucose. Feelings of extreme hunger set in, along with constant thoughts of food. In the second phase, which can last for several weeks, the body begins to consume its own fats, and the organism weakens drastically. In the third phase, the body devours its own proteins, cannibalizing tissues and muscles. Eventually, the skin becomes thin, the eyes become distended, the legs and belly swollen as extreme imbalances lead the body to retain water. Small amounts of effort lead to exhaustion. Along the way, different kinds of diseases can hasten death: scurvy, kwashiorkor, marasmus, pneumonia, typhus, diphtheria, and a wide range of infections and skin diseases caused, directly or indirectly, by lack of food.

The rural Ukrainians deprived of food in the autumn and winter of 1932 began to experience all these stages of hunger in the spring of 1933 – if they had not already done so earlier. Years later some of those who survived sought to describe these terrible months, in written accounts and thousands of interviews. For others who managed to live through this period, the experience was so awful that they were later unable to recall anything about it all. One survivor, a child of eleven at the time, could remember things that caused sadness or disappointment before the famine, even trivial things such as a lost earring. But she had no emotional memory of the famine itself, no horror and no sorrow: 'Probably, my feelings were atrophied by hunger.' She and others have wondered whether famine wasn't somehow deadening, an experience that suppressed emotions and even memory later in life. To some it seemed as if the famine had 'mutilated the immature souls of children'.[3]

Some searched for metaphors to describe what had happened. Tetiana Pavlychka, who lived in Kyiv province, remembered that her sister Tamara 'had a large, swollen stomach, and her neck was long and thin like a bird's neck. People didn't look like people – they were more like starving ghosts.'[4] Another survivor remembered that his mother 'looked like a glass jar, filled with clear spring water. All her body that could be seen ... was see-through and filled with water, like a plastic bag.'[5] A third remembered his brother lying down, 'alive but completely swollen, his body shining as if it were made of glass'.[6] We felt 'giddy', another recalled: 'everything was as if in a fog. There was a horrible pain in our legs, as if someone were pulling the tendons out of them.'[7] Yet another could not rid himself of the memory of a child sitting, rocking its body 'back and forth, back and forth', reciting one endless 'song' in a half voice: 'eat, eat, eat'.[8]

An activist from Russia, one of those sent to Ukraine to help execute the confiscation policy, remembered children too:

All alike: their heads like heavy kernels, their necks skinny as a stork's, every bone movement visible beneath the skin on the arms and legs, the skin itself like yellow gauze stretched over their skeletons. And the faces of those children were old, exhausted, as if they had already lived on the earth for seventy years. And their eyes, Lord![9]

Some survivors specifically recalled the many diseases of starvation and their different physical side effects. Scurvy caused people to feel pain in their joints, to lose their teeth. It also led to night-blindness: people could not see in the dark, and so feared to leave their homes at night.[10] Dropsy – oedema – caused the legs of victims to swell and made their skin very thin, even transparent. Nadia Malyshko, from a village in Dnipropetrovsk province, remembered that her mother 'swelled up, became weak and looked old, though she was only 37. Her legs were shining, and the skin had burst.'[11] Hlafyra Ivanova from Khmelnytskyi province remembered that people turned yellow and black: 'the skin of swollen people grew chapped, and liquid oozed out of their wounds'.[12]

People with swollen legs, covered in sores, could not sit: 'When such a person sat down, the skin broke, liquid began to run down their legs, the smell was awful and they felt unbearable pain.'[13] Children developed swollen bellies, and heads that seemed too heavy for their necks.[14] One woman remembered a girl who was so emaciated that 'one could see how her heart was beating beneath the skin'.[15] M. Mishchenko described the final stages: 'General weakness increases, and the sufferer cannot sit up in bed or move at all. He falls into a drowsy state which may last for a week, until his heart stops beating from exhaustion.'[16]

An emaciated person can die very quickly, unexpectedly, and many did. Volodymyr Slipchenko's sister worked in a school, where she witnessed children dying during lessons – 'a child is sitting at a school desk, then collapses, falls down' – or while playing in the grass outside.[17] Many people died while walking, trying to flee. Another survivor remembered that the roads leading to Donbas were lined with corpses: 'Dead villagers lay on the roads, along the road and paths. There were more bodies than people to move them.'[18]

Those deprived of food were also liable to die suddenly in the act of eating, if they managed to get hold of something to eat. In the spring of 1933, Hryhorii Simia remembered that a terrible stench arose from wheatfields close to the road: hungry people had crawled into the grain stalks to cut off ears of wheat, eaten them and then died: their empty stomachs could no longer digest anything.[19] The same thing happened in the bread lines in the cities. 'There were cases when a person bought bread, ate it and died on the spot, being too exhausted with hunger.'[20] One survivor was tormented by the memory of finding some beets, which he brought to his grandmother. She ate two of them raw and cooked the rest. Within hours she was dead, as her body could not cope with digestion.[21]

For those who remained alive, the physical symptoms were often just the beginning. The psychological changes could be equally dramatic. Some spoke later of a 'psychosis of hunger', though of course such a thing could not be defined or measured.[22] 'From hunger, people's psyches were disturbed. Common sense left them, natural instincts faded,' recalled Petro Boichuk.[23] Pitirim Sorokin, who experienced starvation in the 1921 famine, remembered that after only a week of food deprivation, 'It was very difficult for me to concentrate for any length of time on anything but food. For short periods, by forcing myself, I was able to chase away the "thoughts of hunger" from my consciousness, but they invariably returned and took possession of it.' Eventually, ideas about food 'begin to multiply abundantly in the consciousness, and they acquire a diversity and unprecedented vivacity often reaching the stage of hallucinations'. Other kinds of thoughts 'fade from the field of consciousness, become very vague and uninteresting'.[24]

Over and over, survivors have written and spoken about how personalities were altered by hunger, and how normal behaviour ceased. The desire to eat simply overwhelmed everything else – and familial feelings above all. A woman who had always been kind and generous abruptly changed when food began to run short. She sent her own mother out of her house and told her to go and live with another relative: 'You've lived with us for two weeks,' she told her, 'live with him and do not be a burden to my children.'[25]

Another survivor remembered a young boy searching for extra grain in a field. His sister ran to him and told him to go home because their father had died. The boy replied: 'To hell with him, I want to eat.'[26] A woman told a neighbour that her youngest daughter was dying, and so she had not given the little girl any bread. 'I need to try to support myself, the children will die anyway.'[27] A five-year-old boy whose father had died stole into an uncle's house to find something to eat. Furious, the uncle's family locked him in a cellar where he died as well.[28]

Faced with terrible choices, many made decisions of a kind they would not previously have been able to imagine. One woman told her village that while she would always be able to give birth to other children, she had only one husband, and she wanted him to survive. She duly confiscated the bread her children received at a local kindergarten, and all her children died.[29] A couple put their children in a deep hole and left them there, in order not to have to watch them die. Neighbours heard the children screaming, and they were rescued and survived.[30] Another survivor remembered her mother leaving the house in order not to hear a younger sibling cry.[31]

Uliana Lytvyn, aged eighty at the time she was interviewed, remembered these emotional changes, and especially the disappearance of family feelings – maternal and paternal love – above all else: 'Believe me, famine makes animals, entirely stupefied, of nice, honest people. Neither intellect nor consideration, neither sorrow nor conscience. This is what can be done to kind and honest peasant farmers. When sometimes I dream of that horror, I still cry through the dream.'[32]

Distrust grew too, and indeed had been growing since the beginning of the collectivization and de-kulakization drives a few years earlier. 'Neighbours had been made to spy on neighbours,' wrote Miron Dolot: 'friends had been forced to betray friends; children had been coached to denounce their parents; and even family members avoided meeting each other. The warm traditional hospitality of the villagers had disappeared, to be replaced by mistrust and suspicion. Fear became our constant companion: it was an awesome dread of standing helplessly and hopelessly alone before the monstrous power of the State.'[33]

Iaryna Mytsyk remembered that families who had always left their houses open, even during the years of revolution and civil war, now locked their doors: 'Centuries-old sincerity and generosity did not exist any more. It disappeared with hungry stomachs.'[34] Parents warned their children to beware of neighbours whom they had known all their lives: no one knew who might turn out to be a thief, a spy – or a cannibal. No one wanted others to learn how they had survived either. 'Trust disappeared,' wrote Mariia Doronenko: 'Anyone who got hold of food, or who discovered a means of obtaining food, kept the secret to themselves, refusing to tell even the closest family members.'[35]

Empathy disappeared as well, and not only among the hungriest. The desperation and hysteria of the starving inspired horror and fear, even among those who still had enough to eat. An anonymous letter that eventually found its way into the Vatican archives described the feeling of being around the starving:

In the evening and even in the daytime it is not possible to bring bread home uncovered. The hungry will stop and seize it out of your hands, and often bite your hands or wound them with a knife. I have never seen faces so thin and savage, and bodies so little covered with rags . . . It is necessary to live here to understand and believe the scope of the disaster. Even today, having been to the market, I saw two men dead of hunger whom soldiers threw on a cart on top of each other. How can we live?[36]

As during the Holocaust, the witnesses of intense suffering did not always feel – perhaps could not feel – pity. Instead, they turned their anger on the sufferer.[37] Propaganda encouraged this feeling: the Communist Party loudly and angrily blamed the Ukrainian peasants for their fate, and so did others too. An inhabitant of Mariupol remembered a particularly ugly scene:

One day, as I waited in a queue in front of the store to buy bread, I saw a farm girl of about 15 years of age, in rags, and with starvation looking out of her eyes. She stretched her hand out to everyone who bought bread, asking for a few crumbs. At last she reached the storekeeper. This man must have been some newly arrived stranger who either could not, or would not, speak Ukrainian. He began to berate her, said she was too lazy to work on the farm, and hit her outstretched hand with the blunt edge of a knife blade. The girl fell down and lost a crumb of bread she was holding in the other hand. Then the storekeeper stepped closer, kicked the girl and roared: 'Get up! Go home and get to work!' The girl groaned, stretched out and died. Some in the queue began to weep. The communist storekeeper noticed it and threatened: 'Some are getting too sentimental here. It is easy to spot enemies of the people.'[38]

Hunger also heightened suspicion of strangers and outsiders, even children. The residents of cities became particularly hostile towards any peasants who managed to get through police blockades and enter urban areas in order to beg, or indeed any city-dwellers who could not find anything to eat either. Anastasiia Kh., a child in Kharkiv during the famine, was taken by her father several times to stand outside a cafeteria to receive uneaten scraps of food – until a 'well-dressed man' eventually screamed at them and told them to go away.[39] But she also had the reverse experience. Once, having managed to buy a loaf of bread, she was hurrying home with it. She was stopped by a peasant woman, carrying a baby, who begged her to share it. Thinking of her family, she hurried away: 'No sooner had I walked away than the unfortunate woman keeled over and died. Fear gripped my heart, for it seemed that her wide open eyes were accusing me of denying her bread. They came and took her baby away, which in death she continued to hold in a tight grip. The vision of this dead woman haunted me for a long time afterwards. I was unable to sleep at night, because I kept seeing her before me.'[40]

In these circumstances the rules of ordinary morality no longer made sense. Theft from neighbours, cousins, the collective farm, workplaces became widespread. Among those who suffered, stealing was widely condoned. Neighbours stole chickens from other neighbours, and then defended themselves however they could.[41] People locked their homes from the outside in the daytime and from the inside at night, one anonymous letter-writer complained to the Dnipropetrovsk province committee: 'There is no guarantee that someone won't break in, take your last food and kill you, too. Where to seek help? The militia men are hungry and scared.'[42]

Anybody who worked in a state institution – a collective farm, a school, an office – also stole whatever he or she could. People put grain in their pockets, shoved grain into their shoes, before walking out of public buildings. Others dug secret holes into wooden work implements and hid grain inside them.[43] People stole horses – even from militia headquarters – cows, sheep and pigs, slaughtered them and ate them. In a single district of Dnipropetrovsk province, thirty horses were stolen from collective farms in April and May 1933; in another district thieves stole fifty cows. In some places, peasants were reportedly keeping their cows, if they had them, inside their houses at night.[44]

People also stole seed reserves, which had of course been confiscated from them and were now kept in storage facilities. Often the quantities were small – collective farm workers were regularly caught filling their pockets. But so widespread did this problem become that in March 1933 the Ukrainian authorities issued a special decree instructing the OGPU, militia and activist teams to protect the seeds and punish those caught under the harsh law of 7 August. Special mobile court sessions were set up to hasten prosecution.[45]

No one felt at all guilty anymore about stealing communal property. Of his thefts during the famine period, one man wrote, 'At that time we did not think that this was a big sin, nor did we remember that we probably killed someone by depriving them of food.'[46] Ivan Brynza and his childhood friend, Volodia, stood outside a grain elevator and joined the mad scramble every time some kernels fell to the ground:

> The sacks would rip apart, but the keen-eyed NKVD troops would immediately surround the spot and shout: 'Don't you dare touch socialist property!' The spilled grain was put into new sacks, but a dozen or so grains would always be left behind in the dust. Hungry children would throw themselves onto the dust, trying to scrape up as much of it as possible. But in that 'battle' those children would be beaten and crushed. Weak from hunger, they never got up from the ground.[47]

Sometimes the theft was on a much larger scale. In January 1933 an inspection of bread factories and bakeries in Ukraine revealed that workers all across the republic were hoarding bread and flour on a massive scale, either for personal use or to sell on the black market. As a result, virtually all of the bread available for sale in the official shops was 'of bad quality', containing excessive amounts of air and water, as well as fillers – sawdust, other grains – instead of wheat. In some cases the factories were controlled by 'criminal organizations' that bartered the bread in exchange for other kinds of food products. Account books were also massaged on a massive scale to hide these trades.[48]

This transformation of honest people into thieves was only the beginning. As the weeks passed, the famine literally drove people crazy, provoking irrational anger and more extraordinary acts of aggression. 'The famine was horrible, but that was not the only thing, people became so angry and wild, it was scary to go outside,' recalled one survivor. A boy at the time, he remembered that a neighbour's son teased other children with a loaf of bread and jam that his family had procured. The other children began throwing stones at him, eventually beating him to death. Another boy died in the ensuing battle for the loaf of bread.[49] Adults were no better equipped to cope with the rage brought on by hunger: one survivor remembered that a neighbour became so angered by the sounds of his own children crying for food that he smothered his baby in its cradle, and killed two of his other children by slamming their heads against a wall. Only one of his sons managed to escape.[50]

A similar story was recorded by the secret police in Vinnytsia province, where one farmer, unable to bear the thought of his children starving to death, 'lit a fire in the stove and closed the chimney' in order to kill them: 'The children began to suffocate and cry for help because of the fumes, then he strangled them with his own hands, after which he went to the village council and confessed . . .' The farmer said he had committed the murders because 'there was nothing to eat'. During a subsequent search of his home, no food was found at all.[51]

Vigilantism became widespread. Armed guards would shoot gleaners on sight, and anyone who tried to steal from a warehouse met with the same fate. As the famine worsened, ordinary people also took vengeance on those who stole. Oleksii Lytvynskyi remembered seeing a collective farm boss pick up a boy who had stolen bread and slam his head against a tree – a murder for which he was never held responsible.[52] Hanna Tsivka knew of a woman who killed her niece for stealing a loaf of bread.[53] Mykola Basha's older brother was caught looking for spoiled potatoes in the kitchen garden of a neighbour, who then grabbed him and put him in a cellar filled with waist-high water.[54] Another survivor's aunt was stabbed to death with a pitchfork for stealing scallions from a neighbour's yard.[55]

Sometimes the vigilantism took hold of a whole group. At the 'New Union' collective farm in Dnipropetrovsk province a mob – including the farm chairman, the local veterinarian and the accountant – beat a collective farmer to death for stealing a jug of milk and a few biscuits.[56] When peasants from a nearby village stole a sheep from the collective farm in Rashkova Sloboda, Chernihiv province, a hunt was organized. The farmers from Rashkova Sloboda found the four culprits, surrounded them – and shot them on the spot. Mykola

Opanasenko was a witness to this attack as a child. Later, he had another reflection: 'A bitter question arises: who imbued the peasants' soul with so much animal ferocity that they dealt so mercilessly with people?'[57]

Sometimes the lynch mobs tortured their victims. In Vinnytsia province a mob kept a woman suspected of theft without food and water in a barn for two days before burying her alive. In another Vinnytsia district a twelve-year-old girl, Mariia Sokyrko, was murdered for stealing onions. In Kyiv province the head of a village council 'arrested' two teenage girls accused of theft and burned their arms with matches, stabbed them with needles, and beat them so badly that one died and the other was hospitalized.[58] So common was this kind of behaviour that in June 1933 the Ukrainian government ordered prosecutors to prevent 'mob law' by putting the perpetrators on public trial. Dozens of small-scale 'show trials' took place across Ukraine in June and July, but lynch mobs nevertheless continued to be reported across Ukraine in 1934 and even 1935.[59]

'Animal ferocity' could evolve further. Real insanity of various kinds – hallucinations, psychosis, depression – soon resulted from hunger. A woman whose six children died over three days in May 1933 lost her mind, stopped wearing clothes, unbraided her hair, and told everyone that the 'red broom' had taken her family away.[60] One survivor recalled the horrific story of Varvara, a neighbour who was left alone with two children. At the beginning of 1933, Varvara took her remaining clothes and travelled to a nearby city in the hope of exchanging them for bread. She succeeded, and returned home with a whole loaf. But when she cut the bread, she began to scream: the bread was not a whole loaf, it was stuffed with a paper sack – which meant that once again there was nothing to eat. She took the knife, turned around, stuck it into her son's back and began laughing hysterically; her daughter saw what was happening, and ran for her life.[61]

In time, all of these emotions subsided – to be replaced by complete indifference. Sooner or later, hunger made everyone listless, unable to move or think. People sat on benches in their farmyards, beside the roadside, in their houses – and didn't move. Bustling villages grew quiet, recalled Mykola Proskovchenko, who survived the famine in Odessa province. 'It was a strange silence everywhere. Nobody cried, moaned, complained . . . Indifference was everywhere: people were either swollen or completely exhausted . . . Even a kind of envy was felt toward the dead.'[62] In the spring of 1933, Oleksandra Radchenko wrote in her diary in the middle of the night: 'It is already three o'clock in the morning, meaning that today is 27 April. I am not sleeping. The last days have been filled with a terrible apathy . . .'[63]

'No one feels sorry for anyone,' wrote another survivor, Halyna Budantseva: 'nothing is wished, no one even wants to eat. You wander with no goal in the yard, on the street. After a while, you don't want to walk, there is no strength for that. You lie and wait for death.' She recovered because an uncle came to rescue her. But her sister Tania died on the way to the uncle's village.[64]

Petro Hryhorenko, at that time a student at a military academy, witnessed this indifference when in December 1931 he received an odd letter from his stepmother, alluding to his father's ill health. Alarmed, Petro returned to his village. There he discovered that his father, an enthusiastic proponent of collectivization, was now starving. Petro walked into the office of the local collective farm to inform the officials that he would take his parents away:

> The accountant was a friend of mine from our Komsomol days. He was sitting there alone. 'Good day, Kolia!' I said in greeting. He just sat there, staring at the table. Without even raising his head he said, as if we'd parted five minutes earlier, 'Ah, Petro.' He was completely apathetic. 'So you've come for your father? Now, take him away. Maybe he'll survive. We won't.'[65]

Vasily Grossman described this stage of hunger in *Forever Flowing*:

> In the beginning, starvation drives a person out of the house. In its first stage, he is tormented and driven as though by fire and torn both in the guts and in the soul. And so he tries to escape from this home. People dig up worms, collect grass, and even make the effort to break through and get to the city. Away from home, away from home! And then a day comes when the starving person crawls back into his house. And the meaning of this is that famine, starvation, has won. The

human being cannot be saved. He lies down on his bed and stays there. Not just because he has no strength, but because he has no interest in life and no longer cares about living. He lies there quietly and does not want to be touched. And he does not even want to eat . . . all he wants is to be left alone and for things to be quiet . . .'[66]

Public officials were also shocked by the general indifference. As early as August 1932 a police informer told his contacts that a colleague, a bank employee, had confided in him his 'complete collapse of faith in a better future'. He explained: 'Deep hopelessness can be felt by all urban and rural dwellers, both old and young, party members and non-members of the party. Both intellectuals and the representatives of physical work lose muscle strength and intellectual energy because they think only about how to stop the feeling of hunger in themselves and their children.'[67]

In an extensive report sent to Kaganovich and Kosior in June 1933, a party official working at a machine tractor station in Kamianskyi district reported that in his area people were dying of hunger in the thousands. He listed example after example of people dying in the fields during work, people dying on the way home, people unable even to leave their homes at all. But he too observed the growing indifference. 'People have grown dull, they absolutely do not react,' he wrote. 'Not to mortality, not to cannibalism, not to anything.'[68]

Indifference soon spread to death itself. Traditional Ukrainian funerals had combined church and folk traditions, and included a choir, a meal, the singing of psalms, readings from the Bible, sometimes professional mourners. Now all such rites were banned.[69] Nobody had the strength anymore to dig a grave, hold a ceremony, or play music. Religious practices disappeared along with churches and priests. For a culture that had valued its rituals highly, the impossibility of saying a proper farewell to the dead became another source of trauma: 'There were no funerals,' recalled Kateryna Marchenko. 'There were no priests, requiems, tears. There was no strength to cry.'[70]

One woman remembered her grandfather being buried without a coffin. He was placed in a hole in the ground together with a neighbour and her two sons: 'His children did not cry over him and did not sing, according to a Christian tradition, "Eternal remembrance".'[71]

Another man recalled how his friends treated their dying father: 'We children went to the fields in 1933 and looked for frozen potatoes. Those frozen potatoes we brought home and made 'cookies' from them . . . Once I called on my friends who were just waiting for their 'cookies' [to be ready]. Their father was lying on a bench swollen and unable to get up. He asked his children to give him only one piece and they refused. "Go and find potatoes for yourself," they answered.' The man died that evening.[72]

Another boy was simply rendered helpless:

> Mother had gone away, I was sleeping atop of our stove, and woke before sunrise. 'Dad, I want to eat, Dad!' The house was cold. Dad was not answering. I started to shout. Dawn broke; my father had some foam under his nose. I touched his head – cold. Then a cart arrived, there were corpses in it, lying like sheaves. Two men entered the house, put father on a burlap sack, threw his body on a cart with a swing . . . After that I could not sleep in the house, I slept in stables and haystacks, I was swollen and ragged.[73]

In many cases there were no family members either to care for the dying or to bury the dead at all. Public buildings were quickly turned into primitive mortuaries. In March 1933, Anna S. learned that her school was to be closed due to an 'epidemic of dysentery and typhoid fever'. Desks were removed from the classrooms, hay was strewn on the floor, and the starving were brought in to die, parents and children lying alongside one another.[74] Individual homes sometimes served the same purpose. In Zhytomyr province local authorities broke into two houses when neighbours reported that there had been no smoke from the chimneys for several days. Inside they found the elderly, the adults, the children: 'Dead bodies laid on a stove, on the bench beside, on the bed.' All the corpses were thrown into a well, and dirt was poured in on top of them.[75] Bodies were sometimes not discovered right away. The winter of 1933 was bitter cold, and in many places it was only possible to bury the dead after the ground began to thaw. Dogs and wolves attacked the bodies.[76] That spring, 'the air was filled with the ubiquitous odour of decomposing bodies. The wind carried this odour far and wide, all across Ukraine.'[77]

Train stations, railway tracks and roads also began to accumulate corpses. Peasants who had attempted to escape died where they sat or stood, and were then 'collected as firewood and carried away'.[78] One eyewitness travelled through a region laid waste by famine with her mother in March 1933 and remembered seeing corpses lying or sometimes sitting along the route. 'The coachman tore a piece of burlap he had with him and covered the faces of these dead people.'[79]

Others did not even bother with that. One railway employee, Oleksandr Honcharenko, remembered 'walking along the railroad tracks every morning on the way to work, I would come upon two or three corpses daily, but I would step over them and continue walking. The famine had robbed me of my conscience, human soul and feelings. Stepping over corpses I felt absolutely nothing, as if I were stepping over logs.'[80] Petro Mostovyi remembered the beggars who came to his village seemed 'like ghosts', sat down beside roads or under fences – and died. 'Nobody buried them, our own grief was enough.' To add to the horror, wild cats and dogs gnawed their bodies. A child at the time, Mostovyi was afraid to go to a hamlet near his village because all of its inhabitants had died, and no one was left to bury them. They were left as they were, inside their houses and barns, for many weeks.[81] The result was epidemics of typhus and other diseases.[82]

In the cities, where the authorities still wanted to conceal the horror occurring in the countryside, the men of the OGPU often collected bodies at night and buried them in secret. Between February and June 1933, for example, the OGPU in Kharkiv recorded that it had surreptitiously buried 2,785 corpses.[83] A few years later, during the Great Terror of 1937–8, this secrecy was enforced even further. Mass graves of famine victims were covered up and hidden, and it became dangerous even to know where they were located. In 1938 all the staff of the Lukianivske cemetery in Kyiv were arrested, tried and shot as counter-revolutionary insurgents, probably to prevent them from revealing what they knew.[84]

In larger towns and villages local officials organized teams to collect corpses. Sometimes these teams consisted of Komsomol members.[85] In the late spring of 1933 some were soldiers, sent from outside, who ordered local people to cooperate and keep silent about it.[86] Others were simply able-bodied enough to dig mass graves, and willing to work in exchange for food. One survivor reckoned that she lived through the famine because she had been appointed as a grave-digger and thus received half a loaf of bread and one herring every day.[87] Another recalled that these brigades received bread in exchange for corpses. 'When 40 people died during the day, they received a good fee.'[88] Often, especially in cities such as Kyiv and Kharkiv, the corpse collection teams worked at night, the better to conceal the scale of their task.[89]

Group burials, hastily arranged, occurred without any ceremony at all. 'People were buried without coffins, were simply thrown into the pits and pelted with earth,' recalled one witness.[90] Alternatively, the local burial team dug a grave on the spot where a corpse was lying without trying to identify the person or mark the spot. 'The small hill quickly disappeared after a few heavy rains, overgrew with grass, and no traces were left.'[91] One survivor's grandmother drove a cattle cart from house to house. If she saw ravens, 'that meant there were dead bodies'. When she found individuals not quite dead, she pulled them closer to the door 'so that it would be easier to carry them out' later on.[92] The mass grave sites were often not marked. In some places younger generations, a few years later, could no longer locate them.[93]

Some burial teams may have stretched indifference to the point of cruelty. Many survivors, from various parts of Ukraine, repeat stories of very ill people being buried alive. 'There were cases when they buried half-living people: "Good people, leave me alone. I am not dead," the "corpses" used to cry. "Go to hell! You want us to come tomorrow again?" was the reply.'[94] Another team also took away still-living people, arguing that the next day they would be on another street, so they might as well take their body now, get the 'payment' for each 'corpse' and eat more themselves.[95] Many felt that, once they had dug the mass graves, it didn't matter how they were filled. 'They didn't even shoot, they econo-mized on bullets and pulled living people into the hole.'[96] Even families treated their dying members the same. One grandmother fell ill and lost consciousness. 'When she fell into a sleep-like state, everyone at home thought she was dead. When they came to bury her, however, they noticed that she was still breathing, but they buried her anyway because they said she was going to die anyway. No one was sorry.'[97]

Some, however, managed to escape. One man, Denys Lebid, has described being thrown into a mass grave himself. He tried to get out, but discovered he was too weak. He sat there and waited for death, or for another corpse to fall on top of him. He was eventually rescued by a tractor driver who had come to bulldoze earth over the pit.[98] His story was echoed by that of a woman who was rescued from a mass grave by another woman passing by who heard her screams.[99] Similar stories originate from Cherkasy, Kyiv, Zhytomyr and Vinnytsia provinces, among others.[100]

Anyone who had ever witnessed such a thing – or, worse, experienced it – never forgot. 'I was so frightened by what had happened that I could not talk for several days. I saw dead bodies in my dreams. And I screamed a lot . . .'[101]

The horror, the exhaustion, the inhuman indifference to life and constant exposure to the language of hatred left their mark. Combined with the complete absence of food they also produced, in the Ukrainian countryside, a very rare form of madness: by the late spring and summer, cannibalism was widespread. Even more extraordinarily, its existence was no secret, not in Kharkiv, Kyiv, or Moscow.[102]

Many survivors witnessed either cannibalism or, far more often, necrophagy, the consumption of corpses of people who had died of starvation. But although the phenomenon was widespread, it never became 'normal', and – despite the assertion by the machine tractor station official that people were unaffected by cannibalism – it was rarely treated with indifference. Memories of cannibalism often divide between those who heard stories of it having taking place in other distant villages and those who recall actual incidents. The former, distant in either time or space, do sometimes describe cannibalism as having become 'ordinary'. Ten years after the famine, a traveller in Nazi-occupied Ukraine claimed to have met 'men and women who were openly said to have eaten people . . . the population considers such cases the result of extreme need, without condemning them'.[103] A report from the head of the OGPU in Kyiv province to his superiors in the Ukrainian OGPU also mentions cannibalism becoming a 'habit'. In some villages, 'the view that it is possible to consume human meat grows stronger every day. This opinion spreads especially among hungry and swollen children.'[104]

But those who did actually witness an incident of cannibalism almost always remembered it much differently. Both memoir and documents from the time confirm that cannibalism caused shock and horror, and sometimes led to the intervention of the police or village council.

Larysa Venzhyk, from Kyiv province, remembered that at first there were just rumours, stories 'that children disappear somewhere, that degenerate parents eat their children. It turned out not to be rumours but horrible truth.' On her street two girls, the daughters of neighbours, disappeared. Their brother Misha, aged six, ran away from home. He roamed the village, begging and stealing. When asked why he had left home he said he was afraid: 'Father will cut me up.' The police searched the house, found the evidence, and arrested the parents. As for their remaining son, 'Misha was left to his fate.'[105]

Police also arrested a man in Mariia Davydenko's village in Sumy province. After his wife died, he had gone mad from hunger and eaten first his daughter and then his son. A neighbour noticed that the father was less swollen from hunger than others, and asked him why. 'I have eaten my children,' he replied, 'and if you talk too much, I will eat you.' Backing away, shouting that he was a monster, the neighbour went to the police, who arrested and sentenced the father.[106]

In Vinnytsia province survivors also recalled the fate of Iaryna, who had butchered her own child. She told the story herself: 'Something happened to me. I put the child in a small basin, and he asked: "What are you going to do, Mummy?" I replied: "Nothing, nothing."' But a neighbour who was standing guard over his potatoes outside her window somehow saw what was happening and reported her to the village council. She served a three-year sentence but eventually returned home. Eventually she remarried – but when she told her husband what she had done during the famine, he turned against her.[107] Even many years later, the stigma remained.

Mykola Moskalenko also remembered the horror his own family felt when learning that the children of a neighbour had disappeared. He told his mother about it, and she told the local authorities. Together, a group of villagers gathered around the neighbour's farm: 'We entered her house and asked her where her children were. She said that they died and she had buried them in the field. We went to the field but found nothing. They started a search of her home: the children had been cut up . . . they asked why she had done this, and she answered that her children would not survive anyway, but this way she would.' She was taken away, presumably sentenced.[108]

Stories such as that one spread rapidly and enhanced the atmosphere of threat. Even in the cities, people repeated stories of children being hunted down as food. Sergio Gradenigo, the Italian consul, reported that in Kharkiv parents all brought their children personally to school, and accompanied them at all times, out of fear that starving people were hunting them: 'Children of party leaders and OGPU are especially targeted because they have better clothes than other children. Trade of human meat becomes more active.'[109]

Ukrainian authorities knew about many of the incidents: police reports contained great detail. But Balytsky made special efforts to prevent the stories from spreading. Ukraine's secret police boss warned his subordinates against putting too much information about the famine into writing: 'provide information on the food problems solely to the First Secretaries of the Party Provincial Committees and only orally . . . This is to ensure that written notes on the subject do not circulate among the officials where they might cause rumours . . .'[110]

Nevertheless, the secret police, the ordinary criminal police and other local officials did keep records. One police report from Kyiv province in April 1933 began with 'We have an extraordinary case of cannibalism in the Petrovskyi district':

A kulak woman, aged fifty, from the Zelenky, Bohuslavskyi district, hiding in Kuban since 1932, returned to her home town with her (adult) daughter. Along the road from Horodyshchenska station to Korsun, she lured a passing twelve-year-old boy and slit his throat. The organs and other parts of the body she placed in a bag. In the village of Horodyshche, citizen Sherstiuk, an inhabitant of that place, allowed the woman to spend the night. In a dishonest manner, she pretended that the organs came from a calf, and gave it to the old man to boil and to roast the heart. It was used to feed his whole family, and he ate it too. In the night, intending to use some of the meat which was in the bag, the old man discovered the chopped-up parts of the boy's body. The criminals have been arrested.[111]

Alongside the moral horror, many of the reports also reflect police concern that the stories could spread and have a political impact. In Dnipropetrovsk province the OGPU reported the story of a collective farm member, Ivan Dudnyk, who killed his son with an axe. 'The family is big, it is difficult to stay alive, so I murdered him,' the killer declared. But the police report noted, with approval, that the collective farm members met and adopted a group decision to hold a public trial and 'give Dudnyk capital punishment'.[112] It also noted, with satisfaction, that the villagers had decided to double down on their sowing campaign and increase their output in light of the incident.

Similarly, when a fourteen-year-old boy who murdered his sister for food in the village of Novooleksandrivka, in southeast Ukraine, the OGPU reported with satisfaction that the incident had sparked no 'unhealthy chatter'. All the neighbours believed the boy to be mentally ill, and only feared that he would be returned to the village.[113] In Dnipropetrovsk province a woman who murdered her daughter for food was, the OGPU noted, the wife of a man who had been arrested for refusing to give up his grain. Given that the woman showed signs of being a 'social danger', the police recommended execution.[114]

The real cause of this 'mental illness', or these sudden attacks of 'socially dangerous' emotions, was perfectly obvious to the police as well: people were starving. In Penkivka, the Vinnytsia OGPU reported, a collective farmer had killed two of his daughters and used their flesh for food: 'K. blamed the murder of his children on a long period of starvation. No foodstuffs were found during the search.' In the village of Dubyny another farmer killed both of his daughters too, and 'blamed the famine for committing the murders'. There were, the policemen stated, 'other analogous incidents'.[115]

Throughout the spring of 1933 the numbers of such cases grew. In Kharkiv province the OGPU reported multiple incidents where parents had eaten the flesh of children who had died from starvation, as well as cases where 'starving family members had killed weaker ones, usually children, and used their flesh as food'. Nine such cases were reported in March, fifty-eight in April, 132 in May and 221 in June.[116] In Donetsk province multiple incidents were also observed, again starting in March. 'Iryna Khrypunova strangled her nine-year-old granddaughter and cooked her internal organs. Anton Khrypunov removed his dead eight-year-old sister's internal organs and ate them.' That report concluded almost politely: 'By bringing this to your attention I request you provide appropriate instructions.'[117]

In March the OGPU in Kyiv province were receiving ten or more reports of cannibalism every day.[118] In that month their counter-parts in Vinnytsia province reported six incidents in the previous month of 'cannibalism caused by famine, in which parents killed their children and used their flesh for food'. But these may have been serious underestimates. In one report the OGPU boss of Kyiv province wrote that there were sixty-nine cases of cannibalism between 9 January and 12 March. However, 'these numbers are, obviously, not exact, because in reality there are many more such incidents'.[119]

Certainly, the authorities treated this as a crime, sometimes giving cannibals 'enemy' labels as well. Hanna Bilorus was convicted both of cannibalism and of spreading Polish propaganda, for example; she died in prison in 1933.[120] Secret police files contain multiple records of cannibals who were subsequently imprisoned, executed, or lynched. One very unusual Gulag memoirist has even described an encounter in 1935 with cannibals at the Solovetsky Island prison camp, in the White Sea. Olga Mane was a young Polish woman, arrested crossing the border into the Soviet Union in 1935 (she wanted to study medi-cine in Moscow) and sentenced for spying. After some time in the camp, she was sent to Muksalma, one of the islands in the Solovetsky archipelago. She resisted, because she had heard there were 'Ukrain-ian cannibals', some three hundred of them, on the island. But when she finally met them, she felt differently:

> Shock and horror of the cannibals quickly passed; it was enough to see these unhappy, barefoot, half-naked Ukrainians. They were kept in old monastery buildings: many of them had stomachs swollen from hunger, and most of them were mentally ill. I took care of them, lis-tened to their reminiscences and confidences. They described how their children died of hunger, and how they themselves, very close to starvation, cooked the corpses of their own children and ate them. This happened when they were in a state of shock caused by hunger. Later, when they came to understand what had happened, they lost their minds.

I felt sympathy for them, I tried to be kind, I found warm words for them when they were overcome by attacks of remorse. This helped for some time. They calmed down, started to cry and I cried along with them . . .[121]

Stories of cannibalism were known to the Ukrainian leadership, and to the Moscow leadership too. Kaganovich was, as noted, certainly informed; a Ukrainian Central Committee working group responsible for the spring sowing campaign in 1933 reported back to the party that their work was especially difficult in regions with 'cannibalism' and 'homeless children'.[122] The OGPU continued to report cases of cannibalism well into 1934.[123]

But if either Kharkiv or Moscow ever provided instructions on how to deal with cannibalism, or ever reflected more deeply on its causes, they haven't yet been uncovered. There is no evidence that any action was taken at all. The reports were made, the officials received them, and then they were filed away and forgotten.

12

Survival: Spring and Summer, 1933

I would go to the church up the hill and tear the bark off the linden tree. At home we had buckwheat husks. Mother would sift them, add ground-up linden leaves and bark, and bake biscuits. That's how we ate.

Hryhorii Mazurenko, Kyiv province, 1933[1]

As the gooseberries got bigger, we picked them, even though they weren't ripe. We ate wild geraniums. The acacia tree bloomed. We shook the blossoms off and ate them.

Vira Tyshchenko, Kyiv province, 1933[2]

We grazed on grass and pigweed, like cattle.

Todos Hodun, Cherkasy province, 1933[3]

Even in the face of these physical and psychological changes, even despite hunger, thirst, exhaustion and emaciation, people did their utmost to survive. To do so sometimes required an enormous capacity for evil – many survived in the activist brigades – or an ability to break some of the most fundamental human taboos. But others discovered huge reserves of talent and willpower – or else had the astonishing good luck to be saved by someone who possessed those qualities.

A ten-year-old girl from the Poltava region, observing the disintegration of the adults around her, had the extraordinary idea of abandoning her family. She wrote to her uncle in Kharkiv province:

Dear Uncle! We do not have bread and anything to eat. My parents are exhausted by hunger, they have lain down and do not get up. My mother is blind from hunger and cannot see, I have carried her outside. I want bread very much. Take me, uncle, to Kharkiv to you, because I will die of hunger. Take me, I am small and want to live, and here I will die, because everybody dies . . .[4]

She did not survive. But the same will to live saved others.

To survive, people ate anything. They ate whatever rotten food or scraps that the brigades had overlooked. They ate horses, dogs, cats, rats, ants, turtles. They boiled frogs and toads. They ate squirrels. They cooked hedgehogs over fires, and fried birds' eggs.[5] They ate the bark of oak trees. They ate moss and acorns.[6] They ate leaves and dandelions, as well as marigolds and orach, a kind of wild spinach. They killed crows, pigeons and sparrows.[7] Nadiia Lutsyshyna remembered that 'frogs didn't last long. People caught them all. All the cats were eaten, the pigeons, the frogs; people ate everything. I imagined the scent of delicious food as we ate weeds and beets.'[8]

Women made soup from nettles, and baked pigweed into bread. They pounded acorns, made ersatz flour, and then used the flour to make pancakes.[9] They cooked the buds from linden trees: 'They were good, soft, not bitter,' recalled one survivor.[10] They ate snowdrops, a weed whose roots took the form of an onion and 'seemed sweeter than sugar'.[11] People also made pancakes from leaves and grass.[12] Others mixed acacia leaves and rotten potatoes – often overlooked by the collection brigades – and baked them together to make ersatz *perepichky*, a traditional form of sausage wrapped in bread.[13] The starch inside rotten potatoes could also be scooped out and fried.[14] Nadiia Ovcharuk's aunt made biscuits out of the leaves of linden trees: 'she dried the leaves in the oven, pulled out the veins, and baked biscuits'.[15]

Children ate hemp seeds.[16] People ate the bottom part of river reeds, 'which when young, and close to the root, was sweet like cucumber', though they were denied even those when the authorities trampled and burned the reeds down.[17] In one village people ate the waste products from a slaughterhouse, until those running it poured carbolic acid over the bones and skin. Oksana Zhyhadno and her mother both ate some of the offal anyway, and became ill. Although her mother died, Oksana survived.[18] Many peasants remembered pouring water into the burrows made by field mice in order to wash out the grain stored by the rodents. Others boiled belts and shoes so as to eat the leather.

Just as they knew about the cases of cannibalism, the authorities were also well aware of the extraordinary things that people were trying to eat. A secret police report from March 1933 declared, in a matter-of-fact way, that starving families were eating 'corn cobs and stalks, millet pods, dried straw, herbs, rotten watermelons and beet-roots, potato peelings and acacia pods', as well as cats, dogs and horses.[19] Much of this food made sick people even sicker.

Some survived with less extraordinary types of food consumption, especially if they happened to reside near lakes or rivers. Kateryna Butko, who lived in a village near a river, reckoned that 'without fish, nobody would have survived'.[20] Those who could also used nets to find periwinkles. They boiled them and took the tiny bits of meat out of their shells.[21] Peasants who lived near forests could forage for mushrooms and berries, or trap birds and small animals.

Uncounted numbers of people were saved due to a far more pedestrian reason: they managed to hold on to the family cow. Even in good times cows were important for peasant families, which often had four or more children. But during the famine, possession of a cow, either by individual farmers who had avoided collectivization and confiscation, or by collective farmers who were allowed, as some were, to keep one for private use, was literally a matter of life or death. In hundreds of oral testimonies peasants explain their survival with a single sentence: 'We were saved by our cow.' Most lived off the milk; many, like one family in Kyiv province, used their cow's milk as a form of barter, exchanging it for grain or bread.[22]

Emotions about the cow ran high. Petro Mostovyi in Poltava province remembered that the family cow was so precious that his father and older brother guarded it with a gun and pitchforks.[23] After a thief stole a cow from another peasant in Cherkasy province, the owner learned that it had been slaughtered and that the meat had been stored by one of her neighbours. She marched over to the storehouse and 'put out the eyes of her exhausted enemy with a rake'.[24] To feed their cow, Mariia Pata's family had to take the roof thatch off their house, rip it into small pieces, and soften it with boiling water so that the animal could eat.[25]

Those who did not have a cow often had to rely on others. Random acts of kindness saved some people, as did ties of love and kinship that persisted despite the hunger. In Poltava province Sofiia Zalyvcha and two of her siblings hired themselves out to a collective farm as day labourers. As payment, they received thin soup and 200 grams of bread per day. They ate the soup and saved the bread. Every weekend one of them went home to the family – they had seven additional siblings – and shared the stale bread with their brothers and sisters. Three of the ten children died during the famine, but thanks to the bread or soup the rest survived.[26]

Other children lived because they were adopted by neighbours or relatives. 'My parents' cousin and her husband were leaving for Kharkiv, and they took me and my little sister along ... because of this we survived,' one girl remembered. 'Even today I remember my aunt Marfa with gratitude and warmth as she saved my life in those years of famine,' said another.[27]

Relatives outside Ukraine could help too. Anatolii Bakai's sister, who had moved to the Urals, sent home five kilograms of flour. In an accompanying letter she wrote that there was no famine in the Urals, and that not everybody there even believed there was famine in Ukraine. The flour was not enough to save Anatolii's mother, but it helped keep him alive.[28] Ihor Buhaievych and his grandmother survived in Chernihiv province on dried bread crusts that his mother mailed in packages from Leningrad, where she had managed to find a job. That helped keep them alive until the local post office informed the activist brigade, which began confiscating some of the crusts. Later, Ihor's mother came home and managed to take him to Leningrad herself.[29]

There is anecdotal evidence that some Ukrainian peasants had help from their Jewish neighbours: again, most Jews were not farmers and were therefore not subjected to the deadly requisitions, unless they lived in a blacklisted village. Mariia Havrysh in Vinnytsia province remembered being visited by a Jewish neighbour – 'they were spared because they had no land' – at a time when she was ill, swollen and expecting to die. The woman came over, prepared a meal and fed the whole family, leaving them with some bread and vodka as well, 'thus saving the whole family'.[30] At a time when hatred and suspicion of all kinds were rising, the gesture was a powerful one.

Despite the bans on travel and trade, Ukrainian peasants, as noted, tried both. They crept through cordons and crawled under fences to get into the cities to beg for food. They tried to enter factory towns and industrial worksites. They slipped into the mining towns in Donbas where workers were needed and the foreman might turn a blind eye. They searched near factories for waste that might be edible, for example the debris tossed out by distilleries or packaging plants. They also picked up whatever scraps they could find and tried to sell them. Arthur Koestler, the Hungarian-German writer who was at that time a faithful communist, has left a memorable portrait of a market he saw in Kharkiv in 1933:

> Those who had something to sell squatted in the dust with their goods spread out before them on a handkerchief or scarf. The goods ranged from a handful of rusty nails to a tattered quilt or a pot of sour milk sold by the spoon, flies included. You could see an old woman sitting for hours with one painted Easter egg or one small piece of dried-up goat's cheese before her. Or an old man, his bare feet covered with sores, trying to barter his torn boots for a kilo of black bread and a packet of makhorka tobacco. Hemp slippers, and even soles and heels torn off from boots and replaced by a bandage of rags, were frequent items for barter. Some old men had nothing to sell; they sang Ukrainian ballads and were rewarded by an occasional kopeck. Some of the women had babies lying beside them on the pavement or in their laps; the fly-ridden infant's lips were fastened to the leathery udder from which it seemed to suck bile instead of milk.[31]

The fact that a bazaar – even the barest bazaar – was allowed to exist in urban Ukraine meant that there was, for some people, a lifeline. But the real reason why the cities were less desperate was rationing: workers and bureaucrats received food coupons. These were not available to everybody. According to a 1931 law, all Soviet citizens who worked for the state sector received ration cards. That left out peasants; it also omitted others without formal jobs. In addition, the size of rations was based not only on the importance of the worker, but also of his workplace. Priority went to key industrial regions, and the only one in Ukraine was Donbas. In practice, some 40 per cent of the Ukrainian population therefore received about 80 per cent of the food supplies.[32]

For those not ranked high on the list, rations could be paltry. Visiting Kyiv in 1932, Andrew Cairns, a Canadian agricultural expert, saw two women picking grass in a city park to make soup. They told him that they had rations, but not enough: 'I pointed to the river and remarked that it was very beautiful; they agreed but said they were hungry.' In fact, the women were 'third category' workers who received 125 rubles per month, plus 200 grams of bread a day – about four slices.[33]

The manager of a cooperative store in Kyiv, another 'third category' worker, also told Cairns that he received 200 grams of bread per day and 200 grams for his son, as well as 100 rubles every month. A 'second category' worker got 525 grams of bread each day, and 180 rubles per month. None of that went very far in the municipal bazaars, which sold very little beyond bread, tomatoes and sometimes chicken or dairy products, and all of those at very high prices. Bread could cost five or six rubles a kilo, an egg could cost half a ruble or more, milk two rubles a litre.[34] Peter Egides, a student in Kyiv at the time, received a stipend that was less than the price of a single loaf of bread: 'the situation reached the point where at the age of seventeen I was walking with a cane because I didn't even have the strength to walk'. Egides' grandmother eventually did die of starvation, though she lived in Kyiv as well.[35]

Theoretically, state-run shops should have sold food at lower, more accessible prices. But those shops were empty. Heorhii Sambros, a teacher and state official who kept a diary in those years, has left a memorable description of the shops of Kharkiv. In all of them 'great spaces', once filled from floor to ceiling with products, were either totally empty or filled with nothing but pure alcohol ('bottles of vodka, as if a rainfall, came down to flood the entire city'). Very occasionally they sold food, but it was almost too revolting to contemplate:

> Only in some stores, and on the counter, were [there] the usual 'products', five or six trays or platters of hurriedly prepared dishes. Cold salad, looking like silage, from a rotten, disgusting sauerkraut; a paté from fish remains with soaked cabbage and salty, cut pickles; rarely, pieces of frozen meat with a sauce that looked like shoe paste, soaked

green tomatoes with the smell of a rotten barrel; frozen, sour, filled baked tomatoes with overly peppered, so as not to stink, meat filling, prepared from the remains of some uncertain meat; finally, rarely, such delicacies as boiled eggs or some small fruits, etc. All those dishes (I remember them vividly!) would be put on the counter and were immediately bought out by the buyers.[36]

Andrew Cairns also managed to get into a queue at a shop where he saw 'heavy, warm, soggy bread being sold for 10 rubles per loaf, and a little pork fat at 12 rubles per pound'.[37]

Better-quality food was available in the government canteens attached to every workplace: soups, kasha, occasionally meat. But special certification – a party card or a trade union card – was needed to use them. Sambros, who had neither of these things, befriended a secretary at the educational institute where he worked, and she gave him meal coupons without asking for his membership card: 'at the time I lived, breathed and ate meals "as an outlaw", illegally'. When food shortages grew worse and the institute began to verify who could get meal coupons, he went through an acquaintance to get access to the Ukrainian Writers' House:

> I was aware of the risks: they could have come up to my table, asked for the writer's membership card and shamed me by pulling me out from the table. But there was no other way, I had to take the risk, and thus started frequenting the writers' canteen. I was lucky: I ate there for about 1 1/2 to 2 months and no one asked who I was, not once . . .[38]

Sambros later wangled his way into the Agricultural Academy canteen, and ate there for a few weeks too. As a result, he stayed alive. But he spent most of his waking hours thinking about food: his 'entire salary, almost without exception, went to food'.[39] And he, of course, was far better off than so many others.

Although he was not a peasant, Sambros's experience was in a certain sense typical: paradoxically, the most important source of help for the starving came from Soviet bureaucrats and Soviet bureaucracies. The historian Timothy Snyder has described how state institutions in Nazi-occupied Europe, when they were still functioning, could rescue Jews from the Holocaust, and a parallel story can be told about Stalin's Soviet Union.[40] While the Bolsheviks had systematically destroyed independent institutions, including churches, charities and private companies, state institutions remained – schools, hospitals, orphanages – and some of them were in a position to help. Some of them, theoretically, even had a mandate to do so.

Those best able to help the starving were relatives, parents or children who had jobs inside the system. Petro Shelest, who much later became First Secretary of the Ukrainian Communist Party, wrote a memoir of those years – it began as a diary – which was finally published by his family in 2004. The tragedy of 1933 was clear to him at the time: 'Entire families, even entire villages were starving to death. There were numerous cases of cannibalism . . . It was obviously a crime committed by our government, yet this fact is kept shamefully secret.' In that period Shelest was studying and working as an engineer at an armaments factory. But he was also a Communist Party member in good standing, and that enabled him to send food to his mother. His aid rescued her from starvation in Kharkiv province.[41]

Contacts and friends helped too: one young girl in Poltava province survived the famine because her father had studied on an agricultural course with a man who wound up working in the local government. Surreptitiously, this friend arranged for her family to receive a replacement for their confiscated cow – and thus they lived.[42] Another girl was fortunate enough to have an aunt married to the collective farm chairman: 'I came to her because she had bread, lard and milk. She gave them to me by stealth so that nobody knew.'[43] Often a single person with a job inside the system could save an entire family. Nadiia Malyshko's mother got a job as a cleaner in a school in Dnipropetrovsk province, where the director helped her get a food ration: a quarter-litre of oil and eight kilograms of corn flour every month.[44] Four of seven children in Varvara Horban's family, also in Dnipropetrovsk province, survived because she went to work at a grain elevator and received a small loaf of bread every day.[45]

Those who could not find employment with the state sometimes tried to save their children by turning them over to the state. One mother took her four children to the head office of the local collective farm, declared she could not feed them, renounced responsibility and told the farm chairmen they were now in charge.[46] Halyna Tymosh-chuk's mother in Vinnytsia province made the same decision:

> My mother went to the head of the collective ... and said, 'At least take my two girls. And we'll die, if that's how it has to be.' He was kind and I know he liked mother. And so he said, 'Bring your two children.' And he took us in. His wife was in charge of the nursery, and my sister became her helper. Later, my mother worked at the nursery canteen as a dishwasher. I was still young at the time, only eight. The head of the collective took me into his home. So we survived while others died, all of them, it seems – many, many.[47]

Orphanages were a more common destination. During a three-week period in February 1933, some 105 children were left at the doors of orphanages in the province of Vinnytsia alone.[48] Sometimes it worked: one boy lived through the famine because his mother brought him secretly to an orphanage in the village of Dryzhyna. She told him not to tell anybody that she was alive, as he might not be given food if he wasn't a 'real' orphan. A woman at the orphanage, understanding the situation, also told him not to mention his mother. She protected him, helped him survive the famine and eventually he was reunited with his family.[49] A woman from Poltava province also remained grateful to the end of her life because a teacher in the village school risked her own status and quietly fed her and her siblings, although they were 'children of kulaks'. It wasn't much – broth with no bread, and tiny buckwheat dumplings 'the size of a kidney bean' – but it was enough to keep them all alive.[50]

Across the republic, the sight of starving children wandering the streets did spur the employees of some Soviet institutions into more systematic action. Those who were truly motivated were sometimes able to help, and especially to assist children. Proof that it was possible, at least at a local level, to advocate on behalf of starving orphans comes from a series of letters sent from the party committee boss in Pavlohrad to his superiors in Dnipropetrovsk. In the first, dated 30 March, he described, among other things, the impact of the famine on children:

> Masses of homeless children appeared in our village who have been abandoned by their parents or left behind after their deaths.

According to approximate numbers, there are at least 800 such children. There is a need for two to three special orphanages that will require funds that we do not have in our budget. In the meantime, we are beginning to organize special food supplies for them. For this we need extra stocks of food. I would ask you to please take this into account and direct us according to the correct Soviet policy.[51]

A month later, on 30 April, the Pavlohrad party committee secretary sent in another report. 'By comparison to what I have written to you in previous reports, we have every day a larger and larger increase in homelessness.' In the past two days alone, sixty-five children had been picked up on the streets of the town; local authorities, he explained, had now organized feeding stations in seven places for 710 children. But these measures were insufficient: the district needed extra resources, for all they had was the absolute minimum. Instead, they proposed the creation of orphanages for 1,500 children: 'This matter has now become so urgent, right now, and for so many children, that the sooner we solve it the better results we will achieve towards the goal of liquidating the mass phenomenon of swelling among children, since to leave children in such condition for longer will result in their deaths.'[52] The letter ended with a plea: 'there has been no reaction until now, although this question is extremely serious and demands urgent settlement'.[53] The town did do what it could, and perhaps some children were saved that way.

The situation was far worse in Kharkiv, one of the cities that the starving tried hard to enter. At least where children were concerned, the city authorities did in theory try to help – or at least they acknowledged the scale of the problem. On 30 May the Kharkiv health department reported to the Ukrainian republican authorities a 'large, persistent, ongoing flow of orphans, homeless and starving children into Kharkiv and other large towns in Kharkiv province'. The 1933 budget had provided spaces for 10,000 children in orphanages; the real number was now more than double that, 24,475. A week later over 9,000 more children were picked up off the streets, 700 of them during one night, 27–28 May. Kharkiv province asked for 6.4 million rubles from the state to take care of them, as well as another 450,000 for starving adults.

In practice, these kinds of measures rarely succeeded. A special report filed by the head of the secret police in Vinnytsia, describing the conditions in one of the city's orphanages in May 1933, makes for stark reading:

> The home services picked up children on the street. It is meant to contain 40 children, but more than 100 are now there. The lack of beds and sheets means that two children now share each bed. There are only 67 sheets and 69 blankets. Some blankets are no longer usable. There is also a lack of spoons, plates and other implements. Infants are often left dirty, with crusted eyes and no fresh air. Sometimes children who arrive in satisfactory condition die within two or three months of arrival in the home. The level of mortality is increasing: In March, 32 children died (out of 115), in April, 38 died (out of 134), during the first half of May, 16 (out of 135). Sick children lie beside healthy children, spreading diseases. Employees steal food. The electricity has been cut off, and there is no running water.[54]

In the more distant provinces the situation could be even worse. In the town of Velyka Lepetykha conditions inside the orphanage were so bad that children escaped during the day and wandered into the market to beg and steal food.[55] In Kherson the city's four orphanages were overwhelmed after the number of children nearly doubled in the first three weeks of March, from 480 to 750, mostly because of homeless children picked up off the streets.[56] In Kharkiv the petitions for food and aid meant they failed to come fast enough. The city health department reported in May that most children in the city's overflowing orphanages were weak with hunger. Many had measles and other contagious diseases – and the mortality rate was 30 per cent.[57]

There were also 'orphanages' that hardly deserved that name at all. In 1933, Liubov Drazhevska, at the time a geology student in Kharkiv, went in to her institute to discover that classes were cancelled. The following day she and about forty others were taken by streetcar to the railway station and shown railway carriages filled with children. 'A man wearing a [secret police] uniform, I think, came up to us and said: "For the next few weeks you will be working with these children; you will supervise and feed them." '

Drazhevska entered one of the carriages. 'Some children were in a normal state, more or less, but most of them were very pale and very thin, and many children were swollen from hunger.' She and the others began to serve gruel to the children, though not too much as they were so famished that they could become ill from overeating. Most of them could not explain how they had arrived at the carriages: parents had dropped them off, they had been picked up off the street, they couldn't remember. On the very first day several children died, Drazhevska remembered: 'For the first time in my life I saw people dying, and, of course, this was very difficult.' Others were unbalanced. One girl began screaming: 'Don't cut me up, don't cut me up!' She hallucinated as well, crying out that 'My aunt is weeding beets over there!' Eventually she had to be removed from the car so as not to upset the others.

Drazhevska found the experience unbearable: 'On the whole, I was quite a self-controlled person, but after I came back home that day, I had a fit of hysterics. Before this I did not know what it meant to be a hysteric, but I experienced that then.' Soon she became accustomed to the oddity of the situation, and to the children themselves. She was able to bring them books and paper. She tried to teach them to read. Every day some of them died – but others survived. Eventually, a place was found for them:

> We went by streetcar to a district of Kharkiv, then we had to go very far on foot. It was already dark. The children were five or six years old. They were tired and kept asking me: 'Aunt, where are we going?' But I didn't know. The only thing that I knew was that I was supposed to bring them to the barracks and leave them there. That's all. I don't know what happened to them.[58]

Even with all the deaths and suffering, Drazhevska's story demonstrates a brutal truth: without policemen to organize 'volunteers', without the dirty, underfunded orphanages – even those with dishonest employees and appalling conditions – even more children would have died. The orphanages were terrible. But their very existence saved lives.

The same paradoxical point can be made about another less popular Soviet institution: the Torgsin hard currency shops. As we saw earlier, these shops, first opened in 1930, were originally meant for foreigners who could not legally own rubles. In 1931 they were opened to Soviet citizens, to enable them to exchange whatever foreign money or gold objects they might possess. During the famine years of 1932–3 they expanded in numbers, activity and significance, achieving record sales and creating what some remembered as 'Torgsin gold fever'. In November 1932 the Soviet Politburo decreed that the shops could purchase silver as well as gold, a fact that seemed important enough for the Italian consul to mention in his January 1933 report: 'Now it is said that soon jewellery will be accepted.'[59] At their peak, in 1933, there were 1,500 Torgsin shops, often in prominent places: in Kyiv, there was one on Khreshchatyk street, the most important shopping area in the city.

The expansion was not accidental: the regime knew that famine would bring gold into the state coffers. Following the Torgsin's high turnover in 1932 – in that year the shops brought in 21 tonnes of gold, one and a half times the amount mined by Soviet industry – the state greedily set the 1933 target at more than double that number.[60] The Torgsin income briefly became a crucial factor in Soviet international trade: during the years 1932–5 the gold and other valuable objects that the state obtained through the Torgsins would pay for a fifth of Soviet hard currency expenditure on machinery, raw materials and technology.[61]

For hungry people, the Torgsin shops – often the only place in town where food was readily available – became the focus of dreams and obsession. They attracted stares, curious onlookers and beggars. In 1933 the Welsh journalist Gareth Jones visited one in Moscow. 'Plenty of everything,' he recorded in his notebook'.[62] Malcolm Muggeridge wrote of the 'wistful groups' of people who hung around outside the same shop, staring at the 'tempting pyramids of fruit'.[63] In Bulgakov's novel *The Master and Margarita*, two demons make a memorable appearance in front of the 'glass doors of the Torgsin Store in Smolensk Market', before entering rooms full of 'hundreds of different bolts of richly coloured poplins' where 'racks full of shoes stretched into the distance'.[64]

Away from the capital, most of the Torgsin shops were dark and dirty like other Soviet shops, and operated by rude and angry staff.[65]

Still, many peasants, misled by their consumer goods and by the presence of hard currency, thought that the shops were 'American'.[66] Rumours of what the Torgsin might provide drew one man back from Rostov, in Russia, where he had fled to escape collectivization. Having heard that in Ukraine it was possible to exchange gold for bread, he decided, his son remembered, that it was worth the risk to come home just in order to take his tsarist-era gold coins out of their hiding place and trade them for several kilos of buckwheat and a few loaves of bread.[67]

This long trip was not unusual. Although there were a few mobile Torgsin shops that toured the countryside, hoping to purchase gold, peasants without access to these made major expeditions to reach them in cities and towns. Nadiia Babenko's father gathered the family wedding rings, baptismal crosses and earrings, and walked 200 kilometres from his village, Pylypovychi, to the Torgsin in Kyiv. But it was worth it: he received a pood of flour – 16 kilograms – a litre of oil and two kilograms of buckwheat, which along with frozen potatoes, sorrel, mushrooms, berries and acorns, helped the family survive for the next few weeks.[68]

Not all such journeys ended happily. Thieves hung around Torgsin shops, and robbed or even murdered people as they entered and left. Torgsin staff cheated or mistreated peasants too. Ivan Klymenko and his mother travelled from Krasna Slobidka, a village in Kyiv province, to Khreshchatyk street to sell his grandmother's wedding ring for several scoops of flour. No one had bothered to weigh the ring, so they didn't know if they received a fair deal; once they got home his mother discovered that the flour was mixed with lime. They ate it anyway.[69] Hryhorii Simia went to a Torgsin with his stepfather, who wanted to sell his army medal, a silver Georgian Cross. The seller wouldn't accept it: this particular medal was, the clerk said, only given to 'servants of the tsar' with high positions in the officer corps. Simia's stepfather protested in vain that he'd been an army doctor who treated the wounded regardless of rank. The seller replied: 'So, you treated officers! Upper class! Enemies of the revolution! Yes? Get out of here or I call the police!'[70]

As the famine deepened, some looked for gold wherever they could find it. For centuries Ukrainians had been buried along with their most prized possessions, including jewellery, weapons and crosses. Hunger removed any remaining feeling of respect, and more than one ancient cemetery was robbed, at first only at night but eventually during the daytime too. Since cemeteries were 'Christian', Soviet authorities did not always object to the looting – and in some places they organized it themselves.[71]

At the same time the Soviet regime also began to use the Torgsin shops as a way to encourage friends and relatives of Soviet citizens to contribute hard currency from abroad. In later years all such foreign contacts were forbidden and would be dangerous, even lethal, to maintain. But in 1932–3 the regime's desire for hard currency was such that it allowed people outside the USSR to send 'food transfers' to starving relatives via the shops.[72] Those lucky enough to receive something would have to give the state 25 per cent of the total, and sometimes as much as 50 per cent. But they would then receive coupons that allowed them to buy food at the Torgsin. Transfers arrived from Germany, Poland, Lithuania, France, the United Kingdom and above all the United States.[73] The ethnic German community in Ukraine as well as the Volga region launched letter-writing campaigns aimed at their foreign brethren – Mennonite, Baptist and Catholic – begging for food. Tiny amounts of help could have an enormous impact. The diarist Oleksandra Radchenko, a teacher in the Kharkiv region, received a transfer of three dollars. With that, she obtained '6 kg of wheat flour, 2 kg of sugar, 3 or 4 of rice and 1 kilo of wheat groats at the Torgsin. What a great help to us.'[74]

Although the Torgsin trade saved lives, it also created great bitterness. Many understood the shops in stark terms: they existed to rob starving peasants of what was left of their household wealth. In Odessa an informer told the OGPU he had heard two teachers speculating that peasant wealth might even be the purpose of the famine: 'They have created hunger in order to get more gold and silver to the Torgsin.'[75] In Poltava peasants joked bleakly that the acronym TORGSIN really stood for *Tovarishchi, Revoliutsiia Gibnet, Stalin Istrebliaet Narod!* ('Comrades, the Revolution is Dying, Stalin Exterminates the People!').[76] There was no way to protest against the exploitation of the Torgsin system, except anonymously. The employees of one Torgsin arrived at work one morning to find a placard on the shop door: 'Stalin is an executioner.'[77]

Still, countless families survived thanks to what they were able to sell. 'We sold gold to get corn,' one survivor remembered.[78] Pavlo Chornyi's family sold a great-grandfather's silver medals, earned during the Russian imperial war in the Caucasus in the 1830s.[79] Another woman remembered that her mother had 'some golden things from pre-revolutionary times: She had my father's golden watch, several rings, and so on. Thus, from time to time she went to the Torgsin .. .... For silver and gold my mother received porridge, potatoes or flour. All those products she mixed with different grasses and gave us to eat once a day. In such a way we survived.'[80] Yet another recalled her mother exchanging earrings and her wedding ring for flour, skirts and blouses for beetroot and grain, as well as her dowry – 'fabric, embroidered towels, linen' – for bran or millet.[81]

Those women survived – but they lost a part of themselves in the process. Objects they might have received from their mothers, things that would have connected them to their past, rings and jewellery they might have used or invested in another way – all of these were gone. History, culture, family and identity were destroyed by the famine too, sacrificed in the name of survival.

13
Aftermath

The rye is beginning to ripen
But – and his hair stands on end –
Not many have survived
To see the new harvest.
He won't fall asleep till dawn . . .
Then his mother approaches
And says with sorrow
'My son, it's time to get up,
The sun has risen over the field
We cannot lie peacefully in our graves,
We, the dead, are unable to rest.
Who will care for the precious ears of grain
In the fields, my dear son?'

Mykola Rudenko, 'The Cross', 1976[1]

In the springtime, the Ukrainian countryside is a riot of cherry blossoms, tulip petals, sprouting grass and black mud. Only an hour's drive from Kyiv the villages seem too provincial to have witnessed important historical events. Roads are pockmarked by puddles; some of the rickety cottages still have thatched roofs. Every house has a kitchen garden and many have beehives, chicken coops, and garden sheds filled with tools.

Yet it was in springtime, in this same provincial Ukrainian countryside, that the famine in 1933 reached its peak. Today, that history is there if one looks for it, in the wide fields that once belonged to collective farms, in the overgrown cemeteries, and in the monuments put up since the dissolution of the Soviet Union. Just on the edge of the village of Kodaky, at the point where houses give way to broad fields, local people have erected a piece of black stone. It has a cross-shaped hole cut in the centre and a dedication, 'In memory of the victims of the Holodomor'. In Hrebinky an abandoned mound at the edge of town – a mass grave where famine victims were buried in 1933, then forgotten, then rediscovered – is now encircled by a brick wall and marked, since 1990, with a simple cross.

In Barakhty the famine memorial is hard to miss: a larger-than-life statue of a mourning mother, kneeling beside a cross, at a prominent crossroads in the centre of the village. A list of victims carved into the black granite behind the statue both reveals and conceals. Surnames repeat themselves, showing that the famine wiped out whole families, but Christian names are often missing because records were badly kept:

Bondar, Overko
Bondar, Iosyp
Bondar, Mariia
Bondar, Two Children

The missing names point to a deeper problem. Even in better circumstances, it would have been difficult to keep precise records of the vast numbers of men and women who died on the road, or in train stations, or on the streets of Kyiv. District registrars would have had trouble accounting for everyone who migrated or escaped, or even for every child who survived, by some miracle, in a distant orphanage. But the regime made these problems worse. Although mortality statistics were recorded as accurately as possible in 1933, the authorities, as the next chapter will explain, later altered death registries across Ukraine to hide the numbers of deaths from starvation, and in 1937 scrapped an entire census because of what it revealed.

For all of these reasons, estimates of the numbers of dead have in the past ranged widely, from a few tens of thousands to 2 million, 7 million or even 10 million. But in recent years a team of Ukrainian demographers have looked again at the numbers that were tabulated at the district and provincial level, then passed on to Kharkiv and Moscow, and have come up with better answers.[2] Arguing that 'there was some falsification of cause of death in death certificates, but the number of registered deaths was not tampered with', they have sought to establish reliable numbers of 'excess deaths', meaning the number of people who died above an expected average. They have also looked at 'lost births', or the numbers of births that did not occur, by comparison to what would have been expected, because of the famine.[3] Thanks to their work, agreement is now coalescing around two numbers: 3.9 million excess deaths, or direct losses, and 0.6 million lost births, or indirect losses. That brings the total number of missing Ukrainians to 4.5 million. These figures include all victims, wherever they died – by the roadside, in prison, in orphanages – and are based on the numbers of people in Ukraine before the famine and afterwards.

The total population of the republic at that time was about 31 million people. The direct losses amounted to about 13 per cent of that number.[4] The vast majority of casualties were in the countryside: of the 3.9 million excess deaths, 3.5 million were rural and 400,000 urban. More than 90 per cent of the deaths took place in 1933, and most of those in the first half of the year, with the highest numbers of casualties in May, June and July.[5]

But within those numbers, there are other stories. For one, the statistics show a sharp and notable drop in life expectancy over 1932–4, across a wide range of groups. Before 1932, urban men had a life expectancy at birth of 40 to 46 years, and urban women 47 to 52 years. Rural men had a life expectancy of 42 to 44 years, and rural women 45 to 48 years.

By contrast, Ukrainian men born in 1932, in either the city or countryside, had an average life expectancy of about 30. Women born in that year could expect to live on average to 40. For those born in 1933, the numbers are even starker. Females born in Ukraine in that year lived, on average, to be eight years old. Males born in 1933 could expect to live to the age of five.[6] These extreme statistics reflect, simply, the very high death rates in that year of children.

The new statistical methods are also revealing when applied to Russia. They show that overall the famine touched Russia far less than Ukraine, with an overall 3 per cent 'excess deaths' in rural Russia, as against 14.9 per cent in rural Ukraine. Only a very few regions of Russia were affected by the same patterns of famine as Ukraine: the Volga German region, the Saratov region, Krasnodar and the North Caucasus all had very high death rates in the first half of 1933, corresponding to the political decisions taken that winter. But even in those cases the overall numbers of 'excess deaths' were lower than those in the worst regions of Ukraine.[7]

The general statistics cannot reveal everything. For example, they conceal the story of particular groups within Ukraine, for whom separate accounts were not kept. Anecdotal evidence suggests, for example, that while the ethnic German community suffered greatly, in Ukraine as well as the Volga region, some of its members did get food aid and other forms of help from German sources. Andor Hencke, the German consul in Kyiv from 1933 to 1936, spent much of his first months in Ukraine trying to get food to the German minority community, despite the fact that 'the party authorities and Soviet institutions are essentially unfavorably inclined towards the aid campaign'. He advised ethnic Germans to be discreet and to avoid personal visits to the consulate, so as not to attract attention, but he did communicate with them by post.[8] Equally, as we have seen, there is anecdotal evidence that rural Jews also survived at higher rates because the majority were not farmers and so were not subject to either de-kulakization or collectivization. Jews, Germans and Poles had another advantage too: they were not perceived to be part of the Ukrainian national movement, and thus were not particular targets of the repressive wave of 1932–3, though those groups would become targets later on.

The statistics have also turned up some unexpected stories about the famine in different regions of Ukraine. In the past – going back to the nineteenth century if not further – drought and famine had always hit the southern and eastern steppe regions of the country hardest, as these were most dependent on grain. That was certainly the case in 1921–3 as well as during the smaller famine of 1928. It was also the case during the post-war famine of 1946–7. But in 1932–3 the highest mortality rate was in the Kyiv and Kharkiv provinces, where peasants traditionally grew a wider range of crops, including beets, potatoes and other vegetables, and where historically famine was rare. In Kyiv province death levels in 1932–3 were about 23 per cent higher than they would have been without the Holodomor; in Kharkiv province they were 24 per cent higher. In Vinnytsia and the Moldovan 'autonomous' province the percentage was 13 per cent; in Dnipropetrovsk and Odessa 13 per cent and 14 per cent respectively. In Donetsk province, by contrast, the death rate was only 9 per cent higher in the famine years.[9]

Demographers have offered a range of hypotheses to explain these regional variations, and in at least three exceptional cases good explanations have been found. In theory, for example, peasants living in forested areas should have had greater access to mushrooms, small animals and other sources of food. This environmental factor might explain why Chernihiv province, in northern Ukraine, suffered less than many other parts of the republic. But it cannot explain the high death rates in Kharkiv and Kyiv provinces, which were in mixed forest-steppe regions and which did contain some areas covered by trees or swamp.[10]

Proximity to international borders may also have affected death rates, which were indeed lower in Vinnytsia and Moldova, the two provinces bordering on Poland and Romania, as well as in the westernmost districts of the Kyiv region. Local authorities in these areas, worried about smuggling, discontent and sedition coming from abroad, seem to have hesitated to apply policies with the same degree of cruelty. Peasants who lived in these regions may also have been able to get food through barter, cross-border contacts, and from relatives who lived just on the other side.[11]

The Donetsk region similarly appears to have been a special case. Because, as we have seen, this region was one of the few in Ukraine designated as an industrial 'priority' by the regime, more food was allocated to workers there. More food – relatively speaking – appears to have reached the rural areas too, probably through family connections to the cities. Proximity also meant that peasants in the region found it easier to escape the starving countryside, and to join the proletariat in the mines and factories.

The most intriguing difference, though, is the one remaining between Kyiv and Kharkiv, with very high direct losses, and Dnipropetrovsk and Odessa, where the level of such losses was relatively low. The best explanation appears to be political: both in 1918–20 and 1930–1 the Kyiv and Kharkiv regions witnessed the greatest political resistance, first to the Bolsheviks and then to collectivization. The greatest number of 'terrorist incidents' took place in those regions, as did the largest number of secret police interventions. Andrea Graziosi has argued that the 'impressive geographical, ideological and even personal and "family" continuity between the peasant-based social and national revolts of 1918–20 and those against dekulakization requisitions and collectivization in 1930–1 was strongest in territories where famine reached its harshest peaks'.[12] Although this correlation is not exact – among other things, Makhno's men were very active in southeast Ukraine – it is true that these two provinces, with their proximity to Ukraine's two most culturally important cities, had many links to the nationalist movement. That may explain why repression was cruellest, food aid was scarcest, and death rates were highest.[13]

In other words, the regions 'normally' most affected by drought and famine were less affected in 1932–3 because the famine of those years was not 'normal'. It was a political famine, created for the express purpose of weakening peasant resistance, and thus national identity. And in this, it succeeded.

The Ukrainian famine reached its height in the spring of 1933. Death rates went up in January, and then kept increasing through the spring. But instead of ending abruptly that summer, the tragedy slowly dwindled. 'Excess deaths' continued throughout the rest of 1933 and 1934.

In May the regime finally approved significant food aid for Ukraine – food originally taken, of course, from the peasants themselves – though it was especially targeted at border regions (where fear of outside influence was highest) and in areas where there were not enough healthy people to bring in the harvest.[14] When it finally arrived, the harvest made a difference too. Students, workers and others were rushed to the countryside to make up for lost manpower, and more food became generally available in the countryside as well as the city. Theoretically, the grain collectors had also stopped requisitioning, in accordance with the decree that the Council of Ministers had issued in January. As of that spring, they were supposed to demand a tax – a percentage of the harvest – rather than a fixed amount of grain based on a plan produced in Moscow. In practice, this rule was applied unevenly. In some places peasants were taxed, but in others confiscations continued.[15]

The Central Committee and the Ukrainian government also issued a joint directive in May, on 'halting the mass exile of peasants, reducing the number of arrests and decreasing the number of prisons'. This secret decree, which went out to all party officials as well as the OGPU, courts and prosecutors' offices, reflected a decision to 'stop, as a rule, the use of mass exile and sharp forms of repression in the countryside' and to introduce a less harsh rural regime. There were pragmatic reasons for the change: at the time of the decree 800,000 people were under arrest all across the USSR, prisons and camps were overflowing, and the state could barely cope. In addition, the regime recognized that it would need people to bring in the harvest. But the decree also signalled an end to the harsh treatment of villagers, and thus an end to the policy of food confiscation as well.[16]

As in previous years, there was a procurement campaign in the late summer of 1933. Also as in previous years, there were shortfalls, although in 1933 the conversation about them was far more muted than it had been in the past. In October 1933, Stanislav Kosior, General Secretary of the Ukrainian Communist Party, wrote to Stalin, praising that autumn's harvest, which he noted was an 'improvement' over the previous harvests. However, he admitted that there were still 'problems'. Predicted yields had still not materialized.[17] He also asked for a reduction in the grain procurement plan for Ukraine.

On 18 October 1933 the Soviet Politburo approved this request. Ukraine's required contribution for 1934 was reduced by 415,000 tonnes. A few weeks later Kosior and Pavlo Postyshev, the former Kharkiv party boss and Stalin's envoy in Ukraine, met the Soviet leader – this time in the luxurious setting of his personal train carriage – and he confirmed a further reduction of Ukraine's contribution by 500,000 tonnes. Although the republic was still required to produce a huge quantity of grain to the state, this was an important change.

In acknowledgement of these concessions, the Ukrainian communists also changed their tone. They ceased to criticize the harsh requisitions policy. Instead, in multiple speeches and articles they rallied around the Soviet war against 'nationalism', the scourge that the leadership now blamed for all 'errors' in rural policy. Kosior told a November plenum that 'in some republics of the USSR, in particular in Ukraine, the kulaks' desperate resistance to our victorious socialist offensive led to a growth of nationalism'.

That allusion to 'errors' wasn't strong enough for the leader, however. Stalin personally edited that speech in order to strengthen it: 'in some republics of the USSR, in particular in Ukraine, the main threat is now Ukrainian nationalism that allies with imperialist interventionists'.[18] Stalin drove the point home himself in January 1934 at the Seventeenth Party Congress, remembered as the Congress of Victors. In a long and much-applauded speech he marked the end of the worst famine in Soviet history with a vicious attack on nationalism:

> ... It should be observed that the survivals of capitalism in people's minds are much more tenacious in the sphere of the national question than in any other sphere. They are more tenacious because they are able to disguise themselves well in national costume ...
>
> The deviation towards nationalism reflects the attempts of 'one's own', 'national' bourgeoisie to undermine the Soviet system and to restore capitalism ... It is a *departure* from Leninist internationalism ... [*Stormy applause*][19]

At the same Congress, Postyshev, as the senior Ukrainian communist, took upon himself full responsibility for the 'gross errors and blunders' in Ukrainian agriculture – without mentioning the famine – which he explicitly blamed on nationalism, counter-revolutionaries and invisible foreign forces:

> The CP(B)U [Ukrainian Communist Party] did not take into account all the distinctive characteristics of the class struggle in Ukraine and the peculiarities of the internal situation in the CP(B)U.
>
> What are those characteristics? ...
>
> The first characteristic is that in Ukraine the class enemy masks his activity against socialist construction with the nationalist banner and chauvinist slogans.
>
> The second characteristic is that the Ukrainian kulak underwent a lengthy schooling in struggle against Soviet power, for in Ukraine the civil war was especially fierce and lengthy, given that political banditry was in control of Ukraine for an especially long period.
>
> The third characteristic is that splinter groups of various counter-revolutionary organizations and parties settled in Ukraine more than elsewhere, being attracted to Ukraine on account of its proximity to western borders.

The fourth characteristic is that Ukraine proves to be an object of attraction to various interventionist centres and finds itself under their especially diligent observation.

And, finally, the fifth characteristic is that the deviationists in the CP(B)U in all-Party questions usually allied and continue to ally themselves with the nationalist elements in their ranks, with the deviationists on the nationality question . . .

Unfortunately, the CP(B)U did not draw all those conclusions in full measure. There lies the explanation of its errors and failures both in agriculture and in carrying out Leninist nationality policy in Ukraine . . .[20]

Further concessions followed. In the spring of 1934 there were no requisitions of vegetables. Peasants were allowed to keep the food they had grown inside their remaining private allotments. The Ukrainian leadership now dared to inform Stalin, openly, that some fields would not be sown – there was no one to sow them – and that there was a shortage of seeds, including corn, linen and hemp seeds as well as grain. This time around, Stalin agreed to 'loan' Ukraine seeds as well as food.[21]

Collectivization continued, indeed accelerated: any individual farmers who had survived the famine joined collective farms en masse that spring. This time there was no talk of rebellion, as 151,700 terrified families gave up their homes and property to work for the state. Another 51,800 households joined in the autumn. The demands for grain were quietly relaxed, and the number of arrests in the countryside fell.[22]

Life did not return to 'normal'; it never would. But slowly, Ukrainians stopped dying of hunger.

In the late spring of 1933, Max Harmash, an agricultural specialist from the Dnipropetrovsk region, was recruited by the provincial government to help with sowing the harvest at a collective farm about 25 kilometres from his home. On his first night in the countryside a village councillor directed Harmash to a house where he was told that he could sleep. There he encountered a 'very thin man in rags', who did not answer his greetings. He also found the 'grotesque, half-naked swollen body' of another person lying on a pallet. Rags were strewn about the floor; the stench was unbearable. Harmash backed out of the house, leaving some of his bread for its inhabitants, and ran back to the village council building. There, a watchman told him that there was hardly any food to be found anywhere in the vicinity. Only a few members of the collective farm still had any reserves at all. About half the villagers were already dead. The rest survived by eating cats, dogs and birds.

Horrified and shocked by what he had seen, Harmash fled the dying village as soon as he could. For a long time afterwards he had 'nightmares' and expected severe punishment for abandoning his duties. He was afraid to tell anybody about what had happened. But the punishment never came. Years later he reckoned that the officials who had sent him to the village must have known that there was no grain to sow and no one to sow it, but they had sent for him anyway. Someone had told them to do so, and they were simply fulfilling the task. No one dared to say clearly that the villagers were dying of hunger.[23]

At about the same time Lidiia, a student in Kharkiv, was also sent out to the countryside as part of a labour brigade. She and her companions received accommodation in an empty school building, were warned not to go outside at night and told not to open the door. During the day they went into the fields to weed around the sugar beets. They met no one. But after only a few days their mission was abruptly cut short: 'We returned to Kharkiv at daybreak, but we were not allowed to go home. We were taken to an official building, despite the fact that we were hungry and dirty. When government officials arrived, a girl told me that I had to go to a special department. The manager asked me what I had seen. I said nothing. Then he said "go and don't say anything". Frightened, I never asked the others whether they had been called to the same department.'[24]

Lidiia and Max were witnesses to another facet of the post-famine crisis: in 1933 the Soviet state suddenly faced a drastic shortage of labour in the Ukrainian countryside, which was particularly extreme in some districts. In the Markivka district of Donetsk province, for example, a meeting of village council leaders in December reckoned their prospects were bleak. Some 20,000 people, more than half the population, had perished in the famine. More than 60 per cent of local horses had been killed that year, and 70 per cent of the oxen. Their owners were gone too, one observed: 'Now when you go out into the country you can see villages that are so empty, wolves are living in the houses.' Grain stores were so low that it was impossible to provide collective farm workers with their daily grain ration in exchange for work. The amount of sown land was decreasing, from more than 80,000 hectares in 1931 to 67,000 in 1933.[25]

The brigades of students, workers and party officials sent from the city to the countryside did help somewhat. But this policy now carried some risks: the teams from the urban USSR might get to see, first hand, what had happened in the villages. Like Max, some ran away. Like Lidiia, some had to be monitored. They might go back and describe the scenes of death and devastation, with unknown consequences.

Students and workers could not provide a permanent solution either. For that, the regime needed permanent inhabitants, new people who could live in the countryside and continue to farm. And so, in late 1933, it launched a resettlement programme. Its practical result, in many parts of Ukraine, was the replacement of Ukrainians with Russians, at least as long as the programme – which was not successful – lasted.

By 1933 the Soviet Union already had some experience with moving and resettling people. Hundreds of thousands of kulaks had been moved to the empty northern and eastern regions of the country, as well as to the poorer and emptier districts of Ukraine itself. During the Second World War a range of explicitly ethnic deportations would result in the evictions of whole nationalities, including several Caucasian tribal peoples – the Chechens and the Ingush, the Karachai, the Kalmyks, the Balkars, the Meshketians – as well as the Crimean Tatars and the Volga Germans. In his famous 'Secret Speech' to the party elite in 1956, Nikita Khrushchev denounced these mass population transfers, and joked that 'Ukrainians avoided meeting this fate only because there were too many of them and there was no place to which to deport them. Otherwise, [Stalin] would have deported them also.' The official transcript recorded that this remark sparked 'laughter and animation in the hall'.[26]

Officially, the movement of Russians into Ukraine began as a response to a clear need. Those at the top of the system knew about the drastic labour shortages. In a telegram sent in August 1933, Yakov Yakovlev, the Soviet Commissar for Agriculture, described a collective farm in Melitopol, southeast Ukraine, where 'no more than a third of the households remain ... less than one-fifth with horses'. Single households were labouring under the responsibility for farming 20 hectares of fertile soil by themselves. In western Russia, by contrast, crowded conditions meant that a single family had only one hectare to farm. Stalin responded in a note to Molotov, 'it is necessary to speed up a possible "resettlement of the peasantry"'.[27]

The first phase of the project began with 117,000 Russian peasants – 21,000 households – from Russia and Belarus. They began to arrive in Ukraine in the autumn of 1933. In January and February 1934 a further 20,000 arrived in the depopulated villages of eastern and southern Ukraine, this time coming from Russia as well as other regions of Ukraine.[28] These numbers may be an underestimation, since they include only those who received state assistance to make the trip. Others – an unknown number – simply gathered together what belongings they could take and made the journey from Russia and the other regions on their own, having heard that there was more space and free land in Ukraine. In general, this first wave of arrivals was mostly voluntary – settlers believed they would be given free housing and good food rations, as well as transportation – although some had been evicted from their homes as kulaks or as enemies and so had little choice.

Many were disappointed. They had expected to find accommodation and rich soil. The state had paid for their transportation, including their cattle and tools, given them hot food and rations on their journey, and even promised tax breaks. But the reality proved to be very different, as one woman settler from Zhytomyr province, a child at the time, remembered:

We were evicted from our house too, but we were sent to Horodyshche in Dnipropetrovsk province. That village had died out and we were re-settled there ... In Horodyshche we were given a small room in the hut, we put down some hay and slept on the ground. In the

collective farm they gave out 1 kg of bread for 10 days. We were promised a lot but we have not seen anything of it.[29]

Other surprises lay in store. On arrival, many of the Russians found
the Ukrainian steppe unaccommodating. They did not know how to
start fires with straw and dried grass, as the Ukrainians did. They
were not necessarily welcomed by their new neighbours, who of
course spoke a language they failed to understand. The villages were
empty: even cats and dogs were now quite rare, as Ukrainian planners noted at the end of 1933, which had led to an infestation of mice
in the houses as well as the fields.[30] One settler, writing back to relatives in Russia, found the atmosphere uncanny and strange, though if
he knew that there had been famine, he didn't say so. 'A lot of people
died here,' he wrote instead, 'there were epidemics in 1932. There
were so few of them left that they can't till the land themselves.'
Another noted that 'all the households are destroyed and derelict,
and there is chaos in workplaces. Locals say that it wasn't like that
before, the village used to be orderly. People lived well here . . . the
potatoes grow amazingly well.'[31]

Others began to worry that they would meet the same fate as their
predecessors, particularly when, after a few months' residence, the
things they had been promised gradually disappeared. In 1935 the
new settlers were told that they, like the locals, would have to pay
meat and milk taxes: this too must have seemed an ominous sign.
The records of the Markivka district show that many of the Russian
settlers left in the spring of 1935, and that those who remained were
uneasy. They wrote home, complained about local conditions,
observed that their new neighbours seemed lethargic, half dead. They
had no shoes. They were eating corn husks.[32]

Although the records are probably incomplete, many of those
settlers sent to Ukraine in this first wave of resettlement did indeed
return home within the year. Presumably as a consequence, new
waves of deportation followed. But this second group did not contain
volunteers. According to the deportation orders for the 39,000
'settlers' in February 1935, they were people who had 'not proved
themselves in the strengthening of the border and the collective farm
system', as well as 'nationalistic and anti-Soviet elements'. Many were

from regions of western Ukraine that bordered on foreign countries, including large numbers of ethnic Germans and Poles. The 'fifth column' that the OGPU had described so many times was now removed from the border region for good.

This time the state made far greater efforts to keep the new settlers in place. Secret policemen enlisted locals to help monitor the new arrivals and prevent them from escaping. Those caught trying to leave were punished. This relatively 'successful' resettlement was repeated in 1936, though many of those deported from western Ukraine at this time were sent to distant destinations beyond eastern Ukraine. Some 15,000 Polish and German households – by some accounts 70,000 people – found themselves assigned to Kazakhstan, where famine had also devastated the countryside.[33]

Even at the time these resettlement campaigns were understood to be a form of Russification. Sergio Gradenigo, the observant Italian consul in Kharkiv, reported to Rome a conversation with an unnamed acquaintance who had agreed that the 'Russification of Donbas' was underway. He linked the policy to the closure of Ukrainian-language theatres, the restriction of Ukrainian opera music to just three cities, Kyiv, Kharkiv and Odessa, and the end of Ukrainization.[34] Ordinary people also knew that uninhabited villages were being populated by Russians. 'People said that the authorities wanted to exterminate Ukraine with hunger and settle the land with a Russian population so that Russia will be here,' one eyewitness recalled.[35] An anonymous letter from a resident of Poltava to the *Kommunist* newspaper made the same point: 'The historically unprecedented physical extermination of the Ukrainian nation ... is one of the central goals of the illegal programme of Bolshevik centralism.' This letter was considered important enough to be the topic of a report sent to Stalin himself.[36]

Dramatic as these emergency movements between 1933 and 1936 must have been, they are far less important, in terms of numbers and influence, than the slow-motion movement of Russians into a depopulated Ukraine, and into depleted Ukrainian republican institutions, in subsequent years and decades. Some of them arrived to shore up the Ukrainian Communist Party, which had never recovered from the sweeping arrests of 1933. During and after the famine, the state purged, arrested and even executed tens of thousands of Ukrainian party officials. Often, their replacements came directly from Moscow. In 1933 alone the Soviet Communist Party sent thousands of political cadres, at all levels of the hierarchy, to Ukraine from Russia. By January 1934 only four of the twelve members of the Ukrainian Communist Party Politburo were Ukrainians. Eight of the twelve, in other words, did not speak Ukrainian, which was still the native language of a majority of Ukrainians.[37]

Nor did the purge end there. Three years later the Ukrainian communist leadership became a particular target of the Great Terror, Stalin's nationwide attack on the older members of the Soviet Communist Party. Khrushchev himself famously remembered in his memoir that in 1937–8 the Ukrainian Communist Party was 'purged spotless'.[38] He was certainly in a position to know, since he stage-managed the arrests. Khrushchev, born in a Russian village near the Ukrainian border, grew up in working-class Donbas. Like Kaganovich, he identified with proletarian, Russophone Ukraine, not with the Ukrainian-speaking peasantry. At Stalin's request he returned to Kyiv in 1937, accompanied by a host of secret police troops. After a struggle – the Ukrainian Communist Party at first resisted – he oversaw the arrest of the entire leadership, including Kosior, Chubar and Postyshev. Within months they were all dead; most members of the Ukrainian government were executed in the spring of 1938. Ordinary party members disappeared too: between January 1934 and May 1938 a third of the Ukrainian Communist Party, 167,000 people, were under arrest.[39] In Khrushchev's words, 'it seemed as though not one regional or executive Committee secretary, not one secretary of the council of people's commissars, not even a single deputy was left. We had to start building from scratch.'[40]

By the end of the decade, the purge was complete: at the time of the outbreak of war in 1939 none of the Ukrainian Communist Party leadership had any connection with or sympathy for the national movement or even national communism. By the time the war ended in 1945, the Nazi occupation and the Holocaust devastated the republic and its institutions even further. In the post-war era the party continued to pay lip service to 'Ukrainian' symbols and even language, but at the higher levels it was overwhelmingly Russian speaking. The native Ukrainians who remained in the party were often drawn from the activist groups who had carried out the searches that led to the famine – or, in the years that followed, their children and grandchildren.[41] No one in the party remembered a different Ukraine.

Where the party led, the people followed. Between 1959 and 1970 over a million Russians migrated to Ukraine, drawn to the republic by the opportunities that a population depleted by war, famine and purges had created for energetic new residents. As the Soviet economy industrialized, a network of Russian-speaking industry bosses recruited colleagues from the north. Universities, hospitals and other institutions did the same. At the same time almost all the other minorities still living in Ukraine – the Jews who remained, the Germans, Belarusians, Bulgarians and Greeks – assimilated into the Russian-speaking majority. Peasants who moved from the devastated countryside into the cities often switched from Ukrainian to Russian, in order to get on. As in the nineteenth century, the Russian language offered opportunities and advancement. Ukrainian became simply a 'backwards' language of the provinces.[42]

By the 1970s and 1980s the idea of a mass Ukrainian national movement seemed not just dead but buried. Intellectuals kept the flame alive in a few cities. But most Russians, and many Ukrainians, once again thought of Ukraine as just a province of Russia. Most outsiders failed to distinguish between Russia and Ukraine, if they remembered the name of Ukraine at all.

In the spring of 1933, Mikhail Sholokhov, already then a celebrated writer, sat down at his typewriter in Vyoshenskaya Vstanitsa, a Cossack *stanitsa* in the North Caucasus, and composed a letter to Stalin. It was not the first such missive. As a patriotic and pro-Soviet citizen, Sholokhov had been informing Stalin about the progress of collectivization in Vyoshenskaya Vstanitsa for many months. Perhaps because he had met the Soviet leader in Moscow, he did not fear the consequences. His first missives were short and mostly handwritten, and they often focused on small things he saw going wrong. In 1931 he wrote with concern about the cattle and horses he saw all across the countryside, dying for lack of food. In 1932 he worried that collective farmers were stealing seeds straight out of the sowing machines. He also told the Soviet leader that an order to collectivize livestock had backfired. In some of the local villages 'purchasers' of cattle were beating up peasants and forcibly dragging their livestock away. The peasants fought back and in one village they murdered a requisitioner.

But in the spring of 1933, Sholokhov's tone suddenly grew more urgent: Vyoshenskaya Vstanitsa was in crisis. Stalin needed to know that people were starving to death:

> In this district, as in other districts, collective and individual farmers alike are dying of hunger; adults and children are swollen, and are eating things that no human being should have to eat, starting with carrion and finishing with the bark of oak trees and all kinds of muddy roots.

More details followed. In evocative, literary language, Sholokhov described peasants who refused to work because 'all of our bread sails abroad'. He painted a portrait of the local party secretary, Ovchinnikov, who declared that 'grain must be collected at any price! We'll destroy everything, but we'll grab grain!' He described Ovchinnikov's tactics, including the extortion of seed grain, the confiscation of cows, potatoes, pickled food – all of the tactics that the 1932 decrees had stipulated for both the Northern Caucasus and Ukraine.

Sholokhov also described what happened after the Communist Party purged its lower ranks. Those who lost their party cards were arrested; their families lost access to rationed food, and they began to starve as well. The writer begged Stalin to send some 'authentic' communists to Vyoshenskaya Vstanitsa, ones with the courage to halt the crisis. Using Stalinist language, he called on the Soviet leader to help 'unmask' those who had brutally beaten and tormented the peasants, stolen their grain, and destroyed the agricultural economy of the region.

Stalin's reply was blunt. In two telegrams, as well as a handwritten response, he told Sholokhov he was sorry to hear about these mistakes in the party's work. He offered to send material aid, both to Vyoshenskaya Vstanitsa and the neighbouring Verkhne-Donskii district. But he wasn't entirely sympathetic. He felt the writer's perspective was incomplete. 'You see only one side of the matter,' he told

Sholokhov: 'The grain growers in your region (and not only yours) are conducting sabotage and leaving the Red Army without grain.' These men might look like simple farmers, Stalin explained, but they were in fact waging a quiet, bloodless, but nevertheless effective 'war against Soviet power'. Perhaps the writer was under the impression that they were harmless people. If so, he was gravely mistaken.

Stalin's answer to Sholokhov in the spring of 1933, at the height of the famine, echoed the conspiratorial phrases that he was using in his personal correspondence as well as in speeches and party debates: those who were starving to death were not innocent. On the contrary, they were traitors, they were saboteurs, they were conspiring to undermine the proletarian revolution. They were waging 'a war against Soviet power'.

Whereas, in 1921, the Soviet leadership had spoken of starving peasants as victims, in 1933, Stalin switched the vocabulary. Those who were starving were not victims; they were perpetrators. They were not sufferers; they were responsible for their terrible fate. They had caused the famine, and therefore they deserved to die. From this assessment came the logical conclusion: the state was justified in refusing to help them stay alive.

This was the argument that Stalin would advocate for the rest of his life. He never denied, to Sholokhov or to anyone else, that peasants had died from a famine caused by state policy in 1933, and he certainly never apologized. He clearly read Sholokhov's missives, and took them seriously enough to respond. But he never admitted that any important element of his policy – not collectivization, not grain expropriation, not the searches and shakedowns that had intensified the famine in Ukraine – was wrong. Instead, he placed all responsibility for food shortages and mass deaths firmly onto the shoulders of those who were dying.[43]

This is certainly what he told his party. During the Congress of Victors at the beginning of 1934, where Stalin had denounced nationalism, he also predicted further violence. 'We have defeated the kulaks,' he declared, but the liquidation was not yet complete. Agents of the old regime – 'former people', as he called them – could still do a good deal of harm. More to the point, the party should expect more resistance from these 'moribund classes': 'It is precisely because they are dying and their days are numbered that they will go on from one form of attack to another, sharper form, appealing to the backward sections of the population and mobilizing them against the Soviet regime.'[44]

This was in line with Marxist thinking: the sharpening of contradictions, the creation of greater stress – these were the precursors of revolutionary change. The deaths of millions was not, in other words, a sign that Stalin's policy had failed. On the contrary, it was a sign of success. Victory had been achieved, the enemy had been defeated. As long as the Soviet Union lasted, that view would never be contested.

14

The Cover-Up

There is no actual starvation or deaths from starvation but there is widespread mortality from diseases due to malnutrition.

Walter Duranty, The New York Times, *31 March 1933*

I am almost illiterate and write in a simple manner, but what I write is true and truth, they say, shall overcome evil.

Petro Drobylko, Sumy province, 1933[1]

In 1933 the cities knew that the villages were dying. The leaders and administrators of the Communist Party and the government knew that the villages were dying. The evidence was in front of everyone's eyes: the peasants at the railway stations, the reports coming in from the countryside, the scenes in the cemeteries and morgues. There is no doubt that the Soviet leadership knew it too. In March 1933, Kosior wrote a letter to Stalin in which he explicitly spoke of hunger – Ukraine's provinces were begging the Central Committee for help – and anticipated worse, noting that 'even starvation has not taught good sense to the peasants', who were still too slow in their spring sowing.[2] In April he wrote again, noting the large number of people now joining collective farms: 'the famine has played a large role, having in the first instance hit individual farmers'.[3]

But in the official, Soviet world the Ukrainian famine, like the broader Soviet famine, did not exist. It did not exist in the newspapers, it did not exist in public speeches. Neither national leaders nor local leaders mentioned it – and they never would. Whereas the response to the 1921 famine was a prominent and widely heeded call for international aid, the response to the 1933 famine was total denial, both inside the Soviet Union and abroad, of any serious food shortage. The aim was to make the famine disappear, as if it had never happened. In an era before television and the internet, before open borders and travel, this was easier to achieve than it would have been in the twenty-first century. But even in 1933 the cover-up required an extraordinary effort on the part of numerous people over many years.

The organized denial of the famine began early, before the worst starvation had even begun. From the beginning, its facilitators had a number of different goals. Inside the USSR the cover-up was only partly designed to fool the Soviet public, or at least those who had no direct knowledge of the famine, though at this it probably did not succeed. Rumours were impossible to control, and were even repeated, as Stalin well knew, inside elite Bolshevik families. But letters of protest, which were sent quite frequently from all kinds of people – peasants, officials, bureaucrats – in the years leading up to the famine, soon stopped. There is anecdotal evidence inside the Soviet Union of some effort to control the mail that reached the Red Army. Mariia Bondarenko's brother, a Red Army soldier serving in the Caucasus, told his sister that none of the Ukrainian soldiers received mail from home in 1933. Members of his unit eventually found the withheld letters. Only then had they learned the truth about what was happening to their families.[4] Other soldiers never received letters from home in 1932 or 1933 at all; some recalled that it was as if their families had just disappeared.[5]

Even more effort went into the control of public speech. One Ukrainian Red Army soldier went to serve in 1934, having survived the famine. During one of the 'political instruction' classes that all soldiers had to attend, he asked the teacher a question about the famine. He was sharply rebuked: 'There was no famine and there cannot be, you will be locked up for ten years if you keep talking like this.'[6] Students and workers sent to the countryside to help bring in the 1933 harvest were often told bluntly not to speak of what they had seen. Out of fear many obeyed. We were told to 'sew up our mouths', one remembered.[7] The code of silence was understood by everyone:

> At work no one spoke of the famine or of the bodies in the streets, as if we were all part of a conspiracy of silence. Only with the closest and most trusted of friends would we talk about the terrible news from the villages ... The rumours were confirmed when the townspeople were ordered to the countryside to help with the harvest and saw for themselves whence had come the living skeletons that haunted our city's streets.[8]

The taboo on speaking of the famine in public affected medical workers too. Both doctors and nurses recall being told to 'invent something' for death certificates, or to write down all cases of starvation as the result of 'infectious diseases' or 'cardiac arrest'.[9]

Fear even affected correspondence between officials. In March the secretary of the local government in Dnipropetrovsk wrote a letter to the Central Committee of the Ukrainian Communist Party, complaining that numerous cases of starvation, swelling and deaths from hunger had received no official attention because lower-level officials had failed to report them: 'It was considered to be anti-party, reprehensible even to react to them.' In one case a village party secretary who was himself swollen from hunger had failed to report anything, so afraid was he of censure.[10]

As the emergency passed, official vigilance spread to recordkeepers. In April 1934 the Odessa provincial leadership sent out a note to all the local party committees, warning them about the 'criminally outrageous manner' in which births and deaths were being registered: 'In a number of village councils this work is actually in the hands of class enemies – kulaks, Petliura henchmen, special deportees etc.' Allegedly to increase supervision, the Odessa bosses withdrew death registration books from all village councils, from 1933 'without exception' and from 1932 in some regions as well.[11] Similar orders exist for Kharkiv province, where officials also demanded all death registries from November 1932 until the end of 1933, on the grounds that they were in the hands of 'class-hostile elements' such as kulaks, Petliurites and special deportees.[12]

In reality, both types of document conformed to an identical formula, probably the result of an order from the Ukrainian authorities, and both were intended to destroy evidence of the famine.[13] Although mortality numbers compiled at the provincial and national level did remain in statistical archives, at the village level many records were physically destroyed. Eyewitnesses from Zhytomyr and Chernihiv provinces have described the disappearance of death registries from their villages in 1933–4.[14] In Vinnytsia, Stepan Podolian recalled that his father had been asked to burn the village registry books and rewrite them, eliminating references to hunger.[15]

At the highest levels the cover-up functioned as a form of party discipline: it was a means of controlling officials, even testing their loyalty. To prove their dedication, party members had to accept and endorse the official falsehoods. Roman Terekhov, one of the party bosses in Kharkiv, dared to use the word 'famine' in Stalin's presence and in public during the autumn of 1932, as Terekhov himself later recalled. The Soviet leader's response was harsh: 'You spin this yarn about the famine thinking that you'll intimidate us, but it won't work!' Instead, Stalin told him, 'go to the Writers' Union and write fairy tales for idiots to read'.[16] Terekhov lost his job two weeks later.

An echo of this incident is found in the party conference speeches made over the subsequent year. In many of them Ukrainian communists referred to 'problems' or 'difficulties', but very rarely to 'famine'. Of course they knew it was happening, but in order to survive they had to observe the Kremlin's taboos. Privately, the word remained in use, as we have seen in Kosior's letters to Stalin. But although no written record exists of an order not to use the word 'famine' in public, it is striking how rarely it was used.[17] Instead, Soviet officials used euphemisms. When a Japanese consul in Odessa made an official inquiry about the famine, for example, even he was told 'there are food shortages but no famine'.[18]

The victims were harder to banish. Even after the bodies had been buried in unmarked mass graves, and even after the death registries were altered, there still remained the problem of Soviet statistics. In 1937 the Soviet census bureau set out to count and measure the Soviet population, a vast task made urgent by the need to coordinate central planning. But even as the complex process began – it involved asking millions of people to fill out forms – the Soviet leadership began to be anxious about the possible result. '*Not one figure* from the census can be published', employees of the local statistical offices were told in

December 1936. There was to be '*no* preliminary processing of the raw material' either.[19]

Even so, the final result of the 1937 census was shocking. Newspapers had floated advance stories of growth and a population boom, 'evidence of the great increase in our workers' standard of living' after 'ten years of our heroic fight for socialism'.[20] Statisticians, not wanting to be blamed for sending a negative message, had been filing regular reports of growth too. One preliminary report did cautiously hint that the population levels might turn out to be lower than anticipated in Ukraine, the North Caucasus and the Volga region – 'regions where the resistance of kulaks to collectivization was particularly determined and bitter' – but it devoted little space to the problem. Overall, the projections were optimistic. In 1934 census officials estimated that the population of the USSR stood at 168 million. In 1937 they estimated 170 million or even 172 million.

The real numbers, when they finally arrived, were quite different. The total population figure of the USSR came to 162 million – meaning that (for those who expected 170 million) some eight million people were 'missing'. That inexact number included victims of the famine and their unborn children. It also reflected the genuine chaos of the famine years. The peasants dying by the roadsides, the mass migration, the deportations, the impossibility of keeping accurate statistics in villages where everyone was starving, including public officials – all of these things made the census-takers' job more difficult.[21] In truth, nobody was absolutely sure how many people had really died and how many lived, counted or uncounted. The census-takers had erred on the side of caution.

Rather than accept the result, Stalin abolished it. Meetings were called; expert panels were created. A special Central Committee resolution declared the census badly organized, unprofessional, and a 'gross violation of the basic fundamentals of statistical science'.[22] The journal *Bolshevik* declared that the census had been 'disrupted by contemptible enemies of the people – Trotsky-Bukharinite spies and traitors to the motherland, having slipped at that time into the leadership of the Central Directory of People's Economic Accounting . . . Enemies of the people set themselves the goal of distorting the real number of the population.'[23]

The publication of the 1937 census was halted immediately, and the results never appeared. The statisticians themselves paid the price. The head of the census bureau, Ivan Kraval, at the time a resident of the House on the Embankment, the most exclusive party residence in Moscow, was arrested and executed by firing squad in September. His closest colleagues were also put to death. Repression cascaded downwards to Kazakhstan and Ukraine as well as the Russian provinces, where hundreds of lower-level census officials were sacked from their jobs and sometimes arrested and executed as well. The list of the repressed included not only those directly responsible for the census, but also statisticians who might have had access to the original numbers. Mykhailo Avdiienko, the Kyiv editor of *Soviet Statistics*, was arrested in August and executed in September. Oleksandr Askatin, the head of the economics department at the Ukrainian Academy of Sciences, met the same fate.[24]

By November an entirely new cadre of officials had replaced these men, every one of whom now understood that it was extremely dangerous to produce accurate numbers.[25] A new census was duly commissioned. This time Stalin did not wait for the result. Even before the census had taken place, he declared victory:

> Under the sun of the Great Socialist Revolution an astonishingly rapid, never-before-seen increase in population is taking place. Mighty socialist industry has called into life new professions. Tens of thousands of people, who yesterday were unskilled labourers, today have become qualified masters in the most diverse branches of production. Yesterday's Stakhanovites today have become technicians and engineers. Millions of peasant smallholders, eking out a beggarly life, have become prosperous collective farmers, creators of socialist harvests . . .
> The all-Union census of the population must show all the great changes that have happened in the life of the people, the growth of the cultural and material level of the masses, the increase in the qualification of factory workers and office workers . . .[26]

Stalin got what he ordered: at the Eighteenth Party Congress in March 1939, before the final tally was complete, he announced, with great fanfare, that the Soviet population had indeed reached 170 million.[27]

In due course the statisticians found ways to make the numbers match the rhetoric. They massaged data to mask the high number of prisoners in the north and east of the USSR – the years 1937–9 were a time of major Gulag expansion – and, of course, to hide the ravages of the famine. Census forms for more than 350,000 people residing elsewhere were assigned to Ukraine. Another 375,000 dead souls were allotted to Kazakhstan. As well as altering the totals, the census-takers erased some small national and ethnic groups, and changed the balance of the population in ethnically divided regions to suit Soviet policy. Overall, they boosted the population by at least 1 per cent. For decades afterwards the 1939 census was held up as a model piece of statistical research.[28]

With publication of the 1939 census the great famine vanished not only from the newspapers but from Soviet demography, politics and bureaucracy. The Soviet state never kept any record of the victims, their lives or their deaths. For as long as it existed, it never accepted that they had died at all.

Violence, repression and the census falsification successfully quelled discussion of the famine inside the USSR. But the cover-up of the famine abroad required different tactics. Information was not so easily controlled outside the Soviet Union. Information did cross borders, as did people. In May 1933 a Ukrainian newspaper in Lviv (then a Polish city) published an article denouncing the famine as an attack on the Ukrainian national movement:

> The eastern side of the Zbruch River [the border] now looks like a real military camp that is difficult for a citizen to cross even at night, as in wartime. We are informed of this by refugees who recently managed to wade across the Zbruch . . . they arrived as living skeletons because the famine there is terrible. Even dogs are being killed, and today's slaves of the collective farms are being fed dog meat, for in fertile Ukraine neither bread nor potatoes are to be had.[29]

Other news came from officials and consuls who crossed the border legally as well as from letters mailed from ports, sent via travellers or missed by censors. Ethnic Germans wrote to individuals in the United States and Germany, sometimes to relatives and sometimes to unknown leaders of their religious communities: 'Dear Fathers and Brothers in faraway Germany, a plea from Russia from me of German name . . . I call to you for advice and help and to tell you what is in my grief-stricken heart.'[30] Letters also managed to reach Canada.

These missives had an impact, as did the few refugees. Even as the famine was unfolding, Ukrainians abroad began to protest against it, both peacefully and otherwise. Ethnic Ukrainian politicians brought up the famine at sessions of the Polish parliament, and described it in the Ukrainian-language press.[31] In October 1933, Mykola Lemyk, a member of a Ukrainian nationalist organization in Poland, murdered the secretary of the Soviet consul in Lviv. During his trial in a Polish court, Lemyk, who had been hoping to kill the consul himself, described the murder as revenge for the famine.[32] At the end of that month the Ukrainian community in Poland tried to organize a mass demonstration in protest against the famine, but they were stopped by the Polish government, which feared further violence.[33]

At about the same time, on the other side of the world, the Ukrainian National Council, an organization formed in May 1933, staged street protests in Winnipeg, Canada, and sent a letter to President Roosevelt, enclosing an eyewitness account of the famine.[34] At a meeting held at the Ukrainian church in Winnipeg, diaspora leaders read aloud letters from Ukraine exhorting the public to help Ukraine 'break away' from the USSR.[35] Ukrainians in Brussels, Prague, Bucharest, Geneva, Paris, London and Sofia, among other cities, created action committees that sought, without much luck, to publicize the famine and deliver aid to the starving.[36]

News also filtered out via the Catholic Church. In Poland, Ukrainian Greek-Catholic priests took up collections for victims of the famine in 1933, held a day of mourning and hung black flags on the facades of Ukrainian churches and the local offices of Prosvita, the Ukrainian cultural institute.[37] Polish and Italian diplomats as well as priests with contacts inside the USSR also alerted the Church hierarchy. The Vatican first received a written description of the famine in April 1933, via an anonymous letter smuggled out through the Russian port of Novorossiisk. A second anonymous letter made its way to Rome from the North Caucasus in August. Pope Pius XI ordered both letters published in the Vatican newspaper, *L'Osservatore*

Romano.[38] In that same month the Archbishop of Vienna, Cardinal Innitzer, issued an alarmed appeal. He denounced famine conditions in Russia, and in the 'Ukraine districts of the Soviet Union':

> [they are] accompanied by such cruel phenomena of mass starvation as infanticide and cannibalism ... It is already established that that catastrophe still obtains, even at the time of the new harvest. It will in four months reach a new peak. Once again millions of lives will be lost ... Merely to look on such a situation would be to increase the responsibility of the whole civilized world for mass deaths in Russia. It would mean to bear the guilt of the fact that, at a time when whole sections of the world are almost choked with a surplus of wheat and food, men are starving in Russia.[39]

Later, Innitzer would be the recipient of an unusual form of evidence: a collection of two dozen photographs taken by Alexander Wienerberger, an Austrian engineer who worked at a factory in Kharkiv and smuggled the pictures out over the border. Preserved in the church diocese archive in Vienna, these are still the only verified photographs taken in Ukraine of famine victims in 1933. They show starving people by the sides of roads, empty houses and mass graves. They leave no doubt about the scale of the tragedy.[40] But in 1933 the problem for the Church was not evidence, but politics. A debate broke out inside the Vatican – one faction wanted to send a famine relief mission to the USSR, another preached diplomatic caution. The argument for caution won. Although the Vatican continued to receive information about the famine, the Holy See mostly kept silent in public. Among other things, Hitler's January 1933 electoral victory created a political trap: the hierarchy feared that strong language about the Soviet famine would make it seem as if the Pope favoured Nazi Germany.[41]

Similar arguments took hold elsewhere, shaped by similar political constraints. Many European foreign ministries had superb information about the famine, as it was happening, in real time. Indeed, in 1933, Ukraine was blessed with several extraordinarily observant resident foreigners. Gradenigo, the Italian consul who lived in Kharkiv between 1930 and 1934, understood both the scale of the famine and the impact it had on the Ukrainian national movement.

He did not doubt that 'the hunger is principally the result of a famine organized in order to teach a lesson to the peasants':

> ... The current disaster will lead to the colonization of Ukraine by Russians. It will transform Ukraine's character. In the near future there will be no reason to speak of Ukraine or Ukrainian people, simply because there will be no more 'Ukrainian problem' when Ukraine becomes an indistinguishable part of Russia ...[42]

The German consul in Odessa in 1933 was no less emphatic about the origins of the famine:

> The communist rulers do not let the peasants remember their hardships for too long, achieving this by having one hardship follow the other immediately, and thus, whether one wants to or not, the old fears are forgotten. In the past, if someone in a village was struck by misfortune, entire generations remembered.[43]

Gustav Hilger, a German diplomat in Moscow, later an important adviser on Soviet policy to Hitler (and after that to the CIA), also believed at the time that the famine was artificial:

> It was our impression then that the authorities deliberately refrained from aiding the stricken population, except those organized in collective farms, in order to demonstrate to the recalcitrant peasant that death by starvation was the only alternative to collectivization.[44]

Yet in both Italy and Germany – one already a fascist state, the latter in the course of becoming one – the famine had no impact on official policy. Benito Mussolini personally read and marked up some of the reports from Ukraine, but never said anything in public, perhaps because it was not in the nature of his regime to show pity, or perhaps because the Italians, who concluded a non-aggression treaty with the USSR in September 1933, were more interested in trade.[45] But other than the deliberately discreet effort to help ethnic Germans, and, later, use of the famine in Nazi propaganda, the Germans made no attempt at the time either to protest or to offer aid.

Not all of the reports were believed. Polish diplomats were deeply shocked by the famine – so much so that their accounts were dismissed. Stanislaw Kosnicki, the head of the Kyiv consulate, was rebuked in January 1934 for including too much 'information about famine, misery, persecution of the population, the fight against Ukrainianness etc.'. Polish diplomats, like their colleagues, nevertheless had no doubt that the famine and the repressions were part of a plan: 'Mass arrests and persecutions cannot be explained or justified by peril on the part of the Ukrainian national movement . . . the real cause of the action lies in the planned, far-sighted, long-term policy of the Moscow leaders, who are more and more becoming imperialists, strengthening the political system and borders of the state'.[46]

British diplomats, on the other hand, had no trouble believing the worst stories they heard. They had a whole network of informants, including the Canadian agricultural expert Andrew Cairns, who travelled through Ukraine and the North Caucasus in 1932 on behalf of the Empire Marketing Board. Cairns reported seeing 'rag-clad hungry peasants, some begging for bread, mostly waiting, mostly in vain, for tickets, many climbing on to the steps or joining the crowds on the roof of each car, all filthy and miserable and not a trace of a smile anywhere'.[47] He also concluded that the government's grain export plan was 'ridiculous' and could not be fulfilled.[48]

But the British government not only did not offer aid, it actively discouraged several independent efforts to get food to the starving in 1933, on the grounds that the Soviet government was opposed to such efforts and therefore it was naive to make them. Laurence Collier, head of the Foreign Office Northern Department at the time, also objected to the presence of diaspora Ukrainians in several of the charities: 'anything to do with Ukrainian nationalism was like a red rag to a bull to the Soviet authorities'. Collier understood what was happening – of Cairns' report, he wrote: 'I have seldom read a more convincing document' – but preferred not to ruffle feathers.[49]

Diplomatic silence suited the Soviet leadership, which had good reasons to stop stories about the famine from spreading. Although the Bolshevik goal of world revolution had been pushed into the far distance, it had never been abandoned completely. By 1933 radical political change in Europe once again seemed plausible. The continent was gripped by economic crisis; Hitler had just become Chancellor of Germany. The worsening international situation meant, to the Marxist-Leninist mind, that the final crisis of capitalism must be approaching. In this context, perceptions of the USSR abroad mattered a great deal to Soviet leaders, who hoped to use the crisis to promote the Soviet Union as a superior civilization.

The Soviet leadership also cared about foreign public opinion for domestic reasons. Since 1917, foreigners, from the American communist John Reed to the French writer Anatole France, had been deployed inside the USSR as ballast for propaganda. The writings of foreigners who lauded the achievements of the revolution were published and publicized inside the country, as were the remarks of enthusiastic visitors – communists, writers, intellectuals – who were taken to see Soviet schools, farms and factories. In the wake of the famine, the Soviet leadership encouraged these fellow travellers to dismiss any talk of food shortages – and some of them did.

Their motives were mixed. Some, like the British socialists Beatrice and Sidney Webb, were 'true believers' who wanted some form of socialist revolution in their own countries and sought to use the example of the USSR for their own ends. The Webbs were aware of the famine but downplayed it in order to laud collectivization: 'The experience of the last three harvests seems to justify the claim of the Soviet government that the initial difficulties of this giant transformation have been overcome,' they wrote in 1936. 'There is, indeed, little reason to doubt that the aggregate output of foodstuffs is being increased at a great rate.'[50]

Other visitors seem to have been motivated by vanity, as well as the immense pomp and favour that the USSR could shower upon celebrities. The writer George Bernard Shaw, accompanied by the MP Nancy Astor, celebrated his seventy-fifth birthday at a banquet in Moscow – vegetarian, to accommodate his tastes – in 1931. Having been greeted by welcoming parties and serenaded by brass bands, Shaw was in an expansive mood when he spoke to the audience of Soviet officials and distinguished foreigners.[51] Thanking his hosts, he declared himself the enemy of anti-Soviet rumour-mongers. When friends had heard he was going to Russia, he told the crowd, they had given him tins of food to take on the journey: 'They thought Russia was starving. But I threw all of the food out the window in Poland before I reached the Soviet frontier.'

His audience 'gasped', recalled a journalist in attendance: 'One felt the convulsive reaction in their bellies. A tin of English beef would provide a memorable holiday in the home of any of the workers and intellectuals at the gathering.'[52] A flavour of the cynical weariness with which at least some of the Soviet intelligentsia received these pompous outsiders can be deduced from Andrey Platonov's play, *Fourteen Little Red Huts*. Platonov's play features a visiting foreign intellectual who demands, 'Where can I see socialism? Show it to me at once. Capitalism irritates me.'[53]

In the summer of the famine, the most important real-life version of Platonov's anti-hero was Édouard Herriot, a French Radical politician and former prime minister who was invited to Ukraine at the end of August 1933 specifically to repudiate growing rumours of famine. Herriot's own motivation seems to have been political. Like other 'realist' statesmen in many Western capitals, he wanted to encourage his country's trade relations with the USSR, and he wasn't particularly bothered by the nature of its government. During his two-week trip he visited a model children's colony, saw shops whose shelves had been hastily stocked in advance, rode down the Dnieper River on a boat and met enthusiastic peasants and workers coached especially for the occasion. Before his arrival, Herriot's hotel was hastily refurbished and the staff were given new uniforms.

The highlight of the Frenchman's trip was a visit to a collective farm. Afterwards, he remembered their 'admirably irrigated and cultivated' vegetable gardens. 'I've travelled across Ukraine,' declared Herriot, 'I assure you that I have seen a garden in full bloom'.[54] According to OGPU reports filed afterwards, Herriot did ask about famine, but was assured that any past difficulties were now over.[55] *Pravda* made immediate use of the visit for purposes of domestic propaganda, and proudly stated that Herriot 'categorically contradicted the lies of the bourgeois press in connection with a famine in the USSR', just in case any Soviet citizens had somehow managed to hear them.[56]

The diplomats and one-off visitors did not present a difficult challenge for the Soviet authorities. The Foreign Ministry mandarins were too discreet to voice their opinions. Men like Herriot and Shaw could not speak the language or control their itineraries; it was relatively easy to monitor what they saw and whom they met. By contrast, the manipulation of the foreign press corps in Moscow required a good deal more sophistication. Their movements and conversations could not be completely controlled – and they could not be ordered what to write.

By 1933 the regime already had bad experiences with the more independent-minded members of the press corps. One of these was Rhea Clyman, an extraordinary Canadian who spent four years in Moscow before deciding to drive across the USSR in the company of two American women from Atlanta, arguing with officials at every turn. Clyman was finally stopped in Tbilisi in the summer of 1932 and forcibly deported (the other two women made it to Tashkent before they met the same fate).[57] The result was an enormous headline in the *Toronto Evening Telegram*:

> Telegram Writer Driven from Russia
> Rhea Clyman Exposes Prison Camp Conditions
> Angers Soviet Dictators[58]

Once she knew that she could never return to the USSR, Clyman published a series of luridly written but accurate stories, describing kulak families sent to the far north, the growing food shortages in Ukraine, and the early Gulag camps in Karelia near the Finnish border. She also described the after-effects of collectivization in Ukraine:

> The villages were strangely forlorn and deserted. I could not understand at first. The houses were empty, the doors flung wide open, the roofs were caving in. I felt that we were following in the wake of some hungry horde that was sweeping on ahead of us and laying all these homes bare ... When we had passed ten, fifteen of these villages I began to understand. These were the homes of those thousands of expropriated peasants – the kulaks – I had seen working in the mines and cutting timber in the North. We sped on and on, raising a thick cloud of dust in front and behind, but still those empty houses staring out with unseeing eyes raced on ahead of us.[59]

Although Clyman's writing was embarrassing to the Soviet government, neither she nor her newspaper were sufficiently prestigious to create any stir at a higher level. Her expulsion helped the Soviet state maintain order. It sent a message: the more established, more influential Moscow-based journalists had to be careful if they wanted to keep their jobs.

Indeed, they had to be careful if they wanted to be able to do their jobs at all. At the time, Moscow correspondents needed the state's permission not only to remain in residence but also to file their articles. Without a signature and the official stamp of the press department, the central telegraph office would not send any dispatches abroad. To win that permission, journalists regularly bargained with Foreign Ministry censors over which words they could use, and they kept on good terms with Konstantin Umanskii, the Soviet official responsible for the foreign press corps.[60] William Henry Chamberlin, then the Moscow correspondent for the *Christian Science Monitor*, wrote that the foreign correspondent who refused to soften his commentary 'works under a Sword of Damocles – the threat of expulsion from the country or of the refusal of permission to re-enter it, which of course amounts to the same thing'.[61]

Extra rewards were available to those who played the game particularly well, as the case of Walter Duranty famously illustrates. Duranty was the correspondent for *The New York Times* in Moscow between 1922 and 1936, a role that, for a time, made him relatively rich and famous. Duranty, British by birth, had no ties to the ideological left, adopting rather the position of a hard-headed and sceptical 'realist' trying to listen to both sides of a story. 'It may be objected that the vivisection of living animals is a sad and dreadful thing, and it is true that the lot of kulaks and others who have opposed the Soviet experiment is not a happy one,' he wrote in 1935. But 'in both cases, the suffering inflicted is done with a noble purpose'.[62]

This position made Duranty enormously useful to the regime, which went out of its way to ensure that he lived well in Moscow. He had a large flat, kept a car and a mistress, had the best access of any correspondent, and twice received coveted interviews with Stalin. But the attention he won from his reporting seems to have been the primary motivation for Duranty's flattering coverage of the USSR. Whereas Clyman's writing struck few chords, Duranty's missives from Moscow made him one of the most influential journalists of his time. Many of the men who would become part of Franklin Roosevelt's 'Brains Trust' were looking for new economic ideas and had a deep interest in the Soviet experiment; several had visited Moscow in 1927, where they were granted a six-hour interview with Stalin. Duranty's accounts chimed with their general worldview and attracted wide attention: in 1932 his series of articles on the successes of collectivization and the Five Year Plan won him the Pulitzer Prize. Soon afterwards, Roosevelt, then the governor of New York, invited Duranty to the governor's mansion in Albany, where the Democratic presidential candidate peppered him with queries. 'I asked all the questions this time. It was fascinating,' Roosevelt told another reporter.[63]

But as the famine worsened, controls tightened still further. In 1933 the Foreign Ministry minders, having learned their lesson from Clyman and her companions, began requiring correspondents to obtain permission and submit a proposed itinerary before any journey. All requests to visit Ukraine or the North Caucasus were refused. The sole French correspondent in Moscow received permission to cover Herriot's visit in the summer of 1933 only after he agreed to remain within the party of the former French prime minister, keep to the planned route, and write about nothing other than the events carefully prepared by the Soviet state. The censors also began to watch dispatches for covert reporting on the famine. Some phrases were allowed: 'acute food shortage', 'food stringency', 'food deficit', 'diseases due to malnutrition', but nothing else.[64] In late 1932, Soviet officials even visited Duranty at home, making him nervous.[65]

In that atmosphere few correspondents were inclined to write about the famine, although all of them knew about it. 'Officially, there was no famine,' wrote Chamberlin. But 'to anyone who lived in Russia in 1933 and who kept his eyes and ears open, the historicity of the famine is simply not in question'.[66] Duranty himself discussed the famine with William Strang, a diplomat at the British Embassy, in late 1932. Strang reported back drily that the correspondent for *The New York Times* had been 'waking to the truth for some time', although he had not 'let the great American public into the secret'. Duranty also told Strang that he reckoned 'it quite possible that as many as 10 million people may have died directly or indirectly from lack of food', though that number never appeared in any of his reporting.[67] Duranty's reluctance to write about famine may have been particularly acute: the story cast doubt on his previous, positive (and prize-winning) reporting. But he was not alone. Eugene Lyons, Moscow correspondent for United Press and at one time an enthusiastic Marxist, wrote years later that all foreigners in the city were well aware of what was happening in Ukraine as well as in Kazakhstan and the Volga region:

> The truth is that we did not seek corroboration for the simple reason that we entertained no doubts on the subject. There are facts too large to require eyewitness confirmation ... There was no more need for investigation to establish the mere existence of the Russian famine than investigation to establish the existence of the American depression. Inside Russia the matter was not disputed. The famine was accepted as a matter of course in our casual conversation at the hotels and in our homes. In the foreign colony estimates of famine deaths ranged from one million up; among Russians from three million up . . .[68]

Everyone knew – yet no one mentioned it. Hence the extraordinary reaction of both the Soviet establishment and the Moscow press corps to the journalistic escapade of Gareth Jones.

Jones was a young Welshman, only twenty-seven years old at the time of his journey to the USSR in 1933. Possibly inspired by his mother – as a young woman she had been a governess in the home of John Hughes, the Welsh entrepreneur who founded the city of Donetsk – Jones studied Russian, as well as French and German, at Cambridge University. He then landed a job as a private secretary to David Lloyd George, the former British prime minister. At the same time he began writing about European and Soviet politics as a freelancer, making short trips in and out of the USSR, which put him in a different position from the Moscow correspondents who needed the regime's approval in order to keep their residence permits. On one of those trips, in early 1932 before the travel ban was imposed, Jones journeyed out to the countryside (accompanied by Jack Heinz II, scion of the ketchup empire) where he slept on 'bug-infested floors' in Soviet villages and witnessed the beginnings of the famine. Months later he travelled to Frankfurt-am-Main in the entourage of Adolf Hitler – the first foreign correspondent to have access to the newly elected Chancellor of Germany.[69]

In the spring of 1933, Jones returned to Moscow, this time with a visa granted him largely on the grounds that he worked for Lloyd George (it was stamped 'Besplatno' or 'Gratis', as a sign of official Soviet favour). Ivan Maisky, the Soviet ambassador to London, had been particularly keen to impress Lloyd George and had lobbied on Jones's behalf. Upon arrival, Jones first went around the Soviet capital, meeting with other foreign correspondents and officials. Lyons remembered him as 'an earnest and meticulous little man . . . the sort who carries a note-book and unashamedly records your words as you talk'.[70] Jones met Umanskii, showed him an invitation to pay a visit to the German Consul-General in Kharkiv, outlined a plan to visit a German tractor factory, and asked to visit Ukraine. Umanskii agreed. With that official stamp of approval, Jones set off south.[71]

He boarded the train in Moscow on 10 March. But instead of travelling all the way to Kharkiv, Jones got off the train about forty miles north of the city. Carrying a backpack filled with 'many loaves of white bread, with butter, cheese, meat and chocolate bought with foreign currency from the Torgsin stores', he began to follow the railway track towards the Ukrainian capital.[72] For three days, with no official minder or escort, he walked through more than twenty villages and collective farms, seeing rural Ukraine at the height of the famine, recording his thoughts and impressions in notebooks that were later preserved by his sister:

> I crossed the border from Great Russia into the Ukraine. Everywhere I talked to peasants who walked past. They all had the same story.
>
> 'There is no bread. We haven't had bread for over 2 months. A lot are dying.' The first village had no more potatoes left and the store of *buriak* [beetroot] was running out. They all said: 'The cattle are dying, *nechem kormit'* [there's nothing to feed them with]. We used to feed the world & now we are hungry. How can we sow when we have few horses left? How will we be able to work in the fields when we are weak from want of food?'
>
> Then I caught up [with] a bearded peasant who was walking along. His feet were covered with sacking. We started talking. He spoke in Ukrainian Russian. I gave him [a] lump of bread and of cheese. 'You couldn't buy that anywhere for 20 rubles. There just is no food.'

We walked along and talked. 'Before the War this was all gold. We had horses and cows and pigs and chickens. Now we are ruined . . . We're doomed.'[73]

Jones slept on the floor of peasant huts. He shared his food with people and heard their stories. 'They tried to take away my icons, but I said I'm a peasant, not a dog,' someone told him. 'When we believed in God we were happy and lived well. When they tried to do away with God, we became hungry.' Another man told him he had not eaten meat for a year.

Jones saw a woman making homespun cloth for clothing, and a village where people were eating horse meat.[74] Eventually, he was confronted by a 'militiaman' who asked to see his documents, after which plainclothes policemen, no doubt OGPU, insisted on accompanying him on the next train to Kharkiv and walking him to the door of the German consulate. Jones, 'rejoicing at my freedom, bade him a polite farewell – an anti-climax but a welcome one'.[75]

In Kharkiv he kept making notes. He observed thousands of people queuing in bread lines: 'They begin queuing up 3–4 o'clock in the afternoon to get bread the next morning at 7. It is freezing: many degrees of frost.'[76] Jones spent an evening at the theatre – 'Audience: Plenty of lipstick but no bread' – and spoke to people about the political repression and mass arrests that were rolling across Ukraine at the same time as the famine:

> 'They are cruelly strict now in the factories. If you are absent one day, you are sacked, get your bread card taken away & cannot get a passport.'
>
> 'Life is a nightmare. I cannot go in the tram, it kills my nerves.'
>
> 'It is more terrible than ever. If you say a word now in the factory, you are dismissed. There is no freedom . . .'
>
> 'Everywhere persecution. Everywhere terror. One man we knew said: "My brother died, but he still lies there & we don't know when we'll bury him, for there are queues for the burial."'
>
> 'There is no hope for the future.'[77]

He seems to have tried to call on Umanskii's colleague in Kharkiv, but never managed to speak to him. Quietly, Jones slipped out of the

Soviet Union. A few days later, on 30 March, he appeared in Berlin at a press conference probably arranged by Paul Scheffer, the *Berliner Tageblatt* journalist who had been expelled from the USSR in 1929. Jones declared that a major famine was unfolding across the Soviet Union and issued a statement:

> Everywhere was the cry, 'There is no bread. We are dying.' This cry came from every part of Russia, from the Volga, Siberia, White Russia, the North Caucasus, Central Asia . . .
>
> In the train a Communist denied to me that there was a famine. I flung a crust of bread which I had been eating from my own supply into a spittoon. A peasant fellow-passenger fished it out and ravenously ate it. I threw an orange peel into the spittoon and the peasant again grabbed it and devoured it. The Communist subsided. I stayed overnight in a village where there used to be 200 oxen and where there now are six. The peasants were eating the cattle fodder and had only a month's supply left. They told me that many had already died of hunger. Two soldiers came to arrest a thief. They warned me against travel by night as there were too many 'starving' desperate men.
>
> 'We are waiting for death' was my welcome: 'See, we still have our cattle fodder. Go farther south. There they have nothing. Many houses are empty of people already dead,' they cried.

Jones's press conference was picked up by two senior Berlin-based American journalists, in the *New York Evening Post* ('Famine Grips Russia, Millions Dying, Idle on Rise Says Briton') and the *Chicago Daily News* ('Russian Famine Now as Great as Starvation of 1921, Says Secretary of Lloyd George').[78] Further syndications followed in a wide range of British publications. The articles explained that Jones had taken a 'long walking tour through the Ukraine', quoted his press release, and added details of mass starvation. They noted, as did Jones himself, that he had broken the rules that held back other journalists: 'I tramped through the black earth region,' he wrote, 'because that was once the richest farmland in Russia and because the correspondents have been forbidden to go there to see for themselves what is happening.'[79] Jones went on to publish a dozen further articles in the *London Evening Standard* and *Daily Express*, as well as the *Cardiff Western Mail*.[80]

The authorities who had showered favours on Jones were furious. Maxim Litvinov, the Soviet Foreign Minister, complained angrily to ambassador Maisky, using an acidic literary allusion to Gogol's famous play about a fraudulent bureaucrat:

> It is astonishing that Gareth Johnson [sic] has impersonated the role of Khlestakov and succeeded in getting all of you to play the parts of the local governor and various characters from *The Government Inspector*. In fact, he is just an ordinary citizen, calls himself Lloyd George's secretary and, apparently at the latter's bidding, requests a visa, and you at the diplomatic mission without checking up at all, insist the [OGPU] jump into action to satisfy his request. We gave this individual all kinds of support, helped him in his work, I even agreed to meet him, and he turns out to be an imposter.

In the immediate wake of Jones's press conference, Litvinov proclaimed an even more stringent ban on journalists travelling outside Moscow. Later, Maisky complained to Lloyd George, who, according to the Soviet ambassador's report, distanced himself from Jones, declared that he had not sponsored the trip and had not sent Jones as his representative. What he really believed is unknown, but Lloyd George never saw Jones again.[81]

The Moscow press corps was even angrier. Of course, its members all knew that what Jones had reported was true, and a few were already beginning to look for ways to tell the same story. Malcolm Muggeridge, at the time the correspondent for the *Manchester Guardian* – substituting for Chamberlin, who was out of the country – had just smuggled three articles out of the country via diplomatic bag. The *Guardian* published them anonymously, with heavy cuts made by editors who disapproved of his critique of the USSR, and they were largely ignored: they clashed with bigger stories about Hitler and Germany. But the rest of the press corps, dependent on the goodwill of Umanskii and Litvinov, closed ranks against Jones. Lyons meticulously described what happened:

> Throwing down Jones was as unpleasant a chore as fell to any of us in years of juggling facts to please dictatorial regimes – but throw him down we did, unanimously and in almost identical formulations of

equivocation. Poor Gareth Jones must have been the most surprised human being alive when the facts he so painstakingly garnered from our mouths were snowed under by our denials ... There was much bargaining in a spirit of gentlemanly give-and-take, under the effulgence of Umanskii's gilded smile, before a formal denial was worked out. We admitted enough to soothe our consciences, but in round-about phrases that damned Jones as a liar. The filthy business having been disposed of, someone ordered vodka and *zakuski*'.[82]

Whether or not such a meeting actually ever took place, it does sum up, metaphorically, what happened next. On 31 March, just a day after Jones had spoken out in Berlin, Duranty himself responded. 'Russians Hungry But Not Starving', read the headline of *The New York Times*. Duranty's article went out of its way to mock Jones:

There appears from a British source a big scare story in the American press about famine in the Soviet Union, with 'thousands already dead and millions menaced by death and starvation'. Its author is Gareth Jones, who is a former secretary to David Lloyd George and who recently spent three weeks in the Soviet Union and reached the conclusion that the country was 'on the verge of a terrific smash', as he told the writer. Mr. Jones is a man of a keen and active mind, and he has taken the trouble to learn Russian, which he speaks with considerable fluency, but the writer thought Mr. Jones's judgment was somewhat hasty and asked him on what it was based. It appeared that he had made a forty-mile walk through villages in the neighborhood of Kharkiv and had found conditions sad.

I suggested that that was a rather inadequate cross-section of a big country but nothing could shake his conviction of impending doom.[83]

Duranty continued, using an expression that later became notorious: 'To put it brutally – you can't make an omelette without breaking eggs.' He went on to explain that he had made 'exhaustive inquiries' and concluded that 'conditions are bad, but there is no famine'.

Indignant, Jones wrote a letter to the editor of *The Times*, patiently listing his sources – a huge range of interviewees, including more than twenty consuls and diplomats – and attacking the Moscow press corps:

> Censorship has turned them into masters of euphemism and under-
> statement. Hence they give 'famine' the polite name of 'food shortage'
> and 'starving to death' is softened down to read as 'widespread mor-
> tality from diseases due to malnutrition'.

And there the matter rested. Duranty outshone Jones: he was more
famous, more widely read, more credible. He was also unchallenged.
Later, Lyons, Chamberlin and others expressed regret that they had
not fought harder against him. But at the time nobody came to Jones's
defence, not even Muggeridge, one of the few Moscow correspondents who had dared to express similar views. As for Jones himself, he
was kidnapped and murdered by Chinese bandits while reporting in
Mongolia in 1935.[84]

'Russians Hungry But Not Starving' became the accepted wisdom.
It also coincided nicely with the hard political and diplomatic considerations of the moment. As 1933 turned into 1934 and then 1935,
Europeans grew even more worried about Hitler. Édouard Herriot
was only one of several French politicians, including former prime
ministers Jean-Louis Barthou and Pierre Laval, who believed that the
rise of Nazism required a Franco-Soviet alliance.[85] In the British Foreign Office, Laurence Collier thought a British-Soviet alliance might
be necessary too. In answer to a query by a Member of Parliament,
he explained:

> The truth of the matter is, of course, that we have a certain amount of
> information about famine conditions . . . and that there is no oblig-
> ation on us not to make it public. We do not want to make it public,
> however, because the Soviet government would resent it and our rel-
> ations with them would be prejudiced.[86]

The Poles, who had very detailed information on the famine from
multiple sources, also remained silent. They had signed a non-
aggression pact with the USSR in July 1932; their policy of truce and
cold peace with their Soviet neighbours would backfire badly in
1939.[87]

By the end of 1933 the new Roosevelt administration was actively
looking for reasons to ignore any bad news about the Soviet Union.
The president's team had concluded that developments in Germany

and the need to contain the Japanese meant it was time, finally, for the United States to open full diplomatic relations with Moscow. Roosevelt's interest in central planning and in what he thought were the USSR's great economic successes – the president read Duranty's reporting carefully – encouraged him to believe that there might be a lucrative commercial relationship too.[88] Eventually a deal was struck. Litvinov arrived in New York to sign it – accompanied by Duranty. During a lavish banquet for the Soviet Foreign Minister at the Waldorf Astoria, Duranty was introduced to the 1,500 guests. He stood up and bowed.

Loud applause followed. Duranty's name, the *New Yorker* later reported, provoked 'the only really prolonged pandemonium' of the evening. 'Indeed, one quite got the impression that America, in a spasm of discernment, was recognizing both Russia and Walter Duranty.'[89] With that, the cover-up seemed complete.

15

The Holodomor in History
and Memory

Dear God, calamity again! . . .
It was so peaceful, so serene;
We but began to break the chains
That bind our folk in slavery . . .
When halt! . . . Again the people's blood
Is streaming!

Taras Shevchenko, 'Calamity Again', 1859[1]

In the years that followed the famine, Ukrainians were forbidden to speak about what had happened. They were afraid to mourn publicly. Even if they had dared to do so, there were no churches to pray in, no tombstones to decorate with flowers. When the state destroyed the institutions of the Ukrainian countryside, it struck a blow against public memory as well.

Privately, however, the survivors did remember. They made real or mental notes about what had happened. Some kept diaries, 'locked up in wooden boxes' as one recalled, and hid them beneath floorboards or buried them in the ground.[2] In their villages, within their families, people also told their children what had happened. Volodymyr Chepur was five years old when his mother explained to him that she and his father would give him everything that they had to eat. Even if they did not survive, they wanted him to live so that he could bear witness: 'I must not die, and when I grow up I must tell people how we and our Ukraine died in torment.'[3] Elida Zolotoverkha, the daughter of the diarist Oleksandra Radchenko, also told her children, her grandchildren and then her great-grandchildren to read it and to remember 'the horror that Ukraine had passed through'.[4]

Those words, repeated by so many people in private, left their mark. The official silence gave them almost a secret power. From 1933 onwards such stories became an alternative narrative, an emotionally powerful 'true history' of the famine, an oral tradition that grew and developed alongside the official denials.

Although they lived in a propaganda state where the party controlled public discussion, millions of Ukrainians inside Ukraine knew this alternative narrative. The sense of disjunction, the gap between private and public memory, the gaping hole where the national mourning should have been – these things distressed Ukrainians for decades. After his parents died of starvation in Dnipropetrovsk province, Havrylo Prokopenko could not stop thinking about the famine. He wrote a story about it for school, with an illustration to match. His teacher praised his work but told him to destroy it, for fear it would get him, and her, into trouble. That left him with the feeling that something was wrong. Why could the famine not be mentioned? What was the Soviet state trying to hide? Three decades later, Prokopenko managed to read a poem on a local television station, including a line about 'people black with hunger'. A threatening visit from local authorities followed, but that left him even more convinced that the USSR was responsible for the tragedy.[5]

The absence of commemoration also bothered Volodymyr Samoiliuk. Although he later survived Nazi occupation and fought in the Second World War, nothing ever seemed more tragic to him than the experience of the famine. The memory stayed with him for decades, and he kept waiting for the famine to appear in official history. In 1967 he watched a Soviet television programme about 1933. He stared at the screen, waiting to see a reflection of the horror he remembered. But although he saw clips of the enthusiastic heroes of the first Five Year Plan, the May Day parade, even football matches from that year, 'there was not a word about the horrific famine'.[6]

From 1933 until the late 1980s the silence inside Ukraine was total – with one glaring, painful and complicated exception.

Hitler invaded the Soviet Union on 22 June 1941. By November the Wehrmacht had occupied most of Soviet Ukraine. Not knowing what was to come next, many Ukrainians, even Jewish Ukrainians, at first welcomed the German troops. 'Girls would offer the soldiers flowers and people would offer bread,' one woman recalled. 'We were all so happy to see them. They were going to save us from the Communists who had taken everything and starved us.'[7]

A similar welcome initially greeted the German army in the Baltic states, which had been occupied by the USSR from 1939 until 1941. The Caucasus and Crimea welcomed German troops with enthusiasm as well, though not because the inhabitants were Nazis. De-kulakization, collectivization, mass terror and the Bolshevik attacks on the Church encouraged a naively optimistic view of what the Wehrmacht might bring.[8] In many parts of Ukraine the arrival of the Germans inspired spontaneous de-collectivization. Peasants not only took back land, they destroyed tractors and combine harvesters in a Luddite rage.[9]

The uproar ended quickly – and anyone who hoped for a better life under German occupation had their expectations swiftly dashed. A full account of what happened next is beyond the scope of this book, for the catastrophe inflicted by the Nazis on Ukraine was widespread, violent and brutal on an almost incomprehensible scale. By the time they reached the USSR, the Germans had a lot of experience in destroying other states, and in Ukraine they knew what they wanted to do. The Holocaust began immediately, unfolding not in distant camps but in public. Instead of deportation, the Wehrmacht staged mass executions of Jews as well as Roma in front of their neighbours, at the edge of villages and in forests. Two out of every three Ukrainian Jews died over the course of the war – between 800,000 and a million people – a substantial part of the millions more who died all across the continent.

Hitler's Soviet victims also included more than 2 million Soviet prisoners of war, most of whom died of disease or starvation, many of them on Ukrainian territory. Cannibalism haunted Ukraine once again: at Stalag 306 in Kirovohrad guards reported prisoners eating dead comrades. A witness at Stalag 365 in Volodymyr Volynskyi reported the same.[10] Nazi soldiers and police robbed, beat and arbitrarily murdered other Ukrainians, especially public officials. Slavs, in the Nazi hierarchy, were subhuman *untermenschen*, perhaps one level above the Jews but slated for eventual elimination. Many who had welcomed the Wehrmacht quickly realized that they had exchanged one dictatorship for another, especially when the Germans launched a new wave of deportations. During the course of the war Nazi troops sent more than 2 million Ukrainians to do forced labour in Germany.[11]

Like every occupying power in Ukraine, the Nazis ultimately had only one real interest: grain. Hitler had long claimed that 'the occupation of Ukraine would liberate us from every economic worry', and that Ukrainian territory would ensure 'no one is able to starve us again, like in the last war'. Since the late 1930s his government had been planning to transform that aspiration into reality. Herbert Backe, the sinister Nazi official in charge of food and agriculture, conceived a 'Hunger Plan' whose goals were straightforward: 'the war can only be won if the entire Wehrmacht is fed from Russia in the third year of the war'. But he also concluded that the entire Wehrmacht, as well as Germany itself, could only be fed if the Soviet population were completely deprived of food. As Backe explained in his 'Economic Policy Guidelines' issued in May, as well as in a memorandum circulated to a thousand German officials in June 1941, 'unbelievable hunger' would soon grip Russia, Belarus and the industrial cities of the USSR: Moscow and Leningrad as well as Kyiv and Kharkiv. This famine would not be accidental: the goal was for some 30 million people to 'die out'.[12] The guidelines for the Economics Staff East, which was to be responsible for exploiting conquered territory, put it starkly:

Many tens of millions of people in this territory will become superfluous and will have to die or emigrate to Siberia. *Attempts to rescue the population there from death through starvation by obtaining surpluses from the black earth zone can only be at the expense of supplying Europe. They prevent the possibility of Germany holding out in the war; they prevent Germany and Europe resisting the blockade. With regard to this, absolute clarity must reign.*[13] [emphasis in original]

This was Stalin's policy, multiplied many times: the elimination of whole nations through starvation.

The Nazis never had time to fully implement the 'Hunger Plan' in

Ukraine. But its influence could be felt in their occupation policy. Spontaneous de-collectivization was quickly halted, on the grounds that it would be easier to requisition grain from collective farms. Backe reportedly explained that 'the Germans would have had to introduce the collective farm if the Soviets had not already arranged it'.[14] In 1941 the farms were meant to be turned into 'co-operatives', but that never happened.[15]

Hunger returned too. Stalin's 'scorched earth' policy meant that many of Ukraine's economic assets had already been destroyed by the retreating Red Army. The occupation made the situation worse for those who remained. Just before Kyiv was captured in September, Hermann Göring, the Reich Minister of the Economy, held a meeting with Backe. The two agreed that the city's population should not be allowed to 'devour' food: 'Even if one wanted to feed all the inhabitants of the newly conquered territory, one would be unable to do so.' A few days later Heinrich Himmler of the SS told Hitler that the inhabitants of Kyiv were racially inferior and could be discarded: 'One could easily do without eighty to ninety percent of them.'[16]

In the winter of 1941 the Germans cut off food supplies to the city. Contrary to stereotype, the German authorities were less efficient than their Soviet counterparts: peasant traders did get through the makeshift cordons – they had found it difficult to do so in 1933 – and thousands of people took to the roads and railroads again in search of food. Shortages nevertheless multiplied throughout the occupation zone. Once again, people began to swell, slow down, stare into the distance and die. At least 50,000 people died from starvation in Kyiv that winter. In Kharkiv, which was cordoned off by a Nazi commander, 1,202 people died of hunger in the first two weeks of May 1942; the total deaths from starvation during the occupation amounted to about 20,000.[17]

It was in this context – in hardship and chaos, under brutal occupation, and with a new famine looming – that it became possible, for the first time, to speak openly about the 1933 famine in Ukraine. Circumstances shaped the way the story was told. During the occupation the purpose of the discussion was not to help survivors mourn, recover, create an honest record or learn lessons for the future. Those who hoped for some kind of reckoning with the past were disappointed: many of the peasants who had kept secret diaries of the famine unearthed them and brought them to the offices of provincial newspapers. But 'unfortunately, most of the editors were by now uninterested in those past years, and these valuable chronicles received no publicity'.[18] Instead, those editors – who now owed their jobs, and their lives, to the new dictatorship – mostly published articles in the service of Nazi propaganda. The purpose of the discussion was to justify the new regime.

The Nazis actually knew a good deal about the Soviet famine. German diplomats had described it in their reports to Berlin in great detail while it was taking place; Joseph Goebbels had referred to the famine in a speech at the Nazi Party congress in 1935, where he spoke of 5 million dead.[19] From the moment they arrived, the German occupiers of Ukraine used the famine in their 'ideological work'. They hoped to increase hatred towards Moscow, to remind people of the consequences of Bolshevik rule. They were especially keen to reach rural Ukrainians, whose efforts were required to produce the food needed for the Wehrmacht. Propaganda posters, wall newspapers and cartoons showed unhappy, half-starved peasants. In one an emaciated mother and child stand against a ruined city above the slogan 'This is what Stalin gave Ukraine'. In another an impoverished family sit at a table with no food beneath another slogan: 'Life has become better, comrades, Life has become merrier' – a famous quote from Stalin.[20]

To mark the tenth anniversary of the famine, in 1942–3 – coincidentally the high-water mark of Nazi power in Ukraine – many newspapers published material aimed at winning peasant support. In July 1942, *Ukraïnskiy Khliborob*, an agricultural weekly that reached 250,000 people, published a major article on a 'year of work without the Jew-Bolsheviks':

> All peasants remember well the year of 1933 when hunger mowed people down like grass. In two decades the Soviets turned the land of plenty into the land of hunger where millions perished. The German soldier halted this assault, the peasants greeted the German army with bread and salt, the army that fought for the Ukrainian peasants to work freely.[21]

Other articles followed, and got some traction. A diarist at the time wrote that the Nazi propaganda had a strong impact because some of it was true:

> ... the very look of our people, our houses, our yards, our floors, our toilets, our village councils, the ruins of our churches, the flies, the dirt. In one word – everything that fills Europeans with horror but is ignored by our leaders and their sidekicks who have distanced themselves from ordinary people and the contemporary European standard of living.[22]

A refugee from Poltava told an interviewer immediately after the war that there had been a good deal of discussion of the famine under the occupation. He also remembered that at one point, when it looked as if the Red Army might return, people asked 'And what will those "Reds" of ours bring? A new famine of 1933?'[23]

Like everything else in the Nazi press, these wartime accounts were suffused with anti-semitism. The famine – as well as poverty and repression – was repeatedly blamed on the Jews, an idea that had of course had currency before, but was now enshrined in the occupiers' ideology. One newspaper wrote that the Jews were the only part of the population that did not feel the famine because they bought everything they needed in the Torgsin shops: 'Jews lacked neither gold nor dollars.' Others spoke of Bolshevism itself as a 'Jewish product'.[24] One memoirist recalled that he was shown an anti-semitic propaganda film about the famine in Kyiv during the war. It contained photographs of unearthed corpses, and ended with the murder of a Jewish secret policeman.[25]

The wartime press did manage to publish a tiny number of articles on the famine that had not been specifically designed to fit into the framework of Nazi propaganda. In November 1942, S. Sosnovyi, an agricultural economist, published what may have been the very first quasi-scholarly study of the famine in a Kharkiv newspaper, *Nova Ukraïna*. Sosnovyi's article was free of Nazi jargon, offering a straightforward account of what had happened. The famine, he wrote, had been designed to destroy the Ukrainian peasant opposition to Soviet power. It was not the result of 'natural causes': 'In fact, weather conditions in 1932 were not extraordinary like those, for instance, in 1921.' Sosnovyi also produced the first serious estimate of casualties. Referring to the 1926 and 1939 censuses and other Soviet statistical publications (not the suppressed 1937 census, though he probably knew about it), he concluded that 1.5 million people had died from starvation in Ukraine in 1932, and that 3.3 million died in 1933 – numbers slightly higher than those now widely accepted, but not far off.

Sosnovyi also described, accurately, how the famine had come about, proving that the true story, the 'alternative narrative', was still very much alive a decade after the fact:

> First, they took everything from the collective farm storehouses – everything that farmers earned for their 'work days' (*trudodni*). Then they took forage, seeds, and then they went to the huts and took the last grain from the peasants that they received in advance ... They knew that the area sown was smaller, the amount of grain harvested was lower in 1932 in Ukraine. However, the grain procurement plan was extremely high. Isn't this the first step towards the organization of a famine? During the procurement, Bolsheviks saw there was extremely little grain remaining, yet they carried on and took everything away – this is indeed the way to organize a famine.[26]

Later, similar ideas would form the basis of the argument that the famine had been a genocide, an intentional plan to destroy the Ukrainians as a nation. But in 1942 that term was not yet in use, and even the concept was of no interest to anybody in Nazi-occupied Ukraine.

Sosnovyi's article was dry and analytic, but a poem that accompanied it is evidence that mourning, though suppressed in public, was still taking place. Composed by Oleksa Veretenchenko, 'Somewhere in the Distant Wild North' was part of the *1933* cycle, a series of poems that appeared in *Nova Ukraïna* throughout 1943. Each one struck a different note of pain or nostalgia:

> What has happened to the laughter,
> To the bonfires girls used to light on Midsummer's Eve?
> Where are the Ukrainian villages
> And the cherry orchards by the houses?
> Everything has vanished in a ravenous fire

Mothers are devouring their children,
Madmen are selling human flesh
At the markets.[27]

An echo of those emotions could also be heard in the privacy of people's homes. Because the Soviet and German invasions had effectively united western Ukraine (Galicia, Bukovyna and western Volhynia) with the rest of the country, many western Ukrainians managed to travel east for the first time, recording what they saw and heard. Although the famine had been widely discussed in 1933, it was still a surprise to Bohdan Liubomyrenko, a visitor to central Ukraine during the war, to hear famine stories told over and over again: 'Wherever we visited people, everyone in conversation could not fail to mention, as something very terrible, the days of famine they had lived through.' Sometimes his hosts spoke 'all night long about their horrific experiences':

> The terrifying years of the artificial famine which the government planned with evil gloating against Ukraine in 1932–33 had cut deep into the people's memory. Ten long years had been unable to erase those murderous traces and to disperse the expiring sounds of the innocent children, women and men, of the dying of young people enfeebled by famine. The sad memories still hang like a black haze over the cities and villages, and produce a mortal fear among the witnesses who escaped the starvation.[28]

Ukrainians also began to speak openly about collectivization, resistance and the armed militia that had arrived to repress them in 1930. Many were clear about the political causes of the famine, explaining 'how the peasants were robbed; how everything was confiscated, leaving nothing behind for families, even those with small children. They confiscated everything and exported it to Russia.'[29] Ukrainians elsewhere in the USSR did the same. In the 1980s the writer Svetlana Aleksievich met a female Russian veteran who had served alongside a Ukrainian woman during the war. The woman, a famine survivor who had lost her entire family, told the Russian veteran that she had only survived by eating horse manure: 'I want to defend the Motherland, but I don't want to defend Stalin, that traitor to the revolution.'[30]

Just as they would later on – and just as today – not all the listeners believed these stories. The Russian veteran worried that her comrade was an 'enemy' or a 'spy'. Even the Ukrainian nationalists from Galicia found it hard to grapple with the idea of a state-sponsored famine: 'Frankly, we found it difficult to believe that a government could do such a thing.'[31] The thought that Stalin had deliberately allowed people to starve to death was too horrible, too monstrous, even for those who hated him.

The end of the Second World War did not quite bring a return to the status quo. Inside Ukraine the war altered the language of the regime. Critics of the USSR were no longer mere enemies but 'fascists' or 'Nazis'. Any talk of the famine was 'Hitlerite propaganda'. Memoirs about the famine were buried even deeper in drawers and closets, and discussion of the subject became treasonous. In 1945 one of the most eloquent Holodomor diarists, Oleksandra Radchenko, was literally persecuted for her private writing. During a search of her apartment the secret police confiscated her diary. Following a six-month interrogation, she was charged with having written a 'diary with counter-revolutionary contents'. During her trial she told the judges that 'the main aim of my writings was to devote them to my children. I wrote because after 20 years the children won't believe what violent methods were used to build socialism. The Ukrainian people suffered horrors during 1930–33 . . .' Her appeal fell on deaf ears, and she was sent for a decade to the Gulag, returning to Ukraine only in 1955.[32]

The memory of new horrors overlaid that of 1933 as well. The murder of Kyiv's Jews at the Babi Yar ravine in 1941; the battles for Kursk, Stalingrad, Berlin, all fought with Ukrainian soldiers; the prisoner-of-war camps, the Gulag, the filtration camps for returning deportees, the massacres and the mass arrests, the burnt-out villages and destroyed fields – all of these were now part of Ukraine's story too. In official Soviet historiography 'the Great Fatherland War', as the Second World War came to be called, became the central focus of research and commemoration, while the repression of the 1930s was never discussed. The year 1933 receded behind the years 1941, 1942, 1943, 1944 and 1945.

Even 1946 turned sour, as post-war chaos, a return to harsh requisitioning, a major drought – and, once again, the need for exports, this time to feed Soviet-occupied central Europe – led to further disruptions in food supply. In 1946–7 some 2.5 million tons of Soviet grain were shipped to Bulgaria, Romania, Poland, Czechoslovakia, Yugoslavia and even France. Ukrainians once again went hungry, both in the countryside and the cities, as did others across the USSR. Death tolls related to food deprivation were very high, with many hundreds of thousands suffering from malnutrition.[33]

Outside Ukraine the situation also changed, and in a radically different direction. When the war in Europe ended in May 1945, hundreds of thousands of Ukrainians found themselves, like other Soviet citizens, outside the borders of the USSR. Many were forced labourers, sent to Germany to work in factories and farms. Some had retreated alongside the Wehrmacht, or rather fled to Germany in advance of the returning Red Army: having experienced the famine, they knew they had nothing to gain from the reimposition of Soviet power. Olexa Woropay, an agricultural specialist from Odessa who witnessed the famine, found himself in a 'displaced persons camp' near the German city of Munster, where he and his compatriots were living in 'a huge barracks which was converted from a military garage'. In the winter of 1948, while they waited to be sent on to Canada or Britain, 'there was nothing to do and the evenings were long and dull. To pass the time, people told stories of their experiences'. Woropay wrote them down.[34] A few years later they appeared in London in a small volume called *The Ninth Circle*.

Although it had little impact at the time, *The Ninth Circle* now makes fascinating reading. It reflects the views of people who had been adults during the famine, who still remembered it vividly, and who had had time to reflect on the causes and consequences. Woropay, like Sosnovyi a few years earlier, argued that the famine had been organized deliberately, that Stalin had planned it carefully, and that it was intended from the start to subdue and to 'Sovietize' Ukraine. He described the rebellions that had followed collectivization, and explained what they meant:

> Moscow understood that all this marked the beginning of a further Ukrainian war, and she was afraid, remembering the liberation struggle of 1918–1921. She knew, too, how great a threat an economically

independent Ukraine would be to communism – especially as there still remained in the Ukrainian villages a considerable element which was both nationally conscious and morally strong enough to cherish the idea of an independent, unified Ukraine . . . Red Moscow therefore adopted a most ignominious plan to break the power of resistance of the thirty-five million strong Ukrainian nation. The strength of Ukraine was to be undermined by famine.[35]

Other members of the diaspora concurred. Spontaneously, wherever they found themselves, they began to organize around the famine, to mark it and to commemorate it as a turning point in the history of Ukraine. In 1948, Ukrainians in Germany, many in displaced persons camps, marked the fifteenth anniversary of the famine; in Hanover they organized a demonstration as well as leaflets describing the famine as a 'mass murder'.[36] In 1950 a Ukrainian newspaper in Bavaria reprinted the Sosnovyi article first published in occupied Kharkiv, and repeated its conclusion: the famine had been 'organized' by the Soviet regime.[37]

In 1953 a Ukrainian émigré named Semen Pidhainy went one step further. Born to a Cossack family in Kuban, Pidhainy was a veteran of the Gulag. Arrested and imprisoned in the Solovetskii Island concentration camp, he was released before the Nazi invasion and spent the war working in the city administration of Kharkiv. He wound up in Toronto in 1949, where he dedicated himself to studying and propagating the history of Ukraine. Like the Ukrainians in Germany, his goals were political as well as moral: he wanted to remember, to mourn, but also to draw the West's attention to the brutal and repressive nature of the Soviet regime. In these early years of the Cold War there was still a strong pro-Soviet sentiment in many parts of Europe and North America. Pidhainy and the Ukrainian diaspora dedicated themselves to fighting against it.

In Canada, Pidhainy initiated the founding of the Ukrainian Association of Victims of Russian Communist Terror. He also became a prominent émigré organizer and often spoke to émigré groups, encouraging them to write down their memories, not only of the famine but of life in the USSR. Other émigré institutions did, or had already done, the same. The Ukrainian Cultural and Educational

Centre in Winnipeg, founded in 1944, held a memoir-writing competition in 1947. Although aimed at collecting material about the
Second World War, many of the memoirs submitted concerned the
famine, and the Centre eventually built up a substantial collection.[38]
The Ukrainian community around the world also responded to an
appeal from a diaspora newspaper in Munich for memoirs that would
'serve as a severe accusation of Bolshevik arbitrariness in Ukraine'.[39]

One of the results of these efforts was *The Black Deeds of the
Kremlin*, a book edited by Pidhainy. Eventually comprising two
volumes – the first was published in 1953, on the twentieth anniversary of the famine – the *Black Deeds* contained dozens of memoirs as
well as analysis of the famine and other repressive aspects of the
Soviet regime. Among the authors was Sosnovyi. This time his arguments were shortened and translated into English. Entitled 'The
Truth about the Famine', his essay began bluntly: 'The famine of
1932–33 was needed by the Soviet government to break the backbone
of the Ukrainian opposition to complete Russian domination. Thus,
it was a political move and not the result of natural causes.'[40]

Others described their own experiences. Brief, poignant memoirs
were mixed with longer and more literary reminiscences as well as
drawings and photographs of the dead. G. Sova, who had been an
economist in Poltava, remembered that 'Upon many occasions, I saw
the last ounce of grain, flour and even peas and beans taken away
from the farmers.'[41] I. Kh-ko described how his father 'managed to
conceal some grain in the leggings of his boots' during the search
of their home, but eventually died anyway: 'nobody buried him,
because the dead lay scattered everywhere'.[42]

The editors sent *The Black Deeds of the Kremlin* to libraries across
the country. But like *The Ninth Circle*, the newspaper articles in Canada and the leaflets in Germany, it was studiously ignored by most
Soviet scholars and mainstream academic journals.[43] The mix of
emotive peasant memoir with semi-scholarly essays did not appeal to
professional American historians. Paradoxically, the Cold War did
not help the Ukrainian émigré cause either. The language many of
them were using – 'black deeds' or 'famine as a political weapon' –
sounded too political to many scholars in the 1950s, 1960s and 1970s.
The authors were easily dismissed as 'Cold Warriors' telling tales.

The active suppression of the famine story by Soviet authorities also had, inevitably, a powerful impact on Western historians and writers. The total absence of any hard information about the famine made the Ukrainian claims seem at least highly exaggerated, even incredible. Surely if there had been such a famine then the Soviet government would have reacted to it? Surely no government would stand by while its own people starved?

The Ukrainian diaspora was also undermined by the status of Ukraine itself. Even to serious scholars of Russian history, the notion of 'Ukraine' seemed, in the post-war era, more dubious than ever. Most outsiders knew little of Ukraine's brief, post-revolutionary moment of independence, and even less of the peasant rebellions of 1919 and 1930. Of the arrests and repressions of 1933 they knew nothing at all. The Soviet government encouraged outsiders as well as its own citizens to think of the USSR as a single entity. The official representatives of Ukraine on the world stage were spokesmen for the Soviet Union, and in the post-war West, Ukraine was almost universally considered to be a province of Russia. People calling themselves 'Ukrainian' could seem somehow unserious, much in the way that campaigners for Scottish or Catalan independence once seemed unserious too.

By the 1970s the Ukrainian diaspora in Europe, Canada and the United States was large enough to produce its own historians and journals, and wealthy enough to establish both the Harvard Ukrainian Research Institute and the Canadian Institute for Ukrainian Studies at the University of Alberta in Edmonton. But these efforts were not significant enough to shape the mainstream historical narratives. Frank Sysyn, a leading diaspora scholar, has written that the 'ethnicization' of the field may even have alienated the rest of the scholarly community, because it made Ukrainian history seem a secondary, unworthy pursuit.[44] The memory of the Nazi occupation, and the collaboration of some Ukrainians with the Nazis, also meant that even decades later it was easy to call any advocate of independent Ukraine 'fascist'. The diaspora Ukrainian insistence on their identity even seemed to many North Americans and Europeans to be 'nationalist' and therefore suspicious.

The émigrés could be dismissed as 'notoriously biased', their accounts scorned as 'dubious atrocity tales'. The *Black Deeds* compilation would eventually be described by one prominent scholar of Soviet history as a Cold War 'period piece' with no academic value.[45] But then events began to evolve in Ukraine itself.

In 1980, as the fiftieth anniversary of the famine approached, Ukrainian diaspora groups across North America once again planned to mark the occasion. In Toronto the Ukrainian Famine Research Committee began to film interviews with famine survivors and witnesses across Europe and North America.[46] In New York the Ukrainian Studies Fund commissioned James Mace, a young scholar who had written a doctoral thesis on Ukraine, to launch a major research project at the Harvard Ukrainian Institute.[47] As in the past, conferences were planned, demonstrations were organized, meetings were held in Ukrainian churches and assembly halls in Chicago and Winnipeg. But this time the impact would be different. Pierre Rigoulot, the French historian of communism, has written that 'human knowledge doesn't accumulate like bricks of a wall, which grows regularly, according to the work of the mason. Its development, but also its stagnation or retreat, depends on the social, cultural and political framework.'[48] For Ukraine that framework began to shift in the 1980s, and it would go on changing throughout the decade.

In part, the change in Western perceptions came about thanks to events within Soviet Ukraine, though these were slow in coming. Stalin's death in 1953 had not led to an official reassessment of the famine. In his momentous 'secret speech' in 1956, Stalin's successor, Nikita Khrushchev, attacked the 'cult of personality' that had surrounded the Soviet dictator and denounced Stalin for the murder of hundreds of thousands of people, including many party leaders, in 1937–8. But Khrushchev, who had taken over the Ukrainian Communist Party in 1939, kept silent about both the famine and collectivization. His refusal to speak about it meant that the fate of the peasants remained hard to discern even for dissident intellectuals in the years that followed. In 1969, Roy Medvedev, a high-ranking party insider, mentioned collectivization in *Let History Judge*, the first 'dissident' history of Stalinism. Medvedev described 'tens of thousands' of peasants dying from starvation, but admitted he knew little.

Nevertheless, Khrushchev's 'thaw' opened some cracks in the system. Although historians were unable to touch difficult subjects, sometimes writers could. In 1962 a Soviet literary magazine published Alexander Solzhenitsyn's *A Day in the Life of Ivan Denisovich*, the first honest depiction of the Soviet Gulag. In 1968 another magazine published a short novel by a much lesser known Russian author, Vladimir Tendriakov, in which he wrote of 'Ukrainian kulaks, expropriated and exiled from their homeland', dying in a provincial town square: 'One got used to seeing the dead there in the morning, and the hospital groom, Abram, would come along with his cart and pile the corpses in. Not everyone died. Many of them wandered along the dusty, sordid alleyways, dragging dropsied legs, elephantine and bloodlessly blue, and plucked at every passer-by, begging with dog-like eyes.'[49]

In Ukraine itself the intellectual and literary rejection of Stalinism had a distinctly national flavour. In the less repressive atmosphere of the late 1950s and early 1960s, Ukrainian intellectuals – in Kyiv and Kharkiv and now in Lviv, the formerly Polish territory incorporated into Soviet Ukraine in 1939 – once again began to meet, to write, and to discuss the possibility of a national reawakening. Many had been educated in primary schools that still taught children in Ukrainian, and many had grown up hearing versions of the 'alternative history' of their country from their parents and grandparents. Some began to speak openly about the promotion of the Ukrainian language, Ukrainian literature and a Ukrainian history that differed from the history of Russia.

These muted attempts to resurrect the shadow of a national identity alarmed Moscow. In 1961 seven Ukrainian academics were arrested and tried in Lviv, among them Stepan Virun, who had helped write a pamphlet criticizing 'unjustified repressions accompanied by accusations of nationalism and the annihilation of hundreds of Party and cultural personalities'.[50] Another two dozen went on trial in Kyiv in 1966. Among other 'crimes', one was accused of possessing a book containing an 'anti-Soviet' poem; because it had been printed without the author's name, police had failed to identify the work of Taras Shevchenko (whose works were, at the time, perfectly legal).[51] Shelest, the Ukrainian Communist Party leader, presided over these arrests, though after he lost his position as First Secretary, in 1973, he too came under attack on the grounds that O *Ukraine, Our Soviet Land* 'devotes far too much space to Ukraine's past, its pre-October history, while failing to adequately glorify such epochal events as the triumph of the Great October, the struggle to build socialism'. The book was banned, and Shelest remained in disgrace until 1991.[52]

But by the 1970s the USSR was no longer as cut off from the world as it had once been, and this time around the arrests found an echo. Ukrainian prisoners smuggled news of their cases back to Kyiv; dissidents in Kyiv learned how to contact Radio Liberty or the BBC. By 1971 so much material had leaked out of the USSR that it was possible to publish an edited collection of testimonies from Ukraine, including passionate statements from jailed Ukrainian national activists. In 1974 dissidents published an underground journal that contained several pages on collectivization and the 1932–3 famine. An English-language translation of the journal appeared too, under the title *Ethnocide of Ukrainians in the U.S.S.R.*[53] Soviet analysts and observers in the West slowly became aware that Ukrainian dissidents had a separate and distinct set of grievances. When the Soviet invasion of Afghanistan in 1979 and the election of Ronald Reagan in 1981 brought an abrupt end to the era of détente, a much broader swath of the Western public also refocused on the history of Soviet repression, including repression inside Ukraine.

By the early 1980s the Ukrainian diaspora had also changed. Better established and now better funded – its members no longer poor refugees, but established members of the North American and European middle classes – diaspora organizations could afford to support more substantive projects, and to turn scattered material into books and films. The Canadian interview project evolved into a major documentary: *Harvest of Despair* won awards at film festivals and appeared on Canadian public television in the spring of 1985.

In the United States the public broadcaster's initial reluctance to show the film – it was feared to be too 'right wing' – became controversial. PBS finally broadcast the film in September 1986 as a special episode of 'Firing Line', the programme produced by the conservative columnist and *National Review* editor William Buckley, and followed the broadcast with a debate between Buckley, the historian

Robert Conquest, and the journalists Harrison Salisbury of *The New York Times* and Christopher Hitchens, then of *The Nation*. Much of the debate had nothing to do with the famine itself. Hitchens brought up the topic of Ukrainian anti-semitism. Salisbury focused most of his remarks on Duranty.[54] But a cascade of reviews and articles followed.

An even greater wave of interest accompanied the publication of Conquest's *Harvest of Sorrow*, the most visible fruit of the Harvard documentation project, a few months later. The book (like this one) was written in collaboration with the Harvard Ukrainian Research Institute. Conquest did not have the archives available today. But he worked with Mace to pull together the existing sources: official Soviet documents, memoirs, oral testimony of survivors in the diaspora. *Harvest of Sorrow* finally appeared in 1986 and was reviewed in all major British and American newspapers and in many academic journals – unprecedented, at the time, for a book about Ukraine. Many reviewers expressed astonishment that they knew so little about such a deadly tragedy. In *The Times Literary Supplement* the Soviet scholar Geoffrey Hosking was shocked to discover 'just how much material has accumulated over the years, most of it perfectly accessible in British libraries': 'almost unbelievably, Dr. Conquest's book is the first historical study of what must count as one of the greatest man-made horrors in a century full of them'. Frank Sysyn put it simply: 'No book dealing with Ukraine had ever received such wide notice.'[55]

Not all of the notice was positive: a wide range of professional journals did not review Conquest's book at all, while some North American historians, who saw Conquest both as the representative of a more traditional school of Soviet history as well as a member of the political right, denounced the book in no uncertain terms. J. Arch Getty complained in the *London Review of Books* that Conquest's views had been promoted by the American Enterprise Institute, a conservative think tank, and dismissed his sources as 'partisan' because they were linked to 'Ukrainian émigrés in the West'. Getty concluded that 'in today's conservative political climate, with its "evil empire" discourse, I am sure the book will be very popular'. Then, as now, the historical argument about Ukraine was shaped by domestic

American politics. Although there is no objective reason why the study of the famine should have been considered either 'right wing' or 'left wing' at all, the politics of Cold War academia meant that any scholars who wrote about Soviet atrocities were easily pigeonholed.[56]

Harvest of Sorrow would eventually find an echo inside Ukraine itself, although the authorities tried to block it. Just as the Harvard research project was launching in 1981, a delegation from the UN Mission of the Ukrainian Soviet Socialist Republic visited the university and asked the Ukrainian Research Institute to abandon the project. In exchange, the Institute was offered access to Soviet archives, a great rarity at the time. Harvard refused. After excerpts from Conquest's book appeared in the Toronto *Globe and Mail*, the first secretary to the Soviet Embassy wrote an angry letter to the editor: Yes, some had starved, he claimed, but they were the victims of drought and kulak sabotage.[57] Once the book was published, it proved impossible to keep it away from Ukrainians. In the autumn of 1986 it was read aloud on Radio Liberty, the American-backed, Munich-based radio station, to its listeners inside the USSR.

A more elaborate Soviet response arrived in 1987, with the publication of *Fraud, Famine and Fascism: The Ukrainian Genocide Myth from Hitler to Harvard*. The ostensible author, Douglas Tottle, was a Canadian labour activist. His book described the famine as a hoax invented and propagated by Ukrainian fascists and anti-Soviet groups in the West. Although Tottle acknowledged that poor weather and post-collectivization chaos caused food shortages in those years, he refused to concede that a malevolent state had played any role in spreading starvation. Not only did his book describe the Ukrainian famine as a 'myth', it argued that any accounts of it constituted, by definition, Nazi propaganda. Tottle's book posited, among other things, that the Ukrainian diaspora were all 'Nazis'; that the famine books and monographs constituted an anti-Soviet, Nazi propaganda drive that also had links to Western intelligence; that Harvard University had 'long been a center of anti-communist research, studies and programs' and was linked to the CIA; that Malcolm Muggeridge's writing on the famine was tainted because the Nazis had made use of it; and that Muggeridge himself was a British agent.[58]

The Institute of Party History in both Moscow and Kyiv contributed to Tottle's manuscript; unsigned versions were sent back and forth between their offices and those of the two party Central Committees for corrections and commentary. Soviet diplomats followed the book's publication and progress, and they promoted it where they could.[59] The book eventually attracted a small following: in January 1988 the *Village Voice* published an article, 'In Search of a Soviet Holocaust: A 55-Year-Old Famine Feeds the Right', which used Tottle's work uncritically.[60]

In retrospect, Tottle's book is significant mostly as a harbinger of what was to come, nearly three decades later. Its central argument was built around the supposed link between Ukrainian 'nationalism' – defined as any discussion of Soviet repression in Ukraine, or any discussion of Ukrainian independence or sovereignty – and fascism, as well as American and British intelligence. Much later this same set of links – Ukraine, fascism, the CIA – would be used in the Russian information campaign against the Ukrainian independence and anti-corruption movement of 2014. In a very real sense the groundwork for that campaign was laid in 1987.

Fraud, Famine and Fascism, like other Soviet apologies at the time, conceded that there had been some hunger in Ukraine and Russia in 1932–3, but it attributed mass starvation to the demands of 'modernization', kulak sabotage and alleged bad weather. As with all of the most sophisticated smear campaigns, elements of truth were combined with falsehood and exaggeration. Tottle's book correctly pointed out that some of the photographs which were at that time widely identified with 1933 were actually taken during the famine of 1921. The author correctly identified some bad or misleading reporting from the 1930s as well. Finally, Tottle wrote, correctly, that some Ukrainians had collaborated with the Nazis, and that Nazis had, during their occupation of Ukraine, written and spoken a great deal about the famine.

Although these facts neither diminished the tragedy of 1932–3 nor altered its causes, the 'Nazi' and 'nationalist' associations were intended, simply, to smear anyone who wrote about the famine at all.

To some extent the strategy worked: this Soviet campaign against the Ukrainian memory of the famine, and against the historians of the famine, left a taint of uncertainty. Even Hitchens had felt obligated to mention Ukrainian Nazi collaborators in his discussion of *Harvest of Despair*, and part of the scholarly community would always approach Conquest's book with caution.[61] Without access to archives it was still impossible, in the 1980s, to describe the series of deliberate decisions that had led to the famine in the spring of 1933. It was also impossible to describe the aftermath, the cover-up, or the suppressed census of 1937 in detail.

The research projects that led to both *Harvest of Despair* and *Harvest of Sorrow* nevertheless had a further echo. In 1985 the United States Congress set up a bipartisan commission to investigate the Ukrainian famine, appointing Mace as chief investigator. Its purpose was 'to conduct a study of the 1932–33 Ukrainian famine in order to expand the world's knowledge of the famine and provide the American public with a better understanding of the Soviet system by revealing the Soviet role' in it.[62] The commission took three years to compile its report, a collection of oral and written testimony from survivors in the diaspora, which remains one of the largest ever published in English. When the commission presented its work in 1988, the conclusion was in direct contradiction to the Soviet line: 'There is no doubt,' the commission concluded, that 'large numbers of inhabitants of the Ukraine SSR and the North Caucasus Territory starved to death in a man-made famine in 1932–33, caused by the seizure of the 1932 crop by the Soviet authorities'.

In addition, the commission found that 'Official Soviet allegations of "kulak sabotage", upon which all difficulties were blamed during the Famine, are false'; that the 'Famine was not, as alleged, related to drought'; and that 'attempts were made to prevent the starving from traveling to areas where food was more available'. The commission concluded that 'the Ukrainian famine of 1932–33 was caused by the extraction of agricultural produce from the rural population' and not, in other words, by 'bad weather' or 'kulak sabotage'.[63]

The findings echoed those of Conquest. They also confirmed the authority of Mace, and provided a mountain of new material for other scholars to use in the years that followed. But by the time the commission made its final statement in 1988, the most important debates about the Ukrainian famine were finally beginning to take place not in Europe or North America, but inside Ukraine itself.

On 26 April 1986 some odd, off-the-charts measurements began showing up on radiation-monitoring equipment in Scandinavia. Nuclear scientists across Europe, at first suspecting equipment malfunction, raised the alarm. But the numbers were not a fluke. Within a few days satellite photographs pinpointed the source of the radiation: a nuclear power plant in the city of Chernobyl, in northern Ukraine. Inquiries were made but the Soviet government offered no explanation or guidance. Five days after the explosion a May Day march went ahead in Kyiv, less than eighty miles away. Thousands of people walked through the streets of the Ukrainian capital, oblivious to the invisible radiation in the city's air. The government was well aware of the danger. The Ukrainian Communist Party leader, Volodymyr Shcherbytskyi, arrived late to the march, obviously distressed: the Soviet General Secretary had personally ordered him not to cancel the parade. 'You will put your party card on the table,' Mikhail Gorbachev had told Shcherbytskyi, 'if you bungle the parade.'[64]

Eighteen days after the accident, Gorbachev abruptly reversed his policy. He appeared on Soviet television and announced that the public had a right to know what had happened. Soviet camera crews went to the site, filmed interviews with doctors and local people, and explained what had happened. A bad decision had been made; a turbine test had gone wrong; a nuclear reactor had melted down. Soldiers from all over the Soviet Union had poured concrete over the smouldering remains. Everyone who lived within twenty miles of Chernobyl had abandoned their homes and farms, indefinitely. The death toll, officially listed as thirty-one, actually soared into the thousands, as the men who had shovelled concrete and flown helicopters over the reactor began to die of radiation sickness in other parts of the USSR.

The psychological impact of the accident was no less profound. Chernobyl destroyed the myth of Soviet technical competence – one of the few that many still believed. If the USSR had promised its citizens that communism would guide them into the high-tech future, Chernobyl led them to question whether the USSR could be trusted at all. More importantly, Chernobyl reminded the USSR, and the world, of the stark consequences of Soviet secrecy, even causing Gorbachev himself to reconsider his party's refusal to discuss its past as well as its present. Shaken by the accident, the Soviet leader launched the policy of *glasnost*. Literally translated as 'openness' or 'transparency', *glasnost* encouraged public officials and private individuals to reveal the truth about Soviet institutions and Soviet history, including the history of 1932–3. As a result of this decision, the web of lies woven to hide the famine – the manipulation of statistics, the destruction of death registries, the imprisonment of diarists – would finally unravel.[65]

Inside Ukraine the accident stirred memories of past betrayals and historic catastrophes, leading Ukrainians to challenge their secretive state. On 5 June, just six weeks after the Chernobyl explosion, the poet Ivan Drach rose to speak at a meeting of the official Writers' Union of Ukraine. His words had an unusually emotional edge: Drach's son was one of the young soldiers who had been sent to the accident without proper protective clothing, and he was now suffering from radiation poisoning. Drach himself had been an advocate of nuclear power, on the grounds that it would help modernize Ukraine.[66] Now he blamed the Soviet system both for the nuclear meltdown, the cloak of secrecy that had concealed the explosions, and the chaos that followed. Drach was the first person openly to compare Chernobyl to the famine. Speaking at length, he declared that a 'nuclear lightning bolt had struck at the genotype of the nation':

> Why has the young generation turned away from us? Because we didn't learn to talk openly, to speak the truth about how we lived, and about how we are living now. We have got so used to falsehood . . . When we see Reagan as the head of a commission on the famine of 1933, I wonder, where is the Institute of History when it comes to the truth about 1933?[67]

Party authorities later dismissed Drach's words as an 'emotional outburst', and censored even the internal transcript of the speech. The reference to a 'nuclear lightning bolt' striking at the 'genotype of the nation' – a phrase that was widely misremembered as a direct reference to genocide – was replaced with 'it struck painfully'.[68]

But there was no turning back: Drach's comments had struck a chord among those who heard them at the time, and those who repeated them afterwards. Events gathered pace; very quickly, *glasnost* became real. Gorbachev had intended the policy to reveal the workings of flawed Soviet institutions, with the hope that this would make them function better. Others interpreted *glasnost* more broadly. True stories and factual history began to appear in the Soviet press. The works of Alexander Solzhenitsyn and other chroniclers of the Gulag appeared for the first time in print. Gorbachev became the second Soviet leader, after Khrushchev, to speak openly about 'blank spots' in Soviet history. And unlike his predecessor, Gorbachev made his remarks on television:

> . . . the lack of proper democratization of Soviet society was precisely what made possible both the cult of personality and the violations of the law, arbitrariness and repressions of the 1930s – to be blunt, crimes based on the abuse of power. Many thousands of members of the Party and non-members were subjected to mass repressions. That, comrades, is the bitter truth.[69]

Equally quickly, *glasnost* began to seem insufficient to Ukrainians. In August 1987, Vyacheslav Chornovil, a leading dissident intellectual, wrote a thirty-page open letter to Gorbachev, accusing him of having launched a 'superficial' *glasnost*, one that preserved the 'fictitious sovereignty' of Ukraine and the other non-Russian republics but suppressed their languages, their memories, their true history. Chornovil provided his own list of 'blank spots' in Ukrainian history, naming the people and incidents still left out of official accounts: Hrushevsky, Skrypnyk, Khvylovyi, the mass arrests of intellectuals, the destruction of national culture, the suppression of the Ukrainian language and, of course, the 'genocidal' great famine of 1932–3.[70]

Others followed suit. The Ukrainian chapter of Memorial, the Soviet society for the commemoration of Stalin's victims, began openly collecting testimony and memoirs for the first time. In June 1988 another poet, Borys Oliinyk, stood up at the infamous Nineteenth Party Congress in Moscow – the most open and argumentative ever to take place in history, and the first to be televised live. He raised three issues: the status of the Ukrainian language, the dangers of nuclear power and the famine: 'The reasons for the famine of 1933, which extinguished the lives of millions of Ukrainians, need to be made public, and those responsible for this tragedy [should] be identified by name.'[71]

In that context the Ukrainian Communist Party prepared to respond to the U.S. Congressional Report. Finding itself in a quandary the party decided, as it had so often done in the final, stultifying years of the USSR, to create a committee. Shcherbytskyi tasked scholars at the Ukrainian Academy of Sciences and the Institute of Party History – the organizations behind the publication of *Fraud, Famine and Fascism* – with refuting the general accusations, and in particular with countering the conclusions drawn by the U.S. Congressional Report. Committee members were meant, once again, to produce an official denial. To ensure their success, the historians were given access to archival sources.[72]

The result was unexpected. For many of the scholars the documents were a revelation. They contained precise accounts of the policy decisions, the grain confiscations, the protests of activists, the corpses on city streets, the tragedy of orphans, the terror and the cannibalism. There had been no fraud, the committee concluded. Nor was the 'famine myth' a fascist plot. The famine had been real, it had happened, and it could no longer be denied.

The sixtieth anniversary of the famine, in the autumn of 1993, was like no other that had preceded it. Two years earlier, Ukraine had elected its first president and voted overwhelmingly for independence; the government's subsequent refusal to sign a new union treaty had precipitated the dissolution of the Soviet Union. The Communist Party of Ukraine, in one of its last memorable acts before giving up power, had passed a resolution blaming the 1932–3 famine on the 'criminal course pursued by Stalin and his closest entourage'.[73] Drach and Oliinyk had joined other intellectuals to found Rukh, an independent political party and the first legal manifestation of the national movement since the repressions of the early 1930s. For the first time in history, Ukraine was a sovereign state and acknowledged as such by most of the world.

As a sovereign state, Ukraine was free, by the autumn of 1993, to debate and commemorate its own history. From a mix of motives, former communists and former dissidents were all eager to have a say. In Kyiv the government organized a series of public events. On 9 September the deputy prime minister opened a scholarly conference, underlining the political significance of the famine commemorations. 'Only an independent Ukraine can guarantee that such a tragedy will never be repeated,' he told the audience. James Mace, by then a widely known and admired figure in Ukraine, was also there. He too drew political conclusions: 'I would hope that this commemoration will help Ukrainians remember the danger of political chaos and political dependence on neighboring powers.' President Leonid Kravchuk, a former communist apparatchik, also spoke: 'A democratic form of government protects a people from such misfortunes,' he said. 'If we lose our independence we are destined to forever lag far behind economically, politically and culturally. If this happens, most importantly, we will always face the possibility of repeating those horrible pages in our history, including the famine, which were planned by a foreign power.'[74]

Ivan Drach, the leader of Rukh, called for a broader acknowledgement of the significance of the famine: he demanded that Russians 'repent', and that they follow the example of Germans in acknowledging their guilt. He referred directly to the Holocaust, noting that the Jews had 'forced the whole world to admit its guilt before them'. Although he did not claim that all Ukrainians had been victims – 'Bolshevik marauders in Ukraine mobilized Ukrainians as well' – he did strike a nationalist tone: 'The first lesson which is becoming an integral part of Ukrainian consciousness is that Russia has never had and never will have any other interest in Ukraine beyond the total destruction of the Ukrainian nation.'[75]

The ceremonies continued throughout the weekend. Black streamers hung from government buildings; thousands of people gathered for a memorial service outside St Sofia's Cathedral. But the most moving celebrations were spontaneous. Crowds flocked to Khreshchatyk, Kyiv's central boulevard, where people had put personal documents and photographs on billboards set up at three points along the street. An altar was set up halfway down; visitors left flowers and bread beside it. Civic leaders and politicians from all over

Ukraine laid wreaths at the foot of a new monument. Some brought jars of earth – soil taken from the mass graves of famine victims.[76]

To those who were there, the moment would have seemed definitive. The famine had been publicly recognized and remembered. More than that: after centuries of Russian imperial colonization and decades of Soviet repression, it had been recognized and remembered in a sovereign Ukraine. For better or worse, the famine story had become part of Ukrainian politics and contemporary Ukrainian culture. Children would now study it at school; scholars would piece together the full narrative in archives. Monuments would be built and books would be written. The long process of understanding, interpreting, forgiving, arguing and mourning was about to begin.

Epilogue
The Ukrainian Question
Reconsidered

The mass murder of peoples and of nations that has characterized the advance of the Soviet Union into Europe is not a
new feature of their policy of expansionism . . . Instead, it has
been a long-term characteristic even of the internal policy of
the Kremlin – one which the present masters had ample precedent for in the operations of Tsarist Russia. It is indeed an
indispensable step in the process of 'union' that the Soviet
leaders fondly hope will produce the 'Soviet Man', the 'Soviet
Nation' and to achieve that goal, that unified nation, the
leaders of the Kremlin will gladly destroy the nations and the
cultures that have long inhabited Eastern Europe.
Raphael Lemkin, 'Soviet Genocide in the Ukraine', 1953[1]

Ще не вмерла України і Слава, і Воля
(The glory and the freedom of Ukraine has not yet died)
Ukrainian national anthem

Those who lived through the Ukrainian famine always described it,
once they were allowed to describe it, as an act of state aggression.
The peasants who experienced the searches and the blacklists
remembered them as a collective assault on themselves and their culture. The Ukrainians who witnessed the arrests and murders of
intellectuals, academics, writers and artists remembered them in the
same way, as a deliberate attack on their national cultural elite.

The archival record backs up the testimony of the survivors. Neither crop failure nor bad weather caused the famine in Ukraine. Although the chaos of collectivization helped create the conditions that led to famine, the high numbers of deaths in Ukraine between 1932 and 1934, and especially the spike in the spring of 1933, were not caused directly by collectivization either. Starvation was the result, rather, of the forcible removal of food from people's homes; the roadblocks that prevented peasants from seeking work or food; the harsh rules of the blacklists imposed on farms and villages; the restrictions on barter and trade; and the vicious propaganda campaign designed to persuade Ukrainians to watch, unmoved, as their neighbours died of hunger.

As we have seen, Stalin did not seek to kill *all* Ukrainians, nor did all Ukrainians resist. On the contrary, some Ukrainians collaborated, both actively and passively, with the Soviet project. This book includes many accounts of assaults carried out by neighbours against neighbours, a phenomenon familiar from other mass murders in other places and at other times. But Stalin did seek to physically eliminate the most active and engaged Ukrainians, in both the countryside and the cities. He understood the consequences of both the famine and the simultaneous wave of mass arrests in Ukraine as they were happening. So did the people closest to him, including the leading Ukrainian communists.

At the time it took place, there was no word that could have been used to describe a state-sponsored assault on an ethnic group or nation, and no international law that defined it as a particular kind of crime. But once the word 'genocide' came into use in the late 1940s, many sought to apply it to the famine and the accompanying purges in Ukraine. Their efforts were complicated at the time, and are complicated still, by multiple interpretations of the word 'genocide' – a legal and moral category rather than a historical one – as well as by the convoluted and constantly shifting politics of Russia and Ukraine.

In a very literal sense the concept of 'genocide' has its origins in Ukraine, specifically in the Polish-Jewish-Ukrainian city of Lviv. Raphael Lemkin, the legal scholar who invented the word – combining the Greek word 'genos', meaning race or nation, with the Latin 'cide', meaning killing – studied law at the University of Lviv, then called

Lwów, in the 1920s.[2] The city had previously been Polish until the eighteenth century, then part of the Austro-Hungarian empire. It became Polish after the First World War; Soviet after the Red Army invasion of 1939; German between 1941 and 1944; part of Soviet Ukraine until 1991; and part of independent Ukraine after that. Each change was accompanied by upheaval and sometimes mass violence as new rulers imposed changes in language, culture and law.

Although he left Lviv for Warsaw in 1929, Lemkin wrote in his autobiography that he was inspired to think about genocide by the history of his region, as well as by the brutal emotions that washed over it during the First World War. 'I began to read more history to study whether national, religious or racial groups, as such, were being destroyed,' he wrote. The Turkish assault on the Armenians, 'put to death for no reason other than that they were Christians', moved him in particular to think more deeply about international law and to ask how it could be used to stop such tragedies.[3] His work was made more urgent by the Nazi invasion of Warsaw in 1939, which he immediately understood would involve an assault on the Jews as a group, as well as others. He finally articulated his views in *Axis Rule in Occupied Europe: Laws of Occupation – Analysis of Government – Proposals for Redress*, a book he published in the United States in 1944, having fled occupied Poland. Lemkin defined 'genocide' in *Axis Rule* not as a single act but as a process:

> Generally speaking, genocide does not necessarily mean the immediate destruction of a nation, except when accomplished by mass killings of all members of a nation. It is intended rather to signify a coordinated plan of different actions aiming at the destruction of essential foundations of the life of national groups, with the aim of annihilating the groups themselves. The objectives of such a plan would be disintegration of the political and social institutions, of culture, language, national feelings, religion, and the economic existence of national groups, and the destruction of the personal security, liberty, health, dignity, and even the lives of the individuals belonging to such groups. Genocide is directed against the national group as an entity, and the actions involved are directed against individuals, not in their individual capacity, but as members of the national group.[4]

In *Axis Rule*, Lemkin spoke of different kinds of genocide – political, social, cultural, economic, biological and physical. Separately, in an outline for a history of genocide that he never finished or published, he also listed the techniques which could be used to commit genocide, including among them the desecration of cultural symbols and the destruction of cultural centres such as churches and schools.[5] As broadly defined in Lemkin's published and unpublished work in the 1940s, in other words, 'genocide' certainly included the Sovietization of Ukraine and the Ukrainian famine. He later argued explicitly that this was so. In a 1953 essay entitled 'Soviet Genocide in the Ukraine' Lemkin wrote that the USSR attacked Ukrainian elites precisely because they are 'small and easily eliminated, and so it is upon these groups particularly that the full force of the Soviet axe has fallen, with its familiar tools of mass murder, deportation and forced labour, exile and starvation'.[6]

Had the concept of genocide remained simply an idea in the minds and writings of scholars, there would be no argument today: according to Lemkin's definition, the Holodomor was a genocide – as it is by most intuitive understandings of the word. But the concept of genocide became part of international law in a completely different context: that of the Nuremberg trials and the legal debates which followed.

Lemkin served as adviser to the chief counsel at Nuremberg, Supreme Court Justice Robert Jackson, and, thanks to his advocacy, the term was used at the trial, though it was not mentioned in any of the verdicts. After the Nuremberg trials ended, many felt, for reasons of both morality and *Realpolitik*, that the term ought to be enshrined in the UN's basic documents. But as Norman Naimark and others have argued, international politics, and more specifically Cold War politics, shaped the drafting of the UN convention on genocide far more than the legal scholarship of Lemkin or anyone else.[7]

Initially, a UN General Assembly resolution in December 1946 condemned genocide in language that echoed Lemkin's broad understanding. Genocide was identified as 'a crime under international law ... whether it is committed on religious, racial, political or any other ground'. Early drafts of what would become the UN Convention on the Prevention and Punishment of the Crime of Genocide also included 'political groups' as potential victims of genocide. But the

32-33. Breadlines in Kharkiv.

38-39. Weinerberger took this photograph of the same man – alive and then dead.

40. Two photographs taken by Mykola Bokan, Baturyn, Chernihiv province, and preserved in his police file. The first, from April 1933, includes the caption '300 days without a piece of bread'.

41. Bokan's second photograph, July 1933, includes a memorial to 'Kostya, who died of hunger'. Bokan and his son were arrested for documenting the famine. Both died in the Gulag.

Friday, March 31, 1933   THE EVENING STANDARD

FAMINE RULES RUSSIA

The 5-year Plan Has Killed the Bread Supply

By GARETH JONES

Mr. Jones is one of Mr. Lloyd George's private secretaries. He has just returned from an extensive tour on foot in Soviet Russia. He speaks Russian fluently—and here is the terrible story the peasants told him.

MR. GARETH JONES.

A FEW days ago I stood in a worker's cottage outside Moscow. A father and a son, the father a Russian skilled worker in a Moscow factory, and the son a member of the Young Communist League, stood glaring at one another.

The father, trembling with excitement, lost control of himself and shouted at his Communist son : " It's terrible now. We workers are starving. Look at Chelyabinsk, where I once worked. Disease there is carrying away numbers of us workers and the little food there is uneatable. That is what you have done to our Mother Russia."

The son cried back : " But look at the giants of industry which we have built. Look at the new tractor works. Look at the Dniepostroy. That construction has been worth suffering for."

" Construction indeed ! " was the father's reply. " What's the use of construction when you have destroyed all that's best in Russia ? "

What that worker said at least 96 per cent. of the people of Russia are thinking. There has been construction, but, in the act of building, all that was best in Russia has disappeared. The main result of the Five Year Plan has been the tragic ruin of Russian agriculture. This ruin I saw in its grim reality. I tramped through a number of villages in the snow of March. I saw children with swollen bellies. I slept in peasants' huts, sometimes nine of us in one room. I talked to every peasant I met, and the general conclusion I draw is that the present state of Russian agriculture is already catastrophic but that in a year's time its condition will have worsened tenfold.

What did the peasants say ? There was one cry which resounded everywhere I went, and that was: " There is no bread." The other sentence, which was the *leitmotiv* of my Russian visit, was: " All are swollen." Even within a few miles of Moscow there is no bread left. As I was going through the countryside in that district I chatted to several women who were trudging with empty sacks towards Moscow. They all said : " It is terrible. We have no bread. We have to go all the way to Moscow to get bread and then they will only give us four pounds, which costs three roubles (six shillings nominally). How can a poor man live ? "

" Have you potatoes ? " I asked. Every peasant I asked nodded negatively with sadness.

" What about your cows ? " was my next question. To the Russian peasant the cow means wealth, food and happiness. It is almost the centre-point upon which his life gravitates.

" *The cattle have nearly all died. How can we feed the cattle when we have only fodder to eat ourselves ?* "

" And your horses ? " was the question I asked in every village I visited. The horse is now a question of life and death, for without a horse how can one plough ? And if one cannot plough, how can one sow for the next harvest ? And if one cannot sow for the next harvest, then death is the only prospect in the future.

The reply spelled doom for most of the villages. The peasants said : " Most of our horses have died and we have so little fodder that the remaining ones are scraggy and ill."

If it is grave now and if millions are dying in the villages, as they are, for I did not visit a single village where many had not died, what will it be like in a month's time ? The potatoes left are being counted one by one, but in so many homes the potatoes have long run out. The beet, once used as cattle fodder, may run out in many huts before the new food comes in June, July and August, and many have not even beet.

The situation is graver than in 1921, as all peasants stated emphatically. In that year there was famine in several great regions, but in most parts the peasants could live. It was a localised famine, which had many millions of victims, especially along the Volga. But to-day the famine is everywhere, in the formerly rich Ukraine, in West Russia, in Central Asia, in North Caucasia—everywhere.

What of the towns ? Moscow as yet does not look so stricken, and no one staying in Moscow would have an inkling of what is going on in the countryside, unless he could talk to the peasants who have come hundreds and hundreds of miles to the capital to look for bread. The people in Moscow look warmly clad, and many of the skilled workers, who have their warm meal every day at the factory, are well fed. Some of those who earn very good salaries, or who have special privileges, look even well dressed, but the vast majority of the unskilled workers are feeling the pinch.

I talked to a worker who was hauling a heavy wooden trunk. " It is terrible now," he said. " I get two pounds of bread a day and it is rotten bread. I get no meat, no eggs, no butter. Before the war I used to get a lot of meat and it was cheap. But I haven't had meat for a year. Eggs were only a kopeck each before the war, but now they are a great luxury. I get a little soup, but it is not enough to live on."

And now a new dread visits the Russian worker. That is unemployment. In the last few months very many thousands have been dismissed from factories in many parts of the Soviet Union. I asked one unemployed man what happened to him. He replied: " We are treated like cattle. We are told to get away, and we get no bread card. How can I live ? I used to get a pound of bread a day for all my family, but now there is no bread card. I have to leave the city and make my way out into the countryside where there is also no bread."

The Five Year Plan has built many fine factories. But it is bread that makes factory wheels go round, and the Five Year Plan has destroyed the bread-supplier of Russia.

42. Gareth Jones, *Evening Standard*, 31 March 1933.

43. Walter Duranty (*centre right*) dining sumptuously in his Moscow apartment.

44. Walter Duranty, *The New York Times*, 31 March 1933.

RUSSIANS HUNGRY, BUT NOT STARVING

Deaths From Diseases Due to Malnutrition High, Yet the Soviet Is Entrenched.

LARGER CITIES HAVE FOOD

Ukraine, North Caucasus and Lower Volga Regions Suffer From Shortages.

KREMLIN'S 'DOOM' DENIED

Russians and Foreign Observers In Country See No Ground for Predictions of Disaster.

By WALTER DURANTY.
Special Cable to THE NEW YORK TIMES.

MOSCOW, March 30.—In the middle of the diplomatic duel between Great Britain and the Soviet Union over the accused British engineers there appears from a British source a big scare story in the American press about famine in the Soviet Union, with "thousands already dead and millions menaced by death from starvation."

Its author is Gareth Jones, who a former secretary to David Lloyd George and who recently spent three weeks in the Soviet Union and reached the conclusion that the country was "on the verge of a terrific smash," as he told the writer.

Mr. Jones is a man of a keen and active mind, and he has taken the trouble to learn Russian, which he speaks with considerable fluency, but the writer thought Mr. Jones's judgment was somewhat hasty and asked him on what it was based. It appeared that he had made a forty-mile walk through villages in the neighborhood of Kharkov and had found conditions sad.

I suggested that that was a rather inadequate cross-section of a big country, but nothing could shake his conviction of impending doom.

Predictions of Doom Frequent.

The number of times foreigners, especially Britons, have shaken rueful heads as they composed the Soviet Union's epitaph can scarcely be computed, and in point of fact it has done the Soviet Union incalculable harm since the day when William C. Bullitt's able and honest account of the situation was shelved and negatived during the Versailles Peace Conference by reports that Admiral Kolchak, White Russian leader, had taken Kazan—which he never did—and that the Soviet power was "on the verge of an abyss."

Admiral Kolchak faded. Then General Denikin took Orel and the Soviet Government was on the verge of an abyss again, and General Yudenich "took" Petrograd. But where are Generals Denikin and Yudenich now?

A couple of years ago another British "eyewitness" reported a mutiny in the Moscow garrison and "rows of corpses neatly piled in Theatre Square," and only this week a British news agency revealed a revolt of the Soviet Fifty-fifth Regiment at Dauria, on the Manchurian border. All bunk, of course.

This is not to mention a more regrettable incident of three years ago when an American correspondent discovered half the Ukraine flaming with rebellion and "proved" it by authentic documents eagerly proffered by Rumanians, which documents on examination appeared to relate to events of eight or ten years earlier.

Saw No One Dying.

But to return to Mr. Jones. He told me there was virtually no bread in the villages he had visited and that the adults were haggard, gaunt and discouraged, but that he had seen no dead or dying animals or human beings.

I believed him because I knew it to be correct not only of some parts of the Ukraine but of sections of the North Caucasus and lower Volga regions and, for that matter, Kazakstan, where the attempt to change the stock-raising nomads of the type and the period of Abraham and Isaac into 1933 collective grain farmers has produced the most deplorable results.

It is all too true that the novelty and mismanagement of collective farming, plus the quite efficient conspiracy of Feodor M. Konar and his associates in agricultural commissariats, have made a mess of Soviet food production. [Konar was executed for sabotage.]

But—to put it brutally—you can't make an omelette without breaking eggs, and the Bolshevist leaders are just as indifferent to the casualties that may be involved in their drive toward socialization as any General during the World War who ordered a costly attack in order to show his superiors that he and his division possessed the proper soldierly spirit. In fact, the Bolsheviki are more indifferent because they are animated by fanatical conviction.

Since I talked with Mr. Jones I have made exhaustive inquiries about this alleged famine situation. I have inquired in Soviet commissariats and in foreign embassies with their network of consuls, and I have tabulated information from Britons working as specialists and from my personal connections, Russian and foreign.

Disease Mortality Is High.

All of this seems to me to be more trustworthy information than I could get by a brief trip through any one area. The Soviet Union is too big to permit a hasty study, and it is the foreign correspondent's job to present a whole picture, not a part of it. And here are the facts:

There is a serious food shortage throughout the country, with occasional cases of well-managed State or collective farms. The big cities and the army are adequately supplied with food. There is no actual starvation or deaths from starvation, but there is widespread mortality from diseases due to malnutrition.

In short, conditions are definitely bad in certain sections—the Ukraine, North Caucasus and Lower Volga. The rest of the country is on short rations but nothing worse. These conditions are bad, but there is no famine.

The critical months in this country are February and March, after which a supply of eggs, milk and vegetables comes to supplement the shortage of bread—if, as now, there is a shortage of bread. In every Russian village food conditions will improve henceforth, but that will not answer one really vital question—What about the coming grain crop?

Upon that depends not the future of the Soviet power, which cannot and will not be smashed, but the future policy of the Kremlin. If through climatic conditions, as in 1921, the crop fails, then, indeed, Russia will be menaced by famine. If not, the present difficulties will be speedily forgotten.

45. The Victors: Kaganovich, Stalin, Postyshev, Voroshilov, 1934.

46. The Victims: a mass grave outside Kharkiv, 1933.

USSR, knowing that it could be considered guilty of carrying out genocide against 'political groups' – the kulaks, for example – resisted this broader definition. Instead, the Soviet delegation argued that political groups 'were entirely out of place in a scientific definition of genocide, and their inclusion would weaken the convention and hinder the fight against genocide'. The Soviet delegation sought instead to ensure that the definition of 'genocide' was 'organically bound up with fascism-nazism and other similar race theories'. Lemkin himself began to lobby for this narrower definition, as did others who badly wanted the measure to pass, and feared that the USSR might otherwise block it.[8]

The Convention finally passed in 1948, which was a personal triumph for Lemkin and for many others who had lobbied in its favour. But the legal definition was narrow, and it was interpreted even more narrowly in the years that followed. In practice, 'genocide', as defined by the UN documents, came to mean the physical elimination of an entire ethnic group, in a manner similar to the Holocaust.

The Holodomor does not meet that criterion. The Ukrainian famine was not an attempt to eliminate every single living Ukrainian; it was also halted, in the summer of 1933, well before it could devastate the entire nation. Although Lemkin later argued for an expansion of the term, and even described the Sovietization of Ukraine as the 'classic example of Soviet genocide', it is now difficult to classify the Ukrainian famine, or any other Soviet crime, as genocide in international law.[9] This is hardly surprising, given that the Soviet Union itself helped shape the language precisely in order to prevent Soviet crimes, including the Holodomor, from being classified as 'genocide'.

The difficulty of classifying the Holodomor as a genocide in international law has not stopped a series of Ukrainian governments from trying to do so. The first attempt followed the Orange Revolution of 2004 – a series of street protests in Kyiv against a stolen election, corruption and perceived Russian influence in Ukrainian politics. Those protests led to the election of Viktor Yushchenko, the first president of Ukraine without a Communist Party pedigree. Yushchenko had an unusually strong mandate from the Ukrainian national movement and he used it to promote the study of the famine. He made references to the Holodomor in his inaugural speech and created a National Memory Institute with Holodomor research at its heart. He also lobbied for the United Nations, the Organization of Security and Cooperation in Europe and other international institutions to recognize the Holodomor as a genocide. Under Yushchenko's government, funding for research into the famine expanded dramatically. Dozens of local groups – teachers, students, librarians – joined a national effort to create a Book of Memory, for example, a complete list of famine victims.[10] In January 2010 a Ukrainian court found Stalin, Molotov, Kaganovich, Postyshev, Kosior and others guilty of 'perpetrating genocide'. The court terminated the case on the grounds that the accused were all deceased.[11]

Yushchenko understood the power of the famine as a unifying national memory for Ukrainians, especially because it had been so long denied. He undoubtedly 'politicized' it, in the sense that he used political tools to draw more attention to the story. Some of his own statements about the famine, particularly his claims about the number of casualties, were exaggerated. But he stopped short of using the famine to antagonize Ukraine's Russian neighbours, and he did not describe the famine as a 'Russian' crime against Ukrainians. Indeed, at the seventy-fifth anniversary Holodomor commemoration ceremony in 2008, as on other occasions, Yushchenko went out of his way to avoid blaming the Russian nation for the tragedy:

> We appeal to everyone, above all the Russian Federation, to be true, honest and pure before their brothers in denouncing the crimes of Stalinism and the totalitarian Soviet Union . . . We were all together in the same hell. We reject the brazen lie that we are blaming any one people for our tragedy. This is untrue. There is one criminal: the imperial, communist Soviet regime.[12]

Yushchenko's words were not always heeded by his compatriots. Of course, he was right to blame the famine on Soviet Communist Party policy, not Russian policy: there was no 'Russia', or at least no sovereign Russian state, in 1933. Yet because the Communist Party's 1933 headquarters had been in Moscow, and because Moscow, the capital of post-Soviet Russia, assumed many of the assets of the USSR after 1991, some in Ukraine do now blame 'Russia' for the famine.

The Russian political establishment, which was by the mid-2000s recovering its own imperial ambitions in the region, confused the issue further by choosing to hear Yushchenko's campaign as an attack on Russia, not an attack on the USSR. Pro-Russian groups inside Ukraine followed the Russian state's lead: in 2006 a group of Russian nationalist thugs, led by a member of the local Communist Party, entered the office of Volodymyr Kalinichenko, a historian who wrote about the famine in the Kharkiv region, kicked at locked doors and shouted threats.[13] In 2008 the Russian press denounced the Holodomor commemorations as 'Russophobic' and the Russian president, then Dmitry Medvedev, turned down an invitation to attend, dismissing talk of the 'so-called Holodomor' as 'immoral'.[14] Behind the scenes Medvedev threatened leaders in the region, advising them not to vote for a motion designating the Holodomor as a 'genocide' at the United Nations. According to Prince Andrew of Great Britain, Medvedev told the president of Azerbaijan that he could 'forget about Nagorno-Karabakh,' a region disputed by Azerbaijan and Armenia, unless he voted against a proposal to call the Holodomor a genocide.[15]

The campaign was not just diplomatic. It was accompanied by the emergence of a Russian historical narrative that did not deny the famine, but emphatically downplayed it. There is almost no commemoration of either the Ukrainian or the wider Soviet famine in Russia and very little public debate. To the extent that it is mentioned at all, it is usually part of an argument that clearly denies any particular Ukrainian suffering. In 2008 the Russian scholar Viktor Kondrashin published the most eloquent version of this counter-narrative. *The Famine of 1932–33: The Tragedy of the Russian Village* detailed the horrors of those years in the Russian province of Penza, in the Volga region. Kondrashin did not deny that there had been mass starvation in Ukraine. On the contrary, his work showed that Stalin had launched the brutal process of collectivization, and confirmed that he had ordered the 'thoughtless' confiscation of grain in 1932–3, knowing full well that millions of peasants would die. But Kondrashin also argued that the Ukrainian estimates of Ukrainian death rates were too high, that estimates of famine deaths in the Volga regions had generally been too low, and that Stalin's policies had affected everyone alike. The 'mechanism of the creation of famine was the same', in

Russia and Ukraine, he told an interviewer: 'there were no national differences'.[16]

Kondrashin's argument was partly correct. President Yushchenko is one of many prominent figures who sometimes cite casualty figures for the Holodomor that are too high. Although the Ukrainian scholarly community is now coalescing, with some exceptions, around a number just below 4 million deaths, it is still possible to hear numbers as high as 10 million deaths.[17] Kondrashin may also have been right that Penza province – like Ukraine, a region famous for a civil war-era peasant rebellion that infuriated Lenin in 1918 – was a special target of the Soviet state.[18]

Clearly there is a case for a close examination of the 'special' famine in Penza. There is an even more urgent case for a closer examination of the famine in Kazakhstan, where the very high mortality rate also indicates something much more sinister than negligence. But that should not negate the need for a recognition of the special circumstances of the famine in Ukraine. As this book has shown, the historical record includes decrees directed solely at Ukraine, such as the one closing the Ukrainian border, blacklisting dozens of Ukrainian collective farms and villages, and implicitly linking the grain collection failure to Ukrainization. The demographic record also shows that Ukraine had a higher death toll in those years than any other part of the Soviet Union.

In a public debate with the Ukrainian historian Stanislav Kulchytsky, Kondrashin himself wrote that Stalin saw the food crisis of 1932 as an 'opportunity':

> the famine of 1932–33 and the general economic crisis in Ukraine gave the Stalinist regime an excuse to adopt preventive measures against the Ukrainian national movement and also, in the distant perspective, its possible social base (the intellectuals, the bureaucrats, the peasants).[19]

Since this, more or less, is the argument of most mainstream Ukrainian historians – and of this book – it seems that the gap between the 'Russian' and 'Ukrainian' scholarly interpretations of the famine is not as great as has sometimes been presented.

Nevertheless, politicization of the famine debate has meant that the differences between the public Ukrainian and Russian understandings of the famine have become significant, both in the Russian-Ukrainian context and also within Ukraine itself. Yushchenko spoke often about the famine, and thought carefully about how to commemorate it. But his opponent and successor, Viktor Yanukovych – a 'pro-Russian' president, who had been elected with open Russian financial and political support – abruptly reversed that policy. Yanukovych removed references to the Holodomor from the presidential website, replaced the head of the National Memory Institute with an ex-communist historian, and stopped using the word 'genocide' to describe the famine.

Yanukovych continued to speak of the famine as a 'tragedy' and even as an 'Armageddon', and he frequently used the word 'Holodomor', which implies an artificially created famine. He also continued to hold annual commemoration ceremonies and he did not stop or harass archival researchers, as President Vladimir Putin did in Russia at about the same time, although many had feared that he would.[20] Nevertheless, the president's change of tone and emphasis enraged his political opponents. In particular, his refusal to use the word 'genocide' was widely dismissed as a gesture of deference to Russia (it is notable that President Medvedev did finally visit a Holodomor memorial in Kyiv in 2010, during the Yanukovych presidency, perhaps as a 'reward' for the toned-down language). One group of citizens even tried to take Yanukovych to court for 'genocide denial'.[21] His disastrous presidency further discredited all of his policies, including his downplaying of the famine. He systematically undermined Ukrainian political institutions and engaged in corruption on an extraordinary scale. He fled the country in February 2014 after his police shot more than one hundred protesters dead in Kyiv's Maidan Square, during an extended protest against his rule.

Inevitably, Yanukovych's disgrace left its mark on the public historical debate. Thanks to the politics that swirled around the word 'genocide', it became a kind of identity tag in Ukrainian politics, a term that could mark those who used it as partisans of one political party and those who did not as partisans of another. The problem worsened in the spring of 2014, when the Russian government produced a caricature 'genocide' argument to justify its own behaviour. During the Russian invasions of Crimea and eastern Ukraine,

Russian-backed separatists and Russian politicians both said that their illegal interventions were a 'defence against genocide' – meaning the 'cultural genocide' that 'Ukrainian Nazis' were supposedly carrying out against Russian speakers in Ukraine.

As the conflict between Russia and Ukraine intensified, attacks on the history and historiography also worsened. In August 2015, Russian-backed separatists deliberately destroyed a monument to the victims of the famine in the occupied eastern Ukrainian town of Snizhne – the same place from which separatists had launched the BUK missile a year earlier that brought down Malaysian Airlines flight 17, killing everyone on board.[22] Also in August 2015, Sputnik News, a Russian government propaganda website, published an article in English entitled 'Holodomor Hoax'. The article presented views reminiscent of the old era of denial, called the famine 'one of the 20th century's most famous myths and vitriolic pieces of anti-Soviet Propaganda' and even cited Douglas Tottle's long-discredited book, *Fraud, Famine and Fascism*.[23] The links that Tottle claimed between historians of the famine, alleged Ukrainian Nazis and alleged anti-Soviet forces in the West proved useful again to a Russia that once again sought to discredit Ukrainians as 'Nazis'.[24]

By 2016 the arguments had come full circle. The post-Soviet Russian state was once again in full denial: the Holodomor did not happen, and only 'Nazis' would claim that it did. All these arguments muddied the application of the word 'genocide' so successfully that to use it in any Russian or Ukrainian context has become wearyingly controversial. People feel exhausted by the debate – which was, perhaps, the point of the Russian assault on the historiography of the famine in the first place.

But the genocide debate, so fierce a decade ago, has subsided for other reasons too. The accumulation of evidence means that it matters less, nowadays, whether the 1932–3 famine is called a genocide, a crime against humanity, or simply an act of mass terror. Whatever the definition, it was a horrific assault, carried out by a government against its own people. It was one of several such assaults in the twentieth century, not all of which fit into neat legal definitions. That the famine happened, that it was deliberate, and that it was part of a political plan to undermine Ukrainian identity is becoming more widely accepted, in Ukraine as well as in the West, whether or not an international court confirms it.

Slowly, the debate is also becoming less important to Ukrainians. In truth, the legal arguments about the famine and genocide were often proxies for arguments about Ukraine, Ukrainian sovereignty and Ukraine's right to exist. The discussion of the famine was a way of insisting on Ukraine's right to a separate national history and to its own national memory. But now – after more than a quarter-century of independence, two street revolutions and a Russian invasion that was finally halted by a Ukrainian army – sovereignty is a fact, not a theory that requires historical justification, or indeed any justification at all.

Because it was so devastating, because it was so thoroughly silenced, and because it had such a profound impact on the demography, psychology and politics of Ukraine, the Ukrainian famine continues to shape the thinking of Ukrainians and Russians, both about themselves and about one another, in ways both obvious and subtle. The generation that experienced and survived the famine carried the memories with them for ever. But even the children and grandchildren of survivors and perpetrators continue to be shaped by the tragedy.

Certainly the elimination of Ukraine's elite in the 1930s – the nation's best scholars, writers and political leaders as well as its most energetic farmers – continues to matter. Even three generations later, many of contemporary Ukraine's political problems, including widespread distrust of the state, weak national institutions and a corrupt political class, can be traced directly back to the loss of that first, post-revolutionary, patriotic elite. In 1933 the men and women who could have led the country, the people whom they would have influenced and who would have influenced others in turn, were abruptly removed from the scene. Those who replaced them were frightened into silence and obedience, taught to be wary, careful, cowed. In subsequent years the state became a thing to be feared, not admired; politicians and bureaucrats were never again seen as benign public servants. The political passivity in Ukraine, the tolerance of corruption, and the general wariness of state institutions, even democratic ones – all of these contemporary Ukrainian political pathologies date back to 1933.

The Russification that followed the famine has also left its mark. Thanks to the USSR's systematic destruction of Ukrainian culture and memory, many Russians do not treat Ukraine as a separate nation with a separate history. Many Europeans are only dimly aware that Ukraine exists at all. Ukrainians themselves have mixed and confused loyalties. That ambiguity can translate into cynicism and apathy. Those who do not care much or know much about their nation are not likely to work to make it a better place. Those who do not feel any sense of civic responsibility are less interested in stopping corruption.

Ukraine's contemporary linguistic battles date from the 1930s too. Paradoxically, Stalin reinforced the link between the Ukrainian language and Ukrainian national identity when he tried to destroy them both. As a result linguistic controversies continue to reflect deeper arguments about identity even today. Ukraine is a thoroughly bilingual country – most people speak both Ukrainian and Russian – yet those who prefer one language or the other still regularly complain of discrimination. Riots broke out in 2012 when the Ukrainian state recognized Russian as an 'official' language in several provinces, meaning that it could be used in courts and government offices. In 2014 the post-Maidan Ukrainian government tried to repeal that law, and though the repeal was quickly reversed, Russian-backed 'separatists' used this proposed change to justify their invasion of Ukraine. Russia's challenge, both to the language and to Ukrainian sovereignty, has also created a different kind of popular backlash. In 2005, less than half of Ukrainians used the language as their main form of communication. Ten years later two-thirds preferred Ukrainian to Russian.[25] Thanks to Russian pressure, the nation is unifying behind the Ukrainian language as it has not done since the 1920s.

If the study of the famine helps explain contemporary Ukraine, it also offers a guide to some of the attitudes of contemporary Russia, many of which form part of older patterns. From the time of the revolution, the Bolsheviks knew that they were a minority in Ukraine. To subjugate the majority, they used not only extreme violence, but also virulent and angry forms of propaganda. The Holodomor was preceded by a decade of what we would now call polarizing 'hate speech', language designating some people as 'loyal' Soviet citizens and others as 'enemy' kulaks, a privileged class that would have to be destroyed to make way for the people's revolution. That ideological language justified the behaviour of the men and women who facilitated the famine, the people who confiscated food from starving families, the policemen who arrested and killed their fellow citizens. It also provided them with a sense of moral and political justification. Very few of those who organized the famine felt guilty about having done so: they had been persuaded that the dying peasants were 'enemies of the people', dangerous criminals who had to be eliminated in the name of progress.

Eighty years later, the Russian FSB, the institutional successor of the KGB (itself the successor of the OGPU), continues to demonize its opponents using propaganda and disinformation. The nature and form of hate speech in Ukraine has changed, but the intentions of those who employ it have not. As in the past, the Kremlin uses language to set people against one another, to create first- and second-class citizens, to divide and distract. In 1932–3, Soviet state media described the OGPU troops working with local collaborators as 'Soviet patriots' fighting 'Petliurists', 'kulaks', 'traitors' and 'counter-revolutionaries'. In 2014, Russian state media described Russian special forces carrying out the invasion of Crimea and eastern Ukraine as 'separatist patriots' fighting 'fascists' and 'Nazis' from Kyiv. An extraordinary disinformation campaign, complete with fake stories – that Ukrainian nationalists had crucified a baby, for example – and fake photographs followed, not only inside Russia but on Russian state-sponsored media around the world. Although far more sophisticated than anything Stalin could have devised in an era before electronic media, the spirit of that disinformation campaign was much the same.

Eighty years later, it is possible to hear the echo of Stalin's fear of Ukraine – or rather his fear of unrest spreading from Ukraine to Russia – in the present too. Stalin spoke obsessively about loss of control in Ukraine, and about Polish or other foreign plots to subvert the country. He knew that Ukrainians were suspicious of centralized rule, that collectivization would be unpopular among peasants deeply attached to their land and their traditions, and that Ukrainian nationalism was a galvanizing force, capable of challenging Bolshevism and even destroying it. A sovereign Ukraine could thwart the Soviet project, not only by depriving the USSR of its grain, but also by robbing it of legitimacy. Ukraine had been a Russian colony for centuries, Ukrainian and Russian culture remained closely intertwined, the Russian and Ukrainian languages were closely related. If Ukraine rejected both the Soviet system and its ideology, that rejection could cast doubt upon the whole Soviet project. In 1991 that is precisely what it did.

Russia's current leadership is all too familiar with this history. As in 1932, when Stalin told Kaganovich that 'losing' Ukraine was his greatest worry, the current Russian government also believes that a sovereign, democratic, stable Ukraine, tied to the rest of Europe by links of culture and trade, is a threat to the interests of Russia's leaders. After all, if Ukraine becomes too European – if it achieves anything resembling successful integration into the West – then Russians might ask, why not us? The Ukrainian street revolution of 2014 represented the Russian leadership's worst nightmare: young people calling for the rule of law, denouncing corruption and waving European flags. Such a movement could have been contagious – and so it had to be stopped by whatever means possible. Today's Russian government uses disinformation, corruption and military force to undermine Ukrainian sovereignty just as Soviet governments did in the past. As in 1932, the constant talk of 'war' and 'enemies' also remains useful to Russian leaders who cannot explain stagnant living standards or justify their own privileges, wealth and power.

History offers hope as well as tragedy. In the end, Ukraine was not destroyed. The Ukrainian language did not disappear. The desire for independence did not disappear either – and neither did the desire for democracy, or for a more just society, or for a Ukrainian state that truly represented Ukrainians. When it became possible, Ukrainians expressed these desires. When they were allowed to do so, in 1991, they voted overwhelmingly for independence. Ukraine, as the national anthem proclaims, did not die.

In the end, Stalin failed too. A generation of Ukrainian intellectuals and politicians was murdered in the 1930s, but their legacy lived on. The national aspiration, linked, as in the past, to the aspiration for freedom, was revived in the 1960s; it continued underground in the 1970s and 1980s; it became open again in the 1990s. A new generation of Ukrainian intellectuals and activists reappeared in the 2000s.

The history of the famine is a tragedy with no happy ending. But the history of Ukraine is not a tragedy. Millions of people were murdered, but the nation remains on the map. Memory was suppressed, but Ukrainians today discuss and debate their past. Census records were destroyed, but today the archives are accessible.

The famine and its aftermath left a terrible mark. But although the wounds are still there, millions of Ukrainians are, for the first time since 1933, finally trying to heal them. As a nation, Ukrainians know what happened in the twentieth century, and that knowledge can help shape their future.

Notes

PREFACE

1. V. V. Kondrashin et al., eds., *Golod v SSSR: 1929–1934*, Rossiia XX vek, vol. 1 (Moscow: Mezhdunarodnyi fond 'Demokratiia', 2011), 163–5, citing V. S. Lozyts'kyi, *Holodomor 1932–1933 rokiv: zlochyn vlady – trahediia narodu: dokumenty i materialy* (Kyiv: Heneza, 2008), 37–40.

2. TsDAHOU 1/20/5254 (1932), 1–16, in R. Ia. Pyrih, ed., *Holodomor 1932–1933 rokiv v Ukraïni: Dokumenty i materialy* (Kyiv: Kyievo-Mohylians'ka Akademiia, 2007), 130.

3. Ibid., 134.

4. The word 'Haladamor' appears in Czech publications of the Ukrainian diaspora in the 1930s. 'Holodomor' was probably first used publicly in Ukraine by Oleksii Musiyenko, during a speech at the Writers' Union that was cited in *Literaturna Ukraïna* of 18 February 1988.

5. Hennadii Boriak, 'Sources and Resources on the Famine in Ukraine's Archival System', *Harvard Ukrainian Studies* 27 (2004–5), 117–47.

6. Andrea Graziosi, 'The Soviet 1931–1933 Famines and the Ukrainian Holodomor: Is a New Interpretation Possible, and What Would Its Consequences Be?', *Harvard Ukrainian Studies* 27, no. 1/4 (2004), 100.

7. Tetiana Boriak has summarized their significance in her book *1933: 'I choho vy shche zhyvi?'* (Kyiv: Clio, 2016).

8. Boriak, 'Sources and Resources', 117–47.

INTRODUCTION: THE UKRAINIAN QUESTION

1. Taras Shevchenko, 'Zapovit' ('Testament'), in *Selected Poetry*, trans. John Weir (Kyiv: Ukraine, 1977), 198, available at http://www.infoukes.com/shevchenkomuseum/poetry.htm, accessed 2017.

2. Nikolai Gogol, *Arabesques*, trans. Alexander Tulloch (Ann Arbor, MI: Ardis, 1982), 104.

3. I. M. Dolgorukov, 'Slavny bubny za gorami, ili moe puteshestvie koekuda, 1810 goda: Sochinenie Kniazia Ivana Mikhailovicha Dolgorukago c predisloviem O. M. Bodianskago', *Chteniia v Imperatorskom Obshchestve Istorii i Drevnostei Rossiiskikh pri Moskovskom Universitete* 2 (April–June 1869): glava II 'Materiialy otechestvennye', 46.

4. Serhiy Bilenky, *Romantic Nationalism in Eastern Europe: Russian, Polish and Ukrainian Political Imaginations* (Stanford, CA: Stanford University Press, 2012), 96–7.

5. Ibid., 244, citing Belinskii's review of Mykola Markevych's *Istoriia Malorossii*, found in Belinskii, *Polnoe sobranie sochinenii*, vol. 7 (Moscow: Izdatel'stvo Akademii Nauk, 1953), 60.

6. Aleksandra Efimenko, *Iuzhnaia Rus: Ocherki, issledovaniia i zametki*, vol. 2 (St Petersburg: [publisher unknown] 1905), 219.

7. George Y. Shevelov, *The Ukrainian Language in the First Half of the Twentieth Century, 1900–1941: Its State and Status* (Cambridge, MA: Harvard Ukrainian Research Institute, 1989), 54.

8. Paul Robert Magocsi, *A History of Ukraine: The Land and its Peoples*, 2nd edn (Toronto: University of Toronto Press, 2010), 17.

9. The physical descriptions in Henryk Sienkiewicz's *Trilogy*, a series of nineteenth-century novels set in what is now Ukraine, are actually based on the author's journeys in the United States.

10. Serhii Plokhy, *The Gates of Europe: A History of Ukraine* (New York: Basic Books, 2015), 9.

11. Ibid., 69.

12. Voltaire, *Histoire de Charles XII roy de Suède*, vol. 1 (Basel: Revis, 1756), 171.

13. Shevchenko, 'Zapovit', 198. Also available on the website of the Taras H. Shevchenko Museum and Memorial Park Foundation in Toronto, Canada, accessed 2016, http://www.infoukes.com/shevchenkomuseum/poetry.htm#link3.

14. Magocsi, *A History of Ukraine*, 364.

15. Hennadii Boriak, ed., *Ukraïns'ka identychnist' i movne pytannia v Rosiis'kii imperii: sproba derzhavnoho rehuliuvannia (1847–1914): Zbirnyk dokumentiv i materialiv* (Kyiv: Instytut Istoriï Ukraïny NAN Ukraïny, 2013), 3.

16. Bohdan Krawchenko, *Social Change and National Consciousness in Twentieth-Century Ukraine* (Edmonton, Alberta: Canadian Institute of Ukrainian Studies, 1987), 24.

17. Francis William Wcislo, 'Soslovie or Class? Bureaucratic Reformers and Provincial Gentry in Conflict, 1906–1908', Russian Review 47, no. 1 (1988), 1–24, esp. p. 4; quoted in Andrea Graziosi, Stalinism, Collectivization and the Great Famine, in Holodomor Series (Cambridge, MA: Ukrainian Studies Fund, 2009), 9–10.
18. There are good accounts of the Ukrainian national revival in Orest Subtelny, Ukraine: A History (Toronto: University of Toronto Press, 1988), 221–42; Magocsi, A History of Ukraine, 467–88; and Plokhy, The Gates of Europe, 147–98.
19. Andrea Graziosi, Bol'sheviki i krest'iane na Ukraine, 1918–1919 gody: Ocherk o bol'shevizmakh, natsional-sotsializmakh i krest'ianskikh dvizheniiakh (Moscow: AIRO-XX, 1997), 19–21.
20. Hiroaki Kuromiya, Freedom and Terror in the Donbas: A Ukrainian-Russian Borderland, 1870s–1990s (Cambridge: Cambridge University Press, 1998), 43.
21. Graziosi, Stalinism, Collectivization and the Great Famine, 9–10; Plokhy, The Gates of Europe, 192–3.
22. Richard Pipes, 'Introduction', in Taras Hunczak, ed., The Ukraine, 1917–1921: A Study in Revolution (Cambridge, MA: Harvard University Press, 1977), 3.

1. THE UKRAINIAN REVOLUTION, 1917

1. Robert Paul Browder and Alexander F. Kerensky, eds., The Russian Provisional Government, 1917: Documents (Stanford, CA: Stanford University Press, 1961), 383–5.
2. Leon Trotsky, Sochineniia, Seriia 1: Istoricheskoe podgotovlenie Oktiabria, vol. 3:2 (Moscow: Gosidat, 1925), 202. This is E. H. Carr's translation from A History of Soviet Russia: The Bolshevik Revolution, 1917–1923, vol. 1 (London: Macmillan, 1950).
3. Victor Chernov, The Great Russian Revolution, trans. Philip Mosely (New Haven, CT: Yale University Press, 1936, rpt. New York: Russell and Russell, 1966), 266–7; Thomas M. Prymak, Mykhailo Hrushevsky: The Politics of National Culture (Toronto: University of Toronto Press, 1987), 128–9; Serhii Plokhy, Unmaking Imperial Russia: Mykhailo Hrushevsky and the Writing of Ukrainian History (Toronto: University of Toronto Press, 2005), 17–91.
4. Prymak, Mykhailo Hrushevksy, 129.
5. Plokhy, Unmaking Imperial Russia, 80.
6. Plokhy, The Gates of Europe, 207.

7. All dates in this chapter are according to the 'New Style' (Gregorian) calendar, adopted in February 1918.

8. Subtelny, *Ukraine: A History*, 340.

9. Plokhy, *The Gates of Europe*, 206.

10. 'First Universal of the Ukrainian Central Rada', quoted in Magocsi, *A History of Ukraine*, 473.

11. 'Third Universal of the Ukrainian Central Rada', quoted in ibid., 480.

12. Orlando Figes, *A People's Tragedy: The Russian Revolution, 1891–1924* (London: Pimlico, 1997), 79.

13. Shevelov, *The Ukrainian Language in the First Half of the Twentieth Century*, 78–9.

14. Mark von Hagen, 'The Entangled Eastern Front and the Making of the Ukrainian State: A Forgotten Peace, a Forgotten War and Nation-Building, 1917–1918' (unpublished conference paper), 9; George A. Brinkley, 'Allied Policy and French Intervention in the Ukraine, 1917–1920', in Hunczak, ed., *The Ukraine*, 323–51.

15. Von Hagen, 'The Entangled Eastern Front', 18.

16. Mikhail Bulgakov, *The White Guard*, trans. Marian Schwartz (New Haven, CT: Yale University Press, 2008), 54.

17. Ibid., 67.

18. Arthur E. Adams, *Bolsheviks in the Ukraine: The Second Campaign, 1918–1919* (New Haven, CT: Yale University Press, 1963), 11.

19. Bulgakov, *The White Guard*, 76.

20. Serhii Efremov, *Shchodennyky, 1923–1929* (Kyiv: Hazeta 'Rada', 1997), 379–80.

21. Yuri Shapoval, 'The Symon Petliura Whom We Still Do Not Understand', *Den* 18, last modified 6 June 2006, accessed 2017, http://www.ukemonde.com/petlyura/petlyura_notunder.html.

22. Aleksei Aleksandrovich Gol'denveizer, 'Iz Kievskikh vospominanii, 1917–21', in Iosif Vladimirovich Gessen, ed., *Arkhiv russkoi revoliutsii*, vol. 6 (Berlin: n.p., 1922), 161–303.

23. Adams, *Bolsheviks in the Ukraine*, 81.

24. Gol'denveizer, 'Iz Kievskikh vospominanii', 230–4.

25. Ibid., 232.

26. Bulgakov, *The White Guard*, 59.

27. Richard Pipes, *The Formation of the Soviet Union*, rev. edn (Cambridge, MA: Harvard University Press, 1997), 137.

28. Prymak, *Mykhailo Hrushevksy*, 163.

29. Gol'denveizer, 'Iz Kievskikh vospominanii', 234.

30. Valerii Vasyl'ev, *Politychne kerivnyctvo URSR i SRSR: Dynamika vidnosyn tsentr-subtsentr vlady, 1917–1938* (Kyiv: Instytut Istorii

Ukraïny NAN Ukraïny, 2014), 53–93; Jurij Borys, *The Sovietization of Ukraine 1917–1923: The Communist Doctrine and Practice of National Self-Determination* (Edmonton, Alberta: Canadian Institute of Ukrainian Studies, 1980), 129.

31. Graziosi, *Bol'sheviki i krest'iane na Ukraine*, 20–1.

32. This is argued in Anna Procyk, *Russian Nationalism and Ukraine: The Nationality Policy of the Volunteer Army During the Civil War* (Edmonton, Alberta: Canadian Institute of Ukrainian Studies, 1995).

33. Karl Marx, 'The 18th Brumaire of Louis Bonaparte', in *Karl Marx and Friedrich Engels: Selected Works*, vol. 1 (Moscow: Progress Publishers, 1968), 394–488.

34. V. I. Lenin, *Collected Works*, vol. 10 (Moscow: Progress Publishers, 1965), 40–3.

35. Karl Marx, *The Communist Manifesto* (Charleston, SC: Filiquarian Publishing, 2005), 32.

36. Borys, *The Sovietization of Ukraine*, 30–1.

37. Ibid., 121–38.

38. Josef Stalin, *Works*, vol. 2 (Moscow: Foreign Languages Publishing House, 1954), 303, https://www.marxists.org/reference/archive/stalin/works/1933/01/07.htm. Originally published as 'Natsional'nyi vopros i sotisal'demokratiia', *Prosveshchenie* 3–5 (March–May 1913).

39. From his speech 'Concerning the National Question in Yugoslavia, Speech Delivered in the Yugoslav Commission of the ECCI, March 30, 1925', Stalin, *Works*, vol. 7, 71–2.

40. Steven Kotkin, *Stalin: Paradoxes of Power*, vol. 1 (New York: Penguin Press, 2014), 117.

41. 25 October according to the Julian calendar used in tsarist Russia; 7 November according to the Gregorian calendar, adopted in Russia in 1918.

42. Borys, *The Sovietization of Ukraine*, 174–5; Yaroslav Bilinsky, 'The Communist Takeover of Ukraine', in Hunczak, ed., *The Ukraine*, 113. They are citing a 18 December 1917 (new calendar) *Pravda* article.

43. This policy was a direct harbinger of one pursued by the Russian government in 2014; Bilinsky, 'The Communist Takeover of Ukraine', 113.

44. Borys, *The Sovietization of Ukraine*, 183; John Reshetar, 'The Communist Party of Ukraine and its Role in the Ukrainian Revolution', in Hunczak, ed., *The Ukraine*, 170–1.

45. Borys, *The Sovietization of Ukraine*, 79; Reshetar, 'The Communist Party of Ukraine', 173–4; James Mace, *Communism and the Dilemmas of National Liberation: National Communism in Soviet Ukraine, 1918–1933* (Cambridge, MA: Harvard Ukrainian Research Institute, 1983), 27.

46. Plokhy, *Unmaking Imperial Russia*, 84–5.

47. Mace, *Communism and the Dilemmas of National Liberation*, 26.

48. N. I. Suprunenko, *Ocherki Istorii Grazhdanskoi Voiny i inostrannoi voennoi interventsii na Ukraine* (Moscow: Nauka, 1966), 16.

49. Telegram to Antonov-Ovsienko and Ordzhonikidze, in V. I. Lenin, *Polnoe Sobranie Sochinenii*, vol. 50 (Moscow: Politizdat, 1970), 30. An alternative translation is given in the official English version in Lenin, *Collected Works*, vol. 44, 57–8.

50. Roy A. Medvedev, *Let History Judge: The Origins and Consequences of Stalinism*, first published 1969, rev. and expanded edn, ed. and trans. George Shriver (Oxford: Oxford University Press, 1989), 50.

51. Suprunenko, *Ocherki Istorii Grazhdanskoi Voiny*, 34–5.

52. Borys, *The Sovietization of Ukraine*, 205–6.

53. Ibid., 215.

54. Adams, *Bolsheviks in the Ukraine*, 100.

55. Borys, *The Sovietization of Ukraine*, 221.

56. How this happened is explained at length in Peter Holquist, *Making War, Forging Revolution: Russia's Continuum of Crisis, 1914–1921* (Cambridge, MA: Harvard University Press, 2002), 16–46.

57. M. Philips Price, *My Reminiscences of the Russian Revolution* (London: George Allen & Unwin, 1921), 12–16.

58. Ibid., 78.

59. Ibid., 12–16.

60. George Seldes, *You Can't Print That: The Truth Behind the News, 1918–1928* (New York: Payson & Clark, 1929), 230.

61. Francis Conte, *Christian Rakovski, 1873–1941: A Political Biography* (Boulder, CO: East European Monographs, 1989), 109, citing *Protokoly VIII Konferentsii RKP(b): 3 December 1919* (Moscow: n.p., 1919).

62. Aleksandr Shlikhter, 'Bor'ba za khleb na Ukraine v 1919 godu', *Litopys revoliutsii: Zhurnal istorii KP(b)U ta zhovtnevoi revoliutsii na Ukraini* 2, no. 29 (Berezen'-Kviten', 1928), 97.

63. Holquist, *Making War, Forging Revolution*, 96.

64. Ibid., 248.

65. Alan M. Ball, *Russia's Last Capitalists: The Nepmen, 1921–29* (Berkeley, CA: University of California Press, 1987), 6.

66. Boris Pasternak, *Doctor Zhivago*, trans. Richard Pevear and Larissa Volokhonsky (New York: Pantheon Books, 2010), 175.

67. Bertrand Patenaude, *The Big Show in Bololand: The American Relief Expedition to Soviet Russia in the Famine of 1921* (Stanford, CA: Stanford University Press, 2002), 18–19.

68. Ball, *Russia's Last Capitalists*, 4.

69. Isaac Deutscher, *Stalin: A Political Biography* (London: Oxford University Press, 1949), 195.

70. Price, *My Reminiscences of the Russian Revolution*, 224.

71. Ibid., 260 and 308.

72. Gennadii Bordyugov, 'The Policy and Regime of Extraordinary Measures in Russia under Lenin and Stalin', in *Europe-Asia Studies* 47, no. 4 (June 1995), 617.

73. Vasyl'ev, *Politychne kerivnytstvo URSR i SRSR*, 64–9. Vasyl'ev also underlines the significance of Tsaritsyn for Stalin's later policies.

74. Oleg V. Khlevniuk, *Stalin: New Biography of a Dictator*, trans. Nora Seligman Favorov (New Haven, CT: Yale University Press, 2015), 55–7.

75. Ibid., 57–9.

76. Deutscher, *Stalin*, 204.

77. Pavlo Khrystiuk, *Ukraïns'ka Revoliutsiia: zamitky i materialy do istoriï Ukraïnskoï revoliutsiï, 1917–1920*, vol. 2 (Vienna: n.p., 1921), 136.

78. V. M. Lytvyn et al., *Istoriia ukraïns'koho selianstva: Narysy v 2-kh tomakh*, vol. 2 (Kyiv: Naukova Dumka, 2006), 57.

79. O. S. Rubl'ov and O. P. Reient, *Ukraïns'ki vyzvol'ni zmahannia, 1917–1921 rr.*, vol. 10 (Kyiv: Al'ternatyvy, 1999), 199–205.

80. Borys, *The Sovietization of Ukraine*, 235.

81. Adams, *Bolsheviks in the Ukraine*, 131–2.

82. Volodymyr Serhiichuk et al., *Ukraïns'kyi khlib na eksport, 1932–1933* (Kyiv: PP Serhiichuk M.I., 2006), 3.

83. Shlikhter, 'Bor'ba za khleb na Ukraine', 135.

84. Elias Heifetz, *The Slaughter of the Jews in the Ukraine in 1919* (New York: Thomas Seltzer, 1921), 58.

85. Leon Trotsky, *History of the Russian Revolution*, 3 vols., trans. Max Eastman (Chicago, IL: Haymarket Books, 2008), 229.

86. Vil'iam Noll (William Noll), *Transformatsiia hromadians'koho suspil'stva: Usna istoriia ukraïns'koï selans'koï kul'tury, 1920–30 rokiv* (Kyiv: Rodovid, 1999), 115.

87. Ibid.

88. James Mace, 'The *Komitety Nezamozhnykh Selyan* and the Structure of Soviet Rule in the Ukrainian Countryside, 1920–1933', *Soviet Studies* 35, no. 4 (October 1983), 487–503.

89. Iosyp Nyzhnyk, 'Poka Reserv', COIM Al-1726/2.

90. Shlikhter, 'Bor'ba za khleb na Ukraine', 98.

91. Graziosi, *Bol'sheviki i krest'iane*, 135.

92. Price, *My Reminiscences of the Russian Revolution*, 309–10.

93. Orlando Figes, *Peasant Russia, Civil War: The Volga Countryside in Revolution, 1917–1921* (Oxford: Clarendon Press, 1989), 187.

94. Adams, *Bolsheviks in the Ukraine*, 125–7; Rubl'ov and Reient, *Ukraïns'ki vyzvol'ni zmahannia*, 199–205.

95. Shlikhter, 'Bor'ba za khleb na Ukraine', 135.

96. Holquist, *Making War, Forging Revolution*, 175–80.

97. Ibid., 185.

98. Holquist, ' "Conduct Merciless Mass Terror": Decossackization on the Don, 1919', *Cahiers du monde russe* 38, nos. 1–2 (January–June 1997), 127–62.

99. Shlikhter, 'Bor'ba za khleb na Ukraine', 135.

2. REBELLION, 1919

1. Quoted in Adams, *Bolsheviks in the Ukraine*, 299–300.

2. Bulgakov, *The White Guard*, 301.

3. N. Sukhogorskaya, 'Gulyai-Polye in 1918', Nestor Makhno Archive, accessed 2016, http://www.nestormakhno.info/english/personal/per sonal2.htm.

4. Leon Trotsky, 'Report to the Plenum of the Kharkov Soviet of Workers', Cossacks' and Peasants' Deputies, 14 June 1919', in *How the Revolution Armed: The Military Writings and Speeches of Leon Trotsky*, vol. 2 (London: New Park Publications, 1979), 278.

5. Peter Arshinov, *The History of the Makhnovist Movement (1918–1921)*, trans. Fredy and Lorraine Perlman (London: Freedom Press, 1974), 87–8.

6. Ibid., 273, quoting the pamphlet, 'Comrades in the Red Army!', from June 1920.

7. Stephen Velychenko, *Painting Imperialism and Nationalism Red: The Ukrainian Marxist Critique of Russian Communist Rule in Ukraine* (Toronto: University of Toronto Press, 2015), 177, citing TsDAHOU 57/2/398/12.

8. Heifetz, *The Slaughter of the Jews in the Ukraine*, 59.

9. Adams, *Bolsheviks in the Ukraine*, 149–51.

10. M. Kubanin, *Makhnovshchina: Krest'ianskoe dvizhenie v stepnoi Ukraine v gody grazhdanskoi voiny* (Leningrad: Priboi, 1927), 65–6; see also Adams, *Bolsheviks in the Ukraine*, 151–2.

11. Kubanin, *Makhnovshchina*, 68–9.

12. Adams, *Bolsheviks in the Ukraine*, 299–300.

13. Graziosi, *Bol'sheviki i krest'iane*, 148.

14. Shlikhter, 'Bor'ba za khleb na Ukraine', 106.
15. Rubl'ov and Reient, *Ukraïns'ki vyzvol'ni zmahannia*, 199–210; Graziosi, *Stalinism, Collectivization and the Great Famine*, 21–4.
16. Richard Pipes, *The Formation of the Soviet Union, 1917–1923* (Cambridge, MA: Harvard University Press, 1964), 137.
17. Heinrich Epp, 'The Day the World Ended: December 7, 1919, Steinbach, Russia', trans. D. F. Plett, *Preservings: Newsletter of the Hanover Steinbach Historical Society*, no. 8, part 2 (June 1996), 5–7. Available at http://www.plettfoundation.org/preservings/past-issues, accessed 2017.
18. Michael Palij, *The Anarchism of Nestor Makhno, 1918–1921: An Aspect of the Ukrainian Revolution* (Seattle, WA: University of Washington Press, 1976), 187; Rubl'ov and Reint, *Ukraïns'ki vyzvol'ni zmahannia*, 211–12.
19. Graziosi, *Bol'sheviki i krest'iane*, 147.
20. John Ernest Hodgson, *With Denikin's Armies, Being a Description of the Cossack Counter-Revolution in South Russia, 1918–1920* (London: Temple Bar, 1932), 54–5.
21. Rubl'ov and Reient, *Ukraïns'ki vyzvol'ni zmahannia*, 214–18.
22. Epp, 'The Day the World Ended', 5–7.
23. Hodgson, *With Denikin's Armies*, 54–5.
24. Nizhnik, 'Poka Reserv'.
25. Ibid.
26. Graziosi, *Stalinism, Collectivization and the Great Famine*, 24.
27. Volodymyr Serhiichuk et al., *Pohromy v Ukraïni 1914–1920: vid shtuchnykh stereotypiv do hirkoï pravdy, prykhovuvanoï v radians'kykh arkhivakh* (Kyiv: Vyd-vo im. Oleny Telihy, 1998), 62–3, citing TsDIAUK 1439/1/1552/226.
28. Simon Sebag Montefiore, *The Romanovs* (London: Weidenfeld and Nicolson, 2016), 530.
29. Oleg Budnitskii, *Russian Jews Between the Reds and the Whites, 1917–1920* (Philadelphia, PA: University of Pennsylvania Press, 2012), 225.
30. Serhiichuk, *Pohromy v Ukraïni*, 20–1.
31. Hodgson, *With Denikin's Armies*, 54–5.
32. Henry Abramson, *A Prayer for the Government: Ukrainians and Jews in Revolutionary Times, 1917–1920* (Cambridge, MA: Harvard University Press, 1999), 157.
33. Heifetz, *The Slaughter of the Jews in the Ukraine*, 37.
34. Ibid., 49; for an analysis of the attitudes of the Central Rada and the Directorate towards the Jews, see T. P. Makarenko, 'Evreis'ki pohromy v dobu Ukraïns'koï Revoliutsiï', *Naukovi Pratsi Istorychnoho fakul'tetu Zaporiz'koho Natsional'noho Universytetu* XXXV (2013), 116–19.

35. Serhiichuk, *Pohromy v Ukraïni*, 26–30; Richard Pipes, ed., *The Unknown Lenin: From the Secret Archive* (New Haven: Yale University Press, 1996), 117.
36. Nahum Gergel, 'The Pogroms in Ukraine in 1918–1921', *YIVO Annual of Jewish Social Science* 6 (1951), 245.
37. Heifetz, *The Slaughter of the Jews in the Ukraine*, 235–6.
38. Sergei Ivanovich Gusev-Orenburgskii, *Kniga o Evreiskikh pogromakh na Ukraine v 1919 g.* (Petrograd: Z. I. Grzhebina, 1920), 118–21.
39. Ibid., 119–20.
40. Serhiichuk, *Pohromy v Ukraïni*, 118–19.
41. Le Comité Commémoratif Simon Petliura, *Documents sur les Pogroms en Ukraine et l'assassinat de Simon Petliura à Paris* (Paris: Librairie du Trident, 1927); Henry Abramson, *A Prayer for the Government: Ukrainians and Jews in Revolutionary Times, 1917–1920* (Cambridge, MA: Harvard University Press, 1999), 157.
42. Jan Borkowski, ed., *Rok 1920: Wojna Polsko-Radziecka we wspomnieniach i innych dokumentach* (Warsaw: Państwowy Instytut Wydawniczy, 1990), 128–9.
43. Jozef Piłsudski and Mikhail Nikolaevich Tukhachevskii, *Year 1920 and its Climax: Battle of Warsaw During the Polish-Soviet War, 1919–1920* (London: Piłsudski Institute of London, 1972), 13.
44. For a full account, see Adam Zamoyski, *Warsaw 1920: Lenin's Failed Conquest of Europe* (London: Harper Perennial, 2009).
45. Borys, *The Sovietization of Soviet Ukraine*, 293–5.
46. Graziosi, *Stalinism, Collectivization and the Great Famine*, 22–3.
47. The words of Grigorii Petrovskii, quoted in Terry Martin's *Affirmative Action Empire: Nations and Nationalism in the Soviet Union, 1923–1939* (Ithaca, NY: Cornell University Press), 78.

3. FAMINE AND TRUCE: THE 1920S

1. 'Letter to Molotov', 19 March 1922, in Richard Pipes, ed., *The Unknown Lenin: From the Secret Archive* (New Haven, CT: Yale University Press, 1999), 152–3.
2. Quoted in George Luckyj, 'Mykola Khvylovy, a Defiant Ukrainian Communist', in Katherine Bliss Eaton, ed., *Enemies of the People: The Destruction of Soviet Literary, Theater, and Film Arts in the 1930s* (Evanston, IL: Northwestern University Press, 2002), 170.
3. Stanislav Kul'chyts'kyi, *Holodomor 1932–1933 rr. iak henotsyd: trudnoshchi usvidomlennia* (Kyiv: Naukova Dumka, 2008), 51.

4. Vladyslav Verstiuk, 'Novyi etap revoliutsiino-viis'kovoho protybor-stva v Ukraïni', in Volodymyr Lytvyn, ed., Ukraïna: Politychna Istoria XX-pochatok-XXI stolitia (Kyiv: Parlaments'ke vydavnytstvo, 2007), 392–430; Iurii Shapoval, 'Vsevolod Balickij, bourreau et victime', Cahiers du monde russe, vol. 44, nos. 2–3 (2003), 375.

5. Lyudmyla Hrynevych, Holod 1928–1929 rr. v radians'kii Ukraïni (Kyiv: Instytut Istoriï Ukraïny NAN Ukraïny, 2013), 307–8, citing TsDAVOU 2/2/40 (1921), 33, and RDVA 40442/3/2 (1920), 16, 25.

6. H. H. Fisher, The Famine in Soviet Russia, 1919–1923: The Oper-ations of the American Relief Administration (New York: Macmillan, 1927), 497.

7. Andrea Graziosi, A New, Peculiar State: Explorations in Soviet History (Westport, CT: Praeger, 2000), 75.

8. Stalin, Works, vol. 4, 311.

9. S. V. Iarov, 'Krest'ianskie volneniia na Severo-Zapade Sovetskoi Rossii v 1918–1919 gg.', in V. P. Danilov and T. Shanin, eds., Krest'ianovedenie. Teoriia. Istoriia. Sovremennost', Ezhegodnik 1996 (Moscow: Aspekt Press, 1996), 134–59.

10. Both quotes in Mace, Communism and the Dilemmas of National Liberation, 67.

11. Graziosi, A New, Peculiar State, 78, citing V. Danilov and T. Shanin, eds., Krest'ianskoe vosstanie v Tambovskoi gubernii v 1919–1921 gg. Antonovshchina: Dokumenty i materialy (Tambov: Aspekt Press, 1994), 52–5.

12. DAZhO (Zhytomyr) F. R-1520/4828 (1931), 9–16.

13. Richard Pipes, Russia under the Bolshevik Regime (New York: Vintage Books, 1995), 390.

14. TsDAVOU 337/1/8085 (1929), 26.

15. Fisher, The Famine in Soviet Russia, 497.

16. Vitalii Petrovych Kyrylenko, 'Holod 1921–1923 rokiv u pivdennii Ukraïni' (dissertation, Mykolaivs'kyi Natsional'nyi Universytet imeni V. O. Sukhomlyns'koho, 2015), 158–60.

17. Pipes, Russia under the Bolshevik Regime, 411.

18. Ibid., 412.

19. R. G. Tukudzh'ian, T. V. Pankova-Kozochkina, 'Golod 1921–1922 gg. i 1932–1933 gg. na iuge Rossii: sravnitel'no-istoricheskii analiz', in N. I. Bondar and O. V. Matveev, eds., Istoricheskaia pamiat' nasele-niia iuga Rossii o golode 1932–33: materialy nauchno-prakticheskoi konferentsii (Krasnodar: Isd-vo Traditsiia, 2009), 84.

20. TsDAVOU 337/1/8085 (1929), 27–8.

21. T. O. Hryhorenko, 'Holod 1921–1923 rokiv na Cherkashchyni', in *Holod v Ukraïni u pershii polovyni XX stolittia: prychyny ta naslidky (1921–1923, 1932–1933, 1946–1947) Materialy mizhnarodnoï naukovoï konferentsiï* (Kyiv: 20–21 November 2013), 38–9; Kyrylenko, 'Holod 1921–1923 rokiv u pivdennii Ukraïni', 101.

22. TsDAVOU 337/1/8085 (1929), 38–40.

23. Donald S. Day, 'Woman Reveals Vast Horror of Russian Famine', *Chicago Tribune* (15 August 1921), 5.

24. Patenaude, *The Big Show in Bololand*, 55.

25. Ibid., 59.

26. In the North Caucasus, for example, see Tukudzh'ian, Pankova-Kozochkina, 'Golod 1921–1922 gg. i 1932–1933 gg. na iuge Rossii', 85.

27. This is the observation of Bertrand Patenaude in *The Big Show in Bololand*, 27.

28. TsDAHOU 1/6/29 (1922), 30.

29. Ibid., 27–30.

30. Ibid., 39–41.

31. Pipes, *Russia under the Bolshevik Regime*, 416.

32. Patenaude, *The Big Show in Bololand*, 55.

33. Pipes, *Russia under the Bolshevik Regime*, 417.

34. Ibid., 418–19.

35. Fisher, *The Famine in Soviet Russia*, 535.

36. In fact, there were two Ukrainian famine committees. The first, set up in the spring of 1921, contained several prominent non-Bolshevik politicians. It was quickly dissolved and replaced with a more reliably pro-Soviet famine committee. See O. M. Movchan, 'Komisii ta komitety dopomohy holoduiuchym v USRR', in *Entsyklopediia istoriï Ukraïny*, V. A. Smolii et al., eds., vol. 4 (Kyiv: Naukova Dumka, 2003–13), 471–3.

37. Stanislav Kul'chyts'kyi and O. M. Movchan, *Nevidomi storinky holodu 1921–1923 rr. v Ukraïni* (Kyiv: Instytut Istoriï Ukraïny NAN Ukraïny, 1993), 26.

38. Lenin, *Collected Works*, vol. 45, 302–3.

39. TsDAHOU 1/20/397 (1929), 1–2.

40. G. V. Zhurbelyuk, 'Metodyka istoryko-pravovykh doslidzhen problemy holodu 1921–23 rr. v Ukraïni: Rozvinchannia Mifiv', in Hryhorenko, *Holod v Ukraïni u pershii polovyni XX stolittia*, 53.

41. Fisher, *The Famine in Soviet Russia*, 263.

42. Patenaude, *The Big Show in Bololand*, 96–9; Fisher, *The Famine in Soviet Russia*, 250.

43. TsDAHOU 1/6/29/ (1929), 56.

44. O. I. Syrota, 'Holod 1921–1923 rokiv v Ukraïni ta ioho ruinivni naslidky dlia ukraïns'koho narodu', in *Holod v Ukraïni u pershii polovyni XX stolittia: prychyny ta naslidky (1921–1923, 1932–1933, 1946–1947)*, 146.

45. TsDAHOU 1/6/29 (1929), 6; see also Patenaude, *The Big Show in Bololand*, 101.

46. The American Joint Distribution Committee online archives, *Records of the American Jewish Joint Distribution Committee of the Years 1921–1932*, Folder 76, file NY_AR2132_00855, Minutes of the Meeting of the European Executive Council, 12 November 1921.

47. Ibid., Folder 49, File NY_AR2132_04249, Letter on behalf of J. H. Cohen.

48. Fisher, *The Famine in Soviet Russia*, 271–5.

49. Ibid., 266.

50. See, for example, Zhurbeliuk, 'Metodyka istoryko-pravovykh doslidzhen' problemy holodu 1921–1923 rr. v Ukraïni', 51–8; also Kul'chyts'kyi, *Holodomor 1932–1933 rr. iak henotsyd*, 140–70.

51. Kyrylenko, 'Holod 1921–1923 rokiv u pivdennii Ukraïni', 118–29.

52. TsDAHOU 1/6/29 (1929), 36–9.

53. Ibid., 16–17.

54. Pipes, ed., *The Unknown Lenin*, 152–3.

55. Ibid.

56. Pipes, *Russia under the Bolshevik Regime*, 411.

57. Kyrylenko, 'Holod 1921–1923 rokiv u pivdennii Ukraïni', 130–9.

58. Patenaude, *The Big Show in Bololand*, 197–8.

59. Iurii Mytsyk et al., eds., *Ukraïns'kyi holokost 1932–1933: svidchennia tykh, khto vyzhyv*, vol. 6 (Kyiv: Kyievo-Mohylians'ka Akademiia, 2008), 599.

60. V. A. Smolii et al., *'Ukraïnizatsiia' 1920–1930-kh rokiv: peredumovy, zdobutky, uroky* (Kyiv: Instytut Istoriï Ukraïny NAN Ukraïny, 2003), 15.

61. Pipes, *Russia under the Bolshevik Regime*, 369.

62. Lenin, *Collected Works*, vol. 33, 62.

63. Martin, *The Affirmative Action Empire*, 78–9.

64. Hennadii Yefimenko, 'Bolshevik Language Policy as a Reflection of the Ideas and Practice of Communist Construction, 1919–1933', *The Battle for Ukrainian: A Comparative Perspective*, eds. Michael S. Flier and Andrea Graziosi (Cambridge, MA: Harvard Ukrainian Research Institute, 2017), 173.

65. Yefimenko, 'Bolshevik Language Policy', 170.

66. Ibid.

67. Ball, *Russia's Last Capitalists*, 45–8.

68. Borys, *The Sovietization of Soviet Ukraine*, 249–50.

69. Shevelov, *The Ukrainian Language in the First Half of the Twentieth Century*, 86.

70. Mace, *Communism and the Dilemmas of National Liberation*, 197–8.

71. Smolii, 'Ukraïnizatsiia' *1920–1930-kh rokiv*, 28, citing *Desiatyi s'ezd RKP(b)*: Stenog. Ochtet. – M. (1963), 202–3.

72. The *Borotbysty*, the Left Socialist Revolutionaries, joined the Communist Party (Bolsheviks) of Ukraine, the CP(B)U. The remaining Social Democrats joined another group, the Communist Party, which existed until 1924.

73. Mace, *Communism and the Dilemmas of National Liberation*, 89, citing A. I. Bychkova et al., eds., *Kulturne budivnytstvo v Ukraïnskii RSR, cherven 1941–1950: zbirnyk dokumentiv i materialiv*, vol. 1 (Kyiv: Naukova Dumka, 1989), 229–32, 242–7.

74. Plokhy, *Unmaking Imperial Russia*, 225.

75. Ibid., 216–31; Prymak, *Mykhailo Hrushevsky*, 208–12.

76. Plokhy, *Unmaking Imperial Russia*, 234; Prymak, *Mykhailo Hrushevsky*, 208–12.

77. Iurii I. Shapoval, 'The Mechanisms of the Informational Activity of the GPU-NKVD', *Cahiers du monde russe* 22 (April–December 2001), 207–30.

78. Plokhy, *Unmaking Imperial Russia*, 266.

79. Ibid., 233; Prymak, *Mykhailo Hrushevsky*, 208–12.

80. Prymak, *Mykhailo Hrushevsky*, 212.

81. Natella Voiskounski, 'A Renaissance Assassinated', *Galeriya* 2 (2012) (35), accessed 23 April 2017, http://www.tretyakovgallerymagazine.com/articles/2-2012-35/renaissance-assassinated.

82. George S. Luckyj, *Literary Politics in the Soviet Ukraine, 1917–1934* (New York: Columbia University Press, 1990), 47–9.

83. Ibid., 46.

84. Olga Bertelsen, 'The House of Writers in Ukraine, the 1930s: Conceived, Lived, Perceived', *The Carl Beck Papers in Russian and East European Studies* 2302 (2013), 13–14.

85. Shevelov, *The Ukrainian Language in the First Half of the Twentieth Century*, 131–6.

86. Martin, *The Affirmative Action Empire*, 213, 281.

87. Ibid., 282–5.

88. Matthew Pauly, *Breaking the Tongue: Language, Education, and Power in Soviet Ukraine, 1923–1934* (Toronto: University of Toronto Press, 2014), 66–7.

89. Smolii et al., *'Ukraïnizatsiia' 1920–1930-kh rokiv*, 7–8.

90. Pauly, *Breaking the Tongue*, 4.

91. Petro G. Grigorenko, *Memoirs*, trans. Thomas R. Whitney (New York: W. W. Norton, 1982), 14.

92. Ibid., 15–16.

93. Hiroaki Kuromiya, *The Voices of the Dead: Stalin's Great Terror in the 1930s* (New Haven, CT: Yale University Press, 2007), 108–9.

94. Pauly, *Breaking the Tongue*, 60–1.

95. Ibid., 259–63.

96. Ibid., 146.

97. Ibid., 229–30.

98. The sources for this section are Shapoval, 'Vsevolod Balickij, bourreau et victime', and Iurii Shapoval, Volodymyr Prystaiko and Vadym Zolotar'ov, *ChK-GPU-NKVD v Ukraïni: osoby, fakty, dokumenty* (Kyiv: Abrys, 1997), 25–43.

99. Shapoval, 'Vsevolod Balickij, bourreau et victime', 373.

100. Ibid., 376.

101. In fact, GPU (the State Political Directorate) was the name for the secret police forces starting from February 1922 when it was part of the People's Commissariat for Internal Affairs. From November 1923 it became the OGPU (the Joint, or All-Union, State Political Directorate) under the direct control of the Council of People's Commissars. But the two names were and still are often used interchangeably to describe the police in this era, before they were again renamed in 1934. For purposes of simplicity and ease of understanding, this book will simply use OGPU.

4. THE DOUBLE CRISIS, 1927–9

1. Quoted in Lynne Viola, V. P. Danilov, N. A. Ivnitskii and Denis Kozlov, *The War Against the Peasantry, 1927–1930: The Tragedy of the Soviet Countryside*, trans. Steven Shabad (New Haven, CT: Yale University Press, 2005), 22–3.

2. Elena Osokina, *Our Daily Bread: Socialist Distribution and the Art of Survival in Stalin's Russia, 1927–1941*, trans. Kate Transchel and Greta Bucher (London and New York: Routledge, 2005), 16.

3. TsDAVOU 337/1/8085 (1929), 61–76.

4. E. H. Carr and R. W. Davies, *A History of Soviet Russia: Foundations of a Planned Economy, 1926–1929*, vol. 1 (London: Macmillan, 1978), 943, table 7; Kotkin, *Stalin: Paradoxes of Power*, 662.

5. TsA FSB RF 2/5/386 (1928), 1–3, 15–45, reproduced in Viola et al., eds., *The War Against the Peasantry*, 34–44.

6. Paul Scheffer, *Seven Years in Soviet Russia*, trans. Arthur Livingstone (New York: Macmillan, 1932), 64.

7. Eugene Lyons, *Assignment in Utopia* (New York: Harcourt, Brace, 1937), 97.

8. TsA FSB RF 66/1/174 (1927), 162, in Viola et al., eds., *The War Against the Peasantry*, 22–3.

9. Christopher Andrew and Vasili Mitrokhin, *The Mitrokhin Archive: The KGB in Europe and the West* (London: Allen Lane, 1999), 48–9, citing Christopher Andrew and Oleg Gordievsky, *KGB: The Inside Story of its Foreign Operations from Lenin to Gorbachev* (London: Sceptre, 1991), 126, and Roger Faligot and Rémi Kauffer, *As-tu vu Crémet?* (Paris: Seuil, 1991).

10. Timothy Snyder, *Sketches from a Secret War: A Polish Artist's Mission to Liberate Soviet Ukraine* (New Haven, CT: Yale University Press, 2005), 45–8.

11. James Harris, *The Great Fear: Stalin's Terror of the 1930s* (Oxford: Oxford University Press, 2016), 106–7.

12. Robert Tucker, *Stalin in Power: The Revolution from Above, 1928–1941* (New York: W. W. Norton, 1992), 75.

13. Liudmyla Hrynevych, 'The Price of Stalin's "Revolution from Above": Anticipation of War among the Ukrainian Peasantry', trans. Marta Olynyk, *Key Articles on the Holodomor Translated from Ukrainian into English*, Holodomor Research and Education Consortium, http://holodomor.ca/translated-articles-on-the-holodomor.

14. TsA FSB RF 2/6/567 (1927), 1–5, in Viola et al., eds., *The War Against the Peasantry*, 32.

15. RGASPI, 17/3/666 (1927), 10–12, in ibid., 32–4.

16. RTsKhIDNI, 17/3/667 (1928), 10–12, reproduced in V. Danilov, R. Manning and L. Viola, eds., *Tragediia sovetskoi derevni. Kollektivizatsiia i raskulachivanie: dokumenty i materialy v 5 tomakh, 1927–193*, vol. 1 (Moscow: Rossiiskaia polit. Entsiklopediia, 1999), 136–7.

17. V. M. Lytvyn et al., *Ekonomichna istoriia Ukraïny: Istoryko-ekonomichne doslidzhennia*, vol. 2 (Kyiv: Instytut Istoriï Ukraïny NAN Ukraïny, 2011), 223–4.

18. *Izvestiia TsK KPSS*, 1991, no. 5 (1928), 195–6, in Danilov et al., eds., *Tragediia sovetskoi derevni*, vol. 1, 147.

19. TsA FSB RF 2/6/53 (1928), 87–94, in A. Berelovich and V. Danilov, eds., *Sovetskaia derevnia glazami VChK-OGPU-NKVD, 1918–1939:*

Dokumenty i materialy v 4-kh tomakh, vol. 2 (Moscow: ROSSP'EN, 1998–2005), 655–6.

20. TsA FSB RF 2/6/567 (1928), 109–13, in ibid., vol. 2, 653–4.

21. *Izvestiia* TsK KPSS, 1991, no. 5 (1928), 201–2, in Danilov et al., eds., *Tragediia sovetskoi derevni*, vol. 1, 156–7.

22. TsA FSB RF 2/6/596 (1928), 150–1, in Berelovich and Danilov, eds., *Sovetskaia derevnia glazami VChK—OGPU-NKVD*, vol. 2, 661–3.

23. Maurice Hindus, *Red Bread: Collectivization in a Russian Village* (Bloomington, IN: Indiana University Press, 1988), 60.

24. Ibid., 159.

25. Mikhail Sholokhov, *Virgin Soil Upturned*, trans. Stephen Garry (London: W. & J. Mackay, 1977), 23.

26. Kotkin, *Stalin: Paradoxes of Power*, 672, citing *Izvestiia* TsK KPSS, 1991, no. 6, 203–5, and RGASPI, 558/11/118, 23–6.

27. R. W. Davies, *The Soviet Collective Farm, 1929–1930* (Cambridge, MA: Harvard University Press, 1980), 71.

28. Harris, *The Great Fear*, 86.

29. Khlevniuk, *Stalin: New Biography of a Dictator*, 103.

30. *Izvestiia* TsK KPSS, 1991, no. 7 (1928), 179, in Danilov et al., eds., *Tragediia sovetskoi derevni*, vol. 1, 158.

31. J. Arch Getty and Oleg V. Naumov, *The Road to Terror: Stalin and the Self-Destruction of the Bolsheviks, 1932–1939* (New Haven, CT: Yale University Press, 2002), 41.

32. RTsKhIDNI 17/2/375 chast' II (1928), 50 ob.–66 ob., in Danilov et al., eds., *Tragediia sovetskoi derevni*, vol. 1, 272–355, esp. 319–54.

33. V. P. Danilov, 'Bukharin and the Countryside', in A. Kemp-Welch, ed., *The Ideas of Nikolai Bukharin* (Oxford: Oxford University Press, 1992), 76.

34. This is Martin's point in *The Affirmative Action Empire*, 23, 75–124.

35. Mykola Khvylovyi, *The Cultural Renaissance in Ukraine: Polemical Pamphlets, 1925–1926*, trans. and ed. Myroslav Shkandrij (Edmonton, Alberta: Canadian Institute of Ukrainian Studies, 1986), 222; also quoted in Martin, *The Affirmative Action Empire*, 215.

36. Bertelsen, 'The House of Writers in Ukraine', 4.

37. Martin, *The Affirmative Action Empire*, 288; TsA FSB RF 2/7/525 (1928), 126–7, in Berelovich and Danilov, eds., *Sovetskaia derevnia glazami VChK-OGPU-NKVD*, vol. 2, 817.

38. Martin, *The Affirmative Action Empire*, 212, 215–16, 224.

39. Stalin, *Works*, vol. 8, 162.

40. Shapoval, 'Vsevolod Balickij, bourreau et victime', 379–80, 392.

41. Vasyl' Danylenko, ed., *Ukraïns'ka intelihentsiia i vlada: zvedennia sektrenoho viddilu DPU USRR 1927–1929 rr.* (Kyiv: Tempora, 2012), 25–8.

42. Iurii Shapoval, 'Zhyttia ta smert' Mykoly Khvyl'ovoho: u svitli rozsekrechenykh dokumentiv HPU', in *Z arkhiviv VUChK, HPU, NKVD, KHB* 2, nos. 30/31 (2008): 316–17.

43. Martin, *The Affirmative Action Empire*, 224.

44. Ibid., 225.

45. Shapoval, 'Vsevolod Balickij, bourreau et victime', 383, citing HDA SBU, Kiev, FPI, 1.2.

46. Plokhy, *Unmaking Imperial Russia*, 262–3.

47. Shapoval, 'The Mechanisms of the Informational Activity of the GPU-NKVD', 207–8.

48. Danylenko, *Ukraïns'ka intelihentsiia i vlada*, 61, 63, 68–9, 97.

49. Mace, *Communism and the Dilemmas of National Liberation*, 114.

50. Lyons, *Assignment in Utopia*, 115.

51. Ibid., 116–17.

52. Stephen Kotkin's *Stalin: Paradoxes of Power* has a very good summary of the Shakhty show trial, 687–704.

53. Sheila Fitzpatrick, *Education and Social Mobility in the Soviet Union, 1921–1934* (Cambridge: Cambridge University Press, 1979, 2002), 113.

54. All the victims were rehabilitated in 1989 after a court concluded that the case had been fabricated. See Iurii Shapoval, 'The Case of the "Union for the Liberation of Ukraine": A Prelude to the Holodomor', *Holodomor Studies* 2, no. 2 (Summer–Autumn 2010), 163; on the first 'SVU' see Alexander Motyl, *The Turn to the Right: The Ideological Origins and Development of Ukrainian Nationalism, 1919–1929* (New York: Columbia University Press, 1980), 10–11.

55. Olga Bertelsen and Myroslav Shkandrij, 'The Secret Police and the Campaign against Galicians in Soviet Ukraine, 1929–1934', *Nationalities Papers: The Journal of Nationalism and Ethnicity* 42, no. 1 (2014), 37–62.

56. Shapoval, 'The Case of the "Union for the Liberation of Ukraine"', 158–60.

57. Mace, *Communism and the Dilemmas of National Liberation*, 275.

58. Pauly, *Breaking the Tongue*, 261–3.

59. HDA SBU 13/370/9/142–55, reproduced in Danylenko, *Ukraïns'ka intelihentsiia i vlada*, 470–1.

60. I. M. Prelovs'ka, *Dzherela z istoriï Ukraïns'koi Aftokefal'noï Pravoslavnoï Tserkvy, 1921–1930 – Ukraïns'koï Pravoslavnoï Tserkvy, 1930–1939* (Kyiv: Instytut Ukraïns'koï Arkheohrafiï ta Dzhereloznavstva im. M. C. Hrushevs'koho, 2013), 498–9.

61. Shapoval, 'The Case of the "Union for the Liberation of Ukraine"', 157–8.

62. Ibid., 172.

63. Ibid., 166–7.

64. Kost Turkalo, 'The SVU Trial', in S. O. Pidhainy, ed., *The Black Deeds of the Kremlin: A White Book*, vol. 1 (Toronto: Basilian Press, 1953), 309–14.

65. Myroslav Shkandrij and Olga Bertelsen, 'The Soviet Regime's National Operations in Ukraine, 1929–1934', *Canadian Slavonic Papers* 55, nos. 3/4 (September–December 2013), 420.

66. A. H. Korolev, 'Institut nauchnoi i prakticheskoi veterinarii narkomzema USSR v gody repressii', *Istoriia nauky i biohrafistyka: Elektronne naukove fakhove vydannia – mizhvidomchyi tematychnyi zbirnyk: Natsional'na Akademiia Ahrarnykh Nauk, Natsional'na Naukova Sil's'kohospodars'ka Biblioteka* 3 (2007), http://inb.dnsgb.com.ua.

67. Shkandrij and Bertelsen, 'The Soviet Regime's National Operations in Ukraine', 437–47.

68. Stalin, 'Concerning the National Question in Yugoslavia', speech delivered in the Yugoslav Commission of the ECCI, 30 March 1925, in Stalin, *Works*, vol. 7, 71–2.

69. Martin, *The Affirmative Action Empire*, 147.

70. Andrea Graziosi, 'Collectivisation, révoltes paysannes et politiques gouvernementales (à travers les rapports du GPU d'Ukraine de février–mars 1930)', *Cahiers du monde russe* 35, no. 3 (July–September 1994), 439–40.

71. HDA SBU 13/370/1 (1927), 15–26, in Danylenko, *Ukraïns'ka intelihentsiia i vlada*, 46.

72. HDA SBU 13/370/2 (1927), 106–18, in ibid., 119–20.

73. HDA SBU 13/370/1 (1927), 107–21, in ibid., 78–9.

74. HDA SBU 13/370/4 (1927), 55–74, in ibid., 213–14.

75. Hrynevych, 'The Price of Stalin's "Revolution from Above"', 4.

76. Ibid., 4–5.

77. TsA FSB RF 2/6/25 (1928), 1–66, in Berelovich and Danilov, eds., *Sovetskaia derevnia glazami VChK-OGPU-NKVD*, vol. 2, p. 816; see also all of vol. 2, 780–817.

78. Quoted in V. M. Danylenko et al., eds., *Pavlohrads'ke povstannia, 1930: dokumenty i materialy* (Kyiv: Ukraïns'kyi Pys'mennyk, 2009), 14–15.

79. Lyons, *Assignment in Utopia*, 99.

80. TsA FSB RF 2/6/597 (1928), 22–7, in Danilov, *Tragediia sovetskoi derevni*, vol. 1, 195–200.

81. Hrynevych, *Holod 1928–1929 rr. u radians'kii Ukraïni*, 238–9.

82. Ibid., 90, 232–6, 238–40.

83. TsA FSB RF 2/6/597 (1928), 6–20, in Berelovich and Danilov, eds., *Sovetskaia derevnia glazami VChK-OGPU-NKVD*, vol. 2, 666.

84. Hrynevych, 'The Price of Stalin's "Revolution from Above"', 5.

85. Ibid., 6.

86. Shkandrij and Bertelsen, 'The Soviet Regime's National Operations in Ukraine', 425.

87. RTsKhIDNI 82/2/136 (1928), 1–55, in Danilov, *Tragediia sovetskoi derevni*, vol. 1, 172–92.

88. TsA FSB RF 2/6/599 (1928), 292–9, in Berelovich and Danilov, eds., *Sovetskaia derevnia glazami VChK-OGPU-NKVD*, vol. 2, 723–31.

89. Quoted in Danylenko, *Pavlohrads'ke povstannia*, 14–15.

90. Ibid., 318.

91. TsA FSB RF 2/6/597 (1928), 126–35, in Berelovich and Danilov, eds., *Sovetskaia derevnia glazami VChK-OGPU-NKVD*, vol. 2, 672–82.

5. COLLECTIVIZATION: REVOLUTION IN THE COUNTRYSIDE, 1930

1. P. V., 'Collective Farming', in Pidhainy, *The Black Deeds of the Kremlin*, 213.

2. Lyons, *Assignment in Utopia*, 283.

3. Miron Dolot, *Execution by Hunger: The Hidden Holocaust* (New York: W. W. Norton, 1984), 1–2. Dolot is a pseudonym: the writer's real name was Simon Starow.

4. 'Schedule A, vol. 37, Case 622/(NY)1719 (interviewer W. T., type A4). Female, 53, Ukrainian, Kolkhoznik', July 1951, Harvard Project on the Soviet Social System, Slavic Division, Widener Library, Harvard University, 52.

5. 'Schedule B, vol. 7, Case 67 (interviewer J. R.)', Harvard Project on the Soviet Social System, Slavic Division, Widener Library, Harvard University, 12.

6. Stanislav Kul'chyts'kyi, ed., *Narysy povsiakdennoho zhyttia radians'koi Ukraïny v dobu NEPu (1921–1928 rr.) kolektyvna monohrafiia v 2-kh chastynakh*, vol. 2 (Kyiv: Instytut Istoriï Ukraïny NAN Ukraïny, 2010), 183.

7. Kotkin, *Stalin: Paradoxes of Power*, 672, citing *Izvestiia TsK KPSS*, 1991, no. 6, 203–5, and RGASPI, 558/11/118, 23–6.

8. There were three basic types of collective farm (*kolkhoz*): the commune, the artel and the association for joint cultivation of land (TOZ or SOZ). In addition, there were state-owned farms (*sovkhoz*). R. W. Davies, *The Soviet Collective Farm* (Cambridge, MA: Harvard University Press, 1980), 68.

9. For a general description of collective farm life, see Sheila Fitzpatrick, *Stalin's Peasants: Resistance and Survival in the Russian Village after Collectivization* (Oxford: Oxford University Press, 1994), 128–51.

10. Stalin, 'God velikogo pereloma', *Pravda* (7 November 1929), in Danilov et al., eds., *Tragediia sovetskoi derevni*, vol. 1, 741–2.

11. RtsKhIDNI 17/2/441, vols. 1 and 2; summarized in Robert Conquest, *The Harvest of Sorrow: Soviet Collectivization and the Terror-Famine* (New York: Oxford University Press, 1986), 112–14; and Lynne Viola, *Peasant Rebels under Stalin: Collectivization and the Culture of Peasant Resistance* (Oxford: Oxford University Press, 1996), 24–6.

12. Dolot, *Execution by Hunger*, 6.

13. Lynne Viola, *The Best Sons of the Fatherland: Workers in the Vanguard of Soviet Collectivization* (New York: Oxford University Press, 1987), 31, 62.

14. Ibid., 64.

15. Lev Kopelev, *To Be Preserved Forever*, trans. Anthony Austin (New York: Lippincott, 1977), 11.

16. Hindus, *Red Bread*, 1.

17. Sholokhov, *Virgin Soil Upturned*, 84.

18. Viola, *The Best Sons of the Fatherland*, 76.

19. Antonina Solovieva, 'Sent by the Komsomol', in Sheila Fitzpatrick and Yuri Slezkine, eds., *In the Shadow of Revolution: Life Stories of Russian Women from 1917 to the Second World War* (Princeton, NJ: Princeton University Press, 2000), 237.

20. Tracy McDonald, 'A Peasant Rebellion in Stalin's Russia: The Pitelinskii Uprising, Riazan 1930', *Journal of Social History* 35, no. 1 (Fall 2001), 125–46.

21. Noll, *Transformatsiia hromadians'koho suspil'stva*, 180.

22. 'Case History LH38: Oleksandr Honcharenko, Cherkasy oblast'', in U.S. Congress, *Investigation of the Ukrainian Famine, 1932–1933*, Report to Congress/Commission on the Ukraine Famine, adopted by the Commission 19 April 1988, submitted to Congress 22 April 1988, James E. Mace, ed. (Washington, D.C.: U.S. G.P.O., 1988), 317.

23. TsA FSB RF 2/9/21 (1930), 393–4, in Lynne Viola and V. P. Danilov, eds., *The War Against the Peasantry, 1927–1930: The Tragedy of the*

Soviet Countryside, trans. Steven Shabad (New Haven, CT: Yale University Press, 2005), 219.

24. Solovieva, 'Sent by the Komsomol', in Fitzpatrick and Slezkine, eds., *In the Shadow of Revolution*, 236–7.

25. Pasha Angelina, 'The Most Important Thing', in Fitzpatrick and Slezkine, eds., *In the Shadow of Revolution*, 310.

26. RTsKhIDNI 85/1/118 (1930), 1–13, reproduced in Graziosi, 'Collectivisation, révoltes paysannes et politiques gouvernementales', 476.

27. DAZhO (Zhytomyr) 1520/4828 (1931), 9–16.

28. Graziosi, 'Collectivisation, révoltes paysannes et politiques gouvernementales', 450. This use of 'criminal elements' not only had precedents in 1919–20, it remained part of the Soviet tactical arsenal: the NKVD would rely on criminal networks when creating new secret police forces in occupied Central Europe after 1945.

29. Ibid., 449, citing 'Sergo Ordzhonikidze, "Stenogramma" (Sténogramme) du rapport au noyau militant restraint (aktiv) du parti du district de Herson, 24 mars 1930'; and R. W. Davies, *The Socialist Offensive: The Collectivization of Agriculture 1929–30* (London: Macmillan, 1980), 225.

30. Noll, *Transformatsiia hromadians'koho suspil'stva*, 126.

31. TsA FSB RF 2/8/344 (1930), 344–56, in Danilov, *Tragediia sovetskoi derevni*, vol. 2, 336–42.

32. Testimony of Stepanyda Melentiïvna Khyria, in Mytsyk et al., eds., *Ukraïns'kyi holokost*, vol. 1, 87.

33. 'Case History LH57: Mikhail Frenkin, Baku', in U.S. Congress, *Investigation of the Ukrainian Famine*, Report to Congress, 363.

34. Testimony of Nicolas Chymych, in U.S. Congress and Commission on the Ukraine Famine, *Investigation of the Ukrainian Famine, 1932–1933: Second Interim Report*, meetings and hearings of and before the Commission on the Ukraine Famine held in 1987: hearing, San Francisco, California, 10 February 1987; hearing, Phoenix, Arizona, 13 February 1987; hearing and meeting, Washington, D.C., 30 April 1987; hearing, Philadelphia, Pennsylvania, 5 June 1987 (Washington, D.C.: U.S. G.P.O.: For sale by the Supt. of Docs. U.S. G.P.O., 1988), 126–8.

35. Testimony of Valentin Kochno, in ibid., 18.

36. Dolot, *Execution by Hunger*, 8.

37. Graziosi, 'Collectivisation, révoltes paysannes et politiques gouvernementales', 439–40.

38. Ekaterina Olitskaia, 'My Reminiscences', in Fitzpatrick and Slezkine, eds., *In the Shadow of Revolution*, 39–40.

39. TsDAZhR Ukraïny 539/7/71 (1929), 139, reproduced in Stanislav Kul'chyts'kyi et al., *Kolektivizatsiia i holod na Ukraïni, 1929–1933: zbirnyk dokumentiv i materialiv* (Kyiv: Naukova Dumka, 1992), 106–7.

40. Lynne Viola explains that the *podkulachnik* was thought to be animated by kulak 'essence', even though he owned no property (Viola, *Peasant Rebels Under Stalin*, 34).

41. Hindus, *Red Bread*, 45–6.

42. Otto J. Pohl, Eric J. Schmaltz and Ronald J. Vossler, ' "In our hearts we felt the sentence of death": Ethnic German Recollections of Mass Violence in the USSR, 1928–48', *Journal of Genocide Research* 11, no. 2 (2009), 325–7 and 343.

43. TsA FSB RF 2/8/40 (1930), 6–17, in Danilov, *Tragediia sovetskoi derevni*, vol. 2, 292–303.

44. GARF 9414/1/1944 (1930), 17–25, in Viola and Danilov, eds., *The War Against the Peasantry*, 240–1.

45. TsA FSB RF 2/8/3 (1930), 2, in Berelovich, *Sovetskaia derevnia glazami VChK-OGPU–NKVD*, vol. 3, 71.

46. Dolot, *Execution by Hunger*, 18–19.

47. RGAE 7446/1/283 (1930), 13–18, in Danilov et al., eds., *Tragediia sovetskoi derevni*, vol. 2, 292–303.

48. Testimony of Anastasia Shpychka, in L. B. Kovalenko and Volodymyr Maniak, eds., *33-i Holod: narodna knyha-memorial* (Kyiv: Radians'kyi Pys'mennyk, 1991), 53.

49. TsA FSB RF 2/8/678 (1930), 163–5, in Danilov et al., eds., *Tragediia sovetskoi derevni*, vol. 2, 141–4.

50. Testimony of Kylyna Vasylivna Dykun, in Mytsyk et al., eds., *Ukraïns'kyi holokost*, vol. 1, 89.

51. RGAE 7446/1/283 (1930), 13–18, in Danilov et al., eds., *Tragediia sovetskoi derevni*, vol. 2, 198–203.

52. Testimony of Maria Leshchenko, in Kovalenko and Maniak, eds., *33-i Holod*, 522.

53. RGASPI 17/3/779/ (1930), 18–20, in Danilov et al., eds. *Tragediia sovetskoi derevni*, vol. 2, 303–5.

54. 'Case History LH46: anonymous, Dnipropetrovs'k area', in U.S. Congress, *Investigation of the Ukrainian Famine*, Report to Congress, 339–41.

55. Testimony of Olena Davydivna Demchenko, in Kovalenko and Maniak, eds., *33-i Holod*, 505–6.

56. Dolot, *Execution by Hunger*, 25.

57. TsA FSB RF 2/8/40 (1930), 6–17, in Viola and Danilov, eds., *The War Against the Peasantry*, 281.

58. Testimony of Ivan Samsonovych, in Kovalenko and Maniak, eds., *33-i Holod*, 503–4.

59. Testimony of Mykola Demydovych Fenenko, in Kovalenko and Maniak, eds., *33-i Holod*, 540–2.

60. Noll, *Transformatsiia hromadians'koho suspil'stva*, 124.

61. TsA FSB RF 2/8/823 (1930), 342–51, in Viola and Danilov, eds., *The War Against the Peasantry*, 248.

62. Noll, *Transformatsiia hromadians'koho suspil'stva*, 155.

63. Testimony of Henrikh Pidvysotsky, in Kovalenko and Maniak, eds., *33-i Holod*, 78.

64. TsDAZhR Ukraïny 27/11/543 (1930), 215.

65. RGAE 7446/1/283 (1930), 13–18, in Danilov et al., eds., *Tragediia sovetskoi derevni*, vol. 2, 198–203.

66. Sheila Fitzpatrick, 'The Great Departure: Rural-Urban Migration in the Soviet Union, 1929–1933', in William G. Rosenberg and Lewis H. Siegelbaum, eds., *Social Dimensions of Soviet Industrialization* (Bloomington, IN: Indiana University Press, 1993), 22–5. In footnote 56, Fitzpatrick writes that Rykov remarked that 'the kulaks are fleeing from the raions not yet affected by total collectivization, anticipating that even if there is not total collectivization in their region today, there will be tomorrow'. *Desiataia Ural'skaia oblastnaia konferentsiia Vsesoiuznoi Kommunisticheskoi Partii (bol'shevikov)* (Sverdlovsk, 1930), Bulletin no. 7, 19.

67. Kuromiya, *Freedom and Terror in the Donbas*, 35–41.

68. 'Case History LH38: Oleksandr Honcharenko, Cherkasy oblast'', in U.S. Congress, *Investigation of the Ukrainian Famine*, Report to Congress, 317.

69. Noll, *Transformatsiia hromadians'koho suspil'stva*, 155–6.

70. TsA FSB RF 2/8/678 (1930), 163–5, in Danilov et al., eds., *Tragediia sovetskoi derevni*, vol. 2, 161–3.

71. N. A. Ivnitskii, *Kollektivizatsiia i raskulachivanie, nachalo 30-kh gg.* (Moscow: Interpraks, 1994), 122–37; also V. N. Zemskov, 'Spetsposelentsy (po dokumentam NKVD-MVD-SSSR)', *Sotsiologicheskie Issledovaniia* 11 (1990), 4.

72. N. A. Morozov, *GULAG v Komi Krae, 1929–1956* (Syktyvkar: Syktyvkarskii Gosudarstvennyi Universitet, 1997), 104.

73. RGASPI 17/3/775 (1930), 15–16, in Danilov et al., eds., *Tragediia sovetskoi derevni*, vol. 2, 174–5.

74. Ivnitskii, *Kollektivizatsiia i raskulachivanie*, 122–37; also Zemskov, 'Spetsposelentsy (po dokumentakm NKVD-MVD-SSSR)', 4.

75. Anne Applebaum, *Gulag: A History* (New York: Doubleday, 2003), 46–50.

76. James Harris, 'The Growth of the Gulag: Forced Labor in the Urals Region, 1929–31', *The Russian Review* 56, no. 2 (1997), 265–80.

77. Noll, *Transformatsiia hromadians'koho suspil'stva*, 125.

78. Ibid., 269–71.

79. 'Case History LH38: Oleksandr Honcharenko, Cherkasy oblast'', in U.S. Congress, *Investigation of the Ukrainian Famine*, Report to Congress, 325–9.

80. See for example the testimony of Vasyl' Pavlovych Nechyporenko and Iakiv Antonovych Dziubyshyn in Mytsyk et al., eds., *Ukraïns'kyi holokost*, vol. 1, 163, and vol. 2, 116; and 'Testimony of Mr. Sviatoslav Karavansky', in U.S. Congress, *Investigation of the Ukrainian Famine, 1932–1933: First Interim Report of Meetings and Hearings of and Before the Commission on the Ukraine Famine*, meeting and hearing 8 October 1988 (Washington, D.C.: U.S. G.P.O., 1987), 79; as well as 'Case History LH8', 'Case History LH46' and 'Case History SW34', all in U.S. Congress, *Investigation of the Ukrainian Famine*, Report to Congress, 256, 345 and 386.

81. Oleksandra Bykovets, 'Interview with Oleksandra Bykovets' (Sviatoslav Novytskyi, 1 September 1983) excerpted from the archives of the copyright holder, UCRDC.

82. Testimony of Larysa Donchuk, in U.S. Congress, *Investigation of the Ukrainian Famine, 1932–1933*, second report, 138.

83. Olesia Stasiuk, 'The Deformation of Ukrainian Folk Culture During the Holodomor Years', trans. Marta Olynyk, in *Key Articles on the Holodomor Translated from Ukrainian into English, Holodomor Research and Education Consortium*, 12–13, http://holodomor.ca/translated-articles-on-the-holodomor.

84. Noll, *Transformatsiia hromadians'koho suspil'stva*, 340–87.

85. TsDAHOU 1/20/3108 (1930), 1.

86. Hiroaki Kuromiya, *The Voices of the Dead: Stalin's Great Terror in the 1930s* (New Haven, CT: Yale University Press, 2007), 109.

87. Ibid., 110.

88. Boleslaw Szczesniak, *The Russian Revolution and Religion: A Collection of Documents Concerning the Suppression of Religion by the Communists, 1917–1925* (Notre Dame, IN: University of Notre Dame Press, 1959), 158; Alla Kyrydon, 'Ruinuvannia kul'tovykh sporud

(1920–1930-ti rr.): porushennia tradytsiinoï rytmolohiï prostoru', in *Ukraïns'kyi Istorychnyi Zhurnal* 22, no. 6 (2013), 91–102.

89. McDonald, 'A Peasant Rebellion in Stalin's Russia', 125–46.

90. Testimony of Mykola Ievhenovych Petrenko, in Kovalenko and Maniak, eds., *33-i Holod*, 460.

91. Grigorenko, *Memoirs*, 39.

92. Noll, *Transformatsiia hromadians'koho suspil'stva*, 251–4.

93. Stasiuk, 'The Deformation of Ukrainian Folk Culture During the Holodomor Years'.

94. Noll, *Transformatsiia hromadians'koho suspil'stva*, 242–50.

95. Lytvyn, *Ekonomichna istoriia Ukraïny*, vol. 2, 231–2, 261.

6. REBELLION, 1930

1. Quoted in Viola, *Peasant Rebels Under Stalin*, 132.

2. Ibid., 134.

3. RTsKhIDNI 85/1/118 (1930), 1–13, reproduced in Graziosi, 'Collectivisation, révoltes paysannes et politiques gouvernementales', 477.

4. Sholokhov, *Virgin Soil Upturned*, 157.

5. Alec Nove, *An Economic History of the USSR, 1917–1991* (New York: Penguin, 1992), 186.

6. RTsKhIDNI 85/1/120 (1930), 1–18, reproduced in Graziosi, 'Collectivisation, révoltes paysannes et politiques gouvernementales', 538.

7. RTsKhIDNI 85/1/118 (1930), 1–13, reproduced in ibid., 479.

8. TsGANKh SSSR 7446/5/87 (1930), 35–9, in V. P. Danilov and N. A. Ivnitskii, eds., *Dokumenty svidetel'stvuiut: iz istorii derevni nakanune i v khode kollektivizatsii, 1927–1932 gg.* (Moscow: Politizdat, 1989), 305.

9. 'Testimony of Mr. Valentin Kochno', in U.S. Congress, *Investigation of the Ukrainian Famine: First Interim Report*, 119–20.

10. 'Testimony of Dr. Valentyna Sawchuck of Hamtramck, Michigan', in U.S. Congress, *Investigation of the Ukrainian Famine: First Interim Report*, 144.

11. TsA FSB RF 2/8/232 (1930), 101, 101a, in Berelovich, *Sovetskaia derevnia glazami VChK-OGPU-NKVD*, vol. 3:1, 220–1.

12. Viola, *Peasant Rebels Under Stalin*, 59–60.

13. Andrea Graziosi, 'The Great Famine of 1932–33: Consequences and Implications', *Harvard Ukrainian Studies* 25, nos. 3/4 (Fall 2001), 162.

14. Viola, *Peasant Rebels Under Stalin*, 53.

15. D. D. Goichenko, *Krasnyi apokalipsis: skvoz' raskulachivanie i golo-domor: memuary svidetelia* (Kyiv: Ababahalamaha, 2013), 29–31.

16. Testimony of Olena Doroshenko, in O. M. Veselova and O. F. Nikiliev, *Pam'iat' narodu: Henotsyd v Ukraïni holodom 1932–1933 rokiv: svidchennia*, 2 vols. (Kyiv: Vydavnychnyi dim 'Kalyta', 2009), vol. 1, 408.

17. Viola, *Peasant Rebels Under Stalin*, 55–7.

18. Pohl, ' "In Our Hearts We Felt the Sentence of Death" ', 336.

19. 'Case History SW34: anonymous, Kyiv oblast'', in U.S. Congress, *Investigation of the Ukrainian Famine*, Report to Congress, 392.

20. Testimony of Maria Makukha (Chukut), in ibid., vol. 1, 129.

21. Testimony of Kateryna Laksha, in ibid., vol. 2, 66–7.

22. Ibid.

23. TsA FSB RF 2/8/232 (1930), 72, in Berelovich, *Sovetskaia derevnia glazami VChK-OGPU-NKVD*, vol. 3:1, 219–20.

24. Pasha Angelina, 'The Most Important Thing', in Fitzpatrick and Slezkine, *In the Shadow of Revolution*, 310.

25. TsA FSB RF 2/8/23 (1930), 2–13, and 2/8/23 (1930), 45–65, in Berelovich, *Sovetskaia derevnia glazami VChK-OGPU-NKVD*, vol. 3:1, 144–50, 180–9.

26. Josef Stalin, 'Dizzy with Success: Concerning Questions of the Collective-Farm Movement', *Pravda*, 2 March 1930, reproduced in *Works*, vol. 12, 197–205.

27. Ibid.

28. RGASPI 17/3/779 (1930), 18–20, in Danilov, *Tragediia sovetskoi derevni*, vol. 2, 303–5.

29. Viola, *Peasant Rebels Under Stalin*, 3.

30. Dolot, *Execution by Hunger*, 84.

31. Testimony of Ivan Hazhyman, in Mytsyk, *Ukraïns'kyi holokost*, vol. 3, 113.

32. 'Case History LH38: Oleksandr Honcharenko, Cherkasy oblast'', in U.S. Congress, *Investigation of the Ukrainian Famine*, Report to Congress, 325–9.

33. 'Testimony of Mr. Zinovii Turkalo', in U.S. Congress, *Investigation of the Ukrainian Famine: First Interim Report*, 96.

34. TsA FSB RF 2/8/679 (1930), 23, in Berelovich, *Sovetskaia derevnia glazami VChK-OGPU-NKVD*, vol. 3:1, 420–6.

35. Testimony of Leonida Fedorivna Tkachuk, in Mytsyk, *Ukraïns'kyi holokost*, vol. 2, 50–1.

36. 'Case History LH38: Oleksandr Honcharenko', 325.

37. Pohl, ' "In Our Hearts We Felt the Sentence of Death" ', 336.
38. TsA FSB RF 2/8/679 (1930), 23, in Berelovich, *Sovetskaia derevnia glazami VChK-OGPU-NKVD*, vol. 3:1, 424.
39. Ibid., 421.
40. Viola, *Peasant Rebels Under Stalin*, 183.
41. TsA FSB RF 2/8/679 (1930), 23, in Berelovich, *Sovetskaia derevnia glazami VChK-OGPU-NKVD*, vol. 3:1, 420–6.
42. 'Case History LH57: Mikhail Frenkin, Baku', in U.S. Congress, *Investigation of the Ukrainian Famine*, Report to Congress, 359–65.
43. Viola, *Peasant Rebels Under Stalin*, 103–5, 135–6.
44. RTsKhIDNI 85/1/118 (1930), 1–13, reproduced in Graziosi, 'Collectivisation, révoltes paysannes et politiques gouvernementales', 474–83.
45. TsDAHOU 1/20/3191 (1930), 37.
46. TsA FSB RF 2/8/232 (1930), 101, 101a, in Berelovich, *Sovetskaia derevnia glazami VChK-OGPU-NKVD*, vol. 3:1, 220–1.
47. TsA FSB RF 2/8/23 (1930), 2–13, in ibid., vol. 3:1, 144–50.
48. TsA FSB RF 2/8/23 (1930), 45–65, in ibid., vol. 3:1, 180–9.
49. Iurii Shapoval, Vadym Zolotar'ov and Volodymyr Prystaiko, *ChK-GPU-NKVD v Ukraïni: osoby, fakty, dokumenty* (Kyiv: Abrys, 1997), 39.
50. TsDAHOU 1/20/3154 (1930), 11.
51. TsA FSB RF 2/8/232 (1930), 115, 1150b, in Berelovich, *Sovetskaia derevnia glazami VChK-OGPU-NKVD*, vol. 3:1, 221–2; RTsKhIDNI 85/1/119 (1930), 1–2, reproduced in Graziosi, 'Collectivisation, révoltes paysannes et politiques gouvernementales', 549–50.
52. TsDAHOU 1/20/3154 (1930), 11.
53. The Pavlohrad material comes from Danylenko et al., eds., *Pavlohrads'ke povstannia, 1930: dokumenty i materialy* (Kyiv: Ukrains'kyi Pys'mennyk, 2009).
54. Palij, *The Anarchism of Nestor Makhno*, 46–51.
55. RTsKhIDNI 85/1/120 (1930), 1–18, reproduced in Graziosi, 'Collectivisation, révoltes paysannes et politiques gouvernementales', 537.
56. Ibid., 537–8.
57. RTsKhIDNI 85/1/118 (1930), 43–9, reproduced in ibid., 577–8.
58. TsA FSB RF 2/8/232 (1930), 115, 1150b, in Berelovich, *Sovetskaia derevnia glazami VChK-OGPU-NKVD*, vol. 3:1, 222.
59. Martin, *Affirmative Action Empire*, 294–5.
60. Shapoval, 'The Case of the "Union for the Liberation of Ukraine" ', 178–9.
61. Ibid.

7. COLLECTIVIZATION FAILS, 1931–2

1. RTsKhIDNI 82/2/139 (1932), 145–51, in Martin, *The Affirmative Action Empire*, 298.

2. R. W. Davies and S. G. Wheatcroft, *The Years of Hunger: Soviet Agriculture, 1931–33* (London and New York: Palgrave Macmillan, 2009), 1–4.

3. RGASPI 17/2/60 (1931), 89, tipografskii ekz.; KPSS v rezoliutsiiakh, Izd. 9–3. T.5.C. 233–4, in Danilov et al., eds., *Tragediia sovetskoi derevni*, vol. 2, 773–4.

4. TsA FSB RF 2/8/328 (1930), 336–45, in ibid., vol. 2, 530–6.

5. TsDAZhR Ukraïny 27/11/104 (1930), 75–80, in Kul'chyts'kyi, *Kolektyvizatsiia i holod na Ukraïni*, 226–30.

6. This is Lynne Viola's term, used in *Peasant Rebels Under Stalin*, 205–10.

7. RGAE 7486/37/132 (1930), 59–60, in Danilov et al., eds., *Tragediia sovetskoi derevni*, vol. 2, 467–72.

8. Diana Bojko and Jerzy Bednarek, *Holodomor: The Great Famine in Ukraine 1932–1933*, from the series *Poland and Ukraine in the 1930s–1940s: Unknown Documents from the Archives of the Secret Services* (Warsaw: Institute of National Remembrance, Commission of the Prosecution of Crimes against the Polish Nation, 2009), 70–1.

9. The best account of harvest statistics as well as the controversy around them is in Davies and Wheatcroft, *The Years of Hunger*, 442–7. See also A. V. Bashkin, 'Urozhai tridtsatykh ili ukradennye dostizheniia', *Istoricheskie materialy*, accessed 2017, http://istmat.info/node/21358.

10. Serhiichuk et al., *Ukraïns'kyi khlib na eksport*, 3–4.

11. Elena Osokina, *Zoloto dlia industrializatsii: Torgsin* (Moscow: ROSSPEN, 2009), 17–102.

12. Serhiichuk et al., *Ukraïns'kyi khlib na eksport*, 5–6.

13. Ibid., 7.

14. Sheila Fitzpatrick, 'The Boss and His Team: Stalin and the Inner Circle, 1925–33', in Stephen Fortescue, ed., *Russian Politics from Lenin to Putin* (Basingstoke: Palgrave Macmillan, 2010), 62–3.

15. RGASPI 588/1/5388 (1930), 1160b, 1210b, in Kondrashin et al., eds., *Golod v SSSR*, vol. 1:1, 340; RGASPI 588/11/75 (1930), 15, in Danilov et al., eds., *Tragediia sovetskoi derevni*, vol. 2, 577.

16. RGAE 8043/11/12 (1930), 22–220b, in Kondrashin et al., eds., *Golod v SSSR*, vol. 1:1, 350.

17. RGASPI 17/162/9 (1930), 74, in ibid., vol. 1:1, 351.

18. Figures from Andrea Graziosi, *L'Unione Sovietica 1914–1991* (Bologna: Il mulino, 2011), table 1.

19. Davies and Wheatcroft, *The Years of Hunger*, 48–78.

20. RGASPI 631/5/54 (1931), 25–45, in Danilov et al., eds., *Tragediia sovetskoi derevni*, vol. 3, 137–40.

21. RGAE 8043/1/7 (1931), 61, in Kondrashin et al., eds., *Golod v SSSR*, vol. 1:1, 405–6.

22. RGASPI 17/167/31 (1931), 105, in ibid.

23. RGAE 7486/37/166 (1931), 230–7; RGAE 8043/1/48 (1931), 106–9, 116–30; AP RF 3/40/77 (1931), 186; and various other archival documents, all reproduced in ibid., vol. 1:1, 488–515.

24. RGASPI 17/167/29 (1931), 43, in ibid., vol. 1:1, 344.

25. A. V. Bashkin, 'Urozhai tridtsatykh ili ukradennye dostizheniia'.

26. RGAE 8043/11/17 (1930), 208, in Kondrashin et al., eds., *Golod v SSSR*, vol. 1:1, 230.

27. RGASPI 17/167/28 (1931), 108, in ibid., vol. 1:1, 258.

28. RGASPI 631/5/60 (1931), 32–40, in ibid., vol. 1:1, 536–7.

29. RGASPI 17/2/484 (1931), 43–61, in Danilov et al., eds., *Tragediia sovetskoi derevni*, vol. 3, 198–206.

30. Bojko and Bednarek, *Holodomor*, 82–9.

31. RGASPI 17/167/32 (1931), 119, in Kondrashin et al., eds., *Golod v SSSR*, vol. 1:1, 536.

32. RGASPI 17/2/484 (1931), 43–61, in Danilov et al., eds., *Tragediia sovetskoi derevni*, vol. 3, 198–206.

33. Davies and Wheatcroft, *The Years of Hunger*, 100–1, citing RGASPI 82/2/137 (1932), 30–94.

34. RGASPI 17/26/42 (1932), 193–6, in Danilov et al., eds., *Tragediia sovetskoi derevni*, vol. 3, 227–30.

35. TsDAHOU 1/20/5362 (1932), 3; and TsDAHOU 1/6/235 (1932), 82, in Pyrih, ed., *Holodomor*, 65–6.

36. At this time the Moldovan Autonomous Soviet Socialist Republic was part of Ukraine. The Moldovan ASSR was established in 1940, after the USSR conquered an additional chunk of Romanian territory. The former Moldovan ASSR is now Transnistria, a disputed region of Moldova.

37. AP RF 3/40/80 (1932), 45–51, in Kondrashin et al., eds., *Golod v SSSR*, vol. 1:2, 158–61.

38. Bojko and Bednarek, *Holodomor*, 108.

39. Kondrashin et al., eds., *Golod v SSSR*, vol. 1:2, 163–5, citing Lozyts'kyi, *Holodomor 1932–1933 rokiv v Ukraïni*, 37–40.

40. Kondrashin et al., eds., *Golod v SSSR*, vol. 1:2, 163–5.

41. Ibid.

42. TsA FSB RF 2/10/169 (1932), 1–57, in Berelovich et al., eds., *Sovetskaia derevnia glazami VChK-OGPU-NKVD*, vol. 3:2, 64–91.

43. RGASPI 631/5/74 (1932), 36, in Kondrashin et al., eds., *Golod v SSSR*, vol. 2, 83–4.

44. N. F. Shnaika to Stalin, TsDAHOU 1/20/5254 (1932), 1–16, in Pyrih, ed., *Holodomor*, 133.

45. A. F. Banivs'kyi to Stalin, in ibid., 132.

46. Boiko to Stalin, in ibid., 135.

47. For example, HDA SBU 13/429/40 (1932), 126–47, in V. M. Danylenko et al., eds., *Holodomor 1932–1933 rokiv v Ukraïni za dokumentamy HDA SBU: anotovanyi dovidnyk* (L'viv: Tsentr Doslidzhen' Vyzvol'noho Rukhu, 2010), 278.

48. RGASPI 17/42/50 (1932), 54, in Kondrashin, et al., eds., *Golod v SSSR*, vol. 1:2, 225.

49. TsDAHOU 1/20/5255 (1932), 52–52sv, in Pyrih, ed., *Holodomor*, 169–70.

50. TsDAHOU 1/16/8 (1932), 203–4, in ibid., 93.

51. Bojko and Bednarek, *Holodomor*, 111–12.

52. Dmytro Zlepko, *Der Ukrainische Hunger-Holocaust: Stalins verschwiegener Völkermord 1932/33 an 7 Millionen ukrainischen Bauern im Spiegel geheimgehaltener Akten des deutschen Auswärtigen Amtes: eine Dokumentation* (Sonnenbühl: Verlag Helmut Wild, 1988), 95–7.

53. TsA FSB RF 2/11/1449 (1932), 144–6, in Danilov et al., eds., *Tragediia sovetskoi derevni*, vol. 3, 361–2.

54. 'Dosvid Proskurivshchyny i Koziatynshchyny v borot'bi za tsukrovii buriak', *Visti VUTsVK* (Kharkiv, 6 June 1932), cited in Vasyl Marochko and Olha Movchan, *Holodomor 1932–1933 rokiv v Ukraïni: khronika* (Kyiv: Kyievo-Mohylians'ka Akademiia, 2008), 87.

55. TsDAHOU 1/20/5255 (1932), 4, in Pyrih, ed., *Holodomor*, 70.

56. TsDAHOU 1/6/8 (1932), 203–4, in ibid., 92–3.

57. Serhiichuk et al., *Ukraïns'kyi khlib na eksport*, 78–81.

58. AP RF 3/61/794 (1932), 1–5, in Kondrashin et al., eds., *Golod v SSSR*, vol. 1:2, 227–9.

59. RGASPI 17/162/12 (1932), 85, in Pyrih, ed., *Holodomor*, 113.

60. RGASPI 17/162/12 (1932), 115, in ibid., 139–40.

61. TsDAHOU 1/16/8 (1932), 236, in ibid., 118.

62. TsDAHOU 1/1/378 (1932), 143–51; TsDAHOU 1/1/381 (1932), 63–8, in S. A. Kokin, Valerii Vasyl'ev and Nicolas Werth, eds., *Partiino-*

Radians'ke kerivnytstvo USRR pid chas Holodomoru 1932–33 rr.: vozhdi, pratsivnyky, aktyvisty: zbirnyk dokumentiv ta materialiv (Kyiv: Instytut Istoriï Ukraïny NAN Ukraïny, 2013), 58–74.

63. AP RF 3/61/794 (1932), 18, in Kondrashin et al., eds., *Golod v SSSR*, vol. 1:2, 229.

64. RGASPI 558/11/43 (1932), 70, in Marochko and Movchan, *Holodomor 1932–1933 rokiv v Ukraïni*, 72.

65. Terry Martin, 'Famine Initiators and Directors: Personal Papers: The 1932–33 Ukrainian Terror: New Documentation on Surveillance and the Thought Process of Stalin', in Isajiw W. Wsevolod, ed., *Famine-Genocide in Ukraine, 1932–33* (Toronto: UCRDC, 2003), 107–8.

66. RGASPI 82/2/139 (1932), 162–5, in Pyrih, ed., *Holodomor*, 197–9.

67. Ibid.

68. RGASPI 82/2/139 (1932), 144–53, in ibid., 200–5.

69. RGASPI 558/11/769 (1932), 40–2, in Kondrashin et al., eds., *Golod v SSSR*, vol. 1:2, 242–3.

70. RGASPI 558/11/769 (1932), 77–8, in ibid., vol. 1:2, 243.

71. RGAPSI 81/3/99 (1932), 62–3, in ibid., vol. 1:2, 244.

72. RGASPI 558/11/740/61 (1932), 174, in Pyrih, ed., *Holodomor*, 207.

73. RGASPI 17/162/12 (1932), 180–1, in ibid., 208.

74. TsDAHOU 1/20/5259 (1932), 19, in ibid., 208.

75. Serhiichuk et al., *Ukraïns'kyi khlib na eksport*, 9–10.

76. Testimony of Mykola Kostyrko, in James E. Mace and Leonid Heretz, *Investigation of the Ukrainian Famine, 1932–1933*. Oral history project of the Commission on the Ukraine Famine, 3 vols. (Washington, D.C.: U.S. G.P.O., 1990), vol. 2, 1,057–80.

77. Bojko and Bednarek, *Holodomor*, 55.

78. Serhiichuk et al., *Ukraïns'kyi khlib na eksport*, 11.

79. Andrea Graziosi, *L'Urss di Lenin e Stalin: storia dell'Unione Sovietica, 1914–1945* (Bologna: Il mulino, 2007), 334, table 8.1.

80. Osokina, *Zoloto dlia industrializatsiï*, 540, table 25.

81. RGASPI 558/11/740/41 (1932), in Pyrih, ed., *Holodomor*, 225.

82. Kokin et al., eds., *Partiino-Radians'ke kerivnytstvo USRR pid chas Holodomoru*, 36–7.

83. Ibid., 38–9.

84. Ibid., 43–4.

85. Ibid., 47.

86. Ibid., 52–7.

87. Vasyl'ev, *Politychne kerivnytstvo URSR i SRSR*, 242.

88. Kokin, *Partiino-Radians'ke kerivnytstvo USRR pid chas Holodomoru*, 63–4.

89. RGASPI 558/11/78/16 (1932), in Pyrih, ed., *Holodomor*, 231.

90. TsDAHOU 1/6/236/85 (1932), in ibid.

91. RGASPI 17/3/891 (1932), 52–5; RGAPSI 558/11/78 (1932), 16; and RGASPI 558/11/78 (1932), 12, all in Pyrih, ed., *Holodomor*, 229–32.

92. RGASPI 558/11/78 (1932), 12, in ibid., 232.

93. S3 SSSR 1932 no. 52, str. 312, in Kondrashin et al., eds., *Golod v SSSR*, vol. 1:2, 321–4.

94. RGASPI 81/3/99 (1932), 115–19, in O. V. Khlevniuk et al., eds., *Stalin i Kaganovich: perepiska, 1931–1936 gg.* (Moscow: ROSSPEN, 2001), 244–5; TsDAHOU 1/20/5381 (1932), 11–12, in Pyrih, ed., *Holodomor*, 270.

95. Davies and Wheatcroft, *The Years of Hunger*, 158.

96. Timothy Snyder, *Bloodlands: Europe Between Hitler and Stalin* (New York: Basic Books, 2010), 37.

97. RGASPI 81/3/99 (1932), 106–13, in Khlevniuk et al., eds., *Stalin i Kaganovich*, 235–6.

98. RGASPI 81/3/100 (1932), 137–40, in ibid., 240–1.

99. RGASPI 17/3/2014 (1932), 33–4, in *Tragediia sovetskoi derevni*, vol. 3, 453–4.

100. Sergei Maskudov, 'Victory over the Peasant', in *Hunger by Design: The Great Ukrainian Famine and Its Soviet Context*, ed. Halyna Hryn (Cambridge, MA: Harvard Ukrainian Research Institute, 2008), 60–2.

101. Conquest, *The Harvest of Sorrow*, 226.

102. Pidhainy, *The Black Deeds of the Kremlin*, vol. 1, 205.

103. Graziosi, *L'Urss di Lenin e Stalin*, 333; Davies and Wheatcroft, *The Years of Hunger*, 166–8.

104. Applebaum, *Gulag*, 582–3.

105. Susanna Pechora, interview with Anne Applebaum, 1999.

106. Martin, 'Famine Initiators and Directors', 110.

107. The full list, which was circulated again in November, is dozens of pages long; Valentyna Borysenko, V. M. Danylenko, Serhij Kokin et al., eds., *Rozsekrechena pam'iat': Holodomor 1932–1933 rokiv v Ukraïni v dokumentakh GPU-NKVD* (Kyiv: Stylos, 2007), 193–263, citing HDA SBU 16/25/3 (1952), 4–68; Martin, 'Famine Initiators and Directors', 111.

108. RTsKhIDNI 82/2/139 (1932), 145–51, trans. and repr. in Martin, *The Affirmative Action Empire*, 298.

109. Shapoval, 'Vsevolod Balickij, bourreau et victime', 369–99.

110. RTsKhIDNI 82/2/139 (1932), 145–51, trans. and repr. in Martin, *The Affirmative Action Empire*, 298 (emphasis in the original).

8. FAMINE DECISIONS, 1932: REQUISITIONS, BLACKLISTS AND BORDERS

1. Maxim Gorky, *On the Russian Peasant* (Berlin: I. P. Ladyzhnikov, 1922), 27.
2. Simon Sebag Montefiore, *Stalin: The Court of the Red Tsar* (New York: Knopf, 2004), 107–8.
3. Svetlana Allilueva, *Twenty Letters to a Friend (Dvadtsat' Pisem k Drugu)*, trans. Priscilla Johnson McMillan (New York: Harper Perennial, Reprint Edition, 2016), 105.
4. G. A. Tokaev, *Betrayal of an Ideal* (Bloomington, IN: Indiana University Press, 1955), 161.
5. Miklos Kun, *Stalin: An Unknown Portrait* (Budapest: Central European University Press, 2003), 204; Montefiore, *Stalin*, 86–90.
6. Montefiore, *Stalin*, 90.
7. Ibid., 84.
8. Ibid., 87.
9. Getty and Naumov, *The Road to Terror*, 47.
10. Tucker, *Stalin in Power*, 209–12.
11. Getty and Naumov, *The Road to Terror*, 53–8.
12. Arkadii Vaksberg, *Tsaritsa dokazatel'stv: Vyshinskii i ego zhertvy* (Moscow: Kniga i Biznes, 1992), 68.
13. Ibid., 66–7.
14. Ibid., 69.
15. See Getty and Naumov, *The Road to Terror*, and Robert Conquest, *The Great Terror: Stalin's Purge of the Thirties*, rev. edn (London: Macmillan, 1968), among others.
16. Martin, *The Affirmative Action Empire*, 299.
17. TsDAHOU 1/6/236 (1932), 8–9, in Pyrih, ed., *Holodomor*, 127.
18. Davies and Wheatcroft, *The Years of Hunger*, 10–11.
19. Ibid., 171.
20. Bashkin, 'Urozhai tridtsatykh ili ukradennye dostizheniia'.
21. RGASPI 82/2/141/6, in Pyrih, ed., *Holodomor*, 355–6.
22. TsDAHOU 1/6/237/207–16, in ibid., 388–95.
23. RGASPI 81/3/215/1–24; RGASPI 81/3/232/62, in ibid., 496–514.
24. TsDAGO Ukraïny 1/20/5384/23, in ibid., trans. Bandera, 71.
25. TsDAHOU 1/6/237/207–16, in ibid., 388–95.
26. Ibid.
27. TsDAHOU 1/20/6339 (1933), 25, in ibid., 569.
28. Kul'chyts'kyi, *Holodomor 1932–1933 rr. iak henotsyd*, 294–305.

29. S3 SSSR 1933 no. 38, str. 228, in Kondrashin et al., eds., *Golod v SSSR*, vol. 3, 54–5.

30. S. V. Kul'chyts'kyi, 'Comments at UNAS (National Academy of Sciences) Institute of History of Ukraine Seminar', presented at the Institute of History of Ukraine Seminar, Kyiv, 19 April 2016.

31. Serhiichuk et al., *Ukraïns'kyi khlib na eksport*, 13 and 138.

32. Graziosi, *L'Urss di Lenin e Stalin*, 334, table 8.1. Gold exports would eventually rise, as desperate peasants traded their gold to the state for grain.

33. RGAE 413/13/595 (1933), 47–8, from the *Elektronnyi arkhiv Ukraïns'koho vyzvol'noho rukhu*, accessed 2017, http://avr.org.ua/get PDFasFile.php/arhupa/rgae-413-13-595-0-047.pdf.

34. Heorhii Papakin, *Donbas na 'chornii doshtsi', 1932–1933: Naukovo-populiarnyi narys* (Kyiv: Instytut Istoriï Ukraïny NAN Ukraïny, 2014), 9–11.

35. Heorhii Papakin, 'Blacklists as an Instrument of the Famine-Genocide of 1932–1933 in Ukraine', trans. Marta Olynyk, *Key Articles on the Holodomor Translated from Ukrainian into English*, Holodomor Research and Education Consortium, 2–3, http://holodomor.ca/ translated-articles-on-the-holodomor.

36. '"Chorna Doshka" *Bil'shovyk Poltavshchyny*, 12 Veresnia, 1932', *Ofitsiinyi veb-portal Derzhavnoï Arkhivnoï Sluzhby Ukraïny*, http:// www.archives.gov.ua/Archives/Reestr/Foto-Poltava.php.

37. Papakin, 'Blacklists as an Instrument of the Famine-Genocide of 1932–1933 in Ukraine', 5–6.

38. Heorhii Papakin, *'Chorna doshka': antyselians'ki represiï, 1932–1933* (Kyiv: Instytut Istoriï Ukraïny NAN Ukraïny, 2013), 336. The numbers of districts changed frequently in the 1930s, but in 1932–3 it was 392, according to Oleg Wolowyna's demography team at the Institute of Demography and Social Research of the Ukrainian National Academy of Sciences and the Harvard Ukrainian Research Institute.

39. Institut Demografii Natsional'nogo Issledovatel'skogo Universiteta 'Vysshaia Shkola Ekonomiki', 'Vsesoiuznaia perepis' naseleniia 1926 goda: Natsional'nyi sostav naseleniia po regionam RSFSR: Severo-Kavkazskii krai/Kubanskii okrug', *Demoskop weekly: elektronnaia versiia biulletenia Naselenie i obshchestvo* 719–20 (6–19 March 2017), http://demoscope.ru/weekly/ssp/rus_nac_26.php?reg=862.

40. Papakin, *Donbas na 'chornii doshtsi'*, 12.

41. Bondar and Matveev, *Istoricheskaia pamiat' naseleniia Iuga Rossii o golode 1932–1933*, 101–3.

42. Ibid., 61.

43. Papakin, *Donbas na 'chornii doshtsi'*, 12.

44. Papakin, 'Blacklists as an Instrument of the Famine-Genocide of 1932–1933 in Ukraine', 8.

45. Papakin, *'Chorna doshka'*, 335.

46. Papakin, 'Blacklists as an Instrument of the Famine-Genocide of 1932–1933 in Ukraine', 11.

47. HDA SBU 13/429/40 (1932), 126–47, in Danylenko et al., eds., *Holodomor 1932–1933 rokiv v Ukraïni za dokumentamy HDA SBU*, 278.

48. TsA FSB RF 2/10/169 (1932), 1–57, in Berelovich et al., eds., *Sovetskaia derevnia glazami VChK-OGPU-NKVD*, 64–91.

49. APRF 3/30/189 (1932), 7–10, in Pyrih, ed., *Holodomor*, 615–16.

50. HDA SBU, *Kolektsiia dokumentiv 'Holodomor 1932–1933 rr. v Ukraïni'*, in ibid., 709.

51. 'Schedule A, vol. 36, Case 333/(NY)1582 (Interviewer J. F., Type A4) Male, 29, Ukrainian, Student and Worker', 1–8 July 1951, Harvard Project on the Soviet Social System, Slavic Division, Widener Library, Harvard University, 24.

52. TsDAHOU 1/20/5255 (1932), 16–17, in Pyrih, ed., *Holodomor*, 108–9.

53. TsDAHOU 1/20/5255 (1932), 68–9, in ibid., 253.

54. Testimony of Olena Davydivna Demchenko, in Kovalenko and Maniak, eds., *33-i Holod*, 506.

55. APRF 3/50/189 (1933), 7–10, in Pyrih, ed., *Holodomor*, 615–16.

56. Testimony of Ihor Vasyliovych Buhaievych, in Kovalenko and Maniak, eds., *33-i Holod*, 454–7.

57. Andrea Graziosi, *Lettere da Kharkov. La carestia in Ucraina e nel Caucaso del nord nei rapporti diplomatici italiani 1923–33* (Turin: Einaudi, 1991), 144–6, reproduced in Ukrainian in Pyrih, ed., *Holodomor*, 606–7.

58. DATO 176/1/9 (1932), 3–3v, in Bojko and Bednarek, *Holodomor*, 201.

59. Ibid., 203.

60. DATO 231/1/2067 (1932), 324, in ibid., 231.

61. Testimony of Lydia A., in U.S. Congress and Commission on the Ukraine Famine, *Investigation of the Ukrainian Famine, 1932–1933: Second Interim Report*, 139.

62. Testimony of Ivan Oransky, in ibid., 130.

63. Testimony of an anonymous woman, in ibid., 25.

64. TsDAHOU 1/20/6274 (1933), 185–90, in Pyrih, ed., *Holodomor*, 763.

65. TsDAHOU 1/20/5254 (1932), 1–16, in ibid., 134.

66. RGASPI 558/11/45 (1932), 108–9, in Danilov et al., eds., *Tragediia sovetskoi derevni*, vol. 3, 634–5.

67. RGASPI 17/3/2030 (1932), 17, and 17/42/72 (1932), 109–11, in ibid., 636–8, 644.
68. RGASPI 17/3/907 (1932), 9; and *Kommunist* (Kharkiv, 1 January 1933), in Marochko and Movchan, *Holodomor 1932–1933 rokiv v Ukraïni*, 154, 180.
69. Lev Kopelev, *The Education of a True Believer*, trans. Gary Kern (London: Wildwood House, 1981), 258.
70. APRF 3/30/189 (1933), 26–7, in Pyrih, ed., *Holodomor*, 636.
71. HDA SBU, *Kolektsiia dokumentiv 'Holodomor 1932–1933 rr. v Ukraïni'*, in ibid., 709.
72. Jan Jacek Bruski, 'In Search of New Sources: Polish Diplomatic and Intelligence Reports on the Holodomor', *Holodomor and Gorta mór: Histories, Memories and Representations of Famine in Ukraine and Ireland*, eds. Christian Noack, Lindsay Janssen and Vincent Comerford (London: Anthem Press, 2014), 223.
73. Mytsyk et al., eds., *Ukraïns'kyi holokost*, vol. 7, 538.
74. Testimony of Halyna Budantseva, in Kovalenko and Maniak, eds., *33-i Holodd*, 485.
75. Testimony of Varvara Dibert, in U.S. Congress and Commission on the Ukraine Famine, *Investigation of the Ukrainian Famine, 1932–1933: First Interim Report*, 73–4.
76. Testimony of Halyna Ivanivna Kyrychenko, in Mytsyk, *Ukraïns'kyi holokost*, vol. 2, 100–1.
77. Testimony of Mariia Polikarpivna Umans'ka, in Ukraïns'kyi Instytut natsional'noï pam'iati and V. Iushchenko, eds., *Natsional'na Knyha pam'iati zhertv Holodomoru 1932–1933 rokiv v Ukraïni* (Kyiv: Vydavnytstvo im. Oleny Telihy, 2008), 93.
78. Testimony of Olena Artemivna Kobylko, in O. M. Veselova and O. F. Nikiliev, *Pam'iat' narodu: Henotsyd v Ukraïni holodom 1932–1933 rokiv: svidchennia*, 2 vols. (Kyiv: Vydavnychnyi dim 'Kalyta', 2009), vol. 1, 570.
79. Kopelev, *The Education of a True Believer*, 258.

9. FAMINE DECISIONS, 1932:
THE END OF UKRAINIZATION

1. Quoted in Luckyj, *Literary Politics in Soviet Ukraine*, 228.
2. Martin, *The Affirmative Action Empire*, 306.
3. Sarah Cameron, 'The Kazakh Famine of 1932–33: Current Research and New Directions', *East/West: Journal of Ukrainian Studies* 3, no. 2

(2016), 117–32; Niccolo Piancola, 'Sacrificing the Kazakhs: The Stalinist Hierarchy of Consumption and the Great Famine in Kazakhstan of 1931–33', paper presented at the Slavic-Eurasian Research Centre, 10–11 July 2014, Hokkaido University, Sapporo, Japan.

4. RGASPI 17/3/9.11/42–4, in Pyrih, ed., *Holodomor*, 475–7.

5. Martin, *The Affirmative Action Empire*, 303, citing RTsKhIDNI 17/3/910 (1932).

6. RGASPI 17/3/911/43, in Pyrih, ed., *Holodomor*, 480.

7. HDA SBU Donetsk 4924f/4–13, in Bojko and Bednarek, *Holodomor*, 207–15.

8. Lozyts'kyi, *Holodomor 1932–1933 rokiv*, 134.

9. HDA SBU 16/25/3 (1951), 105, in Borysenko, ed., *Rozsekrechena pam'iat'*, 425–6.

10. Martin, *The Affirmative Action Empire*, 346.

11. Vasyl'ev, *Politychne kerivnytstvo URSR i SRSR*, 332–3.

12. HDA SBU 16/25/3 (1932), 109, in Kokin et al., eds., *Partiino-Radians'ke kerivnytstvo USRR pid chas Holodomoru*, 160.

13. HDA SBU 6/--/75165 (1964), 84–5, in ibid., 193–5.

14. DADO 19/1/20 (1932), 69–70, in ibid., 165.

15. HDA SBU 6/--/75165 (1964), 88–90, in ibid., 196–8.

16. Ibid., 196–8; TsDAHOU 1/16/9 (1932), 59–61, in Pyrih, ed., *Holodomor*, 396–7.

17. RGASPI 17/162/14 (1932), 17, in Pyrih, ed., *Holodomor*, 407.

18. HDA SBU 16/25/3 (1932), 69–100, in Danylenko et al., eds., *Holodomor 1932–1933 rokiv v Ukraïni za dokumentamy HDA SBU*, 60–1.

19. HDA SBU 42/9/-- (1932), 52–5, in Borysenko, ed., *Rozsekrechena pam'iat'*, 428–9.

20. V. Pryluts'kyi, 'Opir molodi politytsi bil'shovyts'koho rezhymu ta represyvni zakhody proty neï v USRR (1928–1936 rr.)', *Z arkhiviv VUChK-GPU-NKVD-KGB* 2/4 (13/15) (2000), 94.

21. HDA SBU 16/25/3 (1951), 111–51, in Borysenko, Danylenko, Kokin, et al., eds., *Rozsekrechena pam'iat'*, 430–72 (exact quote on 431).

22. Ibid., 430–72 and 520–8; for an example of Makhno see 359, for 'active' and 'former Petliurites' see 431–2.

23. HDA SBU 1607 (1932), 10, and HDA SBU 6852 (1932), 8, both in Pyrih, ed., *Holodomor*, 539–41.

24. HDA SBU 9/666/-- (1933), 56, 58–62, 63, in Borysenko, Danylenko, Kokin, et al., eds., *Rozsekrechena pam'iat'*, 512–16.

25. HDA SBU 9/36 (1933), 36a, in Bojko and Bednarek, *Holodomor*, 266–75.

26. Timothy Snyder, *Bloodlands*, 42.

27. TsDAHOU 1/20/5242 (1932), 5–10, in Kokin, *Partiino-Radians'ke kerivnitstvo USRR pid chas Holodomoru*, 210–29.

28. Plokhy, *Unmaking Imperial Russia*, 268–73.

29. Hennadii Iefymenko and L. Iakubova, 'Natsional'ni vidnosyny v radians'kii Ukraïni (1923–1938)', in V. M. Lytvyn et al., eds., *Natsional'ne pytannia v Ukraïni XX–pochatku XXI st.: istorychni narysy* (Kyiv: Nika-Tsentr, 2012), 222–3.

30. Martin, *The Affirmative Action Empire*, 348.

31. Hrihorii Kostiuk, *Stalinizm v Ukraïni* (Kyiv: Vyd-vo Smoloskyp, 1995), 192–6.

32. Ibid., 192–6.

33. Iurii Shapoval, 'Fatal'na Ambivalentnist', *Krytyka: mizhnarodnyi ohliad knyzhok ta idei* (May 2015), https://krytyka.com/ua/articles/fatalna-ambivalentnist.

34. Ibid.

35. Pauly, *Breaking the Tongue*, 241–2.

36. Ibid., 258–66.

37. L. D. Iakubova, *Etnichni menshyny v suspil'no-politychnomu ta kul'turnomu zhytti USRR, 20-i – persha polovyna 30-kh rr. XX st.* (Kyiv: Instytut Istoriï Ukraïny NAN Ukraïny, 2002), 126–31.

38. S. V. Kul'chyts'kyi, 'Holodomor in the Ukrainian Countryside', in *After the Holodomor: The Enduring Impact of the Great Famine on Ukraine*, eds. Andrea Graziosi, Lubomyr Hajda and Halyna Hryn (Cambridge, MA: Harvard Ukrainian Research Institute, 2013), 9.

39. Ibid.

40. Iakubova, *Etnichni menshyny v suspil'no-politychnomu ta kul'turnomu zhytti USRR*, 126–31.

41. H. Koval'chuk, 'Dyrektory Vsenarodnoï Biblioteky Ukraïny (20-30-ti rr.)', *Z arkhiviv VUChK GPU NKVD KGB* 2/4 (13/15) (2000), 179–206.

42. O. Rubl'ov and O. V. Iurkova, 'Instytut Istoriï Ukraïny NAN Ukraïny: vikhy istoriï (1936–2006 rr.)', ed. V. A. Smolii, *Urkaïns'kyi Istorychnyi Zhurnal* 6 (2006), 5–7.

43. Iurii Shapoval, *Ukraïna 20–50 rr.: Storinky nenapysanoï istoriï* (Kyiv: Naukova Dumka, 1993), 126–31.

44. S. A. Tokarev, 'Represiï proty vykladachiv Nizhyns'koho Pedahohichnoho Instytutu v 1930-kh rr.', *Z arkhiviv VUChK GPU NKVD KGB* 1/2 (2013), 146–69.

45. Martin, *The Affirmative Action Empire*, 363.

46. Pauly, *Breaking the Tongue*, 332–9.

47. Martin, *The Affirmative Action Empire*, 363.

48. Hanna Skrypnyk, *Etnohrafichni muzeï Ukraïny: Stanovlennia i rozvytok* (Kyiv: Naukova Dumka, 1989).

49. Alla Kyrydon, 'Ruinuvannia kul'tovykh sporud', 91–102.

50. M. M. Kholostenko, 'Arkitekturnaia rekonstruktsiia Kieva', *Arkitektura SSSR* 12 (1934), 19.

51. A. G. Molokin, 'Proektirovanie Pravitel'stvennogo Tsentra USSR v Kieve', *Arkitektura SSSR* 9 (1935), 11.

52. Titus D. Hewryk, *Vtracheni arkhitekturni pam'iatky Kyieva* (New York-Kyiv: Ukrainian Museum, 1991).

53. Ibid.

54. Serhii Bilokin', 'Masovyi teror iak zasib derzhavnoho upravlinnia v SRSR (1917–1941)', *Dzhereloznavche doslidzhennia* 2 (Drohobych: 'Kolo', 2013), 452–90.

55. Ibid., 519–22.

56. Shevelov, *The Ukrainian Language in the First Half of the Twentieth Century*, 154–8.

57. Ibid., 160–7, quote on 167.

10. FAMINE DECISIONS, 1932:
THE SEARCHES AND THE SEARCHERS

1. Vasilii Grossman, *Everything Flows*, trans. Robert and Elizabeth Chandler (New York: New York Review Classic Books, 2009).

2. Boriak, *1933*, 684.

3. Ibid., 685–6.

4. For hundreds of examples see Valentyna Borysenko, *Svicha pam'iati: Usna istoriia pro henotsyd ukraïntsiv u 1932–1933 rokakh* (Kyiv: Stylos, 2007). Also published in English as *A Candle in Remembrance: An Oral History of the Ukrainian Genocide of 1933–34 (Svicha pam'iati)*, trans. Mark Tarnawsky (New York: Ukrainian Women's League of America, 2010). For this chapter, I used the Ukrainian version of the book.

5. Testimony of Ol'ha Viktorivna Tsymbaliuk, in ibid., 229.

6. Testimony of Anastasiia Mykolaïvna Pavlenko, in ibid., 130–1.

7. Testimony of Larysa Fedorivna Venzhyk (née Shevchuk), in ibid., 137–8.

8. Testimony of Mariia Patrivna Bendryk, in ibid., 247.

9. Testimony of Leonid Iukhymovych Vernydub, in Ukraïns'kyi Instytut natsional'noï pam'iati and Yushchenko, eds., *Natsional'na Knyha pam'iati zhertv Holodomoru*, 65.

10. Testimony of Mariia Myronivna Kozhedub, in Borysenko, *Svicha pam'iati*, 269.

11. Roman Dzwonkowski and Petro Iashchuk, *Głód i represje wobec ludności polskiej na Ukrainie 1932–1947: relacje* (Lublin: Tow. Nauk. Katolickiego Uniwersytetu Lubelskiego, 2004), 160.

12. Testimony of Petro Kuz'mych Mostovyi, in Kovalenko and Maniak, eds., *33-i Holod*, 495.

13. Testimony of Hanna Oleksandrivna Maslianchuk, in Borysenko, *Svicha pam'iati*, 91.

14. Testimony of Paraskeva Vasylivna Kolos, in ibid., 268.

15. Testimony of Mykola Ivanovych Patrynchuk, in ibid., 114.

16. Testimony of Valentyn Kochno, in U.S. Congress, *Investigation of the Ukrainian Famine, 1932–1933: First Interim Report*, 119–20.

17. Testimony of Hanna Omelianivna Flashkina, in Borysenko, *Svicha pam'iati*, 237.

18. Testimony of Anastasiia Mykolaïvna Pavlenko, in ibid., 130.

19. Testimony of Natalia Stepanivna Kuzhel, in ibid., 269.

20. Testimony of Mykhailo Pavlovych Havrylenko, in ibid., 208.

21. Testimony of an anonymous woman, in United States Congress and Commission on the Ukraine Famine, *Investigation of the Ukrainian Famine, 1932–1933: Report to Congress*. Report adopted by the Commission, 19 April 1988, submitted to Congress, 22 April 1988 (Washington, D.C.: U.S. G.P.O.: For sale by Supt. of Docs., U.S. G.P.O., 1988), 341–2, 346.

22. Testimony of Mykola Petrovych Khmel'nyk, in Borysenko, *Svicha pam'iati*, 98.

23. Testimony of Tetiana Tymofiïvna Kotenko, in Veselova and Nikiliev, *Pam'iat' narodu*, vol. 1, 645.

24. Testimony of Halyna Hryhorivna Kovtun, in Borysenko, *Svicha pam'iati*, 257.

25. Testimony of Hanna Iakivna Onoda, in A. V. Karas, *Svidchennia ochevydtsiv pro holod 1930–40-kh rr. na Sivershchyni* (Hlukhiv: RVV HDPU, 2008), 49.

26. Lev Kopelev, 'Interview with Lev Kopelev', 1981, Harvest of Despair Series, excerpted from the archives of the copyright holder, UCRDC.

27. Testimony of Hanna Semenivna Sukhenko, in Borysenko, *Svicha pam'iati*, 149.

28. Testimony of Ihor Vasyliovych Buhaievych, in Kovalenko and Maniak, eds., *33-i Holod*, 454–7.

29. Testimony of Halyna Omel'chenko, in Ukraïns'kyi Instytut natsional'noï pam'iati and Yushchenko, eds., *Natsional'na knyha pam'iati zhertv Holodomoru*, 87.

30. Testimony of Mykola Mylov, in Mytsyk et al., eds., *Ukraïns'kyi holokost*, vol. 3, 129–30.

31. RGASPI 81/3/215 (1932), 1–24, in Pyrih, ed., *Holodomor*, 497.

32. Pavlo Ivanovych Sylka, in Kovalenko and Maniak, eds., *33-i Holod*, 492.

33. Testimony of Kateryna Stepanivna Tsokol, in ibid., 63.

34. Testimony of Lidia Vasylivna Poltavets', in Mytsyk et al., eds., *Ukraïns'kyi holokost*, vol. 2, 215–16.

35. Daria Mattingly, 'Idle, Drunk and Good-for-Nothing: The Cultural Memory of Holodomor Rank-and-File Perpetrators', in Anna Wylegała and Małgorzata Głowacka-Grajper, eds., *The Burden of Memory: History, Memory and Identity in Contemporary Ukraine* (Bloomington, IN: Indiana University Press, 2017).

36. Testimony of Petro Serhiiovych Voitiuk, in Borysenko, *Svicha pam'iati*, 96.

37. Testimony of Volodymyr Ivanovych Teslia, in Veselova and Nikiliev, *Pam'iat' narodu*, vol. 2, 665–7.

38. Testimony of an anonymous woman, in Kovalenko and Maniak, eds., *33-i Holod*, 127.

39. Kopelev, *The Education of a True Believer*, 233.

40. Testimony of Ivan Leonidovych Prymak, in Mytsyk, *Ukraïns'kyi holokost*, vol. 1, 99.

41. Testimony of an anonymous woman, in Ukraïns'kyi Instytut natsional'noi pam'iati and Iushchenko, eds., *Natsional'na Knyha pam'iati zhertv Holodomoru*, 66.

42. Pidhainy, ed., *The Black Deeds of the Kremlin*, vol. 1, 201.

43. Testimony of Ivan J. Danylenko, in U.S. Congress, *Investigation of the Ukrainian Famine, 1932–1933: First Interim Report*, 77.

44. Testimony of Hryhorii Antonovych Harashchenko, in Borysenko, *Svicha pam'iati*, 178–9.

45. Testimony of Anna Pylypiuk, in U.S. Congress, *Investigation of the Ukrainian Famine, 1932–1933: First Interim Report*, 111–12.

46. Kostiantyn Mochul's'kyi, 'I Was Eight Years Old', trans. Marta Olynyk for the Holodomor Research and Education Consortium, original available in Kostiantyn Mochul's'kyi, 'Meni bulo visim lit', *Kryms'ka svitlytsia* 12 (Simferopol', 21 March 2003), 6.

47. Testimony of Anastasiia Kh., in U.S. Congress, *Investigation of the Ukrainian Famine, 1932–1933: First Interim Report*, 158.

48. Testimony of Varvara Svyrydivna Moroz, in Karas, *Svidchennia ochevydtsiv pro holod 1930–40-kh rr. na Sivershchyni*, 51.
49. Testimony of Hnat Fedorovych Myroniuk, in Ukraïns'kyi Instytut natsional'noï pam'iati and Yushchenko, eds., *Natsional'na knyha pam'iati zhertv Holodomoru*, 64.
50. Testimony of Ivan Tarasiuk, in Veselova and Nikiliev, *Pam'iat' narodu*, vol. 2, 656.
51. Testimony of Mykhailo Oleksandrovych Balanovskyi, in ibid., vol. 1, 95–9.
52. Testimony of Hryhorii Moroz, in Ukraïns'kyi Instytut natsional'noi pam'iati and Iushchenko, eds., *Natsional'na Knyha pam'iati zhertv Holodomoru*, 74–5.
53. Testimony of Hanna Andriïvna Talanchuk, in Mytsyk et al., eds., *Ukraïns'kyi holokost*, vol. 2, 184.
54. Boriak, *1933*, 682–4.
55. Tamara Demchenko, 'Svidchennia pro Holodomor iak dzherelo vyvchennia fenomenu stalins'kykh aktyvistiv', in *Problemy istoriï Ukraïny: fakty sudzhennia, poshuky: Mizhvidomchyi zbirnyk naukovykh prats'*, vol. 19, no. 2 (Kyiv: Naukova Dumka, 2010), 71–81.
56. Viola, *The Best Sons of the Fatherland*, 206–9.
57. RGASPI 81/3/215 (1932), 1–24, in Pyrih, ed., *Holodomor*, 504–5.
58. Mattingly, 'Idle, Drunk and Good-for-Nothing'.
59. Testimony of Maria N., in U.S. Congress, *Investigation of the Ukrainian Famine, 1932–1933: First Interim Report*, 152–4.
60. Victor Kravchenko, *I Chose Freedom: The Personal and Political Life of a Soviet Official*, trans. Rhett R. Ludwikowski (London: Robert Hale, 1946), 75.
61. Ibid., 92.
62. Ibid., 91.
63. Ibid., 63, 74.
64. Kopelev, *The Education of a True Believer*, 235.
65. Georges Simenon, 'Peuples qui ont faim', in *Mes Apprentissages: Reportages 1931–1946*, ed. Francis Lacassin (Paris: Omnibus, 2001), 903–4.
66. Andrei Platonovich Platonov, *Fourteen Little Red Huts and Other Plays*, trans. Robert Chandler, Jesse Irwin and Susan Larsen (New York: Columbia University Press, 2016), 104.
67. Lev Kopelev, Ukrainian Canadian Research and Documentation Centre interview.
68. Ibid.
69. Mattingly, 'Idle, Drunk and Good-for-Nothing'.

70. Testimony of Halyna B., in U.S. Congress, *Investigation of the Ukrainian Famine, 1932–1933: First Interim Report*, 125.

71. Kopelev, *The Education of a True Believer*, 245.

72. Testimony of Vasyl' Onufriïenko, in Ukraïns'kyi Instytut natsional'noi pam'iati and Iushchenko, eds., *Natsional'na knyha pam'iati zhertv Holodomoru*, 91.

73. Valerii Vasyl'ev and Iurii I. Shapoval, *Komandyry velykoho holodu: Poïzdky V. Molotova i L. Kahanovycha v Ukraïnu ta Pivnichnyi Kavkaz, 1932–1933 rr.* (Kyiv: Heneza, 2001), 317.

74. Testimony of Mykola Hryhorovych Musiichuk, in Veselova and Nikiliev, *Pam'iat' narodu*, vol. 2, 76.

75. Mattingly, 'Idle, Drunk and Good-for-Nothing'.

76. Testimony of Vira Karpivna Kyryrchenko, in Mytsyk et al., eds., *Ukraïns'kyi holokost*, vol. 7, 180.

77. Boriak, *1933*, 185, 229, 387, 605.

78. Noll, *Transformatsiia hromadians'koho suspil'stva*, 170–1.

79. Mattingly, 'Idle, Drunk and Good-for-Nothing'.

80. Graziosi, 'Collectivisation, révoltes paysannes et politiques gouvernementales', 442–3.

81. DAZhO (Zhytomyr) F. R-1520/4828 (1931), 9–16.

82. Testimony of Maryna Matviïvna Korobs'ka, in Mytsyk et al., eds., *Ukraïns'kyi holokost*, vol. 1, 110.

83. TsDAHOU 1/20/5394 (1932), 3542, in Pyrih, ed., *Holodomor*, 441.

84. RGASPI 17/42/81 (1932), 103–5, in Danilov, *Tragediia sovetskoi derevni*, 640–2.

85. Testimony of Kateryna Ielyzarivna Iaroshenko, in Veselova and Nikiliev, *Pam'iat' narodu*, vol. 2, 881–2.

86. Testimony of Nataliia Arsentiïvna Talanchuk, in Mytsyk et al., eds., *Ukraïns'kyi holokost*, vol. 3, 61.

87. Testimony of Pavlo Kostenko, in ibid., vol. 5, 181.

88. Testimony of Father Tymofii Minenko, in Mytsyk et al., eds., *Ukraïns'kyi holokost*, vol. 3, 145.

89. Mattingly, 'Idle, Drunk and Good-for-Nothing'.

90. Testimony of Vasyl' Vasyl'ovych Bashtanenko, in Mytsyk et al., eds., *Ukraïns'kyi holokost*, vol. 1, 138.

91. TsDAHOU 1/6/238/32–6, in M. M. Starovoitov and V. V. Mykhailychenko, *Holodomor na Luhanshchyni 1932–1933 rr.: Naukovo-dokumental'ne vydannia* (Kyiv: Stylos, 2008), 65–8.

92. Plokhy, *Unmaking Imperial Russia*, 269–70.

93. All of the material on the Richyts'kyi case comes from Kokin et al., eds., *Partiino-Radians'ke kerivnytstvo USRR pid chas Holodomoru*,

289–444, and by the same authors, 'Dokumenty orhaniv VKP(b) ta DPU USRR pro nastroï i modeli povedinky partiino–radians'kykh pratsivnykiv u respublitsi, 1932–33 rr.', *Z arkhiviv VUChK GPU NKVD KGB* 1–2 (40–1) (2013), 392–400.

94. RGASPI 81/3/215 (1932), 1–24, in Pyrih, ed., *Holodomor*, 504–5.

95. S. A. Kokin, Valerii Vasyl'ev and Nicolas Werth, eds., 'Dokumenty orhaniv VKP(b) ta DPU USRR pro nastroï i modeli povedinky partiino-radïans'kykh pratsivnykiv u respublitsi, 1932–33 rr.', *Z arkhiviv VUChK GPU NKVD KGB* 1–2, nos. 40–1 (2013), 392.

11. STARVATION: SPRING AND SUMMER, 1933

1. Testimony of Mariia Hnativna Dziuba, in Mytsyk, *Ukraïns'kyi holokost*, 10 vols. (Kyiv: Kyievo-Mohylians'ka Akademiia, 2004), vol. 1, 262.

2. Quoted in Conquest, *The Harvest of Sorrow*, 143.

3. Testimony of Mariia Andronivna Zapasko-Pryimak, in Kovalenko and Maniak, eds., *33-i Holod*, 354–5.

4. Testimony of Tetiana Pawlichka, in U.S. Congress, *Investigation of the Ukrainian Famine, 1932–1933: First Interim Report*, 75.

5. Testimony of Mykola Stepanovych Pud, in Kovalenko and Maniak, eds., *33-i Holod*, 567–8.

6. Testimony of Hanna Stepanivna Iurchenko in ibid., 536.

7. Ukraïns'kyi Instytut natsional'noi pam'iati and Iushchenko, eds., *Natsional'na knyha pam'iati zhertv Holodomoru*, 115.

8. Testimony of Anastasiia Maksymivna Kucheruk, in Kovalenko and Maniak, eds., *33-i Holod*, 148.

9. Borysenko, *A Candle in Remembrance*, 47.

10. Testimony of Zadvornyi Volodymyr Fedorovych, in Kovalenko and Maniak, eds., *33-i Holod*, 164.

11. Testimony of Nadiia Iosypivna Malyshko (née Sol'nychenko), in Mytsyk, *Ukraïns'kyi holokost*, vol. 1, 27.

12. Testimony of Hlafyra Pavlivna Ivanova, in Ukraïns'kyi Instytut natsional'noi pam'iati and Iushchenko, eds., *Natsional'na Knyha pam'iati zhertv Holodomoru*, 97.

13. Testimony of Anastasiia Maksymivna Kucheruk, in Kovalenko and Maniak, eds., *33-i Holod*, 149.

14. Ibid., 148.

15. Testimony of Nina Ivanivna Marusyk, in ibid., 157.

16. Pidhainy, ed., *The Black Deeds of the Kremlin*, vol. 1, 303.

17. Testimony of Volodymyr Pavlovych Slipchenko, in Kovalenko and Maniak, eds., *33-i Holod*, 88.
18. Testimony of Oleksij Keis, in U.S. Congress and Commission on the Ukraine Famine, *Investigation of the Ukrainian Famine, 1932–1933: Second Interim Report*, 22.
19. Testimony of Hryhorii Fedorovych Sim'ia, in Kovalenko and Maniak, eds., *33-i Holod*, 510–11.
20. Testimony of Oleksandr Honcharenko, in U.S. Congress and Commission on the Ukraine Famine, *Investigation of the Ukrainian Famine, 1932–1933: Second Interim Report*, 333–4.
21. Testimony of Dmytro Zakharovych Kalenyk, in Kovalenko and Maniak, *33-i Holod*, 31.
22. Pidhainy, ed., *The Black Deeds of the Kremlin*, vol. 1, 305.
23. Testimony of Petro Kyrylovych Boichuk, in Ukraïns'kyi Instytut natsional'noi pam'iati and Iushchenko, eds., *Natsional'na Knyha pam'iati zhertv Holodomoru*, 95.
24. Pitirim Sorokin, *Hunger as a Factor in Human Affairs* (Gainesville, FL: University of Florida Press, 1975), 73.
25. Testimony of Mykola Ivanovych Opanasenko, in Kovalenko and Maniak, eds., *33-i Holod*, 526.
26. Testimony of Oleksii Iuriiovych Kurinnyi and Oksana Iukhymivna Hryhorenko, in Mytsyk et al., eds., *Ukraïns'kyi holokost*, vol. 2, 200.
27. From the diary of O. Radchenko, in Pyrih, ed., *Holodomor*, 1,013.
28. Testimony of Nadiia Dmytrivna Lutsyshyna, in Borysenko, *A Candle in Remembrance*, 88.
29. Testimony of Iaryna Vasylivna Kaznadzei, in Mytsyk et al., eds., *Ukraïns'kyi holokost*, vol. 6, 160.
30. Testimony of Anton Tykhonovych Bredun, in Mytsyk et al., eds., *Ukraïns'kyi holokost*, vol. 1, 88.
31. Testimony of Halyna Spyrydonivna Mashyntseva, in ibid., vol. 1, 117–18.
32. Testimony of Uliana Fylymonivna Lytvyn, in Kovalenko and Maniak, eds., *33-i Holod*, 98.
33. Dolot, *Execution by Hunger*, 92.
34. Testimony of Iaryna Petrivna Mytsyk, in Kovalenko and Maniak, eds., *33-i Holod*, 299.
35. Testimony of Mariia Mykolaïvna Doronenko (née Puntus), in Mytsyk et al., eds., *Ukraïns'kyi holokost*, vol. 1, 27.
36. Athanasius D. McVay and Lubomyr Y. Luciuk, eds., *The Holy See and the Holodomor: Documents from the Secret Vatican Archives on the*

Great Famine of 1932–33 in Soviet Ukraine (Toronto: The Kashtan Press, 2011), 5.

37. Dariusz Stola makes this point. Quoted in Anne Applebaum, *Iron Curtain: The Crushing of Eastern Europe, 1944–1956* (New York and London: Doubleday and Allen Lane, 2012), 141.

38. Pidhainy, ed., *The Black Deeds of the Kremlin*, vol. 1, 284.

39. Testimony of Anastasiia Kh., in U.S. Congress, *Investigation of the Ukrainian Famine, 1932–1933: First Interim Report*, 156–7.

40. Ibid.

41. Testimony of Oleksandra Fedotivna Molchanova, in Mytsyk et al., eds., *Ukraïns'kyi holokost*, vol. 1, 91.

42. N. R. Romanets', 'Borot'ba z samosudamy v Ukraïns'komu seli, 1933–1935 rr.', *Naukovi pratsi istorychnoho fakul'tetu Zaporis'koho Natsional'noho Universytetu* XXIX (2010), 186.

43. Testimony of Ihor Vasyl'ovych Buhaevych, in Kovalenko and Maniak, eds., *33-i Holod*, 455–6.

44. Romanets', 'Borot'ba z samosudamy v Ukraïns'komu seli', 186; citing DADO 1520/3/36/(1933), 674 and 1,127, and TsDAHOU 1/20/6395 (1933), 107.

45. Ibid., 186–7.

46. Testimony of Motrona Andriïvna Krasnoshchok, in Mytsyk et al., eds., *Ukraïns'kyi holokost*, vol. 6, 284–5.

47. Ivan Brynza, 'I Was Dying amidst Fields of Grain', in *Zlochyn*, ed. Petro Kardash (Melbourne-Kyiv: Vyd-vo Fortuna, 2003), trans. Marta Olynyk for the Holodomor Research and Education Consortium.

48. From the diary of O. Radchenko, in Pyrih, ed., *Holodomor*, 1,125.

49. Testimony of Motrona Andriïvna Krasnoshchok, in Mytsyk et al., eds., *Ukraïns'kyi holokost*, vol. 6, 284–5.

50. Testimony of Maksym Petrovych Bozhyk, in Kovalenko and Maniak, eds., *33-i Holod*, 126.

51. TsDAHOU 1/20/6274 (1933), 146–8, in Pyrih, ed., *Holodomor*, 750.

52. Testimony of Oleksii Semenovych Lytvyns'kyi, in Borysenko, *A Candle in Remembrance*, 148–9.

53. Testimony of Hanna Oleksandrivna Tsivka, in Mytsyk et al., eds., *Ukraïns'kyi holokost*, vol. 1, 116.

54. Testimony of Mykola Lavrentiiovych Basha, in Karas, *Svidchennia ochevydtsiv*, 30.

55. Testimony of Stephen C., in U.S. Congress *Investigation of the Ukrainian Famine, 1932–1933: First Interim Report*, 126–7.

56. Romanets', 'Borot'ba z samosudamy v Ukraïns'komu seli', 188; citing DADO 19/1/1494 (1933), 109.

57. Testimony of Mykola Ivanovych Opanasenko, in Kovalenko and Maniak, eds., *33-i Holod*, 526.

58. Romanets', 'Borot'ba z samosudamy v Ukraïns'komu seli', 189; citing DADO 1520/3/37 (1933), 104.

59. Romanets', 'Borot'ba z samosudamy v Ukraïns'komu seli', 190; citing DADO 1520/3/35 (1933), 4, TsDAHOU 1/20/6580 (1934), 107, and TsDAHOU 1/20/6777 (1935), 113.

60. Testimony of Marfa Pavlivna Honcharuk, in Kovalenko and Maniak, eds., *33-i Holod*, 29.

61. Testimony of Ol'ha Kocherkevych, in Veselova and Nikiliev, *Pam'iat' narodu*, vol. 1, 651–2.

62. Testimony of Mykola Romanovych Proskovchenko, in Mytsyk et al., eds., *Ukraïns'kyi holokost*, vol. 3, 128.

63. Diary of Oleksandra Radchenko, in Bohdan Klid and Alexander J. Motyl, *The Holodomor Reader: A Sourcebook on the Famine of 1932–33 in Ukraine* (Toronto: Canadian Institute of Ukrainian Studies Press, 2012), 182.

64. Testimony of Halyna Kyrylivna Budantseva (née Piven'), in Kovalenko and Maniak, eds., *33-i Holod*, 485.

65. Petro Hryhorenko, interview by Slavko Novytskyi, UCRDC.

66. Grossman, *Everything Flows*, 136.

67. HDA SBU 65/6352/1 (1932), 444–6, in Danylenko et al., eds., *Holodomor 1932–1933 rokiv v Ukraïni za dokumentamy HDA SBU*, 283.

68. TsDAHOU 1/20/6276 (1933), 55–60, in Pyrih, ed., *Holodomor*, 888.

69. Noll, *Transformatsiia hromadians'koho suspil'stva*, 296–300.

70. Testimony of Kateryna Romanivna Marchenko, in Veselova and Nikiliev, *Pam'iat' narodu*, vol. 2, 11–12.

71. Testimony of Mariia Ivanivna Korniichuk, in Kovalenko and Maniak, eds., *33-i Holod*, 490.

72. 'Schedule A, vol. 36, Case 333/(NY)1582 (Interviewer J. F., Type A4) Male, 29, Ukrainian, Student and Worker', 1–8 July 1951, Harvard Project on the Soviet Social System, Slavic Division, Widener Library, Harvard University, 25.

73. Testimony of Vasyl' Iosypovych Huzenko, in Karas, *Svidchennia ochevydtsiv*, 54–5.

74. Testimony of Anna S., in U.S. Congress and Commission on the Ukraine Famine, *Investigation of the Ukrainian Famine, 1932–1933: Second Interim Report*, 26–7.

75. Testimony of Mykola Iakovych Kovtun, in Kovalenko and Maniak, eds., *33-i Holod*, 313.

76. Testimony of Paraskeva Serhiivna Pidlubna, in Borysenko, *A Candle in Remembrance*, 186.

77. Testimony of Tetiana Pawlichka, in U.S. Congress, *Investigation of the Ukrainian Famine, 1932–1933: First Interim Report*, 75–6.

78. Testimony of M. Barkov, in Veselova and Nikiliev, *Pam'iat' narodu*, vol. 1, 108.

79. Testimony of Larysa Vasylivna Vasyl'chenko, in Kovalenko and Maniak, eds., *33-i Holod*, 477–8.

80. Testimony of Oleksandr Honcharenko, in U.S. Congress and Commission on the Ukraine Famine, *Investigation of the Ukrainian Famine, 1932–1933: Second Interim Report*, 332–3.

81. Testimony of Petro Kuz'mych Mostovyi, in Kovalenko and Maniak, eds., *33-i Holod*, 495.

82. Noll, *Transformatsiia hromadians'koho suspil'stva*, 183.

83. Oleg Bazhan and Vadym Zolotar'ov, 'Konveier Smerti v chasy "Velykoho Teroru" v Ukrayïni: Tekhnologiia rozstriliv, vykonavtsi, misstia pokhovan'', *Kraieznavstvo* 1 (2014), 192.

84. Ibid., 193–4.

85. Testimony of Varvara Dibert, in U.S. Congress, *Investigation of the Ukrainian Famine, 1932–1933: First Interim Report*, 73.

86. Testimony of Leonid A., in ibid., 132–3.

87. Testimony of an anonymous woman, in Kovalenko and Maniak, eds., *33-i Holod*, 508.

88. Testimony of Mykola Iakovych Pishyi, in ibid., 266.

89. Testimony of Larysa Donchuk, in U.S. Congress and Commission on the Ukraine Famine, *Investigation of the Ukrainian Famine, 1932–1933: Second Interim Report*, 138.

90. Testimony of Oleksandra Mykhailivna Krykun (née Reznichenko), in Kovalenko and Maniak, eds., *33-i Holod*, 524.

91. Testimony of Ivan Pavlovych Vasianovych, in ibid., 551–3.

92. Testimony of Vira Prokopivna Kadiuk, in ibid., 346.

93. Daria Mattingly, 'Oral History Project of the School Students of Tororyshche', 2007, from her private collection.

94. 'Schedule A, vol. 36, Case 333', Harvard Project on the Soviet Social System, Slavic Division, Widener Library, Harvard University, 25.

95. Testimony of Liuba Arionivna, in Kovalenko and Maniak, eds., *33-i Holod*, 280.

96. Testimony of Mariia Ievlampiïvna Petrenko, in Mytsyk et al., eds., *Ukraïns'kyi holokost*, vol. 2, 187.

97. Testimony of Stephen C., in U.S. Congress *Investigation of the Ukrainian Famine, 1932–1933: First Interim Report*, 126–7.

98. Testimony of Denys Mykytovych Lebid', in Kovalenko and Maniak, eds., *33-i Holod*, 306.

99. Testimony of Fedir Dmytrovych Zavads'kyi, in ibid., 268.

100. See testimonies in ibid., 98, 327–9, 335 and 340; and Veselova and Nikiliev, *Pam'iat' narodu*, vol. 1, 401, 427, 454.

101. Testimony of Anna Pylypiuk, in U.S. Congress *Investigation of the Ukrainian Famine, 1932–1933: First Interim Report*, 111–12.

102. This, again, is the letter to Kosior and Kaganovich. TsDAHOU 1/20/6276 (1933), 55–60, in Pyrih, ed., *Holodomor*, 888.

103. Karel Berkhoff, 'The Great Famine in Light of the German Invasion and Occupation', in Halyna Hryn and Lubomyr Hadja, eds., *After the Holodomor: The Enduring Impact of the Great Famine of Ukraine* (Cambridge, MA: Harvard Ukrainian Research Institute, 2014).

104. TsDAHOU 1/20/6274 (1933), 185–90, in Pyrih, ed., *Holodomor*, 763.

105. Testimony of Larysa Fedorivna Venzhyk, in Borysenko, *A Candle in Remembrance*, 138–9.

106. Testimony of Mariia Pavlivna Davydenko, in Karas, *Svidchennia ochevydtsiv*, 9.

107. Testimony of Iaryna, in Kovalenko and Maniak, eds., *33-i Holod*, 69.

108. Testimony of Mykola Oleksiiovych Moskalenko, in Karas, *Svidchennia ochevydtsiv*, 56.

109. Andrea Graziosi, *Lysty z Kharkova: Holod v Ukraïni ta na Pivnichnomu Kavkazi v povidomlenniakh italiis'kykh dyplomativ 1932–33 roky* (Kharkiv: Folio, 2007), 125–7.

110. Nicolas Werth, 'Keynote Address for the Holodomor Conference, Harvard Ukrainian Research Institute, 17–18 November 2008', in Hryn and Hajda, eds., *After the Holodomor*, xxxiv.

111. TsDAHOU 1/20/6275 (1933), 124–31, in Ukraïns'kyi Instytut natsional'noï pam'iati and V. I. Ul'iachenko, eds., *Natsional'na knyha pam'iati zhertv Holodomoru 1932–1933 rokiv v Ukraïni: Kyïvs'ka oblast'* (Bila Tserkva: Bukva, 2008), 1,291.

112. DADO 1520/3/9 (1933), 431, in Ukraïns'kyi Instytut natsional'noï pam'iati and E. I. Borodin et al., eds., *Natsional'na knyha pam'iati zhertv Holodomoru 1932–1933 rokiv v Ukraïni: Dnipropetrovs'ka oblast'* (Dnipropetrovsk: ART-PRES, 2008), 1,111.

113. DADO 710/2/2 (1933), 18–19, in Ukraïns'kyi Instytut natsional'noï pam'iati and T. T. Dmytrenko, eds., *Natsional'na knyha pam'iati zhertv Holodomoru 1932–1933 rokiv v Ukraïni: Kirovohrads'ka oblast'* (Kirovohrad: TOV 'Imeks LTD', 2008), 853–4.

114. Ukraïns'kyi Instytut natsional'noi pam'iati and F. H. Turchenko, eds., *Natsional'na Knyha pam'iati zhertv Holodomoru 1932–1933*

rokiv v Ukraïni: Zaporiz'ka oblast' (Zaporizhzhia: Dyke Pole, 2008), 777.

115. TsDAHOU 1/20/6274 (1933), 146–8, in Pyrih, ed., *Holodomor*, 750–1.

116. TsDAHOU 1/20/6276 (1933), 39–46, in ibid., 877.

117. Derzhavnyi Arkhiv Donets'koi Oblasti 326/1/130 (1933), 47, in ibid., 822–3.

118. Davies and Wheatcroft, *The Years of Hunger*, 422.

119. TsDAHOU 1/20/6274 (1933), 185–90, in Ukraïns'kyi Instytut natsional'noi pam'iati and Ul'iachenko, eds., *Natsional'na Knyha pam'iati zhertv Holodomoru: Kyïvs'ka oblast'*, 1,287.

120. HDA SBU, 6/75501-fp.

121. Interview with Olga Mane, HREC/UCRDC Ukrainian Canadian Research and Documentation Centre.

122. TsDAHOU 1/20/6274 (1933), 95–9, in ibid., 1,284.

123. Romanets', 'Borot'ba z samosudamy v Ukraïns'komu seli', 190.

12. SURVIVAL: SPRING AND SUMMER, 1933

1. Testimony of Hryhorii Ivanovych Mazurenko, in Borysenko, *A Candle in Remembrance*, 165.

2. Testimony of Vira Mykhailivna Tyshchenko, in ibid., 147.

3. Testimony of Todos Khomovych Hodun, in ibid., 231.

4. Letter from Khoma Riabokon', in D. F. Solovei, *Skazaty pravdu: Try pratsi pro Holodomor 1932–1933 rr.* (Kyiv-Poltava: Instytut Istoriï Ukraïny NAN Ukraïny, 2005), 77.

5. See, for example, the testimony of Ivan Oleksiiovych Maksymenko, in Karas, *Svidchennia ochevydtsiv*, 32–3; the testimony of Mariia Andrivna Oliinyk (née Liakhimets'), in Mytsyk et al., eds., *Ukraïns'kyi holokost*, vol. 1, 108–9; the testimonies of Nadiia Dmytrivna Lutsyshyna and Larysa Fedorivna Shevchuk (née Venzhuk), in Borysenko, *A Candle in Remembrance*, 88 and 137–41; the testimony of Ivan Pavlovych Vasianovych, in Kovalenko and Maniak, eds., *33-i Holod*, 552–3. See also, as a general reference, Oleksa Riznykiv, *Ïdlo 33-ho: slovnyk holodomoru* (Odessa: Iurydychna literatura, 2003).

6. Testimony of Mariia Pavlivna Davydenko, in Karas, *Svidchennia ochevydtsiv*, 10.

7. See the testimony of Oleksandra Vasylivna Sykal, in ibid., 35; also, the testimonies of Lida Oleksandrivna Kolomiiets' and Mykola Mykhailovych Ostroverkh, in Borysenko, *A Candle in Remembrance*, 99 and 222.

8. Testimony of Nadiia Dmytrivna Lutsyshyna, in ibid., 99.

9. Testimony of Mykola Demydovych Fenenko, in Kovalenko and Maniak, eds., *33-i Holod*, 542.

10. Testimony of Mariia Vasylivna Pykhtina, in Borysenko, *A Candle in Remembrance*, 189.

11. Testimony of Halyna Spyrydonivna Mashyntseva, in Mytsyk et al., eds., *Ukraïns'kyi holokost*, vol. 1, 117–18.

12. Testimony of Petro Kuz'mych Mostovyi, in Kovalenko and Maniak, eds., *33-i Holod*, 495.

13. Testimony of Mariia Semenivna Pata, in Karas, *Svidchennia ochevydtsiv*, 6.

14. Testimony of Vira Illivna Petukh, in ibid., 52.

15. Testmony of Nadiia Zakharivna Ovcharuk, in Borysenko, *A Candle in Remembrance*, 103.

16. Testimony of Kseniia Afanasiïvna Maliar, in Karas, *Svidchennia ochevydtsiv*, 56–7.

17. Testimony of Oksana Andriïvna Zhyhadno, in Borysenko, *A Candle in Remembrance*, 151.

18. Ibid., 152.

19. TsDAHOU 1/20/6274 (1933), 149–58, in Pyrih, ed., *Holodomor*, 156–9.

20. Testimony of Kateryna Prokopivna Butko, in Borysenko, *A Candle in Remembrance*, 143.

21. Testimony of Mykola Hryhorovych Sobrach, in Karas, *Svidchennia ochevydtsiv*, 28–30.

22. Testimony of Liubov Andriïvna Orliuk, in Borysenko, *A Candle in Remembrance*, 158.

23. Testimony of Petro Kuz'mych Mostovyi, in Kovalenko and Maniak, eds., *33-i Holod*, 495.

24. Testimony of Hnat Fedorovych Myroniuk, in Ukraïns'kyi Instytut natsional'noï pam'iati and Iushchenko, *Natsional'na knyha pam'iati zhertv Holodomoru*, 64.

25. Testimony of Mariia Semenivna Pata, in Karas, *Svidchennia ochevydtsiv*, 10–11.

26. Testimony of Sofiia Iakivna Zalyvcha, in Kovalenko and Maniak, eds., *33-i Holod*, 472.

27. Testimony of Dmytro Dmytruk and Mykola Shvedchenko, in Oksana Kis, 'Defying Death: Women's Experience of the Holodomor, 1932–33', *Aspasia* 7 (2013), 54.

28. Testimony of Anatolii Stepanovych Bakai, in Kovalenko and Maniak, eds., *33-i Holod*, 484–5.

29. Testimony of Ihor Vasyliovych Buhaievych, in ibid., 454–7.

30. Testimony of Mariia Terenivna Havrysh, in Borysenko, *A Candle in Remembrance*, 80–1.

31. Arthur Koestler, *The Invisible Writing: An Autobiography* (New York: Macmillan, 1954), 55–6.

32. Oleh Wolowyna, Serhii Plokhy, Nataliia Levchuk, Omelian Rudnytskyi, Pavlo Shevchuk and Alla Kovbasiuk, 'Regional Variations of 1932–34 Famine Losses in Ukraine', *Canadian Studies in Population* 43, nos. 3/4 (2016), 175–202.

33. Marco Carynnyk, Bohdan S. Kordan and Lubomyr Y. Luciuk, eds., *The Foreign Office and the Famine: British Documents on Ukraine and the Great Famine of 1932–1933* (Kingston, Ontario: Limestone Press, 1988), 104–65.

34. Ibid.

35. Interview with Peter Egides, conducted by Marco Carynnyk in Toronto on November 1981. From the archives of the Ukrainian Canadian Research and Documentation Centre, Toronto.

36. HDA SBU 6/68805-FP, vols. 6 and 8, cited in Bojko and Bednarek, *Holodomor: The Great Famine in Ukraine*, 607.

37. Carynnyk et al., eds., *The Foreign Office and the Famine*, 107.

38. Bojko and Bednarek, *Holodomor*, 608.

39. Ibid., 609.

40. Timothy Snyder, *Black Earth: The Holocaust as History and Warning* (New York: Tim Duggan Books, 2015), 249.

41. Petro Shelest, *Spravzhnii sud istorii shche poperedu: Spohady, shchodennyky, dokumenty, materialy*, ed. V. Baran, O. Mandebura, Yu. Shapoval and H. Yudynkova. (Kyiv: Heneza, 2004), 64–5.

42. Testimony of Ielyzaveta Petrivna Radchenko, in Kovalenko and Maniak, eds., *33-i Holod*, 492.

43. Testimony of Kylyna Vasylivna Dykun, in Mytsyk et al., eds., *Ukraïns'kyi holokost*, vol. 1, 90.

44. Testimony of Nadiia Iosypivna Malyshko (Sol'nychenko), in ibid., vol. 1, 27.

45. Testimony of Varvara Stepanivna Horban', in ibid., vol. 1, 29–30.

46. Kis, 'Defying Death', 55.

47. Testimony of Halyna Pavlivna Tymoshchuk, in Borysenko, *A Candle in Remembrance*, 96.

48. DAVO 136/3/74 (1933), 4–4, in Ukraïns'kyi Instytut natsional'noi pam'iati and V. P. Latsyba, eds., *Natsional'na knyha pam'iati zhertv Holodomoru 1932–1933 rokiv v Ukraïni: Vinnyts'ka oblast'* (Vinnytsia: DP 'DFK', 2008), 1,191.

49. Testimony of Stepan Kharytonovych Vasiuta, in Kovalenko and Maniak, eds., *33-i Holod*, 465–6.

50. Testimony of Mariia Ivanivna Korniichuk, in ibid., 489–90.

51. TsDAHOU 1/20/6277 (1933), 233–5, in Pyrih, ed., *Holodomor*, 798–800.

52. TsDAHOU 1/20/6275 (1933), 182–6, in ibid., 833–5.

53. Ibid.

54. DAVO 136/3/71 (1933), 127–9, in Ukraïns'kyi Instytut natsional'noi pam'iati and Latsyba, eds., *Natsional'na knyha pam'iati zhertv Holodomoru*, 1,245.

55. DAKhO, 104/1/123 (1933), 2, in Ukraïns'kyi Instytut natsional'noi pam'iati and S. H. Vodotyka, *Natsional'na knyha pam'iati zhertv Holodomoru 1932–1933 rokiv v Ukraïni: Khersons'ka oblast'*, eds. I. P. Iukhnovs'kyi et al. (Kherson: Vydavnytstvo 'Naddniprians'ka pravda', 2008), 527.

56. DAKhO, 116/1/141 (1933), 19–22, in ibid.

57. DAKhO, P-1962/1/973 (1933), 9, in Pyrih, ed., *Holodomor*, 841–2.

58. Drazhevs'ka Liubov, 'Interview with Liubov Drazhevska', conducted on 22 July 1983 in New York by Sviatoslav Novytsky, UCRDC.

59. RGASPI 17/162/14 (1932), 17, in Pyrih, ed., *Holodomor*, 412; Graziosi, *Lysty z Kharkova*, 128–30.

60. Osokina, *Zoloto dlia industrializatsii*, 96.

61. Ibid., 227.

62. Lubomyr Y. Luciuk, *Tell Them We Are Starving: The 1933 Diaries of Gareth Jones* (Kingston, Ontario: Kashtan Press, 2015), 103.

63. Malcolm Muggeridge, *Winter in Moscow* (Boston, MA: Little Brown, 1934), 146.

64. Bulgakov, *The Master and Margarita*, 391–2.

65. Okosina, *Zoloto dlia industrializatsii*, 250–1, 255, 293.

66. Testimony of Vira Iosypivna Kapynis, in Mytsyk et al., eds., *Ukraïns'kyi holokost*, vol. 7, 193.

67. Testimony of Ivan Iakovych Khomenko, in Veselova and Nikiliev, *Pam'iat' narodu*, vol. 2, 746.

68. Testimony of Nadiia Illivna Babenko, in Kovalenko and Maniak, eds., *33-i Holod*, 558–59.

69. Testimony of Ivan Kyrylovych Klymenko, in Mytsyk et al., eds., *Ukraïns'kyi holokost*, vol. 6, 142–5.

70. Testimony of Hryhorii Fedorovych Sim'ia, in Kovalenko and Maniak, eds., *33-i Holod*, 510–11.

71. Tetiana Yevsieieva, 'The Activities of Ukraine's Union of Militant Atheists during the Period of All-Out Collectivization, 1929–1933', trans.

Marta Olynyk, *Key Articles on the Holodomor Translated from Ukrainian into English,* Holodomor Research and Education Consortium, http://holodomor.ca/translated-articles-on-the-holodomor.

72. Osokina, *Zoloto dlia Industrializatsiï,* 151–3.
73. Ibid., 162–3.
74. Diary of Oleksandra Radchenko, in Klid and Motyl, *The Holodomor Reader,* 182.
75. HDA SBU 13/40/-- (1932), 167–73, in Bojko and Bednarek, *Holodomor,* 91.
76. Testimony of Ihor Vasyl'iovych Buhaevych, in Kovalenko and Maniak, eds., *33-i Holod,* 454.
77. Testimony of Hryhorii Pavlovych Novykov, in ibid., 530.
78. 'Schedule A, vol. 32, Case 91/(NY)1124 (interviewer M. S., type A4) Female, 56, Great Russian, Stenographer', 1–3 June 1951, Harvard Project on the Soviet Social System, Slavic Division, Widener Library, Harvard University, 65.
79. Testimony of Pavlo Feodosiiovych Chornyi, in Mytsyk et al., eds., *Ukraïns'kyi holokost,* vol. 1, 92.
80. 'Schedule A, vol. 36, Case 333 (NY) 1582 (interviewer J. F., type A4). Male, 29, Ukrainian, student and worker. Harvard Project on the Soviet Social System, Slavic Division, Widener Library, Harvard University, 26. See for more, https://iiif.lib.harvard.edu/manifests/view/drs:5608007$1i.
81. Kis, 'Defying Death', 53.

13. AFTERMATH

1. Mykola Rudenko, 'The Cross', trans. Marco Carynnyk, in Wasyl Hryshko, *The Ukrainian Holocaust of 1933* (Toronto: Bahriany Foundation, 1983), 135–6.
2. Oleh Wolowyna's research project on the demographic characteristics and consequences of the 1932–3 famine in the Soviet Union, especially in Ukraine and Russia, has been sponsored by the Institute of Demography and Social Research of the Ukrainian National Academy of Sciences and the Harvard Ukrainian Research Institute, with a grant from the Fulbright Foundation.
3. Quotation is from Oleh Wolowyna, letter to the author, 29 April 2017.
4. Omelian Rudnytskyi, Nataliia Levchuk, Oleh Wolowyna, Pavlo Shevchuk and Alla Kovbasiuk, 'Demography of a Man-Made Human Catastrophe: The Case of Massive Famine in Ukraine, 1932–33', *Canadian Studies in Population* 42, nos. 1–2 (2015), 53–80.

5. Wolowyna et al., 'Regional Variations of 1932–1934 Famine Losses in Ukraine', 175–202.

6. Rudnytskyi et al., 'Demography of a Man-Made Human Catastrophe', 65.

7. Oleh Wolowyna, 'Monthly Distribution of 1933 Famine Losses in Ukraine and Russia at the Regional Level', unpublished paper.

8. HDA SBU 13/--/23 (1933), 237–47, in Bojko and Bednarek, *Holodomor*, 495–500.

9. Wolowyna et al., 'Regional Variations of 1932–1934 Famine Losses in Ukraine', 187.

10. Serhii Plokhy, 'Mapping the Great Famine', *MAPA: Digital Atlas of Ukraine, Harvard Ukrainian Research Institute*, 5–7, accessed 2017, http://gis.huri.harvard.edu/images/pdf/MappingGreatUkrainian Famine.pdf.

11. Wolowyna et al., 'Regional Variations of 1932–1934 Famine Losses in Ukraine', 188; Plokhy, 'Mapping the Great Famine', 19.

12. Andrea Graziosi, 'The Impact of Holodomor Studies on the Understanding of the USSR', in Andrij Makukh and Frank S. Sysyn, eds., *Contextualizing the Holodomor: The Impact of Thirty Years of Ukrainian Famine Studies* (Edmonton, Alberta: Canadian Institute of Ukrainian Studies, 2015), 52.

13. Plokhy, 'Mapping the Great Famine', 16–19.

14. TsDAHOU 1/20/6278/20, in Pyrih, ed., *Holodomor*, 852.

15. Stanislav V. Kul'chyts'kyi, 'Comments at UNAS (National Academy of Sciences) Institute of History of Ukraine Seminar', presented at the Institute of History of Ukraine Seminar, Kyiv, 19 April 2016.

16. RGASPI 17/163/981/229–38, in Danilov et al., eds., *Tragediia sovetskoi derevni*, 952–7.

17. Valerii Vasyl'ev, 'Osoblyvosti polityky kerivnytstva VKP(b) u sil's'komu hospodarstvi URSR (Kinets' 1933–1934 rr.)', *Ukraïns'kyi selianyn: pratsi Naukovo-doslidnoho Instytutu Selianstva* 10 (2006), 342–8.

18. H. Iefimenko and L. Iakubova, 'Natsional'ni vidnosyny v radians'kii Ukraïni (1923–1938)', in V. M. Lytvyn et al., eds., *'Natsional'ne pytannia v Ukraïni XX-pochatku XXI st.: istorychni narysy* (Kyiv: Nika-Tsentr, 2012), 209–27.

19. Stalin, *Works*, vol. 13, 268–370, cited in Klid and Motyl, *The Holodomor Reader*, 265–6.

20. Ibid., 266–8.

21. Vasyl'ev, 'Osoblyvosti polityky kerivnytstva VKP(b) u sil's'komu hospodarstvi URSR', 342–8.

22. Ibid., 342–8.

23. Testimony of Max Harmash, in U.S. Congress and Commission on the Ukraine Famine, *Investigation of the Ukrainian Famine, 1932–1933: Second Interim Report*, 44–6.

24. Testimony of Lidiia A., in ibid., 140–1.

25. H. Iefimenko, 'Lykhovisni 30-ti roky na Markivshchyni', in Stanislav V. Kul'chyts'kyi and O. M. Veselova, eds., *Holod-henotsyd 1933 roku v Ukraïni: istoryko-politolohichnyi analiz sotsial'-no-demohrafichnykh ta moral'no-psykholohichnykh naslidkiv: mizhnarodna naukovo-teoretychna konferentsiia, Kyiv, 28 lystopada 1998 r.: materialy: Instytut Istoriï Ukraïny (Natsional'na Akademiia Nauk Ukraïny): Asotsiatsiia doslidnykiv holodomoriv v Ukraïni* (Kyiv: Vyd-vo M. P. Kots', 2000), 348–56.

26. Nikita Sergeevich Khrushchev, *The 'Secret' Speech Delivered to the Closed Session of the Twentieth Congress of the Communist Party of the Soviet Union*, ed. Bertrand Russell Peace Foundation (Nottingham: Spokesman Books for the Bertrand Russell Peace Foundation, 1976).

27. H. Iefimenko, 'Resettlements and Deportations during the Post-Holodomor Years (1933–1936): A Raion-by-Raion Breakdown', trans. Marta Olynyk, unpublished translation by the Holodomor Research and Education Consortium, 16, citing RGAPSI 11/64/39 (1933). The original can be found at H. Iefimenko, 'Pereselennia ta deportatsiï v postholodomorni roky (1933–1936): poraionnyi zriz', *Problemy Istoriï Ukraïny: fakty, sudzhennia, poshuky: Mizhvidomchyi zbirnyk naukovykh prats'* 22 (2013), 136–66.

28. Ibid., 3–4.

29. Daria Mattingly, 'Oral History Project of the School Students of Tororyshche', 2007, from the private collection of Daria Mattingly.

30. TsDAHOU, 1/20/6375/63–4.

31. Iefimenko, 'Lykhovisni 30-ti roky na Markivshchyni', 348–56.

32. Ibid.

33. Iefimenko, 'Resettlements and Deportations during the Post-Holodomor Years', 28–9.

34. Andrea Graziosi, '"Lettres de Kharkov": La famine en Ukraine et dans le Caucase du Nord (à travers les rapports des diplomates italiens, 1932–1934)', *Cahiers du monde russe et soviétique* 30, no. 1 (1989), 70.

35. Testimony of Iakiv Petrovych Pasichnyk, in Borysenko, *A Candle in Remembrance*, 254.

36. RGASPI 81/3/131 (1933), 43–62, in Marochko and Movchan, *Holodomor 1932–1933 rokiv v Ukraïni*, 256.

37. Bohdan Krawchenko, *Social Change and National Consciousness in Twentieth-Century Ukraine* (Edmonton, Alberta: Canadian Institute of Ukrainian Studies, 1987), 146.

38. Nikita Khrushchev, *Khrushchev Remembers*, trans. Strobe Talbott (Boston, MA: Little, Brown, 1970), 108.

39. Krawchenko, *Social Change and National Consciousness in Twentieth-Century Ukraine*, 148. Of the famine-era leaders only Petrovskyi survived, deprived of his property and his privileges, in Moscow exile.

40. Khrushchev, *Khrushchev Remembers*, 108.

41. This is the conclusion of Daria Mattingly's unpublished PhD thesis.

42. Krawchenko, *Social Change and National Consciousness in Twentieth-Century Ukraine*, 174–5.

43. The entire Sholokhov-Stalin correspondence can be found in Iu.G. Murin, ed., *Pisatel' i vozhd': perepiska M.A. Sholokhova s I.V. Stalinym 1931–1951 gody: sbornik dokumentov iz lichnogo arkhiva I.V. Stalina* (Moscow: Raritet, 1997).

44. Stalin, *Works*, vol. 13, 210–12.

14. THE COVER-UP

1. Petro Drobylko, 'The Cursed Thirties', in Pidhainy, ed., *The Black Deeds of the Kremlin*, vol. 1, 278.

2. PA IIP pri TsK Kompartii Ukrainy 1/101/1243 (1933), 159–63, 172, in R. Ia. Pyrih, ed., *Holod 1932–1933 rokiv na Ukraïni: ochyma istorykiv, movoiu dokumentiv* (Kyiv: Politvydav Ukraïny, 1990), 441–4; not to be confused with *Holodomor 1932–1933* by the same author.

3. APRF 3/40/87/52–64, cited in Kondrashin et al., eds., *Golod v SSSR*, vol. 2, 695–701.

4. Testimony of Mariia Bondarenko, in Kovalenko and Maniak, eds., *33-i Holod*, 90.

5. Testimony of Serhii Fedotovych Kucheriavyi, in Veselova and Nikiliev, *Pam'iat' narodu*, vol. 1, 720.

6. Testimony of Vasyl' Patsiuk Babanka, in Kovalenko and Maniak, eds., *33-i Holod*, 104.

7. Testimony of Iryna Pavlivna N., in Mytsyk et al., eds., *Ukraïns'kyi holokost*, vol. 1, 98.

8. Testimony of A. Butkovska, in U.S. Congress and Commission on the Ukraine Famine, *Investigation of the Ukrainian Famine, 1932–1933: Second Interim Report*, 25.

9. Testimony of Oleksa Voropai, in Veselova and Nikiliev, *Pam'iat' narodu*, vol. 1, 266.

10. TsDAHOU 1/20/6277 (1933), 105–11, in Pyrih, ed., *Holodomor*, 724–5.

11. *Derzhavnyi Arkhiv Odes'koï Oblasti* P-2009/1/4 (1933), 91–2, with thanks to Hennadii Boriak.

12. DAKhO, 3683/2/2 (1933), 52, online at *Holodomor 1932–1933 rr. Kharkivs'ka oblast'*, accessed 2017, http://www.golodomor.kharkov.ua/docsmod.php?docpage=1&doc=772.

13. Anne Applebaum, 'Interview with Professor Hennadii Boriak, Deputy Director, Institute of History of Ukraine, National Academy of Sciences of Ukraine', 25 February 2017.

14. Testimony of Dmytro Koval'chuk, in Veselova and Nikiliev, *Pam'iat' narodu*, vol. 1, 590; testimony of Volodymyr Tkachenko, in Kovalenko and Maniak, *33-i Holod*, 532.

15. Testimony of Stepan Podolian, in Kovalenko and Maniak, eds., *33-i Holod*, 110–11.

16. U.S. Congress and Commission on the Ukraine Famine, *Investigation of the Ukrainian Famine, 1932–1933: Report to Congress*, 46.

17. Applebaum, 'Interview with Andrea Graziosi', February 2014.

18. HDA SBU, Odessa --/66/5 (1932), 2,579–2,579v, in Bojko and Bednarek, *Holodomor*, 227.

19. Catherine Merridale, 'The 1937 Census and the Limits of Stalinist Rule', *The Historical Journal* 39, no. 1 (1 March 1996), 226.

20. Ibid., 230.

21. Ibid., 235–40.

22. A. G. Volkov, 'Perepis' naseleniia SSSR 1937 goda: Istoriia i materialy/Ekspress-informatsiia', *Istoriia Statistiki* 3–5, no. chast' II (1990), 16–18.

23. I. Sautin, 'The National Census – a Duty of the Whole People', trans. 'Seventeen Moments in Soviet History, an Online Archive of Primary Sources', *Bol'shevik* 23–24 (23 December 1938), http://soviethistory.msu.edu/1939-2/the-lost-census/the-lost-census-texts/duty-of-the-whole-people.

24. Interview with Oleh Wolowyna, April 2016.

25. Volkov, 'Perepis' naseleniia SSSR 1937 goda', 16–18.

26. 'Seventeen Moments in Soviet History, an Online Archive of Primary Sources', trans., 'The All-Union Census – a Most Important Govern-

ment Task', *Pravda* (lead article), 29 November 1938, http://soviethistory.msu.edu/1939-2/the-lost-census/the-lost-census-texts/duty-of-the-whole-people.

27. Mark Tolts, 'The Soviet Censuses of 1937 and 1939: Some Problems of Data Evaluation', presented at the International Conference on Soviet Population in the 1920s and 1930s, Toronto, 1995, 4.

28. Ibid., 9–10.

29. Stepan Baran, 'Z nashoï trahediï za Zbruchem', *Dilo* (Lviv) 21, May 1933.

30. Leonard Leshuk, *Days of Famine, Nights of Terror: First-Hand Accounts of Soviet Collectivization 1928–1934* (Washington, D.C.: Europa University Press, 2000), 121.

31. Robert Kuśnierz, *Ukraina w Latach Kolektywizacji i Wielkiego Głodu (1929–1933)* (Toruń: Grado, 2006), 214–17.

32. Testimony of Myroslav Prokop, in Mytsyk et al., eds., *Ukraïns'kyi holokost*, vol. 5, 107–10; Kuśnierz, *Ukraina w Latach Kolektywizacji*, 215.

33. Kuśnierz, *Ukraina w Latach Kolektywizacji*, 220.

34. S. Sipko, 'The Winnipeg Free Press and the Winnipeg Tribune: A Report for the Holodomor Research and Education Consortium', December 2013, excerpted from the archives of the copyright holder, the Ukrainian Canadian Research and Documentation Centre, 5.

35. 'Policy of Soviet Regime Scored by Ukrainians Here – Responsible for Millions of Deaths from Starvation, It Is Claimed', *Winnipeg Free Press* (8 September 1933), 5.

36. Kuśnierz, *Ukraina w Latach Kolektywizacji*, 221–7.

37. DATO 231/1/2067 (1933), 38-41, in Bojko and Bednarek, *Holodomor*, 504–5.

38. McVay and Luciuk, *The Holy See and the Holodomor*, ix, 5.

39. 'Cardinal Asks Aid in Russian Famine', *The New York Times* (20 August 1933).

40. 'Ukrains'kyi Holodomor ochyma avstriitsia', *Radio Svoboda*. Last modified 28 April 2017, accessed 2017. http://www.radiosvoboda.org/a/holodomor-ukraine-1933/25177046.html. Some of the photographs were published in Dr Ewald Ammende, *Muss Russland hungern? Menschen- und Völkerschicksale in der Sowjetunion* (Vienna: Braumüller, 1935). Wienerberger himself published a memoir: *Hart auf Hart [Hard Times] 15 Jahre Ingenieur in Sowjetrußland. Ein Tatsachenbericht* (Salzburg: Pustet, 1939).

41. McVay and Luciuk, *The Holy See and the Holodomor*, viii–xiv.

42. Graziosi, ' "Lettres de Kharkov" ', 57–61.

43. HDA SBU 13/1611 (1933), 41-4, in Bojko and Bednarek, *Holodomor*, 507.

44. Gustav Hilger and Alfred G. Meyer, *The Incompatible Allies: A Memoir-History of German-Soviet Relations, 1918–1941* (New York: Macmillan, 1953), 256.

45. Graziosi, ' "Lettres de Kharkov" ', 7.

46. Bruski, 'In Search of New Sources', 222–4.

47. Carynnyk et al., eds., *The Foreign Office and the Famine*, 105.

48. Ibid., 135.

49. Ibid., 329, 397.

50. Beatrice Webb and Sidney Webb, *Is Soviet Communism a New Civilisation?* (London: The Left Review, 1936), 29.

51. Stanley Weintraub, 'GBS and the Despots', *The Times Literary Supplement Online* (22 August 2011). http://www.the-tls.co.uk/articles/public/gbs-and-the-despots.

52. Lyons, *Assignment in Utopia*, 430.

53. Andrei Platonovich Platonov, *Fourteen Little Red Huts and Other Plays*, trans. Robert Chandler, Jesse Irwin and Susan Larsen (New York: Columbia University Press, 2016), 92.

54. Etienne Thevenin, 'France, Germany and Austria Facing the Famine of 1932–1933 in Ukraine', presented at the James Mace Memorial Panel, IAUS Congress, Donetsk, Ukraine (6 June 2005). http://www.colley.co.uk/garethjones/ukraine2005/Etienne%20Thevein%20%20English%20translation.pdf.

55. TsDAHOU 1/20/6204 (1933), in Marochko and Movchan, *Holodomor 1932–1933 rokiv v Ukraïni*, 257.

56. Quoted in Thevenin, 'France, Germany and Austria', 8.

57. Alva Christiansen, 'American Girls Seized, Expelled from Turkestan', *Chicago Daily Tribune* (23 January 1933).

58. Rhea Clyman, 'Writer Driven From Russia', *Toronto Evening Telegram* (20 September 1932).

59. Rhea Clyman, 'Children Lived on Grass', *Toronto Evening Telegram* (16 May 1933).

60. Lyons, *Asignment in Utopia*, 573–5.

61. William Henry Chamberlin, 'Soviet Taboos', *Foreign Affairs* 13, no. 3 (1935), 431.

62. Walter Duranty, *I Write as I Please* (New York: Simon and Schuster, 1935), 304.

63. Amity Shlaes, *The Forgotten Man: A New History of the Great Depression* (London: Pimlico, 2009), 47–84, 133.

64. Chamberlin, 'Soviet Taboos', 433.

65. Carynnyk et al., eds., *The Foreign Office and the Famine*, 209.

66. Chamberlin, 'Soviet Taboos', 432–3.

67. Carynnyk et al., eds., *The Foreign Office and the Famine*, 202–9.
68. Lyons, *Assignment in Utopia*, 574.
69. Biographical details from Ray Gamache, *Gareth Jones: Eyewitness to History* (Cardiff: Welsh Academic Press, 2013).
70. Lyons, *Assignment in Utopia*, 575.
71. Jones's diary was preserved by his sister at her home in Wales, rediscovered by his grand-nephew, Nigel Colley, and published as Gareth Jones, *Tell Them We Are Starving: The 1933 Diaries of Gareth Jones*, ed. Lubomyr Y. Luciuk (Kingston, Ontario: Kashtan Press, 2015).
72. Gareth Jones, 'Soviet Confiscate Part of Workers' Wages', *Daily Express* (5 April 1933), 8.
73. Luciuk, *Tell Them We Are Starving*, 131.
74. Ibid., 184–6.
75. Gareth Jones, 'Fate of Thrifty in USSR: Gareth Jones Tells How Communists Seized All Land and Let Peasants Starve', *Los Angeles Examiner* (14 January 1935).
76. Luciuk, ed., *Tell Them We Are Starving*, 190.
77. Ibid., 204.
78. Gareth Jones, 'Famine Grips Russia, Millions Dying. Idle on Rise, Says Briton', *Chicago Daily News and Evening Post Foreign Service* (29 March 1933), 1; Edgar Ansel Mowrer, 'Russian Famine Now as Great as Starvation of 1921, Says Secretary of Lloyd George', *Chicago Daily News Foreign Service* (29 March 1933), 2; Gamache, *Gareth Jones: Eyewitness to History*, 183.
79. Gareth Jones, 'Press Release quoted in "Famine Grips Russia Millions Dying. Idle on Rise, Says Briton"', *Evening Post Foreign Service* (29 March 1933).
80. Nigel Linsan Colley, '"1933 Newspaper Articles". Gareth Jones – Hero of Ukraine', accessed 2017, http://www.garethjones.org/overview/articles1933.htm.
81. Teresa Cherfas, 'Reporting Stalin's Famine: Jones and Muggeridge: A Case Study in Forgetting and Rediscovery', *Kritika: Explorations in Russian and Eurasian History* 14, no. 4 (August 2013), 775–804.
82. Lyons, *Assignment in Utopia*, 572, 575–6.
83. Walter Duranty, 'Russians Hungry But Not Starving', *The New York Times* (31 March 1933).
84. Margaret Siriol Colley, *Gareth Jones: A Manchukuo Incident* (Newark, NJ: N. L. Colley, 2001).
85. Thevenin, 'France, Germany and Austria', 9.
86. Carynnyk et al., eds., *The Foreign Office and the Famine*, 329, 397.

87. Snyder, *Bloodlands*, 50.
88. Sally J. Taylor, *Stalin's Apologist: Walter Duranty, the New York Times's Man in Moscow* (New York: Oxford University Press, 1990), xx.
89. Aleck Woollcott quoted in Taylor, *Stalin's Apologist*, 191.

15. THE HOLODOMOR IN HISTORY AND MEMORY

1. http://taras-shevchenko.infolike.net/poem-calamity-again-taras-shevchenko-english-translation-by-john-weir.html. Originally published in Taras Shevchenko, *Zibrannia tvoriv*, vol. 2 (Kyiv, 2003), 303, trans. John Wier.
2. Olexa Woropay, *The Ninth Circle: In Commemoration of the Victims of the Famine of 1933* (Cambridge, MA: Harvard Ukrainian Studies Fund, 1983), 16.
3. Testimony of Volodymyr Mykolaiovych Chepur, in Veselova and Nikiliev, *Pam'iat' narodu*, vol. 2, 758.
4. Mytsyk et al., eds., *Ukraïns'kyi holokost*, vol. 4, 374.
5. Testimony of Havrylo Prokopenko, in Kovalenko and Maniak, eds., *33-i Holod*, 196–7.
6. Testimony of Volodymyr Samoiliuk, in ibid., 95–6.
7. Karel Berkhoff, *Harvest of Despair: Life and Death in Ukraine under Nazi Rule* (Cambridge, MA: Belknap Press, 2004), 20.
8. O. O. Zakharchenko, 'Natsysts'ka propahanda pro zlochyny Stalinshchyny naperedodni i na pochatku Druhoï Svitovoï Viiny', *Naukovyi visnyk Mykolaïvs'koho Derzhavnoho Universytetu*, Istorychni nauky 21 (2008), available online at http://www.nbuv.gov.ua/old_jrn/Soc_Gum/Nvmdu.
9. Berkhoff, *Harvest of Despair*, 117.
10. Snyder, *Bloodlands*, 179–80.
11. Berkhoff, *Harvest of Despair*, 253.
12. Lizzie Collingham, *The Taste of War: World War II and the Battle for Food* (New York: Penguin Press, 2012), 35–7; Snyder, *Bloodlands*, 160–3.
13. Alex J. Kay, 'German Economic Plans for the Occupied Soviet Union and their Implementation', in Timothy Snyder and Ray Brandon, eds., *Stalin and Europe: Imitation and Domination, 1928–1953* (Oxford: Oxford University Press, 2014), 171.
14. Snyder, *Bloodlands*, 164.
15. Kay, 'German Economic Plans for the Occupied Soviet Union and their Implementation', 176.

16. Berkhoff, *Harvest of Despair*, 165.
17. Kay, 'German Economic Plans for the Occupied Soviet Union and their Implementation', 106; Snyder, *Bloodlands*, 174.
18. Woropay, *The Ninth Circle*, 16.
19. Joseph Goebbels, 'Communism with the Mask Off', trans. the Nazi Party, *Nazi and East German Propaganda Online Archive*, last modified 13 September 1935, http://research.calvin.edu/german-propaganda-archive/goebmain.htm; A. I. Kudriachenko, ed., *Holodomor v Ukraïni 1932–1933 rokiv za dokumentamy politychnoho arkhivu Ministerstva Zakordonnykh Sprav Federatyvnoï Respubliky Nimechchyna* (Kyiv: Natsional'nyi Instytut Stratehichnykh Doslidzhen', 2008).
20. O. O. Maievs'kyi, 'Politychni plakat i karykatura, iak zasoby ideolohichnoï borot'by v Ukraïni 1939–1945 rr.', PhD dissertation, Instytut Istoriï Ukraïny Natsional'na Akademiia Nauk Ukraïny (2016), 277–8.
21. V. Kotorenko, 'Rik pratsi v sil's'komu hospodarstvi bez zhydobol'shevykiv', *Ukraïnskyi Khliborob* 7 (July 1942), 2, cited in O. O. Zakharchenko, 'Agrarna polityka Natsystiv na okupovanyii terytoriï Ukraïny', *Istoricheskaia Pamiat' (Odessa)* 2 (2000), 45–6.
22. Oleksandr Dovzhenko, *Ukraïna v ohni: Kinopovist', shchodennyk* (Kyiv: Rad. Pys'mennyk, 1990), 200.
23. Berkhoff, 'The Great Famine in Light of the German Invasion and Occupation', 168.
24. Ibid., 166.
25. Ibid., 167.
26. Bohdan Klid, 'Daily Life under Soviet Rule and the Holodomor in Memoirs and Testimonies of the Late 1940s: Some Preliminary Assessments', presented at the Canadian Association of Slavists 2015 Annual Conference, Ottawa, Ontario, 26 May 2015, citing S. Sosnovyi's *Nova Ukraïna* (8 November 1942).
27. Oleksa Veretenchenko, 'Somewhere in the Distant Wild North', from the series of poems *1933*, published in *Nova Ukraïna* between 1942 and 1943, translated by the Ukrainian Canadian Congress, Toronto Branch, and available at http://faminegenocide.com/commemoration/poetry/2003-1933.htm.
28. Berkhoff, 'The Great Famine in Light of the German Invasion and Occupation', 169.
29. Ibid., 171.
30. Svetlana Aleksievich, *U Voiny ne zhenskoe litso* (Moscow: Vremia, 2013), 11.

31. Berkhoff, 'The Great Famine in Light of the German Invasion and Occupation', 169.

32. Volodymyr Viatrovych, 'Oleksandra Radchenko: Persecuted for her Memory', Stichting Totalitaire Regimes en hun Slachtoffers, project of the Platform of European Memory and Conscience, http://www.sgtrs. nl/data/files/Radchenko%20Oekraine.pdf.

33. Elena Zubkova, *Russia after the War: Hopes, Illusions and Disappointments, 1945–1957*, trans. Hugh Ragsdale (London and New York: Routledge, 2015), 40–50; Stephen Wheatcroft, 'The Soviet Famine of 1946–47, the Weather and Human Agency in Historical Perspective', *Europe-Asia Studies* 64, no. 6 (August 2012), 987–1,005.

34. Woropay, *The Ninth Circle*, 16–17.

35. Ibid., xviii.

36. 'Zum 15 Jahrestag Der Furchtbaren, Durch Das blutdürstige Kommunistische Moskau Organisikhten Hungersnot in der Ukraine', Oseredok Project, Holodomor Research and Education Consortium. Flyers in Ukrainian, English, and German, distributed by Ukrainian participants at an 11 April 1948 demonstration in Hanover, Germany, on the occasion of the fifteenth anniversary of the Famine of 1932–3 in Ukraine. Original, typed, http://holodomor.ca/oseredok-project.

37. S. Sosnovyi, 'Pravda pro velykyi holod na Ukraïni v 1932–1933 rokakh', *Ukraïns'ki visti* (7 February 1948), 4.

38. Klid, 'Daily Life under Soviet Rule'.

39. Ibid.

40. Pidhainy, ed., *The Black Deeds of the Kremlin*, vol. 1, 222–6.

41. Ibid., vol. 1, 243–4.

42. Ibid., vol. 1, 239.

43. Bohdan Klid, 'The Black Deeds of the Kremlin: Sixty Years Later', *Genocide Studies International* 8 (2014), 224–35.

44. Frank Sysyn, 'The Ukrainian Famine of 1932–33: The Role of the Ukrainian Diaspora in Research and Public Discussion', in Levon Chorbajian and George Shirinian, eds., *Studies in Comparative Genocide* (New York: St. Martin's Press, 1999), 182–216.

45. Klid, '*The Black Deeds of the Kremlin*: Sixty Years Later', 229.

46. Now the Ukrainian Canadian Research and Documentation Centre: www.ucrdc.org/History.html.

47. Frank Sysyn, 'Thirty Years of Research on the Holodomor: A Balance Sheet', in Frank Sysyn and Andrij Makuch, eds., *Contextualizing the Holodomor: The Impact of Thirty Years of Ukrainian Famine Studies* (Toronto: Canadian Institute of Ukrainian Studies, 2015), 4.

48. Pierre Rigoulot, *Les Paupières Lourdes: Les Français face au Goulag: Aveuglements et Indignations* (Paris: Éditions universitaires, 1991), 1–10.

49. Vladimir Tendriakov, 'Konchina', *Moskva* 3 (1968), 37.

50. Michael Browne, ed., *Ferment in the Ukraine: Documents by V. Chornovil, I. Kandyba, L. Lukyanenko, V. Moroz and Others* (New York: Praeger Publishers, 1971), 46.

51. Ibid., 9.

52. Iurii Shapoval, 'Petro Shelest: 100th Anniversary of the Birth of One of Ukraine's Most Spectacular Political Figures', *Den [The Day]* (4 March 2008), originally published in Russian as 'Stoletnii Shelest: 14 fevralia ispolniaetsia 100 let odnomu iz samykh koloritnykh rukovoditelei USSR', *Den* (8 February 2008).

53. *Ethnocide of Ukrainians in the U.S.S.R.: An Underground Journal from Soviet Ukraine*, compiled by Maksym Sahaydak, trans. Olena Saciuk and Bohdan Yasen (Baltimore, MD: Smoloskyp Publishers, 1976).

54. John Corry, 'TV Reviews: "Firing Line" Discussion on "Harvest of Depression"', *The New York Times* (24 September 1986).

55. Sysyn, 'Thirty Years of Research on the Holodomor', 4.

56. Ibid., 7.

57. Ibid., 4.

58. Douglas Tottle, *Fraud, Famine, and Fascism: The Ukrainian Genocide Myth from Hitler to Harvard* (Toronto: Progress Books, 1987), 57, 76–7, 123, 133.

59. Lyudmyla Hrynevych, 'Vid zaperechuvannia do vymushenoho vyznannia: pro mekhanizmy vkhodzhennia temy holodu 1932–1933 rr. v ofitsiinyi publichnyi prostir u SRSR ta URSR naprykintsi 1980-kh rr.', *Problemy istorii Ukraïny: fakty, sudzhennia, poshuky: Mizhvidomchyi zbirnyk naukovykh prats'* 18 (spetsial'nyi: Holod 1932–3 rokiv-henotsyd ukrains'koho narodu) (2008), 232–44; Tottle, *Fraud, Famine, and Fascism*.

60. Jeff Coplon, 'In Search of a Soviet Holocaust: A 55-Year-Old Famine Feeds the Right', *Village Voice* (12 January 1988).

61. Sysyn, 'Thirty Years of Research on the Holodomor', 9–10.

62. U.S. Congress and Commission on the Ukraine Famine, *Investigation of the Ukrainian Famine, 1932–1933: Report to Congress*, v.

63. Ibid., vi–viii.

64. Plokhy, *The Gates of Europe*, 310.

65. 'What Chernobyl Did: Not Just a Nuclear Explosion', *Economist* (27 April 1991), pp. 21–3 (the anonymous author was Anne Applebaum).

66. Plokhy, *The Gates of Europe*, 309–10.
67. Ivan Drach, 'Vystup na IX Z'ïzdi Pys'mennykiv Ukraïny', in Oleksandr Lytvyn, ed., *Polityka: Statti, Dopovidi, Vystupy, Interv'iu* (Kyiv: Tovarystvo 'Ukraïna', 1997), 310.
68. Bohdan Nahaylo, *The Ukrainian Resurgence* (Toronto: University of Toronto Press, 1999), 62–3; see also 'Conversation with Ivan Drach', interview by Boriak Hennadii, 7 November 2016.
69. David Remnick, *Lenin's Tomb: The Last Days of the Soviet Empire* (New York: Random House, 1993), 50.
70. Nahaylo, *The Ukrainian Resurgence*, 89–91.
71. Ibid., 137.
72. Georgiy Kasianov, 'Revisiting the Great Famine of 1932–1933: Politics of Memory and Public Consciousness (Ukraine after 1991)', in Michal Kopecek, ed., *Past in the Making: Historical Revisionism in Central Europe after 1989* (Budapest: Central European University Press, 2007), 197–220.
73. Nahaylo, *The Ukrainian Resurgence*, 249.
74. Marta Kolomayets, 'Ukraine's People Recall National Tragedy of Famine-Holocaust', *Ukrainian Weekly* 61, no. 38 (19 September 1993), 1.
75. Catherine Wanner, *Burden of Dreams: History and Identity in Post-Soviet Ukraine* (University Park, PA: Pennsylvania State University Press, 1998), 154–7.
76. Ibid.

EPILOGUE: THE UKRAINIAN QUESTION RECONSIDERED

1. Raphael Lemkin, 'Soviet Genocide in the Ukraine', unpublished talk, 1953, Raphael Lemkin Papers, The New York Public Library, Manuscripts and Archives Division, Astor, Lenox and Tilden Foundations, Raphael Lemkin ZL-273. Reel 3. Available at https://www.uccla.ca/SOVIET_GENOCIDE_IN_THE_UKRAINE.pdf.
2. Two excellent books have recently expanded popular knowledge of Lemkin. See Samantha Power, *A Problem from Hell* (New York: Basic Books, 2002), and Philippe Sands, *East West Street: On the Origins of 'Genocide' and 'Crimes Against Humanity'* (New York: Knopf, 2016).
3. Raphael Lemkin, *Totally Unofficial: The Autobiography of Raphael Lemkin* (New Haven, CT, and London: Yale University Press, 2013), 19–21.

4. Raphael Lemkin, *Axis Rule in Occupied Europe: Laws of Occupation – Analysis of Government – Proposals for Redress* (Washington, D.C.: Carnegie Endowment for International Peace, 1944), 79–95.

5. Now published in Raphael Lemkin, *Lemkin on Genocide*, ed. Steven Leonard Jacobs (Lanham, MD: Lexington Books, 2012).

6. Lemkin, 'Soviet Genocide in the Ukraine'.

7. This is Naimark's argument in Norman M. Naimark, *Stalin's Genocides* (Princeton, NJ: Princeton University Press, 2010).

8. Ibid., 24.

9. Lemkin, 'Soviet Genocide in the Ukraine'.

10. Georgiy Kasianov, 'Holodomor and the Politics of Memory in Ukraine after Independence', in Vincent Comeford, Lindsay Jansen and Christian Noack, eds., *Holodomor and Gorta Mor: Histories, Memories and Representations of Famine in Ukraine and Ireland* (London: Anthem Press, 2014), 167–88.

11. 'Ruling in the criminal proceedings over genocide in Ukraine in 1932–1933', *Human Rights in Ukraine*, http://khpg.org/en/index.php?id=1265217823.

12. 'Ukraine Commemorates Holodomor', *Moscow Times* (24 November 2008).

13. Zenon Zawada, 'Eastern Ukrainians Fight to Preserve the Holodomor's Memory', *Ukrainian Weekly* 67/7 (15 February 2009), 3.

14. Cathy Young, 'Remember the Holodomor', *Weekly Standard* (8 December 2008).

15. U.S. Diplomatic Cable, 'Candid Discussion with Prince Andrew on the Kyrgyz Economy and the "Great Game" (29 October 2008)', *WikiLeaks*, https://wikileaks.org/plusd/cables/08BISHKEK1095_a.html.

16. Ella Maksimova, 'Istorik Viktor Kondrashin: "Ne Rossiia ubivala Ukrainu, Vozhd' – svoi narod"', *Izvestiia* (22 October 2008).

17. Wolowyna et al., 'Regional Variations of 1932–34 Famine Losses in Ukraine', 175–202.

18. Infamously, Lenin was so angered by the peasants of Penza in 1918 that he called for them to be 'pitilessly suppressed'. He wrote a famous telegram about the Penza rebellion, which finished with a list of instructions:
'Hang (and make sure that the hanging takes place in full view of the people) no fewer than one hundred known landlords, rich men, bloodsuckers.
Publish their names.
Seize all their grain . . .'

Robert W. Service, *Lenin: A Biography* (London: Papermac, 2001), 365.

19. V. V. Kondrashin and S. V. Kul'chyts'kyi, 'O Samom Glavnom: professor Stanislav Kul'chitskii i ego rossiiskii kollega Viktor Kondrashin: chem byl Golodomor 1932–1933 godov?', *Den'* (Kyiv, 3 June 2008).

20. Alexander J. Motyl, 'Yanukovych and Stalin's Genocide', *Ukraine's Orange Blues* in *World Affairs Journal Online* (29 November 2012) http://www.worldaffairsjournal.org/blog/alexander-j-motyl/yanukovych-and-stalin%E2%80%99s-genocide.

21. 'Ukrainian Sues Yanukovych over Famine Statement,' *Radio Free Europe Radio Liberty*, last modified 15 June 2010, http://www.rferl.org/amp/Ukrainian_Sues_Yanukovych_Over_Famine_Statement/2072294.html.

22. Halya Coynash, 'Kremlin's Proxies Purge Memory of Victims of Holodomor and Political Repression', *Human Rights in Ukraine: Information Website of the Kharkiv Human Rights Protection Group* (18 August 2015), http://khpg.org/en/index.php?id=1439816093.

23. Ekaterina Blinova, 'Holodomor Hoax: Joseph Stalin's Crime that Never Took Place', *Sputnik News* (9 August 2015), https://sputniknews.com/politics/201508091025560345; see also Cathy Young, 'Russia Denies Stalin's Killer Famine', *Daily Beast* (31 October 2015), http://www.thedailybeast.com/articles/2015/10/31/russia-denies-stalin-s-killer-famine.html.

24. In a peculiar sign of the times, newcoldwar.org, a website devoted to undermining 'the great injustices ... committed by the government installed in Kiev in February [2014] against the whole Ukrainian people' created a link to the writings of Mark Tauger, an American academic. Tauger argues that the Ukrainian famine of 1932–3 was caused by poor weather and plant diseases (for which there is no archival evidence) and thus, by definition, was not a 'genocide'. 'Archive of Writings of Professor Mark Tauger on the Famine Scourges of the Early Years of the Soviet Union', *The New Cold War: Ukraine and Beyond* (23 June 2015).https://www.newcoldwar.org/archive-of-writings-of-professor-mark-tauger-on-the-famine-scourges-of-the-early-years-of-the-soviet-union.

25. Ievgen Vorobiov, 'Why Ukrainians Are Speaking More Ukrainian', *Foreign Policy* (26 June 2015). http://foreignpolicy.com/2015/06/26/why-ukrainians-are-speaking-more-ukrainian.

Selected Bibiliography

ARCHIVES
Canada

UCRDC   Ukrainian Canadian Research and Documentation Centre

Russia/Soviet Union

Archives, some no longer in use, that provided documents cited in collections and monographs:

APRF   Arkhiv Prezidenta Rossiiskoi Federatsii (Archive of the President of the Russian Federation)

GARF   Gosudarstvennyi arkhiv Rossiiskoi Federatsii (State Archive of the Russian Federation)

RGAE   Rossiiskii gosudarstvennyi arkhiv ekonomiki (Russian State Archive of Economics)

RGASPI   Rossiiskii gosudarstvennyi arkhiv sotsial'no-politicheskoi istorii (Russian State Archive of Socio-Political History)

RGVA   Rossiiskii gosudarstvennyi voennyi arkhiv (Russian State Military Archive)

RTsKhIDNI   Rossiiskii tsentr khraneniia i izucheniia dokumentov noveishei istorii (Russian Centre for the Storage and Study of Contemporary History). This archive has now been merged with RGASPI.

TsA FSB RF   Tsentral'nyi arkhiv Federal'noi sluzhby bezopasnosti Rossiiskoi Federatsii (Central Archive of the Federal Security Service of the Russian Federation)

TsGANKh   Tsentral'nyi gosudarstvennyi arkhiv narodnogo khoziaistva SSSR (Central State Archive of the National Economy of the USSR); the old name for the RGAE.

Ukraine

Archives, some no longer in use, which were used by the author or which provided documents cited in collections and monographs:

DADO — Derzhavnyi arkhiv Dnipropetrovs'koï oblasti (State Archive of the Dnipropetrovsk Oblast)

DADskO — Derzhavni Arkhiv Donets'koi Oblasti

DAKhO — Derzhavnyi arkhiv Khersons'koï oblasti (State Archive of Kherson Oblast)

DATO — Derzhavnyi arkhiv Ternopil's'koï oblasti (State Archive of Ternopil' Oblast)

DAVO — Derzhavnyi arkhiv Vinnyts'koï oblasti (State Archive of Vinnytsia Oblast)

DAZhO — Derzhavnyi arkhiv Zhytomyrs'koï oblasti (State Archive of Zhytomyr Oblast)

HDA SBU — Haluzevyi derzhavnyi arkhiv Sluzhby Bezpeky Ukraïny (State Archive of the Security Service of Ukraine)

PA — Arkhiv Instytutu Istoriï Partiï (Archive of the Institute of the History of the Party); this archive has been renamed TsDAHOU

TsDAHOU — Tsentral'nyi derzhavnyi arkhiv hromads'kykh ob'ednan' Ukraïny (Central State Archive of Public Organizations of Ukraine)

TsDAVOU — Tsentral'nyi derzhavnyi arkhiv vyshchykh orhaniv vlady ta upravlinnia (Central State Archive of Supreme Bodies of Power and Government of Ukraine)

TsDAZhR — Tsentral'nyi derzhavnyi arkhiv Zhovtnevoï Revoliutsiï Ukraïns'koï Radians'koï Sotsialistychnoï Respubliky (Central State Archive of the October Revolution, Ukrainian Soviet Socialist Republic); this archive has been renamed TsDAVOU.

EDITED DOCUMENT COLLECTIONS

Berelovich, Alexis, V. A., and Institut rossiiskoi istorii (Rossiiskaia Akademiia Nauk), eds. *Sovetskaia derevnia glazami VChK-OGPU-NKVD, 1918–1939: dokumenty i materialy.* 4 vols. Moscow: ROSSPEN, 1998–2012.

Bojko, Diana, and Jerzy Bednarek. *Holodomor: The Great Famine in Ukraine 1932–1933*, from the series *Poland and Ukraine in the 1930s–1940s: Unknown Documents from the Archives of the Secret Services.* Warsaw: Institute of National Remembrance, Commission of the Prosecution of Crimes against the Polish Nation, 2009.

Borkowski, Jan, ed. *Rok 1920: Wojna Polsko-Radziecka we wspomnieniach i innych dokumentach.* Warsaw: Państwowy Instytut Wydawniczy, 1990.

Borysenko, Valentyna, V. N. Danylenko, Serhij Kokin, et al., eds., *Rozsekrechena pam'iat': Holodomor 1932–1933 rokiv v Ukraïni v dokumentakh GPU-NKVD.* Kyiv: Stylos, 2007.

Carynnyk, Marco, Bohdan S. Kordan, and Lubomyr Y. Luciuk, eds. *The Foreign Office and the Famine: British Documents on Ukraine and the Great Famine of 1932–1933.* Kingston, Ontario: Limeston Press, 1988.

Colley, Nigel Linsan. ' "1933 Newspaper Articles". Gareth Jones – Hero of Ukraine', accessed 11 January 2017. http://www.garethjones.org/over view/articles1933.htm.

Danilov, V., R. Manning, and L. Viola, eds. *Tragediia sovetskoi derevni, kollektivizatsiia i raskulachivanie: dokumenty i materialy v 5 tomakh, 1927–1939.* 5 vols. Moscow: Rossiiskaia polit. Entisklopediia, 1999–2006.

——, and N. A. Ivnitskii, eds. *Dokumenty svidetel'stvuiut: iz istorii derevni nakanune i v khode kollektivizatsii, 1927–1932 gg.* Moscow: Politizdat, 1989.

Danylenko, V. M. et al., eds. *Holodomor 1932–1933 rokiv v Ukraïni za dokumentamy HDA SBU: anotovanyi dovidnyk.* L'viv: Tsentr Doslidzhen' Vyzvol'noho Rukhu, 2010.

——. *Pavlohrads'ke povstannia, 1930: dokumenty i materialy.* Kyiv: Ukraïns'kyi Pys'mennyk, 2009.

Graziosi, Andrea. *Lettere da Kharkov. La carestia in Ucraina e nel Caucaso del nord nei rapporti diplomatici italiani 1923–33.* Turin: Einaudi, 1991. http://www.ibs.it/lettere-da-kharkov-carestia-in-libro-vari/e/9788806121822.

——. ' "Lettres de Kharkov": La famine en Ukraine et dans le Caucase du Nord (à travers les rapports des diplomates italiens, 1932–1934)', *Cahiers du monde russe et soviétique* 30, no. 1 (1989). http://www.persee.fr/doc/cmr_0008-0160_1989_num_30_1_2176.

——. *Lysty z Kharkova: Holod v Ukraïni ta na Pivnichnomu Kavkazi v povidomlenniakh italiis'kykh dyplomativ 1932–33 roky.* Kharkiv: Folio, 2007.

Khlevniuk, O. V. et al., eds. *Stalin i Kaganovich: perepiska, 1931–1936 gg.* Moscow: ROSSPEN, 2001.

Kokin, S. A., Valerii Vasyl'ev, and Nicolas Werth, eds. 'Dokumenty orhaniv VKP(b) ta DPU USRR pro nastroï i modeli povedinky partiino-radians'kykh pratsivnykiv u respublitsi, 1932–33 rr.', *Z arkhiviv VUChK-GPU-NKVD-KGB* 1–2, nos. 40–1 (2013).

——. *Partiino-Radians'ke kerivnytstvo USRR pid chas Holodomoru 1932–33 rr.: vozhdi, pratsivnyky, aktyvisty: zbirnyk dokumentiv ta materialiv*. Kyiv: Instytut Istoriï Ukraïny NAN Ukraïny, 2013.

Kondrashin, V. V. et al., eds. *Golod v SSSR: 1929–1934*. Rossiia XX vek. Moscow: Mezhdunarodnyi fond 'Demokratiia', 2011.

Kudriachenko, A. I., ed. *Holodomor v Ukraïni 1932–1933 rokiv za dokumentamy politychnoho arkhivu ministerstva zakordonnykh sprav Federatyvnoï Respubliky Nimechchyna*. Kyiv: Natsional'nyi Instytut Stratehichnykh Doslidzhen', 2008.

Kul'chyts'kyi, Stanislav, ed. *Kolektyvizatsiia i holod na Ukraïni, 1929–1933: zbirnyk dokumentiv i materialiv*. Kyiv: Naukova Dumka, 1992.

Kuśnierz, Robert. *Pomór w 'raju bolszewickim'. Głód na Ukrainie w latach 1932-1933 w świetle polskich dokumentów dyplomatycznych i dokumentów wywiadu*. Toruń: Wydawnictwo Adam Marszałek, 2009.

Le Comité Commémoratif Simon Petliura. *Documents sur les Pogroms en Ukraine et l'assassinat de Simon Petliura à Paris*. Paris: Librairie du Trident, 1927.

Lenin, V. I. *Collected Works*. Moscow: Progress Publishers, 1965.

Lozyts'kyi, V. S. *Holodomor 1932–1933 rokiv v Ukraïni: zlochyn vlady – trahediia narodu: dokumenty i materialy*. Kyiv: Heneza, 2008.

Pyrih, R. Ia., ed. *Holodomor 1932–1933 rokiv v Ukraïni: Dokumenty i materialy*. Kyiv: Kyievo-Mohylians'ka Akademiia, 2007.

Shapoval, Iurii, Vadym Zolotar'ov, and Volodymyr Prystaiko. *ChK-GPU-NKVD v Ukraïni: osoby, fakty, dokumenty*. Kyiv: Abrys, 1997.

Stalin, Josef. *Works*. 13 vols. Moscow: Foreign Languages Publishing House, 1954. http://www.marxists.org/reference/archive/stalin/works/1933/01/07.htm.

Szczesniak, Boleslaw. *The Russian Revolution and Religion: A Collection of Documents Concerning the Suppression of Religion by the Communists, 1917–1925*. Notre Dame, IN: University of Notre Dame Press, 1959.

Volkov, A. G. 'Perepis' naseleniia SSSR 1937 goda: Istoriia i materialy/Ekspress-informatsiia', *Istoriia Statistiki* 3–5, no. chast' II (1990), 6–63.

MEMOIRS AND ORAL HISTORY COLLECTIONS

Borysenko, Valentyna. *A Candle in Remembrance: An Oral History of the Ukrainian Genocide of 1933–34 (Svicha Pam'iati)*, trans. Mark Tarnawsky. New York: Ukrainian Women's League of America, 2010.

———. *Svicha pam'iati: Usna istoriia pro henotsyd ukraïntsiv u 1932–1933 rokakh*. Kyiv: Stylos, 2007.

Dolot, Miron. *Execution by Hunger: The Hidden Holocaust*. New York: W. W. Norton, 1985.

Duranty, Walter. *I Write as I Please*. New York: Simon and Schuster, 1935.

Epp, Heinrich. 'The Day the World Ended: Dec. 7, 1919, Steinbach, Russia', trans. D. F. Plett, *Preservings: Newsletter of the Hanover Steinbach Historical Society*, no. 8, part 2 (June 1996), 5–7.

Harvard Project on the Soviet Social System Online. Fung Library, Harvard University, http://nrs.harvard.edu/urn-3:FHCL:fun00001.

Jones, Gareth. *Tell Them We Are Starving: The 1933 Diaries of Gareth Jones*, ed. Lubomyr Y. Luciuk (Kingston, Ontario: Kashtan Press, 2015).

Karas, A. V. *Svidchennia ochevydtsiv pro holod 1930–40-kh rr. na Siovershchyni*. Hlukhiv: RVV HDPU, 2008.

Kopelev, Lev. *The Education of a True Believer*, trans. Gary Kern. London: Wildwood House, 1981.

———. *To Be Preserved Forever*, trans. Anthony Austin. New York: Lippincott, 1977.

Kovalenko, L. B., and Volodymyr Maniak, eds. *33-i Holod: narodna knyha-memorial*. Kyiv: Radians'kyi Pys'mennyk, 1991.

Kravchenko, Victor. *I Chose Freedom: The Personal and Political Life of a Soviet Official*, trans. Rhett R. Ludwikowski. London: Robert Hale, 1946.

Lemkin, Raphael. *Totally Unofficial: The Autobiography of Raphael Lemkin*. New Haven, CT, and London: Yale University Press, 2013.

Leshuk, Leonard. *Days of Famine, Nights of Terror: First-Hand Accounts of Soviet Collectivization 1928–1934*. Washington, D.C.: Europa University Press, 2000.

Lyons, Eugene. *Assignment in Utopia*. New York: Harcourt, Brace, 1937.

Mytsyk, Iurii et al., eds. *Ukraïns'kyi holokost 1932–1933: svidchennia tykh, khto vyzhyv*. 10 vols. Kyiv: Kyievo-Mohylians'ka Akademiia, 2004–14.

Price, M. Philips. *My Reminiscences of the Russian Revolution*. London: George Allen & Unwin, 1921.

Ukraïns'kyi Instytut Natsional'noï Pam'iati, and V. Iushchenko, eds. *Natsional'na knyha pam'iati zhertv Holodomoru 1932–1933 rokiv v Ukraïni.* Kyiv: Vydavnytstvo 'Oleny Telihy', 2008.

——, and E. I. Borodin et al., eds. *Natsional'na knyha pam'iati zhertv Holodomoru 1932–1933 rokiv v Ukraïni: Dnipropetrovs'ka oblast'.* Dnipropetrovsk: ART-PRES, 2008.

——, and T. T. Dmytrenko, eds. *Natsional'na knyha pam'iati zhertv Holodomoru 1932–1933 rokiv v Ukraïni: Kirovohrads'ka oblast'.* Kirovohrad: TOV 'Imeks LTD', 2008.

——, and V. P. Latsyba, eds. *Natsional'na knyha pam'iati zhertv Holodomoru 1932–1933 rokiv v Ukraïni: Vinnyts'ka oblast'.* Vinnytsia: DP 'DFK', 2008.

——, and F. H. Turchenko, eds. *Natsional'na knyha pam'iati zhertv Holodomoru 1932–1933 rokiv v Ukraïni: Zaporiz'ka oblast'.* Zaporizhzhia: Dyke Pole, 2008.

——, and V. I. Ul'iachenko, eds. *Natsional'na knyha pam'iati zhertv Holodomoru 1932–1933 rokiv v Ukraïni: Kyïvs'ka oblast'.* Bila Tserkva: Bukva, 2008.

——, and S. H. Vodotyka. *Natsional'na knyha pam'iati zhertv Holodomoru 1932–1933 rokiv v Ukraïni: Khersons'ka oblast',* eds. I. P. Iukhnovs'kyi et al. Kherson: Vydavnytstvo 'Naddniprians'ka pravda', 2008.

United States Congress, and Commission on the Ukraine Famine. *Investigation of the Ukrainian Famine, 1932–1933: Report to Congress.* Adopted by the Commission, 19 April 1988, submitted to Congress, 22 April 1988. Washington, D.C.: U.S. G.P.O.: For sale by Supt. of Docs., U.S. G.P.O., 1988.

——. *Investigation of the Ukrainian Famine, 1932–1933: First Interim Report.* Meetings and hearings of and before the Commission on the Ukraine Famine held in 1986: organizational meeting, Washington, D.C., 23 April 1986: meeting and hearing, Washington, D.C., 8 October 1986: hearing, Glen Spey, New York, 26 October 1986: hearing, Chicago, Illinois, 7 November 1986: hearing, Warren, Michigan, 24 November 1986. Washington, D.C.: U.S. G.P.O.: For sale by the Supt. of Docs., U.S. G.P.O., 1987.

——. *Investigation of the Ukrainian Famine, 1932–1933: Second Interim Report.* Meetings and hearings of and before the Commission on the Ukraine Famine held in 1987: hearing, San Francisco, California, 10 February 1987; hearing, Phoenix, Arizona, 13 February 1987; hearing and meeting, Washington, D.C., 30 April 1987; hearing, Philadelphia,

Pennsylvania, 5 June 1987. Washington, D.C.: U.S. G.P.O.: For sale by the Supt. of Docs., U.S. G.P.O., 1988.

——, James E. Mace, and Leonid Heretz. *Investigation of the Ukrainian Famine, 1932–1933*. Oral history project of the Commission on the Ukraine Famine. Washington, D.C.: U.S. G.P.O., 1990.

Veselova, O. M., and O. F. Nikiliev. *Pam'iat' narodu: Henotsyd v Ukraïni holodom 1932–1933 rokiv: svidchennia*. 2 vols. Kyiv: Vydavnychyi dim 'Kalyta', 2009.

Woropay, Olexa. *The Ninth Circle: In Commemoration of the Victims of the Famine of 1933*. Cambridge, MA: Harvard Ukrainian Studies Fund, 1983.

SELECTED SECONDARY SOURCES

Adams, Arthur E. *Bolsheviks in the Ukraine: The Second Campaign, 1918–1919*. New Haven, CT: Yale University Press, 1963.

Applebaum, Anne. *Gulag: A History*. New York: Doubleday, 2003.

Arshinov, Peter. *The History of the Makhnovist Movement (1918–1921)*, trans. Fredy and Lorraine Perlman. London: Freedom Press, 1974.

Ball, Alan M. *Russia's Last Capitalists: The Nepmen, 1921–29*. Berkeley, CA: University of California Press, 1987.

Berkhoff, Karel. 'The Great Famine in Light of the German Invasion and Occupation', in *After the Holodomor: The Enduring Impact of the Great Famine of Ukraine*, eds. Andrea Graziosi, Lubomyr Hajda, and Halyna Hryn. Cambridge, MA: Harvard Ukrainian Research Institute, 2014.

——. *Harvest of Despair: Life and Death in Ukraine under Nazi Rule*. Cambridge, MA: Belknap Press, 2004.

Bilenky, Serhiy. *Romantic Nationalism in Eastern Europe: Russian, Polish and Ukrainian Political Imaginations*. Stanford, CA: Stanford University Press, 2012.

Bondar, N. I., and O. V. Matveev. *Istoricheskaia pamiat' naseleniia iuga Rossii o golode 1932–33: materialy nauchno-prakticheskoi konferentsii*. Krasnodar: Isd-vo Traditsiia, 2009.

Boriak, Hennadii. 'Sources and Resources on the Famine in Ukraine's Archival System', *Harvard Ukrainian Studies* 27, nos. 2004–5 (2008), 117–47.

Boriak, Tetiana. *1933: 'I choho vy shche zhyvi?'* Kyiv: Clio, NAN Ukraïny, 2016.

Borys, Jurij. *The Sovietization of Ukraine 1917–1923: The Communist Doctrine and Practice of National Self-Determination*. Edmonton, Alberta: Canadian Institute of Ukrainian Studies, 1980.

Bulgakov, Mikhail. *White Guard*, trans. Marian Schwartz. New Haven, CT: Yale University Press, 2008.

Carr, E. H., and R. W. Davies. *A History of Soviet Russia: Foundations of a Planned Economy, 1926–1929.* 4 vols. London: Macmillan, 1978.

Chamberlin, William Henry. 'Soviet Taboos', *Foreign Affairs* 13, no. 3 (1935), 431–40.

Cherfas, Teresa. 'Reporting Stalin's Famine: Jones and Muggeridge: A Case Study in Forgetting and Rediscovery', *Kritika: Explorations in Russian and Eurasian History* 14, no. 4 (August 2013), 775–804.

Colley, Margaret Siriol. *Gareth Jones: A Manchukuo Incident.* Newark, NJ: N. L. Colley, 2001.

Collingham, Lizzie. *The Taste of War: WWII and the Battle for Food.* New York: Penguin Press, 2012.

Comeford, Vincent, Lindsay Jansen and Christian Noack, eds. *Holodomor and Gorta Mor: Histories, Memories and Representations of Famine in Ukraine and Ireland.* London: Anthem Press, 2014.

Conquest, Robert. *The Great Terror: Stalin's Purge of the Thirties*, rev. edn. London: Macmillan, 1968.

——. *The Harvest of Sorrow: Soviet Collectivization and the Terror-Famine.* New York: Oxford University Press, 1986.

Danylenko, Vasyl', ed. *Ukraïns'ka intelihentsiia i vlada: zvedenniia sekretnooho viddilu DPU USRR 1927–1929 rr.* Kyiv: Tempora, 2012.

Davies, R. W. *The Socialist Offensive: The Collectivization of Agriculture 1929–30.* London: Macmillan, 1980.

——, and S. G. Wheatcroft. *The Years of Hunger: Soviet Agriculture, 1931–1933.* London and New York: Palgrave Macmillan, 2009.

Duranty, Walter. 'Russians Hungry But Not Starving', *The New York Times*, 31 March 1933.

Figes, Orlando. *Peasant Russia, Civil War: The Volga Countryside in Revolution, 1917–1921.* Oxford: Clarendon Press, 1989.

——. *A People's Tragedy: The Russian Revolution, 1891–1924.* London: Pimlico, 1997.

——. *The Whisperers: Private Life in Stalin's Russia.* New York: Metropolitan Books, 2007.

Fisher, H. H. *The Famine in Soviet Russia, 1919–1923: The Operations of the American Relief Administration.* New York: Macmillan, 1927.

Fitzpatrick, Sheila. *Education and Social Mobility in the Soviet Union, 1921–1934.* Cambridge: Cambridge University Press, 1979, 2002.

——. 'The Great Departure: Rural-Urban Migration in the Soviet Union, 1929–1933', in *Social Dimensions of Soviet Industrialization*, eds.

William G. Rosenberg and Lewis H. Siegelbaum. Bloomington, IN: Indiana University Press, 1993.

Gamache, Ray. *Gareth Jones: Eyewitness to History*. Cardiff: Welsh Academic Press, 2013.

Gergel, Nahum. 'The Pogroms in Ukraine in 1918–1921', *YIVO Annual of Jewish Social Science* 6 (1951).

Getty, J. Arch, and Oleg V. Naumov. *The Road to Terror: Stalin and the Self-Destruction of the Bolsheviks, 1932–1939*. New Haven, CT: Yale University Press, 2002.

Graziosi, Andrea. *A New, Peculiar State: Explorations in Soviet History*. Westport, CT: Praeger, 2000.

——. *Bol'sheviki i krest'iane na Ukraine, 1918–1919 gody: Ocherk o bol'shevizmakh, natsional-sotsializmakh i krest'ianskikh dvizheniiakh*. Moscow, AIRO-XX, 1997.

——. 'Collectivisation, révoltes paysannes et politiques gouvernementales (à travers les rapports du GPU d'Ukraine de février–mars 1930)', *Cahiers du monde russe* 35, no. 3 (July–September 1994), http://www.persee.fr/doc/cmr_0008-0160_1989_num_30_1_2176.

——. *Stalinism, Collectivization and the Great Famine*, in Holodomor Series. Cambridge, MA: Ukrainian Studies Fund, 2009.

——. 'The Great Famine of 1932–1933: Consequences and Implications', *Harvard Ukrainian Studies* 25, nos. 3/4 (Fall 2001), 157–65.

——. 'The Soviet 1931–1933 Famines and the Ukrainian Holodomor: Is a New Interpretation Possible, and What Would Its Consequences Be?', *Harvard Ukrainian Studies* 27, nos. 1/4 (2004–5), 97–115.

——. *L'Unione Sovietica 1914–1991*. Bologna: Il mulino, 2011.

——. *L'Urss di Lenin e Stalin: storia dell'Unione Sovietica, 1914–1945*. Bologna: Il mulino, 2007.

Grossman, Vasilii. *Everything Flows*, trans. Robert and Elizabeth Chandler. New York: New York Review Classic Books, 2009.

Heifetz, Elias. *The Slaughter of the Jews in the Ukraine in 1919*. New York: Thomas Seltzer, 1921.

Hindus, Maurice. *Red Bread: Collectivization in a Russian Village*. Bloomington, IN: Indiana University Press, 1988.

Hosking, Geoffrey A. *Russia: People and Empire, 1552–1917*. Cambridge, MA: Harvard University Press, 1997.

Hryn, Halyna, and Lubomyr Hajda, eds. *After the Holodomor: The Enduring Impact of the Great Famine of Ukraine*. Cambridge, MA: Harvard Ukrainian Research Institute, 2013.

Hrynevych, Lyudmyla. *Holod 1928–1929 rr. u radians'kii Ukraïni*. Kyiv: Instytut Istoriï Ukraïny NAN Ukraïny, 2013.

——. 'The Price of Stalin's "Revolution from Above": Anticipation of War among the Ukrainian Peasantry', trans. Marta Olynyk. *Key Articles on the Holodomor Translated from Ukrainian into English*, Holodomor Research and Education Consortium. http://holodomor.ca/translated-articles-on-the-holodomor.

——. 'Vid zaperechuvannia do vymushenoho vyznannia: pro mekhanizmy vkhodzhennia temy holodu 1932–1933 rr. v ofitsiinyi publichnyi prostir u SRSR ta URSR naprykintsi 1980-kh rr', *Problemy istoriï Ukraïny: fakty sudzhennia, poshuky: Mizhvidomchyi zbirnyk naukovykh prats'* 18 (spetsial'nyi vypusk: Holod 1932–1933 rokiv–henotsyd ukraïns'koho narodu) (2008), 232–44.

Hunczak, Taras, ed. *The Ukraine, 1917–1921: A Study in Revolution*. Cambridge, MA: Distributed by Harvard University Press for the Harvard Ukrainian Research Institute, 1977.

Iakubova, L. D. *Etnichni menshyny v suspil'no-politychnomu ta kul'turnomu zhytti USRR, 20-i – persha polovyna 30-kh rr. XX st.* Kyiv: Instytut Istoriï Ukraïny NAN Ukraïny, 2006.

Iefimenko, H. 'Lykhovisni 30-ti roky na Markivshchyni', in *Holod-henotsyd 1933 roku v Ukraïni: istoryko-politolohichnyi analiz sotsial'-no-demohrafichnykh ta moral'no-psykholohichnykh naslidkiv: mizhnarodna naukovo-teoretychna konferentsiia, Kyiv, 28 lystopada 1998 r.: materialy: Instytut Istoriï Ukraïny (Natsional'na Akademiia Nauk Ukraïny): Asotsiatsiia doslidnykiv holodomoriv v Ukraïni.*, ed. Stanislav Vladyslavovych Kul'chyts'kyi and O. M. Veselova. Kyiv: Vyd-vo M.P. Kots', 2000.

——. 'Pereselennia ta deportatsii v postholodomorni roky (1933–1936): poraionnyi zriz', *Problemy istorii Ukraïny: fakty, sudzhennia, poshuky: Mizhvidomchyi zbirnyk naukovykh prats'* 22 (2013), 136–66.

——, and L. Iakubova. 'Natsional'ni vidnosyny v radians'kii Ukraïni (1923–1938)', in *Natsional'ne pytannia v Ukraïni XX-pochatku XXI st.: istorychni narysy*, eds. V. M. Lytvyn et al. Kyiv: Nika-Tsentr, 2012.

Ivnitskii, N. A. *Kollektivizatsiia i raskulachivanie, nachalo 30-kh gg.* Moscow: Interpraks, 1994.

Jones, Gareth. 'Famine Grips Russia, Millions Dying, Idle on Rise, Says Briton', *Chicago Daily News and Evening Post Foreign Service*, 29 March 1933.

——. 'Fate of Thrifty in USSR: Gareth Jones Tells How Communists Seized All Land and Let Peasants Starve', *Los Angeles Examiner*, 14 January 1935.

——. 'Press Release. Quoted in "Famine Grips Russia, Millions Dying, Idle on Rise, Says Briton', *Evening Post Foreign Service*, 29 March 1933.

——. 'Soviet Confiscate Part of Workers' Wages', *Daily Express*, 5 April 1933.

Kasianov, Georgiy. 'Holodomor and the Politics of Memory in Ukraine after Independence', in *Holodomor and Gorta Mor: Histories, Memories and Representations of Famine in Ukraine and Ireland*, eds. Vincent Comeford, Lindsay Jansen, and Christian Noack, 167–88. London: Anthem Press, 2014.

——. 'Revisiting the Great Famine of 1932–1933: Politics of Memory and Public Consciousness (Ukraine after 1991)', in *Past in the Making: Historical Revisionism in Central Europe after 1989*, ed. Michal Kopecek, 197–220. Budapest: Central European University Press, 2007.

Khlevniuk, Oleg V. *Stalin: New Biography of a Dictator*, trans. Nora Seligman Favorov. New Haven, CT: Yale University Press, 2015.

Klid, Bohdan. 'Daily Life Under Soviet Rule and the Holodomor in Memoirs and Testimonies of the Late 1940s: Some Preliminary Assessments', presented at the Canadian Association of Slavists 2015 Annual Conference, Ottawa, Ontario, 26 May 2015.

——. 'The Black Deeds of the Kremlin: Sixty Years Later', *Genocide Studies International* 8 (2014), 224–35.

Kondrashin, Viktor, *Golod 1932–1933 godov. Tragediia rossiyskoi derevni*, Moscow: ROSSPEN, 2008

——, and S. V. Kul'chyts'kyi. 'O Samom Glavnom: professor Stanislav Kul'chitskii i ego rossiiskii kollega Viktor Kondrashin: chem byl Golodomor 1932–1933 godov?' *Den'*, Kyiv, 3 June 2008.

Kotkin, Stephen. *Stalin: Paradoxes of Power*, vol. 1. New York: Penguin Press, 2014.

Kubanin, M. *Makhnovshchina: Krest'ianskoe dvizhenie v stepnoi Ukraine v gody grazhdanskoi voiny*. Leningrad: Priboi, 1927.

Kul'chyts'kyi, Stanislav V. 'Comments at UNAS (National Academy of Sciences) Institute of History of Ukraine Seminar', presented at the Institute of History of Ukraine Seminar, Kyiv, 19 April 2016.

——. *Holodomor 1932–1933 rr. iak henotsyd: trudnoshchi usvidomlennia*. Kyiv: Nash chas, 2008.

——. *Chervony vyklyk. Istoriia komunizmu v Ukraini vid joho narodzhennia do zahybel*, vols. 1–3. Kyiv: Tempora, 2013–17.

——. 'Holodomor in the Ukrainian Countryside', in *After the Holodomor: The Enduring Impact of the Great Famine on Ukraine*, eds. Andrea

Graziosi, Lubomyr Hajda, and Halyna Hryn. Cambridge, MA: Harvard Ukrainian Research Institute, 2013.

——. 'Holodomor u pratsiakh ukraïns'kykh radians'kykh istorykiv 1956–1987 rr', *Istoriia v suchasnii shkoli: naukovo-metodychnyi zhurnal*, no. 10 (146) (2013), 29–31.

——. *Narysy povsiakdennoho zhyttia radians'koï Ukraïny v dobu NEPu (1921–1928 rr.) Kolektyvna monohrafiia v 2-kh chastynakh*. 2 vols. Kyiv: Instytut Istoriï Ukraïny NAN Ukraïny, 2010.

——, and O. M. Movchan. *Nevidomi storinky holodu 1921–1923 rr. v Ukraïni*. Kyiv: Instytut Istoriï Ukraïny NAN Ukraïny, 1993.

Kuromiya, Hiroaki. *Freedom and Terror in the Donbas: A Ukrainian-Russian Borderland, 1870s–1990s*. Cambridge: Cambridge University Press, 1998.

Kyrydon, Alla. 'Ruinuvannia kul'tovykh sporud (1920–1930-ti rr.): porushennia tradytsiinoï rytmolohiï prostoru', *Ukraïns'kyi Istorichnyi Zhurnal* 22, no. 6 (2013), 91–102.

Kyrylenko, Vitalii Petrovych. 'Holod 1921–1923 rokiv u pivdennii Ukraïni', dissertation, Mykolaïvs'kyi Natsional'nyi Universytet imeni V. O. Sukhomlyns'koho, 2015.

Lemkin, Raphael. *Axis Rule in Occupied Europe: Laws of Occupation – Analysis of Government – Proposals for Redress*. Washington, D.C.: Carnegie Endowment for International Peace, 1944.

——. *Lemkin on Genocide*, ed. Steven Leonard Jacobs, Lanham, MD: Lexington Books, 2012.

——. 'Soviet Genocide in the Ukraine', unpublished talk, 1953, Raphael Lemkin Papers, New York Public Library, Manuscripts and Archives Division, Astor, Lenox and Tilden Foundations, Raphael Lemkin ZL-273. Reel 3. Available at https://www.uccla.ca/SOVIET_GENOCIDE_IN_THE_UKRAINE.pdf.

Lytvyn, V. M. et al., eds. *Ukraïna: Politychna Istoriia XX pochatok-XXI stolittia*. Kyiv: Parlaments'ke vydavnytstvo, 2007.

Mace, James. *Communism and the Dilemmas of National Liberation: National Communism in Soviet Ukraine, 1918–1933*. Cambridge, MA: Harvard Ukrainian Research Institute, 1983.

Magocsi, Paul Robert. *A History of Ukraine: The Land and its Peoples*, 2nd edn. Toronto: University of Toronto Press, 2010.

Marochko, Vasyl', and Olha Movchan. *Holodomor 1932–1933 rokiv v Ukraïni: khronika*. Kyiv: Kyievo-Mohylians'ka Akademiia, 2008.

Marples, David. *Holodomor: Causes of the Famine of 1932–1933 in Ukraine*. Saskatoon, Saskatchewan: Heritage Press, 2011.

Martin, Terry. 'Famine Initiators and Directors: Personal Papers: The 1932–33 Ukrainian Terror: New Documentation on Surveillance and the Thought Process of Stalin', in *Famine-Genocide in Ukraine, 1932–33*, ed. Isajiw W. Wsevolod. Toronto: Ukrainian Canadian Research and Documentation Centre, 2003.

——. *The Affirmative Action Empire: Nations and Nationalism in the Soviet Union, 1923–1939*. Ithaca, NY: Cornell University Press, 2001.

Maskudov, Sergei. 'Victory over the Peasantry', in *Hunger by Design: The Great Ukrainian Famine and its Soviet Context*, ed. Halyna Hryn. Cambridge, MA: Harvard Ukrainian Research Institute, 2008.

Mattingly, D. 'Idle, Drunk and Good-for-Nothing: Cultural Memory of the Holodomor Rank-and-File Perpetrators', in *The Burden of Memory: History, Memory and Identity in Contemporary Ukraine*, eds. Anna Wylegała and Małgorzata Głowacka-Grajper. Bloomington, IN: Indiana University Press, 2017.

Medvedev, Roy Aleksandrovich. *Let History Judge: The Origins and Consequences of Stalinism*, first published 1969, rev. and expanded edn, ed. and trans. George Shriver. Oxford: Oxford University Press, 1989.

Merridale, Catherine. *Night of Stone: Death and Memory in Twentieth-Century Russia*. New York: Viking, 2001.

——. 'The 1937 Census and the Limits of Stalinist Rule', *The Historical Journal* 39, no. 1 (1 March 1996).

Montefiore, Simon Sebag. *Stalin: The Court of the Red Tsar*. New York: Knopf, 2004.

——. *The Romanovs*. London: Weidenfeld and Nicolson, 2016.

Motyl, Alexander. *The Turn to the Right: The Ideological Origins and Development of Ukrainian Nationalism, 1919–1929*. New York: Columbia University Press, 1980.

Naimark, Norman M. *Stalin's Genocides*. Princeton, NJ: Princeton University Press, 2010.

Noll, Vil'iam. *Transformatsiia hromadians'koho suspil'stva: Usna istoriia ukraïns'koï selians'koï kul'tury, 1920–30 rokiv*. Kyiv: Rodovid, 1999.

Osokina, Elena Aleksandrovna. *Zoloto dlia industrializatsii: Torgsin*. Moscow: ROSSPEN, 2009.

——. *Our Daily Bread: Socialist Distribution and the Art of Survival in Stalin's Russia, 1927–1941*, trans. Kate Transchel and Greta Bucher. London and New York: Routledge, 2005.

Palij, Michael. *The Anarchism of Nestor Makhno, 1918–1921: An Aspect of the Ukrainian Revolution*. Seattle, WA: University of Washington Press, 1976.

Papakin, Heorhii V. *'Chorna doshka': antyselians'ki represiï, 1932–1933*. Kyiv: Instytut Istoriï Ukraïny NAN Ukraïny, 2013.

——. 'Blacklists as an Instrument of the Famine-Genocide of 1932–1933 in Ukraine', trans. Marta Olynyk. *Key Articles on the Holodomor Translated from Ukrainian into English*, Holodomor Research and Education Consortium. http://holodomor.ca/translated-articles-on-the-holodomor.

——. *Donbas na 'chornii doshtsi', 1932–1933: Naukovo-populiarnyi narys*. Kyiv: Instytut Istoriï Ukraïny NAN Ukraïny, 2014.

Pasternak, Boris. *Doctor Zhivago*, trans. Richard Pevear and Larissa Volokhonsky. New York: Pantheon Books, 2010.

Patenaude, Bertrand. *The Big Show in Bololand: The American Relief Expedition to Soviet Russia in the Famine of 1921*. Stanford, CA: Stanford University Press, 2002.

Pauly, Matthew D. *Breaking the Tongue: Language, Education, and Power in Soviet Ukraine, 1923–1924*. Toronto: University of Toronto Press, 2014.

Pidhainy, S. O., ed. *The Black Deeds of the Kremlin: A White Book*, 2 vols. Toronto: Basilian Press, 1953.

Pipes, Richard. *Russia under the Bolshevik Regime*. New York: Vintage Books, 1995.

——, ed. *The Unknown Lenin: From the Secret Archive*. New Haven, CT: Yale University Press, 1999.

Platonov, Andrei Platonovich. *Fourteen Little Red Huts and Other Plays*, trans. Robert Chandler, Jesse Irwin, and Susan Larsen. New York: Columbia University Press, 2016.

Plokhy, Serhii. 'Mapping the Great Famine', *MAPA: Digital Atlas of Ukraine, Harvard Ukrainian Research Institute*, accessed 23 April 2017. http://gis.huri.harvard.edu/images/pdf/MappingGreatUkrainianFamine.pdf.

——. *The Gates of Europe: A History of Ukraine*. New York: Basic Books, 2015.

——. *Unmaking Imperial Russia: Mykhailo Hrushevsky and the Writing of Ukrainian History*. Toronto: University of Toronto Press, 2005. http://www.deslibris.ca/ID/418634.

Pohl, Otto J., Eric J. Schmaltz, and Ronald J. Vossler. ' "In Our Hearts We Felt the Sentence of Death": Ethnic German Recollections of Mass Violence in the USSR, 1928–48', *Journal of Genocide Research* 11, no. 2 (2009), 325–7.

Power, Samantha. *A Problem from Hell*. New York: Basic Books, 2002.

Prymak, Thomas M. *Mykhailo Hrushevsky: The Politics of National Culture*. Toronto: University of Toronto Press, 1987.

Rigoulot, Pierre. *Les Paupières Lourdes: Les Français face au Goulag: Aveuglements et Indignations.* Paris: Éditions universitaires, 1991.

Riznykiv, Oleksa. *Ïdlo 33-ho: slovnyk holodomoru.* Odesa: Iurydychna literatura, 2003.

Romanets', N. R. 'Borot'ba z samosudamy v Ukraïns'komu seli, 1933–1935 rr', *Naukovi pratsi istorychnoho fakul'tetu Zaporiz'koho Natsional'noho Universytetu*, XXIX (2010), 186–91.

Rubl'ov, Oleksandr Serhiiovych, and Oleksandr Petrovych Reient. *Ukraïns'ki vyzvol'ni zmahannia 1917–1921 rr.* Kyiv: Al'ternatyvy, 1999.

Sands, Philippe. *East West Street: On the Origins of 'Genocide' and 'Crimes Against Humanity'.* New York: Knopf, 2016.

Serhiichuk, Volodymyr et al. *Ukraïns'kyi khlib na eksport, 1932–1933.* Kyiv: PP Serhiichuk M.I., 2006.

——. *Pohromy v Ukraïni 1914–1920: vid shtuchnykh stereotypiv do hirkoï pravdy, prykhovuvanoï v radians'kykh arkhivakh.* Kyiv: Vyd-vo im. O. Telihy, 1998.

Service, Robert W. *Lenin: A Biography.* London: Papermac, 2001.

Shapoval, Iurii (Yuri). 'Fatal'na Ambivalentnist', *Krytyka: mizhnarodnyi ohliad knyzhok ta idei* (May 2015). https://krytyka.com/ua/articles/fatalna-ambivalentnist.

——. 'Petro Shelest: 100th Anniversary of the Birth of One of Ukraine's Most Spectacular Political Figures', *Den* (4 March 2008).

——. 'Stoletnii Shelest: 14 fevralia ispolniaetsia 100 let odnomu iz samykh koloritnykh rukovoditelei USSR', *Den* (8 February 2008).

——. 'The Case of the "Union for the Liberation of Ukraine": A Prelude to the Holodomor', *Holodomor Studies* 2, no. 2 (Summer–Autumn 2010).

——. 'The Mechanisms of the Informational Activity of the GPU-NKVD', *Cahiers du monde russe* 22 (2001), 207–30.

——. 'The Symon Petliura Whom We Still Do Not Understand', *Den* 18, last modified 6 June 2006, accessed 20 April 2017. http://www.uke monde.com/petlyura/petlyura_notunder.html.

——. *Ukraïna 20–50 rr.: Storinky nenapysanoï istoriï.* Kyiv: Naukova Dumka, 1993.

——. 'Vsevolod Balickij, bourreau et victime', *Cahiers du monde russe* 44, nos. 2/3 (2003), 369–99.

——. 'Zhyttia ta smert' Mikoly Khvyl'ovoho: u svitli rozsekrechenykh dokumentiv HPU', *Z arkhiviv VUChK, HPU, NKVD, KHB* 2, nos. 30/31 (2008), 316–17.

Shevelov, George Y. *The Ukrainian Language in the First Half of the Twen-*

tieth Century, 1900–1941: Its State and Status. Cambridge, MA: Harvard Ukrainian Research Institute, 1989.

Shkandrij, Myroslav, and Olga Bertelsen. 'The Soviet Regime's National Operations in Ukraine, 1929–1934', *Canadian Slavonic Papers* 55, nos. 3/4 (September–December 2013), 160–83.

Shlikhter, Aleksandr. 'Bor'ba za khleb na Ukraine v 1919 godu', *Litopys revoliutsiï: Zhurnal istoriï KP(b)U ta Zhovtnevoï revoliutsiï na Ukraïni* 2, no. 29 (1928).

Sholokhov, Mikhail. *Virgin Soil Upturned*, trans. Stephen Garry. London: W. & J. Mackay, 1977.

Sipko, S. 'A Report for the Holodomor Research and Education Consortium', n.p., 2013.

Smolii, V. A. et al. *'Ukraïnizatsiia' 1920–1930-kh rokiv: peredumovy, zdobutky, uroky*. Kyiv: Instytut Istoriï Ukraïny NAN Ukraïny, 2003.

Smolii, Valerii et al. *Istoriia ukraïns'koho selianstva: Narysy v 2-kh tomakh*. 2 vols. Kyiv: Instytut Istoriï Ukraïny NAN Ukraïny, 2006.

Snyder, Timothy. *Black Earth: The Holocaust as History and Warning*. New York: Tim Duggan Books, 2015.

——. *Bloodlands: Europe Between Hitler and Stalin*. New York: Basic Books, 2010.

——. *Sketches from a Secret War: A Polish Artist's Mission to Liberate Soviet Ukraine*. New Haven, CT: Yale University Press, 2005.

——, and Ray Brandon. *Stalin and Europe: Imitation and Domination, 1928–1953*. Oxford: Oxford University Press, 2014.

Sosnovyi, S. 'Pravda pro velykyi holod na Ukraïni v 1932–1933 rokakh', *Ukraïns'ki visti* (7 February 1948).

Subtelny, Orest. *Ukraine: A History*. Toronto: University of Toronto Press, 1988.

Sysyn, Frank. 'The Ukrainian Famine of 1932–33: The Role of the Ukrainian Diaspora in Research and Public Discussion', *Studies in Comparative Genocide*, eds. Levon Chorbajian and George Shirinian. New York: St. Martin's Press, 1999.

——. 'Thirty Years of Research on the Holodomor: A Balance Sheet', *Contextualizing the Holodomor: The Impact of Thirty Years of Ukrainian Famine Studies*, eds. Frank Sysyn and Andrij Makuch. Toronto: Canadian Institute of Ukrainian Studies, 2015.

Taylor, Sally J. *Stalin's Apologist: Walter Duranty, the New York Times's Man in Moscow*. New York: Oxford University Press, 1990.

Thevenin, Etienne. 'France, Germany and Austria Facing the Famine of 1932–1933 in Ukraine', presented at the James Mace Memorial Panel, IAUS Congress, Donetsk, Ukraine, 6 June 2005.

Tottle, Douglas. *Fraud, Famine, and Fascism: The Ukrainian Genocide Myth from Hitler to Harvard.* Toronto: Progress Books, 1987.

Tucker, Robert C. *Stalin in Power: The Revolution from Above, 1928–1941.* New York: W. W. Norton, 1992.

Vasyl'ev, Valerii. 'Osoblyvosti polityky kerivnytstva VKP(b) u sil's'komu hospodarstvi URSR (Kinets' 1933–1934 rr.)', *Ukraïns'kyi selianyn: pratsi Naukovo-doslidnoho Instytutu Selianstva* 10 (2006), 342–8.

——. *Politychne kerivnytstvo URSR i SRSR: Dynamika vidnosyn tsentr-subtsentr vlady 1917–1938.* Kyiv: Instytut Istoriï Ukraïny NAN Ukraïny, 2014.

——, and Iurii I. Shapoval. *Komandyry velykoho holodu: Poïzdky V. Molotova i L. Kahanovycha v Ukraïnu ta Pivnichnyi Kavkaz, 1932–1933 rr.* Kyiv: Heneza, 2001.

Viola, Lynne. *Peasant Rebels Under Stalin: Collectivization and the Culture of Peasant Resistance.* Oxford: Oxford University Press, 1996.

——. *The Best Sons of the Fatherland: Workers in the Vanguard of Soviet Collectivization.* New York: Oxford University Press, 1987.

——, and V. P. Danilov, eds. *The War Against the Peasantry, 1927–1930: The Tragedy of the Soviet Countryside,* trans. Steven Shabad. New Haven, CT: Yale University Press, 2005.

Wolowyna, Oleh, Serhii Plokhy, Nataliia Levchuk, Omelian Rudnytskyi, Pavlo Shevchuk and Alla Kovbasiuk. 'Regional Variations of 1932–34 Famine Losses in Ukraine', *Canadian Studies in Population* 43, nos. 3/4 (2016), 175–202.

Yevsieieva, Tetiana. 'The Activities of Ukraine's Union of Militant Atheists during the Period of All-Out Collectivization, 1929–1933', trans. Marta Olynyk. *Key Articles on the Holodomor Translated from Ukrainian into English,* Holodomor Research and Education Consortium. http://holodomor.ca/translated-articles-on-the-holodomor.

Image Credits

Every effort has been made to contact copyright holders. The publishers will be pleased to make good in future editions any errors or omissions brought to their attention. Numbers refer to plates.

TsDKFFA Ukraïny im. H. S. Pshenychnoho: 12, 16, 17, 18, 19, 20, 21.

TsDKFFA Ukraïny im. H. S. Pshenychnoho: 13, 14, 15, 24, 25. Previously published in Ukraïns'kyi Instytut Natsional'noï Pam'iati, and V. Yushchenko, eds. *Natsional'na knyha pam'iati zhertv Holodomoru 1932–1933 rokiv v Ukraïni.* Kyiv: Vydavnytstvo im. Oleny Telihy, 2008.

TsDKFFA Ukraïny im. H. S. Pshenychnoho: 22, 23. Previously published in Serhii Kokin, Valerii Vasyl'ev, and Nicolas Werth, eds. 'Dokumenty orhaniv VKP(b) ta DPU USRR pro nastroï i modeli povedinky partiino-radians'kykh pratsivnykiv u respublitsi, 1932–33 rr.,' *Z arkhiviv VUChK GPU NKVD KGB* 1–2, nos. 40–1 (2013).

Diözesanarchive, Vienna: 26, 27, 28, 29, 30, 31, 32, 33, 34 35, 36, 37, 38, 45. By permission of Samara Pearce, family of Alexander Weinerberger.

HDA SBU: 39, 40. Previously published in Valentyna Borysenko, ed. *Rozsekrechena pam'iat': Holodomor 1932–1933 rokiv v Ukraïni v dokumentakh GPU-NKVD.* Kyiv: Stylos, 2007.

British Library, London: 42. © British Library Board / Bridgeman Images. As with 44, the columns of the original have been aligned for presentation on the page.

Map 4 was adapted from the MAPA: Digital Atlas of Ukraine program at the Ukrainian Research Institute, Harvard University.

Index